PLAYFAIR
FOOTBALL ANNUAL
2009–2010

62nd edition

Editors: Glenda Rollin
and Jack Rollin

D1593911

headline

Copyright © 2009 HEADLINE PUBLISHING GROUP

First published in 2009
by HEADLINE PUBLISHING GROUP

1

Apart from any use permitted under UK copyright law, this publication may only be reproduced, stored, or transmitted, in any form, or by any means, with prior permission in writing of the publishers or, in the case of reprographic production, in accordance with the terms of licences issued by the Copyright Licensing Agency.

Cover photographs Front and spine: Theo Walcott (Arsenal) – *Mike Egerton/ EMPICS Sport/PA Photos*; back: Tim Cahill (Everton) – *Action Images/Carl Recine.*

ISBN 978 0 7553 1963 3

Typeset by Wearset Ltd, Boldon, Tyne and Wear

Printed and bound in Great Britain by Clays Ltd, St Ives plc

Headline's policy is to use papers that are natural, renewable and recyclable products and made from wood grown in sustainable forests. The logging and manufacturing processes are expected to conform to the environmental regulations of the country of origin.

HEADLINE PUBLISHING GROUP
An Hachette UK Company
338 Euston Road
London NW1 3BH

www.headline.co.uk
www.hachette.co.uk

CONTENTS

EDITORIAL

As England prepares to complete the apparent formality of qualifying for the World Cup in South Africa, thanks to the seven out of seven wins in the qualifying stages, the European Under-21 Championship provided a stern reminder that expectations of success can be cruelly denied. Germany's comfortable 4-0 victory in the final in Sweden again put the way our game is developed in question, dominated as it is by the Premier League.

Oddly enough England has a better record at Under-21 level than in any of the other intermediate competitions. At least two trophies were won in the 1980s, the last of them 25 years ago. Compared with that is a solitary success in the 1992–93 Under-19 championship and none at all in the Under-17s.

On the other hand Germany's triumph in Scandinavia made them the proud possessor of all three current championships! Should we now be looking at the structure of the way young players are encouraged in the Bundesliga, instead of the Premier League?

Inevitably there will be calls for a cull of foreign players in this country. Both UEFA and FIFA have been gunning for us over this score, yet it is ironic that Sepp Blatter, head of the latter organisation praised the move of Cristiano Ronaldo from Manchester United to Real Madrid for £80 million as an indication of the health of the game, then criticised the Premier League for its emphasis on wealth!

Since the Premier League was created from the Football League, it is interesting to note that despite losing its top clubs the Coca Cola Championship has established itself as the fifth best supported competition in Europe. The Bundesliga leads and is followed by the PL, Spain's La Liga and Serie A in Italy.

Of course there are fewer foreign players in Germany compared with England. Again there is plenty of ammunition as a target for the home grown fraternity. Sadly, for purposes of discussion, English football has always had more than its fair share of players unqualified to play for the country. They used to be called Scots, Welsh and Irish and were and still remain an integral part of the English scene.

Nowadays more players enter these shores from abroad and the Premier League attracts the best of them. Ironically of course, with the move of Ronaldo to Spain, we also export the odd one or two. But it seems certain that England's failure to win the Euro tournament for Under-21s will cause some alarm at FA headquarters. Not only the defeat but a comprehensive one at that ended with Germany clear winners.

One of the questions being asked is whether the best of our young players are being asked to play too much football, both at domestic and international level. Success naturally means more matches and a strain on young, developing bodies. In order to progress in tournaments, additional fixtures are inevitable.

Comparing the Bundesliga with the Premier League, the Germans have 18 teams compared with our 20. This is not a huge difference but four more matches here in an already crowded fixture list is another burden.

England's Under-21s fulfilled thirteen commitments in 2008–09. Most of the players were featuring regularly in either the Premier League or Football League, many of them regular choices either in the starting line-up or on the bench. If there was a cull of foreigners would this situation actually get worse?

More domestic opportunities would put a further strain on the overall way in which the international scene is regarded. An overhaul of the system is long overdue and while answers to the many questions posed will not be easily found, a start has to be made sooner rather than later.

The grass roots is the starting point and it seems little point in hacking away at the higher-up branches when the problems lie closer to the ground and top-heavy thinking has to be pruned in order to produce a programme which will ensure overall growth.

CLUB AND OTHER RECORDS DURING 2008–2009

Arsenal Jack Wilshere youngest League player 16 years 256 days v Blackburn Rovers. Theo Walcott is the third Arsenal player to score three goals for England. Ted Drake and Ian Wright were the other two. Andrei Arshavin is the second Arsenal player to score four goals at Anfield. Julio Baptista achieved the same feat for the club.

Barnsley Reuben Noble-Lazarus youngest Football League player at 15 years 45 days.

Bournemouth Steve Fletcher most League appearances 514.

Chelsea 86-game unbeaten home run ended by Liverpool. 1 November: Petr Cech keeps 100th clean sheet. Alex scores 1000th PL goal. Frank Lampard 100th PL goal and Nicolas Anelka hat trick. Ashley Cole collects fifth FA Cup winner's medal (three with Arsenal).

Dagenham & Redbridge Tony Roberts, 39, makes his 400th club appearance. Jon Nurse the first fully capped player with four appearances for Barbados.

Darlington Most capped player Franz Burgmeier (Lichtenstein) with five appearances.

Everton Louis Saha scored fastest FA Cup final goal 25 seconds v Chelsea. But with eight runners-up Everton became the biggest final losers. Jose Baxter youngest League player 16 years 191 days v Blackburn Rovers.

Huddersfield Town Andy Booth scores his 150th League and Cup goal in his last match.

Hull City Nick Barmby scores a goal for his sixth different Premier League team.

Leicester City Matty Fryatt is the first City player to score 20 pre-Christmas goals for 43 years. Most League points in a season 96 in League One.

Liverpool Steven Gerrard becomes the 16th different Liverpool player to score 100 goals.

Manchester City Robinho breaks English transfer record in £32.5 million move from Real Madrid.

Manchester United Ryan Giggs is the only player to score a Premier League goal in each season. Edwin Van der Sar breaks PL clean sheet record with 1311 minutes. Cristiano Ronaldo scores his 100th and 101st goals for the club. Real Madrid pay world record £80 million for Ronaldo.

Millwall Neil Harris breaks Teddy Sheringham's record with 112th League and Cup goal.

Milton Keynes Dons Daniel Powell, 17 years 248 days becomes their youngest scorer. Most League goals in a season 83 League One.

Morecambe Most League points in a season 63 in League Two.

Newcastle United Most capped player Shay Given adds 82 before joining Manchester City.

Portsmouth David James extends his PL record to 547 matches overtaking Gary Speed.

Rochdale Gary Jones most League appearances 345.

Referees Clive Oliver, 48, was in charge of Gillingham v Shrewsbury Town play-off. Son Michael, 24, a day later controlling Scunthorpe United v Millwall.

England David Beckham became England's most capped outfield player with 112.

Spain Equalled Brazil's record of 35 unbeaten matches (32 wins).

LEAGUE REVIEW AND CLUB SECTION

Three in a row for Manchester United and Sir Alex Ferguson was an outstanding achievement. Of course there are always at least two ways at looking at any result, invariably from the viewpoint of the winners and losers. Taking this scenario into consideration, when Liverpool's record in second place is analysed, they must still wonder how they managed to finish just as runners-up.

Unbeaten at home, just two defeats away – at Tottenham and Middlesbrough – scored nine more goals than Manchester United and even managed an incredible 4-1 win at Old Trafford in March when the champions elect were about to suffer their only significant wobble. The following week they crashed at Fulham, finishing with nine players, too.

Yet all this merely serves to underline the achievement of Manchester United, who had the most wretched of starts to the campaign after an ill-conceived and draining pre-season tour of Africa. Cristiano Ronaldo was out injured for the first month of the season. Just one win in the opening four and defeat at Anfield, calls for a striker to be signed and loss of the Super Cup to Zenit.

But following defeat at the Emirates Stadium at the hands of Arsenal on 8 November, which coincided with the last goals Edwin Van der Sar conceded until February in Premier League matches, Sir Alex had sorted it all out at least until Liverpool completed the double over them.

With the squad system ruling and the need to juggle requirements for other domestic and European commitments, it is not surprising to reveal that in Premier League games alone, United called upon the services of no fewer than 33 players. Not one player succeeded in playing in every match. The nearest player to turn out in all matches was the central defender Nemanja Vidic with 33 appearancs including once coming on as a substitute. Ronaldo came next with 32 matches, twice appearing from the bench and was leading scorer with 18 goals. Wayne Rooney hit twelve.

Steven Gerrard with 16 goals, Fernando Torres on 14 led the Liverpool assault, but the Premier's leading marksman was Nicolas Anelka with 19 for Chelsea, who finished third having had a change of manager after mid-season when Felipe Scolari was jetisoned and Guus Hiddink became caretaker at Stamford Bridge. Arsenal had for them an indifferent start and too many drawn matches in mid-season and Aston Villa having threatened to break into the top four were caught for fifth place by Everton.

Fulham did exceptionally well and Roy Hodgson earned much praise for his handling of affairs at Craven Cottage. Tottenham Hotspur also had a change at the helm with Harry Redknapp taking over after the club's worst start in their history. West Ham United finishing comfortably, but Manchester City with the second best home record were too often found wanting on travel.

Wigan Athletic could be satisfied with another solid season and Stoke City confounded their critics in twelfth place. Bolton Wanderers tailed off at the end, Portsmouth also underwent managerial movement as did Blackburn Rovers.

Sunderland's Roy Keane quit and relegation was never far removed from thoughts in the north-east hotbed of football of old which also affected Hull City, Newcastle United and Middlesbrough. Hull after an impressive start won only one game from mid-December but survived somehow, not so Newcastle and Middlesbrough. West Bromwich Albion had suffered the curse of being bottom at the New Year.

Wolves, Birmingham automatically, Burnley – the 43rd different PL team now and back in the top flight after 33 years – from the play-offs won promotion. Norwich City, Southampton and Charlton Athletic were relegated from the Championship, their places being taken by Leicester City, Peterborough United and Scunthorpe United from the play-offs. Demoted from League One were Northampton Town, Crewe Alexandra, Cheltenham Town and Hereford United. Brentford, Exeter City, Wycombe Wanderers and Gillingham from the play-offs replaced them, while the points deduction for Luton Town proved too much and they joined Chester City in the Blue Square Premier. New boys Burton Albion and old hands Torquay United came up.

FA Barclays Premiership

		P	W	D	L	F	A	W	D	L	F	A	W	D	L	F	A	GD	Pts
			Home					**Away**					**Total**						
1	Manchester U	38	16	2	1	43	13	12	4	3	25	11	28	6	4	68	24	44	90
2	Liverpool	38	12	7	0	41	13	13	4	2	36	14	25	11	2	77	27	50	86
3	Chelsea	38	11	4	4	33	12	14	2	3	35	12	25	8	5	68	24	44	83
4	Arsenal	38	11	5	3	31	16	9	7	3	37	21	20	12	6	68	37	31	72
5	Everton	38	8	6	5	31	20	9	6	4	24	17	17	12	9	55	37	18	63
6	Aston Villa	38	7	9	3	27	21	10	2	7	27	27	17	11	10	54	48	6	62
7	Fulham	38	11	3	5	28	16	3	8	11	18	14	11	13	39	34	5	53	
8	Tottenham H	38	10	5	4	21	10	4	4	11	24	35	14	9	15	45	45	0	51
9	West Ham U	38	9	8	2	23	22	5	7	19	23	14	9	15	42	45	–3	51
10	Manchester C	38	13	0	6	40	18	2	5	12	18	32	15	5	18	58	50	8	50
11	Wigan Ath	38	8	5	6	17	18	4	4	11	17	27	12	9	17	34	45	–11	45
12	Stoke C	38	10	5	4	22	15	2	4	13	16	40	12	9	17	38	55	–17	45
13	Bolton W	38	7	5	7	21	21	4	3	12	20	32	11	8	19	41	53	–12	41
14	Portsmouth	38	8	3	8	26	29	2	8	9	12	28	10	11	17	38	57	–19	41
15	Blackburn R	38	6	7	6	22	23	4	4	11	18	37	10	11	17	40	60	–20	41
16	Sunderland	38	6	3	10	21	25	3	6	10	13	29	9	9	20	34	54	–20	36
17	Hull C	38	3	5	11	18	36	5	6	8	21	28	8	11	19	39	64	–25	35
18	Newcastle U	38	5	7	7	24	29	2	6	11	16	30	7	13	18	40	59	–19	34
19	Middlesbrough	38	5	9	5	17	20	2	2	15	11	37	7	11	20	28	57	–29	32
20	WBA	38	7	3	9	26	33	1	5	13	10	34	8	8	22	36	67	–31	32

LEADING GOALSCORERS 2008–09

BARCLAYS PREMIERSHIP

Only goals scored in the same division are included.

	League	Carling Cup	FA Cup	Other	Total
Nicolas Anelka (*Chelsea*)	19	0	4	2	25
Cristiano Ronaldo (*Manchester U*)	18	2	1	5	26
Steven Gerrard (*Liverpool*)	16	0	1	7	24
Fernando Torres (*Liverpool*)	14	0	1	2	17
Frank Lampard (*Chelsea*)	12	2	3	3	20
Darren Bent (*Tottenham H*)	12	1	0	4	17
Dirk Kuyt (*Liverpool*)	12	0	0	3	15
Wayne Rooney (*Manchester U*)	12	0	1	7	20
Robin Van Persie (*Arsenal*)	11	0	4	5	20
John Carew (*Aston Villa*)	11	0	1	3	15
Gabriel Agbonlahor (*Aston Villa*)	11	0	0	1	12
Kevin Davies (*Bolton W*)	11	0	0	0	11
Ricardo Fuller (*Stoke C*)	11	0	0	0	11

In order of total goals:

	League	Carling Cup	FA Cup	Other	Total
Peter Crouch (*Portsmouth*)	10	0	1	4	15

Other matches consist of European games, J Paint Trophy, Community Shield and Football League play-offs. Players listed in order of League goals total.

Coca-Cola Football League Championship

			Home				Away				Total					
		P	W	D	L	F	A	W	D	L	F	A	W	D	L	F	A	GD	Pts

		P	W	D	L	F	A	W	D	L	F	A	W	D	L	F	A	GD	Pts
1	Wolverhampton W	46	15	5	3	44	21	12	4	7	36	31	27	9	10	80	52	28	90
2	Birmingham C	46	14	5	4	30	17	9	9	5	24	20	23	14	9	54	37	17	83
3	Sheffield U	46	12	6	5	35	22	10	8	5	29	17	22	14	10	64	39	25	80
4	Reading	46	12	5	6	40	17	9	9	5	32	23	21	14	11	72	40	32	77
5	Burnley	46	14	4	5	42	23	7	8	8	30	37	21	13	12	72	60	12	76
6	Preston NE	46	16	3	4	39	20	5	8	10	27	34	21	11	14	66	54	12	74
7	Cardiff C	46	14	5	4	40	23	5	12	6	25	30	19	17	10	65	53	12	74
8	Swansea C	46	11	9	3	40	22	5	11	7	23	28	16	20	10	63	50	13	68
9	Ipswich T	46	9	8	6	30	26	9	6	8	32	27	17	15	14	62	53	9	66
10	Bristol C	46	7	13	3	30	23	8	3	12	24	31	15	16	15	54	54	0	61
11	QPR	46	12	7	4	28	19	3	9	11	14	25	15	16	15	42	44	−2	61
12	Sheffield W	46	11	6	6	26	14	5	7	11	25	44	16	13	17	51	58	−7	61
13	Watford	46	11	6	6	42	32	5	4	14	26	40	16	10	20	68	72	−4	58
14	Doncaster R	46	9	5	9	16	18	8	2	13	26	35	17	7	22	42	53	−11	58
15	Crystal Palace	46	9	8	6	26	19	6	4	13	26	36	15	12	19	52	55	−3	57
16	Blackpool	46	5	8	10	25	33	8	9	6	22	25	13	17	16	47	58	−11	56
17	Coventry C	46	8	8	7	26	26	5	7	11	21	32	13	15	18	47	58	−11	54
18	Derby Co	46	9	7	7	31	26	5	5	13	24	41	14	12	20	55	67	−12	54
19	Nottingham F	46	8	8	7	28	25	5	7	11	23	37	13	14	19	50	65	−15	53
20	Barnsley	46	8	7	8	28	24	5	6	12	17	34	13	13	20	45	58	−13	52
21	Plymouth Arg	46	7	5	11	31	35	6	7	10	13	22	13	12	21	44	57	−13	51
22	Norwich C	46	9	4	9	35	28	3	5	15	22	42	12	10	24	57	70	−13	46
23	Southampton	46	4	10	9	23	29	6	5	12	23	40	10	15	21	46	69	−23	45
24	Charlton Ath	46	6	8	9	33	38	2	7	14	19	36	8	15	23	52	74	−22	39

COCA-COLA FOOTBALL LEAGUE CHAMPIONSHIP

	League	Carling Cup	FA Cup	Other	Total
Sylvain Ebanks-Blake (Wolverhampton W)	25	0	0	0	25
Ross McCormack (Cardiff C)	21	1	1	0	23
Jason Scotland (Swansea C)	21	0	3	0	24
Kevin Doyle (Reading)	18	0	0	0	18
Tommy Smith (Watford)	17	0	0	0	17
Rob Hulse (Derby Co)	15	0	3	0	18
Chris Iwelumo (Wolverhampton W)	14	2	0	0	16
Kevin Phillips (Birmingham C)	14	0	0	0	14
Marcus Tudgay (Sheffield W)	14	0	0	0	14
Paul Gallagher (Plymouth Arg) (On loan from Blackburn R.)	13	0	0	0	13

Coca-Cola Football League Division 1

			Home					Away					Total					
		P	W	D	L	F	A	W	D	L	F	A	W	D	L	F	A	GD	Pts
1	Leicester C	46	13	9	1	41	16	14	6	3	43	23	27	15	4	84	39	45	96
2	Peterborough U	46	14	6	3	41	22	12	5	6	37	32	26	11	9	78	54	24	89
3	Milton Keynes D	46	12	4	7	42	25	14	5	4	41	22	26	9	11	83	47	36	87
4	Leeds U	46	17	2	4	49	20	9	4	10	28	29	26	6	14	77	49	28	84
5	Millwall	46	13	6	4	30	21	12	3	8	33	32	25	7	14	63	53	10	82
6	Scunthorpe U	46	13	5	5	44	24	9	5	9	38	39	22	10	14	82	63	19	76
7	Tranmere R	46	15	5	3	41	20	6	6	11	21	29	21	11	14	62	49	13	74
8	Southend U	46	13	8	2	29	20	8	6	9	29	41	21	8	17	58	61	–3	71
9	Huddersfield T	46	9	8	6	32	28	9	6	8	30	37	18	14	14	62	65	–3	68
10	Oldham Ath	46	9	9	5	35	24	7	8	8	31	41	16	17	13	66	65	1	65
11	Bristol R	46	11	4	8	44	29	6	8	9	35	32	17	12	17	79	61	18	63
12	Colchester U	46	7	4	12	21	24	11	5	7	37	34	18	9	19	58	58	0	63
13	Walsall	46	10	3	10	34	36	7	9	7	27	30	17	10	19	61	66	–5	61
14	Leyton Orient	46	6	6	11	24	33	9	5	9	21	24	15	11	20	45	57	–12	56
15	Swindon T	46	8	7	8	37	34	4	10	9	31	37	12	17	17	68	71	–3	53
16	Brighton & HA	46	6	6	11	32	40	7	7	9	23	30	13	13	20	55	70	–15	52
17	Yeovil T	46	6	10	7	26	29	6	5	12	15	37	12	15	19	41	66	–25	51
18	Stockport Co*	46	9	7	7	34	28	7	5	11	25	29	16	12	18	59	57	2	50
19	Hartlepool U	46	8	7	8	45	40	5	4	14	21	39	13	11	22	66	79	–13	50
20	Carlisle U	46	8	7	8	36	32	4	7	12	20	37	12	14	20	56	69	–13	50
21	Northampton T	46	8	8	7	38	29	4	5	14	23	36	12	13	21	61	65	–4	49
22	Crewe Alex	46	8	4	11	30	38	4	6	13	29	44	12	10	24	59	82	–23	46
23	Cheltenham T	46	7	6	10	30	38	2	6	15	21	53	9	12	25	51	91	–40	39
24	Hereford U	46	6	4	13	23	28	3	17	19	51	9	7	30	42	79	–37	34	

Stockport Co deducted 10 points.

LEADING GOALSCORERS 2008–09

COCA-COLA FOOTBALL LEAGUE DIVISION 1

	League	Carling Cup	FA Cup	Other	Total
Simon Cox (Swindon T)	29	1	0	2	32
Rickie Lambert (Bristol R)	29	0	0	0	29
Matty Fryatt (Leicester C)	27	0	4	1	32
Jermaine Beckford (Leeds U)	26	4	3	0	33
Gary Hooper (Scunthorpe U)	24	0	4	2	30
Craig Mackail-Smith (Peterborough U)	23	0	3	0	26
Joel Porter (Hartlepool U)	18	3	2	0	23
Lee Hughes (Oldham Ath)	18	0	0	0	18
Aaron McLean (Peterborough U)	17	0	1	0	18
Paul Hayes (Scunthorpe U)	17	0	0	3	20
Aaron Wilbraham (Milton Keynes D)	16	0	0	1	17
Luciano Becchio (Leeds U)	15	2	2	0	19
Danny Graham (Carlisle U)	15	0	1	0	16
Steve Guinan (Hereford U)	15	0	0	0	15

Coca-Cola Football League Division 2

			Home					Away					Total						
		P	W	D	L	F	A	W	D	L	F	A	W	D	L	F	A	GD	Pts
1	Brentford	46	13	8	2	39	15	10	8	5	26	21	23	16	7	65	36	29	85
2	Exeter C	46	13	5	5	36	25	9	8	6	29	25	22	13	11	65	50	15	79
3	Wycombe W	46	11	9	3	32	16	9	9	5	22	17	20	18	8	54	33	21	78
4	Bury	46	14	4	5	36	19	7	11	5	27	24	21	15	10	63	43	20	78
5	Gillingham	46	12	7	4	38	21	9	5	9	20	34	21	12	13	58	55	3	75
6	Rochdale	46	11	6	6	40	24	8	7	8	30	35	19	13	14	70	59	11	70
7	Shrewsbury T	46	14	6	3	41	16	3	12	8	20	28	17	18	11	61	44	17	69
8	Dagenham & R	46	12	3	8	44	24	7	8	8	33	29	19	11	16	77	53	24	68
9	Bradford C	46	11	10	2	39	18	7	3	13	27	37	18	13	15	66	55	11	67
10	Chesterfield	46	8	8	7	32	28	8	7	8	30	29	16	15	15	62	57	5	63
11	Morecambe	46	9	9	5	29	24	6	9	8	24	32	15	18	13	53	56	-3	63
12	Darlington*	46	11	6	6	33	20	9	6	8	28	24	20	12	14	61	44	17	62
13	Lincoln C	46	6	11	6	26	22	8	6	9	27	30	14	17	15	53	52	1	59
14	Rotherham U*	46	11	6	6	32	21	10	6	7	28	25	21	12	13	60	46	14	58
15	Aldershot T	46	9	10	4	36	31	5	2	16	23	49	14	12	20	59	80	-21	54
16	Accrington S	46	9	5	9	25	24	4	6	13	17	35	13	11	22	42	59	-17	50
17	Barnet	46	7	7	9	30	35	4	6	11	26	39	11	15	20	56	74	-18	48
18	Port Vale	46	6	6	11	23	33	7	3	13	21	33	13	9	24	44	66	-22	48
19	Notts Co	46	6	6	11	22	31	5	8	10	27	38	11	14	21	49	69	-20	47
20	Macclesfield T	46	7	4	12	23	37	6	4	13	22	40	13	8	25	45	77	-32	47
21	Bournemouth*	46	11	6	6	28	15	6	6	11	31	36	17	12	17	59	51	8	46
22	Grimsby T	46	6	7	10	31	28	3	7	13	20	41	9	14	23	51	69	-18	41
23	Chester C	46	7	12	4	34	34	4	6	13	19	47	11	18	17	53	81	-38	37
24	Luton T*	46	7	8	8	34	34	6	9	8	24	31	13	17	16	58	65	-7	26

Darlington deducted 10 points, Rotherham U deducted 17 points, Bournemouth deducted 17 points, Luton T deducted 30 points.

COCA-COLA FOOTBALL LEAGUE DIVISION 2

	League	Carling Cup	FA Cup	Other	Total
Grant Holt (Shrewsbury T)	20	0	1	7	28
Jack Lester (Chesterfield)	20	0	2	1	23
Paul Benson (Dagenham & R)	18	0	1	2	21
Reuben Reid (Rotherham U)	18	1	0	0	19
Adam Le Fondre (Rochdale)	17	0	3	0	20
Simeon Jackson (Gillingham)	17	0	1	3	21
John O'Flynn (Barnet)	17	0	1	0	18
Brett Pitman (Bournemouth)	17	0	0	0	17
Peter Thorne (Bradford C)	17	0	0	0	17
Charlie MacDonald (Brentford)	16	0	2	0	18
Andy Bishop (Bury)	16	0	0	1	17
Ryan Lowe (Chester C)	16	2	0	0	18

FA BARCLAYS PREMIERSHIP

HOME TEAM	Arsenal	Aston Villa	Blackburn R	Bolton W	Chelsea	Everton	Fulham	Hull C	Liverpool	Manchester C
Arsenal	—	0-2	4-0	1-0	1-4	3-1	0-0	1-2	1-1	2-0
Aston Villa	2-2	—	3-2	4-2	0-1	3-3	0-0	1-0	0-0	4-2
Blackburn R	0-4	0-2	—	2-2	0-2	0-0	1-0	1-1	1-3	2-2
Bolton W	1-3	1-1	0-0	—	0-2	0-1	1-3	1-1	0-2	2-0
Chelsea	1-2	2-0	2-0	4-3	—	0-0	3-1	0-0	0-1	1-0
Everton	1-1	2-3	2-3	3-0	0-0	—	1-0	2-0	0-2	1-2
Fulham	1-0	3-1	1-2	2-1	2-2	0-2	—	0-1	0-1	1-1
Hull C	1-3	0-1	1-2	0-1	0-3	2-2	2-1	—	1-3	2-2
Liverpool	4-4	5-0	4-0	3-0	2-0	1-1	0-0	2-2	—	1-1
Manchester C	3-0	2-0	3-1	1-0	1-3	0-1	1-3	5-1	2-3	—
Manchester U	0-0	3-2	2-1	2-0	3-0	1-0	3-0	4-3	1-4	2-0
Middlesbrough	1-1	1-1	0-0	1-3	0-5	0-1	0-0	3-1	2-0	2-0
Newcastle U	1-3	2-0	1-2	1-0	0-2	0-0	0-1	1-2	1-5	2-2
Portsmouth	0-3	0-1	3-2	1-0	0-1	2-1	1-1	2-2	2-3	2-0
Stoke C	2-1	3-2	1-0	2-0	0-2	2-3	0-0	1-1	0-0	1-0
Sunderland	1-1	1-2	0-0	1-4	2-3	0-2	1-0	1-0	0-1	0-3
Tottenham H	0-0	1-2	1-0	2-0	1-0	0-1	0-0	0-1	2-1	2-1
WBA	1-3	1-2	2-2	1-1	0-3	1-2	1-0	0-3	0-2	2-1
West Ham U	0-2	0-1	4-1	1-3	0-1	1-3	3-1	2-0	0-3	1-0
Wigan Ath	1-4	0-4	3-0	0-0	0-1	1-0	0-0	1-0	1-1	2-1

2008–2009 RESULTS

Manchester U	Middlesbrough	Newcastle U	Portsmouth	Stoke C	Sunderland	Tottenham H	WBA	West Ham U	Wigan Ath
2-1	2-0	3-0	1-0	4-1	0-0	4-4	1-0	0-0	1-0
0-0	1-2	1-0	0-0	2-2	2-1	1-2	2-1	1-1	0-0
0-2	1-1	3-0	2-0	3-0	1-2	2-1	0-0	1-1	2-0
0-1	4-1	1-0	2-1	3-1	0-0	3-2	0-0	2-1	0-1
1-1	2-0	0-0	4-0	2-1	5-0	1-1	2-0	1-1	2-1
1-1	1-1	2-2	0-3	3-1	3-0	0-0	2-0	3-1	4-0
2-0	3-0	2-1	3-1	1-0	0-0	2-1	2-0	1-2	2-0
0-1	2-1	1-1	0-0	1-2	1-4	1-2	2-2	1-0	0-5
2-1	2-1	3-0	1-0	0-0	2-0	3-1	3-0	0-0	3-2
0-1	1-0	2-1	6-0	3-0	1-0	1-2	4-2	3-0	1-0
—	1-0	1-1	2-0	5-0	1-0	5-2	4-0	2-0	1-0
0-2	—	0-0	1-1	2-1	1-1	2-1	0-1	1-1	0-0
1-2	3-1	—	0-0	2-2	1-1	2-1	2-1	2-2	2-2
0-1	2-1	0-3	—	2-1	3-1	2-0	2-2	1-4	1-2
0-1	1-0	1-1	2-2	—	1-0	2-1	1-0	0-1	2-0
1-2	2-0	2-1	1-2	2-0	—	1-1	4-0	0-1	1-2
0-0	4-0	1-0	1-1	3-1	1-2	—	1-0	1-0	0-0
0-5	3-0	2-3	1-1	0-2	3-0	2-0	—	3-2	3-1
0-1	2-1	3-1	0-0	2-1	2-0	0-2	0-0	—	2-1
1-2	0-1	2-1	1-0	0-0	1-1	1-0	2-1	0-1	—

COCA-COLA FOOTBALL LEAGUE

HOME TEAM	Barnsley	Birmingham C	Blackpool	Bristol C	Burnley	Cardiff C	Charlton Ath	Coventry C	Crystal Palace	Derby Co
Barnsley	—	1-1	0-1	0-0	3-2	0-1	0-0	1-2	3-1	2-0
Birmingham C	2-0	—	0-1	1-0	1-1	1-1	3-2	0-1	1-0	1-0
Blackpool	1-0	2-0	—	0-1	0-1	1-1	2-0	1-1	2-2	3-2
Bristol C	2-0	1-2	0-0	—	1-2	1-1	2-1	2-0	1-0	1-1
Burnley	1-2	1-1	2-0	4-0	—	2-2	2-1	1-1	4-2	3-0
Cardiff C	3-1	1-2	2-0	0-0	3-1	—	2-0	2-1	2-1	4-1
Charlton Ath	1-3	0-0	2-2	0-2	1-1	2-2	—	1-2	1-0	2-2
Coventry C	1-1	1-0	2-1	0-3	1-3	0-2	0-0	—	0-2	1-1
Crystal Palace	3-0	0-0	0-1	4-2	0-0	0-2	1-0	1-1	—	1-0
Derby Co	0-0	1-1	4-1	2-1	1-1	1-1	1-0	2-1	1-2	—
Doncaster R	0-1	0-2	0-0	1-0	2-1	1-1	0-1	1-0	2-0	2-1
Ipswich T	3-0	0-1	1-1	3-1	1-1	1-2	1-1	2-1	1-1	2-0
Norwich C	4-0	1-1	1-1	1-2	1-1	2-0	1-0	1-2	1-2	1-2
Nottingham F	1-0	1-1	0-0	3-2	1-2	0-1	0-0	1-0	0-2	1-3
Plymouth Arg	1-2	0-1	1-2	0-2	1-2	2-1	2-2	4-0	1-3	0-3
Preston NE	2-1	1-0	0-1	2-0	2-1	6-0	2-1	2-1	2-0	2-0
QPR	2-1	1-0	1-1	2-1	1-2	1-1	2-1	1-1	0-0	0-2
Reading	0-0	1-2	1-0	0-2	3-1	1-1	2-2	3-1	4-2	3-0
Sheffield U	2-1	2-1	2-2	3-0	2-3	0-0	3-1	1-1	2-2	4-2
Sheffield W	0-1	1-1	1-1	0-0	4-1	1-0	4-1	0-1	2-0	0-1
Southampton	0-0	1-2	0-1	0-1	2-2	1-0	2-3	1-1	1-0	1-1
Swansea C	2-2	2-3	0-1	1-0	1-1	2-2	1-1	0-0	1-3	1-1
Watford	1-1	0-1	3-4	2-4	3-0	2-2	1-0	2-1	2-0	3-1
Wolverhampton W	2-0	1-1	2-0	2-0	2-0	2-2	2-1	2-1	2-1	3-0

CHAMPIONSHIP 2008–2009 RESULTS

Doncaster R	Ipswich T	Norwich C	Nottingham F	Plymouth Arg	Preston NE	QPR	Reading	Sheffield U	Sheffield W	Southampton	Swansea C	Watford	Wolverhampton W
4-1	1-2	0-0	1-1	2-0	1-1	2-1	0-1	1-2	2-1	0-1	1-3	2-1	1-1
1-0	2-1	1-1	2-0	1-1	1-2	1-0	1-3	1-0	3-1	1-0	0-0	3-2	2-0
2-3	0-1	2-0	1-1	0-1	1-3	0-3	2-2	1-3	0-2	1-1	1-1	0-2	2-2
4-1	1-1	1-0	2-2	2-2	1-1	1-1	1-4	0-0	1-1	2-0	0-0	1-1	2-2
0-0	0-3	2-0	5-0	0-0	3-1	1-0	1-0	1-0	2-4	3-2	0-2	3-2	1-0
3-0	0-3	2-2	2-0	1-0	2-0	0-0	2-2	0-3	2-0	2-1	2-2	2-1	1-2
1-2	2-1	4-2	0-2	2-0	1-0	2-2	4-2	2-5	1-2	0-0	2-0	2-3	1-3
1-0	2-2	2-0	2-2	0-1	0-0	1-0	0-0	1-2	2-0	4-1	1-1	2-3	2-1
2-1	1-4	3-1	1-2	1-2	1-1	0-0	0-0	1-1	3-0	2-0	0-0	0-0	0-1
0-1	0-1	3-1	1-1	2-1	2-2	0-2	0-2	2-1	3-0	0-1	2-2	1-0	2-3
—	1-0	1-1	0-0	1-0	0-2	2-0	0-1	0-2	1-0	0-2	0-0	1-2	0-1
1-3	—	3-2	2-1	0-0	1-2	2-0	2-0	1-1	1-1	0-3	2-2	0-0	0-2
2-1	2-0	—	2-3	1-0	2-2	0-1	0-2	1-0	0-1	2-2	2-3	2-0	5-2
2-4	1-1	1-2	—	2-0	2-1	2-2	0-0	0-1	2-1	3-1	1-1	3-2	0-1
0-3	1-3	1-2	1-0	—	1-0	1-1	2-2	2-2	4-0	2-0	0-1	2-1	2-2
1-0	3-2	1-0	2-1	1-1	—	2-1	2-1	0-0	1-1	2-3	0-2	2-0	1-3
2-0	1-3	0-1	2-1	0-0	3-2	—	0-0	0-0	3-2	4-1	1-0	0-0	1-0
2-1	0-1	2-0	0-1	2-0	0-0	0-0	—	0-1	6-0	1-2	4-0	4-0	1-0
0-1	2-0	1-0	0-0	2-0	1-0	3-0	0-2	—	1-2	0-0	1-0	2-1	1-3
1-0	0-0	3-2	1-0	0-1	1-1	1-0	1-2	1-0	—	2-0	0-0	2-0	0-1
1-2	2-2	2-0	0-2	0-0	3-1	0-0	1-1	1-2	1-1	—	2-2	0-3	1-2
3-1	3-0	2-1	3-1	1-0	1-0	0-0	2-0	1-1	1-1	3-0	—	3-1	3-1
1-1	2-1	2-1	2-1	1-2	2-1	3-0	2-2	0-2	2-2	2-2	2-0	—	2-3
1-0	0-0	3-3	5-1	0-1	1-3	1-0	0-3	1-1	4-1	3-0	2-1	3-1	—

COCA-COLA FOOTBALL LEAGUE

HOME TEAM	Brighton & HA	Bristol R	Carlisle U	Cheltenham T	Colchester U	Crewe Alex	Hartlepool U	Hereford U	Huddersfield T	Leeds U
Brighton & HA	—	1-1	0-2	3-3	1-2	0-4	2-1	0-0	0-1	0-2
Bristol R	1-2	—	2-3	3-2	0-0	0-0	4-1	6-1	1-2	2-2
Carlisle U	3-1	1-1	—	1-0	0-2	4-2	0-1	1-2	3-0	0-2
Cheltenham T	2-2	2-1	1-1	—	4-3	1-0	2-0	2-3	1-2	0-1
Colchester U	0-1	0-1	5-0	3-1	—	0-1	1-1	1-2	0-0	0-1
Crewe Alex	1-2	1-1	1-2	1-2	2-0	—	0-0	2-1	3-1	2-3
Hartlepool U	1-0	1-1	2-2	4-1	4-2	1-4	—	4-2	5-3	0-1
Hereford U	1-2	0-3	1-0	3-0	0-2	2-0	1-1	—	0-1	2-0
Huddersfield T	2-2	1-1	1-0	2-2	2-2	3-2	1-1	2-0	—	1-0
Leeds U	3-1	2-2	0-2	2-0	1-2	5-2	4-1	1-0	1-2	—
Leicester C	0-0	2-1	2-2	4-0	1-1	2-1	1-0	2-1	4-2	1-0
Leyton Orient	2-1	1-2	0-0	1-2	2-1	1-0	1-0	2-1	1-1	2-2
Millwall	0-1	3-2	1-0	2-0	0-1	0-0	2-0	1-0	2-1	3-1
Milton Keynes D	2-0	2-1	3-1	3-1	1-1	2-2	3-1	3-0	1-1	3-1
Northampton T	2-2	0-0	1-0	4-2	1-2	5-1	3-0	2-1	1-1	2-1
Oldham Ath	1-1	0-2	0-0	4-0	0-1	1-1	2-1	4-0	1-1	1-1
Peterborough U	0-0	5-4	1-0	1-1	2-1	4-2	1-2	2-0	4-0	2-0
Scunthorpe U	2-0	0-2	2-1	3-0	3-0	3-0	3-0	3-0	1-2	1-2
Southend U	0-2	1-0	3-0	2-0	3-3	0-1	3-2	1-0	0-1	1-0
Stockport Co	2-0	3-1	3-0	1-0	1-2	4-3	2-1	4-1	1-1	1-3
Swindon T	0-2	2-1	1-1	2-2	1-3	0-0	0-1	3-0	1-3	1-3
Tranmere R	1-0	2-0	4-1	2-0	3-4	2-0	1-0	2-1	3-1	2-1
Walsall	3-0	0-5	2-1	1-1	2-0	1-1	2-3	1-1	2-3	1-0
Yeovil T	1-1	2-2	1-1	1-0	0-2	3-2	2-3	2-2	1-0	1-1

DIVISION 1 2008–2009 RESULTS

Leicester C	Leyton Orient	Millwall	Milton Keynes D	Northampton T	Oldham Ath	Peterborough U	Scunthorpe U	Southend U	Stockport Co	Swindon T	Tranmere R	Walsall	Yeovil T
3-2	0-0	4-1	2-4	1-1	3-1	2-4	1-4	1-3	1-0	2-3	0-0	0-1	5-0
0-1	2-1	4-2	1-2	1-0	2-0	0-1	1-2	4-2	2-0	2-2	2-0	1-3	3-0
1-2	1-3	2-0	3-2	1-1	1-1	3-3	1-1	2-1	1-2	1-1	1-2	1-1	4-1
0-4	0-1	1-3	3-5	0-1	1-1	3-6	1-2	0-0	2-2	2-0	1-0	0-0	1-0
0-1	1-0	1-2	0-3	2-1	2-2	0-1	0-0	0-1	1-0	3-2	0-1	0-2	1-0
0-3	0-2	0-1	2-2	1-3	0-3	1-1	3-2	3-4	0-3	1-0	2-1	2-1	2-0
2-2	0-1	2-3	1-3	2-0	3-3	1-2	2-3	3-0	0-1	3-3	2-1	2-2	0-0
1-3	2-1	0-2	0-1	0-2	5-0	0-1	1-2	0-1	0-1	1-1	2-2	0-0	1-2
2-3	0-1	1-2	1-3	3-2	1-1	1-0	2-0	0-1	1-1	2-1	1-2	2-1	0-0
1-1	2-1	2-0	2-0	3-0	0-2	3-1	3-2	2-0	1-0	1-0	3-1	3-0	4-0
—	3-0	0-1	2-0	0-0	0-0	4-0	2-2	3-0	1-1	1-1	3-1	2-2	1-0
1-3	—	0-0	1-2	1-3	2-1	2-3	2-2	1-1	0-3	1-2	0-1	0-1	0-1
0-1	2-1	—	0-4	1-0	2-3	2-0	1-2	1-1	1-0	1-1	1-0	3-1	1-1
2-2	1-2	0-1	—	1-0	6-2	1-2	0-2	2-0	1-2	1-2	1-0	0-1	3-0
1-2	1-1	0-0	0-1	—	0-1	1-1	3-3	2-3	4-0	3-4	1-1	0-2	3-0
1-1	1-1	4-3	2-0	2-1	—	1-2	3-0	1-1	3-1	0-0	0-2	3-2	0-2
2-0	3-0	1-0	0-0	1-0	2-2	—	2-1	1-2	1-0	2-2	2-2	1-0	1-3
1-2	2-1	3-2	0-1	4-4	2-0	1-0	—	1-1	2-1	3-3	1-1	1-1	2-0
0-2	3-0	0-1	0-2	1-0	1-2	1-0	2-0	—	1-1	2-1	2-1	2-0	0-1
0-0	0-1	2-2	0-1	1-1	3-1	1-3	0-3	3-1	—	1-1	0-0	1-2	0-0
2-2	0-1	1-2	1-1	2-1	2-0	2-2	4-2	3-0	1-1	—	3-1	3-2	2-3
2-0	0-0	1-3	1-1	4-1	0-1	1-1	2-0	2-2	2-1	1-0	—	2-1	1-1
1-4	0-2	1-2	0-3	3-1	1-2	1-2	2-1	5-2	1-0	2-1	0-1	—	2-0
0-2	0-0	2-0	0-0	1-0	2-2	0-1	1-2	1-2	2-4	1-0	1-0	1-1	—

COCA-COLA FOOTBALL LEAGUE

HOME TEAM	Accrington S	Aldershot T	Barnet	Bournemouth	Bradford C	Brentford	Bury	Chester C	Chesterfield	Dagenham & R
Accrington S	—	0-1	1-1	3-0	2-3	1-1	1-2	0-1	1-0	0-0
Aldershot T	3-1	—	1-1	1-1	3-2	1-1	3-3	2-2	1-1	1-2
Barnet	2-1	0-3	—	1-0	4-1	0-1	1-2	3-1	1-3	1-1
Bournemouth	1-0	2-0	0-2	—	4-1	0-1	2-0	1-0	1-1	2-1
Bradford C	1-1	5-0	3-3	1-3	—	1-1	1-0	0-0	3-2	1-1
Brentford	3-0	3-0	1-0	2-0	2-1	—	1-0	3-0	0-1	2-1
Bury	1-0	2-1	1-0	1-0	1-0	1-0	—	1-1	1-2	2-2
Chester C	2-0	0-1	5-1	0-2	0-0	3-0	1-1	—	1-3	2-2
Chesterfield	1-1	5-1	1-1	1-0	0-2	0-1	1-3	1-1	—	1-1
Dagenham & R	0-0	3-1	2-0	0-1	3-0	3-1	1-3	6-0	3-0	—
Darlington	3-0	2-0	2-2	2-1	2-1	1-3	2-2	1-2	0-0	3-0
Exeter C	2-1	3-2	2-1	1-3	1-0	0-2	0-0	2-0	1-6	2-1
Gillingham	1-0	4-4	0-2	1-0	0-2	1-1	0-0	2-0	2-1	2-1
Grimsby T	0-1	1-0	0-1	3-3	1-3	0-1	1-2	1-3	0-1	1-1
Lincoln C	5-1	0-2	2-0	3-3	0-0	2-2	1-1	1-1	3-1	1-3
Luton T	1-2	3-1	3-1	3-3	3-3	0-1	1-2	1-1	0-0	2-1
Macclesfield T	0-2	4-2	2-1	0-2	0-2	2-0	1-1	3-1	1-1	0-4
Morecambe	1-1	2-0	2-1	0-4	2-1	2-0	0-0	3-1	2-2	1-2
Notts Co	1-1	2-1	2-0	1-1	3-1	1-1	0-1	1-2	0-1	0-3
Port Vale	0-2	0-0	0-0	3-1	0-2	0-3	1-1	3-0	0-1	0-1
Rochdale	3-1	3-1	3-1	1-1	3-0	1-2	1-1	6-1	2-1	0-2
Rotherham U	0-0	1-2	3-4	1-0	0-2	0-0	1-1	3-1	3-0	1-1
Shrewsbury T	2-0	1-0	2-2	4-1	2-0	1-3	1-0	1-0	2-1	2-1
Wycombe W	2-1	3-0	1-1	3-1	1-0	0-0	2-1	2-0	1-1	2-1

	Darlington	Exeter C	Gillingham	Grimsby T	Lincoln C	Luton T	Macclesfield T	Morecambe	Notts Co	Port Vale	Rochdale	Rotherham U	Shrewsbury T	Wycombe W
Darlington	1-0	2-1	0-2	3-1	0-2	0-0	2-0	1-0	1-1	2-0	1-3	1-3	2-1	0-1
Exeter C	2-1	1-0	2-1	2-2	2-0	2-1	1-1	0-2	2-2	1-0	2-4	0-1	0-0	3-2
Gillingham	0-1	0-1	2-2	3-3	3-2	1-1	1-3	1-1	0-4	1-2	2-1	2-0	0-0	1-1
Grimsby T	3-1	0-1	1-1	2-1	0-1	1-1	0-1	0-0	0-1	0-0	4-0	0-0	1-0	3-1
Lincoln C	0-0	4-1	2-2	2-0	1-1	1-1	1-0	4-0	2-1	0-1	2-0	3-0	0-0	1-0
Luton T	1-1	1-1	1-1	4-0	1-1	2-0	1-0	3-1	1-1	2-0	1-2	0-0	1-1	3-3
Macclesfield T	2-2	0-1	4-0	0-2	3-1	1-2	3-0	2-1	2-0	3-0	2-1	1-2	2-1	0-0
Morecambe	1-2	0-0	0-1	1-1	0-2	2-2	0-2	1-2	2-0	1-2	0-2	1-5	1-1	0-2
Notts Co	0-0	2-1	0-1	2-1	1-1	2-2	2-4	1-2	3-1	2-1	3-0	1-0	2-2	0-1
Port Vale	0-1	1-2	2-0	4-0	0-3	2-1	2-1	0-2	6-1	1-1	3-2	1-1	1-2	0-1
Rochdale	—	1-1	1-2	1-0	2-0	5-1	1-2	0-0	1-0	2-1	1-2	1-0	1-1	1-2
Rotherham U	2-0	—	3-0	0-0	2-1	0-1	4-0	2-2	2-2	1-0	4-1	1-1	0-1	1-0
Shrewsbury T	1-0	1-0	—	3-0	1-2	0-1	3-1	5-0	2-2	1-0	1-1	4-0	2-2	1-1
Wycombe W	1-2	2-2	3-0	—	5-1	2-2	0-0	2-3	0-1	3-0	0-0	3-0	1-0	1-1
	0-1	0-1	2-0	1-1	—	0-0	1-0	1-1	1-1	0-1	1-0	0-1	0-0	1-0
	1-2	1-2	0-0	2-1	3-2	—	1-0	1-1	1-1	1-3	1-1	2-4	3-1	0-1
	0-6	1-4	0-1	1-0	1-2	2-1	—	0-1	1-1	0-2	0-1	1-2	3-0	0-0
	1-0	1-1	0-1	1-1	1-1	1-2	4-1	—	1-0	1-1	1-1	1-3	1-0	0-0
	0-0	2-1	0-1	0-2	0-1	0-2	1-1	1-0	—	4-2	1-2	0-3	2-2	0-2
	3-1	1-3	1-3	2-1	0-1	1-3	1-4	2-1	1-2	—	2-1	0-0	1-1	1-1
	0-2	2-2	0-1	2-0	2-2	2-0	1-1	1-1	3-0	1-0	—	1-2	2-1	0-1
	0-1	0-1	2-0	4-1	1-0	1-0	2-0	3-2	2-1	1-0	2-2	—	1-2	0-0
	1-0	1-1	7-0	1-1	0-0	3-0	4-0	0-0	3-2	1-2	1-1	1-0	—	0-1
	1-1	1-1	1-0	0-1	1-0	0-0	4-0	1-1	1-2	4-2	0-1	0-0	1-1	—

ACCRINGTON STANLEY　　　　FL CHAMPIONSHIP 2

Player	Ht	Wt	Birthplace	D.O.B.	Source
Arthur Kenny (G)	6 3	13 08	Bellshill	7 12 78	Partick T
Cavanagh Peter (D)	5 11	11 09	Liverpool	14 10 81	Liverpool
Dunbavin Ian (G)	6 2	10 10	Knowsley	27 5 80	Scarborough
Edwards Phil (D)	5 8	11 03	Kirkby	8 11 85	Wigan Ath
Grant Robert (M)	5 11	12 00	Blackpool	27 3 87	Scholar
King Chris (D)	5 8	10 01	Birkenhead	14 11 80	The New Saints
McConville Sean (F)	5 11	11 09	Burscough	6 3 89	Skelmersdale U
Miles John (F)	5 10	10 08	Fazackerley	28 9 81	Macclesfield T
Mullin John (M)	6 0	11 10	Bury	11 8 75	Tranmere R
Mullin Paul (F)	6 0	12 01	Bury	16 3 74	Radcliffe Borough
Murphy Peter (M)	6 0	11 10	Liverpool	13 2 90	Scholar
Proctor Andy (M)	6 0	12 04	Lancashire	13 3 83	Gt Harwood T
Richardson Leam (D)	5 8	11 04	Blackpool	19 11 79	Leeds
Ryan James (M)	5 8	11 08	Maghull	6 9 88	Liverpool
Turner Chris (F)	5 10	11 10	Manchester	12 8 87	Scholar
Williams Robbie (D)	5 10	12 00	Liverpool	12 4 79	St Dominics

League Appearances: Arthur, K. 42; Bell, J. 5(1); Blundell, G. 2; Cavanagh, P. 28(1); Charnock, K. 33(1); Clarke, J. 12(3); Craney, I. 2; Dunbavin, I. 4; Edwards, P. 46; Gornell, T. 10(1); Grant, R. 6(9); Griffiths, R. 13; Higginbotham, K. 5(7); Kay, A. 1(2); King, C. 27; Kissock, J. 5; Lindfield, C. 17(3); Mahon, C. (2); McConville, S. 2(3); Miles, J. 42(1); Mullin, J. 25(6); Mullin, P. 36; Murdock, C. 20(3); Murphy, P. 1(2); Onibuje, F. (5); Proctor, A. 32(5); Richardson, L. 9(2); Ryan, J. 41(3); Smith, A. (1); Symes, M. 7; Turner, C. 14(8); Williams, R. 18(5); Worrall, D. 1(3).

Goals – League (42): Ryan 10, Mullin P 7, Clarke 5 (1 pen), Gornell 4, Miles 3, Proctor 3, Lindfield 2, Cavanagh 1, Craney 1, Grant 1, Griffiths 1, Murdock 1, Symes 1, Williams 1, own goal 1.

Carling Cup (2): Craney 1, Mullin P 1.

FA Cup (0).

J Paint Trophy (0).

Ground: The Fraser Eagle Stadium, Livingstone Road, Accrington, Lancashire BB5 5BX. Telephone: (0871) 434 1968.

Record Attendance: 4368 v Colchester U, FA Cup 1st rd, 3 January 2004.

Capacity: 5,057.

Manager: John Coleman.

Secretary: Hannah Bailey.

Most League Goals: 96, Division 3 (N) 1954–55.

Highest League Scorer in Season: George Stewart, 35, 1955–56 Division 3(N); George Hudson, 35, 1960–61, Division 4.

Most League Goals in Total Aggregate: George Stewart 136, 1954–58.

Most Capped Player: Romuald Boco, (17), Benin.

Most League Appearances: Jim Armstrong, 260, 1927–34.

Colours: All red.

ALDERSHOT TOWN　　　　FL CHAMPIONSHIP 2

Blackburn Chris (D)	6 0	12 00	Crewe	2 8 82	Swindon T
Bull Nikki (G)	6 1	11 03	Hastings	2 10 81	Hayes
Chalmers Lewis (M)	6 0	12 04	Manchester	4 2 86	Altrincham
Charles Anthony (D)	6 0	12 00	Isleworth	11 3 81	Barnet
Cochrane Justin (M)	5 11	11 07	Hackney	26 1 82	Rushden & D
Day Rhys (D)	6 1	12 08	Bridgend	31 8 82	Mansfield T
Donnelly Scott (M)	5 8	11 10	Hammersmith	25 12 87	QPR

Elvins Rob (F)	6 2	12 04	Alvechurch	17 9 86	WBA
Grant John (F)	5 11	11 00	Manchester	9 8 81	Halifax T
Harding Ben (M)	5 10	11 02	Carshalton	6 9 84	Milton Keynes D
Howell Dean (D)	6 1	12 05	Burton-on-Trent	29 11 80	Rushden & D
Hudson Kirk (F)	6 0	10 10	Rochford	12 12 86	Bournemouth
Hylton Danny (F)	6 0	11 03	London	25 2 89	Youth
Jaimez-Ruiz Michael (G)	6 1	12 00	Merida	12 7 84	Northwood
Mendes Junior (F)	5 10	11 04	Ballam	15 9 76	Notts Co
Morgan Marvin (F)	6 4	12 08	Manchester	18 4 83	Woking
Newman Ricky (D)	5 10	12 06	Guildford	5 8 70	Brentford
Sandell Andy (M)	5 11	11 09	Calne	8 9 83	Salisbury C
Soares Louis (M)	5 11	11 05	Reading	8 1 85	Barnet
Straker Anthony (D)	5 9	11 11	Ealing	23 9 88	Crystal Palace
Winfield Dave (D)	6 3	13 08	Aldershot	24 3 88	Youth

League Appearances: Blackburn, C. 36; Bull, N. 30; Chalmers, L. 19(4); Charles, A. 41; Cochrane, J. 9(1); Davies, S. 37(4); Day, R. 16(1); Donnelly, S. 12(8); Elvins, R. 7(8); Grant, J. 28(7); Harding, B. 29; Howell, D. 14; Hudson, K. 35(8); Hylton, D. 16(13); Jaimez-Ruiz, M. 13(1); Lindegaard, A. 6; McCarthy, A. 3(1); Mendes, J. 1(5); Morgan, M. 22(10); Newman, R. 10(7); Osborne, J. 8; Robinson, J. 19; Sandell, A. 24(5); Soares, L. 30(5); Starosta, B. 3; Straker, A. 29(3); Winfield, D. 9(1).

Goals – League (59): Davies 13 (5 pens), Hudson 11, Morgan 6, Grant 5, Hylton 5, Robinson 4, Harding 3, Soares 3, Charles 2, Sandell 2, Chalmers 1, Donnelly 1, Elvins 1, Lindegaard 1, own goal 1.

Carling Cup (1): Morgan 1.

FA Cup (4): Hudson 2, Grant 1 (pen), Morgan 1.

Trophy (2): Davies 1 (pen), Elvins 1.

Ground: EBB Stadium at the Recreation Ground, High Street, Aldershot GU11 1TW. Telephone: 01252 320211.

Record Attendance: 19,138 v Carlisle U, FA Cup 4th rd (replay) 28 January 1970.

Capacity: 7,100.

Manager: Gary Waddock.

Secretary: Graham Hortop.

Most League Goals: 83, Division 4, 1963–64.

Highest League Scorer in Season: John Dungworth, 26, Division 4, 1978–79.

Most League Goals in Total Aggregate: Jack Howarth, 171, 1965–71 and 1972–77.

Most Capped Player: Louie Soares, 3, Barbados.

Most League Appearances: Murray Brodie, 461, 1970–83.

Honours – Blue Square Premier League: Champions 2007–08. **Setanta Shield:** Winners 2008.

Colours: All red with blue and white trim.

ARSENAL   FA PREMIERSHIP

Adebayor Emmanuel (F)	6 4	11 08	Lome	26 2 84	Monaco
Almunia Manuel (G)	6 3	13 00	Pamplona	19 5 77	Celta Vigo
Arshavin Andrei (F)	5 8	9 11	St Petersburg	29 5 81	Zenit
Ayling Luke (D)			London	25 8 91	Scholar
Barazite Nacer (M)	6 2	13 01	Arnhem	27 5 90	Scholar
Bartley Kyle (D)			Manchester	22 5 91	Scholar
Bendtner Nicklas (F)	6 2	13 00	Copenhagen	16 1 88	Scholar
Bothelo Pedro (D)	6 2	12 00	Salvador	14 12 89	Salamanca
Clichy Gael (D)	5 9	10 04	Toulouse	26 7 85	Cannes
Coquelin Francis (M)	5 10	11 08	Laval	13 5 91	Laval
Cruise Thomas (D)			London	9 3 91	Scholar
Denilson (M)	5 10	11 00	Sao Paulo	16 2 88	Sao Paulo
Diaby Vassirki (M)	6 2	12 04	Paris	11 5 86	Auxerre
Djourou Johan (D)	6 3	13 01	Ivory Coast	18 1 87	Scholar

21

Eastmond Craig (D)			Wandsworth	9 12 90	Scholar
Eboue Emmanuel (D)	5 10	10 03	Abidjan	4 6 83	Beveren
Eduardo (F)	5 10	10 03	Rio de Janeiro	25 2 83	Dinamo Zagreb
Emmanuel-Thomas Jay (M)			Forest Gate	27 12 90	Scholar
Fabianski Lukasz (G)	6 3	13 01	Costrzyn nad Odra	18 4 85	Legia
Fabregas Francesc (M)	5 11	11 01	Vilessoc de Mar	4 5 87	Barcelona
Freeman Luke (F)	6 1	10 00	London	22 3 92	Gillingham
Frimpong Emanuel (M)	5 11	10 07	Ghana	10 1 92	Scholar
Gallas William (D)	5 11	12 10	Asnieres	17 8 77	Chelsea
Gibbs Kieran (M)	5 10	10 02	Lambeth	26 9 89	Scholar
Gilbert Kerrea (D)	5 6	11 06	Hammersmith	28 2 87	Scholar
Henderson Conor (M)	6 1	11 13	Sidcup	8 9 91	Scholar
Hoyte Gavin (D)			Waltham Forest	6 6 90	Scholar
Lansbury Henri (M)			Enfield	12 10 90	Scholar
Mannone Vito (G)	6 0	11 08	Desio	2 3 88	Atalanta
Murphy Rhys (F)	6 1	11 13	Shoreham	6 11 90	
Nasri Samir (M)	5 9	11 11	Marseille	26 6 87	Marseille
Nordtveit Havard (D)			Vats	21 6 90	Vats 94
Perez Fran Merida (M)	5 11	13 00	Barcelona	4 3 90	Scholar
Ramsey Aaron (M)	5 9	10 07	Caerphilly	26 12 90	Cardiff C
Randall Mark (M)	6 0	12 12	Milton Keynes	28 9 89	Scholar
Rasmussen Jonas (M)			Denmark	1 8 91	Scholar
Rosicky Tomas (M)	5 11	11 06	Prague	4 10 80	Borussia Dortmund
Sagna Bakari (D)	5 10	11 05	Sens	14 2 83	Auxerre
Senderos Philippe (D)	6 1	13 10	Geneva	14 2 85	Servette
Silvestre Mikael (D)	6 0	13 12	Chambray les Tours	9 8 77	Manchester U
Simpson Jay (M)	5 11	13 04	London	1 12 88	Scholar
Song Bilong Alexandre (M)	6 4	12 07	Douala	9 9 87	Bastia
Sunu Gilles (F)			Chateauroux	30 3 91	Scholar
Szczesny Wojciech (F)	5 10	11 11	Warsaw	18 4 90	Scholar
Toure Kolo (D)	5 10	13 08	Ivory Coast	19 3 81	ASEC Mimosas
Traore Armand (D)	6 1	12 12	Paris	8 10 89	Monaco
Van Persie Robin (F)	6 0	11 00	Rotterdam	6 8 83	Feyenoord
Vela Carlos (F)	5 9	10 05	Mexico	1 3 89	Celta Vigo
Walcott Theo (F)	5 9	11 01	Compton	16 3 89	Southampton
Watt Sanchez (M)			London	14 2 91	Scholar
Wilshere Jack (M)	5 7	11 03	Stevenage	1 1 92	Scholar

League Appearances: Adebayor, E. 21(5); Almunia, M. 32; Arshavin, A. 12; Bendtner, N. 17(14); Bischoff, A. 1(1); Clichy, G. 30(1); Denilson, 36(1); Diaby, V. 16(8); Djourou, J. 13(2); Eboue, E. 17(11); Fabianski, L. 5(1); Fabregas, F. 22; Gallas, W. 23; Gibbs, K. 6(2); Hoyte, G. 1; Mannone, V. 1; Merida Perez, F. (2); Nasri, S. 28(1); Ramsey, A. 1(8); Randall, M. (1); Sagna, B. 34(1); Silvestre, M. 12(2); Song Billong, A. 23(8); Toure, K. 26(3); Van Persie, R. 24(4); Vela, C. 2(12); Walcott, T. 16(6); Wilshere, J. (1).
Goals – League (68): Van Persie 11 (2 pens), Adebayor 10 (1 pen), Bendtner 9 (1 pen), Arshavin 6, Nasri 6, Denilson 3, Diaby 3, Eboue 3 (1 pen), Fabregas 3, Gallas 2, Silvestre 2, Walcott 2, Clichy 1, Song Billong 1, Toure 1, Vela 1, own goals 4.
Carling Cup (9): Vela 4, Bendtner 2, Simpson 2, Wilshere 1.
FA Cup (13): Van Persie 4, Eduardo 3 (1 pen), Bendtner 1, Eboue 1, Gallas 1, Vela 1, Walcott 1, own goal 1.
Champions League (23): Adebayor 6 (1 pen), Van Persie 5 (3 pens), Gallas 3, Walcott 3, Bendtner 2, Diaby 1, Nasri 1, Ramsey 1, Song Billong 1.
Ground: Emirates Stadium, Highbury House, 75 Drayton Park, Islington, London N5 1BU. Telephone (0207) 619 5003.
Record Attendance: 73,295 v Sunderland, Div 1, 9 March 1935. **Capacity:** 60,355.
Manager: Arsène Wenger.
Secretary: David Miles.
Most League Goals: 127, Division 1, 1930–31.
Highest League Scorer in Season: Ted Drake, 42, 1934–35.

Most League Goals in Total Aggregate: Thierry Henry, 174, 1999–2007.
Most Capped Player: Thierry Henry, 81 (111), France.
Most League Appearances: David O'Leary, 558, 1975–93.
Honours – FA Premier League: Champions – 1997–98, 2001–02, 2003–04. **Football League:** Division 1 Champions – 1930–31, 1932–33, 1933–34, 1934–35, 1937–38, 1947–48, 1952–53, 1970–71, 1988–89, 1990–91. **FA Cup:** Winners – 1929–30, 1935–36, 1949–50, 1970–71, 1978–79, 1992–93, 1997–98, 2001–02, 2002–03, 2004–05. **Football League Cup:** Winners – 1986–87, 1992–93. **European Competitions: European Cup-Winners' Cup:** Winners – 1993–94. **Fairs Cup:** Winners – 1969–70.
Colours: Red shirts with white trim, white shorts, white stockings with red tops.

ASTON VILLA   FA PREMIERSHIP

Agbonlahor Gabriel (F)	5 11	12 05	Birmingham	13 10 86	Scholar
Albrighton Marc (M)	6 2	12 06	Sutton Coldfield	18 11 89	Scholar
Baker Nathan (D)	6 2	11 11	Worcester	23 4 91	Scholar
Bannan Barry (D)	5 10	10 08	Glasgow	1 12 89	Scholar
Barry Gareth (D)	5 11	12 06	Hastings	23 2 81	Trainee
Bevan David (G)	6 2	13 00	Cork	24 6 89	Scholar
Bouma Wilfred (D)	5 10	13 01	Helmond	15 6 78	PSV Eindhoven
Carew John (F)	6 5	15 00	Lorenskog	5 9 79	Lyon
Clark Ciaran (D)	6 2	12 00	Harrow	26 9 89	Scholar
Cuellar Carlos (D)	6 3	13 03	Madrid	23 8 81	Rangers
Dau Thomas (G)			Kitsee	9 8 91	Scholar
Davies Curtis (D)	6 2	11 13	Waltham Forest	15 3 85	WBA
Delfouneso Nathan (F)	6 1	12 04	Birmingham	2 2 91	Scholar
Forrester Harry (M)				2 1 91	Scholar
Friedel Brad (G)	6 3	14 00	Lakewood	18 5 71	Blackburn R
Gardner Craig (M)	5 10	11 13	Solihull	25 11 86	Scholar
Guzan Brad (G)	6 4	14 11	Home Glen	9 9 84	Chivas USA
Halfhuid Arsenio			Voorburg	9 11 91	Excelsior
Harewood Marlon (F)	6 1	13 07	Hampstead	25 8 79	West Ham U
Herd Chris (M)	5 9	11 04	Melbourne	4 4 89	Scholar
Heskey Emile (F)	6 2	13 12	Leicester	11 1 78	Wigan Ath
Hofbauer Dominik (M)			Eggenberg	19 9 90	Scholar
Hogg Jonathan (M)	5 7	10 05	Middlesbrough	6 12 88	Scholar
Knight Zat (D)	6 6	15 02	Solihull	2 5 80	Fulham
Lichaj Eric (M)	5 11	12 07	Denwers Grove	17 11 88	Chicago Magic
Lowry Shane (D)	6 1	13 01	Perth	12 6 89	Scholar
McGurk Adam (F)	5 9	12 13	St Helier	24 1 89	Scholar
Milner James (M)	5 9	11 00	Leeds	4 1 86	Newcastle U
O'Halloran Stephen (D)	6 0	11 07	Cork	29 11 87	Scholar
Osbourne Isaiah (M)	6 2	12 07	Birmingham	5 11 87	Scholar
Parish Elliot (G)			Northampton	20 5 90	Scholar
Petrov Stilian (M)	5 11	13 05	Montana	5 7 79	Celtic
Reo-Coker Nigel (M)	5 8	12 03	Southwark	14 5 84	West Ham U
Roome Matthew (D)			Burton	12 10 89	Scholar
Salifou Moustapha (M)	5 11	10 12	Lome	1 6 83	FC Wil
Shorey Nicky (D)	5 9	10 08	Romford	19 2 81	Reading
Sidwell Steve (M)	5 10	11 00	Wandsworth	14 12 82	Chelsea
Siegrist Benjamin (G)			Basle	31 1 92	Scholar
Simmonds Sam (D)			Birmingham	17 3 90	Scholar
Weimann Andreas (F)			Vienna	5 8 91	Scholar
Young Ashley (M)	5 6	9 06	Stevenage	9 7 85	Watford
Young Luke (D)	6 0	12 04	Harlow	19 7 79	Middlesbrough

League Appearances: Agbonlahor, G. 35(1); Barry, G. 38; Carew, J. 18(9); Cuellar, C. 24(4); Davies, C. 34(1); Delfouneso, N. (4); Friedel, B. 38; Gardner, C. 3(11); Guzan, B. (1); Harewood, M. (6); Heskey, E. 11(3); Knight, Z. 13; Laursen, M. 19;

Milner, J. 31(5); Petrov, S. 36; Reo-Coker, N. 19(7); Routledge, W. (1); Shorey, N. 19(2); Sidwell, S. 11(5); Young, A. 36; Young, L. 33(1).
Goals – League (54): Agbonlahor 11, Carew 11, Young A 7, Barry 5 (4 pens), Milner 3, Sidwell 3, Heskey 2, Davies 1, Knight 1, Laursen 1, Petrov 1, Reo-Coker 1, Young L 1, own goals 6.
Carling Cup (0).
FA Cup (6): Milner 3 (2 pens), Carew 1, Delfouneso 1, Sidwell 1.
UEFA Cup (15): Barry 3 (1 pen), Carew 2, Delfouneso 2, Laursen 2, Agbonlahor 1, Gardner 1, Harewood 1, Petrov 1, Reo-Coker 1, Young A 1.
Inter-Toto Cup (3): Carew 1, Laursen 1, Young A 1.
Ground: Villa Park, Trinity Road, Birmingham B6 6HE. Telephone (0121) 327 2299.
Record Attendance: 76,588 v Derby Co, FA Cup 6th rd, 2 March 1946.
Capacity: 42,573.
Manager: Martin O'Neill.
Secretary: Sharon Barnhurst.
Most League Goals: 128, Division 1, 1930–31.
Highest League Scorer in Season: 'Pongo' Waring, 49, Division 1, 1930–31.
Most League Goals in Total Aggregate: Harry Hampton, 215, 1904–15.
Most Capped Player: Steve Staunton 64 (102), Republic of Ireland.
Most League Appearances: Charlie Aitken, 561, 1961–76.
Honours – Football League: Division 1 Champions – 1893–94, 1895–96, 1896–97, 1898–99, 1899–1900, 1909–10, 1980–81. Division 2 Champions – 1937–38, 1959–60. Division 3 Champions – 1971–72. **FA Cup:** Winners – 1887, 1895, 1897, 1905, 1913, 1920, 1957. **Football League Cup:** Winners – 1961, 1975, 1977, 1994, 1996. **European Competitions: European Cup:** Winners – 1981–82. **European Super Cup:** Winners – 1982–83. **Intertoto Cup:** Winners – 2001, 2008.
Colours: Claret body, blue sleeve shirts, white shorts, sky blue stockings.

BARNET   FL CHAMPIONSHIP 2

Adomah Albert (F)	6 1	11 08	Harrow	13 12 87	Harrow Borough
Akurang Cliff (F)	6 2	12 03	Histon	27 2 81	
Beckwith Rob (G)	6 1	13 12	Hackney	12 9 84	Luton T
Birchall Adam (F)	5 6	10 09	Maidstone	2 12 84	Mansfield T
Bishop Neil (M)	6 1	12 10	Stockton	7 8 81	York C
Breen Gary (D)	6 3	13 03	Hendon	12 12 73	Wolverhampton W
Carew Ashley (M)	6 0	11 00	Lambeth	17 12 85	
Charles Elliott (F)	6 2	13 00	Barnet	23 12 90	Scholar
Devera Joe (D)	6 2	12 00	Southgate	6 2 87	Scholar
Deverdics Nicky (M)	5 11	12 04	Gateshead	24 11 87	Gretna
Gillet Kenny (M)	5 10	12 04	Bordeaux	3 1 86	
Harrison Lee (G)	6 2	11 13	Billericay	12 9 71	Peterborough U
Hart Danny (M)	5 10	11 09	London	26 4 89	
Hendon Ian (D)	6 1	13 05	Ilford	5 12 71	Peterborough U
Hendon Ian (D)	6 1	13 02	Ilford	5 12 71	Peterborough U
Hughes Mark (M)	5 10	12 05	Dungannon	16 9 83	Chester C
Leary Michael (M)	6 0	11 11	Ealing	17 4 83	Luton T
Medley Luke (F)	6 1	13 03	Greenwich	21 6 89	Bradford C
O'Flynn John (F)	5 11	11 11	Cobh	11 7 82	
Porter Max (M)	5 10	12 04	London	29 6 87	Bishop's Stortford
St Aimie Kieron (M)	6 1	13 00	Brent	4 5 89	QPR
Tabiri Joe (M)	5 9	11 09	London	16 10 89	
Yakubu Ishmail (D)	6 1	12 09	Nigeria	8 4 85	Scholar

League Appearances: Adomah, A. 45; Akurang, C. 12(12); Beckwith, R. 5; Birchall, A. 19(20); Bishop, N. 41(3); Black, T. 5; Bolasie, Y. 17(3); Breen, G. 22; Burge, R. 1(1); Carew, A. 10; Charles, E. (5); Cole, J. 10; De Magalhaes, J. 4; Devera, J. 33(1); Deverdics, N. 22(7); Furlong, P. 21; Gillet, K. 28(4); Harrison, L. 20(1); Hart, D. 2(1); Hughes, M. 8(1); Kadoch, R. 11(1); Leary, M. 24(4);

24

Lockwood, M. 12; Medley, L. 5(13); Mitchell, P. 3; Nicolau, N. 12(9); O'Flynn, J. 32(2); Ogogo, A. 7(2); Porter, M. 18(8); St Aimie, K. 1(2); Tabiri, J. 4(3); Thomas, A. 2; Townsend, M. 13; Yakubu, I. 37(1).
Goals – League (56): O'Flynn 17 (3 pens), Adomah 9, Furlong 9, Akurang 3, Bolasie 3, Yakubu 3, Birchall 2, Leary 2, Bishop 1, Carew 1, Devera 1, Deverdics 1, Hart 1, Medley 1, Nicolau 1, Ogogo 1.
Carling Cup (0).
FA Cup (3): Adomah 1, O'Flynn 1, Yakubu 1.
J Paint Trophy (2): Birchall 2.
Ground: Underhill Stadium, Barnet Lane, Barnet, Herts EN5 2DN. Telephone 0208 441 6932.
Record Attendance: 11,026 v Wycombe Wanderers, FA Amateur Cup 4th Round 1951–52. **Capacity:** 5,345.
Manager: Ian Hendon.
Secretary: Andrew Adie.
Most League Goals: 81, Division 4, 1991–92
Highest League Scorer in Season: Dougie Freedman, 24, Division 3, 1994–95.
Most League Goals in Total Aggregate: Sean Devine, 47, 1995–99.
Most Capped Player: Ken Charlery, 4, St. Lucia.
Most League Appearances: Paul Wilson, 263, 1991–2000.
Honours – Football League: GMVC: Winners – 1990–91. **Football Conference:** Winners – 2004–05. **FA Amateur Cup:** Winners 1945–46.
Colours: All black with amber trim.

BARNSLEY   FL CHAMPIONSHIP

Anderson (M)	6 2	12 11	Sao Paulo	29	8 82	Everton
Bogdanovic Daniel (F)	6 2	11 02	Misurata	26	3 80	Lokomotiv Sofia
Butterfield Jacob (D)	5 10	11 00	Manchester	10	6 90	Scholar
Campbell-Ryce Jamal (M)	5 7	12 03	Lambeth	6	4 83	Southend U
Colace Roberto (M)	5 10	11 07	Buenos Aires	6	1 84	Newells Old Boys
Coulson Michael (M)	5 10	10 00	Scarborough	29	4 87	Scarborough
Devaney Martin (M)	5 11	12 00	Cheltenham	1	6 80	Watford
El Haimour Mounir (M)	5 9	10 03	Limoges	22	1 80	Neuchatel Xamax
Foster Stephen (D)	6 0	11 05	Warrington	10	9 80	Burnley
Hassell Bobby (D)	5 10	12 00	Derby	4	6 80	Mansfield T
Heslop Simon (M)	5 11	11 00	York	1	5 87	Scholar
Hume Iain (F)	5 7	11 02	Brampton	31	10 83	Leicester C
Kozluk Rob (D)	5 8	10 02	Mansfield	5	8 77	Sheffield U
Macken Jon (F)	5 11	12 04	Manchester	7	9 77	Derby Co
Moore Darren (D)	6 2	15 07	Birmingham	22	4 74	Derby Co
Muller Heinz (G)	6 4	15 04	Frankfurt-on-Main	30	5 78	Lillestrom
Odejayi Kayode (F)	6 2	12 02	Ibadon	21	2 82	Cheltenham T
Potter Luke (D)	6 2	12 07	Barnsley	13	7 89	Scholar
Steele Luke (G)	6 2	12 00	Peterborough	24	9 84	WBA

League Appearances: Anderson, 33; Bogdanovic, D. 13(3); Butterfield, J. (3); Campbell-Ryce, J. 39(1); Colace, R. 30(4); Coulson, M. (2); Cureton, J. 7(1); Devaney, M. 16(10); El Haimour, M. 8(8); Foster, S. 38; Hammill, A. 9(5); Hassell, B. 34(6); Howard, B. 7; Hume, I. 15; Kozluk, R. 36(1); Leon, D. 15(4); Macken, J. 37(8); Mifsud, M. 11(4); Moore, D. 37(1); Mostto, M. 2(7); Muller, H. 36; Noble-Lazarus, R. (2); Odejayi, K. 7(21); Rigters, M. 4(15); Souza, D. 32(1); Steele, L. 10; Teale, G. 2(1); Teimourian, A. 10(1); Van Homoet, M. 14(3); Whaley, S. 4.
Goals – League (45): Campbell-Ryce 9 (3 pens), Macken 9, Bogdanovic 5 (1 pen), Hume 4, Foster 3, Anderson 2, Cureton 2, Mifsud 2, Hammill 1, Howard 1, Leon 1, Moore 1, Mostto 1, Odejayi 1, Whaley 1, own goals 2.
Carling Cup (0).
FA Cup (0).

Ground: Oakwell Stadium, Grove St, Barnsley, South Yorkshire S71 1ET. Telephone (01226) 211 211.
Record Attendance: 40,255 v Stoke C, FA Cup 5th rd, 15 February 1936. **Capacity:** 23,186.
Manager: Simon Davey.
Secretary: Albert Donald Rowing.
Most League Goals: 118, Division 3 (N), 1933–34.
Highest League Scorer in Season: Cecil McCormack, 33, Division 2, 1950–51.
Most League Goals in Total Aggregate: Ernest Hine, 123, 1921–26 and 1934–38.
Most Capped Player: Gerry Taggart, 35 (50), Northern Ireland.
Most League Appearances: Barry Murphy, 514, 1962–78.
Honours – Football League: Division 3 (N) Champions – 1933–34, 1938–39, 1954–55. **FA Cup:** Winners – 1912.
Colours: Red shirts with white trim, white shorts, red stockings.

BIRMINGHAM CITY   FA PREMIERSHIP

Name		Height		Birthplace	Age		Previous Club
Bent Marcus (F)	6 2	13 03	Hammersmith	19	5 78	Charlton Ath
Carr Stephen (D)	5 9	11 13	Dublin	29	8 76	Newcastle U
Carsley Lee (M)	5 10	12 04	Birmingham	28	2 74	Everton
Doyle Colin (G)	6 5	14 05	Cork	12	8 85	Scholar
Fahey Keith (M)	5 10	12 07	Dublin	15	1 83	Aston Villa
Jerome Cameron (F)	6 1	13 06	Huddersfield	14	8 86	Cardiff C
Johnson Damien (M)	5 9	11 09	Lisburn	18	11 78	Blackburn R
Joyce David (D)	5 10	12 13	County Mayo	8	8 90	Scholar
Larsson Sebastian (M)	5 10	11 00	Eskilstuna	6	6 85	Arsenal
McFadden James (M)	6 0	12 11	Glasgow	14	4 83	Everton
McPike James (F)	5 10	11 02	Birmingham	4	10 88	Scholar
McSheffrey Gary (M)	5 8	10 06	Coventry	13	8 82	Coventry C
Murphy David (D)	6 1	12 03	Hartlepool	1	3 84	Hibernian
Mutch Jordon (M)	5 9	10 03	Birmingham	2	12 91	Derby Co
O'Connor Garry (F)	6 1	12 02	Edinburgh	7	5 83	
Parnaby Stuart (M)	5 11	11 00	Durham	19	7 82	Middlesbrough
Pearce Krystian (D)	6 1	13 05	Birmingham	5	1 90	Scholar
Phillips Kevin (F)	5 7	11 00	Hitchin	25	7 73	WBA
Queudrue Franck (D)	6 1	12 01	Paris	27	8 78	Fulham
Ridgewell Liam (D)	5 10	10 03	Bexley	21	7 84	Aston Villa
Shroot Robin (M)	5 9	11 05	London	26	3 88	Harrow Borough
Taylor Maik (G)	6 4	14 02	Hildeshein	4	9 71	Fulham
Taylor Martin (D)	6 4	15 00	Ashington	9	11 79	Blackburn R
Wilson Jared (D)	5 8	10 10	Cheltenham	24	11 89	Scholar

League Appearances: Agustien, K. 13(5); Bent, M. 16(17); Bouazza, H. 9(7); Bowyer, L. 17; Carr, S. 13; Carsley, L. 41; Costly, C. 3(5); De la Cruz, U. (1); Doyle, C. 1(1); Fahey, K. 15(4); Hunt, N. 9(2); Jaidi, R. 30; Jerome, C. 25(18); Johnson, D. 8(1); Kelly, S. 2(3); Larsson, S. 35(3); McFadden, J. 22(8); McSheffrey, G. 3(3); Murphy, D. 28(2); Nafti, M. 6(5); O'Connor, G. 10(6); Owusu-Abeyie, Q. 12(7); Parnaby, S. 19(2); Phillips, K. 24(12); Quashie, N. 8(2); Queudrue, F. 23(2); Ridgewell, L. 36; Sinclair, S. 8(6); Martin Taylor, 23(1); Maik Taylor, 45; Traore, D. 2(1); Wilson, J. (1).
Goals – League (54): Phillips 14, Jerome 9, O'Connor 6, Fahey 4, McFadden 4 (1 pen), Bent 3, Queudrue 3, Carsley 2, Owusu-Abeyie 2, Bouazza 1, Bowyer 1, Larsson 1, Ridgewell 1, Martin Taylor 1, own goals 2.
Carling Cup (4): Jerome 1, Nafti 1, O'Connor 1, Owusu-Abeyie 1.
FA Cup (0).
Ground: St Andrews Stadium, Birmingham B9 4NH. Telephone (0844) 557 1875.
Record Attendance: 66,844 v Everton, FA Cup 5th rd, 11 February 1939.
Capacity: 30,079.
Manager: Alex McLeish.

Secretary: Julia Shelton.
Most League Goals: 103, Division 2, 1893–94 (only 28 games).
Highest League Scorer in Season: Joe Bradford, 29, Division 1, 1927–28.
Most League Goals in Total Aggregate: Joe Bradford, 249, 1920–35.
Most Capped Player: Kenny Cunningham, 32 (72), Republic of Ireland.
Most League Appearances: Frank Womack, 491, 1908–28.
Honours – Football League: Division 2 Champions – 1892–93, 1920–21, 1947–48, 1954–55, 1994–95. **Football League Cup:** Winners – 1963. **Leyland Daf Cup:** Winners – 1991. **Auto Windscreens Shield:** Winners – 1995.
Colours: Blue shirts with white trim, blue shorts, white stockings.

BLACKBURN ROVERS   FA PREMIERSHIP

Andrews Keith (M)	6 0	12 04	Dublin	13 9 80	Milton Keynes D
Blackman Nick (F)	6 2	11 00	Whitefield	11 11 89	Macclesfield T
Brown Jason (G)	5 11	13 03	Southwark	18 5 82	Gillingham
Bunn Mark (G)	6 0	12 02	Camden	16 11 84	Northampton T
Bussmann Bjorn (G)	6 0	12 00	Germany	18 3 91	Scholar
Derbyshire Matt (F)	5 10	11 01	Gt Harwood	14 4 86	Great Harwood T
Diouf El Hadji (F)	5 11	11 11	Dakar	15 1 81	Sunderland
Doran Aaron (M)	5 7	12 00	Ireland	13 5 91	Scholar
Dunn David (M)	5 9	12 03	Gt Harwood	27 12 79	Birmingham C
Emerton Brett (M)	6 1	13 05	Bankstown	22 2 79	Feyenoord
Fielding Frank (G)	5 11	12 00	Blackburn	4 4 88	Scholar
Flynn Jonathan (D)	5 8	11 00		18 11 89	
Gallagher Paul (F)	6 1	12 00	Glasgow	9 8 84	Trainee
Grella Vince (M)	6 0	12 06	Melbourne	5 10 79	Torino
Gunning Gavin (D)			Dublin	26 1 91	Scholar
Hanley Grant (D)				20 11 91	Scholar
Haworth Andrew (M)	5 11	11 10	Lancaster	28 11 88	Scholar
Judge Alan (F)	6 0	13 09	Dublin	11 11 88	
Khizanishvili Zurab (D)	6 1	12 08	Tbilisi	6 10 81	Rangers
Marshall Marcus (F)	5 10	11 06	Hammersmith	7 10 89	
McCarthy Benny (F)	6 0	12 08	Cape Town	12 11 77	Porto
Morrissey Gearoid (M)				17 11 91	Scholar
Nelsen Ryan (D)	5 11	14 02	New Zealand	18 10 77	DC United
Olsson Martin (D)	5 7	11 00	Sweden	17 5 88	Hogaborg
Pedersen Morten (F)	5 11	11 00	Vadso	8 9 81	Tromso
Potts Michael (F)				26 11 91	Scholar
Reid Steven (M)	6 0	12 07	Kingston	10 3 81	Millwall
Rigters Maceo (F)	5 10	14 07	Amsterdam	22 1 84	NAC Breda
Roberts Jason (F)	6 1	13 06	Park Royal	25 1 78	Wigan Ath
Robinson Paul (G)	6 1	14 07	Beverley	15 10 79	Tottenham H
Samba Christopher (D)	6 5	13 03	Creteil	28 3 84	Hertha Berlin
Santa Cruz Julio (F)	6 0	12 04	Asuncion	12 5 90	Cerro Porteno
Santa Cruz Roque (F)	6 2	13 12	Asuncion	16 8 81	Bayern Munich
Treacy Keith (M)	5 11	11 11	Dublin	13 9 88	Scholar
Warnock Stephen (D)	5 7	11 09	Ormskirk	12 12 81	Liverpool

League Appearances: Andrews, K. 27(6); Brown, J. 3(1); Derbyshire, M. 5(12); Diouf, E. 13(1); Doran, A. (3); Dunn, D. 7(8); Emerton, B. 19(1); Fowler, R. 1(2); Givet, G. 14; Grella, V. 15(2); Khizanishvili, Z. 3(2); McCarthy, B. 18(10); Mokoena, A. 9(9); Nelsen, R. 35; Olsson, M. 6(3); Ooijer, A. 30(2); Pedersen, M. 32(1); Reid, S. 4; Roberts, J. 20(6); Robinson, P. 35; Samba, C. 35; Santa Cruz, R. 17(3); Simpson, D. 10(2); Treacy, K. 2(10); Tugay, K. 15(14); Villanueva, C. 6(7); Vogel, J. (1); Warnock, S. 37.
Goals – League (40): McCarthy 10 (4 pens), Roberts 7, Andrews 4, Santa Cruz 4, Warnock 3, Derbyshire 2, Ooijer 2, Samba 2, Diouf 1, Dunn 1, Emerton 1, Nelsen 1, Pedersen 1, Tugay 1.

Carling Cup (10): Derbyshire 3, McCarthy 2, Emerton 1, Olsson 1, Santa Cruz 1, Villaneuva 1, own goal 1.
FA Cup (5): McCarthy 1, Mokoena 1, Samba 1, Santa Cruz 1, Villaneuva 1.
Ground: Ewood Park, Blackburn, Lancashire BB2 4JF. Telephone (0871) 702 1875.
Record Attendance: 62,522 v Bolton W, FA Cup 6th rd, 2 March 1929. **Capacity:** 31,367.
Manager: Sam Allardyce.
Secretary: Andrew Pincher.
Most League Goals: 114, Division 2, 1954–55.
Highest League Scorer in Season: Ted Harper, 43, Division 1, 1925–26.
Most League Goals in Total Aggregate: Simon Garner, 168, 1978–92.
Most Capped Player: Henning Berg, 58 (100), Norway.
Most League Appearances: Derek Fazackerley, 596, 1970–86.
Honours – FA Premier League: Champions – 1994–95. **Football League:** Division 1 Champions – 1911–12, 1913–14. Division 2 Champions – 1938–39. Division 3 Champions – 1974–75. **FA Cup:** Winners – 1884, 1885, 1886, 1890, 1891, 1928.
Football League Cup: Winners – 2002. **Full Members' Cup:** Winners – 1986–87.
Colours: Blue and white halved shirts, white shorts, white stockings.

BLACKPOOL   FL CHAMPIONSHIP

Adam Charlie (M)	6 1	12 00	Dundee	10 12 85	Rangers
Barker Shaun (D)	6 2	12 08	Nottingham	19 9 82	Rotherham U
Burgess Ben (F)	6 3	14 04	Buxton	9 11 81	Hull C
Coid Danny (D)	5 11	11 07	Liverpool	3 10 81	Trainee
Crainey Stephen (D)	5 9	10 06	Glasgow	22 6 81	Leeds U
Edwards Rob (D)	6 1	11 10	Telford	25 12 82	Wolverhampton W
Evatt Ian (D)	6 3	13 12	Coventry	19 11 81	QPR
Gilks Matthew (G)	6 3	13 12	Rochdale	4 6 82	Norwich C
John-Baptiste Alex (D)	6 0	11 11	Sutton-in-Ashfield	31 1 86	Mansfield T
Martin Joe (M)	6 0	12 13	Dagenham	29 11 88	Tottenham H
McPhee Stephen (F)	5 7	11 05	Glasgow	5 6 81	Hull C
Mitchley Danny (F)	5 10	10 08	Liverpool	7 10 89	Scholar
Nardiello Daniel (F)	5 11	11 04	Coventry	22 10 82	QPR
Ormerod Brett (F)	5 11	11 12	Blackburn	18 10 76	Preston NE
Rachubka Paul (G)	6 2	13 04	California	21 5 81	Huddersfield T
Southern Keith (M)	5 10	12 06	Gateshead	24 4 81	Everton
Taylor-Fletcher Gary (F)	5 11	12 06	Liverpool	4 6 81	Huddersfield T
Vaughan David (M)	5 7	11 00	Rhuddlan	18 2 83	Real Sociedad

League Appearances: Adam, C. 13; Aluko, S. (1); Barker, S. 42(1); Blackman, N. 2(3); Broomes, M. (1); Burgess, B. 25(4); Camara, M. 14; Campbell, D. 20; Coid, D. 13(5); Crainey, S. 15(2); Dickinson, L. 5(2); Edwards, R. 35(1); Evatt, I. 33; Fox, D. 15(7); Gilks, M. 4(1); Gow, A. 10(7); Hammill, A. 14(8); Harte, I. 4; Hendrie, L. 5(1); Hughes, L. 2(1); John-Baptiste, A. 21; Jorgensen, C. 21(11); Kabba, S. 12(5); Mahon, A. 1; Marshall, P. 1(1); Martin, J. 10(5); McPhee, S. (5); Mitchley, D. (2); Nardiello, D. (2); Nemeth, K. (1); O'Donovan, R. 11(1); Ormerod, B. 7(8); Owens, G. 1(7); Rachubka, P. 42; Rehman, Z. (3); Reid, K. 7; Small, W. 4(1); Southern, K. 34(1); Taylor-Fletcher, G. 34(4); Vaughan, D. 26(7); Walton, S. (1); Wright, J. 3.
Goals – League (47): Campbell 9 (3 pens), Burgess 6 (2 pens), Gow 5 (1 pen), Taylor-Fletcher 5, Dickinson 4, Southern 3, Adam 2, Edwards 2, Kabba 2, Ormerod 2, Blackman 1, Evatt 1, Hammill 1, Hughes 1, John-Baptiste 1, Small 1, Vaughan 1.
Carling Cup (0).
FA Cup (0).
Ground: Bloomfield Road, Seasiders Way, Blackpool FY1 6JJ. Telephone (0871) 221 953.
Record Attendance: 38,098 v Wolverhampton W, Division 1, 17 September 1955.
Capacity: 9,491.

Manager: Ian Holloway.
Secretary: Matt Williams.
Most League Goals: 98, Division 2, 1929–30.
Highest League Scorer in Season: Jimmy Hampson, 45, Division 2, 1929–30.
Most League Goals in Total Aggregate: Jimmy Hampson, 246, 1927–38.
Most Capped Player: Jimmy Armfield, 43, England.
Most League Appearances: Jimmy Armfield, 568, 1952–71.
Honours – Football League: Division 2 Champions – 1929–30. **FA Cup:** Winners –
1953. **Anglo-Italian Cup:** Winners – 1971. **LDV Vans Trophy:** Winners – 2002, 2004.
Colours: Tangerine shirts with white trim, white shorts, tangerine stockings with
white tops.

BOLTON WANDERERS   FA PREMIERSHIP

Al-Habsi Ali (G)	6 4	12 06	Oman	30 12 81	Lyn
Basham Chris (M)	5 11	12 08	Stafford	20 7 88	Scholar
Bogdan Adam (G)	6 4	14 02	Budapest	27 9 87	
Cahill Gary (D)	6 2	12 06	Dronfield	19 12 85	Aston Villa
Cohen Tamir (M)	5 11	11 09	Israel	4 3 84	Maccabi Netanya
Davies Kevin (F)	6 0	12 10	Sheffield	26 3 77	Southampton
Davies Mark (M)	5 11	11 08	Wolverhampton	18 2 88	Wolverhampton W
Dzemaili Blerim (M)	5 10	11 07	Tetovo	12 4 86	Zurich
Elmander Johan (F)	6 1	11 13	Alingsas	27 5 81	Toulouse
Gardner Ricardo (D)	5 9	11 00	St Andrews	25 9 78	Harbour View
Harsanyi Zoltan (D)	6 1	12 00	Bratislava	1 6 87	Senec
Hunt Nicky (D)	6 1	13 08	Westhoughton	3 9 83	Scholar
Jaaskelainen Jussi (G)	6 3	12 10	Mikkeli	19 4 75	VPS
McCann Gavin (M)	5 11	11 00	Blackpool	10 1 78	Aston Villa
Muamba Fabrice (M)	6 1	11 10	Kinshasa	6 4 88	Birmingham C
Mustapha Riga (F)	5 10	11 00	Accra	10 10 81	Levante
O'Brien Andy (D)	6 2	11 13	Harrogate	29 6 79	Portsmouth
O'Brien Joey (M)	6 0	10 13	Dublin	17 2 86	Scholar
Obadeyi Temitope (F)	5 10	11 09	Coventry	29 10 89	Scholar
Samuel JLloyd (D)	5 11	11 04	Trinidad	29 3 81	Aston Villa
Shittu Dan (D)	6 2	16 03	Lagos	2 9 80	Watford
Steinsson Gretar (D)	6 2	12 04	Siglufjordur	9 1 82	AZ
Taylor Matthew (D)	5 11	12 03	Oxford	27 11 81	Portsmouth
Vaz Te Ricardo (F)	6 2	12 07	Lisbon	1 10 86	Scholar

League Appearances: Basham, C. 4(7); Cahill, G. 33; Cohen, T. 3(1); Davies, K.
37(1); Davies, M. 8(2); Elmander, J. 30; Gardner, R. 18(11); Helguson, H. (1);
Jaaskelainen, J. 38; Makukula, A. 4(2); McCann, G. 30(3); Muamba, F. 33(5);
Mustapha, R. 2(15); Nolan, K. 20; O'Brien, A. 30(4); O'Brien, J. 5(2); Obadeyi, T.
(3); Puygrenier, S. 5(2); Samuel, J. 38; Shittu, D. 9(1); Smolarek, E. 1(11); Steins-
son, G. 37; Taylor, M. 33(1); Vaz Te, R. (2).
Goals – League (41): Davies K 11, Taylor 10, Elmander 5, Gardner 4, Cahill 3,
Steinsson 3, Basham 1, Cohen 1, O'Brien A 1, Puygrenier 1, own goal 1.
Carling Cup (1): Nolan 1.
FA Cup (1): Smolarek 1.
Ground: The Reebok Stadium, Burnden Way, Lostock, Bolton, Lancashire BL6
6JW. Telephone Bolton (0844) 871 2932.
Record Attendance: 69,912 v Manchester C, FA Cup 5th rd, 18 February 1933.
Capacity: 28,101.
Manager: Gary Megson.
Secretary: Simon Marland.
Most League Goals: 100, Division 1, 1996–97.
Highest League Scorer in Season: Joe Smith, 38, Division 1, 1920–21.
Most League Goals in Total Aggregate: Nat Lofthouse, 255, 1946–61.
Most Capped Player: Mark Fish, 34 (62), South Africa.

29

Most League Appearances: Eddie Hopkinson, 519, 1956–70.
Honours – Football League: Division 1 Champions – 1996–97. Division 2 Champions – 1908–09, 1977–78. Division 3 Champions – 1972–73. **FA Cup:** Winners – 1923, 1926, 1929, 1958. **Sherpa Van Trophy:** Winners – 1989.
Colours: White shirts with blue shoulder trim, blue shorts, white stockings.

AFC BOURNEMOUTH   FL CHAMPIONSHIP 2

Player						
Anderton Darren (M)	6 2	13 04	Southampton	3	3 72	Wolverhampton W
Bartley Marvyn (M)	6 1	12 04	Reading	4	7 86	Hampton & Richmond B
Bradbury Lee (F)	6 0	12 07	Isle of Wight	3	7 75	Southend U
Connell Alan (F)	6 0	12 00	Enfield	5	2 83	Brentford
Cooper Shaun (D)	5 10	10 05	Newport (IW)	5	10 83	Portsmouth
Cummings Warren (D)	5 9	11 08	Aberdeen	15	10 80	Chelsea
Feeney Liam (M)	5 10	12 02	Hammersmith	24	1 87	Salisbury C
Fletcher Steve (F)	6 2	14 09	Hartlepool	26	7 72	Crawley T
Garry Ryan (D)	6 0	11 05	Hornchurch	29	9 83	Arsenal
Goulding Jeff (F)	6 2	11 11	Sutton	13	5 84	Fisher Ath
Guyett Scott (D)	6 2	13 06	Ascot	20	1 76	Yeovil T
Hollands Danny (M)	6 0	12 00	Ashford	6	11 85	Chelsea
Igoe Sammy (M)	5 6	10 00	Staines	30	9 75	Bristol R
Jalal Shwan (G)	6 2	14 02	Baghdad	14	8 83	Peterborough U
McQuoid Josh (M)	5 9	10 10	Southampton	15	12 89	Scholar
Molesley Mark (M)	6 1	12 07	Hillingdon	11	3 81	Grays Ath
Partington Joe (M)	5 11	11 13	Portsmouth	1	4 90	Scholar
Pearce Jason (D)	5 11	12 00	Hampshire	6	12 87	Portsmouth
Pitman Brett (M)	6 0	11 00	Jersey	31	1 88	St Paul's, Jersey
Pryce Ryan (G)	6 0	11 09	Bournemouth	20	9 89	Scholar
Robinson Anton (M)	5 9	10 03	Harrow	17	2 86	Weymouth
Tindall Jason (M)	6 1	11 09	Stepney	15	11 77	Weymouth

League Appearances: Anderton, D. 17(1); Bartley, M. 27(6); Bradbury, L. 28(6); Button, D. 4; Connell, A. 6(6); Cooper, S. 35(2); Cummings, W. 27(5); Feeney, L. 6(8); Fletcher, S. 19(2); Garry, R. 21(4); Goulding, J. 14(13); Guyett, S. 21(4); Hollands, D. 39(3); Igoe, S. 22(6); Jalal, S. 41; Lindfield, C. 1(2); McQuoid, J. 5(11); Molesley, M. 22(7); Osei-Kuffour, J. 2; Partington, J. 6(5); Pearce, J. 44; Pettefer, C. 1(1); Pitman, B. 29(10); Preston, C. 2; Pryce, R. 1; Rankine, M. 3; Robinson, A. 16(1); Sappleton, R. 1(2); Sturrock, B. 1(3); Symes, M. 3(2); Thomson, J. 6; Tindall, J. (2); Tubbs, M. 6(2); Wagstaff, S. 3(2); Ward, J. 16(5); Webb, G. (1); Wiggins, R. 12(1).
Goals – League (59): Pitman 17 (2 pens), Bradbury 6 (1 pen), Hollands 6, Fletcher 4, Molesley 4, Pearce 4, Feeney 3, Goulding 3, Pearce 2, Bartley 1, Igoe 1, Lindfield 1, Partington 1, Robinson 1, Sappleton 1, Thomson 1, Tubbs 1, Ward 1, own goals 2.
Carling Cup (1): Osei-Kuffour 1.
FA Cup (1): Pearce 1.
J Paint Trophy (4): Anderton 1, Goulding 1, Hollands 1, Igoe 1.
Ground: Dean Court, Kings Park, Bournemouth BH7 7AF. Telephone (01202) 726 300.
Record Attendance: 28,799 v Manchester U, FA Cup 6th rd, 2 March 1957.
Capacity: 10,375 (with temporary stand) 9,776 (without).
Manager: Eddie Howe.
Secretary: Neil Vacher (Football Administrator).
Most League Goals: 88, Division 3 (S), 1956–57.
Highest League Scorer in Season: Ted MacDougall, 42, 1970–71.
Most League Goals in Total Aggregate: Ron Eyre, 202, 1924–33.
Most Capped Player: Gerry Peyton, 7 (33), Republic of Ireland.
Most League Appearances: Steve Fletcher, 514, 1992–2007; 2008–09.

Honours – Football League: Division 3 Champions – 1986–87. **Associate Members' Cup:** Winners – 1984.
Colours: Red shirts with black trim, black shorts, black stockings.

BRADFORD CITY　　　　　　FL CHAMPIONSHIP 2

Ainge Simon (D)	6 1	12 02	Bradford	18	2 88	Scholar
Arnison Paul (D)	5 10	10 12	Hartlepool	18	9 77	Carlisle U
Boulding Mick (F)	5 10	11 05	Sheffield	8	2 76	Mansfield T
Boulding Rory (F)	6 0	12 02	Sheffield	21	7 88	Mansfield T
Bower Mark (D)	5 10	11 00	Bradford	23	1 80	Trainee
Brandon Chris (M)	5 8	10 00	Bradford	7	4 76	Huddersfield T
Bullock Lee (M)	6 0	11 04	Stockton	22	5 81	Hartlepool U
Clarke Matthew (D)	6 3	12 07	Leeds	18	12 80	Darlington
Colbeck Joe (M)	5 10	10 12	Bradford	29	11 86	Scholar
Conlon Barry (F)	6 3	14 00	Drogheda	1	10 78	Mansfield T
Convey Matthew (G)	6 1	11 12	Oman	5	11 89	Scholar
Daley Omar (M)	5 7	10 03	Jamaica	25	4 81	Charleston Battery
Furman Dean (M)	6 0	11 08	Cape Town	22	6 88	Rangers
Heckingbottom Paul (D)	6 0	13 01	Barnsley	17	7 77	Barnsley
Lee Graeme (D)	6 2	13 07	Middlesbrough	31	5 78	Doncaster R
McLaren Paul (M)	6 0	13 04	High Wycombe	17	11 76	Tranmere R
McLaughlin Jon (G)	6 2	13 00	Edinburgh	9	9 87	Harrogate Railway
Nix Kyle (F)	5 6	9 10	Sydney	21	1 86	Sheffield U
O'Brien Luke (D)	5 9	12 01	Halifax	11	9 88	Scholar
Osborne Leon (F)	5 10	10 10	Doncaster	28	10 89	Scholar
Sharry Luke (M)	5 10	12 12	Leeds	9	3 90	Scholar
Taylforth Sean (F)	5 11	10 03	Chester	10	3 89	Scholar
Thorne Peter (F)	6 1	13 13	Manchester	21	6 73	Norwich C
Topp Willy (F)	5 9	11 04	Temuco	4	3 86	Universitario
Wetherall David (D)	6 3	13 12	Sheffield	14	3 71	Leeds U

League Appearances: Ainge, S. 1; Arnison, P. 25(2); Boulding, M. 35(9); Boulding, R. 1; Bower, M. (3); Brandon, C. 4(3); Bullock, L. 15(8); Clarke, M. 42; Clarke, T. 4(2); Colbeck, J. 19(9); Conlon, B. 15(15); Daley, O. 26(2); Evans, R. 45; Furman, D. 26(6); Gillespie, K. 2(1); Heckingbottom, P. 9; Jones, S. 25(2); Law, N. 30(3); Lee, G. 44; McLaren, P. 32(2); McLaughlin, J. 1; Moncur, T. 11(3); Mullin, P. 5(1); Nix, K. 6(10); O'Brien, L. 34(1); O'Grady, C. (2); Osborne, L. 1(1); Rehman, Z. 16(1); Sharry, L. (1); Thorne, P. 32(5); Topp, W. (2).
Goals – League (66): Thorne 17, Boulding M 12, Conlon 10 (3 pens), Furman 4, Bullock 3, Daley 3, Jones 3, Law 3, McLaren 3, Clarke M 2, Colbeck 2, Lee 2, O'Brien 1, own goal 1.
Carling Cup (0).
FA Cup (3): Boulding M 1, Daley 1, Lee 1.
J Paint Trophy (1): Conlon 1.
Ground: Cral Window Stadium, Valley Parade, Bradford BD8 7DY. Telephone 01274 773 335.
Record Attendance: 39,146 v Burnley, FA Cup 4th rd, 11 March 1911. **Capacity:** 25,136.
Manager: Stuart McCall.
Secretary: Jon Pollard.
Most League Goals: 128, Division 3 (N), 1928–29.
Highest League Scorer in Season: David Layne, 34, Division 4, 1961–62.
Most League Goals in Total Aggregate: Bobby Campbell, 121, 1981–84, 1984–86.
Most Capped Player: Jamie Lawrence, (42), Jamaica.
Most League Appearances: Cec Podd, 502, 1970–84.
Honours – Football League: Division 2 Champions – 1907–08. Division 3 Champions – 1984–85. Division 3 (N) Champions – 1928–29. **FA Cup:** Winners – 1911.

Colours: Claret and amber striped shirts with claret sleeves, black shorts, black stockings.

BRENTFORD FL CHAMPIONSHIP 1

Ademola Moses (F)	5 6	10 08	Croydon	18 2 89	Croydon Ath
Bean Marcus (M)	5 11	11 06	Hammersmith	2 11 84	Blackpool
Brown Simon (G)	6 2	15 00	Chelmsford	3 12 76	Colchester U
Charles Darius (M)	5 11	11 10	Ealing	10 12 87	Scholar
Dickson Ryan (M)	5 10	11 05	Saltash	14 12 86	Plymouth Arg
Elder Nathan (F)	6 1	13 12	Hornchurch	5 4 85	Brighton & HA
Hunt David (M)	5 11	11 09	Dulwich	10 9 82	Shrewsbury T
Ide Charlie (M)	5 8	10 06	Sunbury	10 5 88	Scholar
MacDonald Charlie (F)	5 8	12 10	Southwark	13 2 81	Southend U
Montague Ross (F)	6 0	12 11	Isleworth	1 11 88	Scholar
O'Connor Kevin (F)	5 11	12 00	Blackburn	24 2 82	Trainee
Osborne Karleigh (M)	6 2	12 08	Southall	19 3 88	Scholar
Pead Craig (M)	5 9	11 06	Bromsgrove	15 9 81	Walsall
Phillips Mark (D)	6 2	11 00	Lambeth	27 1 82	Millwall
Poole Glenn (M)	5 7	11 04	Essex	3 2 81	Rochdale
Powell Darren (D)	6 2	13 07	Hammersmith	10 3 76	Derby Co
Smith Gary (M)	5 8	10 09	Middlesbrough	30 1 84	Milton Keynes D
Williams Marvin (M)	5 11	11 06	London	12 8 87	Yeovil T
Wood Sam (M)	6 0	11 05	London	6 2 88	Bromley

League Appearances: Ademola, M. (8); Andersen, M. 1; Artus, F. (1); Bean, M. 43(1); Bennett, A. 44; Bowditch, D. 8(1); Brown, S. (1); Clarke, B. 8; Connell, A. 1(1); Dickson, R. 31(8); Elder, N. 18(9); Halls, J. 22(1); Hamer, B. 45; Hunt, D. 10(10); Johnson, B. 7(3); MacDonald, C. 38; Newton, A. 30(5); O'Connor, K. 25(3); Osborne, K. 19(4); Pead, C. 5(1); Phillips, M. 28(5); Poole, G. 18(8); Powell, D. 3(1); Rhodes, J. 14; Scannell, D. 1(1); Smith, G. 2(2); Spencer, D. 3(2); Williams, Marvin 21(13); Williams, S. 5(6); Wilson, J. 14; Wood, S. 37(3); Wright, J. 5.
Goals – League (65): MacDonald 16 (3 pens), Bean 9, Rhodes 7, Clarke 6 (1 pen), Elder 6, Poole 5 (2 pens), Osborne 4, Bowditch 2, Hunt 2, Williams S 2, Bennett 1, Dickson 1, Newton 1, Phillips 1, Spencer 1, Wood 1.
Carling Cup (0).
FA Cup (4): MacDonald 2, Elder 1, Marvin Williams 1.
J Paint Trophy (4): Poole 2 (1 pen), O'Connor 1, Marvin Williams 1.
Ground: Griffin Park, Braemar Road, Brentford, Middlesex TW8 0NT. Telephone (0845) 3456 442.
Record Attendance: 38,678 v Leicester C, FA Cup 6th rd, 26 February 1949.
Capacity: 12,400.
Manager: Andy Scott.
Secretary: Lisa Hall.
Most League Goals: 98, Division 4, 1962–63.
Highest League Scorer in Season: Jack Holliday, 38, Division 3 (S), 1932–33.
Most League Goals in Total Aggregate: Jim Towers, 153, 1954–61.
Most Capped Player: John Buttigieg, 22 (98), Malta.
Most League Appearances: Ken Coote, 514, 1949–64.
Honours – Football League: Championship 2 Winners – 2008–09. Division 2 Champions – 1934–35. Division 3 Champions – 1991–92, 1998–99. Division 3 (S) Champions – 1932–33. Division 4 Champions – 1962–63.
Colours: Red and white striped shirts with red sleeves, black shorts, black stockings.

BRIGHTON & HOVE ALBION FL CHAMPIONSHIP 1

Carole Sebastien (M)	5 7	11 05	Pontoise	8 9 72	Darlington
Cox Dean (M)	5 4	9 08	Haywards Heath	12 8 87	Scholar

Davies Craig (F)	6 2	13 05	Burton-on-Trent	9 1 86	Oldham Ath
Dixon Jonny (F)	5 9	11 01	Murcia	16 1 84	Aldershot T
El-Abd Adam (D)	5 10	13 05	Brighton	11 9 84	Scholar
Elphick Tommy (M)	5 11	11 07	Brighton	7 9 87	Scholar
Forster Nicky (F)	5 9	11 05	Caterham	8 9 73	Hull C
Hart Gary (F)	5 9	12 03	Harlow	21 9 76	Stansted
Hawkins Colin (D)	6 1	12 06	Galway	17 8 77	Coventry C
Jarrett Jason (M)	6 1	13 10	Bury	14 9 79	Preston NE
Kuipers Michels (G)	6 2	15 00	Amsterdam	26 6 74	Bristol R
Livermore David (M)	5 11	12 02	Edmonton	20 5 80	Hull C
Lynch Joel (D)	6 1	12 10	Eastbourne	3 10 87	Scholar
McLeod Kevin (M)	5 11	11 00	Liverpool	12 9 80	Colchester U
McNulty Jim (D)	6 1	12 00	Liverpool	13 2 85	Stockport co
Murray Glenn (F)	6 1	12 12	Maryport	25 9 83	Rochdale
Virgo Adam (D)	6 2	13 12	Brighton	25 1 83	Colchester U
Whing Andrew (D)	6 0	12 00	Birmingham	20 9 84	Coventry C

League Appearances: Andersen, M. 5; Andrew, C. 3(6); Anyinsah, J. 10(1); Bangura, A. 6; Birchall, C. 8(1); Borrowdale, G. 11(1); Carole, S. 5(7); Cook, S. (2); Cox, D. 32(8); Davies, C. 10(6); Dicker, G. 9; Dixon, J. (1); El-Abd, A. 25(6); Elphick, T. 38(1); Fleetwood, S. 5(6); Forster, N. 26(4); Fraser, T. 18(9); Hart, G. 7(4); Hawkins, C. 17; Heath, M. 6; Hinshelwood, A. 11(3); Jarrett, J. 11(2); Johnson, B. 10; Kuipers, M. 28; Livermore, D. 12(4); Loft, D. 7(5); Lynch, J. (2); Mayo, K. (2); McLeod, K. 11(10); McNulty, J. 5; Murray, G. 18(5); Owusu, L. 13(1); Richards, M. 23; Robinson, J. (5); Savage, R. 6; Sullivan, J. 13; Thomson, S. 17; Thornton, K. 4(8); Virgo, A. 36; Whing, A. 40.
Goals – League (55): Forster 12 (3 pens), Murray 11 (2 pens), Owusu 7, Cox 4, Johnson 4, Virgo 3, Andrew 2, Davies 1, Dicker 1, Elphick 1, Fleetwood 1, Fraser 1, Heath 1, Hinshelwood 1, McNulty 1, Richards 1, Robinson 1, own goals 2.
Carling Cup (7): Virgo 2, Anyinsah 1, Elphick 1, Forster 1, Murray 1, Richards 1.
FA Cup (4): Cox 1, Forster 1, Fraser 1, McLeod 1.
J Paint Trophy (6): Forster 2 (1 pen), Anyinsah 1, Livermore 1, McLeod 1, Virgo 1 (pen).
Ground: Withdean Stadium, Tongdean Lane, Brighton, East Sussex BN1 5JD. Telephone (01273) 695 400 (admin offices 44 North Road, Brighton).
Record Attendance: 36,747 v Fulham, Division 2, 27 December 1958 (at Goldstone Ground).
Capacity: 8,850.
Manager: Russell Slade.
Secretary: Derek J. Allan.
Most League Goals: 112, Division 3 (S), 1955–56.
Highest League Scorer in Season: Peter Ward, 32, Division 3, 1976–77.
Most League Goals in Total Aggregate: Tommy Cook, 114, 1922–29.
Most Capped Player: Steve Penney, 17, Northern Ireland.
Most League Appearances: 'Tug' Wilson, 509, 1922–36.
Honours – Football League: Division 2 Champions – 2001–02. Division 3 Champions – 2000–01. Division 3 (S) Champions – 1957–58. Division 4 Champions – 1964–65.
Colours: Blue and white striped shirts, white sleeves with blue trim, white shorts, white stockings.

BRISTOL CITY   FL CHAMPIONSHIP

Adebola Dele (F)	6 3	12 08	Lagos	23 6 75	Coventry C
Akinde John (F)			London	9 7 89	Ebbsfleet U
Artus Frankie (M)	6 0	11 02	Bristol	27 9 88	Scholar
Basso Adriano (G)	6 1	11 07	Jundiai	18 4 75	Woking
Carey Louis (D)	5 10	12 09	Bristol	20 1 77	Trainee
Elliott Marvin (M)	6 0	12 02	Wandsworth	15 9 84	Millwall

33

Fontaine Liam (D)	5 11	11 09	Beckenham	7 1 86	Fulham
Henderson Stephen (G)	6 3	11 00	Dublin	2 5 88	Aston Villa
Johnson Lee (M)	5 6	10 07	Newmarket	7 6 81	Hearts
Maynard Nicky (F)	5 11	11 00	Winsford	11 12 86	Crewe Alex
McAllister Jamie (D)	5 10	11 00	Glasgow	26 4 78	Hearts
McCombe Jamie (D)	6 5	12 05	Scunthorpe	1 1 83	Lincoln C
McIndoe Michael (M)	5 8	11 00	Edinburgh	2 12 79	Wolverhampton W
Orr Bradley (M)	6 0	11 11	Liverpool	1 11 82	Newcastle U
Plummer Tristan (F)	5 6	10 07	Bristol	30 1 90	Scholar
Ribeiro Christian (D)	5 11	12 02	Neath	14 12 89	Scholar
Skuse Cole (M)	6 1	11 05	Bristol	29 3 86	Scholar
Sproule Ivan (M)	5 8	11 09	Castlederg	18 2 81	Hibernian
Styvar Peter (F)	5 11	12 04	Roznava	13 8 80	
Trundle Lee (F)	6 0	11 06	Liverpool	10 10 76	Swansea C
Walker Jordan (D)			Bristol	1 8 89	Scholar
Weale Chris (G)	6 2	13 01	Chard	9 2 82	Yeovil T
Williams Gavin (M)	5 10	11 05	Pontypridd	20 6 80	Ipswich T
Wilson Brian (D)	5 10	11 00	Manchester	9 5 83	Cheltenham T
Wilson James (D)	6 2	11 05	Newport	26 2 89	Scholar

League Appearances: Adebola, D. 32(7); Akinde, J. 1(6); Basso, A. 43; Brooker, S. (4); Carey, L. 28; Elliott, M. 24(4); Fontaine, L. 41(1); Henderson, S. (1); Iriekpen, I. 4(5); John, S. 13(11); Johnson, L. 43(1); Maynard, N. 34(9); McAllister, J. 35; McCombe, J. 24(4); McIndoe, M. 43(2); Murray, S. (3); Noble, D. 5(4); Orr, B. 37(1); Skuse, C. 29(4); Sproule, I. 18(20); Styvar, P. 2(8); Trundle, L. 4(15); Weale, C. 3(2); Webster, A. 2(3); Williams, G. 24(11); Wilson, B. 17(3); Wilson, J. (2).
Goals – League (54): Maynard 11 (1 pen), Adebola 10, McIndoe 6 (1 pen) Elliott 3, Johnson 3, Sproule 3, Williams 3, Brooker 2, Fontaine 2, John 2, Skuse 2, Trundle 2, Akinde 1, McAllister 1, McCombe 1, Noble 1, Orr 1 (pen).
Carling Cup (3): Brooker 1, Carey 1, Wilson B 1.
FA Cup (0).
Ground: Ashton Gate Stadium, Bristol BS3 2EJ. Telephone (0871) 222 6666.
Record Attendance: 43,335 v Preston NE, FA Cup 5th rd, 16 February 1935.
Capacity: 21,804.
Manager: Gary Johnson.
Secretary: Michelle McDonald.
Most League Goals: 104, Division 3 (S), 1926–27.
Highest League Scorer in Season: Don Clark, 36, Division 3 (S), 1946–47.
Most League Goals in Total Aggregate: John Atyeo, 314, 1951–66.
Most Capped Player: Billy Wedlock, 26, England.
Most League Appearances: John Atyeo, 597, 1951–66.
Honours – Football League: Division 2 Champions – 1905–06. Division 3 (S) Champions – 1922–23, 1926–27, 1954–55. **Welsh Cup:** Winners – 1934. **Anglo-Scottish Cup:** Winners – 1977–78. **Freight Rover Trophy:** Winners – 1985–86. **LDV Vans Trophy:** Winners – 2002–03.
Colours: Red shirts with white trim, white shorts, red stockings.

BRISTOL ROVERS   FL CHAMPIONSHIP 1

Anthony Byron (D)	6 1	11 02	Newport	20 9 84	Cardiff C
Campbell Stuart (M)	5 10	10 00	Corby	9 12 77	Grimsby T
Clough Charlie (M)	6 2	12 07	Taunton	3 9 90	Scholar
Coles Danny (D)	6 1	11 05	Bristol	31 10 81	Hull C
Duffy Darryl (F)	5 11	12 01	Glasgow	16 4 84	Swansea C
Elliott Steve (D)	6 1	14 00	Derby	29 10 78	Blackpool
Green Mike (G)	6 1	13 01	Bristol	23 07 89	Scholar
Haldane Lewis (F)	6 0	11 03	Trowbridge	13 3 85	Scholar
Hughes Jeff (D)	6 1	11 00	Larne	29 5 85	Crystal Palace
Hunt Ben (F)	6 1	12 07	London	23 1 90	West Ham U

Kite Alex (D)   6 0   12 05   Kent   7 3 89   Scholar
Lambert Rickie (F)   6 2   14 08   Liverpool   16 2 82   Rochdale
Lescott Aaron (M)   5 8   10 09   Birmingham   2 12 78   Stockport Co
Lines Chris (M)   6 2   12 00   Bristol   30 11 85   Filton College
Osei-Kuffour Jo (F)   5 8   11 11   Edmonton   17 11 81   Bournemouth
Phillips Steve (G)   6 1   11 10   Bath   6 5 78   Bristol C
Pipe David (M)   5 9   12 01   Caerphilly   5 11 83   Notts Co
Reece Charlie (M)   5 11 11 03   Birmingham   8 9 88   Scholar
Rigg Sean (F)   5 9   12 01   Bristol   1 10 88   Scholar
Williams Andy (F)   5 11 11 09   Hereford   14 8 86   Hereford U

League Appearances: Anthony, B. 29(1); Campbell, S. 42(2); Coles, D. 5; Disley, C. 33(11); Duffy, D. 28(15); Elliott, S. 39; Green, R. 23(3); Hinton, C. 19(6); Hughes, J. 43; Hunt, B. (12); Jacobson, J. 6(16); Lambert, R. 43(2); Lescott, A. 43(1); Lines, C. 44(1); Osei-Kuffour, J. 26(15); Phillips, S. 46; Pipe, D. 36(3); Reece, C. 1; Rigg, S. (8); Williams, A. (4).
Goals – League (79): Lambert 29 (5 pens), Duffy 13, Osei-Kuffour 11, Hughes 6, Lines 4, Disley 3, Elliott 3, Lescott 3, Anthony 2, Coles 1, Hinton 1, Pipe 1, Williams 1, own goal 1.
Carling Cup (0).
FA Cup (0).
J Paint Trophy (0).
Ground: The Memorial Stadium, Filton Avenue, Horfield, Bristol BS7 0BF. Telephone (0117) 909 6648.
Record Attendance: 9,464 v Liverpool, FA Cup 4th rd, 8 February 1992 (Twerton Park). 38,472 v Preston NE, FA Cup 4th rd, 30 January 1960 (Eastville). 12,011 v WBA, FA Cup 6th rd, 9 March 2008 (Memorial Stadium).
Capacity: 11,626.
Manager: Paul Trollope.
Secretary: Rod Wesson.
Most League Goals: 92, Division 3 (S), 1952–53.
Highest League Scorer in Season: Geoff Bradford, 33, Division 3 (S), 1952–53.
Most League Goals in Total Aggregate: Geoff Bradford, 242, 1949–64.
Most Capped Player: Vitalijs Astafjevs, 31 (142), Latvia.
Most League Appearances: Stuart Taylor, 546, 1966–80.
Honours – Football League: Division 3 (S) Champions – 1952–53. Division 3 Champions – 1989–90.
Colours: Blue and white quartered shirts, white shorts, white stockings.

BURNLEY   FA PREMIERSHIP

Alexander Graham (D)   5 10   12 07   Coventry   10 10 71   Preston NE
Berisha Besart (M)   5 11   11 12   Pristina   29 7 85   Hamburg
Blake Robbie (F)   5 9   12 00   Middlesbrough   4 3 76   Leeds U
Caldwell Steve (D)   5 11   11 05   Stirling   12 9 80   Sunderland
Carlisle Clarke (D)   6 2   14 11   Preston   14 10 79   Watford
Duff Michael (D)   6 3   12 10   Belfast   11 1 78   Cheltenham T
Eagles Chris (M)   5 10   11 07   Hemel Hempstead 19 11 85   Manchester U
Elliott Wade (M)   5 10   10 03   Southampton   14 12 78   Bournemouth
Gudjohnsson Joey (M)   5 9   12 04   Akranes   25 5 80   AZ
Jensen Brian (G)   6 4   16 09   Copenhagen   8 6 75   WBA
Jordan Stephen (D)   6 1   13 00   Warrington   6 3 82   Manchester C
Kalvenes Christian (D) 6 0   11 11   Bergen   8 3 77   Dundee U
Kay Adam (M)   5 10   11 02   Burnley   29 9 89   Scholar
MacDonald Alex (F)   5 7   11 04   Warrington   14 4 90   Scholar
McCann Chris (M)   6 1   11 11   Dublin   21 7 87   Scholar
McDonald Kevin (M)   6 2   13 03   Carnoustie   4 11 88   Dundee
Paterson Martin (F)   5 9   10 11   Tunstall   13 5 87   Scunthorpe U
Penny Diego (G)   6 6   12 00   Lima   22 4 84   Coromel Bolognesi

35

Rodriguez Jay (F)   6 0   12 00 Burnley   27 7 89 Scholar
Thompson Steven (F) 6 2   12 05 Paisley   14 10 78 Cardiff C
Van der Schaaf Remco (D) 6 1   12 02 Ten Boer   28 2 78 Vitesse

League Appearances: Akinbiyi, A. 1(10); Alexander, G. 46; Anderson, R. 4; Blake, R. 33(13); Caldwell, S. 45; Carlisle, C. 36; Duff, M. 22(5); Eagles, C. 30(13); Elliott, W. 41(1); Gudjonsson, J. 20(19); Jensen, B. 45; Jordan, S. 26(1); Kalvenes, C. 21; MacDonald, A. (3); Mahon, A. (8); McCann, C. 44; McDonald, K. 9(16); Paterson, M. 39(4); Penny, D. 1; Rodriguez, J. 2(23); Thompson, S. 23(11); Van der Schaaf, R. 1; Williams, R. 17.
Goals – League (72): Paterson 12, Alexander 9 (8 pens), Blake 8, Eagles 8, Thompson 7, Gudjonsson 6, McCann 6, Elliott 4, Carlisle 3, Caldwell 2, Rodriguez 2, Duff 1, Kalvenes 1, Mahon 1, McDonald 1, own goal 1.
Carling Cup (13): Paterson 5, McCann 2, McDonald 2, Rodriguez 2, Akinbiyi 1, Blake 1.
FA Cup (7): Thompson 3, Alexander 1 (pen), Elliott 1, Paterson 1, Rodriguez 1.
Play-Offs (4): Alexander 1 (pen), Elliott 1, Paterson 1, Thompson 1.
Ground: Turf Moor, Harry Potts Way, Burnley, Lancashire BB10 4BX. Telephone (0871) 221 1882.
Record Attendance: 54,775 v Huddersfield T, FA Cup 3rd rd, 23 February 1924.
Capacity: 22,610.
Manager: Owen Coyle.
Football Secretary: Pauline Scott
Most League Goals: 102, Division 1, 1960–61.
Highest League Scorer in Season: George Beel, 35, Division 1, 1927–28.
Most League Goals in Total Aggregate: George Beel, 179, 1923–32.
Most Capped Player: Jimmy McIlroy, 51 (55), Northern Ireland.
Most League Appearances: Jerry Dawson, 522, 1907–28.
Honours – Football League: Division 1 Champions – 1920–21, 1959–60. Division 2 Champions – 1897–98, 1972–73. Division 3 Champions – 1981–82. Division 4 Champions – 1991–92. **FA Cup:** Winners – 1913–14. **Anglo-Scottish Cup:** Winners – 1978–79.
Colours: Claret shirts with blue sleeves, white shorts, claret stockings.

BURTON ALBION   FL CHAMPIONSHIP 2

Austin Ryan (D)   6 3   13 07 Stoke   15 11 84 Crewe Alex
Banim Jody (F)   5 8   13 01 Manchester   1 4 78 Droylsden
Buxton Jake (D)   5 11 13 01 Sutton-in-Ashfield 4 3 85 Mansfield T
Corbett Andrew (M) 6 0   11 05 Worcester   20 2 82 Nuneaton B
Deeney Saul (G)   6 1   11 07 Derry   23 3 83 Hucknall T
Gilroy Keith (M)   5 10 10 12 Sligo   8 7 83 Darlington
Goodfellow Marc (M) 5 10 10 01 Swadlincote 20 9 81 Bury
Harrad Shaun (F)   5 10 12 04 Nottingham 11 12 84 Notts Co
Holmes Danny (M)   6 0   11 13 Burton-on-Trent 17 11 86 Port Vale
James Tony (M)   6 3   14 02 Cardiff   9 10 78 Weymouth
McGrath John (M)   5 10 10 03 Limerick   27 3 80 Tamworth
Morris Lee (M)   5 10 11 02 Driffield   30 4 80 Yeovil T
Pearson Greg (F)   6 0   11 00 Birmingham 3 4 85 Bishop's Stortford
Poole Kevin (G)   5 10 11 11 Bromsgrove 21 7 63 Derby Co
Simpson Michael (M) 5 8   11 07 Nottingham 28 7 74 Leyton Orient
Stride Darren (M)   6 0   13 05 Burton-on-Trent 28 9 75
Webster Aaron (D) 6 2   12 02 Burton-on-Trent 19 12 80

League Appearances: Armstrong, 1+2; Austin, 19+15; Bailey, 6+4; Banim, 8+7; Brayford, 6; Butler, 3+9; Buxton, 41; Byrne, 3+4; Corbett, 45; Deeney, 8; Gilroy, 38+1; Goodfellow, 18+12; Harrad, 28+13; Holmes, 6+10; James, 29; McGrath, 46; Morris, 16+13; Newby, 10+12; Pearson, 34+6; Poole, 38; Simmons, 1+1; Simpson, 40+1; Stride, 17+12; Webster, 36+2; Yates, 9+1.

36

Goals – League (81): Pearson 18 (7 pens), Harrad 15 (3 pens), Morris 7, Webster 7, Goodfellow 6, McGrath 6, Gilroy 5, Simpson 3, Austin 2, Butler 2, Corbett 2, Stride 2, Armstrong 1, Brayford 1, Buxton 1, Yates 1, own goals 2.
FA Cup (0).
Ground: Pirelli Stadium, Princess Way, Burton-on-Trent, Staffordshire DE13 0AR. Telephone: (01283) 565 938.
Record attendance: 6,192 v Oxford U Blue Square Premier 17 April 2009.
Capacity: 6,350 (2,034 seated).
Manager: Paul Peschisolido.
Football Secretary: Fleur Robinson.
Most Appearances: Darren Stride, 635.
Honours: Conference: Champions – 2008–09. **Southern League Cup:** Winners – 1964, 1997, 2000. **Northern Premier League:** Champions – 2001–02. **Northern Premier League Shield:** 1983. **Challenge Cup:** Winners – 1983. **Birmingham Senior Cup:** Winners – 1954, 1997. **Staffordshire Senior Cup:** Winners – 1956. **Midland Floodlit Cup:** Winners – 1976.
Colours: Yellow shirts with black insert, black shorts, black stockings.

BURY   FL CHAMPIONSHIP 2

Anane Ricky (D)	6 1	12 03	Manchester	12 1 91	Scholar
Baker Richie (M)	5 7	11 10	Burnley	29 12 87	Preston NE
Barry-Murphy Brian (M)	6 1	13 01	Cork	27 7 78	Sheffield W
Belford Cameron (G)	6 1	11 10	Nuneaton	16 10 88	Coventry C
Bishop Andy (F)	6 0	11 00	Stone	19 10 82	York C
Brown Wayne (G)	6 0	13 11	Southampton	14 1 77	Hereford U
Buchanan David (M)	5 8	10 08	Rochdale	6 5 86	Scholar
Cresswell Ryan (D)	5 9	10 05	Rotherham	22 12 87	Sheffield U
Dawson Stephen (M)	5 9	11 09	Dublin	4 12 85	Mansfield T
Dorney Jack (M)	5 9	10 00	Ashton-under-Lyne	9 1 90	Scholar
Futcher Ben (D)	6 7	12 05	Manchester	20 2 81	Peterborough U
Haslam Steven (M)	5 11	10 10	Sheffield	6 9 79	Halifax T
Hurst Glynn (F)	5 10	11 05	Barnsley	17 1 76	Shrewsbury T
Jones Mike (M)	5 11	12 04	Birkenhead	15 8 87	Tranmere R
Morgan Paul (D)	6 0	11 07	Belfast	23 10 78	Lincoln C
Morrell Andy (F)	5 11	12 00	Doncaster	28 9 74	Blackpool
Racchi Danny (D)	5 8	10 04	Halifax	22 11 87	Huddersfield T
Rouse Domaine (F)	5 6	10 10	Stretford	4 7 89	Scholar
Scott Paul (D)	5 11	12 00	Wakefield	5 11 79	Huddersfield T

League Appearances: Baker, R. 6(16); Barry-Murphy, B. 41(1); Belford, C. (1); Bennett, E. 46; Bishop, A. 39(3); Brown, W. 35; Buchanan, D. 46; Cresswell, R. 19(6); Dawson, S. 42(1); Futcher, B. 33(1); Haslam, S. 13; Howell, D. (3); Hurst, G. 16(21); Jevons, P. 3(4); Jones, M. 46; Morrell, A. 31(10); O'Grady, C. 3(3); Racchi, D. (21); Scott, P. 33; Sodje, E. 40(1); Tyler, M. 11; Welsh, J. 3(2).
Goals – League (63): Bishop 16 (5 pens), Morrell 9, Hurst 8, Sodje 7, Jones 4, Bennett 3, Scott 3, Barry-Murphy 2, Dawson 2, Futcher 2, Jevons 2 (2 pens), Cresswell 1, own goals 4.
Carling Cup (0).
FA Cup (0).
J Paint Trophy (1): Bishop 1.
Play-Offs (1): own goal 1.
Ground: Gigg Lane, Bury BL9 9HR. Telephone (0161) 764 4881.
Record Attendance: 35,000 v Bolton W, FA Cup 3rd rd, 9 January 1960. **Capacity:** 11,669.
Manager: Alan Knill.
Secretary: Mrs Jill Neville.
Most League Goals: 108, Division 3, 1960–61.
Highest League Scorer in Season: Craig Madden, 35, Division 4, 1981–82.

Most League Goals in Total Aggregate: Craig Madden, 129, 1978–86.
Most Capped Player: Bill Gorman, 11 (13), Republic of Ireland and (4), Northern Ireland.
Most League Appearances: Norman Bullock, 506, 1920–35.
Honours – Football League: Division 2 Champions – 1894–95, 1996–97. Division 3 Champions – 1960–61. **FA Cup:** Winners – 1900, 1903.
Colours: White shirts, royal blue shorts, white stockings.

CARDIFF CITY   FL CHAMPIONSHIP

Blake Darcy (M)	5 10	12 05	New Tredegar	13 12 88	Scholar
Bothroyd Jay (F)	6 3	14 11	Islington	7 5 82	Wolverhampton W
Burke Chris (M)	5 9	10 10	Glasgow	2 12 83	Rangers
Capaldi Tony (D)	6 0	11 08	Porsgrunn	12 8 81	Plymouth Arg
Commigues Miguel (D)	5 9	11 03	Les Abymes	16 3 82	Swindon T
Dennehy Darren (D)	6 4	12 08	Republic of Ireland	21 9 88	Everton
Enckelman Peter (G)	6 2	12 05	Turku	10 3 77	Blackburn R
Feeney Warren (F)	5 8	12 04	Belfast	17 1 81	Luton T
Gyepes Gabor (D)	6 3	13 01	Hungary	26 6 81	Northampton T
Johnson Roger (D)	6 3	12 02	Ashford	24 4 83	Wycombe W
Kennedy Mark (M)	5 11	11 09	Dublin	15 5 76	Crystal Palace
Ledley Joe (M)	6 0	11 07	Cardiff	23 1 87	Scholar
Marshall David (G)	6 3	13 04	Glasgow	5 3 85	Norwich C
Matthews Adam (M)	5 10	11 02	Swansea	13 1 92	Scholar
McCormack Ross (F)	5 9	11 00	Glasgow	18 8 86	Motherwell
McNaughton Kevin (D)	5 10	10 06	Dundee	28 8 82	Aberdeen
McPhail Steve (M)	5 10	13 03	Westminster	9 12 79	Barnsley
Morris Aaron (D)	6 1	12 05	Cardiff	30 12 89	Scholar
Owusu-Abeyie Quincy (F)	5 11	11 10	Amsterdam	15 4 86	Birmingham C
Parry Paul (M)	5 11	12 12	Newport	19 8 80	Hereford U
Rae Gavin (D)	5 11	10 04	Aberdeen	28 11 77	Rangers
Sak Erwin (G)	6 0		Lublin	15 2 90	Sokol
Scimeca Riccardo (D)	6 1	12 09	Leamington Spa	13 6 75	WBA
Whittingham Peter (M)	5 10	11 06	Nuneaton	8 9 84	Aston Villa

League Appearances: Blake, D. 4(3); Bothroyd, J. 35(4); Burke, C. 8(6); Capaldi, T. 3; Chopra, M. 23(4); Comminges, M. 10(20); Enckelman, P. 11(1); Gyepes, G. 25(2); Heaton, T. 21; Johnson, E. 5(25); Johnson, R. 45; Kennedy, M. 35(1); Konstantopoulos, D. 6; Ledley, J. 40; Loovens, G. 1; McCormack, R. 32(6); McNaughton, K. 39; McPhail, S. 27(5); Owusu-Abeyie, Q. (5); Parry, P. 33(7); Purse, D. 21(2); Rae, G. 39(2); Routledge, W. 9; Scimeca, R. 2(2); Taylor, S. 8; Thompson, S. 1(3); Whittingham, P. 23(10).
Goals – League (65): McCormack 21 (9 pens), Bothroyd 12, Chopra 9 (3 pens), Johnson R 5, Ledley 4, Whittingham 3, Gyepes 2, Johnson E 2, Parry 2, Routledge 2, Burke 1, Rae 1, Thompson 1.
Carling Cup (4): Parry 2, McCormack 1 (pen), Whittingham 1.
FA Cup (2): Ledley 1, McCormack 1.
Ground: Ninian Park, Sloper Rd, Cardiff CF11 8SX (moving to new ground at Leckwith Road, Cardiff CF11 8AZ). Telephone (029) 2022 1001.
Record Attendance: 62,634, Wales v England, 17 October 1959. **Capacity:** 20,324.
Manager: Dave Jones.
Secretary: Jason Turner.
Most League Goals: 95, Division 3, 2000–01.
Highest League Scorer in Season: Robert Earnshaw, 31, Division 2, 2002–03.
Most League Goals in Total Aggregate: Len Davies, 128, 1920–31.
Most Capped Player: Alf Sherwood, 39 (41), Wales.
Most League Appearances: Phil Dwyer, 471, 1972–85.
Honours – Football League: Division 3 (S) Champions – 1946–47; Division 3 Champions – 1992–93. **FA Cup:** Winners – 1926–27 (only occasion the Cup has

38

been won by a club outside England). **Welsh Cup:** Winners – 22 times. **Charity Shield:** Winners 1927.
Colours: Blue shirts with yellow trim, white shorts, white stockings.

CARLISLE UNITED　　　　　FL CHAMPIONSHIP 1

Aldred Tom (D)	6 2	13 02	Bolton	11 9 90	Scholar
Anyinsah Joe (M)	5 8	11 00	Bristol	8 10 84	Preston NE
Blake Jonny (M)	5 8	11 00	Carlisle	4 2 91	Scholar
Bridge-Wilkinson Marc (M)	5 6	11 00	Coventry	16 3 79	Bradford C
Burns Michael (M)	5 10	11 06	Whiston	14 9 88	Liverpool
Cook Andy (F)	6 1	11 04	Bishop Auckland	18 10 90	Scholar
Dobie Scott (F)	6 1	12 05	Workington	10 10 78	Nottingham F
Gowling Josh (D)	6 3	12 08	Coventry	29 11 83	Bournemouth
Graham Danny (F)	5 11	12 05	Gateshead	12 8 85	Middlesbrough
Harte Ian (D)	5 11	12 06	Drogheda	31 8 77	Blackpool
Horwood Evan (D)	6 0	10 06	Billingham	10 3 86	Gretna
Kavanagh Graham (M)	5 10	13 03	Dublin	2 12 73	Sunderland
Keogh Richard (D)	6 0	11 02	Harlow	11 8 86	Bristol C
Livesey Danny (D)	6 3	12 10	Salford	31 12 84	Bolton W
Madine Gary (F)	6 1	12 04	Gateshead	24 8 90	Scholar
Murphy Peter (M)	5 10	12 10	Dublin	27 10 80	Blackburn R
Raven David (D)	6 0	11 04	Birkenhead	10 3 85	Liverpool
Taylor Cleveland (M)	5 8	10 07	Leicester	9 9 83	Scunthorpe U
Thirlwell Paul (M)	5 11	11 04	Springwell Village	13 2 79	Derby Co
Williams Ben (G)	6 0	13 01	Manchester	27 8 82	Crewe Alex

League Appearances: Alnwick, B. 6; Anyinsah, J. 16(3); Birchall, C. (2); Bridge-Wilkinson, M. 20(3); Bridges, M. 12(18); Burns, M. (1); Campion, D. 2; Carlton, D. 12; Dobie, S. 11(19); Gowling, J. 3(1); Graham, D. 39(5); Hackney, S. 16(6); Harte, I. 3; Horwood, E. 22(2); Joyce, L. 4(3); Kane, T. 6(3); Kavanagh, G. 34; Keogh, R. 31(1); Krul, T. 9; Liddle, M. 21(1); Livesey, D. 27; Lumsdon, C. 4(3); Madine, G. (14); Morris, I. 4(2); Murphy, P. 27(1); Myrie-Williams, J. 1(7); Neal, L. 15(1); Raven, D. 41; Rothery, G. 1(1); Smith, G. 1; Smith, J. 11(5); Taylor, C. 37(5); Taylor, G. 5; Thirlwell, P. 33(1); Welsh, J. 2(2); Williams, B. 31.
Goals – League (56): Graham 15 (2 pens), Bridges 7 (1 pen), Bridge-Wilkinson 5 (1 pen), Kavanagh 5, Anyinsah 4, Thirlwell 4, Carlton 3, Dobie 3, Taylor C 3, Neal 2, Hackney 1, Harte 1, Keogh 1, Madine 1, Taylor G 1.
Carling Cup (1): Murphy 1.
FA Cup (3): Graham 1, Kavanagh 1, Madine 1.
J Paint Trophy (2): Bridges 1, Madine 1.
Ground: Brunton Park, Warwick Road, Carlisle CA1 1LL. Telephone (01228) 526 237.
Record Attendance: 27,500 v Birmingham C, FA Cup 3rd rd, 5 January 1957 and v Middlesbrough, FA Cup 5th rd, 7 February 1970. **Capacity:** 16,982.
Manager: Greg Abbott.
Secretary: Sarah McKnight.
Most League Goals: 113, Division 4, 1963–64.
Highest League Scorer in Season: Jimmy McConnell, 42, Division 3 (N), 1928–29.
Most League Goals in Total Aggregate: Jimmy McConnell, 126, 1928–32.
Most Capped Player: Eric Welsh, 4, Northern Ireland.
Most League Appearances: Allan Ross, 466, 1963–79.
Honours – Football League: Division 3 Champions – 1964–65, 1994–95; Championship 2 Champions – 2005–06. **Auto Windscreen Shield:** Winners 1997.
Colours: Blue and white shirts with alternate blue and red sleeves and white trim, blue shorts, blue stockings.

Bailey Nicky (M)	5 10	12 06	Hammersmith	10	6 84	Southend U
Basey Grant (D)	6 2	13 12	Farnborough	30 11 88		Scholar
Burton Deon (F)	5 9	11 09	Ashford	25 10 76		Sheffield W
Christensen Martin (D)	5 11	12 10	Ishoj	23 12 87		Herfolge
Dickson Christopher (F)	5 11	11 00	East Dulwich	28 12 84		Dulwich H
Elliot Rob (G)	6 3	14 10	Chatham	30	4 86	Scholar
Fleetwood Stuart (F)	5 10	12 07	Gloucester	23	4 86	Hereford U
Fofana Beko (F)			Ivory Coast	8	9 88	ASEC Mimosas
Gray Andy (F)	6 1	13 00	Harrogate	15 11 77		Burnley
Hudson Mark (D)	6 1	12 01	Guildford	30	3 82	Crystal Palace
Kouadio Konan (M)			Abidjan	31 12 88		ASEC Mimosas
McLeod Izale (F)	6 1	11 02	Birmingham	15 10 84		Milton Keynes D
Moutaouakil Yassin (D)	5 10	11 05	Nice	18	7 86	Chateauroux
Racon Therry (M)	5 10	10 02	Villen've-St-Georges	1	5 84	Guingamp
Randolph Darren (G)	6 2	14 00	Dublin	12	5 87	Scholar
Sam Lloyd (F)	5 8	10 00	Leeds	27	9 84	Scholar
Semedo Jose (D)	6 0	12 08	Setubal	11	1 85	Sporting Lisbon
Shelvey Jonjo (M)	6 1	11 02	Romford	27	2 92	Scholar
Sinclair Dean (M)	5 10	11 03	St Albans	17 12 84		Barnet
Solly Chris (D)	5 8	10 07	Chatham	20	1 91	Scholar
Spring Matthew (M)	5 11	12 05	Harlow	17 11 79		Luton T
Wagstaff Scott (F)	5 10	10 03	Maidstone	31	3 90	Scholar
Youga Kelly (D)	5 11	12 06	Bangui	22	9 85	Lyon

League Appearances: Ambrose, D. 9(12); Bailey, N. 43; Basey, G. 10(9); Bouazza, H. 22(3); Burton, D. 12(8); Butterfield, D. 12; Cranie, M. 19; Dickson, C. 6(15); Elliot, R. 23; Fortune, J. 17; Gillespie, K. 4(2); Gray, A. 21(6); Holland, M. 18(16); Hudson, M. 43; Kandol, T. 10(3); McEveley, J. 6; McLeod, I. 2; Moutaouakil, Y. 9(2); Murty, G. 8; Primus, L. 10; Racon, T. 19; Randolph, D. 1; Sam, L. 28(10); Semedo, J. 12(6); Shelvey, J. 14(2); Soares, T. 10(1); Solly, C. (1); Spring, M. 12(1); Thomas, J. 1; Todorov, S. 2(11); Tuna, T. (2); Varney, L. 16(2); Waghorn, M. 4(3); Wagstaff, S. (2); Ward, D. 16; Weaver, N. 22; Wright, J. 2; Youga, K. 32(1); Zheng-Zhi, 11(2).

Goals – League (52): Bailey 13, Gray 7 (3 pens), Burton 5 (1 pen), Bouazza 4, Hudson 3, Racon 3, Shelvey 3, Kandol 2, Spring 2, Varney L 2, Holland 1, Primus 1, Soares 1, Todorov 1, Waghorn 1, Youga 1, Zheng-Zhi 1, own goal 1.

Carling Cup (0).

FA Cup (3): Ambrose 1, Dickson 1, Shelvey 1.

Ground: The Valley, Floyd Road, Charlton, London SE7 8BL. Telephone (020) 8333 4000.

Record Attendance: 75,031 v Aston Villa, FA Cup 5th rd, 12 February 1938 (at The Valley). **Capacity:** 27,111.

Manager: Phil Parkinson.

Football Secretary: Chris Parkes.

Most League Goals: 107, Division 2, 1957–58.

Highest League Scorer in Season: Ralph Allen, 32, Division 3 (S), 1934–35.

Most League Goals in Total Aggregate: Stuart Leary, 153, 1953–62.

Most Capped Player: Jonatan Johansson, 41 (88), Finland.

Most League Appearances: Sam Bartram, 583, 1934–56.

Honours – Football League: Division 1 Champions – 1999–2000. Division 3 (S) Champions – 1928–29, 1934–35. **FA Cup:** Winners – 1947.

Colours: Red shirts with white trim, white shorts, red stockings.

CHELSEA   FA PREMIERSHIP

Name	Ht	Wt	Birthplace	Born	Previous Club
Alex (D)	6 2	14 00	Niteroi	17 6 82	PSV Eindhoven
Anelka Nicolas (F)	6 1	13 03	Versailles	14 3 79	Bolton W
Ballack Michael (M)	6 2	13 05	Gorlitz	26 12 76	Bayern Munich
Belletti Juliano (D)	5 9	10 12	Casacvel	20 6 76	Barcelona
Bertrand Ryan (D)	5 10	11 00	Southwark	5 8 89	Scholar
Borini Fabio (F)	5 10	11 02	Bentivoglio	23 3 91	Bologna
Bosingwa Jose (D)	6 0	12 08	Kinshasa	24 8 82	Porto
Bridcutt Liam (M)	5 9	11 07	Reading	8 5 89	Scholar
Cech Petr (G)	6 5	14 03	Plzen	20 5 82	Rennes
Clifford Conor (M)	5 8	10 08	Dublin	1 10 91	Scholar
Cole Ashley (D)	5 8	10 08	Stepney	20 12 80	Arsenal
Cole Joe (M)	5 9	11 07	Islington	8 11 81	West Ham U
Cork Jack (D)	6 0	10 12	Carshalton	25 6 89	Scholar
Cummings Shaun (F)	6 0	11 10	Hammersmith	25 2 89	Scholar
Deco (M)	5 9	11 07	Sao Bernardo do Campo	27 8 77	Barcelona
Di Santo Franko (F)	6 4	13 01	Mendoza	7 4 89	Audax Italiano
Drogba Didier (F)	6 2	13 08	Abidjan	11 3 78	Marseille
Essien Michael (M)	5 10	13 06	Accra	3 12 82	Lyon
Gordon Ben (D)	5 11	12 06	Bradford	2 3 91	Scholar
Hilario (G)	6 2	13 05	San Pedro da Cova	21 10 75	Porto
Hutchinson Sam (D)	6 0	11 07	Slough	3 8 89	Scholar
Ivanovic Branislav (M)	6 0	12 04	Sremska Mitreovica	22 2 84	Lokomotiv Moscow
Kakuta Gael (F)	5 8	10 03	Lille	21 6 91	Lens
Kalou Salomon (F)	6 0	12 02	Oume	5 8 85	Feyenoord
Lampard Frank (M)	6 0	14 01	Romford	20 6 78	West Ham U
Magnay Carl (D)	6 0	11 13	Durham	27 1 89	
Malouda Florent (M)	6 0	11 06	Cayenne	13 6 80	Lyon
Mancienne Michael (D)	6 0	11 09	Isleworth	8 1 88	Scholar
Mellis Jacob (D)	6 0	11 08	Nottingham	8 1 91	Scholar
Mikel John Obi (M)	6 0	13 05	Jos	22 4 87	Lyn
Nielsen Morten (F)	6 3	13 12	Copenhagen	24 2 90	FC Copenhagen
Ofori-Twumasi Nana (D)	5 8	11 09	Accra	15 5 90	Scholar
Paulo Ferreira (D)	6 0	11 13	Cascais	18 1 79	Porto
Philliskirk Daniel (M)	5 10	10 07	Oldham	10 4 91	Scholar
Pizarro Claudio (F)	6 0	12 06	Lima	3 10 78	Bayern Munich
Rajkovic Slobodan (D)	6 5	14 00	Belgrade	3 3 89	OFK Belgrade
Ricardo Carvalho (D)	6 0	12 04	Amarante	18 5 78	Porto
Sahar Ben (F)	5 10	12 05	Holon	10 8 89	Hapoel Tel Aviv
Sarki Emmanuel (M)			Nigeria	26 12 87	
Sawyer Lee (M)	5 10	10 03	Leytonstone	10 9 89	Scholar
Shevchenko Andriy (F)	6 0	11 05	Dvirkivshchyna	29 9 76	AC Milan
Sinclair Scott (F)	5 10	10 00	Bath	26 3 89	Bristol R
Smith Jimmy (M)	6 0	10 03	Newham	7 1 87	Scholar
Stoch Miroslav (F)	5 6	10 01	Nitra	19 10 89	Scholar
Taiwo Tom (M)	5 8	10 07	Leeds	27 2 90	Scholar
Taylor Rhys (G)	6 2	12 08	Neath	7 4 90	
Tejera Rodriguez Sergio (M)	5 11	10 10	Barcelona	28 5 90	Scholar
Terry John (D)	6 1	13 08	Barking	7 12 80	Trainee
Tore Gokhan (M)	5 9	11 09	Cologne	20 1 92	Leverkusen
Van Aanholt Patrick (D)	5 9	10 08	S'Hertogenbosch	3 7 88	Ajax
Woods Michael (M)	6 0	12 07	York	6 4 90	Scholar

League Appearances: Alex, 22(2); Anelka, N. 33(4); Ballack, M. 22(7); Belletti, J. 5(15); Bosingwa, J. 34; Bridge, W. 3(3); Cech, P. 35; Cole, A. 33(1); Cole, J. 14; Cudicini, C. 2; Deco, 17(7); Di Santo, F. (8); Drogba, D. 15(9); Essien, M. 10(1);

Hilario, 1; Ivanovic, B. 11(5); Kalou, S. 17(10); Lampard, F. 37; Malouda, F. 24(7); Mancienne, M. 2(2); Mikel, J. 33(1); Mineiro, (1); Paulo Ferreira, 1(6); Quaresma, R. 1(3); Ricardo Carvalho, 11(1); Sinclair, S. (2); Stoch, M. (4); Terry, J. 35; Wright-Phillips, S. (1).

Goals – League (68): Anelka 19, Lampard 12 (2 pens), Kalou 7, Malouda 6, Drogba 5, Belletti 3, Deco 3, Alex 2, Bosingwa 2, Cole J 2, Ballack 1, Cole A 1, Essien 1, Ricardo Carvalho 1, Terry 1, own goals 2.

Carling Cup (5): Lampard 2 (1 pen), Drogba 1, Kalou 1, Malouda 1.

FA Cup (17): Anelka 4, Ballack 3, Drogba 3, Lampard 3, Kalou 2, Alex 1, Malouda 1.

Champions League (20): Drogba 5, Lampard 3, Anelka 2, Essien 2, Ivanovic 2, Terry 2, Alex 1, Cole J 1, Kalou 1, Malouda 1.

Ground: Stamford Bridge, Fulham Rd, London SW6 1HS. Telephone (0871) 984 1955.

Record Attendance: 82,905 v Arsenal, Division 1, 12 October 1935.

Capacity: 41,841.

Manager: Carlo Ancelotti.

Secretary: David Barnard.

Most League Goals: 98, Division 1, 1960–61.

Highest League Scorer in Season: Jimmy Greaves, 41, 1960–61.

Most League Goals in Total Aggregate: Bobby Tambling, 164, 1958–70.

Most Capped Player: Marcel Desailly, 67 (116), France.

Most League Appearances: Ron Harris, 655, 1962–80.

Honours – FA Premier League: Champions – 2004–05, 2005–06. **Football League:** Division 1 Champions – 1954–55. Division 2 Champions – 1983–84, 1988–89. **FA Cup:** Winners – 1970, 1997, 2000, 2007, 2009. **Football League Cup:** Winners – 1964–65, 1997–98, 2004–05, 2006–07. **Full Members' Cup:** Winners – 1985–86. **Zenith Data Systems Cup:** Winners – 1989–90. **European Cup-Winners' Cup:** Winners – 1970–71, 1997–98. **Super Cup:** Winners – 1999.

Colours: Reflex blue shirts, reflex blue shorts, white stockings with blue trim.

CHELTENHAM TOWN   FL CHAMPIONSHIP 2

Bird David (M)	5 9	12 00	Gloucester	26 12 84	Cinderford T
Brown Scott P (G)	6 2	13 01	Wolverhampton	26 4 85	Bristol C
Diallo Drissa (D)	6 1	11 13	Nouadhibou	4 1 73	Milton Keynes D
Duff Shane (D)	6 1	12 10	Wroughton	2 4 82	Juniors
Emery Josh (M)	5 6	10 09	Ledbury	30 9 90	Scholar
Finnigan John (M)	5 8	10 09	Wakefield	29 3 76	Lincoln C
Gallinagh Andy (D)	5 8	11 08	Sutton Coldfield	16 3 85	Stratford T
Hammond Elvis (F)	5 10	11 02	Accra	6 10 80	Leicester C
Lee Jake (M)	6 0	12 07	Swindon	18 9 91	Scholar
Lewis Theo (M)	5 10	10 12	Oxford	10 8 91	Scholar
Low Josh (M)	6 2	14 03	Bristol	15 2 79	Peterborough U
Puddy Will (G)	5 10	11 07	Salisbury	4 10 87	Scholar
Ridley Lee (D)	5 9	11 11	Scunthorpe	5 12 81	Scunthorpe U
Russell Alex (M)	5 10	11 07	Crosby	17 3 73	Bristol C
Townsend Michael (D)	6 1	13 12	Walsall	17 5 86	Wolverhampton W
Watkins Marley (M)	5 10	10 04	London	17 10 90	Scholar

League Appearances: Antonio, M. 7(2); Armstrong, C. 3(2); Artus, F. 9; Berchiche, Y. 7; Bignall, N. 8(5); Bird, D. 24(3); Brown, S. 35; Caines, G. 5(3); Connor, P. 18(7); Constantine, L. 4(2); Diallo, D. 27; Duff, S. 18(2); Durrant, J. (4); Emery, J. (1); Finnigan, J. 13(4); Fleetwood, S. 6; Gallinagh, A. 30(9); Gill, B. 5(2); Gill, J. 6; Hammond, E. 17(5); Hayes, J. 3(3); Hayles, B. 11(1); Haynes, K. 2(2); Hemmings, A. (1); Higgs, S. 10; Hutton, D. 5(2); Kenton, D. 13; Ledgister, A. (1); Lee, J. 2(1); Lewis, T. (2); Lindegaard, A. 11(4); Low, J. 13(1); Montrose, L. 5; Murray, S. 12(1); Myrie-Williams, J. 5; Owusu, L. 16(6); Payne, S. 9(2); Puddy, W. 1; Ridley, L. 24(3); Rowe-Turner, L. 1; Russell, A. 19(4); Sinclair, D. 2(1);

42

Spencer, D. 5(9); Townsend, M. 23(3); Vincent, A. 16(13); Watkins, M. 4(8); Wesolowski, J. 4; Westlake, I. 22; Westwood, C. 9; Wright, A. 22(1).
Goals – League (51): Owusu 7, Hammond 5 (1 pen), Hayles 4, Artus 3, Spencer 3 (1 pen), Vincent 3 (1 pen), Connor 2, Diallo 2 (1 pen), Fleetwood 2 (1 pen), Murray 2, Westlake 2, Westwood 2, Bignall 1, Bird 1, Caines 1, Constantine 1, Finnigan 1 (pen), Gallinagh 1, Gill B 1, Hutton 1, Kenton 1, Myrie-Williams 1, Payne 1, Townsend 1 (pen), own goals 2.
Carling Cup (3): Gill B 1, Russell 1, Vincent 1.
FA Cup (6): Vincent 2, Finnigan 1 (pen), Montrose 1, Murray 1, Owusu 1 (pen).
J Paint Trophy (1): Low 1.
Ground: The Abbey Business Stadium, Whaddon Road, Cheltenham, Gloucestershire GL52 5NA. Telephone (01242) 573 558.
Record Attendance: at Whaddon Road: 8,326 v Reading, FA Cup 1st rd, 17 November 1956; at Cheltenham Athletic Ground: 10,389 v Blackpool, FA Cup 3rd rd, 13 January 1934.
Capacity: 7,136.
Manager: Martin Allen.
Secretary: Paul Godfrey.
Most League Goals: 66, Division 3, 2001–02.
Highest League Scorer in Season: Julian Alsop, 20, Division 3, 2001–02.
Most League Goals in Total Aggregate: Martin Devaney, 38, 1999–2005.
Most Capped Player: Grant McCann, 7 (22), Northern Ireland.
Most League Appearances: Jamie Victory, 258, 1999–.
Honours – Football Conference: Champions – 1998–99. **FA Trophy:** Winners – 1997–98.
Colours: All red with white trim.

CHESTER CITY   BLUE SQUARE PREMIER

Barry Anthony (M)	5 7	10 00	Liverpool	29 5 86	Yeovil T
Butler Paul (D)	6 2	13 00	Manchester	2 11 72	Leeds U
Danby John (G)	6 2	14 06	Stoke	20 9 83	Kidderminster H
Dinning Tony (M)	6 0	13 05	Wallsend	12 4 75	Stockport Co
Ellams Lloyd (F)	6 2	12 00	Chester	11 1 91	Scholar
Ellison Kevin (M)	6 0	12 00	Liverpool	23 2 79	Tranmere R
Harris Jay (M)	5 7	11 06	Liverpool	15 4 87	Accrington S
Kelly Shaun (D)	6 1	11 04	Southampton	4 7 86	Scholar
Linwood Paul (D)	6 2	13 03	Birkenhead	24 10 83	Tranmere R
Mannix David (M)	5 8	11 06	Winsford	24 9 85	Accrington S
McManus Paul (F)	5 6	10 00	Liverpool	22 4 90	Scholar
Partridge Richie (M)	5 8	11 00	Dublin	12 9 80	Rotherham U
Roberts Kevin (D)	6 2	14 00	Chester	10 3 87	
Rule Glenn (M)	5 11	11 07	Birkenhead	30 11 89	Scholar
Rutherford Paul (M)	5 9	11 07	Moreton	10 7 87	Greenleas
Vaughan James (D)	5 10	12 09	Liverpool	6 12 86	Tranmere R
Vaughan Stephen (D)	5 6	11 11	Liverpool	22 1 85	Liverpool
Wilson Laurence (M)	5 10	10 09	Huyton	10 10 86	Everton

League Appearances: Barry, A. 38(5); Butler, P. 1; Danby, J. 41; Dinning, T. 3(1); Ellams, L. 2(2); Ellison, K. 39; Harris, J. 24(7); Hughes, M. 25(1); Johnson, E. 7(3); Jones, B. 2(13); Kelly, S. 23(4); Linwood, P. 43; Lowe, R. 45; Mannix, D. 10(3); McManus, P. 6(3); Mozika, D. 21(1); Owen, J. 4(3); Partridge, R. 15(13); Platt, K. (1); Roberts, K. 44; Rule, G. 18(4); Rutherford, P. 5(14); Smith, P. (5); Spencer, J. 5; Taylor, P. 2(7); Vaughan, J. 42; Vaughan, S. 7(1); Wilson, L. 34.
Goals – League (43): Lowe 16 (3 pens), Ellison 8, Roberts 4, Linwood 2, Mannix 2, McManus 2, Owen 2, Barry 1, Ellams 1, Johnson 1, Kelly 1, Wilson 1, own goals 2.
Carling Cup (2): Lowe 2 (1 pen).
FA Cup (0).
J Paint Trophy (1): Ellison 1.

Ground: Deva Stadium, Bumpers Lane, Chester CH1 4LT. Telephone (01244) 371 376.
Record Attendance: 20,500 v Chelsea, FA Cup 3rd rd (replay), 16 January 1952 (at Sealand Road).
Capacity: 6,012.
Manager: Mick Wadsworth.
Secretary: Tony Allan.
Most League Goals: 119, Division 4, 1964–65.
Highest League Scorer in Season: Dick Yates, 36, Division 3 (N), 1946–47.
Most League Goals in Total Aggregate: Stuart Rimmer, 135, 1985–88, 1991–98.
Most Capped Player: Angus Eve, 35 (117), Trinidad & Tobago.
Most League Appearances: Ray Gill, 406, 1951–62.
Honours – Conference: Champions – 2003–04. **Welsh Cup:** Winners – 1908, 1933, 1947. **Debenhams Cup:** Winners 1977.
Colours: Blue and white striped shirts, blue shorts, blue stockings.

CHESTERFIELD   FL CHAMPIONSHIP 2

Austin Kevin (D)	6 1	14 08	Hackney	12 2 73	Swansea C
Boden Scott (F)	5 11	11 00	Sheffield	19 12 89	IFK Marlehamn
Bowery Jordan (F)	6 1	12 00	Nottingham	2 7 91	Scholar
Currie Darren (M)	5 11	12 07	Hampstead	29 11 74	Luton T
Downes Aaron (D)	6 3	13 00	Mudgee	15 5 85	Frickley C
Goodall Alan (D)	5 7	11 08	Birkenhead	2 12 81	Luton T
Gray Dan (M)	6 0	11 00	Mansfield	23 11 89	Scholar
Gritton Martin (F)	6 1	12 02	Glasgow	1 6 78	Macclesfield T
Hall Danny (D)	6 0	12 02	Ashton-under-Lyne	14 11 83	Gretna
Harsley Paul (M)	5 8	11 05	Scunthorpe	29 5 78	Port Vale
Kerry Lloyd (M)	6 2	12 04	Chesterfield	22 1 88	Sheffield U
Lee Tommy (G)	6 2	12 00	Keighley	3 1 86	Macclesfield T
Lester Jack (F)	5 9	12 08	Sheffield	8 10 75	Nottingham F
Lowry Jamie (D)	6 0	12 04	Newquay	18 3 87	Scholar
Niven Derek (M)	6 0	12 02	Falkirk	12 12 83	Bolton W
Page Robert (D)	6 0	12 05	Llwynpia	3 9 74	Huddersfield T
Picken Phil (D)	5 9	10 08	Droylsden	12 11 85	Manchester U
Robertson Gregor (D)	6 0	12 04	Edinburgh	19 1 84	Rotherham U
Winter Jamie (M)	5 10	13 10	Dundee	4 8 85	Aberdeen

League Appearances: Algar, B. 1(2); Askham, L. (1); Austin, K. 27(8); Boden, L. 4; Boden, S. 3(8); Bowery, J. (3); Carson, T. 18; Currie, D. 14(13); Downes, A. 40(2); Goodall, A. 21(7); Gray, D. 20(5); Gritton, M. 19(1); Hall, D. 25; Harsley, P. 7(10); Kerry, L. 28(5); Lee, T. 28; Lester, J. 37; Lowry, J. 37(5); McDonald, C. 1(1); Montrose, L. 11(1); Niven, D. 21(10); Page, R. 16; Picken, P. 9(2); Robertson, G. 32(6); Talbot, D. 17; Teixeira, V. (5); Till, P. 14(2); Ward, J. 23; Wilson, J. 15(1); Winter, J. 18(6).
Goals – League (62): Lester 20, Ward 14 (3 pens), Gritton 4, Currie 3, Goodall 3, Kerry 3, Boden S 2, Downes 2, Niven 2, Robertson 2, Talbot 2, Winter 2, Hall 1, Harsley 1, own goal 1.
Carling Cup (0).
FA Cup (6): Lester 2, Ward 2, Winter 2.
J Paint Trophy (2): Kerry 1, Lester 1.
Ground: The Recreation Ground, Chesterfield, Derbyshire S40 4SX. Telephone (01246) 209 765.
Record Attendance: 30,968 v Newcastle U, Division 2, 7 April 1939. **Capacity:** 8,502.
Manager: John Sheridan.
Finance Director: Alan Walters.
Most League Goals: 102, Division 3 (N), 1930–31.
Highest League Scorer in Season: Jimmy Cookson, 44, Division 3 (N), 1925–26.

Most League Goals in Total Aggregate: Ernie Moss, 161, 1969–76, 1979–81 and 1984–86.
Most Capped Player: Walter McMillen, 4 (7), Northern Ireland; Mark Williams, 4 (30), Northern Ireland.
Most League Appearances: Dave Blakey, 613, 1948–67.
Honours – Football League: Division 3 (N) Champions – 1930–31, 1935–36. Division 4 Champions – 1969–70, 1984–85. **Anglo-Scottish Cup:** Winners – 1980–81.
Colours: Blue shirts with white trim, white shorts, white stockings.

COLCHESTER UNITED   FL CHAMPIONSHIP 1

Baldwin Pat (D)	6 3	12 07	City of London	12 11 82	Chelsea
Cousins Mark (G)	6 1	11 03	Chelmsford	9 1 87	Scholar
Coyne Chris (D)	6 2	13 10	Brisbane	20 12 78	Luton T
Elito Medy (M)	6 2	13 00	Kinshasa	20 3 90	Scholar
Gerken Dean (G)	6 1	12 08	Rochford	22 5 85	Scholar
Gillespie Steven (F)	5 9	11 02	Liverpool	4 6 84	Cheltenham T
Guy Jamie (M)	6 1	13 00	Barking	1 8 87	Scholar
Hackney Simon (M)	5 8	9 13	Manchester	5 2 84	Carlisle U
Hammond Dean (M)	6 0	11 09	Hastings	7 3 83	Brighton & HA
Heath Matt (D)	6 4	13 13	Leicester	1 11 81	Leeds U
Ifil Phil (D)	5 10	12 02	Willesden	18 11 86	Tottenham H
Izzet Kem (M)	5 7	10 05	Mile End	29 9 80	Charlton Ath
Jackson Johnnie (M)	6 0	12 08	Camden	15 8 82	Tottenham H
Lockwood Matt (D)	5 11	11 10	Southend	17 10 76	Nottingham F
Maybury Alan (D)	5 8	11 08	Dublin	8 8 78	Leicester C
Perkins David (D)	5 6	11 06	St Asaph	21 6 82	Rochdale
Platt Clive (F)	6 4	12 07	Wolverhampton	27 10 77	Milton Keynes D
Reid Paul (D)	6 2	11 08	Carlisle	18 2 82	Barnsley
Tierney Marc (D)	5 11	11 04	Manchester	7 9 86	Shrewsbury T
Vernon Scott (F)	6 1	11 06	Manchester	13 12 83	Blackpool
White John (M)	5 10	12 01	Maldon	26 7 86	Scholar
Wordsworth Anthony (M)	6 1	12 00	London	3 1 89	Scholar
Yeates Mark (F)	5 8	13 03	Dublin	11 1 85	Tottenham H

League Appearances: Baldwin, P. 35; Borrowdale, G. 4; Corcoran, S. (1); Cousins, M. 9; Coyne, C. 17(2); Easter, J. 5; Elito, M. (5); Gerken, D. 21; Gillespie, S. 8(9); Gobern, L. 5(7); Guy, J. 1(3); Hackney, S. 11(6); Hammond, D. 38(3); Hawley, K. 4; Heath, M. 11(3); Hills, L. 1; Ifil, P. 5(1); Izzet, K. 39(4); Jackson, J. 22(7); Lockwood, M. 5; Maybury, A. 25; Perkins, D. 35(3); Platt, C. 39(4); Reid, P. 25(1); Tierney, M. 26; Trotman, N. 5(1); Vernon, S. 15(18); Vincent, A. 5(1); Walker, J. 16; Wasiu, A. 3(12); White, J. 19(7); Williams, S. 1; Wordsworth, A. 9(21); Yeates, M. 42(1).
Goals – League (58): Yeates 12, Platt 10, Hammond 5 (1 pen), Perkins 5, Gillespie 4 (2 pens), Jackson 4, Vernon 4, Wordsworth 3, Easter 2, Wasiu 2, Izzet 1, Reid 1, Tierney 1, Vincent 1, own goals 3.
Carling Cup (2): Gillespie 1, Keith 1.
FA Cup (0).
J Paint Trophy (3): Perkins 1, Williams 1, Yeates 1.
Ground: Weston Homes Community Stadium, United Way, Colchester, Essex CO4 5UP. Telephone (01206) 755 100.
Record Attendance: 19,072 v Reading, FA Cup 1st rd, 27 November, 1948.
Capacity: 10,000
Manager: Paul Lambert.
Football Secretary: Caroline Pugh.
Most League Goals: 104, Division 4, 1961–62.
Highest League Scorer in Season: Bobby Hunt, 38, Division 4, 1961–62.
Most League Goals in Total Aggregate: Martyn King, 130, 1956–64.
Most Capped Player: Bela Balogh, 2 (9), Hungary.

Most League Appearances: Micky Cook, 613, 1969–84.
Honours – GM Vauxhall Conference: Winners – 1991–92. **FA Trophy:** Winners:
1991–92.
Colours: Royal blue and white striped shirts with white sleeves, royal blue shorts,
royal blue stockings.

COVENTRY CITY   FL CHAMPIONSHIP

Bell David (M)	5 10	11 05	Kettering	21	1 84	Norwich C
Best Leon (F)	6 1	13 03	Nottingham	19	9 86	Southampton
Dann Scott (D)	6 2	12 00	Liverpool	14	2 87	Walsall
Doyle Micky (M)	5 8	11 00	Dublin	8	7 81	Celtic
Eastwood Freddy (F)	5 11	12 04	Epsom	29	10 83	Wolverhampton W
Fox Daniel (D)	5 11	12 06	Crewe	29	5 86	Walsall
Gunnarsson Aron (M)	5 9	11 00	Akureyri	22	9 89	AZ
Hall Marcus (D)	6 1	12 02	Coventry	24	3 76	Stoke C
Ireland Daniel (G)			Sydney	20	1 89	
Konstantopoulos Dimitrios (G)	6 4	14 02	Kalamata	29	11 79	Hartlepool U
McPake James (D)	6 2	12 08	Bellshill	2	6 84	Livingston
Morrison Clinton (F)	6 0	12 00	Tooting	14	5 79	Crystal Palace
Osbourne Isaac (M)	5 9	11 11	Birmingham	22	6 86	Scholar
Simpson Robbie (F)	6 1	11 11	Poole	15	3 85	Cambridge U
Thornton Kevin (M)	5 7	11 00	Drogheda	9	7 86	Scholar
Turner Ben (D)	6 4	14 04	Birmingham	21	1 88	Scholar
Ward Elliot (D)	6 2	13 00	Harrow	19	1 85	West Ham U
Westwood Keiren (G)	6 1	13 10	Manchester	23	10 84	Carlisle U
Wright Stephen (D)	6 0	12 06	Liverpool	8	2 80	Sunderland

League Appearances: Bell, D. 8(1); Best, L. 16(15); Beuzelin, G. 28(7); Cain, A.
(5); Dann, S. 31; Doyle, M. 34(3); Eastwood, F. 37(9); Fox, D. 39; Grandison, J. (2);
Gray, J. 3; Gunnarsson, A. 38(2); Hall, M. 15(8); Henderson, J. 9(1); Marshall, A.
(2); McKenzie, L. 10(9); McPake, J. 3(1); Mifsud, M. 19(7); Morrison, C. 40(5);
Osbourne, I. 20(5); Sawyer, L. 1(1); Simpson, R. 14(19); Tabb, J. 21(1); Thornton,
K. 1(3); Turner, B. 22(2); Walker, A. (2); Ward, E. 33; Westwood, K. 46; Wright, S.
17; Wynter, C. 1.
Goals – League (47): Morrison 10, Fox 5, Ward 5 (4 pens), Eastwood 4, Dann 3,
McKenzie 3, Simpson 3, Tabb 3, Best 2, Doyle 2, Mifsud 2, Bell 1, Beuzelin 1, Gray
1, Gunnarsson 1, Henderson 1.
Carling Cup (5): Morrison 2, Simpson 2, Dann 1.
FA Cup (6): Best 2, Doyle 1, Gunnarsson 1, McKenzie 1, Ward 1.
Ground: The Ricoh Arena, Phoenix Way, Foleshill, Coventry CV6 6GE.
Telephone (0844) 873 1883.
Record Attendance: 28,163 v WBA, FA Cup 5th rd, 16 February 2008 (at The
Ricoh Arena); 51,455 v Wolverhampton W, Division 2, 29 April 1967 (at Highfield
Road). **Capacity:** 32,609.
Manager: Chris Coleman.
Secretary: Pam Hindson.
Most League Goals: 108, Division 3 (S), 1931–32.
Highest League Scorer in Season: Clarrie Bourton, 49, Division 3 (S), 1931–32.
Most League Goals in Total Aggregate: Clarrie Bourton, 171, 1931–37.
Most Capped Player: Magnus Hedman, 44 (58), Sweden.
Most League Appearances: Steve Ogrizovic, 507, 1984–2000.
Honours – Football League: Division 2 Champions – 1966–67. Division 3 Champions
– 1963–64. Division 3 (S) Champions 1935–36. **FA Cup:** Winners – 1986–1987.
Colours: Sky blue and white striped shirts with sky blue sleeves, sky blue shorts,
sky blue stockings.

Name						
Bailey James (M)	6 0	12 05	Bollington	18 9 88	Scholar
Brayford John (D)	5 8	11 02	Stoke	29 12 87	Burton Alb
Clements Chris (M)	5 9	10 05	Birmingham	6 2 90	Scholar
Collis Steve (G)	6 3	12 05	Harrow	18 3 81	Southend U
Donaldson Clayton (F)	6 1	11 07	Bradford	7 2 84	Hibernian
Elding Anthony (F)	6 1	12 02	Boston	16 4 82	Leeds U
Grant Joel (F)	6 0	12 01	Hammersmith	26 8 87	Aldershot T
Jones Billy (D)	5 11	13 00	Shrewsbury	24 3 87	Scholar
Legzdins Adam (G)	6 1	14 02	Stafford	28 11 86	Birmingham C
McManus Scott (D)	6 0	11 00	Manchester	28 5 89	Curzon Ashton
Miller Shaun (F)	5 10	11 08	Alsager	25 9 87	Scholar
Moore Byron (M)	6 0	10 06	Stoke	24 8 88	Scholar
Murphy Luke (M)	6 1	11 05	Macclesfield	21 10 89	Scholar
O'Connor Michael (M)	6 1	11 08	Belfast	6 10 87	Scholar
O'Donnell Daniel (D)	6 2	11 11	Liverpool	10 3 86	Liverpool
Pope Tom (F)	6 3	11 03	Stoke	27 8 85	Lancaster C
Schumacher Steven (M)	5 10	11 00	Liverpool	30 4 84	Bradford C
Shelley Danny (D)	5 9	10 08	Stoke	29 12 90	Scholar
Westwood Ashley (D)	5 10	11 00	Crewe	1 4 90	Scholar
Zola Calvin (F)	6 3	14 06	Kinshasa	31 12 84	Tranmere R

League Appearances: Abbey, G. 4(3); Bailey, J. 24; Baudet, J. 35; Bopp, E. 4(3); Brayford, J. 34(2); Broomes, M. 19; Carrington, M. 12(5); Collis, S. 18; Daniel, C. 9(4); Donaldson, C. 28(9); Elding, A. 10(6); Grant, J. 19(9); Green, S. 2; Jones, B. 38; Lawrence, D. 26; Lunt, K. 2(1); McCready, C. 4(1); McManus, S. 3(3); Miller, S. 18(15); Moore, B. 22(14); Murphy, L. 3(6); O'Connor, M. 23; O'Donnell, D. 22(2); Pope, T. 17(9); Rix, B. 1(3); Ruddy, J. 19; Schumacher, S. 8(7); Sheehan, A. 3; Shelley, D. 3; Sigurdsson, G. 14(1); Tomlinson, S. 9; Westwood, A. (2); Woodards, D. 35(2); Zola, C. 18(9).
Goals – League (59): Pope 10, Donaldson 6, Jones 6 (2 pens), Zola 5, Miller 4, Moore 3, O'Connor 3 (1 pen), Sigurdsson 3 (1 pen), Brayford 2, Carrington 2, Grant 2, Lawrence 2, Schumacher 2, Bopp 1, Daniel 1, Elding 1, McCready 1, McManus 1, Murphy 1, O'Donnell 1, own goals 2.
Carling Cup (5): Elding 2 (1 pen), O'Connor 2 (1 pen), Moore 1.
FA Cup (7): Miller 3, Donaldson 1, Lawrence 1, Murphy 1, Shelley 1.
J Paint Trophy (3): Jones 1, O'Donnell 1, Schumacher 1.
Ground: The Alexandra Stadium, Gresty Road, Crewe, Cheshire CW2 6EB. Telephone (01270) 213 014.
Record Attendance: 20,000 v Tottenham H, FA Cup 4th rd, 30 January 1960.
Capacity: 10,107.
Manager: Gudjon Thordarson.
Secretary: Andrew Blakemore.
Most League Goals: 95, Division 3 (N), 1931–32.
Highest League Scorer in Season: Terry Harkin, 35, Division 4, 1964–65.
Most League Goals in Total Aggregate: Bert Swindells, 126, 1928–37.
Most Capped Player: Clayton Ince, 38 (78), Trinidad & Tobago.
Most League Appearances: Tommy Lowry, 436, 1966–78.
Honours – Welsh Cup: Winners – 1936, 1937.
Colours: Red shirts with yellow trim, white shorts, red stockings.

CRYSTAL PALACE   FL CHAMPIONSHIP

Andrew Calvin (F)	6 0	12 11	Luton	19 12 86	Luton T
Butterfield Danny (D)	5 10	11 06	Boston	21 11 79	Grimsby T
Cadogan Kieron (M)	6 4	12 07	Wandsworth	16 8 90	Scholar

Carle Nick (F)	5 9	12 04	Sydney	23 11 81	Bristol C
Clyne Nathaniel (D)	5 9	10 07	London	5 4 91	Scholar
Comley James (M)	5 10	12 09	London	24 1 91	Scholar
Danns Neil (M)	5 10	10 12	Liverpool	23 11 82	Birmingham C
Derry Shaun (M)	5 10	10 13	Nottingham	6 12 77	Leeds U
Djilali Kieran (M)	6 3	13 02	London	1 1 91	Scholar
Ertl Johannes (D)	6 2	12 08	Graz	13 11 82	FK Austria
Flahavan Darryl (G)	5 11	12 05	Southampton	9 9 77	Southend U
Fonte Jose (D)	6 2	12 08	Penafiel	22 12 83	
Hill Clint (D)	6 0	11 06	Liverpool	19 10 78	Stoke C
Hills Lee (D)	5 10	11 11	Croydon	3 4 90	Scholar
Kuqi Shefki (F)	6 2	13 13	Kosova	10 11 76	Blackburn R
Lawrence Matthew (D)	6 1	12 10	Northampton	14 6 74	Millwall
Lee Alan (F)	6 2	13 09	Galway	21 8 78	Ipswich T
McCarthy Patrick (D)	6 2	13 07	Dublin	31 5 83	Charlton Ath
Moses Victor (F)	5 10	11 07	Lagos	12 12 90	Scholar
Scannell Sean (F)	5 9	11 07	Cork	21 3 89	Scholar
Speroni Julian (G)	6 0	11 00	Buenos Aires	18 5 79	Dundee
Thomas Simon (F)	5 6	12 02	London	21 7 84	Boreham Wood
Wiggins Rhoys (D)	5 8	11 05	Hillingdon	4 11 87	Scholar

League Appearances: Andrew, C. 1(6); Beattie, C. 15; Butterfield, D. 17(9); Cadogan, K. (4); Carle, N. 35(2); Clyne, N. 25(1); Comley, J. 1(3); Danns, N. 14(6); Davis, C. 7; Derry, S. 35(4); Djilali, K. 2(4); Ertl, J. 3(9); Flahavan, D. 1; Fletcher, C. (3); Fonte, J. 36(2); Fonte, R. 5(5); Griffit, L. 2(3); Hill, C. 43; Hills, L. 8(6); Ifill, P. 27(6); Kuqi, S. 20(15); Lawrence, M. 28(4); Lee, A. 10(6); McCarthy, P. 25(2); Moses, V. 19(8); Oster, J. 27(4); Pinney, N. (1); Scannell, S. 16(9); Scowcroft, J. 5(5); Soares, T. 4; Speroni, J. 45; Stokes, A. 11(2); Thomas, S. (1); Watson, B. 18; Wiggins, R. 1.

Goals – League (52): Kuqi 10 (1 pen), Beattie 5, Watson 5 (2 pens), Fonte J 4, Ifill 4, Carle 3 (1 pen), Lee 3, McCarthy 3, Oster 3, Danns 2, Moses 2, Scannell 2, Andrew 1, Butterfield 1, Cadogan 1, Hill 1, Stokes 1, own goal 1.

Carling Cup (2): Carle 1, Oster 1.

FA Cup (5): Ifill 2, Danns 1, Hill 1, Scannell 1.

Ground: Selhurst Park, Whitehorse Lane, London SE25 6PU. Telephone (020) 8768 6000.

Record Attendance: 51,482 v Burnley, Division 2, 11 May 1979. **Capacity:** 26,225.

Manager: Neil Warnock.

Assistant Secretary: Christine Dowdeswell.

Most League Goals: 110, Division 4, 1960–61.

Highest League Scorer in Season: Peter Simpson, 46, Division 3 (S), 1930–31.

Most League Goals in Total Aggregate: Peter Simpson, 153, 1930–36.

Most Capped Player: Aleksandrs Kolinko, 23 (82), Latvia.

Most League Appearances: Jim Cannon, 571, 1973–88.

Honours – Football League: Division 1 – Champions 1993–94. Division 2 Champions – 1978–79. Division 3 (S) 1920–21. **Zenith Data Systems Cup:** Winners – 1991.

Colours: All white with red and blue diagonal stripe shirts.

DAGENHAM & REDBRIDGE   FL CHAMPIONSHIP 2

Arber Mark (D)	6 1	11 09	Johannesburg	9 10 77	Peterborough U
Benson Paul (F)	6 1	11 01	Rochford	12 10 79	White Notley
Charge Daniel (M)	5 11	11 00	Dagenham	1 1 90	Scholar
Cook Anthony (M)	5 7	11 02	London	10 8 89	Croydon Ath
Erskine Emmanuel (F)	6 1	13 06	London	13 1 89	Wingate & Finchley
Foster Danny (D)	5 11	13 02	Enfield	23 9 84	Tottenham H
Gain Peter (M)	5 9	11 07	Hammersmith	11 11 76	Peterborough U
Graham Richard (M)	5 10	11 10	Newry	5 8 79	Barnet
Griffiths Scott (D)	5 9	11 08	London	27 11 85	Aveley

Hogan David (G)	6 0	13 10	Harlow	31	5 89	
Huke Shane (M)	5 11	12 07	Reading	2	10 85	Peterborough U
Montgomery Graeme (M)	6 1	12 00	Dagenham	3	3 88	Wealdstone
Nurse Jon (F)	5 9	12 04	Barbados	28	3 81	Stevenage B
Nwokeji Mark (M)	5 11	11 05	London	30	1 82	Staines T
Okuonghae Magnus (D)	6 3	13 04	Nigeria	16	2 86	Rushden & D
Patterson Marlon (D)	5 9	11 10	London	24	6 83	Yeading
Roberts Tony (G)	6 0	14 11	Bangor	4	8 69	QPR
Rochester Kraig (M)	6 1	13 01	London	3	11 88	Leicester C
Saunders Sam (M)	5 8	11 06	London	29	10 82	Thurrock
Southam Glen (M)	5 9	11 06	Enfield	27	8 80	Bishop's Stortford
Strevens Ben (F)	6 0	12 02	Edgware	24	5 80	Barnet
Taiwo Soloman (M)	6 1	13 02	Lagos	29	4 85	Sutton U
Tejan-Sie Thomas (F)	5 6	11 08	London	23	11 88	Wingate & Finchley
Thomas Wesley (F)	5 10	11 00	Essex	23	1 87	Fisher Ath
Uddin Anwar (D)	6 1	13 07	London	1	11 81	Bristol R

League Appearances: Arber, M. 42; Benson, P. 31(2); Button, D. 3; Charge, D. (1); Foster, D. 38; Gain, P. 30(1); Graham, R. 3(2); Green, D. 2; Griffiths, S. 43(1); Guy, J. 5(4); Hogan, D. (1); Huke, S. (1); Loft, D. 10(1); Montgomery, G. (5); Nurse, J. 16(18); Nwokeji, M. 3(3); Okuonghae, M. 45; Palmer, A. 3; Ritchie, M. 36(1); Roberts, T. 43; Saunders, S. 40; Southam, G. 17(13); Strevens, B. 46(7); Taiwo, S. 39(1); Tejan-Sie, T. (1); Thomas, W. 1(4); Thompson, E. (1); Uddin, A. 10(7).
Goals – League (77): Benson 17, Saunders 14 (1 pen), Strevens 14 (1 pen), Ritchie 11, Nurse 4, Taiwo 4, Arber 3, Nwokeji 3, Foster 2, Okuonghae 2, Green 1, Guy 1, Southam 1.
Carling Cup (1): Taiwo 1.
FA Cup (4): Benson 1, Ritchie 1, Strevens 1, Taiwo 1.
J Paint Trophy (5): Benson 2, Nwokeji 2, Southam 1 (pen).
Ground: London Borough of Barking and Dagenham Stadium, Victoria Road, Dagenham, Essex, RM10 7XR. Telephone (0208) 592 1549.
Record Attendance: 4,791 v Shrewsbury T, FL2, 2 May 2009. **Capacity:** 6,007.
Manager: John L. Still.
Secretary: Terry Grover.
Most League Goals: 77, FL 2, 2008–09.
Highest League Scorer in Season: Paul Benson, 28 Conference 2006–07.
Most League Goals in Total Aggregate: 29, Ben Strevens, 2007–.
Most Capped Player: Jon Nurse, 4, Barbados.
Most League Appearances: Ben Strevens, 92, 2007–.
Honours – Conference: Champions – 2006–07. **Isthmian League (Premier):** Champions 1999–2000.
Colours: Red and blue striped shirts with red sleeves, white shorts, red stockings.

DARLINGTON   FL CHAMPIONSHIP 2

Abbott Pawel (F)	6 2	13 10	York	5	5 82	Swansea C
Austin Neil (D)	5 10	11 09	Barnsley	26	4 83	Barnsley
Barnes Corey (F)	5 8	10 08	Sunderland	1	1 92	Scholar
Blundell Gregg (F)	5 10	11 00	Liverpool	1	1 76	Chester C
Foster Steve (D)	6 1	13 00	Mansfield	3	12 74	Scunthorpe U
Gray Josh (F)	6 1	11 12	South Shields	22	7 91	Scholar
Hardman Lewis (D)	5 10	11 00	Sunderland	12	4 85	Scholar
Kazimierczak Prezemek (G)	6 0	12 02	Lodz	22	2 88	Bolton W
Kennedy Jason (M)	6 1	13 02	Stockton	11	9 86	Middlesbrough
Liversedge Nick (G)	6 1	11 07	Huddersfield	18	7 88	Scholar
Main Curtis (F)	5 9	12 02	South Shields	20	6 92	Scholar
Miller Ian (M)	6 2	12 02	Colchester	23	11 83	Ipswich T
Oakes Andy (G)	6 3	12 04	Northwich	11	1 77	Swansea C
Pocklington Scott (G)	6 2	13 00	Bishop Auckland	18	9 90	Scholar

Poole David (M)	5 8	12 00	Manchester	25 11 84	Stockport Co
Purdie Rob (M)	5 9	11 06	Leicester	28 9 82	Hereford U
Ravenhill Ricky (M)	5 10	11 00	Doncaster	16 1 82	Grimsby T
Ryan Tim (D)	5 10	11 00	Stockport	10 12 74	Boston U
Smith Michael (M)	5 11	11 03	Wallsend	17 10 91	Scholar
Valentine Ryan (D)	5 10	11 05	Wrexham	19 8 82	Wrexham
White Alan (D)	6 0	13 04	Darlington	22 3 76	Notts Co

League Appearances: Abbott, P. 15(3); Austin, N. 29(4); Barnes, C. 2(1); Blundell, G. 2(18); Brown, S. 22; Burgmeier, F. 30(5); Carlton, D. 16(1); Carole, S. 3(3); Clarke, B. 18(2); Flynn, M. 4; Foran, R. 7(2); Fortune, C. 3(4); Foster, S. 34; Gerken, D. 7; Gray, J. 1(4); Griffin, A. 9(8); Groves, D. (1); Hatch, L. 23(3); Hulbert, R. 9(18); Kazimierczak, P. 7(1); Kennedy, J. 44(2); Main, C. 5(13); Miller, I. 16(5); Oakes, A. 10; Poole, D. 18(8); Proudlock, A. 3(5); Purdie, R. 39(1); Ravenhill, R. 37(1); Ryan, T. 21(3); Tremarco, C. 2; Valentine, R. 30(1); White, A. 40.
Goals – League (61): Abbott 8, Clarke B 8 (1 pen), Hatch 8, Purdie 6 (4 pens), Kennedy 5, Carlton 4, Austin 3, Foran 3, Blundell 2, Burgmeier 2, Hulbert 2, Main 2, Ravenhill 2, White 2, Miller 1, Poole 1, own goals 2.
Carling Cup (3): Blundell 1, Clarke B 1, Kennedy 1.
FA Cup (0).
J Paint Trophy (3): White 2, Foster 1.
Ground: Northern Echo Darlington Arena, Neasham Road, Hurworth Moor, Darlington DL2 1DL. Telephone (01325) 387 000.
Record Attendance: 21,023 v Bolton W, League Cup 3rd rd, 14 November 1960.
Capacity: 25,000.
Manager: Colin Todd.
Secretary: Lisa Charlton.
Most League Goals: 108, Division 3 (N), 1929–30.
Highest League Scorer in Season: David Brown, 39, Division 3 (N), 1924–25.
Most League Goals in Total Aggregate: Alan Walsh, 90, 1978–84.
Most Capped Player: Franz Burgmeier, 5 (53), Liechtenstein.
Most League Appearances: Ron Greener, 442, 1955–68.
Honours – Football League: Division 3 (N) Champions – 1924–25. Division 4 Champions – 1990–91. **GM Vauxhall Conference:** Champions – 1989–90.
Colours: Black and white hooped shirts with black sleeves and red trim, black shorts, black stockings.

DERBY COUNTY   FL CHAMPIONSHIP

Addison Miles (D)	6 2	13 03	Newham	7 1 89	Scholar
Albrechtsen Martin (D)	6 1	12 13	Copenhagen	31 3 80	WBA
Atkins Ross (G)	6 0	13 00	Derby	3 11 89	Scholar
Barnes Giles (M)	6 0	12 10	Barking	5 8 88	Scholar
Beardsley Jason (D)	6 0	11 00	Burton	12 7 89	Scholar
Bywater Stephen (G)	6 2	12 08	Manchester	7 6 81	West Ham U
Carroll Roy (G)	6 2	13 12	Enniskillen	30 9 77	Rangers
Commons Kris (M)	5 6	9 08	Mansfield	30 8 83	Nottingham F
Connolly Paul (D)	6 0	11 09	Liverpool	29 9 83	Plymouth Arg
Davies Steve (F)	6 0	12 00	Liverpool	29 12 87	Tranmere R
Davis Claude (D)	6 3	14 04	Kingston	6 3 79	Sheffield U
Dickinson Liam (F)	6 4	14 01	Salford	4 10 85	Stockport Co
Dudley Mark (D)	5 10	12 02	Doncaster	29 1 90	Scholar
Green Paul (M)	5 9	10 02	Pontefract	10 4 83	Doncaster R
Hanson Mitchell (D)	6 1	13 07	Derby	2 9 88	Scholar
Hulse Rob (F)	6 1	12 04	Crewe	25 10 79	Sheffield U
Leacock Dean (D)	6 2	12 04	Croydon	10 6 84	Fulham
McEveley James (D)	6 1	13 13	Liverpool	11 2 85	Blackburn R
Mears Tyrone (D)	5 11	11 10	Stockport	18 2 83	West Ham U
Mendy Arnaud (F)	6 3	13 10	Evreux	10 2 90	

Nyatanga Lewin (D)	6 2	12 08	Burton	18 8 88	Scholar
Pearson Stephen (M)	6 1	11 11	Lanark	2 10 82	Celtic
Porter Chris (F)	6 1	12 09	Wigan	12 12 83	Motherwell
Price Lewis (G)	6 3	13 05	Bournemouth	19 7 84	Ipswich T
Prijovic Aleksander (F)	5 11	13 08	St Gallen	21 4 90	Parma
Savage Robbie (M)	5 11	11 00	Wrexham	18 10 74	Blackburn R
Sterjovski Mile (M)	6 1	12 08	Wollongong	27 5 79	Genclerbirligi
Stewart Jordan (D)	6 0	12 09	Birmingham	3 3 82	Watford
Teale Gary (M)	5 9	11 04	Glasgow	21 7 78	Wigan Ath
Varney Luke (F)	5 11	11 00	Leicester	28 9 82	Charlton Ath
Villa Emanuel (F)	6 0	12 00	Capital Federal	24 2 82	Atlas
Zadkovich Ruben (M)	5 11	11 00	Australia	23 5 86	Notts Co

League Appearances: Addison, M. 28; Albrechtsen, M. 35; Bannan, B. 6(4); Barazite, N. 21(9); Barnes, G. 1(2); Bywater, S. 30(1); Camara, M. 1; Carroll, R. 16; Commons, K. 30(4); Connolly, P. 39(1); Davies, S. 8(11); Davis, C. 6(2); Dudley, M. (1); Ellington, N. 13(14); Eustace, J. 6(3); Green, P. 29; Hulse, R. 42(2); Kazmierczak, P. 12(10); Leacock, D. 10(1); McEveley, J. 13(2); Mears, T. 3; Nyatanga, L. 27(3); O'Brien, M. (1); Pearson, S. 8(4); Pereplotkins, A. 2; Porter, C. 3(2); Powell, D. 5(1); Savage, R. 20(2); Sterjovski, M. 6(9); Stewart, J. 26; Stubbs, A. 1; Teale, G. 24(1); Todd, A. 7(4); Tomkins, J. 5(2); Varney, L. 9(1); Villa, E. 12(18); Zadkovich, R. 2(3).
Goals – League (55): Hulse 15, Commons 5, Davies 3 (1 pen), Ellington 3 (1 pen), Green 3, Porter 3, Albrechtsen 2, Kazmierczak 2, Sterjovski 2, Stewart 2, Villa 2, Addison 1, Bannan 1, Barazite 1, Connolly 1, Eustace 1, Nyatanga 1, Pearson 1, Savage 1, Teale 1, Varney 1, own goals 3.
Carling Cup (14): Ellington 6 (1 pen), Villa 4, Barnes 2 (1 pen), Commons 1, Green 1.
FA Cup (9): Hulse 3, Green 2, Addison 1, Albrechtsen 1, Commons 1, Davies 1 (pen).
Ground: Pride Park Stadium, Derby DE24 8XL. Telephone (0871) 472 1884.
Record Attendance: Pride Park: 33,475 Derby Co Legends v Rangers 9 in a Row Legends, 1 May 2006 (Ted McMinn Benefit). Baseball Ground: 41,826 v Tottenham H, Division 1, 20 September 1969. **Capacity:** 33,597.
Manager: Nigel Clough.
Secretary: Clare Morris.
Most League Goals: 111, Division 3 (N), 1956–57.
Highest League Scorer in Season: Jack Bowers, 37, Division 1, 1930–31; Ray Straw, 37 Division 3 (N), 1956–57.
Most League Goals in Total Aggregate: Steve Bloomer, 292, 1892–1906 and 1910–14.
Most Capped Players: Deon Burton, 42 (59).
Most League Appearances: Kevin Hector, 486, 1966–78 and 1980–82.
Honours – Football League: Division 1 Champions – 1971–72, 1974–75. Division 2 Champions – 1911–12, 1914–15, 1968–69, 1986–87. Division 3 (N) Champions – 1956–57. **FA Cup:** Winners – 1945–46. **Texaco Cup:** Winners 1972.
Colours: White shirts with black trim, black shorts, white stockings.

DONCASTER ROVERS   FL CHAMPIONSHIP

Brooker Stephen (F)	6 0	14 00	Newport Pagnell	21 5 81	Bristol C
Chambers James (D)	5 10	11 11	West Bromwich	20 11 80	Leicester C
Coppinger James (F)	5 7	10 03	Middlesbrough	10 1 81	Exeter C
Elliott Stuart (M)	5 10	11 09	Belfast	23 7 78	Hull C
Fairhust Waide (F)	5 10	10 07	Sheffield	7 5 89	Scholar
Guy Lewis (F)	5 10	10 07	Penrith	27 8 85	Newcastle U
Hayter James (F)	5 9	10 13	Newport (IW)	9 4 79	Bournemouth
Heffernan Paul (F)	5 10	11 00	Dublin	29 12 81	Bristol C
Hird Samuel (D)	5 7	10 12	Askern	7 9 87	Leeds U
Lockwood Adam (D)	6 0	12 07	Wakefield	26 10 81	Yeovil T

51

Mills Matthew (D)	6 3	12 12	Swindon	14 7 86	Manchester C
O'Connor James (D)	5 10	12 05	Birmingham	20 11 84	Bournemouth
Roberts Gareth (D)	5 8	12 00	Wrexham	6 2 78	Tranmere R
Shiels Dean (F)	5 11	9 10	Magherfelt	1 2 85	Hibernian
Smith Ben (G)	6 0	13 00	Newcastle	5 9 86	Stockport Co
Spicer John (M)	5 11	11 07	Romford	13 9 83	Burnley
Stock Brian (M)	5 11	11 02	Winchester	24 12 81	Preston NE
Sullivan Neil (G)	6 2	12 00	Sutton	24 2 70	Leeds U
Van Nieuwstadt Jos (D)	5 9	12 10	Waalwijk	19 11 79	Excelsior
Wellens Richard (M)	5 9	11 06	Manchester	26 3 80	Oldham Ath
Wilson Mark (M)	5 11	12 00	Scunthorpe	9 2 79	Dallas
Woods Gary (G)	6 1	11 00	Kettering	1 10 90	Manchester U
Woods Martin (M)	5 11	11 13	Airdrie	1 1 86	Rotherham U

League Appearances: Ameobi, T. (1); Brooker, S. (1); Byfield, D. 3(12); Chambers, J. 34(3); Coppinger, J. 29(3); Elliott, S. 3(6); Fairhurst, W. (3); Greer, G. (1); Guy, L. 19(10); Hayter, J. 13(14); Heffernan, P. 19(9); Hird, S. 33(4); Lockwood, A. 12(10); LuaLua, K. 2(2); Martis, S. 5; Mills, M. 41; O'Connor, J. 31(1); Price, Jason 11(11); Roberts, G. 27(5); Shiels, D. 6(6); Spicer, J. 26(4); Stock, B. 36; Sullivan, N. 46; Taylor, G. 11(6); Van Nieuwstadt, J. 9(7); Wellens, R. 39; Wilson, M. 15(7); Woods, G. (1); Woods, M. 36(5).
Goals – League (42): Heffernan 10, Stock 6 (4 pens), Coppinger 5, Hayter 4, Wellens 3, Guy 2, Woods M 2, Brooker 1, Hird 1, Martis 1, O'Connor 1, Roberts 1, Shiels 1, Spicer 1, Van Nieuwstadt 1, Wilson 1, own goal 1.
Carling Cup (0).
FA Cup (4): Stock 2, Hird 1, Price 1.
Ground: Keepmoat Stadium, Stadium Way, Lakeside, Doncaster, South Yorkshire DN4 5JW. Telephone (01302) 764 664.
Record Attendance: 37,149 v Hull C, Division 3 (N), 2 October 1948. **Capacity:** 15,231.
Manager: Sean O'Driscoll.
Secretary: David Morris.
Most League Goals: 123, Division 3 (N), 1946–47.
Highest League Scorer in Season: Clarrie Jordan, 42, Division 3 (N) 1946–47.
Most League Goals in Total Aggregate: Tom Keetley, 180, 1923–29.
Most Capped Player: Len Graham, 14, Northern Ireland.
Most League Appearances: Fred Emery, 417, 1925–36.
Honours – Football League: Division 3 Champions – 2003–04. Division 3 (N) Champions – 1934–35, 1946–47, 1949–50. Division 4 Champions – 1965–66, 1968–69. **J Paint Trophy:** Winners – 2006–07. **Football Conference:** Champions – 2002–03.
Colours: Red and white hooped shirts, black shorts, black stockings.

EVERTON   FA PREMIERSHIP

Agard Kieran (F)			Newham	10 10 89	Scholar
Akpan Hope (M)			Liverpool	14 8 91	Scholar
Anichebe Victor (F)	6 1	13 00	Nigeria	23 4 88	Scholar
Arteta Mikel (M)	5 9	10 08	San Sebastian	26 3 82	Real Sociedad
Baines Leighton (D)	5 8	11 00	Liverpool	11 12 84	Wigan Ath
Barnett Moses (D)			London	3 12 90	Arsenal
Baxter Jose (F)	5 10	11 07	Bootle	7 2 92	Academy
Cahill Tim (M)	5 10	10 12	Sydney	6 12 79	Millwall
Codling Lewis (F)			Bootle	11 11 90	Scholar
Coleman Seamus (D)			Donegal	11 10 88	
Craig Nathan (M)			Bangor	25 10 91	Scholar
Duffy Shane (D)			County Derry	1 1 92	Scholar
Fellaini Marouane (M)	6 4	13 05	Brussels	22 11 87	Standard Liege
Gosling Dan (M)	6 0	11 00	Brixham	2 2 90	Plymouth Arg

Hibbert Tony (D)	5 9	11 05	Liverpool	20 2 81	Trainee
Howard Tim (G)	6 3	14 12	North Brunswick	6 3 79	Manchester U
Jagielka Phil (D)	6 0	13 01	Manchester	17 8 82	Sheffield U
Jutkiewicz Lukas (F)	6 1	12 11	Southampton	20 3 89	Swindon T
Kinsella Gerard (M)				30 11 90	Scholar
Krenn George (M)			Austria	4 10 90	Scholar
Lescott Jolean (D)	6 2	13 00	Birmingham	16 8 82	Wolverhampton W
McCarten James (D)			Netherton	8 11 90	Scholar
Nash Carlo (G)	6 5	14 01	Bolton	13 9 73	Wigan Ath
Neville Phil (M)	5 11	12 00	Bury	21 1 77	Manchester U
Osman Leon (F)	5 8	10 09	Billinge	17 5 81	Trainee
Pienaar Steven (M)	5 10	10 06	Westbury	17 3 82	Borussia Dortmund
Rodwell Jack (D)	6 2	12 08	Birkdale	11 3 91	Scholar
Ruddy John (G)	6 3	12 07	St Ives	24 10 86	Cambridge U
Saha Louis (F)	6 1	12 08	Paris	8 8 78	Manchester U
Sheppard Karl (F)			Shelbourne	14 2 91	Scholar
Turner Iain (G)	6 3	12 10	Stirling	26 1 84	Trainee
Vaughan James (F)	5 11	12 08	Birmingham	14 7 88	Scholar
Wallace James (M)			Fazackerly	19 12 91	Scholar
Yakubu Ayegbeni (F)	6 0	14 07	Benin City	22 11 82	Middlesbrough
Yobo Joseph (D)	6 1	13 00	Kano	6 9 80	Marseille

League Appearances: Anichebe, V. 5(12); Arteta, M. 26; Baines, L. 26(5); Baxter, J. 1(2); Cahill, T. 28(2); Castillo, S. 5(4); Fellaini, M. 28(2); Gosling, D. 6(5); Hibbert, T. 16(1); Howard, T. 38; Jacobsen, L. 4(1); Jagielka, P. 33(1); Jo, 11(1); Jutkiewicz, L. (1); Lescott, J. 35(1); Neville, P. 36(1); Nuno Valente, 1(1); Osman, L. 32(2); Pienaar, S. 27(1); Rodwell, J. 9(10); Saha, L. 10(14); Van der Meyde, A. (2); Vaughan, J. 1(12); Yakubu, A. 14; Yobo, J. 26(1).
Goals – League (55): Cahill 8, Fellaini 8, Arteta 6 (2 pens), Osman 6, Saha 6 (1 pen), Jo 5 (1 pen) Lescott 4, Yakubu 4, Pienaar 3, Gosling 2, Anichebe 1, Baines 1, Yobo 1.
Carling Cup (0).
FA Cup (9): Saha 2, Arteta 1 (pen), Cahill 1, Fellaini 1, Gosling 1, Lescott 1, Osman 1, Rodwell 1.
UEFA Cup (3): Castillo 1, Jagielka 1, Yakubu 1.
Ground: Goodison Park, Goodison Road, Liverpool L4 4EL. Telephone (0871) 663 1878.
Record Attendance: 78,299 v Liverpool, Division 1, 18 September 1948. **Capacity:** 40,158.
Manager: David Moyes.
Secretary: David Harrison.
Most League Goals: 121, Division 2, 1930–31.
Highest League Scorer in Season: William Ralph 'Dixie' Dean, 60, Division 1, 1927–28 (All-time League record).
Most League Goals in Total Aggregate: William Ralph 'Dixie' Dean, 349, 1925–37.
Most Capped Player: Neville Southall, 92, Wales.
Most League Appearances: Neville Southall, 578, 1981–98.
Honours – Football League: Division 1 Champions – 1890–91, 1914–15, 1927–28, 1931–32, 1938–39, 1962–63, 1969–70, 1984–85, 1986–87. Division 2 Champions – 1930–31. **FA Cup:** Winners – 1906, 1933, 1966, 1984, 1995. **European Competitions: European Cup-Winners' Cup:** Winners – 1984–85.
Colours: Blue shirts with white trim collar, white shorts, white stockings.

EXETER CITY   FL CHAMPIONSHIP 1

Basham Steve (F)	5 11	12 04	Southampton	2 12 77	Oxford U
Bull Ronnie (D)	5 7	10 12	Hackney	26 12 80	Rushden & D
Carlisle Wayne (M)	6 0	11 06	Lisburn	9 9 79	Leyton Orient
Cozic Bertrand (M)	5 10	12 06	Quimper	18 5 78	Team Bath

Edwards Rob (M)	6 0	12 07	Kendal	1	7 73	Blackpool
Gill Matthew (M)	5 11	11 10	Cambridge	8	11 80	Notts Co
Harley Ryan (D)	5 9	11 00	Bristol	22	1 85	Weston-Super-Mare
Jones Paul (G)	6 3	13 00	Maidstone	28	6 86	Leyton Orient
Logan Richard (F)	6 0	12 05	Bury St Edmunds	4	1 82	Weymouth
McAllister Craig (F)	6 1	11 03	Glasgow	28	6 80	Oxford U
Moxey Dean (D)	5 11	12 00	Exeter	14	1 86	
Panther Manny (F)	6 0	13 07	Glasgow	11	5 84	York C
Saunders Neil (M)	6 0	12 06	Barking	7	5 83	Team Bath
Seaborne Daniel (D)	6 0	11 10	Barnstaple	5	3 87	
Sercombe Liam (M)	5 10	10 10	Exeter	25	4 90	
Shephard Chris (M)	6 3	13 03	Exeter	2	6 90	
Stansfield Adam (F)	5 11	11 02	Plymouth	10	9 78	Hereford U
Stewart Marcus (F)	5 10	11 00	Bristol	7	12 72	Yeovil T
Taylor Matt (D)	6 1	12 04	Ormskirk	30	1 82	Team Bath
Tully Steve (D)	5 9	11 00	Paignton	10	2 80	Weymouth
Watson Ben (F)	5 10	10 11	Brighton	06	12 85	Grays Ath

League Appearances: Archibald-Henville, T. 19; Basham, S. 12(11); Cozic, B. 14(6); Edwards, R. 44; Fleetwood, S. 7(2); Friend, G. 4; Gill, M. 43; Harley, R. 25(6); Jones, P. 46; Logan, R. 18(12); McAllister, C. 8(22); Moxey, D. 41(2); Murray, F. 3(3); Obersteller, J. 3(4); Panther, M. 15(7); Russell, A. 7; Saunders, N. 15(2); Seaborne, D. 31(2); Sercombe, L. 16(13); Shephard, C. (2); Stansfield, A. 32(5); Stewart, M. 35(1); Taylor, M. 29(2); Tully, S. 35(1); Watson, B. 4(8).
Goals – League (65): Stansfield 10, Gill 9 (1 pen), McAllister 7, Stewart 7 (2 pens), Harley 4, Logan 4, Moxey 4, Fleetwood 3, Saunders 3, Basham 2 (1 pen), Panther 2, Sercombe 2, Taylor 2, Watson 2, Seaborne 1, own goals 3.
Carling Cup (1): Moxey 1.
FA Cup (2): Basham 1, Moxey 1.
J Paint Trophy (1): Harley 1.
Ground: St James Park, Stadium Way, Exeter EX4 6PX. Telephone: (01392) 411 243.
Record Attendance: 20,984 v Sunderland, FA Cup 6th rd (replay), 4 March 1931.
Ground Capacity: 8,830.
Manager: Paul Tisdale.
Football Secretary: Mike Radford.
Most League Goals: 88, Division 3 (S), 1932–33.
Highest League Scorer in Season: Fred Whitlow, 33, Division 3 (S), 1932–33.
Most League Goals in Total Aggregate: Tony Kellow, 129, 1976–78, 1980–83, 1985–88.
Most Capped Player: Dermot Curtis, 1 (17), Eire.
Most League Appearances: Arnold Mitchell, 495, 1952–66.
Honours – Division 3 (S) Cup: Winners 1934.
Colours: Red and white broad striped shirts, white sleeves with black trim, black shorts, black stockings.

FULHAM   FA PREMIERSHIP

Anderson Joe (D)				13	10 89	Scholar
Andreasen Leon (D)	6 1	13 03	Aidt Thorso	23	4 83	Werder Bremen
Baird Chris (D)	5 10	11 11	Ballymoney	25	2 82	Southampton
Bouazza Hameur (F)	5 10	12 01	Evry	22	2 85	Watford
Brown Wayne (M)	5 9	12 05	Kingston	6	8 88	Scholar
Davies Simon (M)	5 10	11 07	Haverfordwest	23	10 79	Everton
Dempsey Clinton (M)	6 1	12 02	Nacogdoches	9	3 83	New England R
Etheridge Neil (G)	6 3	14 00	Enfield	7	2 90	Scholar
Etuhu Dickson (M)	6 2	13 04	Kano	8	6 82	Sunderland
Foderingham Wesley (G)			Hammersmith	14	1 91	Scholar
Gera Zoltan (M)	6 0	11 11	Pecs	22	4 79	WBA

Hangeland Brede (D)	6 4	13 05	Houston	20 6 81	FC Copenhagen
Hoesen Danny (F)				15 1 91	Fortuna Sittard
Hughes Aaron (D)	6 0	11 02	Cookstown	8 11 79	Aston Villa
Johnson Andy (F)	5 7	10 09	Bedford	10 2 81	Everton
Johnson Eddie (F)	6 0	12 02	Bunnell	31 3 84	Kansas City Wizards
Kallio Toni (D)	6 4	13 03	Tampere	9 8 78	
Kamara Diomansy (F)	6 0	11 05	Paris	8 11 80	WBA
Konchesky Paul (D)	5 10	11 07	Barking	15 5 81	West Ham U
Leijer Adrian (D)	6 1	12 08	Dubbo	25 3 86	Melbourne Victory
Milsom Robert (D)	5 10	11 05	Redhill	2 1 87	Scholar
Moscatiello Luca (M)				25 5 91	Internazionale
Murphy Danny (M)	5 10	11 09	Chester	18 3 77	Tottenham H
Nevland Erik (F)	5 10	11 12	Stavanger	10 11 77	Groningen
Omozusi Elliot (D)	5 11	12 08	Hackney	15 12 88	Scholar
Osei-Gyan King (M)	6 3	11 11	Ghana	22 12 88	
Owusu Daniel (M)	5 8	10 03	Ghana	13 6 89	
Pantsil John (D)	5 10	12 08	Berekum	15 6 81	West Ham U
Saunders Matthew (M)	5 11	11 05	Chertsey	12 9 89	Scholar
Schwarzer Mark (G)	6 4	14 07	Sydney	6 10 72	Middlesbrough
Seol Ki-Hyun (F)	6 0	11 07	South Korea	8 1 79	Reading
Smalling Chris (D)	6 4	14 02	Greenwich	22 11 89	
Stockdale David (G)	6 3	13 04	Leeds	20 9 85	Darlington
Stoor Fredrik (D)	6 0	12 06	Stockholm	28 2 84	Rosenborg
Teimourian Andranik (M)	5 11	11 07	Tehran	6 3 83	Bolton W
Uwezu Michael (F)	5 6	12 02	Nigeria	12 12 90	
Watts Adam (D)	6 1	11 09	London	4 3 88	Scholar
Zamora Bobby (F)	6 1	11 11	Barking	16 1 81	West Ham U
Zuberbuhler Pascal (G)	6 5	15 08	Frauenfeld	8 1 71	Neuchatel Xamax

League Appearances: Andreasen, L. (6); Baird, C. 3(7); Brown, W. (1); Bullard, J. 18; Dacourt, O. (9); Davies, S. 33; Dempsey, C. 28(7); Etuhu, D. 19(2); Gera, Z. 20(12); Gray, J. (1); Hangeland, B. 37; Hughes, A. 38; Johnson, A. 30(1); Kallio, T. 2(1); Kamara, D. 3(9); Konchesky, P. 36; Milsom, R. (1); Murphy, D. 38; Nevland, E. 4(17); Pantsil, J. 37; Schwarzer, M. 38; Seol, K. 2(2); Smalling, C. (1); Stoor, F. (2); Teimourian, A. (1); Zamora, B. 32(3).
Goals – League (39): Dempsey 7, Johnson 7, Murphy 5 (5 pens), Kamara 4, Nevland 4, Bullard 2, Davies 2, Gera 2, Zamora 2, Etuhu 1, Hangeland 1, Konchesky 1, Seol 1.
Carling Cup (3): Bullard 1, Gera 1, Murphy 1.
FA Cup (9): Johnson 3, Zamorah 2, Davies 1, Dempsey 1, Murphy 1, own goal 1.
Ground: Craven Cottage, Stevenage Road, London SW6 6HH. Telephone: (0870) 442 1222.
Record Attendance: 49,335 v Millwall, Division 2, 8 October 1938. **Capacity:** 26,600.
Manager: Roy Hodgson.
Secretary: Darren Preston.
Most League Goals: 111, Division 3 (S), 1931–32.
Highest League Scorer in Season: Frank Newton, 43, Division 3 (S), 1931–32.
Most League Goals in Total Aggregate: Gordon Davies, 159, 1978–84, 1986–91.
Most Capped Player: Johnny Haynes, 56, England.
Most League Appearances: Johnny Haynes, 594, 1952–70.
Honours – Football League: Division 1 Champions – 2000–01. Division 2 Champions – 1948–49, 1998–99. Division 3 (S) Champions – 1931–32. **European Competitions: Intertoto Cup:** Winners – 2002.
Colours: White shirts with black trim, black shorts, white stockings.

GILLINGHAM   FL CHAMPIONSHIP 1

Ba George (F)	6 1	13 05	Abidjan	24	1 79	
Barcham Andy (F)	5 8	10 11	Basildon	16 12 86		Tottenham H
Bentley Mark (M)	6 2	13 07	Hertford	7	1 78	Southend U
Cumbers Luis (M)	6 0	11 10	Chelmsford	6	9 88	Scholar
Fuller Barry (M)	5 10	11 10	Ashford	25	9 84	Stevenage B
Jackson Simeon (M)	5 10	10 12	Kingston Jam	28	3 87	Rushden & D
Jarrett Albert (M)	6 1	10 07	Sierra Leone	23 10 84		Watford
Julian Alan (G)	6 2	13 07	Ashford	11	3 83	Brentford
King Simon (D)	6 0	13 00	Oxford	11	4 83	Barnet
Lewis Stuart (M)	5 10	11 06	Welwyn	15 10 87		Stevenage B
McCammon Mark (F)	6 2	14 05	Barnet	7	8 78	Doncaster R
Miller Adam (M)	5 11	11 06	Hemel Hempstead	19	2 82	Stevenage B
Murphy Tom (M)	5 11	10 12	Gillingham	19 12 91		Scholar
Nutter John (D)	6 2	12 10	Taplow	13	6 82	Stevenage B
Oli Dennis (F)	6 0	12 00	Newham	28	1 84	Grays Ath
Payne Jack (M)	5 9	9 02	Gravesend	5 12 91		Scholar
Pugh Andy (F)	5 9	12 02	Gravesend	28	1 89	Scholar
Richards Garry (D)	6 3	13 00	Romford	11	6 86	Southend U
Royce Simon (G)	6 2	12 10	Forest Gate	9	9 71	QPR
Weston Curtis (M)	5 11	11 09	Greenwich	24	1 87	Leeds U
Wynter Tom (M)	5 7	11 11	Lewisham	20	6 90	Scholar

League Appearances: Barcham, A. 31(2); Bentley, M. 34(5); Berry, T. 2(3); Crofts, A. 7(2); Cumbers, L. (7); Daniels, C. 5; Fuller, B. 37; Jackson, S. 37(4); Jarrett, A. 11(5); Julian, A. 4; King, S. 43; Lewis, S. 13(8); McCammon, M. 21(10); Miller, A. 32(3); Mills, L. 6(1); Mulligan, G. 12(14); Nutter, J. 43(2); Oli, D. 20(11); Payne, J. (2); Peters, J. 1(2); Pugh, A. (1); Richards, G. 26(10); Royce, S. 42; Southall, N. 28(8); Steer, R. 3(2); Weston, C. 43(2); Wright, J. 5.
Goals – League (58): Jackson 17 (4 pens), Barcham 6, Miller 6 (1 pen), McCammon 5, Weston 5, Oli 4, Southall 3, King 2, Mulligan 2, Richards 2, Bentley 1, Cumbers 1, Daniels 1, Mills 1, own goals 2.
Carling Cup (0).
FA Cup (4): Barcham 3, Jackson 1.
J Paint Trophy (0).
Play-Offs (3): Jackson 3 (1 pen).
Ground: KRBS Priestfield Stadium, Redfern Avenue, Gillingham, Kent ME7 4DD. Telephone (01634) 300 000.
Record Attendance: 23,002 v QPR, FA Cup 3rd rd, 10 January 1948. **Capacity:** 11,440.
Manager: Mark Stimson.
Secretary: Gwen Poynter.
Most League Goals: 90, Division 4, 1973–74.
Highest League Scorer in Season: Ernie Morgan, 31, Division 3 (S), 1954–55; Brian Yeo, 31, Division 4, 1973–74.
Most League Goals in Total Aggregate: Brian Yeo, 135, 1963–75.
Most Capped Player: Mamady Sidibe, 7 (12), Mali.
Most League Appearances: John Simpson, 571, 1957–72.
Honours – Football League: Division 4 Champions – 1963–64.
Colours: Blue with white insert.

GRIMSBY TOWN   FL CHAMPIONSHIP 2

Akpa Akpro Jean-Louis (F)	6 0	10 12	Toulouse	4	1 85	Toulouse
Atkinson Rob (D)	6 1	12 00	Beverley	29	4 87	Barnsley
Bennett Ryan (D)	6 0	13 02	London	4	8 85	Scholar
Bird Matthew (D)	6 0	11 07	Grimsby	31 10 90		Scholar

Bore Peter (M)	5 11	11 04	Grimsby	4 11 87	Scholar
Boshell Danny (M)	5 11	11 09	Bradford	30 5 81	Stockport Co
Boshell Danny (M)	5 11	11 09	Bradford	30 5 81	Stockport Co
Clarke Jamie (D)	6 2	12 03	Sunderland	18 9 82	Boston U
Fuller Josh (M)	5 9	11 00	Grimsby	12 12 80	Scholar
Hegarty Nick (M)	5 10	11 00	Hemsworth	25 6 86	Scholar
Heywood Matt (D)	6 3	14 00	Chatham	26 8 79	Brentford
Jarman Nathan (F)	5 11	11 03	Scunthorpe	19 9 86	Barnsley
Llewellyn Chris (F)	5 11	11 06	Swansea	29 8 79	Wrexham
Lund Jonathan (M)	5 10	11 10	Leeds	1 11 88	
Normington Grant (M)	5 8	12 08	Hull	9 5 90	Scholar
North Danny (F)	5 9	12 08	Grimsby	7 9 87	Scholar
Proudlock Adam (F)	6 0	13 07	Wellington	9 5 81	Darlington
Stockdale Robbie (D)	6 0	11 03	Middlesbrough	30 11 79	Tranmere R

League Appearances: Akpa Akpro, J. 19(1); Ameobi, T. 2; Atkinson, R. 30(1); Barnes, P. 32; Bennett, R. 45; Bore, P. 10(17); Boshell, D. 18(6); Butler, M. 3; Clarke, J. 31(1); Conlon, B. 8(7); Elliott, S. 9(2); Forbes, A. 8(7); Fuller, J. (1); Hegarty, N. 32(3); Henderson, W. 14; Heslop, S. 5(3); Heywood, M. 16(2); Hope, R. 6; Hunt, J. 21(1); Jarman, N. 25(8); Kalala, J. 21; Kamara, M. 1(1); Llewellyn, C. 13(15); Newey, T. 23(1); Normington, G. (1); North, D. 2(13); Proudlock, A. 22(6); Sinclair, D. 9; Stockdale, R. 19(1); Sweeney, P. 8; Taylor, A. 3(3); Till, P. 15(1); Trotter, L. 15; Vidal, J. 2(1); Widdowson, J. 19(1).
Goals – League (51): Proudlock 8 (1 pen), Jarman 6, Bennett 5, Conlon 5 (1 pen), Hegarty 4, Akpa Akpro 3, Forbes 3, Atkinson 2, Boshell 2, Elliott 2, Kalala 2, Till 2 (1 pen), Trotter 2, Bore 1, Clarke 1, North 1, Sinclair 1, Widdowson 1.
Carling Cup (3): Hunt 1, Newey 1, own goal 1.
FA Cup (1): Stockdale 1.
J Paint Trophy (3): Hegarty 1, Jarman 1, North 1.
Ground: Blundell Park, Cleethorpes, North-East Lincolnshire DN35 7PY. Telephone (01472) 605 050.
Record Attendance: 31,651 v Wolverhampton W, FA Cup 5th rd, 20 February 1937. **Capacity:** 9,106.
Manager: Mike Newell.
Chief Executive: Ian Fleming.
Most League Goals: 103, Division 2, 1933–34.
Highest League Scorer in Season: Pat Glover, 42, Division 2, 1933–34.
Most League Goals in Total Aggregate: Pat Glover, 180, 1930–39.
Most Capped Player: Pat Glover, 7, Wales.
Most League Appearances: John McDermott, 647, 1987–2007.
Honours – Football League: Division 2 Champions – 1900–01, 1933–34. Division 3 (N) Champions – 1925–26, 1955–56. Division 3 Champions – 1979–80. Division 4 Champions – 1971–72. **League Group Cup:** Winners – 1981–82. **Auto Windscreens Shield:** Winners – 1997–98.
Colours: Black and white striped shirts, black shorts, white stockings.

HARTLEPOOL UNITED   FL CHAMPIONSHIP 1

Brown James (F)	5 11	11 00	Newcastle	3 1 87	Cramlington J
Clark Ben (D)	6 1	13 11	Shotley Bridge	24 1 83	Sunderland
Collins Sam (D)	6 2	14 03	Pontefract	5 6 77	Hull C
Cook Mark (D)	6 1	12 01	North Shields	7 9 88	Newcastle U
Foley David (F)	5 4	8 09	South Shields	12 5 87	Scholar
Humphreys Richie (M)	5 11	12 07	Sheffield	30 11 77	Cambridge U
Jones Richie (M)	6 0	11 00	Manchester	26 9 86	Manchester U
Liddle Gary (D)	6 1	12 06	Middlesbrough	15 6 86	Middlesbrough
Mackay Michael (F)	6 0	11 08	Durham	11 10 82	Consett
Monkhouse Andrew (M)	6 2	12 06	Leeds	23 10 80	Swindon T
Nelson Michael (D)	6 2	13 03	Gateshead	15 3 82	Bury

Power Alan (M)	5 7	11 06	Dublin	23	1 88	Nottingham F
Robson Matty (D)	5 10	11 02	Durham	23	1 85	Scholar
Rowell Jonny (M)	5 7	11 02	Newcastle	10	9 89	Scholar
Sweeney Anthony (M)	6 0	11 07	Stockton	5	9 83	Scholar
Tymon Matty (F)	5 11	12 04	Middlesbrough	15	4 90	Scholar

League Appearances: Barker, R. (8); Boland, W. 3; Brown, J. 18; Budtz, J. 9(1); Clark, B. 35; Collins, S. 40; Foley, D. 4(19); Guy, L. 4; Henderson, L. 2(6); Humphreys, R. 39(6); Jones, R. 36; Kyle, K. 15; Lange, R. 2(1); Lee-Barrett, A. 37; Liddle, G. 37(6); MacKay, M. 9(14); McCunnie, J. 10(5); Monkhouse, A. 41(3); Nardiello, B. 8(4); Nelson, M. 46; Parker, K. 9; Porter, J. 37(1); Power, A. (4); Robson, M. 14(15); Rowell, J. 3(3); Skarz, J. 5(2); Sweeney, A. 43(1).
Goals – League (66): Porter 18 (6 pens), Brown 6, Monkhouse 6, Kyle 5, Nelson 5, Sweeney 5, Jones 3, Nardiello 3, Clark 2 (2 pens), MacKay 2, Robson 2, Barker 1, Boland 1, Collins 1, Lange 1, own goals 5.
Carling Cup (8): Porter 3, Foley 2, Barker 1, Brown 1, Monkhouse 1.
FA Cup (10): Mackay 2, Porter 2 (1 pen), Brown 1, Foley 1, Liddle 1, Monkhouse 1, Nelson 1, own goal 1.
J Paint Trophy (0).
Ground: Victoria Park, Clarence Road, Hartlepool TS24 8BZ. Telephone (01429) 272 584.
Record Attendance: 17,426 v Manchester U, FA Cup 3rd rd, 5 January 1957.
Capacity: 7,630.
Director of Sport: Chris Turner.
Senior Administrator: Maureen Smith.
Most League Goals: 90, Division 3 (N), 1956–57.
Highest League Scorer in Season: William Robinson, 28, Division 3 (N), 1927–28; Joe Allon, 28, Division 4, 1990–91.
Most League Goals in Total Aggregate: Ken Johnson, 98, 1949–64.
Most Capped Player: Ambrose Fogarty, 1 (11), Republic of Ireland.
Most League Appearances: Wattie Moore, 447, 1948–64.
Honours – Nil.
Colours: White shirts with blue trim, blue shorts, white stockings.

HEREFORD UNITED   FL CHAMPIONSHIP 2

Beckwith Dean (D)	6 3	13 01	Southwark	18	9 83	Gillingham
Diagouraga Toumani (M)	6 2	11 05	Corbeil-Essones	10	6 87	Watford
Done Matt (M)	5 10	10 04	Oswestry	22	6 88	Wrexham
Guinan Stephen (F)	6 1	13 02	Birmingham	24	12 75	Cheltenham T
Gwynne Sam (M)	5 9	11 11	Hereford	17	12 87	Scholar
Jones Craig (M)	6 0	12 02	Hereford	12	12 89	Cardiff C
Macleod Jack (M)	5 8	10 00	Hereford	3	8 88	Carshalton Ath
O'Leary Stephen (M)	6 0	11 09	Barnet	12	2 85	Luton T
Rose Richard (D)	6 0	12 04	Pembury	8	9 82	Gillingham
Smith Ben (M)	5 9	11 09	Chelmsford	23	11 78	Weymouth
Taylor Kris (M)	5 9	11 05	Stafford	12	1 84	Walsall
Veiga Jose Manuel (G)	6 2	12 13	Lisbon	18	12 76	Atherstone T

League Appearances: Ainsworth, L. 7; Antwi-Birago, G. 5; Ashikodi, M. 4(2); Beckwith, D. 22(3); Brandy, F. 14(1); Broadhurst, K. 23(2); Chadwick, N. 5(5); Dennehy, D. 3; Diagouraga, T. 45; Done, M. 24(12); Easton, C. 9(3); Gowling, J. 13; Guinan, S. 40(3); Gulacsi, P. 18; Gwynne, S. 17(4); Hewson, S. 9(1); Hudson-Odoi, B. 10(6); Jackson, R. 24(1); Johnson, S. 8(21); Jones, C. 1(2); Macleod, J. 2(4); Murray, M. 3; Myrie-Williams, J. 15; N'Gotty, B. 8; O'Leary, S. 11(4); Oji, S. 4; Pugh, M. 8(1); Randolph, D. 13; Rose, R. 40(2); Samson, C. 10(1); Smith, B. 29(8); Taylor, K. 38(1); Threlfall, R. 3; Veiga, J. 1; Weale, C. 1; Williams, A. 19(7).

Goals – League (42): Guinan 15 (4 pens), Brandy 4, Ainsworth 3, Hewson 3, Hudson-Odoi 3, Diagouraga 2, Myrie-Williams 2, Williams 2, Beckwith 1, Broadhurst 1, Chadwick 1 (pen), Gwynne 1, O'Leary 1, Pugh 1, Smith 1, Taylor 1.
Carling Cup (1): Ashikodi 1.
FA Cup (1): Taylor 1.
J Paint Trophy (1): Done 1.
Ground: Athletic Ground, Edgar Street, Hereford, Herefordshire HR4 9JU. Telephone (08442) 761 939.
Record Attendance: 18,114 v Sheffield Wed., FA Cup 3rd rd, 4 January 1958.
Capacity: 7,149.
Manager: John Trewick.
Secretary: Mrs Joan Fennessy.
Most League Goals: 86, Division 3, 1975–76.
Highest League Scorer in Season: Dixie McNeil, 35, 1975–76.
Most League Goals in Total Aggregate: Stewart Phillips, 93, 1980–88, 1990–91.
Most Capped Player: Trevor Benjamin, 2, Jamaica.
Most League Appearances: Mel Pejic, 412, 1980–92.
Honours – Football League: Division 3 Champions – 1975–76. **Welsh Cup:** Winners – 1990.
Colours: White shirts, black shorts, white stockings.

HUDDERSFIELD TOWN   FL CHAMPIONSHIP 1

Ainsworth Lionel (F)	5 9	9 10	Nottingham	1 10 87	Watford
Berrett James (M)	5 10	10 13	Halifax	13 1 89	Scholar
Booth Andy (F)	6 1	13 00	Huddersfield	6 12 73	Sheffield W
Butler Andy (D)	6 0	13 00	Doncaster	4 11 83	Scunthorpe U
Clarke Nathan (D)	6 2	12 00	Halifax	30 11 83	Scholar
Clarke Tom (D)	5 11	12 02	Halifax	21 12 87	Scholar
Collins Michael (M)	6 0	10 12	Halifax	30 4 86	Scholar
Craney Ian (M)	5 10	12 00	Liverpool	21 7 82	Accrington S
Denton Tom (F)	6 6	14 00	Shepley	24 7 89	Wakefield
Eastwood Simon (G)	6 2	12 09	Luton	26 6 89	Scholar
Flynn Michael (M)	5 10	13 04	Newport	17 10 80	Blackpool
Glennon Matthew (G)	6 2	13 11	Stockport	8 10 78	St Johnstone
Goodwin Jim (M)	5 9	12 01	Waterford	20 11 81	Scunthorpe U
Jevons Phil (F)	5 11	12 00	Liverpool	1 8 79	Bristol C
Lucketti Chris (D)	6 1	13 06	Rochdale	28 9 71	Sheffield U
Novak Lee (F)	6 0	12 04	Newcastle	28 9 88	Gateshead
Parker Keigan (F)	5 7	10 05	Livingston	8 6 82	Blackpool
Pilkington Anthony (M)	5 11	12 00	Manchester	3 11 87	Stockport Co
Roberts Gary (F)	5 10	11 09	Chester	18 3 84	Ipswich T
Skarz Joe (D)	5 11	13 00	Huddersfield	13 7 89	Scholar
Smithies Alex (G)	6 1	10 01	Huddersfield	25 3 90	Scholar
Williams Robbie (D)	5 10	11 13	Pontefract	2 10 84	Barnsley

League Appearances: Ainsworth, L. 7(7); Beckett, L. (1); Berrett, J. 8(1); Booth, A. 9(11); Broadbent, D. (1); Butler, A. 42; Cadamarteri, D. 24(8); Clarke, N. 38; Clarke, T. 11(4); Collins, M. 34(2); Craney, I. 23(11); Dickinson, L. 13; Eastwood, S. 1; Flynn, M. 18(7); Glennon, M. 18; Goodwin, J. 35(2); Holdsworth, A. 30(4); Jevons, P. 12(11); Jones, S. 2(2); Jutkiewicz, L. 6(1); Kamara, M. (2); Kelly, M. 7; Lucketti, C. 12(1); Parker, K. 14(6); Pilkington, A. 16; Roberts, G. 43; Skarz, J. 9; Smithies, A. 27; Unsworth, D. 4; Werling, D. (3); Williams, R. 31(4); Worthington, J. 12(7).
Goals – League (62): Collins 9, Roberts 9 (1 pen), Booth 8, Dickinson 6, Craney 5, Butler 4, Flynn 4, Clarke N 3, Cadamarteri 2, Jevons 2, Parker 2, Pilkington 2, Berrett 1, Clarke T 1, Goodwin 1, Kelly 1, Skarz 1, own goal 1.
Carling Cup (5): Roberts 2, Flynn 1, Williams 1, Worthington 1.
FA Cup (3): Collins 1, Craney 1, Williams 1.

J Paint Trophy (0).
Ground: The Galpharm Stadium, Stadium Way, Leeds Road, Huddersfield HD1 6PX. Telephone 0870 4444 677.
Record Attendance: 67,037 v Arsenal, FA Cup 6th rd, 27 February 1932 (at Leeds Road); 23,678 v Liverpool, FA Cup 3rd rd, 12 December 1999 (at Alfred McAlpine Stadium).
Capacity: 24,554.
Manager: Lee Clark.
Secretary: Ann Hough.
Most League Goals: 101, Division 4, 1979–80.
Highest League Scorer in Season: Sam Taylor, 35, Division 2, 1919–20; George Brown, 35, Division 1, 1925–26.
Most League Goals in Total Aggregate: George Brown, 142, 1921–29; Jimmy Glazzard, 142, 1946–56.
Most Capped Player: Jimmy Nicholson, 31 (41), Northern Ireland.
Most League Appearances: Billy Smith, 520, 1914–34.
Honours – Football League: Division 1 Champions – 1923–24, 1924–25, 1925–26. Division 2 Champions – 1969–70. Division 4 Champions – 1979–80. **FA Cup:** Winners – 1922.
Colours: Blue and white striped shirts, white shorts, black stockings.

HULL CITY   FA PREMIERSHIP

Ashbee Ian (M)	6 1	13 07	Birmingham	6 9 76	Cambridge U
Atkinson William (M)	5 10	10 07	Beverley	14 10 88	Scholar
Barmby Nick (M)	5 7	11 03	Hull	11 2 74	Leeds U
Boateng George (M)	5 9	12 06	Nkawkaw	5 9 75	Middlesbrough
Brown Wayne (D)	6 0	12 06	Barking	20 8 77	Colchester U
Bullard Jimmy (M)	5 10	11 05	Newham	23 10 78	Fulham
Cooper Liam (D)	6 2	13 07	Hull	30 8 91	Scholar
Cousin Daniel (F)	6 2	12 13	Libreville	7 2 77	Rangers
Dawson Andy (D)	5 10	11 02	Northallerton	20 10 78	Scunthorpe U
Devitt Jamie (F)	5 10	10 05	Dublin	6 6 90	Scholar
Doyle Nathan (M)	5 11	12 06	Derby	12 1 87	Derby Co
Duke Matt (G)	6 5	13 04	Sheffield	16 7 77	Sheffield U
Fagan Craig (F)	5 11	11 11	Birmingham	11 12 82	Derby Co
Featherstone Nicky (F)	5 7	11 03	Goole	22 9 89	Scholar
Folan Caleb (F)	6 2	14 07	Leeds	26 10 82	Wigan Ath
Garcia Richard (F)	5 11	12 01	Perth	4 9 81	Colchester U
Gardner Anthony (D)	6 3	14 00	Stone	19 9 80	Tottenham H
Gardner Steven (D)	5 9	10 09	Hull	12 5 90	Scholar
Geovanni (F)	5 8	10 08	Acaiaca	11 1 80	Manchester C
Halmosi Peter (M)	5 10	10 12	Szombathely	25 9 79	Plymouth Arg
Hughes Bryan (M)	5 10	11 08	Liverpool	19 6 76	Charlton Ath
Kendall Ryan (F)	5 7	10 09	Hull	14 9 89	Trainee
Kilbane Kevin (M)	6 1	13 05	Preston	1 2 77	Wigan Ath
Marney Dean (M)	6 0	11 05	Barking	31 1 84	Tottenham H
Mendy Bernard (D)	5 11	12 02	Evreux	20 8 81	Paris St Germain
Myhill Boaz (G)	6 3	14 06	Modesto	9 11 82	Aston Villa
Oxley Mark (G)	5 11	11 05		2 6 90	Rotherham U
Ricketts Sam (D)	6 1	12 01	Aylesbury	11 10 81	Swansea C
Turner Michael (D)	6 4	13 05	Lewisham	9 11 83	Brentford
Warner Tony (G)	6 4	15 06	Liverpool	11 5 74	Fulham
Woodhead Tom (G)	5 10	12 00	Beverley	9 5 90	Scholar
Zayatte Kamil (D)	6 2	13 10	Conakry	7 3 85	Lens

League Appearances: Ashbee, I. 31; Barmby, N. 13(8); Boateng, G. 21(2); Brown, W. 1; Bullard, J. (1); Cousin, D. 18(9); Dawson, A. 25; Doyle, N. 2(1); Duke, M. 10; Fagan, C. 15(7); Folan, C. 2(13); France, R. 1(1); Garcia, R. 13(10); Gardner, A. 6;

Geovanni, 32(2); Giannakopoulos, S. (2); Halmosi, P. 4(14); Hughes, B. 1(5); Kilbane, K. 15(1); King, M. 19(1); Manucho, 6(7); Marney, D. 26(5); McShane, P. 17; Mendy, B. 15(13); Myhill, B. 28; Ricketts, S. 27(2); Turner, M. 38; Windass, D. 1(4); Zayatte, K. 31(1).
Goals – League (39): Geovanni 8 (1 pen), King 5 (2 pens), Cousin 4, Turner 4, Fagan 3, Manucho 2, Mendy 2, Ashbee 1, Barmby 1, Dawson 1, Folan 1, Garcia 1, McShane 1, Windass 1, Zayatte 1, own goals 3.
Carling Cup (1): Windass 1.
FA Cup (7): Ashbee 1, Barmby 1, Cousin 1, Halmosi 1, Turner 1, Zayatte 1, own goal 1.
Ground: Kingston Communications Stadium, Walton St, Hull HU3 6HU. Telephone (0870) 837 0003.
Record Attendance: 55,019 v Manchester U, FA Cup 6th rd, 26 February 1949 (Boothferry Park); 25,512 v Sunderland, FL C, 28 October 2007 (KC Stadium).
Capacity: 25,404.
Manager: Phil Brown.
Football Secretary: Phil Hough.
Most League Goals: 109, Division 3, 1965–66.
Highest League Scorer in Season: Bill McNaughton, 39, Division 3 (N), 1932–33.
Most League Goals in Total Aggregate: Chris Chilton, 195, 1960–71.
Most Capped Player: Theo Whitmore, 28 (105), Jamaica.
Most League Appearances: Andy Davidson, 520, 1952–67.
Honours – Football League: Division 3 (N) Champions – 1932–33, 1948–49. Division 3 Champions – 1965–66.
Colours: Black and amber striped shirts, black shorts, black stockings.

IPSWICH TOWN   FL CHAMPIONSHIP

Balkestein Pim (D)	6 3	12 00	Gouda	29 4 87	Heerenveen
Bruce Alex (D)	6 0	11 06	Norwich	28 9 84	Birmingham C
Civelli Luciano (M)	6 2	13 01	Capital Federal	6 10 86	Banfield
Counago Pablo (F)	5 11	11 06	Pontevedra	9 8 79	Malaga
Garvan Owen (M)	6 0	10 07	Dublin	29 1 88	Scholar
Haynes Danny (F)	5 11	12 04	Peckham	19 1 88	Scholar
Lisbie Kevin (F)	5 10	11 06	Hackney	17 10 78	Colchester U
McAuley Gareth (D)	6 3	13 00	Larne	5 12 78	Leicester C
Norris David (M)	5 7	11 06	Stamford	22 2 81	Plymouth Arg
Peters Jaime (M)	5 7	10 12	Toronto	4 5 87	Moor Green
Quinn Alan (M)	5 9	10 06	Dublin	13 6 79	Sheffield U
Rhodes Jordan (F)	6 1	11 03	Oldham	5 2 90	Barnsley
Smith Tommy (D)	6 2	12 02	Macclesfield	31 3 90	Scholar
Stead Jon (F)	6 3	13 03	Huddersfield	7 4 83	Sheffield U
Sumulikoski Velice (M)	6 0	12 02	Macedonia	24 1 81	Zenit
Supple Shane (G)	5 11	11 07	Dublin	4 5 87	Scholar
Thatcher Ben (D)	5 10	12 07	Swindon	30 11 75	Charlton Ath
Trotter Liam (M)	6 2	12 02	Ipswich	24 8 88	Scholar
Upson Edward (M)	5 10	11 07	Bury St Edmunds	21 11 89	Scholar
Walters Jon (F)	6 0	12 06	Birkenhead	20 9 83	Chester C
Wright David (D)	5 11	11 01	Warrington	1 5 80	Wigan Ath
Wright Richard (G)	6 2	14 04	Ipswich	5 11 77	West Ham U

League Appearances: Ambrose, D. 6(3); Balkestein, P. 15(5); Bowditch, D. (1); Bruce, A. 25; Campo, I. 14(3); Civelli, L. 8; Counago, P. 26(18); Garvan, O. 22(15); Giovani, 6(2); Harding, D. 1; Haynes, D. 8(16); Lee, A. 2(1); Lisbie, K. 24(17); McAuley, G. 35; Miller, T. 26(6); Naylor, R. 20(3); Norris, D. 35(2); Peters, J. 2(1); Quinn, A. 28(6); Rhodes, J. (2); Richards, M. 1; Smith, T. 2; Stead, J. 26(13); Sumulikoski, V. 22(4); Thatcher, B. 20; Trotter, L. 2(1); Volz, M. 20(2); Walters, J. 30(6); Wickham, C. (2); Wright, D. 34; Wright, R. 46.

Goals – League (62): Stead 12, Counago 9, Garvan 7, Lisbie 6, Miller 5 (2 pens), Walters 5, Giovani 4 (2 pens), Norris 3, Quinn 2, Bruce 1, Campo 1, Trotter 1, Wright D 1, own goals 5.
Carling Cup (7): Haynes 2, Counago 1, Lee 1, Lisbie 1, Miller 1, Walters 1.
FA Cup (4): Bruce 1, Counago 1, Stead 1, Walters 1 (pen).
Ground: Portman Road, Ipswich, Suffolk IP1 2DA. Telephone (01473) 400 500.
Record Attendance: 38,010 v Leeds U, FA Cup 6th rd, 8 March 1975.
Capacity: 30,311.
Manager: Roy Keane.
Secretary: Sally Webb.
Most League Goals: 106, Division 3 (S), 1955–56.
Highest League Scorer in Season: Ted Phillips, 41, Division 3 (S), 1956–57.
Most League Goals in Total Aggregate: Ray Crawford, 204, 1958–63 and 1966–69.
Most Capped Player: Allan Hunter, 47 (53), Northern Ireland.
Most League Appearances: Mick Mills, 591, 1966–82.
Honours – Football League: Division 1 Champions – 1961–62. Division 2 Champions – 1960–61, 1967–68, 1991–92. Division 3 (S) Champions – 1953–54, 1956–57. **FA Cup:** Winners – 1977–78. **European Competitions: UEFA Cup:** Winners – 1980–81.
Colours: Blue and white thin striped shirts, blue sleeves, white shorts, blue stockings.

LEEDS UNITED   FL CHAMPIONSHIP 1

Ankergren Casper (G)	6 3	14 07	Koge	9 11 79	Brondby
Becchio Luciano (F)	6 2	13 05	Cordoba	28 12 83	Merida
Beckford Jermaine (F)	6 2	13 02	Ealing	9 12 83	Wealdstone
Darville Liam (D)				26 10 90	Scholar
Delph Fabian (M)	5 8	10 00	Bradford	21 11 89	Scholar
Elliott Tom (F)	5 10	11 02	Leeds	9 9 89	School
Grella Mike (F)	5 11	12 02	Glen Cove	23 1 87	Duke Univ
Hotchkiss Oliver (M)			Houghton-le-Spring	27 9 89	Scholar
Howson Jonathan (M)	5 11	12 01	Leeds	21 5 88	Scholar
Hughes Andy (M)	5 11	12 01	Stockport	2 1 78	Norwich C
Huntington Paul (D)	6 3	12 08	Carlisle	17 9 87	Newcastle U
Johnson Brad (M)	6 0	12 10	Hackney	28 4 87	Northampton T
Kandol Tresor (F)	6 1	11 05	Banga	20 8 81	Barnet
Kilkenny Neil (M)	5 8	10 08	Enfield	19 12 85	Birmingham C
Martin Alan (G)	6 0	11 11	Glasgow	1 1 89	Motherwell
Michalik Lubomir (D)	6 4	13 00	Cadca	13 8 83	Bolton W
Naylor Richard (D)	6 1	13 07	Leeds	28 2 77	Ipswich T
Parker Ben (D)	5 11	11 06	Pontefract	8 11 87	Scholar
Prutton David (M)	5 10	13 00	Hull	12 9 81	Southampton
Robinson Andy (M)	5 8	11 04	Birkenhead	3 11 79	Swansea C
Rui Marques Manuel (D)	5 11	11 13	Luanda	3 9 77	Maritimo
Sheehan Alan (D)	5 11	11 02	Athlone	14 9 86	Leicester C
Showunmi Enoch (F)	6 3	14 11	Kilburn	21 4 82	Bristol C
Snodgrass Robert (F)	6 0	12 02	Glasgow	7 9 87	Livingston
Sweeney Peter (M)	6 0	12 11	Glasgow	25 9 84	Stoke C
Webb Jonathan (D)	5 10	11 02	Wetherby	15 1 90	
White Aidan (D)			Leeds	10 10 91	Scholar

League Appearances: Ankergren, C. 33; Assoumani, M. 1; Becchio, L. 40(5); Beckford, J. 32(2); Christie, M. 1(3); Delph, F. 40(2); Dickinson, C. 7; Dickinson, L. 4(4); Douglas, J. 42(1); Grella, M. (11); Howson, J. 26(14); Hughes, A. 18(9); Huntington, P. 4; Johnson, B. 7(8); Kilkenny, N. 27(3); Lucas, D. 13; Michalik, L. 15(4); Naylor, R. 22; Parker, B. 23(1); Prutton, D. 8(8); Richardson, F. 21(2); Robinson, A. 20(12); Rui Marques, M. 32; Sheehan, A. 11; Showunmi, E. 3(5); Snodgrass, R. 25(17); Sodje, S. 5; Telfer, P. 14; Trundle, L. 7(3); White, A. 5.

Goals – League (77): Beckford 26, Becchio 15, Snodgrass 9 (1 pen), Delph 6, Howson 4, Kilkenny 4, Robinson 2, Showunmi 2, Christie 1, Douglas 1, Johnson 1, Naylor 1, Rui Marques 1, Sheehan 1, Trundle 1, own goals 2.
Carling Cup (13): Beckford 4, Becchio 2, Robinson 2, Showunmi 2, Snodgrass 2, Douglas 1.
FA Cup (6): Beckford 3, Parker 1, Robinson 1 (pen), own goal 1.
J Paint Trophy (4): Becchio 1, Howson 1, Robinson 1 (pen), Showunmi 1.
Play-Offs (1): Becchio 1.
Ground: Elland Road Stadium, Elland Rd, Leeds LS11 0ES. Telephone (0871) 334 1919.
Record Attendance: 57,892 v Sunderland, FA Cup 5th rd (replay), 15 March 1967.
Capacity: 39,457.
Manager: Simon Grayson.
Most League Goals: 98, Division 2, 1927–28.
Highest League Scorer in Season: John Charles, 42, Division 2, 1953–54.
Most League Goals in Total Aggregate: Peter Lorimer, 168, 1965–79 and 1983–86.
Most Capped Player: Lucas Radebe, 58 (70), South Africa.
Most League Appearances: Jack Charlton, 629, 1953–73.
Honours – Football League: Division 1 Champions – 1968–69, 1973–74, 1991–92. Division 2 Champions – 1923–24, 1963–64, 1989–90. **FA Cup:** Winners – 1972. **Football League Cup:** Winners – 1967–68. **European Competitions: European Fairs Cup:** Winners – 1967–68, 1970–71.
Colours: All white with one vertical blue stripe and blue trim sleeves, white shorts, white stockings.

LEICESTER CITY   FL CHAMPIONSHIP

Name					
Adams Nicky (F)	5 10	11 00	Bolton	16 10 86	Bury
Berner Bruno (M)	6 1	12 13	Zurich	21 11 77	Blackburn R
Campbell Dudley (F)	5 10	11 00	London	12 11 81	Birmingham C
Chambers Ashley (F)	5 10	11 06	Leicester	1 3 90	Scholar
Cisak Aleksander (G)	6 3	14 11	Krakow	19 5 89	Scholar
Clemence Stephen (M)	6 0	12 09	Liverpool	31 3 78	Birmingham C
Dickov Paul (F)	5 6	10 06	Livingston	1 11 72	Manchester C
Dyer Lloyd (M)	5 8	10 03	Birmingham	13 9 82	Milton Keynes D
Edworthy Marc (D)	5 10	11 11	Barnstaple	24 12 72	Derby Co
Fryatt Matty (F)	5 10	11 00	Nuneaton	5 3 86	Walsall
Gradel Max (M)	5 8	12 03	Ivory Coast	30 9 87	Scholar
Hayes Jonathan (M)	5 7	11 00	Dublin	9 7 87	Reading
Hobbs Jack (D)	6 3	13 05	Portsmouth	18 8 88	Liverpool
Howard Steve (F)	6 3	15 00	Durham	10 5 76	Derby Co
King Andy (M)	6 0	11 10	Luton	29 10 88	Scholar
King Craig (F)	5 11	11 12	Chesterfield	6 10 90	Scholar
Logan Conrad (G)	6 0	14 09	Letterkenny	18 4 86	Scholar
Mattock Joe (D)	5 11	11 04	Leicester	15 5 90	Scholar
Morrison Michael (D)	6 0	12 00	Bury St Edmunds	3 3 88	Cambridge U
Oakley Matthew (M)	5 10	12 06	Peterborough	17 8 77	Derby Co
O'Neill Luke (D)			Slough	20 8 91	Scholar
Pentney Carl (G)	6 0	12 00	Leicester	3 2 89	
Porter Levi (F)	5 4	10 05	Leicester	6 4 87	Scholar
Powell Chris (D)	5 11	11 12	Lambeth	8 9 69	Charlton Ath
Rowe-Turner Lathaniel (D)	6 1	13 00	Leicester	12 11 89	Scholar
Sappleton Reneil (M)	5 10	11 13	Kingston	8 12 89	QPR
Tunchev Aleksandar (D)	6 2	13 03	Pazardzhik	10 7 81	CSKA Sofia
Wesolowski James (D)	5 8	11 11	Sydney	25 8 87	Scholar
Worley Harry (D)	6 3	13 00	Warrington	25 11 88	Chelsea

League Appearances: Adams, N. 4(8); Ajdarevic, A. (5); Berner, B. 21(11); Brown, W. 7(2); Bunn, M. 3; Campbell, D. 2(5); Chambers, A. (1); Cleverley, T.

63

10(5); Davies, M. 5(2); Dickov, P. 4(16); Dyer, L. 43(1); Edworthy, M. 5; Fryatt, M. 46; Gilbert, K. 33(1); Gradel, M. 16(11); Hayles, B. 1(9); Henderson, P. 6; Hobbs, J. 39(5); Howard, S. 40(1); King, A. 45; Kisnorbo, P. 5(3); Martin, D. 25; Mattock, J. 25(6); Morrison, M. 32(3); Oakley, M. 45; Pentney, C. (1); Porter, L. 1; Powell, C. 12(5); Stockdale, D. 8; Tunchev, A. 19(1); Warner, T. 4.
Goals – League (84): Fryatt 27 (4 pens), Howard 13 (2 pens), Dyer 10, King A 9, Oakley 8, Berner 3, Morrison 3, Cleverley 2, Dickov 2 (1 pen), Davies 1, Gilbert 1, Gradel 1, Hobbs 1, Mattock 1, Tunchev 1, own goal 1.
Carling Cup (3): Dickov 1, Howard 1, King A 1.
FA Cup (7): Fryatt 4 (1 pen), Dyer 1, Gradel 1, King A 1.
J Paint Trophy (3): Adams 1, Fryatt 1, Howard 1.
Ground: Walkers Stadium, Filbert Way, Leicester LE2 7FL. Telephone (0844) 815 6000.
Record Attendance: 47,298 v Tottenham H, FA Cup 5th rd, 18 February 1928.
Capacity: 32,312.
Manager: Nigel Pearson.
Secretary: Andrew Neville.
Most League Goals: 109, Division 2, 1956–57.
Highest League Scorer in Season: Arthur Rowley, 44, Division 2, 1956–57.
Most League Goals in Total Aggregate: Arthur Chandler, 259, 1923–35.
Most Capped Player: John O'Neill, 39, Northern Ireland.
Most League Appearances: Adam Black, 528, 1920–35.
Honours – Football League: Championship 1 Winners – 2008–09. Division 2 Champions – 1924–25, 1936–37, 1953–54, 1956–57, 1970–71, 1979–80. **Football League Cup:** Winners – 1964, 1997, 2000.
Colours: Blue shirts with white trim, white shorts, blue stockings with white trim.

LEYTON ORIENT   FL CHAMPIONSHIP 1

Ashworth Luke (D)	6 2	12 08	Bolton	4 12 89	Wigan Ath
Baker Harry (M)	5 11	12 04	Bexley Heath	20 9 90	Scholar
Boyd Adam (F)	5 9	10 12	Hartlepool	25 5 82	Luton T
Cave-Brown Andrew (D)	5 10	12 02	Gravesend	5 8 88	Norwich C
Chambers Adam (M)	5 10	11 08	Sandwell	20 11 80	Kidderminster H
Daniels Charlie (M)	6 1	12 12	Harlow	7 9 86	Tottenham H
Demetriou Jason (M)	5 11	10 08	Newham	18 11 87	Scholar
Jarvis Ryan (F)	6 1	11 11	Fakenham	11 7 86	Norwich C
Jones Jamie (G)	6 2	14 05	Kirkby	18 2 89	Everton
Melligan John (M)	5 9	11 02	Dublin	11 2 82	Cheltenham T
Mkandawire Tamika (D)	6 1	12 03	Malawi	28 5 83	Hereford U
Morris Glenn (G)	5 11	11 00	Woolwich	20 12 83	Scholar
Pires Loick (F)	6 3	13 02	Lisbon	20 11 89	Scholar
Purches Stephen (D)	5 11	11 13	Ilford	14 1 80	Bournemouth
Thornton Sean (M)	5 10	11 00	Drogheda	18 5 83	Doncaster R

League Appearances: Ashworth, L. 1(2); Baker, H. 2(2); Boyd, A. 27(6); Cave-Brown, A. 10(3); Chambers, A. 33; Church, S. 12(1); Daniels, C. 21; Dawkins, S. 2(9); Demetriou, J. 42(1); Granville, D. 12; Gray, W. 6(10); Jarvis, R. 15(16); Jeffery, J. (1); Jones, J. 20; McGleish, S. 15(1); Melligan, J. 25(10); Mkandawire, T. 36; Morgan, D. 18(14); Morris, G. 26; Palmer, A. 7(3); Parkin, S. 12(1); Pires, L. (6); Purches, S. 42; Saah, B. 14(1); Smith, J. 15(1); Spence, J. 20; Terry, P. 24(4); Thelwell, A. 23(5); Thornton, S. 26(4).
Goals – League (45): Boyd 9 (3 pens), McGleish 6 (3 pens), Church 5, Mkandawire 5, Morgan D 5, Demetriou 4, Purches 3, Daniels 2, Melligan 2, Chambers 1, Terry 1, Thornton 1, own goal 1.
Carling Cup (1): Boyd 1.
FA Cup (4): Demetriou 2, Granville 1, Melligan 1 (pen).
J Paint Trophy (6): Boyd 2 (2 pens), Jarvis 2, Chambers 1, Melligan 1.

Ground: Matchroom Stadium, Brisbane Road, Leyton, London E10 5NE. Telephone 0871 310 1881.
Record Attendance: 34,345 v West Ham U, FA Cup 4th rd, 25 January 1964.
Capacity: 9,300.
Manager: Geraint Williams.
Secretary: Lindsey Freeman.
Most League Goals: 106, Division 3 (S), 1955–56.
Highest League Scorer in Season: Tom Johnston, 35, Division 2, 1957–58.
Most League Goals in Total Aggregate: Tom Johnston, 121, 1956–58, 1959–61.
Most Capped Players: Tunji Banjo, 7 (7), Nigeria; John Chiedozie, 7 (9), Nigeria; Tony Grealish, 7 (45), Eire.
Most League Appearances: Peter Allen, 432, 1965–78.
Honours – Football League: Division 3 Champions – 1969–70. Division 3 (S) Champions – 1955–56.
Colours: Red shirts with white insert and striped sleeves, red shorts, red stockings.

LINCOLN CITY   FL CHAMPIONSHIP 2

Adams Nathan (M)	5 7	11 00	Lincoln	6 10 91	Scholar
Beevers Lee (D)	6 1	13 00	Doncaster	4 12 83	Boston U
Brown Aaron (M)	5 10	11 11	Bristol	14 3 80	Gillingham
Brown Nat (F)	6 2	12 05	Sheffield	15 6 81	Huddersfield T
Burch Rob (M)	6 2	12 13	Yeovil	8 10 83	Sheffield W
Clarke Shane (D)	6 1	13 03	Lincoln	7 11 87	Scholar
Colman-Carr Luca (D)	5 8	11 02	Epsom	11 1 91	Scholar
Duffy Ayden (M)	5 8	10 12	Kettering	16 11 86	Scholar
Green Paul (D)	5 8	10 04	Birmingham	15 4 87	Aston Villa
Hone Daniel (D)	6 2	12 00	Croydon	15 9 89	Scholar
Hutchinson Andrew (F)	5 7	12 00	Lincoln	10 3 92	Scholar
John-Lewis Leneli (M)	5 10	11 10	Hammersmith	17 5 89	Scholar
Kerr Scott (M)	5 9	10 07	Leeds	11 12 81	Scarborough
Kovacs Janos (D)	6 4	14 10	Budapest	11 9 85	Chesterfield
Miller Kern (D)	5 9	11 03	Boston	2 9 91	Scholar
Mullarkey Sam (F)	5 11	12 03	Lincoln	24 9 87	Grantham T
N'Guessan Dany (M)	6 0	12 13	Ivry-sur-Seine	11 8 87	Boston U
Oakes Stefan (M)	6 1	13 07	Leicester	6 9 78	Wycombe W
Patulea Adrian (F)	5 10	11 04	Targoviste	10 11 84	Petrolul
Swaibu Moses (D)	6 2	11 11	Croydon	9 5 89	Crystal Palace

League Appearances: Adams, N. (2); Beevers, L. 43(1); Brown, A. 33(6); Burch, R. 46; Clarke, S. 13(10); Colman-Carr, L. (1); Duffy, A. (1); Elding, A. 15; Frecklington, L. 25(2); Gall, K. 6(3); Graham, D. 2(7); Green, P. 33; Hone, D. 17(2); Horsfield, G. 14(3); Hutchinson, A. 3(1); John-Lewis, L. 21(6); Kerr, S. 45; King, G. 2(3); Kovacs, J. 45; Miller, K. (1); Mullarkey, S. 7(11); N'Guessan, D. 43(2); O'Connor, M. 9(1); Oakes, S. 21(7); Patulea, A. 17(14); Sinclair, F. 21(2); Swaibu, M. 10; Wright, B. 15(18).
Goals – League (53): Patulea 11, N'Guessan 8 (1 pen), Frecklington 7 (2 pens), John-Lewis 4, Elding 3, Kovacs 3, Beevers 2, Brown A 2, Kerr 2, Wright 2, Green 1, Hone 1, Horsfield 1, Hutchinson 1, Mullarkey 1, O'Connor 1, Oakes 1, own goals 2.
Carling Cup (1): Wright 1.
FA Cup (2): John-Lewis 1, N'Guessan 1.
J Paint Trophy (0).
Ground: Sincil Bank Stadium, Sincil Bank, Lincoln LN5 8LD. Telephone (0870) 899 2005.
Record Attendance: 23,196 v Derby Co, League Cup 4th rd, 15 November 1967.
Capacity: 10,059.
Manager: Peter Jackson.
Football Secretary: Fran Martin.

Most League Goals: 121, Division 3 (N), 1951–52.
Highest League Scorer in Season: Allan Hall, 41, Division 3 (N), 1931–32.
Most League Goals in Total Aggregate: Andy Graver, 144, 1950–55 and 1958–61.
Most Capped Player: Gareth McAuley, 5 (16), Northern Ireland.
Most League Appearances: Grant Brown, 407, 1989–2002.
Honours – Football League: Division 3 (N) Champions – 1931–32, 1947–48, 1951–52. Division 4 Champions – 1975–76. **GM Vauxhall Conference:** Champions – 1987–88.
Colours: Red and white striped shirts, red sleeves, black shorts, red stockings.

LIVERPOOL   FA PREMIERSHIP

Name			Birthplace		Previous Club
Agger Daniel (D)	6 2	12 06	Hvidovre	12 12 84	Brondby
Amoo David (F)			London	23 4 91	Scholar
Anderson Paul (M)	5 9	10 04	Leicester	23 7 88	Hull C
Arbeloa Alvaro (D)	6 0	12 06	Salamanca	17 1 83	La Coruna
Ayala Daniel (D)	6 3	13 01	Seville	7 11 90	Sevilla
Babel Ryan (F)	6 1	12 04	Amsterdam	19 12 86	Ajax
Benayoun Yossi (M)	5 10	11 00	Beer Sheva	6 6 80	West Ham U
Bouzanis Dean (G)	6 1	13 05	Sydney	2 10 90	Sydney
Brouwer Jordy (F)			Den Haag	26 2 88	Ajax
Bruna Gerardo (M)	5 8	10 02	Mendoza	29 1 91	
Carragher Jamie (D)	5 9	12 01	Liverpool	28 1 78	Trainee
Cavalieri Diego (G)	6 3	13 07	Sao Paulo	1 12 82	Palmeiras
Crowther Ryan (M)	5 10	11 01	Stockport	17 9 88	
Darby Stephen (D)	6 1	11 11	Liverpool	6 10 88	Scholar
Degen Philipp (D)	6 0	12 10	Holstein	15 2 83	Bor Dortmund
Dossena Andrea (D)	5 11	12 06	Lodi	11 9 81	Udinese
Duran Vazquez Fransisco (M)			Malaga	28 4 88	Malaga
Eccleston Nathan (F)	5 10	12 00	Manchester	30 12 90	Scholar
El Zhar Nabil (F)	5 9	11 05	Rabat	27 8 86	St Etienne
Fabio Aurelio (M)	5 10	11 11	Sao Carlos	24 9 79	Valencia
Flora Vitor (M)	6 0	12 10	Sao Joaqu	21 2 90	
Flynn Ryan (M)	5 8	10 00	Scotland	4 9 88	Falkirk
Gerrard Steven (M)	6 0	12 05	Whiston	30 5 80	Trainee
Gulacsi Peter (G)	6 3	13 01	Budapest	6 5 90	MTK Budapest
Hammill Adam (M)	5 11	11 07	Liverpool	25 1 88	Scholar
Hansen Martin (G)	6 2	12 07	Denmark	15 6 90	Scholar
Highdale Sean (M)			Liverpool	4 3 91	
Insua Emiliano (D)	5 10	12 08	Buenos Aires	7 1 89	Boca Juniors
Irwin Steven (D)	5 8	10 06	Liverpool	29 9 90	Scholar
Itandje Charles (G)	6 3	13 01	Bobigny	2 11 82	Lens
Kacaniklic Alexander (M)	5 11	10 05	Sweden	13 8 91	Scholar
Kelly Martin (D)	6 3	12 02	Bolton	27 4 90	Scholar
Kuyt Dirk (F)	6 0	12 02	Katwijk	22 7 80	Feyenoord
Leto Sebastian (M)	6 2	12 04	San Vicente	30 8 86	Lanus
Lindfield Craig (F)	6 0	10 05	Wirral	7 9 88	Scholar
Lucas (M)	5 10	11 09	Dourados	9 1 87	Gremio
Martin David (G)	6 1	13 04	Romford	22 1 86	Milton Keynes D
Mascherano Javier (M)	5 10	12 02	San Lorenzo	8 6 84	West Ham U
Mendy Emmanuel (D)	5 11	11 09	Medina Gounass	30 3 90	Murcia
Mihaylov Nikolay (G)	6 3	14 00	Bulgaria	28 6 88	Levski
Nemeth Krisztian (M)	5 10	11 07	Gyor	5 1 89	
N'Gog David (F)	6 3	12 04	Gennevillers	1 4 89	Paris St Germain
Pacheco Daniel (F)	5 6	10 07	Malaga	5 1 91	Barcelona
Palsson Victor (M)	6 1	12 00	Iceland	30 4 91	Aarhus
Plessis Damien (M)	6 3	12 02	Neuvy-sous-Bois	5 3 88	Lyon
Reina Jose (G)	6 2	14 06	Madrid	31 8 82	Villarreal

Riera Alberto (M)	6 1	12 01	Manacor	15 4 82	Espanyol
Roberts Michael (M)			Liverpool	5 12 91	
San Jose Mikel (M)	6 0	12 04	Pamplona	30 5 89	Athletic Bilbao
Saric Craig (F)	6 0	10 09	Wirral	7 9 88	Lleida
Simon Andras (F)	6 0	11 05	Salgotarjan	30 3 90	MTK Budapest
Skrtel Martin (D)	6 3	12 10	Hamdlova	15 12 84	Zenit
Spearing Jay (D)	5 6	11 00	Wirral	25 11 88	Scholar
Threlfall Robbie (D)	5 11	11 00	Liverpool	25 11 88	Scholar
Torres Fernando (F)	5 9	12 03	Madrid	20 3 84	Atletico Madrid
Voronin Andrei (F)	5 11	11 08	Odessa	21 7 79	Leverkusen
Weijl Vincent (F)	6 0	12 04	Amsterdam	11 11 90	AZ
Xabi Alonso (M)	6 0	12 02	Tolosa	25 11 81	Real Sociedad

League Appearances: Agger, D. 15(3); Alonso, X. 27(6); Arbeloa, A. 29; Babel, R. 6(21); Benayoun, Y. 21(11); Carragher, J. 38; Dossena, A. 12(4); El Zhar, N. 1(14); Fabio Aurelio, 19(5); Gerrard, S. 30(1); Hyypia, S. 12(4); Insua, E. 9(1); Keane, R. 16(3); Kuyt, D. 36(2); Lucas, 13(12); Mascherano, J. 27; N'Gog, D. 2(12); Pennant, J. 2(1); Plessis, D. 1; Reina, J. 38; Riera, A. 24(4); Skrtel, M. 20(1); Torres, F. 20(4).
Goals – League (77): Gerrard 16 (4 pens), Torres 14, Kuyt 12, Benayoun 8, Keane 5, Alonso 4 (1 pen), Babel 3, Riera 3, Fabio Aurelio 2, N'Gog 2, Agger 1, Arbeloa 1, Dossena 1, Hyypia 1, Lucas 1, own goals 3.
Carling Cup (4): Agger 1, Hyypia 1, Lucas 1, Plessis 1.
FA Cup (3): Gerrard 1, Riera 1, Torres 1.
Champions League (22): Gerrard 7 (3 pens), Kuyt 3, Keane 2, Torres 2, Babel 1, Benayoun 1, Dossena 1, Fabio Aurelio 1, Lucas 1, N'Gog 1, Riera 1, Xabi Alonso 1 (pen).
Ground: Anfield Stadium, Anfield Road, Liverpool L4 0TH. Telephone (0151) 260 1433.
Record Attendance: 61,905 v Wolverhampton W, FA Cup 4th rd, 2 February 1952.
Capacity: 45,522.
Manager: Rafael Benitez.
Secretary: Ian Silvester.
Most League Goals: 106, Division 2, 1895–96.
Highest League Scorer in Season: Roger Hunt, 41, Division 2, 1961–62.
Most League Goals in Total Aggregate: Roger Hunt, 245, 1959–69.
Most Capped Player: Ian Rush, 67 (73), Wales.
Most League Appearances: Ian Callaghan, 640, 1960–78.
Honours – Football League: Division 1 – Champions 1900–01, 1905–06, 1921–22, 1922–23, 1946–47, 1963–64, 1965–66, 1972–73, 1975–76, 1976–77, 1978–79, 1979–80, 1981–82, 1982–83, 1983–84, 1985–86, 1987–88, 1989–90 (Liverpool have a record number of 18 League Championship wins). Division 2 Champions – 1893–94, 1895–96, 1904–05, 1961–62. **FA Cup:** Winners – 1965, 1974, 1986, 1989, 1992, 2001, 2006. **League Cup:** Winners – 1981, 1982, 1983, 1984, 1995, 2001, 2003. **League Super Cup:** Winners 1985–86. **European Competitions: European Cup:** Winners – 1976–77, 1977–78, 1980–81, 1983–84. **Champions League:** Winners – 2004–05. **UEFA Cup:** Winners – 1972–73, 1975–76, 2001. **Super Cup:** Winners – 1977, 2005.
Colours: All red with white trim.

LUTON TOWN   BLUE SQUARE PREMIER

Asafu-Adjaye Ed (D)	5 11	12 04	London	22 12 88	Scholar
Beavan George (D)	5 9	12 02	Luton	12 1 90	Scholar
Charles Ryan (F)	6 0	12 00	Enfield	30 9 89	Scholar
Craddock Tom (F)	5 11	11 10	Durham	14 10 86	Middlesbrough
Gallen Kevin (F)	5 11	13 05	Hammersmith	21 9 75	Milton Keynes D
Gnakpa Claude (D)	6 0	13 05	Marseille	9 6 83	Peterborough U
Hall Asa (M)	6 2	11 09	Sandwell	29 11 86	Birmingham C
Henderson Ian (F)	5 10	11 06	Thetford	24 1 85	Northampton T
Jarvis Rossi (D)	5 11	11 12	Fakenham	11 3 88	Norwich C

Keane Keith (M)	5 9	11 02	Luton	20 11 86	Scholar
Nicholls Kevin (M)	5 10	11 13	Newham	2 1 79	Preston NE
Pilkington George (D)	5 11	12 05	Rugeley	7 11 81	Port Vale
Roper Ian (D)	6 3	14 00	Nuneaton	20 6 77	Walsall
Talbot Drew (F)	5 11	11 00	Barnsley	19 7 86	Sheffield W

League Appearances: Andrews, W. 1(6); Asafu-Adjaye, E. 17(2); Beavan, G. 3(1); Bower, M. 16; Brill, D. 23; Charles, R. (10); Craddock, T. 27; Davis, S. 22(2); Emanuel, L. 17(3); Gallen, K. 26(3); Gnakpa, C. 19(8); Hall, A. 35(7); Henderson, I. 14(5); Howells, J. 14(14); Jarvis, R. 31(4); Keane, K. 40; Klein-Davies, J. (1); Livermore, D. 18(4); Logan, C. 22; Martin, C. 39(1); McVeigh, P. 9(4); Nicholls, K. 16(3); O'Connor, G. 3; Parkin, S. 15(8); Patrick, J. (2); Pilkington, G. 18; Plummer, T. (5); Price, L. 1; Pugh, M. 3(1); Roper, I. 18(1); Spillane, M. 35(4); Talbot, D. 4(3); Wasiu, A. 2(3); Watson, K. 2(4); Worley, H. 6(2).
Goals – League (58): Martin 11, Craddock 10 (4 pens), Hall 10, Parkin 4, Gallen 3, McVeigh 3 (1 pen), Roper 3, Spillane 3, Bower 1, Charles 1, Davis 1, Emanuel 1, Gnakpa 1, Henderson 1, Jarvis 1, Wasiu 1, own goals 3.
Carling Cup (3): Chambers 1, Jarvis 1, Plummer 1.
FA Cup (1): Spillane 1.
J Paint Trophy (8): Craddock 2, Gnakpa 2, Martin 2, Hall 1, Jarvis 1.
Ground: Kenilworth Road Stadium, 1 Maple Road, Luton, Beds LU4 8AW. Telephone (01582) 411 622.
Record Attendance: 30,069 v Blackpool, FA Cup 6th rd replay, 4 March 1959.
Capacity: 10,226.
Manager: Mick Harford.
Acting Secretary: Gary Sweet.
Most League Goals: 103, Division 3 (S), 1936–37.
Highest League Scorer in Season: Joe Payne, 55, Division 3 (S), 1936–37.
Most League Goals in Total Aggregate: Gordon Turner, 243, 1949–64.
Most Capped Player: Mal Donaghy, 58 (91), Northern Ireland.
Most League Appearances: Bob Morton, 494, 1948–64.
Honours – Football League: Championship 1: Winners – 2004–05. Division 3 Champions – 1981–82. Division 4 Champions – 1967–68. Division 3 (S) Champions – 1936–37. **Football League Cup:** Winners – 1987–88. **Johnstone's Paint Trophy:** Winners – 2008–09.
Colours: White shirts with amber trim, black shorts, white stockings.

MACCLESFIELD TOWN   FL CHAMPIONSHIP 2

Bell Lee (M)	5 11	12 04	Crewe	26 1 83	Mansfield T
Blackman Nick (M)	6 2	11 08	Whitefield	11 11 89	Scholar
Brain Jonny (G)	6 3	13 05	Carlisle	11 2 83	Port Vale
Brisley Shaun (M)	6 2	12 02	Stockport	6 5 90	Scholar
Dennis Kristian (F)	5 11	11 00	Macclesfield	12 3 90	Scholar
Evans Gary (F)	6 0	12 08	Macclesfield	26 4 88	
Flynn Matthew (D)	6 0	11 08	Warrington	10 5 89	Warrington T
Green Francis (F)	5 9	11 04	Nottingham	25 4 80	Boston U
Hadfield Jordan (M)	5 10	11 04	Swinton	12 8 87	Stockport Co
Hessey Sean (D)	5 11	12 08	Whiston	19 9 78	Chester C
Liburd Patrece (D)	5 9	11 05	Basseterr	1 3 88	Dorchester T
Mukendi Vinny (F)	6 2	12 00	Bury	12 3 92	Scholar
Reid Izak (M)	5 5	10 05	Sheffield	08 7 87	Scholar
Rooney John (F)	5 10	12 00	Liverpool	17 12 90	Scholar
Thomas Danny (M)	5 7	10 10	Leamington Spa	1 5 81	Hereford U

League Appearances: Bains, R. 1(1); Bell, L. 37(4); Brain, J. 46; Brisley, S. 38; Brown, N. 29(1); Daniel, C. 8; Deen, A. 19(9); Dennis, K. (3); Dunfield, T. 19(1); Elliott, T. 4(2); Evans, G. 35(5); Flynn, M. 23(5); Fraser-Allen, K. (2); Green, F. 9(15); Gritton, M. 13(8); Hadfield, J. 14(2); Harvey, N. (5); Hessey, S. 29(4); Jen-

68

nings, J. 13(5); Liburd, P. 1; McDonald, C. 2; Millar, C. (2); Morgan, P. 38(1); Mukendi, V. (1); Reid, I. 30(8); Rooney, J. 10(4); Sinclair, E. 14(3); Thomas, D. 24(16); Tolley, J. 14(2); Walker, R. 14(1); Yeo, S. 22(11).
Goals – League (45): Evans 12 (5 pens), Yeo 7 (1 pen), Brown 6, Gritton 5, Green 3, Reid I 2, Rooney 2, Thomas 2, Bell 1, Dennis 1, Dunfield 1, Morgan 1, Sinclair 1, own goal 1.
Carling Cup (3): Brisley 1, Evans 1, Gritton 1.
FA Cup (5): Green 2, Brisley 1, Dunfield 1, Gritton 1.
J Paint Trophy (0).
Ground: Moss Rose Ground, London Road, Macclesfield, Cheshire SK11 0DQ. Telephone (01625) 264 686.
Record Attendance: 9,008 v Winsford U, Cheshire Senior Cup 2nd rd, 4 February 1948. **Capacity:** 6,141.
Manager: Keith Alexander.
Company Secretary: Barrie Darcey.
Most League Goals: 66, Division 3, 1999–2000.
Highest League Scorer in Season: Jon Parkin, 22, League 2, 2004–05.
Most League Goals in Total Aggregate: Matt Tipton, 45, 2002–05; 2006–07.
Most Capped Player: George Abbey, 10(16), Nigeria.
Most League Appearances: Darren Tinson, 263, 1997–2003.
Honours – None.
Colours: Blue shirts with white design, white shorts, blue stockings.

MANCHESTER CITY

FA PREMIERSHIP

Ball David (F)			Whitefield	14 12 89	Scholar
Bellamy Craig (F)	5 9	10 12	Cardiff	13 7 79	West Ham U
Ben Haim Tal (D)	5 11	11 09	Rishon Le Zion	31 3 82	Chelsea
Benali Ahmad (M)			Libya	7 2 92	Scholar
Bojinov Valeri (F)	5 10	12 04	Oriahovizca	15 2 86	Juventus
Bridge Wayne (D)	5 10	12 13	Southampton	5 8 80	Chelsea
Caicedo Felipe (F)	6 1	12 08	Guayaquil	5 9 88	Basle
Clayton Adam (M)	5 9	11 11	Manchester	14 1 89	Scholar
De Jong Nigel (D)	5 8	11 05	Amsterdam	30 11 84	Hamburg
Dunne Richard (D)	6 2	15 12	Dublin	21 9 79	Everton
Elano (M)	5 9	10 03	Iracemapolis	14 6 81	Shakhtar Donetsk
Etuhu Calvin (F)	6 0	12 09	Nigeria	30 5 88	Scholar
Evans Ched (F)	6 0	12 00	Rhyl	28 12 88	Scholar
Garrido Javier (M)	5 10	11 11	Irun	15 3 85	Real Sociedad
Gelson (M)	6 0	11 03	Cape Verde Islands	2 9 86	Sion
Given Shay (G)	6 0	13 03	Lifford	20 4 76	Newcastle U
Hart Joe (G)	6 5	14 05	Shrewsbury	19 4 87	Shrewsbury T
Ireland Stephen (F)	5 8	10 07	Cobh	22 8 86	Scholar
Jo (F)	5 9	11 00	Sao Paulo	20 3 87	CSKA Moscow
Johansen Tobias (G)			Tonsberg	29 8 90	Academy
Johnson Michael (M)	6 0	12 07	Urmston	3 3 88	Scholar
Kay Scott (M)			Manchester	18 9 89	Scholar
Kompany Vincent (D)	6 3	13 05	Uccle	10 4 86	Hamburg
Logan Shaleum (D)	5 8	10 01	Manchester	29 1 88	Scholar
Marshall Paul (M)	6 1	12 03	Manchester	9 7 89	Scholar
McDermott Donal (M)	6 6	12 00	Dublin	19 10 89	Scholar
McDonald Clayton (D)	6 6	16 05	Liverpool	26 12 88	Scholar
McGivern Ryan (D)	5 10	11 07	Newry	8 1 90	Scholar
Mee Ben (D)			Manchester	21 9 89	Scholar
Mentel Filip (G)			Bratislava	2 2 90	Academy
Moore Karl (F)	5 7		Dublin	9 11 88	Scholar
Mwaruwari Benjamin (F)	6 2	12 03	Harare	13 8 78	Portsmouth
Nielsen Gunnar (G)	6 3	14 00	Faeroes	7 10 86	Blackburn R
Onuoha Nedum (D)	6 2	12 04	Warri	12 11 86	Scholar

Petrov Martin (F)	6 0	12 02	Vzatza	15 1 79	Atletico Madrid
Poole James (F)			Stockport	20 3 90	Scholar
Richards Micah (D)	5 11	13 00	Birmingham	24 6 88	Scholar
Robinho (F)	5 8	10 00	Sao Vicente	25 1 84	Real Madrid
Schmeichel Kasper (G)	6 1	13 00	Copenhagen	5 11 86	Scholar
Sturridge Danny (F)	5 11	12 02	Birmingham	1 9 89	Scholar
Timely-Tchuimeni Alex (F)			Monrovia	11 5 91	Cotonsport
Vidal Javan (D)	5 10	10 10	Manchester	10 5 89	Scholar
Weiss Vladimir (M)	5 8	11 02	Bratislava	30 11 89	Academy
Wright-Phillips Shaun (F)	5 5	10 01	Lewisham	25 10 81	Chelsea
Zabaleta Pablo (D)	5 8	10 12	Buenos Aires	16 1 85	Espanyol

League Appearances: Ball, M. 8; Bellamy, C. 7(1); Ben Haim, T. 8(1); Berti, G. (1); Bojinov, V. 2(6); Bridge, W. 16; Caicedo, F. 10(7); Corluka, V. 3; De Jong, N. 16; Dunne, R. 31; Elano, 21(7); Etuhu, K. 2(2); Evans, C. 3(13); Garrido, J. 11(2); Gelson, 3(14); Given, S. 15; Hamann, D. 5(4); Hart, J. 23; Ireland, S. 34(1); Jo, 6(3); Johnson, M. 3; Kompany, V. 34; Logan, S. 1; Mwaruwari, B. 7(1); Onuoha, N. 20(3); Petrov, M. 4(5); Richards, M. 33(1); Robinho, 30(1); Schmeichel, K. (1); Sturridge, D. 3(13); Vassell, D. 6(2); Weiss, V. (1); Wright-Phillips, S. 27; Zabaleta, P. 26(3).
Goals – League (58): Robinho 14 (1 pen), Ireland 9, Elano 6 (4 pens), Wright-Phillips 5, Caicedo 4, Sturridge 4 (1 pen), Bellamy 3, Bojinov 1, Corluka 1, Dunne 1, Evans 1, Garrido 1, Gelson 1, Jo 1, Kompany 1, Mwaruwari 1, Onuoha 1, Richards 1, Zabaleta 1, own goal 1.
Carling Cup (2): Gelson 1, Ireland 1.
FA Cup (0).
UEFA Cup (24): Caicedo 3, Ireland 3, Wright-Phillips 3, Bellamy 2, Elano 2 (1 pen), Jo 2, Mwaruwari 2, Petkov 2, Hamann 1, Onuoha 1, Robinho 1, Vassell 1, own goal 1.
Ground: The City of Manchester Stadium, SportCity, Manchester M11 3FF. Telephone (0870) 062 1894.
Record Attendance: (at Maine Road) 85,569 v Stoke C, FA Cup 6th rd, 3 March 1934 (British record for any game outside London or Glasgow) (at City of Manchester Stadium) 47,304 v Chelsea, FA Premier League, 28 February 2004.
Capacity: 47,726.
Manager: Mark Hughes.
Secretary: Bernard Halford.
Most League Goals: 108, Division 2, 1926–27, 108, Division 1, 2001–02.
Highest League Scorer in Season: Tommy Johnson, 38, Division 1, 1928–29.
Most League Goals in Total Aggregate: Tommy Johnson, 158, 1919–30.
Most Capped Player: Colin Bell, 48, England.
Most League Appearances: Alan Oakes, 565, 1959–76.
Honours – Football League: Division 1 Champions – 1936–37, 1967–68, 2001–02. Division 2 Champions – 1898–99, 1902–03, 1909–10, 1927–28, 1946–47, 1965–66. **FA Cup:** Winners – 1904, 1934, 1956, 1969. **Football League Cup:** Winners – 1970, 1976. **European Competitions: European Cup-Winners' Cup:** Winners – 1969–70.
Colours: Sky blue shirts with white detail, white shorts with sky blue detail, white stockings with sky blue tops.

MANCHESTER UNITED   FA PREMIERSHIP

Amos Ben (G)	6 2	13 00	Macclesfield	10 4 90	Scholar
Anderson (M)	5 8	10 07	Porto Alegre	13 4 88	Porto
Berbatov Dimitar (F)	6 2	12 06	Blagoevgrad	30 1 81	Tottenham H
Brady Robert (F)			Belfast	14 1 92	Scholar
Brandy Febian (F)	5 5	10 00	Manchester	4 2 89	Scholar
Brown Wes (D)	6 1	13 11	Manchester	13 10 79	Scholar
Campbell Frazier (F)	5 11	12 04	Huddersfield	13 9 87	Scholar
Carrick Michael (M)	6 2	13 03	Wallsend	28 7 81	Tottenham H

Name			Birthplace			Prev. Club
Cathcart Craig (D)	6 2	11 06	Belfast	6	2 89	Scholar
Chester James (D)	5 10	11 13	Warrington	23	1 89	Scholar
Cleverley Tom (M)	5 8	10 07	Basingstoke	12	8 89	Scholar
De Laet Ritchie (D)	6 1	12 02	Antwerp	28 11 88		Stoke C
Drinkwater Daniel (M)			Manchester	5	3 90	Scholar
Eckersley Richard (D)	5 9	11 09	Salford	12	3 89	Scholar
Eikrem Magnus (M)			Molde	8	8 90	Scholar
Evans Corry (M)	5 8	10 12	Belfast	30	7 90	Scholar
Evans Jonny (D)	6 2	12 02	Belfast	3	1 88	Scholar
Evra Patrice (D)	5 8	11 10	Dakar	15	5 81	Monaco
Fabio (D)	5 8	10 03	Rio de Janeiro	9	7 90	Fluminense
Ferdinand Rio (D)	6 2	13 12	Peckham	7 11 78		Leeds U
Fletcher Darren (M)	6 0	13 01	Edinburgh	1	2 84	Scholar
Foster Ben (G)	6 2	12 08	Leamington Spa	3	4 83	Stoke C
Gibson Darron (M)	6 0	12 04	Londonderry	25 10 87		Scholar
Giggs Ryan (F)	5 11	11 00	Cardiff	29 11 73		School
Gray David (F)	5 11	11 02	Edinburgh	4	5 88	Scholar
Hargreaves Owen (M)	5 11	11 07	Calgary	20	1 81	Bayern Munich
Heaton Tom (G)	6 1	13 12	Chester	15	4 86	Scholar
Hewson Sam (M)	5 8	11 02	Bolton	28 11 88		Scholar
King Joshua (F)			Oslo	15	1 92	Scholar
Kuszczak Tomasz (G)	6 3	13 03	Krosno Odrzanska	20	3 82	WBA
Macheda Federico (F)	6 0	11 13	Rome	22	8 91	Scholar
Manucho (F)	6 2	13 00	Luanda	7	3 83	Petro Atletico
Martin Lee (M)	5 10	10 03	Taunton	9	2 87	Scholar
Nani (M)	5 9	10 04	Amadora	17 11 86		Sporting Lisbon
Neville Gary (D)	5 11	12 04	Bury	18	2 75	Scholar
O'Shea John (D)	6 3	12 10	Waterford	30	4 81	Waterford
Park Ji-Sung (M)	5 9	11 06	Seoul	25	2 81	PSV Eindhoven
Petrucci Davide (F)			Rome	5 10 91		Scholar
Possebon Rodrigo (M)	6 0	11 13	Sapucaia do Sul	13	2 89	Internacional
Rafael (D)	6 3	12 08	Petropolis	9	7 90	Fluminense
Rooney Wayne (F)	5 10	12 04	Liverpool	24 10 85		Everton
Scholes Paul (M)	5 7	11 00	Salford	16 11 74		Scholar
Simpson Danny (D)	5 9	11 05	Salford	4	1 87	Scholar
Tosic Zoran (F)	5 7	10 12	Zrenjanin	28	4 87	Partizan Belgrade
Van der Sar Edwin (G)	6 5	14 11	Voorhout	29 10 70		Fulham
Vidic Nemanja (D)	6 1	13 02	Uzice	21 10 81		Spartak Moscow
Welbeck Daniel (F)	6 1	11 07	Manchester	26 11 90		Scholar
Zieler Ron-Robert (G)	6 1	11 07	Cologne	12	2 89	Scholar

League Appearances: Anderson, 11(6); Berbatov, D. 29(2); Brown, W. 6(2); Campbell, F. 1; Carrick, M. 24(4); De Laet, R. 1; Eckersley, R. (2); Evans, J. 16(1); Evra, P. 28; Ferdinand, R. 24; Fletcher, D. 25(1); Foster, B. 2; Gibson, D. 1(2); Giggs, R. 15(13); Hargreaves, O. 1(1); Kuszczak, T. 3(1); Macheda, F. 2(2); Manucho, (1); Martin, L. 1; Nani, 7(6); Neville, G. 13(3); O'Shea, J. 20(10); Park, J. 21(4); Possebon, R. (3); Rafael, 12(4); Ronaldo, C. 31(2); Rooney, W. 25(5); Scholes, P. 14(7); Tevez, C. 18(11); Tosic, Z. (2); Van der Sar, E. 33; Vidic, N. 33(1); Welbeck, D. 1(2).

Goals – League (68): Ronaldo 18 (4 pens), Rooney 12, Berbatov 9, Tevez 5, Carrick 4, Vidic 4, Fletcher 3, Giggs 2, Macheda 2, Park 2, Scholes 2, Brown 1, Gibson 1, Nani 1, Rafael 1, Welbeck 1.

Carling Cup (13): Tevez 6 (2 pens), Nani 3, Ronaldo 2, Giggs 1, O'Shea 1.

FA Cup (13): Gibson 2, Nani 2 (1 pen), Tevez 2, Welbeck 2, Berbatov 1, Park 1, Ronaldo 1, Rooney 1, Scholes 1.

Champions League (18): Berbatov 4, Ronaldo 4, Rooney 4, Tevez 2, Giggs 1, O'Shea 1, Park 1, Vidic 1.

FIFA Club World Cup (6): Rooney 3, Fletcher 1, Ronaldo 1, Vidic 1.

Community Shield (0).

Super Cup (1): Vidic 1.

Ground: Old Trafford, Sir Matt Busby Way, Manchester M16 0RA. Telephone (0161) 868 8000.
Record Attendance: 76,962 Wolverhampton W v Grimsby T, FA Cup semi-final. 25 March 1939. **Club record:** 76,098 v Blackburn R, Premier League, 31 March 2007. **Capacity:** 76,212.
Manager: Sir Alex Ferguson CBE.
Secretary: Ken Ramsden.
Most League Goals: 103, Division 1, 1956–57 and 1958–59.
Highest League Scorer in Season: Dennis Viollet, 32, 1959–60.
Most League Goals in Total Aggregate: Bobby Charlton, 199, 1956–73.
Most Capped Player: Bobby Charlton, 106, England.
Most League Appearances: Bobby Charlton, 606, 1956–73.
Honours – FA Premier League: Champions – 1992–93, 1993–94, 1995–96, 1996–97, 1998–99, 1999–2000, 2000–01, 2002–03, 2006–07, 2007–08, 2008–09. **Football League:** Division 1 Champions – 1907–8, 1910–11, 1951–52, 1955–56, 1956–57, 1964–65, 1966–67. Division 2 Champions – 1935–36, 1974–75. **FA Cup:** Winners – 1909, 1948, 1963, 1977, 1983, 1985, 1990, 1994, 1996, 1999, 2004. **Football League Cup:** Winners – 1991–92, 2006, 2009. **European Competitions: European Cup:** Winners – 1967–68. **Champions League:** Winners – 1998–99, 2007–08. **European Cup-Winners' Cup:** Winners – 1990–91. **Super Cup:** Winners – 1991. **Inter-Continental Cup:** Winners – 1999.
Colours: Red shirts, white shorts, black stockings.

MIDDLESBROUGH   FL CHAMPIONSHIP

Name			Birthplace	Birthdate			Previous club
Aliadiere Jeremie (F)	6 0	11 00	Rambouillet	30	3 83	Arsenal
Alves Afonso (F)	6 1	11 09	Belo Horizonte	30	1 81	Heerenveen
Arca Julio (M)	5 9	11 13	Quilmes	31	1 81	Sunderland
Bates Matthew (D)	5 10	12 03	Stockton	10	12 86	Scholar
Bennett Joe (D)	5 10	10 04	Rochdale	28	3 90	Scholar
Digard Didier (M)	6 0	11 13	Gisors	12	7 86	Paris St Germain
Downing Stewart (M)	5 11	10 04	Middlesbrough	22	7 84	Scholar
Emnes Marvin (M)	5 9	10 06	Rotterdam	27	5 88	Sparta Rotterdam
Franks Jonathan (M)	5 9	11 03	Stockton	8	4 90	Scholar
Grounds Jonathan (D)	6 1	13 10	Ingleby Barwick	2	2 88	Scholar
Hines Sebastian (M)	6 2	12 04	Wetherby	29	5 88	Scholar
Hoyte Justin (D)	5 11	11 00	Waltham Forest	20	11 84	Arsenal
Huth Robert (D)	6 3	14 07	Berlin	18	8 84	Chelsea
Johnson Adam (M)	5 9	9 11	Sunderland	14	7 87	Scholar
Johnson John (D)	6 0	12 00	Middlesbrough	16	9 88	Scholar
Jones Brad (G)	6 3	12 01	Armidale	19	3 82	Trainee
McMahon Anthony (D)	5 10	11 04	Bishop Auckland	24	3 86	Scholar
Mido (F)	6 2	14 09	Cairo	23	2 83	Tottenham H
O'Neil Gary (M)	5 10	11 00	Bromley	18	5 83	Portsmouth
Pogatetz Emanuel (D)	6 2	13 05	Steinbock	16	1 83	Graz
Porritt Nathan (M)	5 9	12 00	Middlesbrough	9	1 90	Scholar
Riggott Chris (D)	6 2	13 09	Derby	1	9 80	Derby Co
Shawky Mohamed (M)	5 11	11 11	Port Said	5	10 81	Al-Ahly
Smallwood Richard (M)			Redcar	29	12 90	Scholar
Steele Jason (G)	6 2	12 13	Bishop Auckland	18	8 90	Scholar
Taylor Andrew (D)	5 10	11 04	Hartlepool	1	8 86	Trainee
Tuncay Sanli (F)	5 10	11 00	Sakarya	16	1 82	Fenerbahce
Turnbull Ross (G)	6 4	15 00	Bishop Auckland	4	1 85	Trainee
Walker Josh (M)	5 11	11 13	Newcastle	21	2 89	Scholar
Wheater David (D)	6 4	12 12	Redcar	14	2 87	Scholar
Williams Rhys (D)	6 2	11 05	Perth	14	7 88	Scholar

League Appearances: Aliadiere, J. 27(2); Alves, A. 24(7); Arca, J. 14(4); Bates, M. 15(2); Bennett, J. (1); Digard, D. 15(8); Downing, S. 37; Emnes, M. 3(12); Franks,

72

J. (1); Grounds, J. 2; Hines, S. (1); Hoyte, J. 17(5); Huth, R. 23(1); Johnson, A. 10(16); Johnson, J. (1); Jones, B. 16; King, M. 9(4); McMahon, T. 13; Mido, 5(8); O'Neil, G. 28(1); Pogatetz, E. 27; Riggott, C. 17; Shawky, M. 11(2); Taylor, A. 20(6); Tuncay, S. 30(3); Turnbull, R. 22; Walker, J. 2(4); Wheater, D. 31(1).
Goals – League (28): Tuncay 7, Alves 4 (1 pen) Mido 4, O'Neil 4, Aliadiere 2, King 2, Bates 1, Pogatetz 1, Wheater 1, own goals 2.
Carling Cup (6): Johnson A 2, Aliadiere 1, Digard 1, Emnes 1, Mido 1.
FA Cup (8): Alves 3, Downing 2, Emnes 1, Tuncay 1, Wheater 1.
Ground: Riverside Stadium, Middlesbrough TS3 6RS. Telephone (0844) 499 6789.
Record Attendance: Ayresome Park: 53,536 v Newcastle U, Division 1, 27 December 1949. Riverside Stadium: 34,814 v Newcastle U, FA Premier League, 5 March 2003. **Capacity:** 35,100.
Manager: Gareth Southgate.
Secretary: Karen Nelson.
Most League Goals: 122, Division 2, 1926–27.
Highest League Scorer in Season: George Camsell, 59, Division 2, 1926–27 (Second Division record).
Most League Goals in Total Aggregate: George Camsell, 325, 1925–39.
Most Capped Player: Wilf Mannion, 26, England.
Most League Appearances: Tim Williamson, 563, 1902–23.
Honours – Football League: Division 1 Champions 1994–95. Division 2 Champions 1926–27, 1928–29, 1973–74. **Football League Cup:** Winners – 2004, 2009. **Amateur Cup:** Winners – 1895, 1898. **Anglo-Scottish Cup:** Winners – 1975–76.
Colours: Red shirts with white chestband, red shorts, red stockings.

MILLWALL   FL CHAMPIONSHIP 1

Abdou Nadjim (M)	5 10	11 02	Martigues	13 7 84	Plymouth Arg
Alexander Gary (F)	6 0	13 04	Lambeth	15 8 79	Leyton Orient
Barron Scott (D)	5 9	9 08	Preston	2 9 85	Ipswich T
Bignot Marcus (D)	5 7	11 04	Birmingham	22 8 74	QPR
Bolder Adam (M)	5 9	10 08	Hull	25 10 80	QPR
Craig Tony (D)	6 0	10 03	Greenwich	20 4 85	Crystal Palace
Dunne Alan (D)	5 10	10 13	Dublin	23 8 82	Trainee
Edwards Preston (G)	6 0	12 07	Edmonton	5 9 89	Scholar
Forde David (G)	6 3	13 06	Galway	20 12 79	Cardiff C
Frampton Andrew (D)	5 11	10 10	Wimbledon	3 9 79	Brentford
Fuseini Ali (M)	5 6	9 10	Ghana	7 12 88	Scholar
Grabban Lewis (F)	6 0	11 03	Croydon	12 1 88	Crystal Palace
Grimes Ashley (M)	6 0	11 02	Swinton	9 12 86	Manchester C
Hackett Chris (M)	6 0	11 06	Oxford	1 3 83	Hearts
Harris Neil (F)	5 11	12 09	Orsett	12 7 77	Nottingham F
Laird Marc (M)	6 1	10 07	Edinburgh	23 1 86	Manchester C
Martin David (M)	5 9	10 10	Erith	3 6 85	Crystal Palace
O'Connor Patrick (M)	6 1	13 00	Croydon	5 9 90	Scholar
Robinson Paul (D)	6 1	11 09	Barnet	7 1 82	Scholar
Whitbread Zak (D)	6 2	11 04	Houston	10 1 84	Liverpool

League Appearances: Abdou, N. 31(5); Alexander, G. 29(6); Bakayogo, Z. ; Barron, S. 7(7); Bignot, M. 1; Bolder, A. 28; Brkovic, A. 3(3); Craig, T. 43(1); Duffy, R. 11(1); Dunne, A. 20(4); Easter, J. 2(3); Forbes, A. (2); Forde, D. 46; Frampton, A. 32(5); Fuseini, A. 11(6); Grabban, L. 29(2); Grimes, A. 4(13); Hackett, C. 15(7); Harris, N. 20(15); Henry, J. 15(1); Kandol, T. 16(2); Laird, M. 30(8); Martin, D. 37(7); McLeod, I. 5(2); Moore, K. 2(4); Noel-Williams, G. 1; Pericard, V. 2; Price, J. 6(2); Robinson, P. 26; Smith, R. (1); Spiller, D. (2); Whitbread, Z. 34(4).
Goals – League (63): Alexander 11 (1 pen), Harris 8 (1 pen), Kandol 8, Grabban 6, Laird 5, Martin 4 (1 pen), Abdou 3, Henry 3 (1 pen), Price 3, Craig 2, Grimes 2, McLeod 2 (1 pen), Robinson 2, Brkovic 1, Easter 1, Frampton 1, own goal 1.
Carling Cup (0).

FA Cup (11): Alexander 2, Grimes 2, Harris 2, Barron 1, Frampton 1, Grabban 1, Laird 1, Whitbread 1.
J Paint Trophy (0).
Play-Offs (4): Alexander 2, Abdou 1, Harris 1.
Ground: The Den, Zampa Road, London SE16 3LN. Telephone (020) 7232 1222.
Record Attendance: 20,093 v Arsenal, FA Cup 3rd rd, 10 January 1994. **Capacity:** 19,734.
Manager: Kenny Jackett.
Secretary: Yvonne Haines.
Most League Goals: 127, Division 3 (S), 1927–28.
Highest League Scorer in Season: Richard Parker, 37, Division 3 (S), 1926–27.
Most League Goals in Total Aggregate: Teddy Sheringham, 93, 1984–91 and Neil Harris, 101, 1995–2004; 2006–08.
Most Capped Player: Eamonn Dunphy, 22 (23), Republic of Ireland.
Most League Appearances: Barry Kitchener, 523, 1967–82.
Honours – Football League: Division 2 Champions – 1987–88, 2000–01. Division 3 (S) Champions – 1927–28, 1937–38. Division 4 Champions – 1961–62. **Football League Trophy:** Winners – 1982–83.
Colours: Royal blue shirts with white detail, white shorts, royal blue stockings.

MILTON KEYNES DONS   FL CHAMPIONSHIP 1

Baldock Sam (F)	5 7	10 07	Buckingham	15 3 89	Scholar
Chadwick Luke (M)	5 11	11 08	Cambridge	18 11 80	Norwich C
Chicksen Adam (D)	5 8	11 09	Coventry	1 11 90	Scholar
Gueret Willy (G)	6 1	13 02	Saint Claude	3 8 73	Swansea C
Howell Luke (D)	5 10	10 05	Cuckfield	5 1 87	Gillingham
Leven Peter (M)	5 11	12 13	Glasgow	27 9 83	Chesterfield
Lewington Dean (D)	5 11	11 07	Kingston	18 5 84	Scholar
Llera Miguel (D)	6 3	13 12	Seville	7 8 79	
O'Hanlon Sean (D)	6 1	12 05	Southport	2 1 83	Swindon T
Regan Carl (D)	5 11	11 12	Liverpool	14 1 80	Macclesfield T
Stirling Jude (D)	6 2	11 12	Enfield	29 6 82	Peterborough U
Swailes Danny (D)	6 3	12 06	Bolton	1 4 79	Macclesfield T
Wilbraham Aaron (F)	6 3	12 04	Knutsford	21 10 79	Hull C
Wright Mark (M)	5 11	11 00	Wolverhampton	24 2 82	Walsall

League Appearances: Abbey, N. (1); Andrews, K. 1; Baldock, S. 32(8); Belson, F. 9(4); Chadwick, L. 21(3); Chicksen, A. (1); Cummings, S. 29(3); Flo, T. 2(11); Gallen, K. 1(5); Gerba, A. 16(8); Gleeson, S. 5; Gueret, W. 44; Howell, L. 9(6); Johnson, J. 19(14); Leven, P. 37(3); Lewington, D. 40; Llera, M. 34; Magnay, C. (2); McDermott, D. (1); N'Gala, B. 1(2); Navarro, A. 32(6); O'Hanlon, S. 40; Powell, D. (7); Price, L. 2; Puncheon, J. 26(1); Regan, C. 24(3); Stirling, J. 21(11); Sturm, F. 2(3); Swailes, D. 1; Wilbraham, A. 29(4); Wright, M. 29(3).
Goals – League (83): Wilbraham 16, Baldock 12 (1 pen), Gerba 10, Leven 10 (3 pens), Chadwick 6, Johnson 5, Wright 5, Puncheon 4, O'Hanlon 3, Lewington 2, Llera 2, Stirling 2, Gallen 1, Howell 1, Navarro 1, Powell 1, own goals 2.
Carling Cup (2): Baldock 1, O'Hanlon 1.
FA Cup (1): Johnson 1.
J Paint Trophy (0).
Play-Offs (1): Wilbraham 1.
Ground: Stadiummk, Stadium Way West, Milton Keynes, Buckinghamshire MK9 1FA. Telephone (01908) 622 922.
Record Attendance: 30,115 v Manchester U, FA Premier League, 9 May 1993 (at Selhurst Park). **Capacity:** 21,189.
Manager: Paul Ince.
Head of Football Operations: Kirstine Nicholson.
Most League Goals: 97, Division 3, 1983–84; as Milton Keynes Dons 83, FL 1, 2008–09.

Highest League Scorer in Season: Alan Cork, 29, 1983–84.
Most League Goals in Total Aggregate: Alan Cork, 145, 1977–92.
Most Capped Player: Kenny Cunningham, 40 (72), Republic of Ireland.
Most League Appearances: Alan Cork, 430, 1977–92.
Honours – Football League: Championship 2 Champions – 2007–08. Division 4 Champions – 1982–83. **FA Cup:** Winners – 1987–88. **Johnstone's Paint Trophy:** Winners – 2007–08.
Colours: White shirts, white shorts, white stockings with black tops.

MORECAMBE   FL CHAMPIONSHIP 2

Player			Club		Previous Club
Adams Danny (D)	6 1	14 00	Altrincham	3 1 76	Huddersfield T
Artell Dave (D)	6 3	14 01	Rotherham	22 11 80	Chester C
Bentley Jim (D)	6 1	12 00	Liverpool	11 6 76	Telford U
Curtis Wayne (F)	6 0	14 05	Barrow	6 3 80	Holker Old Boys
Davies Scott (G)	6 0	11 00	Blackpool	27 2 87	Scholar
Drummond Stuart (M)	6 2	13 08	Preston	11 12 75	Shrewsbury T
Duffy Mark (M)	5 9	11 05	Liverpool	7 10 85	Southport
Edge Lewis (G)	6 1	12 10	Lancaster	12 1 87	Blackpool
Hunter Garry (M)	5 7	10 03	Morecambe	1 1 85	Scholar
McLachlan Fraser (M)	5 11	12 11	Manchester	9 11 82	Mansfield T
McStay Henry (D)	6 0	11 11	Co Armagh	6 3 85	Antwerp
Parrish Andy (D)	6 0	11 00	Bolton	22 6 88	Bury
Roche Barry (G)	6 5	14 08	Dublin	6 4 82	Chesterfield
Stanley Craig (M)	6 0	12 06	Coventry	3 3 83	Hereford U
Taylor Aaron (F)	5 8	11 11	Morecambe	9 3 90	
Twiss Michael (F)	5 11	13 05	Salford	26 12 77	Chester C
Wainwright Neil (M)	6 0	12 00	Warrington	4 11 77	Darlington

League Appearances: Adams, D. 39; Artell, D. 35(2); Bentley, J. 45; Blinkhorn, M. 5(6); Carlton, D. 8; Carr, M. 4(3); Curtis, W. 23(9); Drummond, S. 41(3); Duffy, M. 4(5); Howe, R. 35(2); Hunter, G. 23(6); McCann, R. 11(2); McGivern, R. 5; McLachlan, F. 21(6); McStay, H. 17(3); O'Carroll, D. 15(14); Parrish, A. 10(3); Roche, B. 46; Smith, D. (2); Stanley, C. 22(2); Taylor, A. 7(10); Twiss, M. 26(2); Wainwright, N. 32(6); Yates, A. 32.
Goals – League (53): Drummond 10, Howe 10 (1 pen), Curtis 5, O'Carroll 5, Stanley 5, Artell 3, Bentley 3, Twiss 3, Carlton 2, Taylor 2, Duffy 1, Hunter 1, McGivern 1, McStay 1, Wainwright 1.
Carling Cup (0).
FA Cup (4): Taylor 2, Howe 1 (pen), McStay 1.
J Paint Trophy (2): Drummond 1, Howe 1.
Ground: Christie Park, Lancaster Road, Morecambe LA4 5TJ. Telephone (01524) 411 797.
Record Attendance: 9,383 v Weymouth FA Cup 3rd rd, 6 January 1962.
Capacity: 6,030.
Manager: Sammy McIlroy.
Secretary: Neil Marsdin.
Most League Goals: 59, FL 2, 2007–08.
Highest League Scorer in Season: Justin Jackson, 29, 1999–2000.
Most League Goals in Total Aggregate: 12, Stuart Drummond 2007–.
Most League Appearances: 88, Jim Bentley, 2007–.
Honours – Conference: Promoted to Football League (play-offs) 2006–07. **Presidents Cup:** Winners –, 1991–92. **FA Trophy:** Winners 1973–74. **Lancs Senior Cup:** Winners 1967–68. **Lancs Combination:** Champions – 1924–25, 1961–62, 1962–63, 1967–68. **Lancs Combination Cup:** Winners – 1926–27, 1945–46, 1964–65, 1966–67, 1967–68. **Lancs Junior Cup:** Winners – 1927, 1928, 1962, 1963, 1969, 1986, 1987, 1994, 1996, 1999, 2004.
Colours: Red shirts with white sleeves, white shorts, red stockings.

Adjei Samuel (F)	6 1	12 00	Ghana	18 1 92	Jonkoping
Ameobi Foluwashola (F)	6 3	11 13	Zaria	12 10 81	Scholar
Barton Joey (M)	5 11	12 05	Huyton	2 9 82	Manchester C
Bassong Sebastien (D)	6 2	11 07	Paris	9 7 86	Metz
Beye Habib (D)	6 0	12 06	Suresnes	19 10 77	Marseille
Butt Nicky (M)	5 10	11 05	Manchester	21 1 75	Manchester U
Carroll Andy (F)	6 3	13 08	Newcastle	6 1 89	Scholar
Coloccini Fabricio (D)	6 0	12 04	Cordoba	22 1 82	La Coruna
Danquah Frank (F)	5 11	11 07	Amsterdam	4 10 89	Academy
Donaldson Ryan (F)	5 9	11 00		1 5 91	Scholar
Duff Damien (M)	5 9	12 06	Ballyboden	2 3 79	Chelsea
Edgar David (D)	6 2	12 13	Ontario	19 5 87	Scholar
Forster Fraser (G)	6 4	14 00	Newcastle	17 3 88	Scholar
Geremi (M)	5 9	13 01	Bafoussam	20 12 78	Chelsea
Godsmark Jonny (M)	5 6	10 01	Guide Post	3 9 89	Scholar
Guthrie Danny (M)	5 9	11 06	Shrewsbury	18 4 87	Liverpool
Gutierrez Jonas (M)	6 0	11 07	Saenz Pena	5 7 82	Mallorca
Harper Steve (G)	6 2	13 10	Easington	14 3 75	Seaham Red Star
Jose Enrique (D)	6 0	12 00	Valencia	23 1 86	Villarreal
Kadar Tamas (D)	6 0	12 10	Veszprem	14 3 90	Zalaegerszegi
Krul Tim (G)	6 2	11 08	Den Haag	3 4 88	Den Haag
LuaLua Kazenga (F)	5 11	12 00	Kinshasa	10 12 90	Scholar
Martins Obafemi (F)	5 10	11 06	Lagos	28 10 84	Internazionale
McLaughlin Patrick (M)			Larne	14 1 91	
Ngo Baheng Wesley (F)	5 11	11 06	Blanc Mesnil	23 9 89	Le Havre
Nolan Kevin (M)	6 0	14 00	Liverpool	24 6 82	Bolton W
Ranger Nile (F)	6 2	13 03	London	11 4 91	Southampton
Smith Alan (F)	5 10	12 04	Rothwell	28 10 80	Manchester U
Soderberg Ole (G)			Norrkoping	20 7 90	BK Hacken
Taylor Ryan (M)	5 8	10 04	Liverpool	19 8 84	Wigan Ath
Taylor Steven (D)	6 1	13 01	Greenwich	23 1 86	Scholar
Tozer Ben (D)	6 1	13 05	Plymouth	1 3 90	Swindon T
Xisco (F)	6 0	13 03	Palma	26 6 86	La Coruna
Zamblera Fabio (F)	6 3	14 09	Atalanta	7 4 90	Atalanta

League Appearances: Ameobi, S. 14(8); Barton, J. 6(3); Bassong, S. 26(4); Beye, H. 22(1); Butt, N. 33; Cacapa, C. 4(2); Carroll, A. 5(9); Coloccini, F. 34; Duff, D. 28(2); Edgar, D. 7(4); Geremi, 11(4); Given, S. 22; Gonzalez, I. (2); Guthrie, D. 21(3); Gutierrez, J. 23(7); Harper, S. 16; Jose Enrique, 24(2); Lovenkrands, P. 8(4); LuaLua, K. (3); Martins, O. 21(3); Milner, J. 2; N'Zogbia, C. 14(4); Nolan, K. 10(1); Owen, M. 21(7); Smith, A. 4(2); Taylor, R. 8(2); Taylor, S. 25(2); Viduka, M. 6(6); Xisco, 3(2).

Goals – League (40): Martins 8, Owen 8 (1 pen), Ameobi 4 (1 pen), Taylor S 4, Carroll 3, Duff 3, Lovenkrands 3, Guthrie 2 (1 pen), Barton 1 (pen), Edgar 1, N'Zogbia 1, Xisco 1, own goal 1.

Carling Cup (4): Owen 2, Milner 1, own goal 1.

FA Cup (0).

Ground: St James' Park, Newcastle upon Tyne NE1 4ST. Telephone (0191) 201 8400.

Record Attendance: 68,386 v Chelsea, Division 1, 3 Sept 1930. **Capacity:** 52,387.

Manager: TBC.

Most League Goals: 98, Division 1, 1951–52.

Highest League Scorer in Season: Hughie Gallacher, 36, Division 1, 1926–27.

Most League Goals in Total Aggregate: Jackie Milburn, 177, 1946–57.

Most Capped Player: Shay Given, 82 (96), Republic of Ireland.

Most League Appearances: Jim Lawrence, 432, 1904–22.

Honours – Football League: Division 1 – Champions 1904–05, 1906–07, 1908–09, 1926–27, 1992–93. Division 2 Champions – 1964–65. **FA Cup:** Winners – 1910, 1924, 1932, 1951, 1952, 1955. **Texaco Cup:** Winners – 1973–74, 1974–75. **European Competitions: European Fairs Cup:** Winners – 1968–69. **Anglo-Italian Cup:** Winners – 1973. **Intertoto Cup:** Winners – 2006.
Colours: Black and white striped shirts, black shorts with white trim, black stockings.

NORTHAMPTON TOWN   FL CHAMPIONSHIP 2

Akinfenwa Adebayo (F)	5 11	13 07	Nigeria	10 5 82	Millwall
Anya Ikechi (M)	5 5	11 04	Glasgow	3 1 88	Wycombe W
Benjamin Joseph (F)	5 11	11 05	Waltham Forest	8 10 90	Scholar
Coke Gilles (M)	6 0	11 11	London	3 6 86	Mansfield T
Crowe Jason (D)	5 9	10 09	Sidcup	30 9 78	Grimsby T
Davis Liam (M)	5 9	11 07	Wandsworth	23 11 86	Coventry C
Dunn Chris (G)	6 5	13 11	Hammersmith	23 10 87	Scholar
Dyer Alex (M)	5 8	11 07	Wordsley	1 6 90	Scholar
Gilligan Ryan (M)	5 10	11 07	Swindon	18 1 87	Watford
Guttridge Luke (M)	5 6	9 07	Barnstaple	27 3 82	Colchester U
Holt Andy (M)	6 1	12 07	Stockport	21 5 78	Wrexham
Hughes Mark (D)	6 1	13 03	Liverpool	9 12 86	Everton
Jackman Danny (D)	5 4	10 00	Worcester	3 1 83	Gillingham
Osman Abdul (M)	6 0	11 00	Accra	27 2 87	Gretna

League Appearances: Akinfenwa, A. 29(4); Anya, I. 6(8); Benjamin, J. (4); Bignall, N. 1(4); Bunn, M. 3; Clarke, B. 5; Coke, G. 25(7); Constantine, L. 21(11); Crowe, J. 42(1); Davis, L. 21(8); Doig, C. 26(2); Dolman, L. 9(5); Dunn, C. 29; Dyer, A. 5(3); Fielding, F. 12; Gilligan, R. 23(8); Guttridge, L. 23(2); Gyepes, G. 2; Hawley, K. 11; Henderson, I. (3); Hodgkiss, J. 4(1); Holt, A. 28(13); Hughes, M. 41; Jackman, D. 42(1); Larkin, C. 9(12); Little, M. 9; Magnay, C. 2; McGleish, S. 7(2); Osman, A. 34(2); Prijovic, A. 3(7); Rodgers, P. 9(2); Todd, A. 7; Vernon, S. 4(2); Walker, K. 9; Watts, A. 3(2); Zieler, R. 2.
Goals – League (61): Akinfenwa 13 (3 pens) Jackman 8, Crowe 5, Davis 4, Anya 3, Clarke 3 (1 pen), Constantine 3, Gilligan 3, Coke 2, Guttridge 2, Hawley 2, Holt 2, Osman 2, Prijovic 2, Bignall 1, Doig 1, Hughes 1, Larkin 1, McGleish 1, Vernon 1, own goal 1.
Carling Cup (5): Akinfenwa 2 (1 pen), Crowe 1, Guttridge 1, Larkin 1.
FA Cup (3): Crowe 2, McGleish 1.
J Paint Trophy (0).
Ground: Sixfields Stadium, Upton Way, Northampton NN5 5QA. Telephone 01604 683 700.
Record Attendance: (at County Ground): 24,523 v Fulham, Division 1, 23 April 1966; (at Sixfields Stadium): 7,557 v Manchester C, Division 2, 26 September 1998.
Capacity: 7,300.
Manager: Stuart Gray.
Secretary: Norman Howells.
Most League Goals: 109, Division 3, 1962–63 and Division 3 (S), 1952–53.
Highest League Scorer in Season: Cliff Holton, 36, Division 3, 1961–62.
Most League Goals in Total Aggregate: Jack English, 135, 1947–60.
Most Capped Player: Edwin Lloyd Davies, 12 (16), Wales.
Most League Appearances: Tommy Fowler, 521, 1946–61.
Honours – Football League: Division 3 Champions – 1962–63. Division 4 Champions – 1986–87.
Colours: Claret shirts with yellow inserts, white shorts, white stockings.

Adeyemi Thomas (M)	6 1	12 04	Norwich	24 10 91	Scholar
Clingan Sammy (M)	5 11	11 06	Belfast	13 1 84	Nottingham F
Croft Lee (D)	5 11	12 12	Wigan	21 6 85	Manchester C
Cureton Jamie (F)	5 8	10 07	Bristol	28 8 75	Colchester U
Daley Luke (F)			Northampton	10 11 89	Scholar
Doherty Gary (D)	6 2	13 04	Carndonagh	31 1 80	Tottenham H
Drury Adam (D)	5 10	11 08	Cottenham	29 8 78	Peterborough U
Gow Alan (M)	6 0	11 00	Glasgow	9 10 82	Blackpool
Hoolahan Wes (M)	5 6	10 03	Dublin	10 8 83	Blackpool
Killen Chris (F0	6 1	11 07	Wellington	8 10 81	Celtic
Lathrope Damon (M)	5 8	10 02	Stevenage	28 10 89	Scholar
Martin Chris (F)	6 2	12 06	Norwich	4 11 88	Scholar
McDonald Cody (F)	5 10	11 03	Norwich	30 5 86	Dartford
Otsemobor John (D)	5 10	12 07	Liverpool	23 3 83	Crewe Alex
Pattison Matt (M)	5 9	11 00	Johannesburg	27 10 86	Newcastle U
Renton Kris (F)	6 3	12 06	Musselburgh	12 7 90	Scholar
Rudd Declan (G)	6 3	12 06	Norwich	16 1 91	Scholar
Russell Darel (M)	5 10	11 09	Mile End	22 10 80	Stoke C
Smith Korey (M)	5 9	11 01	Welwyn	31 1 91	Scholar
Spillane Michael (M)	5 9	11 10	Cambridge	23 3 89	Scholar
Stefanovic Dejan (D)	6 2	13 01	Belgrade	28 10 74	Fulham

League Appearances: Bell, D. 12(7); Bertrand, R. 37(1); Carney, D. 4(5); Clingan, S. 40; Cort, C. 7(5); Croft, L. 34(7); Cureton, J. 10(12); Daley, L. (3); Doherty, G. 32(2); Drury, A. 10(1); Fotheringham, M. 20(7); Gow, A. 8(5); Grounds, J. 14(2); Hoolahan, W. 27(5); Kennedy, J. 15(1); Killen, C. (4); Koroma, O. 2(3); Lappin, S. 4(1); Lee, A. 6(1); Leijer, A. 1(3); Lita, L. 16; Lupoli, A. 7(10); Marshall, D. 46; McDonald, C. 1(6); Mooney, D. 8(1); Omozusi, E. 20(1); Otsemobor, J. 35(2); Pattison, M. 18(6); Russell, D. 31(7); Shackell, J. 15; Sibierski, A. 13(2); Smith, K. 1(1); Stefanovic, D. 12.
Goals – League (57): Lita 7, Clingan 6 (4 pens), Croft 5, Lupoli 4, Russell 4, Doherty 3, Grounds 3, Mooney 3, Pattison 3, Cureton 2, Hoolahan 2, Kennedy 2, Lee 2, Sibierski 2, Cort 1, Fotheringham 1, McDonald 1, own goals 6.
Carling Cup (0).
FA Cup (1): Lupoli 1.
Ground: Carrow Road, Norwich NR1 1JE. Telephone (01603) 760 760.
Record Attendance: 43,984 v Leicester C, FA Cup 6th rd, 30 March 1963.
Capacity: 26,034.
Manager: Bryan Gunn.
Secretary: Kevan Platt.
Most League Goals: 99, Division 3 (S), 1952–53.
Highest League Scorer in Season: Ralph Hunt, 31, Division 3 (S), 1955–56.
Most League Goals in Total Aggregate: Johnny Gavin, 122, 1945–54, 1955–58.
Most Capped Player: Mark Bowen, 35 (41), Wales.
Most League Appearances: Ron Ashman, 592, 1947–64.
Honours – Football League: Division 1 Champions – 2003–04. Division 2 Champions – 1971–72, 1985–86. Division 3 (S) Champions – 1933–34. **Football League Cup:** Winners – 1962, 1985.
Colours: Yellow shirts with two thin green stripes, green shorts, yellow stockings.

Bengelloun Tarik (M)			Paris	8 2 91	Scholar
Bennett Julian (D)	6 1	13 00	Nottingham	17 12 84	Walsall
Byrne Mark (M)	5 9	11 00	Dublin	9 11 88	Crumlin

Chambers Luke (D)	6 1	11 13	Kettering	28 9 85	Northampton T
Cohen Chris (M)	5 11	10 11	Norwich	5 3 87	Yeovil T
Darnet Mickael (F)			Cagnes-sur-Mer	10 3 90	Cannes
Davies Arron (M)	5 9	11 00	Cardiff	22 6 84	Yeovil T
Diagne Tony (D)			Meulan	17 9 90	Scholar
Earnshaw Robert (F)	5 6	9 09	Mulfulira	6 4 81	Derby Co
Garner Joe (F)	5 10	11 02	Blackburn	12 4 88	Carlisle U
Gibbons Robert (M)			Dublin	8 10 91	Scholar
Heath Joseph (D)	5 11	11 11	Birkenhead	4 10 88	Scholar
McCleary Garath (F)	5 10	12 06	Oxford	15 5 87	Bromley
McGugan Lewis (M)	5 9	11 06	Long Eaton	25 10 88	Scholar
Mitchell Aaron (D)			Nottingham	5 2 90	Scholar
Moloney Brendan (M)	6 1	11 02	Enfield	18 1 89	Scholar
Morgan Wes (D)	6 2	14 00	Nottingham	21 1 84	Scholar
Moussi Guy (M)	6 1	12 11	Bondy	23 1 85	Angers
Newbold Adam (F)	6 0	12 00	Nottingham	16 11 89	Scholar
Perch James (D)	5 11	11 05	Mansfield	29 9 85	Scholar
Redmond Shane (G)	6 0	12 10	Dublin	23 3 89	Scholar
Reid James (M)	5 10	11 04	Nottingham	28 2 90	Scholar
Smith Paul (G)	6 3	14 00	Epsom	17 12 79	Southampton
Thornhill Matt (M)	6 1	13 10	Nottingham	11 10 88	Scholar
Tyson Nathan (F)	5 10	10 02	Reading	4 5 82	Wycombe W
Wilson Kelvin (D)	6 2	12 12	Nottingham	3 9 85	Preston NE

League Appearances: Anderson, P. 24(2); Bennett, J. 10(2); Blackstock, D. 6; Breckin, I. 17(6); Byrne, M. (1); Camp, L. 15; Chambers, L. 32(7); Cohen, C. 41; Cole, A. 5(5); Davies, A. 3(10); Earnshaw, R. 26(6); Fletcher, C. 4(1); Garner, J. 19(9); Gunter, C. 8; Heath, J. 9(1); Lynch, J. 20(3); Martin, L. 9(4); McCleary, G. 14(25); McGugan, L. 25(8); McSheffrey, G. 4; Moloney, B. 9(3); Morgan, W. 42; Moussi, G. 14(1); Newbold, A. (4); Osbourne, I. 7(1); Perch, J. 36(1); Reid, J. (1); Sinclair, E. (3); Smith, P. 28; Thornhill, M. 13(11); Turner, I. 3; Tyson, N. 28(7); Wilson, K. 35(1).
Goals – League (50): Earnshaw 12, Garner 7, McGugan 5 (1 pen), Tyson 5, Perch 3, Thornhill 3, Anderson 2, Blackstock 2, Chambers 2, Cohen 2, Martin 1, McCleary 1, Morgan 1, own goals 4.
Carling Cup (5): Earnshaw 3, Cohen 1, Newbold 1.
FA Cup (6): Earnshaw 2, Tyson 2 (1 pen), Cohen 1, Garner 1.
Ground: The City Ground, Nottingham NG2 5FJ. Telephone (0115) 982 4444.
Record Attendance: 49,946 v Manchester U, Division 1, 28 October 1967.
Capacity: 30,576.
Manager: Billy Davies.
Football Administrator: Jane Carnelly.
Most League Goals: 110, Division 3 (S), 1950–51.
Highest League Scorer in Season: Wally Ardron, 36, Division 3 (S), 1950–51.
Most League Goals in Total Aggregate: Grenville Morris, 199, 1898–1913.
Most Capped Player: Stuart Pearce, 76 (78), England.
Most League Appearances: Bob McKinlay, 614, 1951–70.
Honours – Football League: Division 1 – Champions 1977–78, 1997–98. Division 2 Champions – 1906–07, 1921–22. Division 3 (S) Champions – 1950–51. **FA Cup:** Winners – 1898, 1959. **Football League Cup:** Winners – 1977–78, 1978–79, 1988–89, 1989–90. **Anglo-Scottish Cup:** Winners – 1976–77. **Simod Cup:** Winners – 1989. **Zenith Data Systems Cup:** Winners – 1991–92. **European Competitions: European Cup:** Winners – 1978–79, 1979–80. **Super Cup:** Winners – 1979–80.
Colours: Red shirts, white shorts, red stockings.

NOTTS COUNTY   FL CHAMPIONSHIP 2

| Butcher Richard (M) | 6 0 | 13 01 | Peterborough | 22 1 81 | Peterborough U |
| Canham Sean (F) | 6 1 | 13 01 | Exeter | 26 9 84 | Team Bath |

Clapham Jamie (M)	5 9	11 09	Lincoln	7 12 75	Leicester C
Edwards Mike (D)	6 1	13 01	North Ferriby	25 4 80	Grimsby T
Facey Delroy (F)	6 0	15 02	Huddersfield	22 4 80	Gillingham
Fairclough Ben (F)	5 5	9 10	Nottingham	18 4 89	Nottingham F
Hamshaw Matt (M)	5 10	11 08	Rotherham	1 1 82	Mansfield T
Hoult Russell (G)	6 3	14 09	Ashby	22 11 72	Stoke C
Hunt Steve (D)	6 1	13 05	Southampton	11 11 84	Colchester U
Nowland Adam (M)	5 11	11 06	Preston	6 7 81	Preston NE
Pilkington Kevin (G)	6 1	13 00	Hitchin	8 3 74	Mansfield T
Thompson John (D)	6 0	12 01	Dublin	12 10 81	Oldham Ath
Weston Myles (F)	5 11	12 05	Lewisham	12 3 88	Charlton Ath

League Appearances: Beardsley, J. 11; Butcher, R. 29(5); Canham, S. 7(16); Clapham, J. 40; Edwards, M. 42(1); Facey, D. 44(1); Fairclough, B. 2(6); Forrester, J. 27(3); Forte, J. 15(3); Hamshaw, M. 39(2); Hanson, M. 5; Hoult, R. 16; Hunt, S. 8(3); Johnson, M. 29; Lillis, J. 5; MacKenzie, N. (1); Mayo, P. 10(2); Neal, L. 4; Nowland, A. 16(4); Picken, P. 22; Pilkington, K. 25; Richards, M. (1); Smith, J. 6(7); Strachan, G. 13(5); Tann, A. 9(5); Thompson, J. 35; Wedderburn, N. 3(6); Weir-Daley, S. (10); Weston, M. 44.

Goals – League (49): Facey 9, Forrester 8 (4 pens), Forte 8, Butcher 6, Canham 3, Hamshaw 3, Weston 3, Clapham 2, Edwards 2, Johnson 2, Thompson 2, Strachan 1.

Carling Cup (1): Weston 1.

FA Cup (3): Butcher 1, Canham 1, Smith 1.

J Paint Trophy (1): Butcher 1.

Ground: Meadow Lane Stadium, Meadow Lane, Nottingham NG2 3HJ. Telephone (0115) 952 9000.

Record Attendance: 47,310 v York C, FA Cup 6th rd, 12 March 1955. **Capacity:** 20,300.

Manager: Ian McParland.

General Manager: Tony Cuthbert.

Most League Goals: 107, Division 4, 1959–60.

Highest League Scorer in Season: Tom Keetley, 39, Division 3 (S), 1930–31.

Most League Goals in Total Aggregate: Les Bradd, 125, 1967–78.

Most Capped Player: Kevin Wilson, 15 (42), Northern Ireland.

Most League Appearances: Albert Iremonger, 564, 1904–26.

Honours – Football League: Division 2 Champions – 1896–97, 1913–14, 1922–23. Division 3 Champions – 1997–98. Division 3 (S) Champions – 1930–31, 1949–50. Division 4 Champions – 1970–71. **FA Cup:** Winners – 1893–94. **Anglo-Italian Cup:** Winners – 1995.

Colours: Black and white striped shirts, black shorts, black stockings.

OLDHAM ATHLETIC   FL CHAMPIONSHIP 1

Alessandra Lewis (F)	5 9	11 07	Oldham	8 2 89	Scholar
Allott Mark (M)	5 11	11 07	Manchester	3 10 77	Chesterfield
Black Paul (D)	6 0	12 10	Middleton	18 1 90	Scholar
Brooke Ryan (M)	6 1	11 07	Crewe	4 10 90	Scholar
Eardley Neal (D)	5 11	11 10	Llandudno	6 11 88	Scholar
Fleming Greg (G)	5 11	12 09	Edinburgh	27 9 86	Gretna
Hazell Reuben (D)	5 11	12 05	Birmingham	24 4 79	Chesterfield
Lee Kieran (D)	6 1	12 00	Tameside	22 6 88	Manchester U
Lomax Kelvin (D)	5 10	12 03	Bury	12 11 86	Scholar
O'Grady Chris (F)	6 3	12 04	Nottingham	25 1 86	Rotherham U
Smalley Deane (M)	6 0	11 10	Chadderton	5 9 88	Scholar
Stephens Dale (M)	5 11	11 06	Bolton	12 12 87	Bury
Taylor Chris (M)	5 11	11 00	Oldham	20 12 86	Scholar
Whitaker Danny (M)	5 10	11 00	Manchester	14 11 80	Port Vale
Wolfenden Matthew (M)	5 9	11 01	Oldham	23 7 87	Scholar

League Appearances: Alessandra, L. 12(20); Allott, M. 44(1); Black, P. 2(1); Brooke, R. (1); Budtz, J. 3; Byfield, D. 8; Byrne, R. 3(1); Crossley, M. 21; Davies, C. 5(7); Eardley, N. 31(3); Ferreira, F. (1); Fleming, G. 17(1); Golbourne, S. 7(1); Gregan, S. 38(2); Hazell, R. 43; Hines, S. 4; Hughes, L. 36(1); Jones, D. 23; Kabba, S. 7(1); Lee, K. 6(1); Liddell, A. 18(14); Lomax, K. 27; Maher, K. 21(7); O'Grady, C. 3(10); Ormerod, B. 2(3); Smalley, D. 22(12); Stam, S. 11(2); Supple, S. 5; Taylor, C. 42; Westlake, I. 5; Whitaker, D. 30(9); Windass, D. 9(2); Wolfenden, M. 1(4).
Goals – League (66): Hughes 18, Taylor 10, Liddell 8 (5 pens), Whitaker 6, Alessandra 5, Smalley 5, Allott 3, Hazell 3, Eardley 2 (1 pen), Brooke 1, Byfield 1, Jones D 1, Maher 1, Windass 1, own goal 1.
Carling Cup (0).
FA Cup (2): Taylor 1, Whitaker 1.
J Paint Trophy (1): Whitaker 1.
Ground: Boundary Park, Furtherwood Road, Oldham OL1 2PA. Telephone (0871) 226 2235.
Record Attendance: 46,471 v Sheffield W, FA Cup 4th rd, 25 January 1930.
Capacity: 13,624.
Manager: Dave Penney.
Secretary: Alan Hardy.
Most League Goals: 95, Division 4, 1962–63.
Highest League Scorer in Season: Tom Davis, 33, Division 3 (N), 1936–37.
Most League Goals in Total Aggregate: Roger Palmer, 141, 1980–94.
Most Capped Player: Gunnar Halle, 24 (64), Norway.
Most League Appearances: Ian Wood, 525, 1966–80.
Honours – Football League: Division 2 Champions – 1990–91, Division 3 (N) Champions – 1952–53. Division 3 Champions – 1973–74.
Colours: Blue shirts with white design, blue shorts, white stockings.

PETERBOROUGH UNITED   FL CHAMPIONSHIP

Batt Shaun (F)	6 3	12 08	Luton	22 2 87	Fisher Ath
Blackett Shane (D)	6 0	12 11	Luton	3 10 82	Dagenham & R
Blanchett Danny (M)	5 11	11 12	Derby	12 3 88	Cambridge C
Boyd George (M)	5 10	11 07	Stevenage	2 10 85	Stevenage B
Charnock Kieran (D)	6 1	13 07	Preston	3 8 84	Northwich Vic
Coutts Paul (M)	5 9	11 11	Aberdeen	22 7 88	Cove R
Day Jamie (M)	5 9	10 06	Wycombe	7 5 86	Scholar
Frecklington Lee (M)	5 8	11 00	Lincoln	8 9 85	Lincoln C
Green Dominic (F)	5 6	11 02	London	5 7 89	Dagenham & R
Hatch Liam (F)	6 4	13 09	Hitchin	3 4 84	Barnet
Howe Rene (F)	6 0	14 03	Bedford	22 10 86	Kettering T
Keates Dean (M)	5 6	10 06	Walsall	30 6 78	Walsall
Lee Charlie (M)	5 11	11 07	Whitechapel	5 1 87	Tottenham H
Lewis Joe (G)	6 5	12 10	Bury St Edmunds	6 10 87	Norwich C
Mackail-Smith Craig (F)	6 3	12 04	Hertford	25 2 84	Dagenham & R
Martin Russell (M)	6 0	11 08	Brighton	4 1 86	Wycombe W
McKeown James (G)	6 1	13 07	Birmingham	24 7 89	Scholar
McLean Aaron (F)	5 8	10 03	Hammersmith	25 5 83	Grays Ath
Morgan Craig (D)	6 0	11 00	Asaph	16 6 85	Milton Keynes D
Potter Alfie (M)	5 7	9 06	Peterborough	9 1 89	Millwall
Rendell Scott (F)	6 1	13 00	Ashford	21 10 86	Cambridge U
Rowe Thomas (M)	5 11	12 11	Manchester	1 5 89	Stockport Co
Torres Sergio (M)	6 2	12 04	Mar del Plata	8 11 83	Wycombe W
Tyler Mark (G)	5 11	12 00	Norwich	2 4 77	Trainee
Westwood Chris (D)	5 11	12 10	Dudley	13 2 77	Walsall
Whelpdale Chris (M)	6 0	12 08	Harold Wood	27 1 87	Billericay T
Williams Tom (M)	5 11	12 06	Carshalton	8 7 80	Wycombe W

Wright Ben (F)   6 2   13 05 Basingstoke   10 8 88 Hampton &
    Richmond B
Zakuani Gaby (D)   6 1   12 13 DR Congo   31 5 86 Fulham

League Appearances: Batt, S. 10(20); Blackett, S. 7(4); Blanchett, D. 2(1); Boyd, G. 46; Charnock, K. 2; Chester, J. 5; Coutts, P. 34(3); Crofts, A. 4(5); Day, J. 5; Frecklington, L. 2(5); Green, D. 3(13); Hatch, L. (1); Hyde, M. 5(4); Keates, D. 37(1); Lee, C. 39(5); Lewis, J. 46; Mackail-Smith, C. 43(3); Martin, R. 46; McKeown, J. (1); McLean, A. 39(3); Morgan, C. 26(1); Rendell, S. 2(1); Torres, S. 10(5); Westwood, C. 10(6); Whelpdale, C. 29(10); Williams, T. 22(3); Wright, B. (1); Zakuani, G. 32.
Goals – League (78): Mackail-Smith 23 (3 pens), McLean 18, Boyd 9, Whelpdale 7, Keates 5 (2 pens), Lee 5, Batt 2, Green 1, Martin 1, Rendell 1, Torres 1, Zakuani 1, own goals 4.
Carling Cup (1): Boyd 1.
FA Cup (4): Mackail-Smith 3, McLean 1.
J Paint Trophy (0).
Ground: London Road Stadium, Peterborough PE2 8AL. Telephone (01733) 563 947.
Record Attendance: 30,096 v Swansea T, FA Cup 5th rd, 20 February 1965.
Capacity: 15,460.
Player-Manager: Darren Ferguson.
Secretary: Karen Turner.
Most League Goals: 134, Division 4, 1960–61.
Highest League Scorer in Season: Terry Bly, 52, Division 4, 1960–61.
Most League Goals in Total Aggregate: Jim Hall, 122, 1967–75.
Most Capped Player: James Quinn, 9 (50), Northern Ireland.
Most League Appearances: Tommy Robson, 482, 1968–81.
Honours – Football League: Division 4 Champions – 1960–61, 1973–74.
Colours: Blue shirts with white design, white shorts, blue stockings.

PLYMOUTH ARGYLE   FL CHAMPIONSHIP

Barker Chris (D)	6 2	13 08	Sheffield	2 3 80	QPR
Barnes Ashley (F)	6 0	12 00	Bath	30 10 89	Paulton R
Bolasie Yannick (M)	6 2	13 02	DR Congo	24 5 89	
Clark Chris (F)	5 7	10 05	Aberdeen	15 9 80	
Donnelly George (F)	6 2	13 03	Plymouth	28 5 88	Skelmersdale U
Doumbe Stephen (D)	6 1	12 05	Paris	28 0 79	Hibernian
Duguid Karl (M)	5 11	11 06	Hitchin	21 3 78	Colchester U
Easter Jermaine (F)	5 9	12 02	Cardiff	15 1 82	Wycombe W
Fallon Rory (F)	6 2	11 09	Gisborne	20 3 82	Swansea C
Folly Yoann (M)	5 9	11 04	Togo	6 6 85	Sheffield W
Head Liam (F)				26 1 92	Scholar
Larrieu Romain (G)	6 2	13 00	Mont-de-Marsan	31 8 76	ASOA Valence
Mackie Jamie (F)	5 8	11 00	Dorking	22 9 85	Exeter C
MacLean Steve (F)	5 11	12 06	Edinburgh	23 8 82	Cardiff C
McCrory Damien (M)	6 2	12 10	Limerick	23 2 90	Scholar
McNamee David (D)	5 11	11 02	Glasgow	10 10 80	Coventry C
Noone Craig (M)	6 3	12 07	Fazackerly	17 11 87	Southport
Paterson Jim (M)	5 11	12 13	Bellshill	25 9 79	
Puncheon Jason (M)	5 9	12 05	Croydon	26 6 86	Barnet
Sawyer Gary (D)	6 0	11 08	Bideford	5 7 85	Scholar
Saxton Lloyd (G)	5 11	12 03	Alsager	18 4 90	Scholar
Seip Marcel (D)	6 0	12 04	Wenschoten	5 4 82	Heerenveen
Stack Graham (G)	6 2	12 07	Hampstead	26 9 81	Reading
Summerfield Luke (M)	6 0	11 00	Ivybridge	6 12 87	Scholar
Timar Krisztian (D)	6 3	13 08	Budapest	4 10 79	Ferencvaros
Walton Simon (D)	6 1	13 05	Sherburn-in-Elmet	13 9 87	QPR

League Appearances: Barker, C. 38(2); Barnes, A. 12(3); Cathcart, C. 30(1); Clark, C. 30(6); Donnelly, G. (2); Douala, R. 1(1); Doumbe, S. 21(3); Duguid, K. 39; Easter, J. 2(2); Fallon, R. 26(18); Fletcher, C. 13; Folly, Y. 6(5); Gallagher, P. 36(4); Gray, D. 14; Judge, A. 15(2); Larrieu, R. 41; MacLean, S. 11(10); Mackie, J. 35(8); Marin, N. 1(5); McNamee, D. 5(5); Mpenza, E. 3(6); Noone, C. 3(18); Paterson, J. 7(10); Puncheon, J. 5(1); Sawyer, G. 13; Seip, M. 41; Stack, G. 5; Summerfield, L. 28(1); Timar, K. 13(8); Walton, S. 12(1).
Goals – League (44): Gallagher 13 (2 pens), Fallon 5, Mackie 5, Sawyer 3, Seip 3, Judge 2, MacLean 2, Mpenza 2, Summerfield 2 (2 pens), Barnes 1, Cathcart 1, Doumbe 1, Duguid 1, Fletcher 1, Noone 1, own goal 1.
Carling Cup (0).
FA Cup (1): Duguid 1.
Ground: Home Park, Plymouth, Devon PL2 3DQ. Telephone (01752) 562 561.
Record Attendance: 43,596 v Aston Villa, Division 2, 10 October 1936.
Capacity: 21,118.
Manager: Paul Sturrock.
Secretary: Carole Rowntree.
Most League Goals: 107, Division 3 (S), 1925–26 and 1951–52.
Highest League Scorer in Season: Jack Cock, Division 3 (S), 1926–27.
Most League Goals in Total Aggregate: Sammy Black, 180, 1924–38.
Most Capped Player: Moses Russell, 20 (23), Wales.
Most League Appearances: Kevin Hodges, 530, 1978–92.
Honours – Football League: Division 2 Champions – 2003–04. Division 3 (S) Champions – 1929–30, 1951–52. Division 3 Champions – 1958–59, 2001–02.
Colours: Green shirts with one white sleeve, white shorts, black stockings.

PORTSMOUTH   FA PREMIERSHIP

Ashdown Jamie (G)	6 1	13 05	Reading	30 11 80	Reading
Basinas Angelos (M)	5 11	11 13	Chalkida	31 1 76	AEK Athens
Begovic Asmir (G)	6 6	13 01	Trebinje	20 6 87	La Louviere
Belhadj Nadir (D)	5 9	10 07	Saint-Claude	18 6 82	Lens
Ciftci Nadir (F)	6 1	13 00	Karacan	12 2 92	Scholar
Collins Joe (M)			Southampton	29 10 90	Scholar
Cowan-Hall Paris (F)			London	5 10 90	Scholar
Cranie Martin (D)	6 1	12 09	Yeovil	23 9 86	Southampton
Crouch Peter (F)	6 7	13 03	Macclesfield	30 1 81	Liverpool
Davis Sean (M)	5 10	12 00	Clapham	20 9 79	Tottenham H
Diop Papa Bouba (M)	6 4	14 12	Dakar	28 1 78	Fulham
Distin Sylvain (D)	6 3	14 06	Bagnolet	16 12 77	Manchester C
Gazet DuChattelier Ryan (M)			Richmond (Aus)	17 2 91	Scholar
Hreidarsson Hermann (D)	6 3	12 12	Reykjavik	11 7 74	Charlton Ath
Hughes Richard (M)	6 0	13 03.	Glasgow	25 6 79	Bournemouth
Hurst James (D)			Sutton Coldfield	31 1 92	Scholar
James David (G)	6 4	14 13	Welwyn	1 8 70	Manchester C
Johnson Glen (D)	6 0	13 04	Greenwich	23 8 84	Chelsea
Kaboul Younes (D)	6 2	13 07	St-Julien-en-Genevois	4 1 86	Tottenham H
Kanu Nwankwo (F)	6 5	13 00	Owerri	1 8 76	WBA
Kilbey Tom (M)	6 3	13 08	Waltham Forest	19 10 90	Millwall
Koroma Omar (F)	5 10	12 00	Banjul	22 10 89	Banjul Hawks
Kranjcar Niko (M)	6 1	12 08	Zagreb	13 8 84	Hajduk Split
Mahoto Gautier (M)			Paris	21 2 92	Scholar
Mantyla Tero (M)			Finland	18 4 91	Scholar
Mullins Hayden (D)	5 11	11 12	Reading	27 3 79	West Ham U
Mvuemba Arnold (M)	5 8	10 07	Alencon	28 1 85	Rennes
Nlundulu Gael (F)				29 4 92	Scholar
Nugent Dave (F)	5 11	12 13	Liverpool	2 5 85	Preston NE
O'Brien Liam (G)			Brent	30 11 91	Scholar

Primus Linvoy (D)	5 10	12 04	Forest Gate	14 9 73	Reading
Reynolds Callum (D)			Luton	10 11 89	Scholar
Ritchie Matt (M)	5 8	11 00	Portsmouth	10 9 89	Scholar
Stewart Jon (G)	6 1	13 09	Harlesden	13 3 89	Weymouth
Subotic Danijel (F)	6 1	13 00	Basle	31 1 89	Scholar
Utaka John (F)	5 9	11 02	Enugu	8 1 82	Rennes
Ward Joel (D)	6 2	11 13		29 10 89	Scholar
Wilson Marc (M)	6 2	12 07	Belfast	17 8 87	Scholar

League Appearances: Basinas, A. 3; Begovic, A. 2; Belhadj, N. 21(8); Campbell, S. 32; Crouch, P. 38; Davis, S. 31(1); Defoe, J. 17(2); Diarra, L. 11(1); Diop, P. 15(1); Distin, S. 38; Gekas, T. (1); Hreidarsson, H. 19(4); Hughes, R. 17(3); James, D. 36; Johnson, G. 29; Kaboul, Y. 17(3); Kanu, N. 3(14); Kranjcar, N. 16(5); Little, G. 4(1); Mullins, H. 15(2); Mvuemba, A. 1(5); Nugent, D. 13(3); Pamarot, N. 11(5); Pennant, J. 9(4); Primus, L. (1); Thomas, J. (3); Traore, A. 14(5); Utaka, J. 4(14); Wilson, M. 2(1).
Goals – League (38): Crouch 10, Defoe 8 (2 pens), Johnson 3, Kranjcar 3, Nugent 3, Belhadj 2, Hreidarsson 2, Davis 1, Kaboul 1, Kanu 1, Traore A 1, Utaka 1, own goals 2.
Carling Cup (0).
FA Cup (2): Crouch 1, Kranjcar 1.
UEFA Cup (11): Crouch 4, Defoe 2, Diarra 1, Hreidarsson 1, Kaboul 1, Kanu 1, Mvuemba 1.
Community Shield (0).
Ground: Fratton Park, Frogmore Road, Portsmouth, Hampshire PO4 8RA. Telephone (02392) 731 204.
Record Attendance: 51,385 v Derby Co, FA Cup 6th rd, 26 February 1949.
Capacity: 20,688.
Manager: Paul Hart.
Secretary: Paul Weld.
Most League Goals: 97, Division 1, 2002–03.
Highest League Scorer in Season: Guy Whittingham, 42, Division 1, 1992–93.
Most League Goals in Total Aggregate: Peter Harris, 194, 1946–60.
Most Capped Player: Jimmy Dickinson, 48, England.
Most League Appearances: Jimmy Dickinson, 764, 1946–65.
Honours – Football League: Division 1 Champions – 1948–49, 1949–50, 2002–03. Division 3 (S) Champions – 1923–24. Division 3 Champions – 1961–62, 1982–83.
FA Cup: Winners – 1939, 2008.
Colours: Blue shirts with yellow trim, blue shorts, blue stockings.

PORT VALE   FL CHAMPIONSHIP 2

Anyon Joe (G)	6 1	12 11	Poulton-le-Fylde	29 12 86	Scholar
Chapman Luke (M)	6 1	11 10	Cannock	10 3 91	Scholar
Collins Lee (D)	6 1	11 10	Telford	23 9 83	Wolverhampton W
Davidson Ross (M)	6 2	11 05	Burton	6 9 89	Scholar
Dodds Louis (F)	5 10	12 04	Leicester	8 10 86	Leicester C
Edwards Paul (M)	5 11	10 12	Manchester	1 1 80	Oldham Ath
Glover Danny (M)	6 0	11 02	Crewe	24 10 89	Scholar
Griffith Anthony (M)	6 0	12 00	Huddersfield	28 10 86	Doncaster R
Howland David (M)	5 11	10 08	Ballynahinch	17 9 86	Birmingham C
Lawrie James (F)	6 0	12 05	Dindonald	18 12 90	Scholar
Malbon Anthony (M)	5 8	11 00	Stoke	14 10 91	Scholar
Martin Chris (G)	6 0	13 05	Mansfield	21 7 90	Scholar
McCombe John (D)	6 2	13 00	Pontefract	7 5 85	Hereford U
Owen Gareth (D)	6 1	11 07	Cheadle	21 9 82	Stockport Co
Prosser Luke (M)	6 3	10 05	Hertfordshire	28 5 88	Scholar
Richards Marc (F)	6 2	12 06	Wolverhampton	8 7 82	Barnsley
Richman Simon (M)	5 11	11 12	Ormskirk	2 6 90	Scholar

Stockley Sam (D)	6 0	12 08	Tiverton	5 9 77	Wycombe W
Taylor Rob (D)	5 7	11 05	Nuneaton	16 1 85	Nuneaton B
Thompson Steve (F)	5 7	11 11	Peterlee	15 4 89	Scholar

League Appearances: Ahmed, A. 4(1); Anyon, J. 36; Brammer, D. 13; Brown, S. 18; Collins, L. 39; Davidson, R. 15(8); Dodds, L. 37(7); Edwards, P. 29(2); Gall, K. 7; Glover, D. 11(12); Griffith, A. 37(1); Howland, D. 35(5); Lawrie, J. 8(10); MacKenzie, N. 2; Malbon, A. (1); Marshall, P. 13; Martin, C. 10(1); McCombe, J. 30(1); McCrory, D. 10(2); Owen, G. 12; Perry, K. 9(6); Prosser, L. 24(2); Richards, M. 30; Richman, S. 20(17); Rodgers, L. 10(5); Slater, C. 6; Stockley, S. 21(1); Taiwo, T. 2(2); Taylor, R. 10(10); Thompson, S. 5(12); Tudor, S. 3(2).
Goals – League (44): Richards 10 (1 pen), Dodds 7, Richman 5, Glover 3, Rodgers 3, Taylor 3, Howland 2, Lawrie 2, McCombe 2, Thompson 2, Ahmed 1, Brown S 1, Collins 1, Marshall 1, Prosser 1.
Carling Cup (1): Rodgers 1.
FA Cup (5): Dodds 3, Howland 1, Richards 1.
J Paint Trophy (0).
Ground: Vale Park, Hamil Road, Burslem, Stoke-on-Trent ST6 1AW. Telephone (01782) 655 800.
Record Attendance: 49,768 v Aston Villa, FA Cup 5th rd, 20 February 1960.
Capacity: 18,982.
Manager: Micky Adams.
Secretary: Bill Lodey.
Most League Goals: 110, Division 4, 1958–59.
Highest League Scorer in Season: Wilf Kirkham 38, Division 2, 1926–27.
Most League Goals in Total Aggregate: Wilf Kirkham 154, 1923–29, 1931–33.
Most Capped Player: Chris Birchall, 22 (32), Trinidad & Tobago.
Most League Appearances: Roy Sproson, 761, 1950–72.
Honours – Football League: Division 3 (N) Champions – 1929–30, 1953–54. Division 4 Champions – 1958–59. **Autoglass Trophy:** Winners – 1993. **LDV Vans Trophy:** Winners – 2001.
Colours: Black and white striped shirts, black shorts, black stockings.

PRESTON NORTH END   FL CHAMPIONSHIP

Barton Adam (M)	5 11	12 01	Blackburn	7 1 91	Scholar
Brown Chris (F)	6 3	13 01	Doncaster	11 12 84	Norwich C
Carter Darren (M)	6 2	12 11	Solihull	18 12 83	WBA
Chaplow Richard (M)	5 9	9 03	Accrington	2 2 85	WBA
Chilvers Liam (D)	6 2	12 08	Chelmsford	6 11 81	Colchester U
Collins Dominic (D)			Preston	15 4 91	Scholar
Davidson Callum (D)	5 10	11 00	Stirling	25 6 76	Leicester C
Elliott Stephen (F)	5 8	11 07	Dublin	6 1 84	Wolverhampton W
Hart Michael (M)	5 10	11 06	Bellshill	10 2 80	
Hawley Karl (F)	5 8	12 02	Walsall	6 12 81	Carlisle U
Henderson Wayne (G)	5 11	12 02	Dublin	16 9 83	Brighton & HA
Jones Billy (M)	5 11	13 00	Shrewsbury	24 3 87	Crewe Alex
Lonergan Andrew (G)	6 2	13 00	Preston	19 10 83	Scholar
Mawene Youl (D)	6 1	13 00	Caen	16 7 79	Derby Co
Mayor Danny (M)			Preston	18 10 90	Scholar
McKenna Paul (M)	5 8	11 00	Eccleston	20 10 77	Trainee
Mellor Neil (F)	6 0	14 00	Sheffield	4 11 82	Liverpool
Neal Chris (G)	6 2	12 04	St Albans	23 10 85	Scholar
Nicholson Barry (M)	5 7	9 01	Dumfries	24 8 78	Aberdeen
Nolan Eddie (D)	6 0	13 05	Waterford	5 8 88	Blackburn R
Parkin Jon (F)	6 4	13 07	Barnsley	30 12 81	Stoke C
Sedgwick Chris (M)	6 0	12 01	Sheffield	28 4 80	Rotherham U
St Ledger-Hall Sean (D)	6 0	11 09	Birmingham	28 12 84	Peterborough U
Trotman Neal (D)	6 3	13 08	Levenshulme	11 3 87	Oldham Ath

| Wallace Ross (M) | 5 6 | 9 12 | Dundee | 23 5 85 | Sunderland |
| Whaley Simon (M) | 5 10 | 11 11 | Bolton | 7 6 85 | Bury |

League Appearances: Brown, C. 15(15); Brown, W. 6; Carter, D. 8(10); Chaplow, R. 21(4); Chilvers, L. (1); Davidson, C. 18(2); Davies, A. 5; Elliott, S. 23(14); Hart, M. 5(1); Hawley, K. (5); Hill, M. 1; Jarrett, J. (3); Jones, B. 44; Lonergan, A. 46; Mawene, Y. 38(3); McEveley, J. 7; McKenna, P. 44; Mellor, N. 20(13); Nicholson, B. 27(10); Nolan, E. 18(3); Parkin, J. 30(9); Sedgwick, C. 38(2); St Ledger-Hall, S. 46; Wallace, R. 34(5); Whaley, S. 7(14); Williamson, L. 5.
Goals – League (66): Parkin 11, Mellor 10 (2 pens), Brown C 6, Elliott 6, St Ledger-Hall 5, Wallace 5, Davidson 4 (4 pens), Chaplow 3, Jones 3, Nicholson 3, Mawene 2, McKenna 2, Sedgwick 1, Whaley 1, Williamson 1, own goals 3.
Carling Cup (2): Mellor 2.
FA Cup (0).
Play-Offs (1): St Ledger-Hall 1.
Ground: Deepdale, Sir Tom Finney Way, Preston PR1 6RU. Telephone (0844) 856 1964.
Record Attendance: 42,684 v Arsenal, Division 1, 23 April 1938. **Capacity:** 23,408.
Manager: Alan Irvine.
Secretary: Janet Parr.
Most League Goals: 100, Division 2, 1927–28 and Division 1, 1957–58.
Highest League Scorer in Season: Ted Harper 37, Division 2, 1932–33.
Most League Goals in Total Aggregate: Tom Finney, 187, 1946–60.
Most Capped Player: Tom Finney, 76, England.
Most League Appearances: Alan Kelly, 447, 1961–75.
Honours – Football League: Division 1 Champions – 1888–89 (first champions), 1889–90. Division 2 Champions – 1903–04, 1912–13, 1950–51, 1999–2000. Division 3 Champions – 1970–71, 1995–96. **FA Cup:** Winners – 1889, 1938.
Colours: White shirts, blue shorts, white stockings.

QUEENS PARK RANGERS　　　FL CHAMPIONSHIP

Agyemang Patrick (F)	6 1	12 00	Walthamstow	29 9 80	Preston NE
Ainsworth Gareth (M)	5 10	12 05	Blackburn	10 5 73	Cardiff C
Alberti Matteo (M)	5 10	11 05	Chievo Verona	4 8 88	
Balanta Angelo (F)	5 10	11 11	Colombia	1 7 90	Scholar
Blackstock Dexter (F)	6 2	13 03	Oxford	20 5 86	Southampton
Borrowdale Gary (D)	6 0	12 01	Sutton	16 7 85	Coventry C
Buzsaky Akos (M)	5 11	11 09	Hungary	7 5 82	Plymouth Arg
Camp Lee (G)	5 11	11 11	Derby	22 8 84	Derby Co
Cerny Radek (G)	6 1	14 02	Prague	18 2 74	Tottenham H
Connolly Matthew (D)	6 1	11 03	Barnet	24 9 87	Arsenal
Cook Lee (M)	5 8	11 10	Hammersmith	3 8 82	Fulham
Delaney Damien (D)	6 3	14 00	Cork	20 7 81	Hull C
Ephraim Hogan (F)	5 9	10 06	Islington	31 3 88	West Ham U
German Antonio (F)	5 10	12 03	London	26 12 91	Scholar
Gorkss Kaspars (D)	6 3	13 05	Riga	6 11 81	Blackpool
Hall Fitz (D)	6 3	13 00	Leytonstone	20 12 80	Wigan Ath
Helguson Heidar (F)	5 10	12 09	Akureyri	22 8 77	Bolton W
Leigertwood Mikele (D)	6 1	11 04	Enfield	12 11 82	Sheffield U
Lopez Jordi (M)	6 0	12 02	Granollers	28 2 81	Santander
Mahon Gavin (M)	5 11	13 07	Birmingham	2 1 77	Watford
Ramage Peter (D)	6 3	11 02	Whitley Bay	22 11 83	Newcastle U
Rose Romone (M)	5 9	11 05	Pennsylvania	19 1 90	Scholar
Routledge Wayne (M)	5 6	11 02	Sidcup	7 1 85	Aston Villa
Rowlands Martin (M)	5 9	10 10	Hammersmith	8 2 79	Brentford
Stewart Damion (D)	6 3	13 08	Kingston	8 8 80	Harbour View
Vine Rowan (F)	5 11	12 10	Basingstoke	21 9 82	Birmingham C

League Appearances: Agyemang, P. 11(9); Alberti, M. 6(6); Balanta, A. 2(8); Blackstock, D. 26(10); Buzsaky, A. 5(6); Camp, L. 4; Cerny, R. 42; Connolly, M. 31(4); Cook, L. 28(6); Delaney, D. 35(2); Di Carmine, S. 15(12); Ephraim, H. 16(11); German, A. (3); Gorkss, K. 30(1); Hall, F. 18(6); Helguson, H. 15(5); Ledesma, E. 11(6); Leigertwood, M. 36(6); Lopez, J. 7(3); Mahon, G. 29(6); Miller, L. 11(2); Parejo, D. 10(4); Ramage, P. 30(1); Rose, R. (2); Routledge, W. 18(1); Rowlands, M. 20(4); Stewart, D. 37; Taarabt, A. 5(2); Tommasi, D. 5(2); Vine, R. 3(2).

Goals – League (42): Blackstock 11, Helguson 5 (1 pen), Agyemang 2, Alberti 2, Di Carmine 2, Hall 2, Leigertwood 2, Mahon 2, Rowlands 2, Stewart 2, Balanta 1, Buzsaky 1, Cook 1, Delaney 1, Ephraim 1, Ledesma 1, Lopez 1, Routledge 1, Taarabt 1, Vine 1.

Carling Cup (8): Ledesma 3, Stewart 2, Balanta 1, Blackstock 1, Delaney 1.

FA Cup (1): Di Carmine 1.

Ground: Loftus Road Stadium, South Africa Road, Shepherds Bush, London W12 7PA. Telephone (020) 8743 0262.

Record Attendance: 35,353 v Leeds U, Division 1, 27 April 1974. **Capacity:** 18,682.

Manager: Jim Magilton.

Most League Goals: 111, Division 3, 1961–62.

Highest League Scorer in Season: George Goddard, 37, Division 3 (S), 1929–30.

Most League Goals in Total Aggregate: George Goddard, 172, 1926–34.

Most Capped Player: Alan McDonald, 52, Northern Ireland.

Most League Appearances: Tony Ingham, 519, 1950–63.

Honours – Football League: Division 2 Champions – 1982–83. Division 3 (S) Champions – 1947–48. Division 3 Champions – 1966–67. **Football League Cup:** Winners – 1966–67.

Colours: Blue and white hooped shirts, white shorts, white stockings.

READING   FL CHAMPIONSHIP

Andersen Mikkel (G)	6 5	12 08	Herlev	17 12 88	AB Copenhagen
Antonio Michail (M)	6 0	11 11	London	28 3 90	Tooting & M
Armstrong Chris (D)	5 9	11 00	Newcastle	5 8 82	Sheffield U
Bignall Nicholas (F)	5 10	11 12	Reading	11 7 90	Scholar
Bikey Andre (D)	6 0	12 08	Douala	8 1 85	Lokomotiv Moscow
Bozanic Oliver (M)	6 0	12 00	Melbourne	8 1 89	Central Coast M
Church Simon (F)	6 0	13 04	Wycombe	10 12 88	Scholar
Cisse Kalifa (M)	6 2	12 11	Orleans	1 9 84	Boavista
Davies Scott (M)	5 11	12 00	Dublin	10 3 88	Wycombe W
Doyle Kevin (F)	5 11	12 06	Adamstown	18 9 83	Cork C
Federici Adam (G)	6 2	14 02	Nowra	31 1 85	
Gunnarsson Brynjar (M)	6 1	12 01	Reykjavik	16 10 75	Watford
Hahnemann Marcus (G)	6 3	16 04	Seattle	15 6 72	Fulham
Hamer Ben (G)	5 11	12 04	Reading	20 11 87	Crawley T
Harper James (M)	5 10	11 02	Chelmsford	9 11 80	Arsenal
Henry James (M)	6 1	11 11	Woodley	10 6 89	Scholar
Hunt Noel (F)	5 8	11 05	Waterford	26 12 82	Dundee U
Hunt Steve (M)	5 9	10 10	Port Laoise	1 8 80	Brentford
Ingimarsson Ivar (D)	6 0	12 07	Reykjavik	20 8 77	Wolverhampton W
Karacan Jem (M)	5 10	11 13	Lewisham	21 2 89	Scholar
Kebe Jimmy (M)	6 2	11 07	Vitry-sur-Seine	19 1 84	Boulogne
Kelly Julian (D)	5 8	11 04	London	6 9 89	Scholar
Long Shane (F)	5 10	11 02	Kilkenny	22 1 87	Cork C
Matejovsky Marek (M)	5 10	11 00	Brandys nad Labem	20 12 81	Mlada Boleslav
McCarthy Alex (G)	6 1	11 12	Reading	3 12 89	Scholar
Mooney David (F)	6 0	12 01	Dublin	30 10 84	Cork C
Pearce Alex (D)	6 0	11 10	Reading	9 11 88	Scholar
Robson-Kanu Hal (F)	5 7	11 08	Hammersmith	21 5 89	
Rosenior Liam (D)	5 10	11 05	Wandsworth	9 7 84	Fulham

Sigurdsson Gylfi (M) 6 1 12 02 Reykjavik   9 9 89 Scholar
Tabb Jay (M)   5 7 10 00 Tooting   21 2 84 Coventry C

League Appearances: Armstrong, C. 40; Bikey, A. 23(2); Cisse, K. 24(12); Convey, B. 3(3); Doyle, K. 39(2); Duberry, M. 27; Federici, A. 14(1); Gunnarsson, B. 13(14); Hahnemann, M. 32; Harding, D. 3; Harper, J. 28(6); Henry, J. 3(4); Hunt, N. 27(10); Hunt, S. 41(5); Ingimarsson, I. 26; Karacan, J. 15; Kebe, J. 38(3); Kelly, J. 4(3); Kitson, D. 9(1); Lita, L. 6(4); Little, G. 5(3); Long, S. 11(26); Matejovsky, M. 11(11); Pearce, A. 13(3); Rosenior, L. 42; Sonko, I. 3; Tabb, J. 6(3).
Goals – League (72): Doyle 18, Hunt N 11, Long 9 (1 pen), Hunt S 6 (4 pens), Cisse 5, Bikey 3, Sonko 3, Gunnarsson 2, Kebe 2, Kitson 2, Armstrong 1, Federici 1, Harper 1, Ingimarsson 1, Karacan 1, Lita 1, Matejovsky 1, Pearce 1, own goals 3.
Carling Cup (9): Henry 4 (1 pen), Hunt N 2, Hunt S 1, Karacan 1, Pearce 1.
FA Cup (0).
Play-Offs (0).
Ground: The Madejski Stadium, Junction 11, M4, Reading, Berkshire RG2 0FL. Telephone (0118) 968 1100.
Record Attendance: Elm Park: 33,042 v Brentford, FA Cup 5th rd, 19 February 1927; Madejski Stadium: 24,122 v Aston villa, Premiership, 10 February 2007.
Capacity: 24,082.
Manager: Brendan Rodgers.
Secretary: Sue Hewett.
Most League Goals: 112, Division 3 (S), 1951–52.
Highest League Scorer in Season: Ronnie Blackman, 39, Division 3 (S), 1951–52.
Most League Goals in Total Aggregate: Ronnie Blackman, 158, 1947–54.
Most Capped Player: Jimmy Quinn, 17 (46), Northern Ireland.
Most League Appearances: Martin Hicks, 500, 1978–91.
Honours – Football League: Championship Champions – 2005–06. Division 2 Champions – 1993–94. Division 3 Champions – 1985–86. Division 3 (S) Champions – 1925–26. Division 4 Champions – 1978–79. **Simod Cup:** Winners – 1987–88.
Colours: Blue and white hooped shirts, white shorts, blue stockings.

ROCHDALE   FL CHAMPIONSHIP 2

Buckley Will (F)   6 0 13 00 Burnley   12 8 88 Curzon Ashton
D'Laryea Nathan (D)   5 10 12 02 Manchester   3 9 85 Manchester C
Dagnall Chris (F)   5 8 12 03 Liverpool   15 4 86 Tranmere R
Higginbotham Kallum (F) 5 11 10 10 Manchester   15 6 89 Oldham Ath
Holness Marcus (D)   6 0 12 02 Oldham   8 12 88 Scholar
Jones Gary (M)   5 11 12 05 Birkenhead   3 6 77 Barnsley
Keltie Clark (M)   5 11 11 08 Newcastle   31 8 83 Darlington
Kennedy Tom (D)   5 10 11 01 Bury   24 6 85 Bury
Le Fondre Adam (F)   5 9 11 04 Stockport   2 12 86 Stockport Co
McArdle Rory (D)   6 1 11 05 Sheffield   1 5 87 Sheffield W
McEvilly Lee (F)   6 0 13 00 Liverpool   15 4 82 Cambridge U
Ramsden Simon (D)   6 0 12 06 Bishop Auckland 17 12 81 Grimsby T
Rundle Adam (M)   5 8 11 01 Durham   8 7 84 Mansfield T
Russell Sam (G)   6 0 10 13 Middlesbrough   4 10 82 Darlington
Shaw Jon (F)   6 0 13 01 Sheffield   10 11 83 Halifax T
Stanton Nathan (D)   5 9 12 06 Nottingham   6 5 81 Scunthorpe U
Thompson Joe (M)   6 0   9 07 Rochdale   5 3 89 Scholar
Toner Ciaran (M)   6 1 12 02 Craigavon   30 6 81 Grimsby T

League Appearances: Adams, N. 12(2); Buckley, W. 28(9); Dagnall, C. 25(15); Fielding, F. 23; Flitcroft, D. (1); Higginbotham, K. 3(4); Holness, M. 4(4); Jones, G. 28; Jones, M. 7(2); Keltie, C. 26(5); Kennedy, T. 45; Lambert, K. (1); Le Fondre, A. 28(16); Madine, G. 1(2); McArdle, R. 41; McEvilly, L. 4(12); Newey, T. 1(1); Ramsden, S. 25(3); Rhodes, J. 5; Rundle, A. 32(12); Russell, S. 23; Shaw, J. 5(1);

88

Stanton, N. 39; Thompson, J. 21(9); Thorpe, L. 18(10); Toner, C. 32(5); Wiseman, S. 30(2).
Goals – League (70): Le Fondre 18 (7 pens), Buckley 10, Dagnall 7, Rundle 7, McEvilly 5, Thompson 5, Thorpe 5, Kennedy 4 (2 pens), McArdle 2, Rhodes 2, Adams 1, Higginbotham 1, Keltie 1 (pen), Shaw 1, Toner 1.
Carling Cup (0).
FA Cup (4): Le Fondre 3, Dagnall 1.
J Paint Trophy (2): Dagnall 1, Thorpe 1.
Play-Offs (1): Dagnall 1.
Ground: Spotland Stadium, Sandy Lane, Rochdale OL11 5DS. Telephone (01706) 644 648.
Record Attendance: 24,231 v Notts Co, FA Cup 2nd rd, 10 December 1949.
Capacity: 10,199.
Manager: Keith Hill.
Secretary: Colin Garlick.
Most League Goals: 105, Division 3 (N), 1926–27.
Highest League Scorer in Season: Albert Whitehurst, 44, Division 3 (N), 1926–27.
Most League Goals in Total Aggregate: Reg Jenkins, 119, 1964–73.
Most Capped Player: Leo Bertos, 6 (23), New Zealand.
Most League Appearances: Gary Jones, 345, 1998–2001; 2003–.
Honours – None.
Colours: Black and blue striped shirts, white shorts, blue stockings.

ROTHERHAM UNITED　　　　FL CHAMPIONSHIP 2

Barker Richard (F)	6 0	14 03	Sheffield	30 5 75	Hartlepool U
Brogan Stephen (D)	5 7	10 04	Rotherham	12 4 88	Scholar
Broughton Drewe (F)	6 3	12 01	Hitchin	25 10 78	Milton Keynes D
Burchill Mark (F)	5 8	11 09	Broxburn	18 8 80	Dunfermline Ath
Cahill Tom (F)	5 10	12 08	Derby	21 11 86	Matlock T
Cann Steven (G)	6 2	12 06	South Africa	20 1 88	Derby Co
Cummins Michael (M)	6 0	13 06	Dublin	1 6 78	Darlington
Fenton Nick (D)	6 0	10 02	Preston	23 11 79	Grimsby T
Green Jamie (F)	5 7	10 07	Doncaster	18 8 89	Scholar
Harrison Danny (M)	5 11	12 04	Liverpool	4 11 82	Tranmere R
Holmes Peter (M)	5 11	11 13	Bishop Auckland	18 11 80	Luton T
Hudson Mark (M)	5 10	11 03	Bishop Auckland	24 10 80	Huddersfield T
Joseph Marc (D)	6 0	12 05	Leicester	10 11 76	Blackpool
Lynch Mark (D)	5 11	11 03	Manchester	2 9 81	Yeovil T
Mills Pablo (D)	5 11	11 04	Birmingham	27 5 84	Derby Co
Newsham Mark (M)	5 10	9 11	Hatfield	24 3 87	Scholar
Nicholas Andrew (D)	6 2	12 08	Liverpool	10 10 83	Swindon T
Reid Reuben (F)	6 0	12 02	Bristol	26 7 88	Brentford
Sharps Ian (D)	6 3	13 05	Warrington	23 10 80	Tranmere R
Taylor Jason (M)	6 1	11 03	Ashton-under-Lyne	28 1 87	Stockport Co
Taylor Ryan (F)	6 2	10 10	Rotherham	4 5 88	Scholar
Todd Andrew (M)	6 0	11 03	Nottingham	22 2 79	Accrington S
Tonge Dale (D)	5 10	10 06	Doncaster	7 5 85	Barnsley
Warrington Andy (G)	6 3	12 13	Sheffield	10 6 76	Bury
Yates Jamie (F)	5 7	11 01	Sheffield	24 12 88	Scholar

League Appearances: Barker, R. 4(9); Brogan, S. (1); Broughton, D. 33(7); Burchill, M. 10(14); Cann, S. (1); Clarke, J. 7(4); Cummins, M. 30(5); Fenton, N. 45; Garcia, O. 2; Green, J. 29(2); Harrison, D. 27(6); Holmes, P. 2(1); Hudson, D. 35(7); Joseph, M. 13(12); Lynch, M. 7(1); Mills, P. 34(1); Nicholas, A. 19; Reid, R. 38(3); Rhodes, A. 14(4); Sharps, I. 45; Stockdale, D. 8; Taylor, J. 9(6); Taylor, R. 16(17); Thomas, S. 2; Tonge, D. 39; Warrington, A. 38; Yates, J. (3).

Goals – League (60): Reid 18 (3 pens), Broughton 6, Burchill 5 (3 pens), Hudson 5, Cummins 4, Sharps 4, Taylor R 4, Clarke 2, Lynch 2, Rhodes 2, Barker 1, Fenton 1, Green 1, Harrison 1, Mills 1, Taylor J 1, Tonge 1, own goal 1.
Carling Cup (5): Broughton 1, Fenton 1, Harrison 1, Reid 1, Rhodes 1.
FA Cup (1): Cummins 1.
J Paint Trophy (7): Broughton 2, Fenton 1, Harrison 1, Hudson 1, Sharps 1, Tonge 1.
Ground: Don Valley Stadium, Worksop Road, Sheffield, South Yorkshire S9 3TL. Telephone (08444) 140 737.
Record Attendance: 25,170 v Sheffield U, Division 2, 13 December 1952. **Capacity:** 25,000.
Manager: Mark Robins.
Secretary: J. Pilmner.
Most League Goals: 114, Division 3 (N), 1946–47.
Highest League Scorer in Season: Wally Ardron, 38, Division 3 (N), 1946–47.
Most League Goals in Total Aggregate: Gladstone Guest, 130, 1946–56.
Most Capped Player: Shaun Goater, 14 (36), Bermuda.
Most League Appearances: Danny Williams, 459, 1946–62.
Honours – Football League: Division 3 Champions – 1980–81. Division 3 (N) Champions – 1950–51. Division 4 Champions – 1988–89. **Auto Windscreens Shield:** Winners – 1996.
Colours: Red shirts with white design, white shorts, red stockings.

SCUNTHORPE UNITED   FL CHAMPIONSHIP

Byrne Cliff (D)	6 0	12 11	Dublin	27	4 82	Sunderland
Crosby Andy (D)	6 2	13 07	Rotherham	3	3 73	Oxford U
Forte Jonathan (M)	6 0	12 02	Sheffield	25	7 86	Sheffield U
Hayes Paul (F)	6 0	12 12	Dagenham	20	9 83	Barnsley
Hooper Gary (F)	5 10	12 07	Loughton	26	1 88	Southend U
Hurst Kevan (M)	5 10	11 07	Chesterfield	27	8 85	Sheffield U
Lillis Joshua (G)	6 2	12 09	Scunthorpe	24	6 87	Scholar
May Ben (F)	6 2	12 12	Gravesend	10	3 84	Millwall
McCann Grant (M)	5 10	11 00	Belfast	14	4 80	Barnsley
Milne Kenny (D)	6 2	12 08	Stirling	26	8 79	Falkirk
Mirfin David (D)	6 3	13 00	Sheffield	18	4 85	Huddersfield T
Morris Ian (M)	6 0	11 05	Dublin	27	2 87	Leeds U
Murphy Joe (G)	6 2	13 06	Dublin	21	8 81	Sunderland
Slocombe Sam (G)	6 0	11 11	Scunthorpe	5	6 88	
Sparrow Matt (M)	5 11	11 06	Wembley	3	10 81	Scholar
Thompson Gary (M)	6 0	14 02	Kendal	24	11 80	Morecambe
Togwell Sam (D)	5 11	12 04	Beaconsfield	14	10 84	Barnsley
Williams Marcus (D)	5 10	10 07	Doncaster	8	4 86	Scholar
Winn Peter (M)	6 0	11 09	Cleethorpes	19	12 88	Scholar
Woolford Martyn (M)	6 0	11 09	Pontefract	13	10 85	York C
Wright Andrew (M)	6 1	13 07	Southport	15	1 85	West Virginia Univ

League Appearances: Byrne, C. 43; Crosby, A. 3(1); Forte, J. 1(7); Hayes, P. 39(5); Hooper, G. 45; Hurst, K. 13(7); Iriekpen, H. 14(2); Lansbury, H. 12(4); Lillis, J. 4(1); May, B. 5(18); McCann, G. 43; Mills, J. 13(1); Milne, K. 1; Mirfin, D. 32(1); Morris, I. 4(16); Murphy, J. 42; Odejayi, K. 1(5); Pearce, K. 36(3); Sparrow, M. 27(9); Thompson, G. 15(9); Togwell, S. 34(6); Trotter, L. 4(8); Williams, M. 26; Woolford, M. 32(7); Wright, A. 17(11).
Goals – League (82): Hooper 24, Hayes 17 (4 pens), McCann 9 (3 pens), Iriekpen 4, Lansbury 4, Sparrow 4, Woolford 4, Thompson 3, Byrne 2, Hurst 2, May 2, Togwell 2, Morris 1, Odejayi 1, Trotter 1, own goals 2.
Carling Cup (0).
FA Cup (7): Hooper 4, Hurst 1, May 1, Togwell 1.

J Paint Trophy (12): Hayes 3, Hooper 2, McCann 1, May 1, Mirfin 1, Morris 1, Pearce 1, Togwell 1, Woolford 1.
Play-Offs (4): Sparrow 2, Woolford 2.
Ground: Glanford Park, Doncaster Road, Scunthorpe DN15 8TD. Telephone (0871) 221 1899.
Record Attendance: Old Showground: 23,935 v Portsmouth, FA Cup 4th rd, 30 January 1954. Glanford Park: 8,906 v Nottingham F, FL 1, 10 March 2007.
Capacity: 9,088.
Manager: Nigel Adkins BSc. (Hons).
General Manager: Jamie Hammond.
Most League Goals: 88, Division 3 (N), 1957–58.
Highest League Scorer in Season: Barrie Thomas, 31, Division 2, 1961–62.
Most League Goals in Total Aggregate: Steve Cammack, 110, 1979–81, 1981–86.
Most Capped Player: Dave Mulligan, 1(20), New Zealand.
Most League Appearances: Jack Brownsword, 595, 1950–65.
Honours – Football League: FL 1 Champions – 2006–07; Division 3 (N) Champions – 1957–58.
Colours: Claret shirts with blue design, white cuffs on sleeves, claret shorts, claret stockings.

SHEFFIELD UNITED   FL CHAMPIONSHIP

Name			Birthplace		Date	Previous Club
Abdi Liban (F)			Somalia	5 10 88		Scholar
Bennett Ian (G)	6 0	12 10	Worksop	10 10 71		Leeds U
Carney David (M)	5 11	11 00	Sydney	30 11 83		Oldham Ath
Chapman Adam (M)			Doncaster	29 11 89		Scholar
Cotterill David (F)	5 9	11 02	Cardiff	4 12 87		Wigan Ath
Geary Derek (D)	5 6	10 08	Dublin	19 6 80		Sheffield W
Haber Justin (G)	5 11	12 00	Malta	9 6 81		Haidari
Henderson Darius (F)	6 3	14 03	Sutton	7 9 81		Watford
Hendrie Lee (M)	5 10	11 00	Birmingham	18 5 77		Aston Villa
Howard Brian (M)	5 8	11 00	Winchester	23 1 83		Barnsley
Jihai Sun (D)	5 9	12 02	Dalian	30 9 77		Manchester C
Kenny Paddy (G)	6 0	15 10	Halifax	17 5 78		Bury
Kilgallon Matt (D)	6 2	12 11	York	8 1 84		Leeds U
Law Nicky (M)	5 10	11 06	Nottingham	29 3 88		Scholar
Montgomery Nick (M)	5 8	12 08	Leeds	28 10 81		Scholar
Morgan Chris (D)	6 0	13 06	Barnsley	9 11 77		Barnsley
Naughton Kyle (M)	5 11	11 07	Sheffield	11 11 88		Scholar
Naysmith Gary (D)	5 9	12 01	Edinburgh	16 11 78		Everton
Quinn Stephen (M)	5 6	9 08	Dublin	4 4 86		Scholar
Robertson Jordan (F)	6 0	12 06	Sheffield	12 2 88		Scholar
Sharp Billy (F)	5 9	11 00	Sheffield	5 2 86		Scunthorpe U
S-Latef Zeyn (F)			Sweden	22 7 90		Scholar
Speed Gary (M)	5 10	12 10	Deeside	8 9 69		Bolton W
Walker Kyle (D)	5 10	11 07	Sheffield	28 5 90		Scholar
Ward Jamie (M)	5 5	9 04	Birmingham	12 5 86		Chesterfield
Wedgbury Sam (D)			West Bromwich	26 2 89		Worcester C

League Appearances: Beattie, C. 1(12); Beattie, J. 21(2); Bennett, I. 2; Bromby, L. 6(6); Cotterill, D. 17(7); Dyer, N. 3(4); Ehiogu, U. 11(5); Geary, D. (1); Gillespie, K. (1); Halford, G. 31(10); Henderson, D. 25(7); Hendrie, L. (5); Howard, B. 22(4); Jihai, S. 11(1); Kenny, P. 44; Kilgallon, M. 39(1); Lupoli, A. 2(7); Montgomery, N. 26(2); Morgan, C. 40(1); Naughton, K. 39(1); Naysmith, G. 37(2); O'Toole, J. 5(4); Quinn, S. 43; Sharp, B. 17(5); Speed, G. 17; Spring, M. 8(3); Stead, J. (1); Stokes, A. 5(7); Tonge, M. 4; Walker, K. 2; Ward, J. 7(9); Webber, D. 21(15).

Goals – League (64): Beattie J 12 (5 pens), Quinn S 7, Henderson 6, Cotterill 4 (4 pens), Halford 4, Sharp 4, Webber 4, Speed 3 (1 pen), Howard 2, Lupoli 2, Morgan

2, Ward 2, Beattie C 1, Bromby 1, Dyer 1, Ehiogu 1, Kilgallon 1, Naughton 1, O'Toole 1, Spring 1, own goals 4.
Carling Cup (5): Henderson 1, Hendrie 1, Naughton 1, Quinn S 1, Webber 1 (pen).
FA Cup (8): Halford 3, Sharp 2, Hendrie 1, Naughton 1, Webber 1.
Play-Offs (2): Halford 1, Howard 1.
Ground: Bramall Lane, Cherry Street, Sheffield S2 4SU. Telephone (0871) 995 1899.
Record Attendance: 68,287 v Leeds U, FA Cup 5th rd, 15 February 1936.
Capacity: 32,500.
Manager: Kevin Blackwell.
Secretary: Donna Fletcher.
Most League Goals: 102, Division 1, 1925–26.
Highest League Scorer in Season: Jimmy Dunne, 41, Division 1, 1930–31.
Most League Goals in Total Aggregate: Harry Johnson, 205, 1919–30.
Most Capped Player: Billy Gillespie, 25, Northern Ireland.
Most League Appearances: Joe Shaw, 629, 1948–66.
Honours – Football League: Division 1 Champions – 1897–98. Division 2 Champions – 1952–53. Division 4 Champions – 1981–82. **FA Cup:** Winners – 1899, 1902, 1915, 1925.
Colours: Red and white striped shirts, black shorts, black stockings.

SHEFFIELD WEDNESDAY   FL CHAMPIONSHIP

Beevers Mark (D)	6 4	13 00	Barnsley	21 11 89	Scholar
Boden Luke (F)	6 1	12 00	Sheffield	26 11 88	Scholar
Buxton Lewis (D)	6 1	13 11	Newport (IW)	10 12 83	Stoke C
Clarke Leon (F)	6 2	14 02	Birmingham	10 2 85	Wolverhampton W
Esajas Etienne (F)	5 7	10 03	Amsterdam	4 11 84	Vitesse
Grant Lee (G)	6 3	13 01	Hemel Hempstead	27 1 83	Derby Co
Gray Michael (D)	5 8	10 07	Sunderland	3 8 74	Wolverhampton W
Hinds Richard (D)	6 2	12 02	Sheffield	22 8 80	Scunthorpe U
Jameson Aaron (G)	6 3	13 00	Sheffield	7 11 89	Scholar
Jeffers Francis (F)	5 10	11 02	Liverpool	25 1 81	Blackburn R
Johnson Jermaine (M)	6 0	12 08	Kingston	25 6 80	Bradford C
Lekaj Rocky (M)	5 10	10 05	Kosovo	12 10 89	Scholar
McAllister Sean (M)	5 8	10 07	Bolton	15 8 87	Scholar
O'Donnell Richard (G)	6 2	13 05	Sheffield	12 9 89	Scholar
O'Connor James (M)	5 8	11 00	Dublin	1 9 79	Burnley
Simek Frankie (D)	6 0	11 06	St Louis	13 10 84	Arsenal
Sodje Akpo (F)	6 2	12 08	Greenwich	31 1 81	Port Vale
Spurr Tommy (D)	6 1	11 05	Leeds	13 9 87	Scholar
Tudgay Marcus (F)	5 10	12 04	Worthing	3 2 83	Derby Co
Wood Richard (D)	6 3	12 03	Ossett	5 7 85	Scholar

League Appearances: Beevers, M. 30(4); Boden, L. 2(10); Burton, D. 9(8); Buxton, L. 32; Clarke, L. 20(9); Esajas, E. 18(4); Gilbert, P. 8; Grant, L. 46; Gray, M. 13; Hinds, R. 13(1); Jeffers, F. 20(11); Johnson, J. 29(8); Lekaj, R. (2); McAllister, S. 37(3); McMahon, T. 14(1); Modest, N. 1(3); O'Connor, J. 35(6); Potter, D. 17; Simek, F. 4(2); Slusarski, B. 4(3); Small, W. 6(13); Smith, J. 3(9); Sodje, A. 2(9); Spurr, T. 41; Tudgay, M. 42; Varney, L. 3(1); Watson, S. 15(7); Wood, R. 42.
Goals – League (51): Tudgay 14 (2 pens), Clarke 8 (1 pen), Esajas 3, Jeffers 3 (1 pen), Johnson 3, McAllister 3, Watson 3, Potter 2, Sodje 2, Spurr 2, Varney 2, Burton 1, Buxton 1, McMahon 1, Slusarski 1, Small 1, own goal 1.
Carling Cup (2): Esajas 2.
FA Cup (1): Spurr 1.
Ground: Hillsborough, Sheffield S6 1SW. Telephone (0871) 995 1867.
Record Attendance: 72,841 v Manchester C, FA Cup 5th rd, 17 February 1934.
Capacity: 39,812.
Manager: Brian Laws.
Company Secretary: Paul Johnson.
Most League Goals: 106, Division 2, 1958–59.

Highest League Scorer in Season: Derek Dooley, 46, Division 2, 1951–52.
Most League Goals in Total Aggregate: Andrew Wilson, 199, 1900–20.
Most Capped Player: Nigel Worthington, 50 (66), Northern Ireland.
Most League Appearances: Andrew Wilson, 501, 1900–20.
Honours – Football League: Division 1 Champions – 1902–03, 1903–04, 1928–29, 1929–30. Division 2 Champions – 1899–1900, 1925–26, 1951–52, 1955–56, 1958–59.
FA Cup: Winners – 1896, 1907, 1935. **Football League Cup:** Winners – 1990–91.
Colours: Blue and white striped shirts, black shorts, black stockings.

SHREWSBURY TOWN   FL CHAMPIONSHIP 2

Ashton Neil (M)	5 8	12 04	Liverpool	15 1 85	Tranmere R
Bevan Scott (G)	6 6	15 10	Southampton	16 9 79	Kidderminster H
Cansdell-Sherriff Shane (D)	5 11	11 08	Sydney	10 11 82	Tranmere R
Constable James (F)	6 2	12 12	Malmesbury	4 10 84	Kidderminster H
Coughlan Graham (D)	6 2	13 07	Dublin	18 11 74	Rotherham U
Davies Ben (M)	5 10	12 08	Birmingham	27 5 81	Chester C
Dunfield Terry (M)	5 11	12 04	Vancouver	20 2 82	Macclesfield T
Garner Glyn (G)	6 2	13 11	Pontypool	9 12 86	Leyton Orient
Herd Ben (D)	5 9	10 12	Welwyn	21 6 85	Watford
Hibbert Dave (F)	6 2	12 00	Eccleshall	28 1 86	Preston NE
Holt Grant (F)	6 1	14 02	Carlisle	12 4 81	Nottingham F
Humphrey Chris (M)	5 10	10 08	Walsall	19 9 87	WBA
Jackson Mike (D)	6 0	13 08	Runcorn	4 12 73	Blackpool
Langmead Kelvin (M)	6 1	12 00	Coventry	23 3 85	Preston NE
Leslie Steve (M)	5 11	12 10	Shrewsbury	5 11 87	Scholar
McIntyre Kevin (M)	6 0	11 10	Liverpool	23 12 77	Macclesfield T
Moss Darren (D)	5 10	11 00	Wrexham	24 5 81	Crewe Alex
Murray Paul (M)	5 9	10 08	Carlisle	30 8 76	Gretna
Pugh Marc (M)	5 11	11 04	Burnley	2 4 87	Bury
Riza Omer (F)	5 9	11 00	Edmonton	8 11 79	Trabzonspor

League Appearances: Ashikodi, M. 4(4); Ashton, N. 24(7); Cansdell-Sherriff, S. 27(4); Chadwick, N. 9(6); Coughlan, G. 42; Daniels, L. 38; Davies, B. 42; Dunfield, T. 15(2); Garner, G. 4; Gilks, M. 4; Herd, B. 20(1); Hibbert, D. 9(14); Hindmarch, S. (3); Holt, G. 43; Humphrey, C. 24(13); Hunt, D. (2); Jackson, M. 21; Labadie, J. 1; Langmead, K. 29(4); Leslie, S. 12(15); McIntyre, K. 25(1); Moss, D. 28(1); Murray, P. 31(1); Pugh, M. (7); Riza, O. (2); Sigurdsson, G. 4(1); Symes, M. 1(7); Thornton, S. 5; Tierney, M. 18; Walker, R. 16(11); White, J. 3(6); Worrall, D. 7(2).
Goals – League (61): Holt 20 (9 pens), Davies 12, Walker 5, Coughlan 4, Hibbert 3, Cansdell-Sherriff 2, Chadwick 2, Humphrey 2, Jackson 2, Murray 2, Symes 2, Ashikodi, Sigurdsson, Thornton, White 1, own goal 1.
Carling Cup (0).
FA Cup (1): Holt 1.
J Paint Trophy (14): Holt 7, McIntyre 2, Cansdell-Sherriff 1, Coughlan 1, Davies 1, Leslie 1, Walker 1.
Play-Offs (1): McIntyre 1.
Ground: ProStar Stadium, Oteley Road, Shrewsbury, Shropshire SY2 6ST. Telephone (0871) 811 8800.
Record Attendance: 18,917 v Walsall, Division 3, 26 April 1961; 8,429 v Bury, FL 2, Play-off semi final, 7 May 2009 (ProStar Stadium). **Capacity:** 10,000.
Manager: Paul Simpson.
Secretary/General Manager: Jonathan Harris.
Most League Goals: 101, Division 4, 1958–59.
Highest League Scorer in Season: Arthur Rowley, 38, Division 4, 1958–59.
Most League Goals in Total Aggregate: Arthur Rowley, 152, 1958–65 (completing his League record of 434 goals).

Most Capped Player: Jimmy McLaughlin, 5 (12), Northern Ireland; Bernard McNally, 5, Northern Ireland.
Most League Appearances: Mickey Brown, 418, 1986–91; 1992–94; 1996–2001.
Honours – Football League: Division 3 Champions – 1978–79, 1993–94. **Welsh Cup:** Winners – 1891, 1938, 1977, 1979, 1984, 1985.
Colours: Blue shirts with amber design, blue shorts, blue stockings.

SOUTHAMPTON   FL CHAMPIONSHIP 1

Bialkowski Bartosz (G)	6 3	12 10	Braniewo	6 7 87	Gornik Zabrze
Davis Kelvin (G)	6 1	14 09	Bedford	29 9 76	Sunderland
Dyer Nathan (M)	5 5	9 00	Trowbridge	29 11 87	Scholar
Euell Jason (F)	5 11	11 13	Lambeth	6 2 77	Middlesbrough
Forecast Tommy (G)	6 2	12 08	Newham	15 10 86	Tottenham H
Gillett Simon (M)	5 6	11 07	Oxford	6 11 85	Scholar
Gobern Oscar (M)	5 11	10 10	Birmingham	26 1 91	Scholar
Holmes Lee (M)	5 8	10 06	Mansfield	2 4 87	Derby Co
James Lloyd (M)	5 11	11 01	Bristol	16 2 88	Scholar
Lallana Adam (M)			Southampton	10 5 88	Scholar
Lancashire Oliver (D)	6 1	11 10	Basingstoke	13 12 88	Scholar
McGoldrick David (F)	6 1	11 10	Nottingham	29 11 87	Notts Co
McLaggon Kane (F)	6 2	12 05	Barry	21 9 90	Scholar
Mills Joseph (F)	5 9	11 00	Swindon	30 10 89	Scholar
Molyneux Lee (D)	5 10	11 07	Liverpool	24 2 89	Scholar
Paterson Matthew (F)	5 10	10 10	Glasgow	18 10 89	Scholar
Perry Chris (D)	5 8	11 03	Carshalton	26 4 73	Luton T
Poke Michael (G)	6 1	13 12	Staines	21 11 85	Trainee
Pulis Anthony (M)	5 10	11 13	Bristol	21 7 84	Stoke C
Rasiak Grzegorz (F)	6 2	13 10	Szczecin	12 1 79	Tottenham H
Saganowski Marek (F)	5 10	12 04	Lodz	31 10 78	Troyes
Schneiderlin Morgan (M)	5 11	11 11	Zellwiller	8 11 89	Strasbourg
Surman Andrew (M)	6 0	11 09	Johannesburg	20 8 86	Trainee
Thomas Wayne (D)	6 2	14 12	Gloucester	17 5 79	Burnley
Thomson Jake (M)	5 11	11 05	Southsea	12 5 89	Scholar
White Jamie (F)	5 8	10 07	Southampton	21 9 89	Scholar
Wotton Paul (D)	5 11	12 00	Plymouth	17 8 77	Plymouth Arg
Wright-Phillips Bradley (F)	5 10	11 00	Lewisham	12 3 85	Manchester C

League Appearances: Cork, J. 22(1); Davis, K. 46; Dyer, N. 1(3); Euell, J. 18(6); Gasmi, R. (4); Gillett, S. 23(4); Gobern, O. 4(2); Holmes, L. 11; James, L. 40(1); John, S. 4(3); Lallana, A. 34(6); Lancashire, O. 10(1); Liptak, Z. (7); McGoldrick, D. 45(1); McLaggon, K. 1(6); Mills, J. 6(2); Molyneux, L. 4; Paterson, M. 1(10); Pearce, A. 6(3); Pekhart, T. 2(7); Perry, C. 38(2); Robertson, J. 8(2); Saeijs, J. 20; Saganowski, M. 14(5); Schneiderlin, M. 23(7); Skacel, R. 28; Smith, R. 7(6); Surman, A. 44; Svensson, M. 4; Thomson, J. 6(4); White, J. 2(1); Wotton, P. 18(11); Wright-Phillips, B. 16(17).
Goals – League (46): McGoldrick 12 (2 pens), Surman 7 (1 pen), Saganowski 6, Wright-Phillips 6, Euell 2, Pearce 2, Perry 2, Saeijs 2, Lallana 1, McLaggon 1, Paterson 1, Pekhart 1, Robertson 1, Skacel 1, own goal 1.
Carling Cup (6): Holmes 2, McGoldrick 2 (1 pen), John 1, Lallana 1.
FA Cup (0).
Ground: St Mary's Stadium, Britannia Road, Southampton SO14 5FP. Telephone (0845) 688 9448.
Manager: TBC.
Record Attendance: 32,104 v Liverpool, FA Premier League, 18 January 2003.
Capacity: 32,689.
Secretary: Liz Coley.
Most League Goals: 112, Division 3 (S), 1957–58.
Highest League Scorer in Season: Derek Reeves, 39, Division 3, 1959–60.

Most League Goals in Total Aggregate: Mike Channon, 185, 1966–77, 1979–82.
Most Capped Player: Peter Shilton, 49 (125), England.
Most League Appearances: Terry Paine, 713, 1956–74.
Honours – Football League: Division 3 (S) Champions – 1921–22. Division 3 Champions – 1959–60. **FA Cup:** Winners – 1975–76.
Colours: Red and white striped shirts, black shorts, white stockings.

SOUTHEND UNITED　　　　　FL CHAMPIONSHIP 1

Barnard Lee (F)	5 10	10 10	Romford	18	7 84	Tottenham H
Barrett Adam (D)	6 1	12 09	Dagenham	29 11 79		Bristol R
Betsy Kevin (M)	6 1	12 00	Seychelles	20	3 78	Bristol C
Christophe Jean-Francois (M)	6 1	13 01	Creil	13	6 82	Portsmouth
Clarke Peter (D)	6 0	12 10	Southport	3	1 82	Blackpool
Francis Simon (D)	6 3	14 00	Nottingham	16	2 85	Sheffield U
Freedman Dougie (F)	5 9	12 05	Glasgow	21	1 74	Crystal Palace
Grant Anthony (M)	5 10	11 01	Lambeth	4	6 87	Chelsea
Herd Johnny (M)	5 9	12 00	Huntingdon	3 10 89		Welling U
Joyce Ian (G)	6 3	13 07	Kinnelon	12	7 85	Watford
Laurent Francis (F)	6 3	14 00	Paris	6	1 86	Mainz
Masters Clark (G)	6 2	13 12	Hastings	31	5 87	Brentford
McCormack James (M)	5 9	11 09	Dublin	10	1 84	Preston NE
Mildenhall Steve (G)	6 4	14 01	Swindon	13	5 78	Yeovil T
Moussa Franck (M)	5 8	10 08	Brussels	24	9 87	Scholar
O'Keefe Stuart (M)	5 8	10 00	Norwich	4	3 91	Ipswich T
Revell Alex (F)	6 3	13 00	Cambridge	7	7 83	Brighton & HA
Sankofa Osei (D)	6 0	12 04	London	19	3 85	Charlton Ath
Scannell Damian (M)	5 10	11 07	Croydon	28	4 85	Eastleigh
Walker James (F)	5 10	11 10	Hackney	25 11 87		Charlton Ath

League Appearances: Ademeno, C. 1(1); Bailey, N. 1; Barnard, L. 24(11); Barrett, A. 45; Betsy, K. 28(13); Christophe, J. 29(4); Clarke, P. 43; Dervite, D. 18; Federici, A. 10; Feeney, L. (1); Francis, S. 37(8); Freedman, D. 12(4); Furlong, P. 1(2); Grant, A. 23(12); Harding, D. 19; Herd, J. 5(1); Joyce, I. 2(1); Laurent, F. 10(11); McCormack, A. 26(8); Mildenhall, S. 34; Milsom, R. 6; Moussa, F. 25(1); O'Keefe, S. 1(2); Revell, A. 19(4); Robinson, T. 20(1); Robson-Kanu, H. 12(2); Sankofa, O. 23(4); Sawyer, L. 11(1); Scannell, D. 6(13); Stanislas, J. 6; Walker, J. 9(8).
Goals – League (58): Barnard 11 (3 pens), Robinson T 7 (1 pen), Freedman 5, Christophe 4, Clarke 4, Revell 4, Betsy 3, Laurent 3, Barrett 2, McCormack 2, Moussa 2, Robson-Kanu 2, Walker 2, Grant 1, Harding 1, Sawyer 1, Scannell 1, Stanislas 1, own goals 2.
Carling Cup (0).
FA Cup (9): Stanislaus 2, Walker 2, Barrett 1, Christophe 1, Clarke 1, Francis 1, Laurent 1.
J Paint Trophy (2): Sawyer 2.
Ground: Roots Hall Stadium, Victoria Avenue, Southend-on-Sea SS2 6NQ. Telephone (01702) 304 050.
Record Attendance: 31,090 v Liverpool FA Cup 3rd rd, 10 January 1979. **Capacity:** 12,260.
Manager: Steve Tilson.
Secretary: Helen Norbury.
Most League Goals: 92, Division 3 (S), 1950–51.
Highest League Scorer in Season: Jim Shankly, 31, 1928–29; Sammy McCrory, 1957–58, both in Division 3 (S).
Most League Goals in Total Aggregate: Roy Hollis, 122, 1953–60.
Most Capped Player: George Mackenzie, 9, Eire.
Most League Appearances: Sandy Anderson, 452, 1950–63.

Honours – Football League: Championship 1 Champions – 2005–06. Division 4 Champions – 1980–81.
Colours: Navy blue shirts, sky blue neck, black sleeves, black shorts, black stockings.

STOCKPORT COUNTY   FL CHAMPIONSHIP 1

Baker Carl (M)	6 2	12 06	Prescot	26 12 82	Morecambe
Dicker Gary (M)	6 0	12 00	Dublin	31 7 86	Birmingham C
Edwards Declan (M)			London	23 12 89	Galway U
Johnson Oli (F)	5 11	12 04	Wakefield	6 11 87	Nostell MW
Mainwaring Matty (M)	5 11	12 02	Salford	28 3 90	Preston NE
Mullins John (D)	5 11	12 07	Hampstead	6 11 85	Mansfield T
Pilkington Danny (F)	5 9	11 10	Blackburn	25 5 90	Mysercough Coll
Raynes Michael (M)	6 4	12 00	Wythenshawe	15 10 87	Scholar
Rose Michael (D)	5 11	12 04	Salford	28 7 82	Yeovil T
Tansey Greg (M)	6 1	12 03	Huyton	21 11 88	Scholar
Thompson Josh (D)	6 4	12 00	Bolton	25 2 91	Scholar
Thompson Peter (F)	5 9	13 06	Belfast	2 5 84	Linfield
Tunnicliffe James (D)	6 4	12 03	Denton	17 1 89	Scholar
Turnbull Paul (F)	5 10	11 07	Stockport	23 1 89	Scholar
Vincent James (M)	5 11	11 00	Glossop	27 9 89	Scholar
Williams Owain fon (G)	6 1	12 10	Gwynedd	17 3 87	Crewe Alex

League Appearances: Baker, C. 15(7); Blizzard, D. 30(1); Davies, C. 9; Dicker, G. 22(3); Ennis, P. (2); Fisher, T. (1); Fojut, J. 3; Forster, F. 6; Gleeson, S. 17(4); Halls, A. 4(1); Johnson, O. 9(15); Kane, T. 3; Logan, C. 7; Mainwaring, M. 17(4); McNeil, M. 15(4); McNulty, J. 26; McSweeney, L. 28(8); Mooney, D. 2; Mullins, J. 31(2); O'Grady, C. 17(1); Owen, G. 8; Pilkington, A. 22(2); Pilkington, D. (3); Raynes, M. 34(1); Rose, M. 23(4); Rowe, D. (3); Rowe, T. 42(2); Tansey, G. 9(3); Taylor, J. 5(3); Thompson, J. 6(3); Thompson, P. 12(7); Threlfall, R. 1(1); Tunnicliffe, J. 27(3); Turnbull, P. 15(19); Vincent, J. 8(8); Williams, O. 33.
Goals – League (59): Rowe T 7, Johnson 6, Davies 5 (1 pen), Pilkington A 5, McSweeney 4, Baker 3, Blizzard 3, McNeil 3, Mullins 3, Raynes 3, Thompson 3, Gleeson 2, O'Grady 2, Vincent 2, Mainwaring 1, McNulty 1, Tansey 1, Taylor 1, Turnbull 1, own goals 3.
Carling Cup (0).
FA Cup (7): Davies 1, Dicker 1, Gleeson 1, McNeil 1, Pilkington A 1, Rose 1, Vincent 1.
J Paint Trophy (1): McSweeney 1.
Ground: Edgeley Park, Hardcastle Road, Edgeley, Stockport, Cheshire SK3 9DD. Telephone (0161) 286 8888 (ext. 257).
Record Attendance: 27,833 v Liverpool, FA Cup 5th rd, 11 February 1950.
Capacity: 10,641.
Manager: Gary Ablett.
Secretary (acting): Rachael Moss.
Most League Goals: 115, Division 3 (N), 1933–34.
Highest League Scorer in Season: Alf Lythgoe, 46, Division 3 (N), 1933–34.
Most League Goals in Total Aggregate: Jack Connor, 132, 1951–56.
Most Capped Player: Jarkko Wiss, 9 (43), Finland.
Most League Appearances: Andy Thorpe, 489, 1978–86, 1988–92.
Honours – Football League: Division 3 (N) Champions – 1921–22, 1936–37. Division 4 Champions – 1966–67.
Colours: Reflex blue shirts with one broad white band, white shorts, white stockings.

STOKE CITY

FA PREMIERSHIP

Beattie James (F)	6 1	13 06	Lancaster	27 2 78 Sheffield U
Cort Leon (D)	6 3	13 01	Bermondsey	11 9 79 Crystal Palace
Cresswell Richard (F)	6 0	11 08	Bridlington	20 9 77 Leeds U
Davies Andrew (D)	6 2	12 03	Stockton	17 12 84 Southampton
Delap Rory (M)	6 0	11 10	Sutton Coldfield	6 7 76 Sunderland
Diagne-Faye Aboulaye (D)	6 2	13 10	Dakar	26 2 78 Newcastle U
Diao Salif (M)	6 1	13 03	Kedougou	10 2 77 Liverpool
Dickinson Carl (D)	6 0	12 00	Swadlincote	31 3 87 Scholar
Etherington Matthew (M)	5 10	10 12	Truro	14 8 81 West Ham U
Faye Amdy (M)	6 1	12 06	Dakar	12 3 77 Charlton Ath
Fuller Ricardo (F)	6 3	13 03	Kingston	31 10 79 Southampton
Griffin Andy (D)	5 9	10 10	Billinge	7 3 79 Derby Co
Griffin Andy (D)	5 8	10 10	Wigan	17 3 79 Derby Co
Higginbotham Danny (D)	6 1	12 03	Manchester	29 12 78 Sunderland
Kitson David (F)	6 3	12 07	Hitchin	21 1 80 Reading
Lawrence Liam (M)	5 11	11 03	Retford	14 12 81 Sunderland
Olofinjana Seyi (M)	6 4	11 10	Lagos	30 6 80 Wolverhampton W
Pugh Danny (M)	6 0	12 10	Manchester	19 10 82 Preston NE
Shawcross Ryan (D)	6 3	13 03	Chester	4 10 87 Manchester U
Shotton Ryan (D)	6 3	13 05	Stoke	30 9 88 Scholar
Sidibe Mamady (F)	6 4	12 02	Bamako	18 12 79 Gillingham
Simonsen Steve (G)	6 2	14 00	South Shields	3 4 79 Everton
Soares Tom (M)	6 0	11 04	Reading	10 7 86 Crystal Palace
Sonko Ibrahima (D)	6 3	13 07	Bignola	22 1 81 Reading
Sorensen Thomas (G)	6 5	14 00	Odense	12 6 76 Aston Villa
St Louis-Hamilton Danzelle (G)	6 4	15 00	Stevenage	5 5 90 Scholar
Tonge Michael (M)	6 0	11 10	Manchester	7 4 83 Sheffield U
Wedderburn Nathanial (M)	6 1	13 05	Wolverhampton	30 6 91 Scholar
Whelan Glenn (M)	5 11	12 07	Dublin	13 1 84 Sheffield W
Wilkinson Andy (D)	5 11	11 00	Stone	6 8 84 Scholar

League Appearances: Beattie, J. 16; Camara, H. (4); Cort, L. 9(2); Cresswell, R. 11(18); Davies, A. (2); Delap, R. 34; Diagne-Faye, A. 36; Diao, S. 18(2); Dickinson, C. 3(2); Etherington, M. 12(2); Faye, A. 18(3); Fuller, R. 25(9); Griffin, A. 17(3); Higginbotham, D. 28; Kelly, S. 2(4); Kitson, D. 10(6); Lawrence, L. 18(2); Olofinjana, S. 14(4); Pericard, V. 1(3); Pugh, D. 9(8); Shawcross, R. 28(2); Sidibe, M. 17(5); Simonsen, S. 3(2); Soares, T. 5(2); Sonko, I. 7(7); Sorensen, T. 35(1); Tonge, M. 1(9); Whelan, G. 21(5); Wilkinson, A. 20(2).
Goals – League (38): Fuller 11 (2 pens), Beattie 7 (1 pen), Diagne-Faye 3, Lawrence 3 (1 pen), Shawcross 3, Sidibe 3, Delap 2, Olofinjana 2, Higginbotham 1 (pen), Whelan 1, own goals 2.
Carling Cup (7): Whelan 2, Cresswell 1, Parkin 1, Pericard 1, Pugh 1, Sidibe 1.
FA Cup (0).
Ground: Britannia Stadium, Stanley Matthews Way, Stoke-on-Trent ST4 4EG. Telephone (0871) 663 2008.
Record Attendance: 51,380 v Arsenal, Division 1, 29 March 1937 (at Victoria Ground). **Capacity:** 28,383.
Manager: Tony Pulis.
Football Administrator: Eddie Harrison.
Most League Goals: 92, Division 3 (N), 1926–27.
Highest League Scorer in Season: Freddie Steele, 33, Division 1, 1936–37.
Most League Goals in Total Aggregate: Freddie Steele, 142, 1934–49.
Most Capped Player: Gordon Banks, 36 (73), England.
Most League Appearances: Eric Skeels, 506, 1958–76.

Honours – Football League: Division 2 Champions – 1932–33, 1962–63, 1992–93. Division 3 (N) Champions – 1926–27. **Football League Cup:** Winners – 1971–72. **Autoglass Trophy:** Winners – 1992. **Auto Windscreens Shield:** Winners – 2000. **Colours:** Red and white striped shirts, white shorts, royal blue stockings.

SUNDERLAND
FA PREMIERSHIP

Anderson Russell (D)	5 11	10 09	Aberdeen	25 10 78	Aberdeen
Bardsley Phillip (D)	5 11	11 13	Salford	28 6 85	Manchester U
Carson Trevor (G)	6 0	14 11	Downpatrick	5 3 88	Scholar
Chandler Jamie (M)	5 7	11 02	South Shields	24 3 89	Scholar
Chopra Michael (F)	5 9	10 10	Newcastle	23 12 83	Cardiff C
Colback Jack (M)	5 9	11 05	Newcastle	24 10 89	Scholar
Collins Danny (D)	6 2	12 00	Buckley	6 8 80	Chester C
Cook Jordan (M)	5 10	10 10	Hetton-le-Hole	20 3 90	Scholar
Dowson David (F)	5 10	12 00	Bishop Auckland	12 9 88	Scholar
Edwards Carlos (M)	5 8	11 02	Port of Spain	24 10 78	Luton T
Ferdinand Anton (D)	6 2	11 00	Peckham	18 2 85	West Ham U
Fulop Marton (G)	6 6	14 07	Budapest	3 5 83	Tottenham H
Gordon Craig (G)	6 4	12 02	Edinburgh	31 12 82	Hearts
Halford Greg (D)	6 4	12 10	Chelmsford	8 12 84	Reading
Healy David (F)	5 8	10 09	Downpatrick	5 8 79	Fulham
Henderson Jordan (M)	6 0	10 07	Sunderland	17 6 90	Scholar
Hourihane Conor (M)	6 0	11 05	Cork	2 2 91	Scholar
Jones Kenwyne (F)	6 2	13 06	Trinidad & Tobago	5 10 84	Southampton
Kay Michael (D)	6 0	11 05	Shotley Bridge	12 9 89	Scholar
Leadbitter Grant (M)	5 9	11 06	Sunderland	7 1 86	Trainee
Liddle Michael (D)	5 6	11 00	London	25 12 89	Scholar
Luscombe Nathan (M)	5 8	11 09	Gateshead	6 11 89	Scholar
Malbranque Steed (M)	5 7	11 09	Mouscron	6 1 80	Tottenham H
McCartney George (D)	5 11	11 02	Belfast	29 4 81	West Ham U
McShane Paul (D)	6 0	11 05	Wicklow	6 1 86	WBA
Meyler David (M)	6 3	13 03	Cork	25 5 89	Cork C
Murphy Daryl (F)	6 2	13 12	Waterford	15 3 83	Waterford
Mvoto Jean-Yves (D)	6 4	14 00	Paris	6 9 88	Paris St Germain
Nosworthy Nayron (D)	6 0	12 08	Brixton	11 10 80	Gillingham
O'Donovan Roy (F)	5 10	11 07	Cork	10 8 85	Cork C
Reid Andy (M)	5 9	12 08	Dublin	29 7 82	Charlton Ath
Richardson Kieran (M)	5 9	11 13	Greenwich	21 10 84	Manchester U
Stokes Anthony (F)	5 11	11 06	Dublin	25 7 88	Arsenal
Tainio Teemu (M)	5 9	11 09	Tornio	27 11 79	Tottenham H
Waghorn Martyn (F)	5 9	13 01	South Shields	23 1 90	Scholar
Weir Robbie (M)	5 9	11 07	Belfast	12 12 88	Scholar
Whitehead Dean (M)	5 11	11 02	Oxford	12 1 82	Oxford U

League Appearances: Bardsley, P. 27(1); Ben Haim, T. 5; Chimbonda, P. 13; Chopra, M. 1(5); Cisse, D. 29(6); Collins, D. 35; Davenport, C. 7(1); Diouf, E. 11(3); Edwards, C. 6(16); Ferdinand, A. 31; Fulop, M. 26; Gordon, C. 12; Healy, D. (10); Henderson, J. (1); Higginbotham, D. 1; Jones, K. 25(4); Leadbitter, G. 12(11); Malbranque, S. 34(2); McCartney, G. 16; McShane, P. (3); Miller, L. 1(2); Murphy, D. 6(17); Nosworthy, N. 16; Reid, A. 20(12); Richardson, K. 31(1); Stokes, A. (2); Tainio, T. 18(3); Waghorn, M. 1; Whitehead, D. 30(4); Yorke, D. 4(3).
Goals – League (34): Cisse 10 (1 pen), Jones 10, Richardson 4, Chopra 2, Leadbitter 2, Collins 1, Healy 1, Malbranque 1, Reid 1, own goals 2.
Carling Cup (5): Stokes 2, Bardsley 1, Healy 1, Jones 1.
FA Cup (3): Cisse 1, Healy 1, Jones 1.
Ground: Stadium of Light, Sunderland, Tyne and Wear SR5 1SU. Telephone (0871) 911 1200.

Record Attendance: 75,118 v Derby Co, FA Cup 6th rd replay, 8 March 1933 (Roker Park). 48,353 v Liverpool, FA Premier League, 13 April 2002 (Stadium of Light). **Capacity:** 49,000.
Manager: Steve Bruce.
Club Secretary: Margaret Byrne.
Most League Goals: 109, Division 1, 1935–36.
Highest League Scorer in Season: Dave Halliday, 43, Division 1, 1928–29.
Most League Goals in Total Aggregate: Charlie Buchan, 209, 1911–25.
Most Capped Player: Charlie Hurley, 38 (40), Republic of Ireland.
Most League Appearances: Jim Montgomery, 537, 1962–77.
Honours – Football League: Championship – Winners – 2004–05, 2006–07. Division 1 Champions – 1891–92, 1892–93, 1894–95, 1901–02, 1912–13, 1935–36, 1995–96, 1998–99. Division 2 Champions – 1975–76. Division 3 Champions – 1987–88. **FA Cup:** Winners – 1937, 1973.
Colours: Red and white striped shirts, black shorts, black stockings.

SWANSEA CITY   FL CHAMPIONSHIP

Name	Ht	Wt	Birthplace	Birthdate	Previous
Allen Joe (M)	5 6	9 10	Carmarthen	14 3 90	Scholar
Bauza Guillem (F)	5 11	12 01	Palma de Mallorca	25 10 84	Espanyol
Bessone Fede (D)	5 11	11 13	Cordoba	23 1 84	Gimnastic
Bodde Ferrie (M)	5 10	12 06	Delft	4 5 82	Den Haag
Bond Chad (F)	6 0	11 00	Neath	20 4 87	Scholar
Britton Leon (M)	5 6	10 00	Merton	16 9 82	West Ham U
Butler Thomas (M)	5 7	12 00	Dublin	25 4 81	Hartlepool U
Collins Matthew (M)	5 9	11 07	Merthyr	31 3 86	Fulham
Evans Scott (M)	6 0	11 07	Swansea	6 1 89	Manchester C
Gomez Jordi (M)	5 10	11 09	Barcelona	24 5 85	Espanyol
Gower Mark (M)	5 11	11 12	Edmonton	5 10 78	Southend U
Jones Chris (F)	5 9	11 00	Swansea	12 9 89	Scholar
MacDonald Shaun (M)	6 1	11 04	Swansea	17 6 88	Scholar
Monk Garry (D)	6 1	13 00	Bedford	6 3 79	Barnsley
Morgan Kerry (M)	5 10	11 03	Merthyr	31 10 88	Scholar
O'Leary Kristian (M)	6 0	12 09	Port Talbot	30 8 77	Trainee
Orlandi Andrea (M)	6 0	12 01	Barcelona	3 8 84	Alaves
Painter Marcos (D)	5 11	12 04	Solihull	17 8 86	Birmingham C
Pintado Gorka (F)	5 11	11 11	San Sebastian	24 3 78	Grenada
Pratley Darren (M)	6 1	11 00	Barking	22 4 85	Fulham
Rangel Angel (D)	5 11	11 09	Tortosa	28 10 82	Terrassa
Scotland Jason (F)	5 8	11 10	Morvant	18 2 79	St Johnstone
Serran Albert (D)	6 0	12 10	Barcelona	17 7 84	Espanyol
Tate Alan (D)	6 1	13 05	Easington	2 9 82	Manchester U
Tudur-Jones Owain (M)	6 2	12 00	Bangor	15 10 84	Bangor C
Williams Ashley (D)	6 0	11 02	Wolverhampton	23 8 84	Stockport Co

League Appearances: Allen, J. 17(6); Bauza, G. 4(11); Bessone, F. 13(2); Bodde, F. 17; Brandy, F. (14); Britton, L. 42(1); Butler, T. 20(9); Collins, M. 2(1); De Vries, D. 40; Dyer, N. 13(4); Gomez, J. 38(6); Gower, M. 32(4); Konstantopoulos, D. 4; Krysiak, A. 2; Macdonald, S. 2(3); Monk, G. 40; O'Halloran, S. 2; Orlandi, A. 6(5); Painter, M. 11; Pintado, G. 9(31); Pratley, D. 33(4); Rangel, A. 39(1); Scotland, J. 39(6); Serran, A. 10(3); Tate, A. 21(4); Tudur Jones, O. 4(5); Williams, A. 46.
Goals – League (63): Scotland 21 (5 pens), Gomez 12 (1 pen), Bodde 7, Pintado 5, Pratley 4, Bauza 2, Dyer 2, Williams 2, Allen 1, Butler 1, Monk 1, Orlandi 1, Rangel 1, Tate 1, own goals 2.
Carling Cup (5): Gomes 2 (1 pen), MacDonald 2, Pintado 1.
FA Cup (6): Scotland 3 (1 pen), Bauza 1, Dyer 1, Pintado 1.
Ground: Liberty Stadium, Morfa, Swansea SA1 2FA. Telephone (01792) 616 600.
Record Attendance: 32,796 v Arsenal, FA Cup 4th rd, 17 February 1968 (at Vetch Field). **Capacity:** 20,520.

Manager: Paulo Sousa.
Secretary: Jackie Rockey.
Most League Goals: 90, Division 2, 1956–57.
Highest League Scorer in Season: Cyril Pearce, 35, Division 2, 1931–32.
Most League Goals in Total Aggregate: Ivor Allchurch, 166, 1949–58, 1965–68.
Most Capped Player: Ivor Allchurch, 42 (68), Wales.
Most League Appearances: Wilfred Milne, 585, 1919–37.
Honours – Football League: Championship 1 – Winners – 2007–08, Division 3 Champions – 1999–2000. Division 3 (S) Champions – 1924–25, 1948–49. **Autoglass Trophy:** Winners – 1994, 2006. **Football League Trophy:** Winners – 2006. **Welsh Cup:** Winners – 11 times.
Colours: All white.

SWINDON TOWN   FL CHAMPIONSHIP 1

Aljofree Hasney (D)	6 0	12 00	Manchester	11 7 78	Plymouth Arg
Amankwaah Kevin (D)	6 1	12 12	Harrow	19 5 82	Swansea C
Casal Kasali Yinka (D)	6 1	12 08	London	21 10 87	Cambuur
Cox Simon (M)	5 10	10 12	Reading	28 4 87	Reading
Easton Craig (M)	5 11	11 03	Bellshill	26 2 79	Leyton Orient
Hammonds Kurt (M)			Wakefield	6 12 90	Scholar
Ifil Jerel (D)	6 1	12 11	Wembley	27 6 82	Watford
Kanyuka Patrick (D)	6 0	12 06	Kinshasa	19 7 87	QPR
Kennedy Callum (M)	6 1	12 10	Cheltenham	6 1 89	Scholar
Lescinel Jean-Francois (M)	6 2	12 04	Cayenne	2 10 86	Guingamp
Macklin Lloyd (M)	5 9	12 03	Camberley	2 8 91	
Marshall Mark (M)	5 7	10 07	Manchester (Jam)	9 5 86	Eastleigh
McGovern John-Paul (M)	5 10	12 02	Glasgow	3 10 80	Milton Keynes D
McNamee Anthony (M)	5 6	10 03	Kensington	13 7 84	Watford
Morrison Sean (D)	6 4	14 00	Plymouth	8 1 91	Plymouth Arg
Paynter Billy (F)	6 1	14 01	Liverpool	13 7 84	Southend U
Peacock Lee (F)	6 0	12 08	Paisley	9 10 76	Sheffield W
Scott Mark (M)	5 9	12 04	Cheltenham	14 3 86	
Smith Phil (G)	6 0	15 02	Harrow	14 12 79	Crawley T
Timlin Michael (M)	5 8	11 08	Lambeth	19 3 85	Fulham

League Appearances: Aljofree, H. 17(1); Allen, C. 2(2); Amankwaah, K. 26(5); Brezovan, P. 21; Casal, K. 4(1); Corr, B. 2(9); Cox, S. 45; Easton, C. 14(9); Greer, G. 19; Ifil, J. 28(2); Joyce, B. 1; Kanyuka, P. 16; Kennedy, C. 3(1); Lescinel, J. 2(3); Macklin, L. 2(3); Marshall, M. (12); McGovern, J. 22(4); McNamee, A. 30(13); Morrison, S. 18(2); Nalis, L. 18(6); Paynter, B. 42; Peacock, L. 17(10); Pook, M. 11(3); Razak, H. (3); Robson-Kanu, H. 20; Smith, J. 34(4); Smith, P. 25; Sturrock, B. 2(8); Timlin, M. 38(3); Tudur-Jones, O. 11; Vincent, J. 18.
Goals – League (68): Cox 29 (6 pens), Paynter 11, Smith J 5 (2 pens), Robson-Kanu 4, Amankwaah 2, Corr 2, Easton 2, McGovern 2, Peacock 2, Timlin 2, Greer 1, Ifil 1, Kanyuka 1, Morrison 1, Tudur-Jones 1, own goals 2.
Carling Cup (2): Cox 1, Paynter 1.
FA Cup (0).
J Paint Trophy (4): Cox 2, Ifil 1, Peacock 1.
Ground: The County Ground, County Road, Swindon, Wiltshire SN1 2ED. Telephone (0871) 423 6433.
Record Attendance: 32,000 v Arsenal, FA Cup 3rd rd, 15 January 1972. **Capacity:** 14,225.
Manager: Danny Wilson.
Secretary: Louise Fletcher.
Most League Goals: 100, Division 3 (S), 1926–27.
Highest League Scorer in Season: Harry Morris, 47, Division 3 (S), 1926–27.
Most League Goals in Total Aggregate: Harry Morris, 216, 1926–33.
Most Capped Player: Rod Thomas, 30 (50), Wales.

Most League Appearances: John Trollope, 770, 1960–80.
Honours – Football League: Division 2 Champions – 1995–96. Division 4 Champions – 1985–86. **Football League Cup:** Winners – 1968–69, 2007–08. **Anglo-Italian Cup:** Winners – 1970.
Colours: All red with white inserts on shirt.

TORQUAY UNITED   FL CHAMPIONSHIP 2

Adams Steve (D)	6 0	12 04	Plymouth	25 9 80	Swindon T
Benyon Elliot (F)	5 9	10 01	High Wycombe	29 8 87	Bristol C
Bevan Scott (G)	6 6	15 04	Southampton	19 9 79	Shrewsbury T
Brough Michael (M)	5 9	11 07	Nottingham	1 8 81	Forest Green R
Carayol Mustapha (M)	5 9	11 11	Banjul	10 6 89	Milton Keynes D
Carlisle Wayne (M)	5 7	11 00	Lisburn	9 9 79	Exeter C
Christie Iyseden (F)	6 0	12 02	Coventry	14 11 76	Stevenage B
D'Sane Roscoe (F)	5 7	10 12	Epsom	16 10 80	Accrington S
Ellis Mark (D)	6 2	12 04	Plymouth	30 9 88	Bolton W
Green Matthew (F)	5 8	10 05	Bath	13 5 87	Cardiff C
Hargreaves Chris (M)	5 11	12 02	Cleethorpes	12 5 72	Oxford U
Hodges Lee (M)	6 0	12 02	Epping	4 9 73	Plymouth Arg
Mansell Lee (M)	5 9	10 10	Gloucester	23 9 82	Oxford U
Nicholson Kevin (M)	5 8	11 05	Derby	2 10 80	Forest Green R
Rice Martin (G)	5 9	12 00	Exeter	7 3 86	Exeter C
Robertson Chris (D)	6 3	11 09	Dundee	11 10 86	Sheffield U
Sills Tim (F)	6 2	12 02	Romsey	10 9 79	Hereford U
Stevens Danny (F)	5 10	11 07	Enfield	26 11 86	Luton T
Thompson Tyrone (M)	5 9	11 02	Sheffield	8 5 81	Crawley T
Todd Chris (D)	6 1	11 09	Swansea	22 8 81	Exeter C
Wroe Nicky (M)	5 11	10 01	Sheffield	28 9 85	York C

League Appearances: Adams, 1+2; Benyon, 17+17; Bevan, 34; Brough, 2+1; Carayol, 14+16; Carlisle, 34+3; Charran, 0+1; Christie, 2+4; D'Sane, 22+5; Ellis, 8+1; Green, 15+14; Hargreaves, 44; Hodges, 31+4; Mansell, 41+1; Nicholson, 38+2; Poke, 12+1; Robertson, 27+3; Sills, 43+2; Stevens, 15+14; Sturrock, 6+1; Thompson, 17+6; Todd, 16; Woods, 27; Wroe, 40; Yeoman, 0+1.
Goals – League (72): Sills 14 (3 pens), Benyon 9, D'Sane 9, Carlisle 8 (1 pen), Wroe 6, Stevens 5, Green 4, Hargreaves 4, Nicholson 3, Robertson 3, Sturrock 2, Christie 1, Ellis 1, Thompson 1, Todd 1, Woods 1.
FA Cup (9): Sills 4, Benyon 2, Thompson 2, Green 1.
Play-Offs (4): Sills 2, Hargreaves 1, Wroe 1.
Ground: Plainmoor Ground, Torquay, Devon TQ1 3PS. Telephone (01803) 328 666.
Record Attendance: 21,908 v Huddersfield T, FA Cup 4th rd, 29 January 1955.
Capacity: 6,117.
Manager: Paul Buckle.
Secretary: Ann Sandford.
Most League Goals: 89, Division 3 (S), 1956–57.
Highest League Scorer in Season: Sammy Collins, 40, Division 3 (S), 1955–56.
Most League Goals in Total Aggregate: Sammy Collins, 204, 1948–58.
Most Capped Player: Rodney Jack, (71), St Vincent.
Most League Appearances: Dennis Lewis, 443, 1947–59.
Honours – None.
Colours: Yellow shirts, yellow shorts, yellow stockings.

TOTTENHAM HOTSPUR   FA PREMIERSHIP

Alnwick Ben (G)	6 0	12 09	Prudhoe	1 1 87	Sunderland
Archibald-Henville Troy (D)	6 2	13 03	Newham	4 11 88	Scholar

Assou-Ekotto Benoit (D)	5 10	11 00	Douala	24 3 84	Lens
Bale Gareth (D)	6 0	11 10	Cardiff	16 7 89	Southampton
Bent Darren (F)	5 11	12 07	Wandsworth	6 2 84	Charlton Ath
Bentley David (F)	5 10	11 03	Peterborough	27 8 84	Blackburn R
Berchiche Yuri (D)			Resideus	10 2 90	Athletic Bilbao
Boateng Kevin-Prince (M)	6 0	11 09	Berlin	6 3 87	Hertha Berlin
Bostock John (M)	5 10	11 11	Romford	13 10 91	Crystal Palace
Butcher Callum (D)			Rochford	26 2 91	Scholar
Butcher Lee (G)	6 0	12 13	Waltham Forest	11 10 88	Arsenal
Button David (G)	6 3	13 00	Stevenage	27 2 89	Scholar
Chimbonda Pascal (D)	5 11	11 11	Les Abymes	21 2 79	Wigan Ath
Corluka Vedran (D)	6 3	13 03	Zagreb	9 2 86	Manchester C
Cudicini Carlo (G)	6 1	12 08	Milan	6 9 73	Chelsea
Dawson Michael (D)	6 2	12 02	Northallerton	18 11 83	Nottingham F
Defoe Jermain (F)	5 7	10 04	Beckton	7 10 82	Portsmouth
Dervite Dorian (D)	6 3	13 06	Lille	25 7 88	
Gilberto (F)	5 11	12 04	Rio de Janeiro	28 2 77	Hertha Berlin
Giovani (F)	5 8	12 03	Monterrey	11 5 89	Barcelona
Gomes Heurelho (G)	6 3	12 13	Joao Pinheiro	15 2 81	PSV Eindhoven
Gunter Chris (D)	5 11	11 02	Newport	21 7 89	Cardiff C
Huddlestone Tom (M)	6 2	11 02	Nottingham	28 12 86	Derby Co
Hutton Alan (D)	6 1	11 05	Glasgow	30 11 84	Rangers
Jansson Oscar (G)	6 0	12 13	Orebro	23 12 90	Karlslund
Jenas Jermaine (M)	5 11	11 00	Nottingham	18 2 83	Newcastle U
Keane Robbie (F)	5 9	12 06	Dublin	8 7 80	Leeds U
King Ledley (D)	6 2	14 05	Bow	12 10 80	Trainee
Lennon Aaron (M)	5 6	10 03	Leeds	16 4 87	Leeds U
Livermore Jake (M)			Enfield	14 11 89	Scholar
Mason Ryan (M)	5 9	10 00	Enfield	13 6 91	Scholar
Modric Luka (M)	5 8	10 03	Zadar	9 9 85	Dinamo Zagreb
Mpuku Paul-Jose (M)			Kinshasa	19 4 92	Scholar
O'Hara Jamie (M)	5 11	12 04	Dartford	25 9 86	Scholar
Obika Jonathan (F)	6 0	12 00	Enfield	12 9 90	Scholar
Palacios Wilson (D)	5 10	11 11	La Ceiba	29 7 84	Wigan Ath
Parrett Dean (M)	5 10	11 04	Hampstead	16 11 91	Scholar
Pavlyuchenko Roman (F)	6 2	12 04	Mostovskoy	15 12 81	Spartak Moscow
Pekhart Tomas (F)			Susice	26 5 89	
Rose Danny (M)	5 8	11 11	Doncaster	2 7 90	Scholar
Smith Adam (D)	5 8	10 05	Leytonstone	29 4 91	Scholar
Taarabt Adel (M)	5 9	10 12	Berre-l'Etang	24 5 89	
Townsend Andros (M)	6 0	12 00	Whipps Cross	16 7 91	Scholar
Woodgate Jonathan (D)	6 2	12 06	Middlesbrough	22 1 80	Middlesbrough
Zokora Didier (D)	5 11	12 04	Abidjan	14 12 80	St Etienne

League Appearances: Assou-Ekotto, B. 29; Bale, G. 12(4); Bent, D. 21(12); Bentley, D. 20(5); Berbatov, D. (1); Boateng, K. (1); Campbell, F. 1(9); Chimbonda, P. 1(2); Corluka, V. 33(1); Cudicini, C. 4; Dawson, M. 13(3); Defoe, J. 6(2); Gilberto, 1; Giovani, 2(4); Gomes, H. 34; Gunter, C. 2(1); Huddlestone, T. 14(8); Hutton, A. 5(3); Jenas, J. 28(4); Keane, R. 14; King, L. 24; Lennon, A. 26(9); Modric, L. 34; O'Hara, J. 6(9); Palacios, W. 11; Pavlyuchenko, R. 19(9); Taarabt, A. (1); Woodgate, J. 34; Zokora, D. 24(5).

Goals – League (45): Bent 12 (1 pen), Keane 5 (2 pens), Lennon 5, Pavlyuchenko 5, Jenas 4, Defoe 3, Modric 3, Bentley 1, Campbell 1, Dawson 1, King 1, O'Hara 1, Woodgate 1, own goals 2.
Carling Cup (14): Pavlyuchenko 6 (1 pen), Campbell 2, O'Hara 2, Bent 1, Dawson 1, Defoe 1, own goal 1.
FA Cup (4): Pavlyuchenko 3 (1 pen), Modric 1.
UEFA Cup (11): Bent 4, Huddlestone 2, Bentley 1, Giovani 1, Modric 1, O'Hara 1, own goal 1.

102

Ground: White Hart Lane, Bill Nicholson Way, 748 High Road, Tottenham, London N17 0AP. Telephone (0844) 499 5000.
Record Attendance: 75,038 v Sunderland, FA Cup 6th rd, 5 March 1938.
Capacity: 36,534.
Manager: Harry Redknapp.
Secretary: John Alexander.
Most League Goals: 115, Division 1, 1960–61.
Highest League Scorer in Season: Jimmy Greaves, 37, Division 1, 1962–63.
Most League Goals in Total Aggregate: Jimmy Greaves, 220, 1961–70.
Most Capped Player: Pat Jennings, 74 (119), Northern Ireland.
Most League Appearances: Steve Perryman, 655, 1969–86.
Honours – Football League: Division 1 Champions – 1950–51, 1960–61. Division 2 Champions – 1919–20, 1949–50. **FA Cup:** Winners – 1901 (as non-League club), 1921, 1961, 1962, 1967, 1981, 1982, 1991. **Football League Cup:** Winners – 1970–71, 1972–73, 1998–99, 2007–08. **European Competitions: European Cup-Winners' Cup:** Winners – 1962–63. **UEFA Cup:** Winners – 1971–72, 1983–84.
Colours: White shirts with black inserts and trim on sleeves, black shorts, white stockings with two black hoops.

TRANMERE ROVERS   FL CHAMPIONSHIP 1

Barnett Charlie (M)	5 7	11 07	Liverpool	19 9 88	Liverpool
Chorley Ben (M)	6 3	13 02	Sidcup	30 9 82	Milton Keynes D
Coyne Danny (G)	6 0	13 00	Prestatyn	27 8 73	Burnley
Cresswell Aaron (D)	5 7	10 05	Liverpool	15 12 89	Scholar
Curran Craig (F)	5 11	11 11	Liverpool	23 8 89	Scholar
Edds Gareth (D)	5 11	11 01	Sydney	3 2 81	Milton Keynes D
Goodison Ian (D)	6 1	12 06	St James, Jam	21 11 72	Seba U
Gornell Terry (F)	5 11	12 04	Liverpool	16 12 89	Scholar
Jennings Steven (M)	5 7	11 07	Liverpool	28 10 84	Scholar
Kay Antony (D)	5 11	11 08	Barnsley	21 10 82	Barnsley
Macauley Josh (F)	6 0	12 00	Liverpool	2 3 91	Scholar
Moore Ian (F)	5 11	12 00	Birkenhead	26 8 76	Hartlepool U
Savage Bas (F)	6 3	13 08	London	7 1 82	Millwall
Shuker Chris (M)	5 5	9 03	Liverpool	9 5 82	Barnsley
Taylor Andy (D)	5 11	11 07	Blackburn	14 3 86	Blackburn R
Taylor Ash (M)	6 0	12 00	Chester	2 9 89	Scholar

League Appearances: Achterberg, J. 7; Antwi-Birago, G. 4(1); Barnett, C. 25(4); Burns, R. (2); Chorley, B. 45; Coyne, D. 39; Cresswell, A. 8(5); Curran, C. 7(8); Edds, G. 22(12); Goodison, I. 33; Gornell, T. 4(6); Greenacre, C. 6(7); Henry, P. 1; Holmes, D. 1; Jennings, S. 44; Johnson, J. 4; Kay, A. 44; Macauley, J. (1); Mayor, D. 3; Moore, I. 40(2); O'Callaghan, G. 4(2); Savage, B. 38(4); Shotton, R. 33; Shuker, C. 23(5); Sonko, E. 29(6); Taylor, Andy 38(1); Taylor, Ash 1; Wilson, M. 4(1).
Goals – League (62): Kay 11, Moore 10 (3 pens), Savage 9, Shotton 5, Sonko 5, Barnett 3, Curran 3, Jennings 3 (1 pen), Shuker 3, Edds 2, Greenacre 2, Chorley 1, Cresswell 1, Goodison 1, Gornell 1, Andy Taylor 1, own goal 1.
Carling Cup (0).
FA Cup (2): Kay 1, Shuker 1.
J Paint Trophy (4): Moore 1, Shotton 1, Shuker 1, Sonko 1.
Ground: Prenton Park, Prenton Road West, Birkenhead, Merseyside CH42 9PY. Telephone (0871) 221 2001.
Record Attendance: 24,424 v Stoke C, FA Cup 4th rd, 5 February 1972.
Capacity: 16,587.
Manager: John Barnes.
Secretary: Mick Horton.
Most League Goals: 111, Division 3 (N), 1930–31.
Highest League Scorer in Season: Bunny Bell, 35, Division 3 (N), 1933–34.

Most League Goals in Total Aggregate: Ian Muir, 142, 1985–95.
Most Capped Player: John Aldridge, 30 (69), Republic of Ireland.
Most League Appearances: Harold Bell, 595, 1946–64 (incl. League record 401 consecutive appearances).
Honours – Football League: Division 3 (N) Champions – 1937–38. **Welsh Cup:** Winners – 1935. **Leyland Daf Cup:** Winners – 1990.
Colours: All white with one sky blue sleeve and one dark blue cuff on reverse.

WALSALL   FL CHAMPIONSHIP 1

Bradley Mark (D)	6 0	11 05	Dudley	14 1 88	Scholar
Craddock Josh (M)	5 11	10 08	Wolverhampton	5 3 91	Scholar
Davies Richard (M)	5 11	11 05	Wolverhampton	15 5 90	Scholar
Deeney Troy (F)	5 11	12 00	Birmingham	29 6 88	Chelmsley T
Gerrard Anthony (D)	6 2	13 07	Liverpool	6 2 86	Everton
Gilmartin Rene (G)	6 5	13 06	Islington	31 5 87	St Patrick's BC
Ibehre Jabo (F)	6 2	13 13	Islington	28 1 83	Leyton Orient
Ince Clayton (G)	6 3	13 02	Trinidad	13 7 72	Coventry C
Mattis Dwayne (M)	6 1	11 12	Huddersfield	31 7 81	Barnsley
Nicholls Alex (F)	5 10	11 00	Stourbridge	19 12 87	Scholar
Palmer Chris (M)	5 7	11 00	Derby	16 10 83	Wycombe W
Roberts Steve (D)	6 1	11 02	Wrexham	24 2 80	Doncaster R
Sansara Netan (D)	6 0	12 00	Walsall	3 8 89	Scholar
Smith Emmanuel (M)	6 2	12 03	Birmingham	8 11 88	Scholar
Taundry Richard (D)	5 9	12 10	Walsall	15 2 89	Scholar
Weston Rhys (D)	6 1	12 12	Kingston	27 10 80	Port Vale
Zaaboub Sofiane (D)	5 11	11 09	Melun	23 1 83	Swindon T

League Appearances: Adkins, S. (1); Boertien, P. 25(6); Bradley, M. 16(12); Craddock, J. (2); Davies, R. (3); Deeney, T. 37(8); Demontagnac, I. 2(8); Gerrard, A. 42; Gilmartin, R. 10(1); Grigg, W. (1); Hughes, S. 32; Ibehre, J. 35(4); Ince, C. 36; Mattis, D. 33(4); Nicholls, A. 38(7); Palmer, C. 41(3); Reich, M. 9(10); Ricketts, M. 25(3); Roberts, S. 15; Sansara, N. 7(3); Shroot, R. (5); Smith, M. 22(4); Taundry, R. 27(11); Weston, R. 30(1); Williams, S. (5); Zaaboub, S. 24(5).
Goals – League (61): Deeney 12, Ibehre 10, Ricketts 9 (2 pens), Nicholls 6, Mattis 4, Demontagnac 3, Gerrard 3, Reich 3 (1 pen), Hughes 2, Palmer 1, Roberts 1, Weston 1, Williams S 1, own goals 3.
Carling Cup (1): Ricketts 1.
FA Cup (1): Ricketts 1.
J Paint Trophy (2): Ibehre 1, Ricketts 1.
Ground: Banks's Stadium, Bescot Crescent, Walsall WS1 4SA. Telephone (0871) 221 0442.
Record Attendance: 11,037 v Wolverhampton W, Division 1, 11 January 2003.
Capacity: 11,300.
Manager: Chris Hutchings.
Secretary: Roy Whalley.
Most League Goals: 102, Division 4, 1959–60.
Highest League Scorer in Season: Gilbert Alsop, 40, Division 3 (N), 1933–34 and 1934–35.
Most League Goals in Total Aggregate: Tony Richards, 184, 1954–63; Colin Taylor, 184, 1958–63, 1964–68, 1969–73.
Most Capped Player: Mick Kearns, 15 (18), Republic of Ireland.
Most League Appearances: Colin Harrison, 467, 1964–82.
Honours – Football League: FL 2 Champions – 2006–07. Division 4 Champions – 1959–60.
Colours: Red shirts with white cuffs on sleeves, white shorts, red stockings with white tops.

Avinel Cedric (D)	6 2	13 03	Paris	11	9 86	Creteil
Bangura Al Hassan (M)	5 8	10 07	Sierra Leone	24	1 88	Scholar
Bennett Dale (D)				6	1 90	Scholar
Bromby Leigh (D)	5 11	11 06	Dewsbury	2	6 80	Sheffield U
Cauna Aleksandrs (M)	5 8	10 05	Daugavpils	19	1 88	
Cowie Don (M)	5 5	8 05	Inverness	15	2 83	Inverness CT
DeMerit Jay (D)	6 1	13 05	Wisconsin	4	12 79	Northwood
Doyley Lloyd (D)	5 10	12 05	Whitechapel	1	12 82	Scholar
Ellington Nathan (F)	5 10	13 01	Bradford	2	7 81	WBA
Eustace John (M)	5 11	11 12	Solihull	3	11 79	Stoke C
Gibson Billy (M)	6 2	11 08	Harrow	30	9 90	Scholar
Harley Jon (D)	5 8	10 03	Maidstone	26	9 79	Burnley
Henderson Liam (F)	5 11	12 02	Gateshead	28	12 89	Hartlepool U
Hodson Lee (D)			Watford	2	10 91	Scholar
Hoskins Will (F)	5 9	11 11	Nottingham	6	5 86	Rotherham U
Jenkins Ross (M)	5 11	12 06	Watford	9	11 90	Scholar
Kiernan Robert (D)	6 1	11 13	Watford	13	1 91	Scholar
Lee Richard (G)	6 0	13 03	Oxford	5	10 82	Scholar
Loach Scott (G)	6 1	13 01	Nottingham	27	5 88	Lincoln C
Mariappa Adrian (D)	5 10	11 12	Harrow	3	10 86	Scholar
McAnuff Jobi (M)	5 11	11 05	Edmonton	9	11 81	Crystal Palace
O'Toole John (M)	6 2	13 07	Harrow	30	9 88	
Oshodi Eddie (D)	6 3	12 07	Brentford	14	1 92	Scholar
Parkes Jordan (D)	6 0	12 00	Watford	26	7 89	Scholar
Priskin Tamas (F)	6 1	11 07	Komarno	27	6 86	Gyor
Robinson Theo (M)	5 11	11 00	Birmingham	22	1 89	Scholar
Sadler Matthew (D)	5 11	11 08	Birmingham	26	2 85	Birmingham C
Searle Stuart (G)	6 3	12 04	Wimbledon	27	2 79	Basingstoke T
Smith Tommy (M)	5 8	11 04	Hemel Hempstead	22	5 80	Derby Co
Williamson Lee (M)	5 10	10 04	Derby	7	6 82	Rotherham U
Williamson Michael (D)	6 4	13 03	Stoke	8	11 83	Wycombe W
Young Lewis (M)	5 10	11 02	Stevenage	27	9 89	Scholar

League Appearances: Ainsworth, L. 1(6); Bangura, A. (2); Bridcutt, L. 4(2); Bromby, L. 19(3); Cauna, A. 2(3); Cork, J. 18(1); Cowie, D. 10; DeMerit, J. 31(1); Doyley, L. 35(2); Eustace, J. 14(3); Francis, D. (4); Harley, J. 32(5); Henderson, L. (5); Hodson, L. (1); Hoskins, W. 16(16); Hoyte, G. 6(1); Jenkins, R. 28(1); Lee, R. 9(1); Loach, S. 30(1); Mariappa, A. 37(2); McAnuff, J. 34(6); O'Toole, J. 14(8); Parkes, J. 1; Poom, M. 7; Priskin, T. 32(4); Rasiak, G. 12(9); Robinson, T. (3); Rose, D. 3(4); Sadler, M. 15; Smith, T. 43(1); Sodje, S. 1; Stepanov, A. (1); Ward, D. 9; Williamson, L. 26(8); Williamson, M. 17; Young, L. (1).
Goals – League (68): Smith 17 (4 pens), Priskin 12, Rasiak 8, O'Toole 7, Hoskins 4, Cowie 3, McAnuff 3, Eustace 2, Williamson L 2, Cauna 1, Harley 1, Jenkins 1, Mariappa 1, Ward 1, Williamson M 1, own goals 4.
Carling Cup (6): Francis 1, Hoskins 1, O'Toole 1, Priskin 1, Williamson L 1, own goal 1.
FA Cup (6): Rasiak 2, Cork 1, DeMerit 1, Hoskins 1, Priskin 1.
Ground: Vicarage Road Stadium, Vicarage Road, Watford, Hertfordshire WD18 0ER. Telephone (0845) 442 1881.
Record Attendance: 34,099 v Manchester U, FA Cup 4th rd (replay), 3 February 1969. **Capacity:** 19,920.
Manager: Malky Mackay.
Secretary: Michelle Ives.
Most League Goals: 92, Division 4, 1959–60.
Highest League Scorer in Season: Cliff Holton, 42, Division 4, 1959–60.

Most League Goals in Total Aggregate: Luther Blissett, 148, 1976–83, 1984–88, 1991–92.
Most Capped Player: John Barnes, 31 (79), England and Kenny Jackett, 31, Wales.
Most League Appearances: Luther Blissett, 415, 1976–83, 1984–88, 1991–92.
Honours – Football League: Division 2 Champions – 1997–98. Division 3 Champions – 1968–69. Division 4 Champions – 1977–78.
Colours: Yellow shirts with red collar, black shorts, yellow stockings.

WEST BROMWICH ALBION   FA CHAMPIONSHIP

Barnett Leon (D)	6 0	12 04	Stevenage	30 11 85	Luton T
Beattie Craig (F)	6 0	11 07	Glasgow	16 1 84	Celtic
Bednar Roman (F)	6 3	13 03	Prague	26 3 83	Hearts
Borja Valero (M)	5 9	11 07	Madrid	12 1 85	Mallorca
Brunt Chris (M)	6 1	13 04	Belfast	14 12 84	Sheffield W
Carson Scott (G)	6 3	14 00	Whitehaven	3 9 85	Liverpool
Cech Marek (D)	6 0	11 09	Trebisov	26 1 83	Porto
Clement Neil (D)	6 0	12 03	Reading	3 10 78	Chelsea
Daniels Luke (G)	6 1	12 10	Bolton	5 1 88	Manchester U
Dorrans Graham (F)	5 9	11 07	Glasgow	5 5 87	Livingston
Greening Jonathan (M)	5 11	11 00	Scarborough	2 1 79	Middlesbrough
Kiely Dean (G)	6 1	14 00	Salford	10 10 70	Portsmouth
Kim Do-Heon (M)	5 9	11 07	Incheon	14 7 82	Seongnam
Koren Robert (M)	5 9	11 03	Ljubljana	20 9 80	Lillestrom
Labadie Josh (M)	5 7	11 02	London	31 8 90	Scholar
MacDonald Sherjill (F)	6 0	12 06	Amsterdam	20 11 84	Hereford U
Martis Shelton (D)	6 0	11 11	Willemstad	29 11 82	Darlington
Meite Abdoulaye (D)	6 1	12 13	Paris	6 10 80	Bolton W
Miller Ishmael (F)	6 3	14 00	Manchester	5 3 87	Manchester C
Moore Luke (F)	5 11	11 13	Birmingham	13 2 86	Aston Villa
Morrison James (M)	5 10	10 06	Darlington	25 5 86	Middlesbrough
Olsson Jonas (D)	6 4	12 08	Landskrona	10 3 83	NEC Nijmegen
Robinson Paul (D)	5 9	11 12	Watford	14 12 78	Watford
Teixeira Felipe (F)	5 9	10 10	Paris	2 10 80	Academica
Worrall David (M)	6 0	11 03	Manchester	12 6 90	Bury
Zuiverloon Gianni (D)	5 10	11 00	Rotterdam	30 12 86	Heerenveen

League Appearances: Barnett, L. 10(1); Beattie, C. 1(6); Bednar, R. 12(14); Borja Valero, 27(3); Brunt, C. 28(6); Carson, S. 35; Cech, M. 3(5); Donk, R. 14(2); Dorrans, G. 5(3); Fortune, M. 17; Greening, J. 33(1); Hoefkens, C. 6(4); Kiely, D. 3; Kim, D. 9(7); Koren, R. 34(1); MacDonald, S. 5; Martis, S. 6(1); Meite, A. 18; Menseguez, J. 3(4); Miller, I. 11(4); Moore, L. 5(16); Morrison, J. 29(1); Mulumbu, Y. 2(4); Olsson, J. 28; Pele, 1(2); Robinson, P. 35; Simpson, J. 9(4); Teixeira, F. 1(9); Wood, C. (2); Zuiverloon, G. 33.
Goals – League (36): Brunt 8 (1 pen), Bednar 6 (2 pens), Fortune 5, Miller 3, Morrison 3 Greening 2, Olsson 2, Beattie 1, Koren 1, Menseguez 1, Moore 1, Simpson 1, own goals 2.
Carling Cup (1): Koren 1.
FA Cup (6): Kim 1, Koren 1, Olsson 1, Robinson 1, Simpson 1, Zuiverloon 1.
Ground: The Hawthorns, West Bromwich, West Midlands B71 4LF. Telephone (0871) 271 1100.
Record Attendance: 64,815 v Arsenal, FA Cup 6th rd, 6 March 1937. **Capacity:** 28,003.
Head Coach: Roberto Di Matteo.
Secretary: Darren Eales.
Most League Goals: 105, Division 2, 1929–30.
Highest League Scorer in Season: William 'Ginger' Richardson, 39, Division 1, 1935–36.
Most League Goals in Total Aggregate: Tony Brown, 218, 1963–79.

Most Capped Player: Stuart Williams, 33 (43), Wales.
Most League Appearances: Tony Brown, 574, 1963–80.
Honours – Football League: Division 1 Champions – 1919–20. Championship winners – 2007–08. Division 2 Champions – 1901–02, 1910–11. **FA Cup:** Winners – 1888, 1892, 1931, 1954, 1968. **Football League Cup:** Winners – 1965–66.
Colours: Navy blue and white striped shirts, white shorts, white stockings.

WEST HAM UNITED   FA PREMIERSHIP

Name			Place			Club
Abdullah Ahmed (F)			Saudi Arabia	12	11 91	Scholar
Ashton Dean (F)	6 2	14 07	Crewe	24	11 83	Norwich C
Behrami Valon (M)	6 0	11 02	Kosovka Mitrovika	19	4 85	Lazio
Boa Morte Luis (F)	5 9	12 06	Lisbon	4	8 77	Fulham
Cole Carlton (F)	6 3	14 02	Croydon	12	11 83	Chelsea
Collins James (D)	6 2	14 05	Newport	23	8 83	Cardiff C
Collison Jack (M)	6 0	13 10	Watford	2	10 88	Scholar
Davenport Calum (D)	6 4	14 00	Bedford	1	1 83	Tottenham H
Dixon Terry (F)			Holloway	15	1 90	Tottenham H
Dyer Kieron (M)	5 8	10 01	Ipswich	29	12 78	Newcastle U
Eyjolfsson Holmar (D)			Iceland	6	8 90	
Faubert Julien (M)	5 10	11 08	Le Havre	1	8 83	Bordeaux
Gabbidon Daniel (D)	6 0	13 05	Cwmbran	8	8 79	Cardiff C
Green Robert (G)	6 3	14 09	Chertsey	18	1 80	Norwich C
Hines Zavon (F)	5 10	10 07	Jamaica	27	12 88	Scholar
N'Gala Bondz (D)	6 0	12 00	Newham	13	9 89	Scholar
Neill Lucas (D)	6 0	12 03	Sydney	9	3 78	Blackburn R
Noble Mark (M)	5 11	12 00	West Ham	8	5 87	Scholar
Nsereko Savio (M)	5 9	11 07	Kampala	27	7 89	Brescia
Parker Scott (M)	5 9	11 10	Lambeth	13	10 80	Newcastle U
Payne Josh (M)	6 0	11 09		25	11 90	Scholar
Quashie Nigel (M)	6 0	13 10	Peckham	20	7 78	WBA
Sears Freddie (F)	5 8	10 01	Hornchurch	27	11 89	Scholar
Spector Jonathan (D)	6 0	12 08	Arlington	1	3 86	Manchester U
Spence Jordan (M)	5 11	11 13	Woodford	24	5 90	Scholar
Stanislas Junior (M)	6 0	12 00	Kidbrooke	26	11 89	Scholar
Stech Marek (G)	6 3	14 00	Prague	28	1 90	Scholar
Tomkins James (D)	6 3	11 10	Basildon	29	3 89	Scholar
Upson Matthew (D)	6 1	11 04	Stowmarket	18	4 79	Birmingham C

League Appearances: Ashton, D. 4; Behrami, V. 24; Bellamy, C. 13(3); Boa Morte, L. 13(14); Bowyer, L. 4(2); Cole, C. 26(1); Collins, J. 17(1); Collison, J. 16(4); Davenport, C. 7; Di Michele, D. 22(8); Dyer, K. 1(6); Etherington, M. 8(5); Faubert, J. 15(5); Green, R. 38; Ilunga, H. 35; Kovac, R. 8(1); Lopez, W. (5); McCartney, G. (1); Mullins, H. 5(12); Neill, L. 34; Noble, M. 28(1); Nsereko, S. 1(9); Parker, S. 28; Payne, J. (2); Sears, F. 4(13); Spector, J. 4(5); Stanislas, J. 7(2); Tomkins, J. 11(1); Tristan, D. 8(6); Upson, M. 37.
Goals – League (42): Cole 10, Bellamy 5, Di Michele 4, Collison 3, Noble 3 (1 pen), Tristan 3, Ashton 2, Etherington 2, Stanislas 2, Behrami 1, Davenport 1, Kovac 1, Mullins 1, Neill 1, Parker 1, Tomkins 1, own goal 1.
Carling Cup (4): Bowyer 1, Cole 1, Hines 1, Reid 1.
FA Cup (6): Ilunga 2, Noble 2 (2 pens), Behrami 1, Cole 1.
Ground: The Boleyn Ground, Upton Park, Green Street, London E13 9AZ. Telephone (020) 8548 2748.
Record Attendance: 42,322 v Tottenham H, Division 1, 17 October 1970. **Capacity:** 35,303.
Manager: Gianfranco Zola.
Secretary: Peter Barnes.
Most League Goals: 101, Division 2, 1957–58.
Highest League Scorer in Season: Vic Watson, 42, Division 1, 1929–30.

Most League Goals in Total Aggregate: Vic Watson, 298, 1920–35.
Most Capped Player: Bobby Moore, 108, England.
Most League Appearances: Billy Bonds, 663, 1967–88.
Honours – Football League: Division 2 Champions – 1957–58, 1980–81. **FA Cup:** Winners – 1964, 1975, 1980. **European Competitions: European Cup-Winners' Cup:** Winners – 1964–65. **Intertoto Cup:** Winners – 1999.
Colours: Claret shirts with light blue sleeves and white collar, white shorts, white stockings.

WIGAN ATHLETIC   FA PREMIERSHIP

Bouaouzan Rachid (M)	5 6	11 02	Rotterdam	20	2 84	Sparta Rotterdam
Boyce Emmerson (D)	6 0	12 06	Aylesbury	24	9 79	Crystal Palace
Bramble Titus (D)	6 2	13 10	Ipswich	31	7 81	Newcastle U
Brown Michael (M)	5 9	12 04	Hartlepool	25	1 77	Fulham
Cattermole Lee (M)	5 10	11 13	Stockton	21	3 88	Middlesbrough
Cho Won-Hee (M)	5 10	11 07	Seoul	17	4 83	Suwon Blue Wings
Cywka Tomasz (M)	5 10	11 09	Gliwice	27	6 88	Gwarek Zabrze
De Ridder Daniel (M)	5 11	10 12	Amsterdam	6	3 84	Birmingham C
Edman Erik (D)	5 10	12 04	Huskvarna	11	11 78	Rennes
Figueroa Maynor (D)	5 11	12 02	Jutiapa	2	5 83	Victoria La Ceiba
Holt Joe (F)	5 8	11 07	Liverpool	1	2 90	Scholar
Kapo Olivier (M)	6 1	12 06	Abidjan	27	9 80	Birmingham C
King Marlon (F)	5 10	12 10	Dulwich	26	4 80	Watford
Kingson Richard (G)	6 3	13 10	Accra	13	6 78	Birmingham C
Kirkland Chris (G)	6 5	14 05	Leicester	2	5 81	Liverpool
Koumas Jason (M)	5 10	11 02	Wrexham	25	9 79	WBA
Kupisz Tomasz (M)	5 11	12 00	Radom	2	1 90	Piaseczno
Melchiot Mario (D)	6 2	11 09	Amsterdam	4	11 76	Rennes
N'Zogbia Charles (M)	5 9	11 00	Le Havre	28	5 86	Newcastle U
Pollitt Mike (G)	6 4	15 03	Farnworth	29	2 72	Rotherham U
Pollitt Mike (G)	6 4	15 03	Farnworth	29	2 72	Rotherham U
Rodallega Hugo (F)	5 11	11 05	El Carmelo	25	7 85	Necaxa
Routledge Jon (M)	5 7	11 05	Liverpool	23	11 89	Liverpool
Scharner Paul (D)	6 3	13 03	Prugstall	11	3 80	Brann
Valencia Luis Antonio (M)	5 11	12 09	Lago Agrio	4	8 85	Villarreal
Watson Ben (M)	5 10	10 11	Camberwell	9	7 85	Crystal Palace

League Appearances: Boyce, E. 26(1); Bramble, T. 35; Brown, M. 18(7); Camara, H. 3(14); Cattermole, L. 33; Cho, W. 1; De Ridder, D. 5(13); Edman, E. (2); Figueroa, M. 38; Heskey, E. 20; Kapo, O. 10(9); Kilbane, K. 3(7); Kingson, R. 3(1); Kirkland, C. 32; Koumas, J. 5(11); McManaman, C. (1); Melchiot, M. 33(1); Mido, 10(2); N'Zogbia, C. 13; Palacios, W. 21; Pollitt, M. 3; Rodallega, H. 9(6); Routledge, J. (1); Scharner, P. 27(2); Sibierski, A. (3); Taylor, R. 11(1); Valencia, L. 31; Watson, B. 6(4); Zaki, A. 22(7).
Goals – League (34): Zaki 10 (4 pens), Heskey 3, Rodallega 3, Valencia 3, Camara 2, Mido 2 (1 pen), Taylor 2, Watson 2, Boyce 1, Bramble 1, Cattermole 1, Figueroa 1, Kapo 1, N'Zogbia 1, own goal 1.
Carling Cup (8): Camara 3, Cattermole 1, Kapo 1, Kupisz 1, Scharner 1, Zaki 1.
FA Cup (1): Camara 1.
Ground: JJB Stadium, Robin Park, Newtown, Wigan WN5 0UZ. Telephone (01942) 774 000.
Record Attendance: 27,526 v Hereford U, FA Cup 2nd rd, 12 December 1953 (at Springfield Park). **Capacity:** 25,138.
Manager: Roberto Martinez.
Secretary: Stuart Hayton.
Most League Goals: 84, Division 3, 1996–97.
Highest League Scorer in Season: Graeme Jones, 31, Division 3, 1996–97.
Most League Goals in Total Aggregate: Andy Liddell, 70, 1998–2004.

Most Capped Player: Lee McCulloch, 11(15), Scotland.
Most League Appearances: Kevin Langley, 317, 1981–86, 1990–94.
Honours – Football League: Division 2 Champions – 2002–03. Division 3 Champions – 1996–97. **Freight Rover Trophy:** Winners – 1984–85. **Auto Windscreens Shield:** Winners – 1998–99.
Colours: Blue and white shirts with blue sleeves, blue shorts, white stockings.

WOLVERHAMPTON WANDERERS   FA PREMIERSHIP

Bennett Elliott (M)	5 9	10 13	Telford	18 12 88	Scholar
Bennett Kyle (M)			Telford	9 9 90	
Berra Christophe (D)	6 1	12 10	Edinburgh	31 1 85	Hearts
Collins Neill (D)	6 3	12 06	Irvine	2 9 83	Sunderland
Ebanks-Blake Sylvan (F)	5 10	13 04	Cambridge	29 3 86	Plymouth Arg
Edwards Dave (M)	5 11	11 04	Shrewsbury	3 2 86	Luton T
Elokobi George (D)	5 10	13 02	Cameroon	31 1 86	Colchester U
Foley Kevin (D)	5 9	11 11	Luton	1 11 84	Luton T
Friend George (D)	6 2	13 01	Dorchester	19 10 87	Exeter C
Gleeson Stephen (M)	6 2	11 00	Dublin	3 8 88	Scholar
Hemmings Ashley (M)	5 8	11 06	Wolverhampton	3 3 91	Scholar
Hennessey Wayne (G)	6 0	11 06	Anglesey	24 1 87	Scholar
Henry Karl (M)	6 0	11 02	Wolverhampton	26 11 82	Stoke C
Hill Matt (D)	5 7	12 06	Bristol	26 3 81	Preston NE
Ikeme Carl (G)	6 2	13 09	Sutton Coldfield	8 6 86	Scholar
Iwelumo Chris (F)	6 3	15 03	Coatbridge	1 8 78	Charlton Ath
Jarvis Matthew (M)	5 8	11 10	Middlesbrough	22 5 86	Gillingham
Jones Daniel (D)	6 2	13 00	Rowley Regis	14 7 86	Scholar
Jones David (M)	5 11	10 10	Southport	4 11 84	Derby Co
Keogh Andy (F)	6 0	11 00	Dublin	16 5 86	Scunthorpe U
Kightly Michael (F)	5 9	11 09	Basildon	24 1 86	Grays Ath
Little Mark (D)	6 1	12 11	Worcester	20 8 88	Scholar
Murray Matt (G)	6 4	13 10	Solihull	2 5 81	Trainee
Potter Darren (M)	6 1	11 05	Liverpool	21 12 84	Liverpool
Shackell Jason (D)	6 4	13 06	Stevenage	27 9 83	Norwich C
Stearman Richard (D)	6 2	10 08	Wolverhampton	19 8 87	Leicester C
Vokes Sam (F)	6 1	13 10	Southampton	21 10 89	Bournemouth
Ward Darren (D)	6 3	11 04	Kenton	13 9 78	Crystal Palace
Ward Stephen (F)	5 11	12 01	Dublin	20 8 85	Bohemians

League Appearances: Berra, C. 15; Collins, N. 20(3); Craddock, J. 17; Ebanks-Blake, S. 41; Edwards, C. 5(1); Edwards, D. 23(21); Elokobi, G. 3(1); Foley, K. 45; Friend, G. 4(2); Gray, M. 4(4); Harewood, M. 2(3); Hemmings, A. (2); Hennessey, W. 34(1); Henry, K. 42(1); Hill, M. 13; Ikeme, C. 12; Iwelumo, C. 25(6); Jarvis, M. 21(7); Jones, David 31(3); Keogh, A. 21(21); Kightly, M. 37(1); Mancienne, M. 8(2); Quashie, N. 3; Reid, K. 3(5); Shackell, J. 3(9); Stearman, R. 32(5); Vokes, S. 4(32); Ward, D. (1); Ward, S. 38(4).
Goals – League (80): Ebanks-Blake 25 (6 pens), Iwelumo 14 (1 pen), Kightly 8, Vokes 6, Keogh 5, Collins 4, David Jones 4 (1 pen), Edwards D 3, Jarvis 3, Craddock 1, Foley 1, Gray 1, Reid 1, Stearman 1, own goals 3.
Carling Cup (3): Iwelumo 2, Davies 1.
FA Cup (3): Vokes 2, Keogh 1.
Ground: Molineux, Waterloo Road, Wolverhampton WV1 4QR. Telephone (0871) 222 2220.
Record Attendance: 61,315 v Liverpool, FA Cup 5th rd, 11 February 1939.
Capacity: 28,565.
Manager: Mick McCarthy.
Secretary: Richard Skirrow.
Most League Goals: 115, Division 2, 1931–32.
Highest League Scorer in Season: Dennis Westcott, 38, Division 1, 1946–47.

Most League Goals in Total Aggregate: Steve Bull, 250, 1986–99.
Most Capped Player: Billy Wright, 105, England (70 consecutive).
Most League Appearances: Derek Parkin, 501, 1967–82.
Honours – Football League: Championship Winners – 2008–09. Division 1 Champions – 1953–54, 1957–58, 1958–59. Division 2 Champions – 1931–32, 1976–77. Division 3 (N) Champions – 1923–24. Division 3 Champions – 1988–89. Division 4 Champions – 1987–88. **FA Cup:** Winners – 1893, 1908, 1949, 1960. **Football League Cup:** Winners – 1973–74, 1979–80. **Texaco Cup:** Winners – 1971. **Sherpa Van Trophy:** Winners – 1988.
Colours: Old gold shirts with black trim, black shorts, old gold stockings with black tops.

WYCOMBE WANDERERS　　　FL CHAMPIONSHIP 1

Antwi Will (D)	6 2	12 08	Epsom	19 10 82	Aldershot T
Ashton Nathan (D)	5 8	9 07	Plaistow	30 1 87	Fulham
Bloomfield Matt (M)	5 9	11 00	Ipswich	8 2 84	Ipswich T
Doherty Tom (M)	5 8	10 06	Bristol	17 3 79	QPR
Grant Gavin (F)	5 11	11 00	Middlesex	27 3 84	Millwall
Harrold Matt (F)	6 1	11 10	Leyton	25 7 84	Southend U
Holt Gary (M)	6 0	12 00	Irvine	9 3 73	Nottingham F
Hunt Lewis (D)	5 11	12 09	Birmingham	25 8 82	Southend U
Johnson Leon (D)	6 1	13 05	Shoreditch	10 5 81	Gillingham
McCracken David (D)	6 2	11 06	Glasgow	16 10 81	Dundee U
Moncur TJ (D)	5 10	12 08	Hackney	23 9 87	Fulham
Mousinho John (D)	6 1	12 07	Buckingham	30 4 86	Brentford
Oliver Luke (D)	6 6	14 05	Hammersmith	1 5 84	Stevenage B
Phillips Matthew (M)	6 0	12 10	Aylesbury	13 3 91	Scholar
Pittman Jon-Paul (F)	5 9	11 00	Oklahoma City	24 10 86	Crawley T
Shearer Scott (G)	6 3	12 00	Glasgow	15 2 81	Bristol R
Spence Lewis (M)	5 9	11 02	Lambeth	29 10 87	Crystal Palace
Woodman Craig (D)	5 9	10 11	Tiverton	22 12 82	Bristol C
Young Jamie (G)	5 11	13 00	Brisbane	25 8 85	Reading
Zebroski Chris (F)	6 1	11 08	Swindon	29 10 86	Millwall

League Appearances: Akinde, J. 11; Antwi, W. 4(2); Ashton, N. (11); Balanta, A. 9(2); Beavon, S. 2(6); Bloomfield, M. 15(5); Casement, C. 12; Church, S. 6(3); Crooks, L. 2; Doherty, T. 34; Grant, G. 9(1); Harrold, M. 28(9); Holt, G. 33; Hunt, L. 20; Johnson, L. 29; McCracken, D. 39; McGleish, S. 10(5); Moncur, T. (2); Mousinho, J. 21(13); Moussa, F. 7(2); Oliver, L. 1(7); Phillips, M. 18(19); Pittman, J. 11(6); Rice, R. (1); Sawyer, L. 8(1); Shearer, S. 29; Sinclair, F. 9; Spence, L. 21(9); Stech, M. 2; Vieira, M. 2(12); Williamson, M. 22; Woodman, C. 46; Young, J. 15; Zebroski, C. 31(2).
Goals – League (54): Harrold 9 (2 pens), Akinde 7, Zebroski 7, Balanta 3, McGleish 3 (2 pens), Phillips 3, Pittman 3, Williamson 3, Johnson 2, Mousinho 2, Spence 2, Vieira 2, Holt 1, Hunt 1, McCracken 1, Sawyer 1, Woodman 1, own goals 3.
Carling Cup (0).
FA Cup (4): Harrold 3, Phillips 1.
J Paint Trophy (0).
Ground: Adams Park, Hillbottom Road, Sands, High Wycombe HP12 4HJ. Telephone (01494) 472 100.
Record Attendance: 9,921 v Fulham, FA Cup 3rd rd, 9 January 2002.
Capacity: 10,000.
Manager: Peter Taylor.
Secretary: Keith Allen.
Most League Goals: 72, Championship 2, 2005–06.
Highest League Goalscorer in Season: Scott McGleish, 25, 2007–08.
Most League Goals in Total Aggregate: Nathan Tyson, 42, 2005–06.
Most Capped Player: Mark Rogers, 7, Canada.
Most League Appearances: Steve Brown, 371, 1994–2004.

Honours – GM Vauxhall Conference: Winners – 1993. **FA Trophy:** Winners – 1991, 1993.
Colours: Light blue and dark blue quartered shirts, light blue shorts, light blue stockings.

YEOVIL TOWN   FL CHAMPIONSHIP 1

Alcock Craig (D)	5 8	11 00	Truro	8 12 87	Scholar
Brown Aaron (D)	6 4	14 07	Birmingham	23 6 83	Reading
Downes Aiden (F)	5 8	11 07	Dublin	24 7 88	Everton
Jones Nathan (M)	5 6	10 06	Rhondda	28 5 73	Brighton & HA
McCollin Andre (F)	5 7	10 06		8 7 87	Fisher Ath
Murtagh Kieran (M)	6 0	12 00	Wapping	29 10 88	Fisher Ath
Peltier Lee (F)	5 10	12 00	Liverpool	11 12 86	Liverpool
Roberts Gary (M)	5 8	10 05	Chester	4 2 87	Crewe Alex
Schofield Danny (F)	5 10	11 02	Doncaster	10 4 80	Huddersfield T
Skiverton Terry (D)	6 1	13 06	Mile End	26 6 75	Wycombe W
Smith Nathan (D)	5 11	12 00	Enfield	11 1 87	Potters Bar T
Tomlin Gavin (F)	6 0	12 02	Brentford	21 8 83	Yeading
Wagenaar Josh (G)	6 0	14 02	Grimsby, Can	26 2 85	Lyngby
Way Darren (M)	5 7	11 00	Plymouth	21 11 79	Swansea C

League Appearances: Alcock, C. 25(5); Begovic, A. 14; Bircham, M. 3; Brown, A. 16(7); Dayton, J. (2); Downes, A. 15(9); Forbes, T. 38; Hutchins, D. 8(1); Jones, N. 14(7); Macdonald, S. 4; Maguire, D. 1; McCollin, A. (11); Murtagh, K. 16(10); Noble, D. 2; Noel-Williams, G. 6; Obika, J. 10; Owen, G. 7; Owusu, L. (4); Peltier, L. 34(1); Prijovic, A. 4; Rendell, S. 5; Roberts, G. 27(3); Rodgers, L. 10(12); Schofield, D. 34(5); Skiverton, T. 25; Smith, N. 32(1); Tomlin, G. 29(13); Townsend, A. 10; Wagenaar, J. 22(1); Warne, P. 38(6); Way, D. 15; Weale, C. 10; Welsh, A. 23(14); Worthington, J. 9.
Goals – League (41): Tomlin 7, Obika 4, Schofield 4, Warne 4, Brown A 3, Rodgers 3, Macdonald 2, Roberts 2, Skiverton 2, Way 2, Alcock 1, McCollin 1, Owusu 1, Peltier 1, Smith 1, Townsend 1, Weale 1, own goal 1.
Carling Cup (2): Tomlin 1, Warne 1.
FA Cup (1): Skiverton 1.
J Paint Trophy (2): Bircham 1, Tomlin 1 (pen).
Ground: Huish Park, Lufton Way, Yeovil, Somerset BA22 8YF. Telephone (01935) 423 662.
Record Attendance: 9,527 v Leeds U, FL 1, 25 April 2008 (16,318 v Sunderland at Huish). **Capacity:** 9,665.
Manager: Terry Skiverton.
Secretary: Jean Cotton.
Most League Goals: 90, FL 2, 2004–05.
Highest League Goalscorer in Season: Phil Jevons, 27, 2004–05.
Most League Goals in Total Aggregate: Phil Jevons, 42, 2004–06.
Most Capped Player: Andrejs Stolcers, 1 (81), Latvia and Arron Davies, 1, Wales.
Most League Appearances: Terry Skiverton, 195, 2003–.
Honours – Football League: Championship 2 – Winners 2004–05. **Football Conference:** Champions – 2002–03. **FA Trophy:** Winners 2001–02.
Colours: Green and white hooped shirts, green shorts, white stockings.

LEAGUE POSITIONS: FA PREMIER from 1992–93 and DIVISION 1 1983–84 to 1991–92

	2007-08	2006-07	2005-06	2004-05	2003-04	2002-03	2001-02	2000-01	1999-2000	1998-99	1997-98	1996-97	1995-96
Arsenal	3	4	4	2	1	2	1	2	2	2	1	3	5
Aston Villa	6	11	16	10	6	16	8	8	6	6	7	5	4
Barnsley	–	–	–	–	–	–	–	–	–	–	19	–	–
Birmingham C	19	–	18	12	10	13	–	–	–	–	–	–	–
Blackburn R	7	10	6	15	15	6	10	–	–	19	6	13	7
Bolton W	16	7	8	6	8	17	16	–	–	–	18	–	20
Bradford C	–	–	–	–	–	–	–	20	17	–	–	–	–
Charlton Ath	–	19	13	11	7	12	14	9	–	18	–	–	–
Chelsea	2	2	1	1	2	4	6	6	5	3	4	6	11
Coventry C	–	–	–	–	–	–	–	19	14	15	11	17	16
Crystal Palace	–	–	–	18	–	–	–	–	–	–	20	–	–
Derby Co	20	–	–	–	–	–	19	17	16	8	9	12	–
Everton	5	6	11	4	17	7	15	16	13	14	17	15	6
Fulham	17	16	12	13	9	14	13	–	–	–	–	–	–
Ipswich T	–	–	–	–	–	–	18	5	–	–	–	–	–
Leeds U	–	–	–	–	19	15	5	4	3	4	5	11	13
Leicester C	–	–	–	–	18	–	20	13	8	10	10	9	–
Liverpool	4	3	3	5	4	5	2	3	4	7	3	4	3
Luton T	–	–	–	–	–	–	–	–	–	–	–	–	–
Manchester C	9	14	15	8	16	9	–	18	–	–	–	–	18
Manchester U	1	1	2	3	3	1	3	1	1	1	2	1	1
Middlesbrough	13	12	14	7	11	11	12	14	12	9	–	19	12
Millwall	–	–	–	–	–	–	–	–	–	–	–	–	–
Newcastle U	12	13	7	14	5	3	4	11	11	13	13	2	2
Norwich C	–	–	–	19	–	–	–	–	–	–	–	–	–
Nottingham F	–	–	–	–	–	–	–	–	–	20	–	20	9
Notts Co	–	–	–	–	–	–	–	–	–	–	–	–	–
Oldham Ath	–	–	–	–	–	–	–	–	–	–	–	–	–
Oxford U	–	–	–	–	–	–	–	–	–	–	–	–	–
Portsmouth	8	9	17	16	13	–	–	–	–	–	–	–	–
QPR	–	–	–	–	–	–	–	–	–	–	–	–	19
Reading	18	8	–	–	–	–	–	–	–	–	–	–	–
Sheffield U	–	18	–	–	–	–	–	–	–	–	–	–	–
Sheffield W	–	–	–	–	–	–	–	–	19	12	16	7	15
Southampton	–	–	–	20	12	8	11	10	15	17	12	16	17
Stoke C	–	–	–	–	–	–	–	–	–	–	–	–	–
Sunderland	15	–	20	–	–	20	17	7	7	–	–	18	–
Swindon T	–	–	–	–	–	–	–	–	–	–	–	–	–
Tottenham H	11	5	5	9	14	10	9	12	10	11	14	10	8
Watford	–	20	–	–	–	–	–	–	20	–	–	–	–
WBA	–	–	19	17	–	19	–	–	–	–	–	–	–
West Ham U	10	15	9	–	–	18	7	15	9	5	8	14	10
Wigan Ath	14	17	10	–	–	–	–	–	–	–	–	–	–
Wimbledon	–	–	–	–	–	–	–	–	18	16	15	8	14
Wolverhampton W	–	–	–	–	20	–	–	–	–	–	–	–	–

1994-95	1993-94	1992-93	1991-92	1990-91	1989-90	1988-89	1987-88	1986-87	1985-86	1984-85	1983-84	
12	4	10	4	1	4	1	6	4	7	7	6	Arsenal
18	10	2	7	17	2	17	–	22	16	10	10	Aston Villa
–	–	–	–	–	–	–	–	–	–	–	–	Barnsley
–	–	–	–	–	–	–	–	–	21	–	20	Birmingham C
1	2	4	–	–	–	–	–	–	–	–	–	Blackburn R
–	–	–	–	–	–	–	–	–	–	–	–	Bolton W
–	–	–	–	–	–	–	–	–	–	–	–	Bradford C
–	–	–	–	–	19	14	17	19	–	–	–	Charlton Ath
11	14	11	14	11	5	–	18	14	6	6	–	Chelsea
16	11	15	19	16	12	7	10	10	17	18	19	Coventry C
19	–	20	10	3	15	–	–	–	–	–	–	Crystal Palace
–	–	–	–	20	16	5	15	–	–	–	–	Derby Co
15	17	13	12	9	6	8	4	1	2	1	7	Everton
–	–	–	–	–	–	–	–	–	–	–	–	Fulham
22	19	16	–	–	–	–	–	–	20	17	12	Ipswich T
5	5	17	1	4	–	–	–	–	–	–	–	Leeds U
21	–	–	–	–	–	–	–	20	19	15	15	Leicester C
4	8	6	2	1	2	1	2	1	2	2	1	Liverpool
–	–	–	20	18	17	16	9	7	9	13	16	Luton T
17	16	9	5	5	14	–	–	21	15	–	–	Manchester C
2	1	1	2	6	13	11	2	11	4	4	4	Manchester U
–	–	21	–	–	–	18	–	–	–	–	–	Middlesbrough
–	–	–	–	–	20	10	–	–	–	–	–	Millwall
6	3	–	–	–	–	20	8	17	11	14	–	Newcastle U
20	12	3	18	15	10	4	14	5	–	20	14	Norwich C
3	–	22	8	8	9	3	3	8	8	9	3	Nottingham F
–	–	–	21	–	–	–	–	–	–	–	21	Notts Co
–	21	19	17	–	–	–	–	–	–	–	–	Oldham Ath
–	–	–	–	–	–	21	18	18	–	–	–	Oxford U
–	–	–	–	–	–	19	–	–	–	–	–	Portsmouth
8	9	5	11	12	11	9	5	16	13	19	5	QPR
–	–	–	–	–	–	–	–	–	–	–	–	Reading
–	20	14	9	13	–	–	–	–	–	–	–	Sheffield U
13	7	7	3	–	18	15	11	13	5	8	–	Sheffield W
10	18	18	16	14	7	13	12	12	14	5	2	Southampton
–	–	–	–	–	–	–	–	–	–	22	18	Stoke C
–	–	–	19	–	–	–	–	–	–	21	13	Sunderland
–	22	–	–	–	–	–	–	–	–	–	–	Swindon T
7	15	8	15	10	3	6	13	3	10	3	8	Tottenham H
–	–	–	–	–	–	20	9	12	11	11	–	Watford
–	–	–	–	–	–	–	–	–	22	12	17	WBA
14	13	–	22	–	–	19	16	15	3	16	9	West Ham U
–	–	–	–	–	–	–	–	–	–	–	–	Wigan Ath
9	6	12	13	7	8	12	7	6	–	–	–	Wimbledon
–	–	–	–	–	–	–	–	–	–	–	22	Wolverhampton W

LEAGUE POSITIONS: DIVISION 1 from 1992–93, CHAMPIONSHIP from 2004–05 and DIVISION 2 1983–84 to 1991–92

	2007-08	2006-07	2005-06	2004-05	2003-04	2002-03	2001-02	2000-01	1999-2000	1998-99	1997-98	1996-97	1995-96
Aston Villa	–	–	–	–	–	–	–	–	–	–	–	–	–
Barnsley	18	20	–	–	–	–	23	16	4	13	–	2	10
Birmingham C	–	2	–	–	–	–	5	5	5	4	7	10	15
Blackburn R	–	–	–	–	–	–	2	11	–	–	–	–	–
Blackpool	19	–	–	–	–	–	–	–	–	–	–	–	–
Bolton W	–	–	–	–	–	–	3	6	6	–	1	–	–
Bournemouth	–	–	–	–	–	–	–	–	–	–	–	–	–
Bradford C	–	–	–	–	23	19	15	–	–	2	13	21	–
Brentford	–	–	–	–	–	–	–	–	–	–	–	–	–
Brighton & HA	–	–	22	20	–	23	–	–	–	–	–	–	–
Bristol C	4	–	–	–	–	–	–	–	–	24	–	–	–
Bristol R	–	–	–	–	–	–	–	–	–	–	–	–	–
Burnley	13	15	17	13	19	16	7	7	–	–	–	–	–
Bury	–	–	–	–	–	–	–	–	–	22	17	–	–
Cambridge U	–	–	–	–	–	–	–	–	–	–	–	–	–
Cardiff C	12	13	11	16	13	–	–	–	–	–	–	–	–
Carlisle U	–	–	–	–	–	–	–	–	–	–	–	–	–
Charlton Ath	11	–	–	–	–	–	–	–	1	–	4	15	6
Chelsea	–	–	–	–	–	–	–	–	–	–	–	–	–
Colchester U	24	10	–	–	–	–	–	–	–	–	–	–	–
Coventry C	21	17	8	19	12	20	11	–	–	–	–	–	–
Crewe Alex	–	–	22	21	18	–	22	14	19	18	11	–	–
Crystal Palace	5	12	6	–	6	14	10	21	15	14	–	6	3
Derby Co	–	3	20	4	20	18	–	–	–	–	–	–	2
Fulham	–	–	–	–	–	–	–	1	9	–	–	–	–
Gillingham	–	–	–	22	21	11	12	13	–	–	–	–	–
Grimsby T	–	–	–	–	–	24	19	18	20	11	–	22	17
Huddersfield T	–	–	–	–	–	–	–	22	8	10	16	20	8
Hull C	3	21	18	–	–	–	–	–	–	–	–	–	–
Ipswich T	8	14	15	3	5	7	–	–	3	3	5	4	7
Leeds U	–	24	5	14	–	–	–	–	–	–	–	–	–
Leicester C	22	19	16	15	–	2	–	–	–	–	–	–	5
Luton T	–	23	10	–	–	–	–	–	–	–	–	–	24
Manchester C	–	–	–	–	–	–	1	–	2	–	22	14	–
Middlesbrough	–	–	–	–	–	–	–	–	–	–	2	–	–
Millwall	–	–	23	10	10	9	4	–	–	–	–	–	22
Newcastle U	–	–	–	–	–	–	–	–	–	–	–	–	–
Norwich C	17	16	9	–	1	8	6	15	12	9	15	13	16
Nottingham F	–	–	–	23	14	6	16	11	14	–	1	–	–
Notts Co	–	–	–	–	–	–	–	–	–	–	–	–	–
Oldham Ath	–	–	–	–	–	–	–	–	–	–	–	23	18
Oxford U	–	–	–	–	–	–	–	–	23	12	17	–	–
Peterborough U	–	–	–	–	–	–	–	–	–	–	–	–	–
Plymouth Arg	10	11	14	17	–	–	–	–	–	–	–	–	–
Port Vale	–	–	–	–	–	–	–	–	23	21	19	8	12
Portsmouth	–	–	–	–	–	1	17	20	18	19	20	7	21
Preston NE	15	7	4	5	15	12	8	4	–	–	–	–	–
QPR	14	18	21	11	–	–	–	23	10	20	21	9	–

1994-95	1993-94	1992-93	1991-92	1990-91	1989-90	1988-89	1987-88	1986-87	1985-86	1984-85	1983-84	
-	-	-	-	-	-	-	2	-	-	-	-	Aston Villa
6	18	13	16	8	19	7	14	11	12	11	14	Barnsley
-	22	19	-	-	-	23	19	19	-	2	-	Birmingham C
-	-	-	6	19	5	5	5	12	19	5	6	Blackburn R
-	-	-	-	-	-	-	-	-	-	-	-	Blackpool
3	14	-	-	-	-	-	-	-	-	-	-	Bolton W
-	-	-	-	-	22	12	17	-	-	-	-	Bournemouth
-	-	-	-	23	14	4	10	13	-	-	-	Bradford C
-	-	22	-	-	-	-	-	-	-	-	-	Brentford
-	-	-	23	6	18	19	-	22	11	6	9	Brighton & HA
23	13	15	17	9	-	-	-	-	-	-	-	Bristol C
-	-	24	13	13	-	-	-	-	-	-	-	Bristol R
22	-	-	-	-	-	-	-	-	-	-	-	Burnley
-	-	-	-	-	-	-	-	-	-	-	-	Bury
-	-	23	5	-	-	-	-	-	-	-	-	Cambridge U
-	-	-	-	-	-	-	-	-	-	21	15	Cardiff C
-	-	-	-	-	-	-	-	-	20	16	7	Carlisle U
15	11	12	7	16	-	-	-	-	2	17	13	Charlton Ath
-	-	-	-	-	-	1	-	-	-	-	1	Chelsea
-	-	-	-	-	-	-	-	-	-	-	-	Colchester U
-	-	-	-	-	-	-	-	-	-	-	-	Coventry C
-	-	-	-	-	-	-	-	-	-	-	-	Crewe Alex
-	1	-	-	-	-	3	6	6	5	15	18	Crystal Palace
9	6	8	3	-	-	-	-	1	-	-	20	Derby Co
-	-	-	-	-	-	-	-	-	22	9	11	Fulham
-	-	-	-	-	-	-	-	-	-	-	-	Gillingham
10	16	9	19	-	-	-	-	21	15	10	5	Grimsby T
-	-	-	-	-	-	-	23	17	16	13	12	Huddersfield T
-	-	-	24	14	21	15	14	6	-	-	-	Hull C
-	-	-	1	14	9	8	8	5	-	-	-	Ipswich T
-	-	-	-	-	1	10	7	4	14	7	10	Leeds U
-	4	6	22	13	15	13	-	-	-	-	-	Leicester C
16	20	20	-	-	-	-	-	-	-	-	-	Luton T
-	-	-	-	-	-	2	9	-	-	3	4	Manchester C
1	9	-	2	7	21	-	3	-	21	19	17	Middlesbrough
12	3	7	15	5	-	-	1	16	9	-	-	Millwall
-	-	1	20	11	3	-	-	-	-	-	3	Newcastle U
-	-	-	-	-	-	-	-	-	1	-	-	Norwich C
-	2	-	-	-	-	-	-	-	-	-	-	Nottingham F
24	7	17	-	4	-	-	-	-	-	20	-	Notts Co
14	-	-	-	1	8	16	10	3	8	14	19	Oldham Ath
-	23	14	21	10	17	17	-	-	-	1	-	Oxford U
-	24	10	-	-	-	-	-	-	-	-	-	Peterborough U
-	-	-	22	18	16	18	16	7	-	-	-	Plymouth Arg
17	-	-	24	15	11	-	-	-	-	-	-	Port Vale
18	17	3	9	17	12	20	-	2	4	4	16	Portsmouth
-	-	-	-	-	-	-	-	-	-	-	-	Preston NE
-	-	-	-	-	-	-	-	-	-	-	-	QPR

LEAGUE POSITIONS: DIVISION 1 from 1992–93, CHAMPIONSHIP from 2004–05 and DIVISION 2 1983–84 to 1991–92 (cont.)

	2007-08	2006-07	2005-06	2004-05	2003-04	2002-03	2001-02	2000-01	1999-2000	1998-99	1997-98	1996-97	1995-96
Reading	–	–	1	7	9	4	–	–	–	–	24	18	19
Scunthorpe U	23	–	–	–	–	–	–	–	–	–	–	–	–
Sheffield U	9	–	2	8	8	3	13	10	16	8	6	5	9
Sheffield W	16	9	19	–	–	22	20	17	–	–	–	–	–
Shrewsbury T	–	–	–	–	–	–	–	–	–	–	–	–	–
Southampton	20	6	12	–	–	–	–	–	–	–	–	–	–
Southend U	–	22	–	–	–	–	–	–	–	–	–	24	14
Stockport Co	–	–	–	–	–	–	24	19	17	16	8	–	–
Stoke C	2	8	13	12	11	21	–	–	–	–	–	–	–
Sunderland	–	1	–	1	3	–	–	–	–	–	23	12	4
Swansea C	–	–	–	1	–	–	–	–	–	1	3	–	1
Swindon T	–	–	–	–	–	–	–	24	17	18	19	–	–
Tranmere R	–	–	–	–	–	–	–	24	13	15	14	11	13
Walsall	–	–	–	–	22	17	18	–	22	–	–	–	–
Watford	6	–	3	18	16	13	14	9	–	5	–	–	23
WBA	1	4	–	–	2	–	2	6	21	12	10	16	11
West Ham U	–	–	–	6	4	–	–	–	–	–	–	–	–
Wigan Ath	–	–	–	2	7	–	–	–	–	–	–	–	–
Wimbledon	–	–	–	–	24	10	9	8	–	–	–	–	–
Wolverhampton W	7	5	7	9	–	5	3	12	7	7	9	3	20

LEAGUE POSITIONS: DIVISION 2 from 1992–93, LEAGUE 1 from 2004–05 and DIVISION 3 1983–84 to 1991–92

	2007-08	2006-07	2005-06	2004-05	2003-04	2002-03	2001-02	2000-01	1999-2000	1998-99	1997-98	1996-97	1995-96
Aldershot	–	–	–	–	–	–	–	–	–	–	–	–	–
Barnet	–	–	–	–	–	–	–	–	–	–	–	–	–
Barnsley	–	–	5	13	12	19	–	–	–	–	–	–	–
Birmingham C	–	–	–	–	–	–	–	–	–	–	–	–	–
Blackpool	–	3	19	16	14	13	16	–	22	14	12	7	3
Bolton W	–	–	–	–	–	–	–	–	–	–	–	–	–
Bournemouth	21	19	17	8	9	–	21	7	16	7	9	16	14
Bradford C	–	22	11	11	–	–	–	–	–	–	–	–	6
Brentford	–	24	3	4	17	16	3	14	17	–	21	4	15
Brighton & HA	7	18	–	–	4	–	1	–	–	–	–	–	23
Bristol C	–	2	9	7	3	3	7	9	9	–	2	5	13
Bristol R	16	–	–	–	–	–	–	21	7	13	5	17	10
Burnley	–	–	–	–	–	–	–	–	2	15	20	9	17
Bury	–	–	–	–	–	–	22	16	15	–	–	1	–
Cambridge U	–	–	–	–	–	–	24	19	19	–	–	–	–
Cardiff C	–	–	–	–	–	6	4	–	21	–	–	–	–
Carlisle U	4	8	–	–	–	–	–	–	–	–	23	–	21
Cheltenham T	19	17	–	–	–	21	–	–	–	–	–	–	–

1994-95	1993-94	1992-93	1991-92	1990-91	1989-90	1988-89	1987-88	1986-87	1985-86	1984-85	1983-84	
2	–	–	–	–	–	–	22	13	–	–	–	Reading
–	–	–	–	–	–	–	–	–	–	–	–	Scunthorpe U
8	–	–	–	–	2	–	21	9	7	18	–	Sheffield U
–	–	–	3	–	–	–	–	–	–	–	2	Sheffield W
–	–	–	–	–	22	18	18	17	8	8	–	Shrewsbury T
–	–	–	–	–	–	–	–	–	–	–	–	Southampton
13	15	18	12	–	–	–	–	–	–	–	–	Southend U
–	–	–	–	–	–	–	–	–	–	–	–	Stockport Co
11	10	–	–	–	24	13	11	8	10	–	–	Stoke C
20	12	21	18	–	6	11	–	20	18	–	–	Sunderland
–	–	–	–	–	–	–	–	–	–	21	–	Swansea C
21	–	5	8	21	4	6	12	–	–	–	–	Swindon T
5	5	4	14	–	–	–	–	–	–	–	–	Tranmere R
–	–	–	–	–	–	24	–	–	–	–	–	Walsall
7	19	16	10	20	15	4	–	–	–	–	–	Watford
19	21	–	–	23	20	9	20	15	–	–	–	WBA
–	–	2	–	2	7	–	–	–	–	–	–	West Ham U
–	–	–	–	–	–	–	–	–	–	–	–	Wigan Ath
–	–	–	–	–	–	–	–	–	3	12	–	Wimbledon
4	8	11	11	12	10	–	–	–	–	22	–	Wolverhampton W

1994-95	1993-94	1992-93	1991-92	1990-91	1989-90	1988-89	1987-88	1986-87	1985-86	1984-85	1983-84	
–	–	–	–	–	24	20	–	–	–	–	–	Aldershot
–	24	–	–	–	–	–	–	–	–	–	–	Barnet
–	–	–	–	–	–	–	–	–	–	–	–	Barnsley
1	–	–	2	12	7	–	–	–	–	–	–	Birmingham C
12	20	18	–	–	23	19	10	9	12	–	–	Blackpool
–	–	2	13	4	6	10	–	21	18	17	10	Bolton W
19	17	17	8	9	–	–	–	1	15	10	17	Bournemouth
14	7	10	16	8	–	–	–	–	–	1	7	Bradford C
2	16	–	1	6	13	7	12	11	10	13	20	Brentford
16	14	9	–	–	–	–	2	–	–	–	–	Brighton & HA
–	–	–	–	2	11	5	6	9	5	–	–	Bristol C
4	8	–	–	–	1	5	8	19	16	6	5	Bristol R
–	6	13	–	–	–	–	–	–	–	21	12	Burnley
–	–	–	21	7	5	13	14	16	20	–	–	Bury
20	10	–	–	1	–	–	–	–	–	24	–	Cambridge U
22	19	–	–	21	16	–	–	–	22	–	–	Cardiff C
–	–	–	–	–	–	–	–	22	–	–	–	Carlisle U
–	–	–	–	–	–	–	–	–	–	–	–	Cheltenham T

LEAGUE POSITIONS: DIVISION 2 from 1992–93, LEAGUE 1 from 2004–05 and DIVISION 3 1983–84 to 1991–92 (cont.)

	2007-08	2006-07	2005-06	2004-05	2003-04	2002-03	2001-02	2000-01	1999-2000	1998-99	1997-98	1996-97	1995-96
Chester C	–	–	–	–	–	–	–	–	–	–	–	–	–
Chesterfield	–	21	16	17	20	20	18	–	24	9	10	10	7
Colchester U	–	–	2	15	11	12	15	17	18	18	–	–	–
Crewe Alex	20	13	–	–	–	2	–	–	–	–	–	6	5
Darlington	–	–	–	–	–	–	–	–	–	–	–	–	–
Derby Co	–	–	–	–	–	–	–	–	–	–	–	–	–
Doncaster R	3	11	8	10	–	–	–	–	–	–	–	–	–
Exeter C	–	–	–	–	–	–	–	–	–	–	–	–	–
Fulham	–	–	–	–	–	–	–	–	–	1	6	–	–
Gillingham	22	16	14	–	–	–	–	–	3	4	8	11	–
Grimsby T	–	–	–	–	21	–	–	–	–	–	3	–	–
Hartlepool U	15	–	21	6	6	–	–	–	–	–	–	–	–
Huddersfield T	10	15	4	9	–	22	6	–	–	–	–	–	–
Hull C	–	–	–	2	–	–	–	–	–	–	–	–	24
Leeds U	5	–	–	–	–	–	–	–	–	–	–	–	–
Leyton Orient	14	20	–	–	–	–	–	–	–	–	–	–	–
Lincoln C	–	–	–	–	–	–	–	–	23	–	–	–	–
Luton T	24	–	–	1	10	9	–	22	13	12	17	3	–
Macclesfield T	–	–	–	–	–	–	–	–	–	24	–	–	–
Manchester C	–	–	–	–	–	–	–	–	–	–	3	–	–
Mansfield T	–	–	–	–	23	–	–	–	–	–	–	–	–
Middlesbrough	–	–	–	–	–	–	–	–	–	–	–	–	–
Millwall	17	10	–	–	–	–	–	1	5	10	18	14	–
Newport Co	–	–	–	–	–	–	–	–	–	–	–	–	–
Northampton T	9	14	–	–	–	24	20	18	–	22	4	–	–
Nottingham F	2	4	7	–	–	–	–	–	–	–	–	–	–
Notts Co	–	–	–	–	23	15	19	8	8	16	–	24	4
Oldham Ath	8	6	10	19	15	5	9	15	14	20	13	–	–
Oxford U	–	–	–	–	–	–	–	24	20	–	–	–	2
Peterborough U	–	–	–	23	18	11	17	12	–	–	–	21	19
Plymouth Arg	–	–	–	–	1	8	–	–	–	–	22	19	–
Port Vale	23	12	13	18	7	17	14	11	–	–	–	–	–
Preston NE	–	–	–	–	–	–	–	–	1	5	15	15	–
QPR	–	–	–	–	2	4	8	–	–	–	–	–	–
Reading	–	–	–	–	–	–	2	3	10	11	–	–	–
Rotherham U	–	23	20	–	–	22	–	–	2	–	–	23	16
Rushden & D	–	–	–	–	22	–	–	–	–	–	–	–	–
Scunthorpe U	–	1	12	–	–	–	–	–	23	–	–	–	–
Sheffield U	–	–	–	5	16	–	–	–	–	–	–	–	–
Sheffield W	–	–	–	–	–	–	–	–	–	–	–	–	–
Shrewsbury T	–	–	–	–	–	–	–	–	–	–	–	22	18
Southend U	6	–	1	–	–	–	–	–	–	–	24	–	–
Stockport Co	–	–	–	24	19	14	–	–	–	–	–	2	9
Stoke C	–	–	–	–	–	5	5	6	8	–	–	–	–
Sunderland	–	–	–	–	–	–	–	–	–	–	–	–	–
Swansea C	1	7	6	–	–	–	–	23	–	–	–	–	22
Swindon T	13	–	23	12	5	10	13	20	–	–	–	–	1
Torquay U	–	–	–	21	–	–	–	–	–	–	–	–	–
Tranmere R	11	9	18	3	8	7	12	–	–	–	–	–	–

1994-95	1993-94	1992-93	1991-92	1990-91	1989-90	1988-89	1987-88	1986-87	1985-86	1984-85	1983-84	
23	–	24	18	19	16	8	15	15	–	–	–	Chester C
–	–	–	–	–	–	22	18	17	17	–	–	Chesterfield
3	–	–	–	22	12	–	–	–	–	–	–	Colchester U
–	–	–	24	–	–	–	–	23	13	–	–	Crewe Alex
–	–	–	–	–	–	–	–	–	3	7	–	Darlington
–	–	–	–	–	–	24	13	11	14	–	–	Derby Co
–	22	19	20	16	–	–	–	–	–	–	24	Doncaster R
–	21	12	9	21	20	4	9	18	–	–	–	Exeter C
–	–	–	–	–	–	23	13	5	5	4	8	Fulham
–	23	16	11	–	–	–	–	–	–	–	–	Gillingham
–	–	–	–	3	–	–	22	–	–	–	–	Grimsby T
–	–	–	–	–	–	–	–	–	–	–	–	Hartlepool U
5	11	15	3	11	8	14	–	–	–	–	–	Huddersfield T
8	9	20	14	–	–	–	–	–	–	3	4	Hull C
–	–	–	–	–	–	–	–	–	–	–	–	Leeds U
24	18	7	10	13	14	–	–	–	–	22	11	Leyton Orient
–	–	–	–	–	–	–	–	21	19	14	–	Lincoln C
–	–	–	–	–	–	–	–	–	–	–	–	Luton T
–	–	–	–	–	–	–	–	–	–	–	–	Macclesfield T
–	–	–	–	–	–	–	–	–	–	–	–	Manchester C
–	–	22	–	24	15	15	19	10	–	–	–	Mansfield T
–	–	–	–	–	–	–	–	2	–	–	–	Middlesbrough
–	–	–	–	–	–	–	–	–	–	2	9	Millwall
–	–	–	–	–	–	–	23	19	18	13	–	Newport Co
–	–	–	–	22	20	6	–	–	–	–	–	Northampton T
–	–	–	–	–	–	–	–	–	–	–	–	Nottingham F
–	–	–	–	3	9	4	7	8	–	–	–	Notts Co
7	–	–	–	–	–	–	–	–	–	–	1	Oldham Ath
15	–	–	6	–	–	–	–	–	–	–	–	Oxford U
21	3	14	–	–	–	–	–	2	15	19	–	Peterborough U
–	2	3	–	–	–	3	11	12	–	–	23	Plymouth Arg
–	–	21	17	17	19	6	16	–	–	–	16	Port Vale
–	–	–	–	–	–	–	–	–	–	23	16	Preston NE
–	–	–	–	–	–	–	–	–	–	–	–	QPR
–	1	8	12	15	10	18	–	–	1	9	–	Reading
17	15	11	–	23	9	–	21	14	14	12	18	Rotherham U
–	–	–	–	–	–	–	–	–	–	–	–	Rushden & D
–	–	–	–	–	–	–	–	–	–	–	21	Scunthorpe U
–	–	–	–	–	2	–	–	–	–	–	3	Sheffield U
–	–	–	–	–	–	–	–	–	–	–	–	Sheffield W
18	–	–	22	18	11	–	–	–	–	–	–	Shrewsbury T
–	–	–	–	2	–	21	17	–	–	–	22	Southend U
11	4	6	5	14	–	–	–	–	–	–	–	Stockport Co
–	–	1	4	14	–	–	–	–	–	–	–	Stoke C
–	–	–	–	–	–	–	1	–	–	–	–	Sunderland
10	13	5	19	20	17	12	–	–	24	20	–	Swansea C
–	–	–	23	–	–	–	–	3	–	–	–	Swindon T
–	–	23	–	–	–	–	–	–	–	–	–	Torquay U
–	–	–	–	5	4	–	–	–	–	–	–	Tranmere R

LEAGUE POSITIONS: DIVISION 2 from 1992–93, LEAGUE 1 from 2004–05 and DIVISION 3 1983–84 to 1991–92 (cont.)

	2007-08	2006-07	2005-06	2004-05	2003-04	2002-03	2001-02	2000-01	1999-2000	1998-99	1997-98	1996-97	1995-96
Walsall	12	–	24	14	–	–	–	4	–	2	19	12	11
Watford	–	–	–	–	–	–	–	–	–	–	1	13	–
WBA	–	–	–	–	–	–	–	–	–	–	–	–	–
Wigan Ath	–	–	–	–	1	10	6	4	6	11	–	–	–
Wimbledon	–	–	22†	20†	–	–	–	–	–	–	–	–	–
Wolverhampton W	–	–	–	–	–	–	–	–	–	–	–	–	–
Wrexham	–	–	–	22	13	–	23	10	11	17	7	8	8
Wycombe W	–	–	–	–	24	18	11	13	12	19	14	18	12
Yeovil T	18	5	15	–	–	–	–	–	–	–	–	–	–
York C	–	–	–	–	–	–	–	–	–	21	16	20	20

†As Milton Keynes D

LEAGUE POSITIONS: DIVISION 3 from 1992–93, LEAGUE 2 from 2004–05 and DIVISION 4 1983–84 to 1991–92

	2007-08	2006-07	2005-06	2004-05	2003-04	2002-03	2001-02	2000-01	1999-2000	1998-99	1997-98	1996-97	1995-96
Accrington S	17	20	–	–	–	–	–	–	–	–	–	–	–
Aldershot	–	–	–	–	–	–	–	–	–	–	–	–	–
Barnet	12	14	18	–	–	–	–	24	6	16	7	15	9
Blackpool	–	–	–	–	–	–	7	–	–	–	–	–	–
Bolton W	–	–	–	–	–	–	–	–	–	–	–	–	–
Boston U	–	23	11	16	11	15	–	–	–	–	–	–	–
Bournemouth	–	–	–	–	–	4	–	–	–	–	–	–	–
Bradford C	10	–	–	–	–	–	–	–	–	–	–	–	–
Brentford	14	–	–	–	–	–	–	–	–	1	–	–	–
Brighton & HA	–	–	–	–	–	–	1	11	17	23	23	–	–
Bristol C	–	–	–	–	–	–	–	–	–	–	–	–	–
Bristol R	–	6	12	12	15	20	23	–	–	–	–	–	–
Burnley	–	–	–	–	–	–	–	–	–	–	–	–	3
Bury	13	21	19	17	12	7	–	–	–	–	–	–	3
Cambridge U	–	–	–	24	13	12	–	–	–	2	16	10	16
Cardiff C	–	–	–	–	–	–	–	2	–	3	21	7	22
Carlisle U	–	–	1	–	23	22	17	22	23	23	–	3	–
Cheltenham T	–	–	5	14	14	–	4	9	8	–	–	–	–
Chester C	22	18	15	20	–	–	–	–	24	14	14	6	8
Chesterfield	8	–	–	–	–	–	–	3	–	–	–	–	–
Colchester U	–	–	–	–	–	–	–	–	–	–	4	8	7
Crewe Alex	–	–	–	–	–	–	–	–	–	–	–	–	–
Dagenham & R	20	–	–	–	–	–	–	–	–	–	–	–	–

*Record expunged

	1994-95	1993-94	1992-93	1991-92	1990-91	1989-90	1988-89	1987-88	1986-87	1985-86	1984-85	1983-84
Walsall	–	–	–	–	24	–	3	8	6	11	6	–
Watford	–	–	–	–	–	–	–	–	–	–	–	–
WBA	–	–	4	7	–	–	–	–	–	–	–	–
Wigan Ath	–	–	23	15	10	18	17	7	4	4	16	15
Wimbledon	–	–	–	–	–	–	–	–	–	–	–	2
Wolverhampton W	–	–	–	–	–	1	–	–	–	23	–	–
Wrexham	13	12	–	–	–	–	–	–	–	–	–	–
Wycombe W	6	–	–	–	–	–	–	–	–	–	–	–
Yeovil T	–	–	–	–	–	–	–	–	–	–	–	–
York C	9	5	–	–	–	–	–	23	20	7	8	–

	1994-95	1993-94	1992-93	1991-92	1990-91	1989-90	1988-89	1987-88	1986-87	1985-86	1984-85	1983-84
Accrington S	–	–	*	23	22	–	–	–	6	16	13	5
Aldershot	–	–	–	–	–	–	–	–	–	–	–	–
Barnet	11	–	3	7	–	–	–	–	–	–	–	–
Blackpool	–	–	4	5	–	–	–	–	–	–	2	6
Bolton W	–	–	–	–	–	–	–	3	–	–	–	–
Boston U	–	–	–	–	–	–	–	–	–	–	–	–
Bradford C	–	–	–	–	–	–	–	–	–	–	–	–
Leeds U	–	–	–	–	–	–	–	–	–	–	–	–
Brentford	–	–	–	–	–	–	–	–	–	–	–	–
Brighton & HA	–	–	–	–	–	–	–	–	–	–	–	–
Bristol C	–	–	–	–	–	–	–	–	–	–	–	–
Bristol R	–	–	–	–	–	–	–	–	–	–	–	4
Burnley	–	–	–	1	6	16	16	10	22	14	–	–
Bury	4	13	7	–	–	–	–	–	–	–	4	15
Cambridge U	–	–	–	–	–	6	8	15	11	22	–	–
Cardiff C	–	–	1	9	13	–	–	2	13	–	–	–
Carlisle U	1	7	18	22	20	8	12	23	–	–	–	–
Cheltenham T	–	–	–	–	–	–	–	–	–	–	–	–
Chester C	–	2	–	–	–	–	–	–	–	2	16	24
Chesterfield	3	8	12	13	18	7	–	–	–	–	1	13
Colchester U	10	17	10	–	–	24	22	9	5	6	7	8
Crewe Alex	–	3	6	6	–	–	3	17	17	12	10	16
Dagenham & R	–	–	–	–	–	–	–	–	–	–	–	–

LEAGUE POSITIONS: DIVISION 3 from 1992–93, LEAGUE 2 from 2004–05 and DIVISION 4 1983–84 to 1991–92 (cont.)

	2007-08	2006-07	2005-06	2004-05	2003-04	2002-03	2001-02	2000-01	1999-2000	1998-99	1997-98	1996-97	1995-96
Darlington	6	11	8	8	18	14	15	20	4	11	19	18	5
Doncaster R	–	–	–	–	1	–	–	–	–	–	24	19	13
Exeter C	–	–	–	–	–	23	16	19	21	12	15	22	14
Fulham	–	–	–	–	–	–	–	–	–	–	–	2	17
Gillingham	–	–	–	–	–	–	–	–	–	–	–	–	2
Grimsby T	16	15	4	18	–	–	–	–	–	–	–	–	–
Halifax T	–	–	–	–	–	–	24	23	18	10	–	–	–
Hartlepool U	–	2	–	–	–	2	7	4	7	22	17	20	20
Hereford U	3	16	–	–	–	–	–	–	–	–	–	24	6
Huddersfield T	–	–	–	–	4	–	–	–	–	–	–	–	–
Hull C	–	–	–	–	2	13	11	6	14	21	22	17	–
Kidderminster H	–	–	23	16	11	10	16	16	–	–	–	–	–
Leyton Orient	–	–	3	11	19	18	18	5	19	6	11	16	21
Lincoln C	15	5	7	6	7	6	22	18	15	–	3	9	18
Luton T	–	–	–	–	–	–	2	–	–	–	–	–	–
Macclesfield T	19	22	17	5	20	16	13	14	13	–	2	–	–
Maidstone U	–	–	–	–	–	–	–	–	–	–	–	–	–
Mansfield T	23	17	16	13	5	–	3	13	17	8	12	11	19
Morecambe	11	–	–	–	–	–	–	–	–	–	–	–	–
Newport Co	–	–	–	–	–	–	–	–	–	–	–	–	–
Northampton T	–	–	2	7	6	–	–	–	3	–	–	4	11
Notts Co	21	13	21	19	–	–	–	–	–	–	1	–	–
Oxford U	–	–	23	15	9	8	21	–	–	–	–	–	–
Peterborough U	2	10	9	–	–	–	–	–	5	9	10	–	–
Plymouth Arg	–	–	–	–	–	1	12	12	13	–	–	–	4
Port Vale	–	–	–	–	–	–	–	–	–	–	–	–	–
Preston NE	–	–	–	–	–	–	–	–	–	–	–	–	1
Reading	–	–	–	–	–	–	–	–	–	–	–	–	–
Rochdale	5	9	14	9	21	19	5	8	10	19	18	14	15
Rotherham U	9	–	–	–	–	–	–	–	2	5	9	–	–
Rushden & D	–	–	24	22	–	1	6	–	–	–	–	–	–
Scarborough	–	–	–	–	–	–	–	–	–	24	6	12	23
Scunthorpe U	–	–	–	2	22	5	8	10	–	4	8	13	12
Shrewsbury T	18	7	10	21	–	24	9	15	22	15	13	–	–
Southend U	–	–	–	4	17	17	12	11	16	18	–	–	–
Stockport Co	4	8	22	–	–	–	–	–	–	–	–	–	–
Swansea C	–	–	–	3	10	21	20	–	1	7	20	5	–
Swindon T	–	3	–	–	–	–	–	–	–	–	–	–	–
Torquay U	–	24	20	–	3	9	19	21	9	20	5	21	24
Tranmere R	–	–	–	–	–	–	–	–	–	–	–	–	–
Walsall	–	1	–	–	–	–	–	–	–	–	–	–	–
Wigan Ath	–	–	–	–	–	–	–	–	–	–	–	1	10
Wimbledon	1†	4†	–	–	–	–	–	–	–	–	–	–	–
Wolverhampton W	–	–	–	–	–	–	–	–	–	–	–	–	–
Wrexham	24	19	13	–	–	3	–	–	–	–	–	–	–
Wycombe W	7	12	6	10	–	–	–	–	–	–	–	–	–
Yeovil T	–	–	–	1	8	–	–	–	–	–	–	–	–
York C	–	–	–	–	24	10	14	17	20	–	–	–	–

†As Milton Keynes D

1994-95	1993-94	1992-93	1991-92	1990-91	1989-90	1988-89	1987-88	1986-87	1985-86	1984-85	1983-84	
20	21	15	–	1	–	24	13	–	–	3	14	Darlington
9	15	16	21	11	20	23	–	–	–	–	2	Doncaster R
22	–	–	–	–	1	13	22	14	21	18	–	Exeter C
8	–	–	–	–	–	–	–	–	–	–	–	Fulham
19	16	21	11	15	14	–	–	–	–	–	–	Gillingham
–	–	–	–	–	2	9	–	–	–	–	–	Grimsby T
–	–	22	20	22	23	21	18	15	20	21	21	Halifax T
18	–	–	–	3	19	19	16	18	7	19	23	Hartlepool U
16	20	17	17	17	17	15	19	16	10	5	11	Hereford U
–	–	–	–	–	–	–	–	–	–	–	–	Huddersfield T
–	–	–	–	–	–	–	–	–	–	–	–	Hull C
–	–	–	–	–	–	–	–	–	–	–	–	Kidderminster H
–	–	–	–	–	–	6	8	7	5	–	–	Leyton Orient
12	18	8	10	14	10	10	–	24	–	–	–	Lincoln C
–	–	–	–	–	–	–	–	–	–	–	–	Luton T
–	–	–	–	–	–	–	–	–	–	–	–	Macclesfield T
–	–	–	18	19	5	–	–	–	–	–	–	Maidstone U
6	12	–	3	–	–	–	–	–	3	14	19	Mansfield T
–	–	–	–	–	–	–	–	–	–	–	–	Morecambe
–	–	–	–	–	–	24	–	–	–	–	–	Newport Co
17	22	20	16	10	–	–	–	1	8	23	18	Northampton T
–	–	–	–	–	–	–	–	–	–	–	–	Notts Co
–	–	–	–	–	–	–	–	–	–	–	–	Oxford U
–	–	–	4	9	17	7	10	17	11	7	–	Peterborough U
–	–	–	–	–	–	–	–	–	–	–	–	Plymouth Arg
–	–	–	–	–	–	–	–	–	4	12	–	Port Vale
5	5	–	–	–	–	–	2	23	–	–	3	Preston NE
–	–	–	–	–	–	–	–	–	–	–	3	Reading
15	9	11	8	12	12	18	21	21	18	17	22	Rochdale
–	–	2	–	–	1	–	–	–	–	–	–	Rotherham U
–	–	–	–	–	–	–	–	–	–	–	–	Rushden & D
21	14	13	12	9	18	5	12	–	–	–	–	Scarborough
7	11	14	5	8	11	4	4	8	15	9	–	Scunthorpe U
–	1	9	–	–	–	–	–	–	–	–	–	Shrewsbury T
–	–	–	3	–	3	9	20	–	–	–	–	Southend U
–	–	–	–	2	4	20	20	19	11	22	12	Stockport Co
–	–	–	–	–	–	–	6	12	–	–	–	Swansea C
–	–	–	–	–	–	–	–	–	1	8	17	Swindon T
13	6	19	–	7	15	14	5	23	24	24	9	Torquay U
–	–	–	–	–	–	2	14	20	19	6	10	Tranmere R
2	10	5	15	16	–	–	–	–	–	–	–	Walsall
14	19	–	–	–	–	–	–	–	–	–	–	Wigan Ath
–	–	–	–	–	–	–	–	–	–	–	–	Wimbledon
–	–	–	–	–	–	–	1	4	–	–	–	Wolverhampton W
–	–	2	14	24	21	7	11	9	13	15	20	Wrexham
–	4	–	–	–	–	–	–	–	–	–	–	Wycombe W
–	–	–	–	–	–	–	–	–	–	–	–	Yeovil T
–	–	4	19	21	13	11	–	–	–	–	1	York C

LEAGUE CHAMPIONSHIP HONOURS

FA PREMIER LEAGUE

Maximum points: 126

	First	Pts	Second	Pts	Third	Pts
1992–93	Manchester U	84	Aston Villa	74	Norwich C	72
1993–94	Manchester U	92	Blackburn R	84	Newcastle U	77
1994–95	Blackburn R	89	Manchester U	88	Nottingham F	77

Maximum points: 114

1995–96	Manchester U	82	Newcastle U	78	Liverpool	71
1996–97	Manchester U	75	Newcastle U*	68	Arsenal*	68
1997–98	Arsenal	78	Manchester U	77	Liverpool	65
1998–99	Manchester U	79	Arsenal	78	Chelsea	75
1999–00	Manchester U	91	Arsenal	73	Leeds U	69
2000–01	Manchester U	80	Arsenal	70	Liverpool	69
2001–02	Arsenal	87	Liverpool	80	Manchester U	77
2002–03	Manchester U	83	Arsenal	78	Newcastle U	69
2003–04	Arsenal	90	Chelsea	79	Manchester U	75
2004–05	Chelsea	95	Arsenal	83	Manchester U	77
2005–06	Chelsea	91	Manchester U	83	Liverpool	82
2006–07	Manchester U	89	Chelsea	83	Liverpool*	68
2007–08	Manchester U	87	Chelsea	85	Arsenal	83
2008–09	Manchester U	90	Liverpool	86	Chelsea	83

FOOTBALL LEAGUE CHAMPIONSHIP

Maximum points: 138

2004–05	Sunderland	94	Wigan Ath	87	Ipswich T††	85
2005–06	Reading	106	Sheffield U	90	Watford	81
2006–07	Sunderland	88	Birmingham C	86	Derby Co	84
2007–08	WBA	81	Stoke C	79	Hull C	75
2008–09	Wolverhampton W	90	Birmingham C	83	Sheffield U††	80

DIVISION 1

Maximum points: 138

1992–93	Newcastle U	96	West Ham U*	88	Portsmouth††	88
1993–94	Crystal Palace	90	Nottingham F	83	Millwall††	74
1994–95	Middlesbrough	82	Reading††	79	Bolton W	77
1995–96	Sunderland	83	Derby Co	79	Crystal Palace††	75
1996–97	Bolton W	98	Barnsley	80	Wolverhampton W††	76
1997–98	Nottingham F	94	Middlesbrough	91	Sunderland††	90
1998–99	Sunderland	105	Bradford C	87	Ipswich T††	86
1999–00	Charlton Ath	91	Manchester C	89	Ipswich T	87
2000–01	Fulham	101	Blackburn R	91	Bolton W	87
2001–02	Manchester C	99	WBA	89	Wolverhampton W††	86
2002–03	Portsmouth	98	Leicester C	92	Sheffield U††	80
2003–04	Norwich C	94	WBA	86	Sunderland††	79

FOOTBALL LEAGUE CHAMPIONSHIP 1

Maximum points: 138

2004–05	Luton T	98	Hull C	86	Tranmere R††	79
2005–06	Southend U	82	Colchester U	79	Brentford††	76
2006–07	Scunthorpe U	91	Bristol C	85	Blackpool	83
2007–08	Swansea C	92	Nottingham F	82	Doncaster R	80
2008–09	Leicester C	96	Peterborough U	89	Milton Keynes D††	87

DIVISION 2
Maximum points: 138

	First	Pts	Second	Pts	Third	Pts
1992–93	Stoke C	93	Bolton W	90	Port Vale††	89
1993–94	Reading	89	Port Vale	88	Plymouth Arg††	85
1994–95	Birmingham C	89	Brentford††	85	Crewe Alex††	83
1995–96	Swindon T	92	Oxford U	83	Blackpool††	82
1996–97	Bury	84	Stockport Co	82	Luton T††	78
1997–98	Watford	88	Bristol C	85	Grimsby T	72
1998–99	Fulham	101	Walsall	87	Manchester C	82
1999–00	Preston NE	95	Burnley	88	Gillingham	85
2000–01	Millwall	93	Rotherham U	91	Reading††	86
2001–02	Brighton & HA	90	Reading	84	Brentford*††	83
2002–03	Wigan Ath	100	Crewe Alex	86	Bristol C††	83
2003–04	Plymouth Arg	90	QPR	83	Bristol C††	82

FOOTBALL LEAGUE CHAMPIONSHIP 2
Maximum points: 138

		Pts		Pts		Pts
2004–05	Yeovil T	83	Scunthorpe U*	80	Swansea C	80
2005–06	Carlisle U	86	Northampton T	83	Leyton Orient	81
2006–07	Walsall	89	Hartlepool U	88	Swindon T	85
2007–08	Milton Keynes D	97	Peterborough U	92	Hereford U	88
2008–09	Brentford	85	Exeter C	79	Wycombe W*	78

DIVISION 3
Maximum points: 126

1992–93	Cardiff C	83	Wrexham	80	Barnet	79
1993–94	Shrewsbury T	79	Chester C	74	Crewe Alex	73
1994–95	Carlisle U	91	Walsall	83	Chesterfield	81

Maximum points: 138

1995–96	Preston NE	86	Gillingham	83	Bury	79
1996–97	Wigan Ath*	87	Fulham	87	Carlisle U	84
1997–98	Notts Co	99	Macclesfield T	82	Lincoln C	75
1998–99	Brentford	85	Cambridge U	81	Cardiff C	80
1999–00	Swansea C	85	Rotherham U	84	Northampton T	82
2000–01	Brighton & HA	92	Cardiff C	82	Chesterfield¶	80
2001–02	Plymouth Arg	102	Luton T	97	Mansfield T	79
2002–03	Rushden & D	87	Hartlepool U	85	Wrexham	84
2003–04	Doncaster R	92	Hull C	88	Torquay U*	81

* Won or placed on goal average (ratio)/goal difference.
†† Not promoted after play-offs. ¶ 9 pts deducted for irregularities.

FOOTBALL LEAGUE
Maximum points: a 44; b 60

1888–89a	Preston NE	40	Aston Villa	29	Wolverhampton W	28
1889–90a	Preston NE	33	Everton	31	Blackburn R	27
1890–91a	Everton	29	Preston NE	27	Notts Co	26
1891–92b	Sunderland	42	Preston NE	37	Bolton W	36

DIVISION 1 to 1991–92
Maximum points: a 44; b 52; c 60; d 68; e 76; f 84; g 126; h 120; k 114.

1892–93c	Sunderland	48	Preston NE	37	Everton	36
1893–94c	Aston Villa	44	Sunderland	38	Derby Co	36
1894–95c	Sunderland	47	Everton	42	Aston Villa	39

	First	Pts	Second	Pts	Third	Pts
1895–96c	Aston Villa	45	Derby Co	41	Everton	39
1896–97c	Aston Villa	47	Sheffield U*	36	Derby Co	36
1897–98c	Sheffield U	42	Sunderland	37	Wolverhampton W*	35
1898–99d	Aston Villa	45	Liverpool	43	Burnley	39
1899–1900d	Aston Villa	50	Sheffield U	48	Sunderland	41
1900–01d	Liverpool	45	Sunderland	43	Notts Co	40
1901–02d	Sunderland	44	Everton	41	Newcastle U	37
1902–03d	The Wednesday	42	Aston Villa*	41	Sunderland	41
1903–04d	The Wednesday	47	Manchester C	44	Everton	43
1904–05d	Newcastle U	48	Everton	47	Manchester C	46
1905–06e	Liverpool	51	Preston NE	47	The Wednesday	44
1906–07e	Newcastle U	51	Bristol C	48	Everton*	45
1907–08e	Manchester U	52	Aston Villa*	43	Manchester C	43
1908–09e	Newcastle U	53	Everton	46	Sunderland	44
1909–10e	Aston Villa	53	Liverpool	48	Blackburn R*	45
1910–11e	Manchester U	52	Aston Villa	51	Sunderland*	45
1911–12e	Blackburn R	49	Everton	46	Newcastle U	44
1912–13e	Sunderland	54	Aston Villa	50	Sheffield W	49
1913–14e	Blackburn R	51	Aston Villa	44	Middlesbrough*	43
1914–15e	Everton	46	Oldham Ath	45	Blackburn R*	43
1919–20f	WBA	60	Burnley	51	Chelsea	49
1920–21f	Burnley	59	Manchester C	54	Bolton W	52
1921–22f	Liverpool	57	Tottenham H	51	Burnley	49
1922–23f	Liverpool	60	Sunderland	54	Huddersfield T	53
1923–24f	Huddersfield T*	57	Cardiff C	57	Sunderland	53
1924–25f	Huddersfield T	58	WBA	56	Bolton W	55
1925–26f	Huddersfield T	57	Arsenal	52	Sunderland	48
1926–27f	Newcastle U	56	Huddersfield T	51	Sunderland	49
1927–28f	Everton	53	Huddersfield T	51	Leicester C	48
1928–29f	Sheffield W	52	Leicester C	51	Aston Villa	50
1929–30f	Sheffield W	60	Derby Co	50	Manchester C*	47
1930–31f	Arsenal	66	Aston Villa	59	Sheffield W	52
1931–32f	Everton	56	Arsenal	54	Sheffield W	50
1932–33f	Arsenal	58	Aston Villa	54	Sheffield W	51
1933–34f	Arsenal	59	Huddersfield T	56	Tottenham H	49
1934–35f	Arsenal	58	Sunderland	54	Sheffield W	49
1935–36f	Sunderland	56	Derby Co*	48	Huddersfield T	48
1936–37f	Manchester C	57	Charlton Ath	54	Arsenal	52
1937–38f	Arsenal	52	Wolverhampton W	51	Preston NE	49
1938–39f	Everton	59	Wolverhampton W	55	Charlton Ath	50
1946–47f	Liverpool	57	Manchester U*	56	Wolverhampton W	56
1947–48f	Arsenal	59	Manchester U*	52	Burnley	52
1948–49f	Portsmouth	58	Manchester U*	53	Derby Co	53
1949–50f	Portsmouth*	53	Wolverhampton W	53	Sunderland	52
1950–51f	Tottenham H	60	Manchester U	56	Blackpool	50
1951–52f	Manchester U	57	Tottenham H*	53	Arsenal	53
1952–53f	Arsenal*	54	Preston NE	54	Wolverhampton W	51
1953–54f	Wolverhampton W	57	WBA	53	Huddersfield T	51
1954–55f	Chelsea	52	Wolverhampton W*	48	Portsmouth*	48
1955–56f	Manchester U	60	Blackpool*	49	Wolverhampton W	49
1956–57f	Manchester U	64	Tottenham H*	56	Preston NE	56
1957–58f	Wolverhampton W	64	Preston NE	59	Tottenham H	51
1958–59f	Wolverhampton W	61	Manchester U	55	Arsenal*	50
1959–60f	Burnley	55	Wolverhampton W	54	Tottenham H	53

	First	Pts	Second	Pts	Third	Pts
1960–61f	Tottenham H	66	Sheffield W	58	Wolverhampton W	57
1961–62f	Ipswich T	56	Burnley	53	Tottenham H	52
1962–63f	Everton	61	Tottenham H	55	Burnley	54
1963–64f	Liverpool	57	Manchester U	53	Everton	52
1964–65f	Manchester U*	61	Leeds U	61	Chelsea	56
1965–66f	Liverpool	61	Leeds U*	55	Burnley	55
1966–67f	Manchester U	60	Nottingham F*	56	Tottenham H	56
1967–68f	Manchester C	58	Manchester U	56	Liverpool	55
1968–69f	Leeds U	67	Liverpool	61	Everton	57
1969–70f	Everton	66	Leeds U	57	Chelsea	55
1970–71f	Arsenal	65	Leeds U	64	Tottenham H*	52
1971–72f	Derby Co	58	Leeds U*	57	Liverpool*	57
1972–73f	Liverpool	60	Arsenal	57	Leeds U	53
1973–74f	Leeds U	62	Liverpool	57	Derby Co	48
1974–75f	Derby Co	53	Liverpool*	51	Ipswich T	51
1975–76f	Liverpool	60	QPR	59	Manchester U	56
1976–77f	Liverpool	57	Manchester C	56	Ipswich T	52
1977–78f	Nottingham F	64	Liverpool	57	Everton	55
1978–79f	Liverpool	68	Nottingham F	60	WBA	59
1979–80f	Liverpool	60	Manchester U	58	Ipswich T	53
1980–81f	Aston Villa	60	Ipswich T	56	Arsenal	53
1981–82g	Liverpool	87	Ipswich T	83	Manchester U	78
1982–83g	Liverpool	82	Watford	71	Manchester U	70
1983–84g	Liverpool	80	Southampton	77	Nottingham F*	74
1984–85g	Everton	90	Liverpool*	77	Tottenham H	77
1985–86g	Liverpool	88	Everton	86	West Ham U	84
1986–87g	Everton	86	Liverpool	77	Tottenham H	71
1987–88h	Liverpool	90	Manchester U	81	Nottingham F	73
1988–89k	Arsenal*	76	Liverpool	76	Nottingham F	64
1989–90k	Liverpool	79	Aston Villa	70	Tottenham H	63
1990–91k	Arsenal†	83	Liverpool	76	Crystal Palace	69
1991–92g	Leeds U	82	Manchester U	78	Sheffield W	75

No official competition during 1915–19 and 1939–46; Regional Leagues operating.
* Won or placed on goal average (ratio)/goal difference.
† 2 pts deducted

DIVISION 2 to 1991–92

Maximum points: a 44; b 56; c 60; d 68; e 76; f 84; g 126; h 132; k 138.

1892–93a	Small Heath	36	Sheffield U	35	Darwen	30
1893–94b	Liverpool	50	Small Heath	42	Notts Co	39
1894–95c	Bury	48	Notts Co	39	Newton Heath*	38
1895–96c	Liverpool*	46	Manchester C	46	Grimsby T*	42
1896–97c	Notts Co	42	Newton Heath	39	Grimsby T	38
1897–98c	Burnley	48	Newcastle U	45	Manchester C	39
1898–99d	Manchester C	52	Glossop NE	46	Leicester Fosse	45
1899–1900d	The Wednesday	54	Bolton W	52	Small Heath	46
1900–01d	Grimsby T	49	Small Heath	48	Burnley	44
1901–02d	WBA	55	Middlesbrough	51	Preston NE*	42
1902–03d	Manchester C	54	Small Heath	51	Woolwich A	48
1903–04d	Preston NE	50	Woolwich A	49	Manchester U	48
1904–05d	Liverpool	58	Bolton W	56	Manchester U	53
1905–06e	Bristol C	66	Manchester U	62	Chelsea	53
1906–07e	Nottingham F	60	Chelsea	57	Leicester Fosse	48
1907–08e	Bradford C	54	Leicester Fosse	52	Oldham Ath	50

127

	First	Pts	Second	Pts	Third	Pts
1908–09e	Bolton W	52	Tottenham H*	51	WBA	51
1909–10e	Manchester C	54	Oldham Ath*	53	Hull C*	53
1910–11e	WBA	53	Bolton W	51	Chelsea	49
1911–12e	Derby Co*	54	Chelsea	54	Burnley	52
1912–13e	Preston NE	53	Burnley	50	Birmingham	46
1913–14e	Notts Co	53	Bradford PA*	49	Woolwich A	49
1914–15e	Derby Co	53	Preston NE	50	Barnsley	47
1919–20f	Tottenham H	70	Huddersfield T	64	Birmingham	56
1920–21f	Birmingham*	58	Cardiff C	58	Bristol C	51
1921–22f	Nottingham F	56	Stoke C*	52	Barnsley	52
1922–23f	Notts Co	53	West Ham U*	51	Leicester C	51
1923–24f	Leeds U	54	Bury*	51	Derby Co	51
1924–25f	Leicester C	59	Manchester U	57	Derby Co	55
1925–26f	Sheffield W	60	Derby Co	57	Chelsea	52
1926–27f	Middlesbrough	62	Portsmouth*	54	Manchester C	54
1927–28f	Manchester C	59	Leeds U	57	Chelsea	54
1928–29f	Middlesbrough	55	Grimsby T	53	Bradford PA*	48
1929–30f	Blackpool	58	Chelsea	54	Oldham Ath	53
1930–31f	Everton	61	WBA	54	Tottenham H	51
1931–32f	Wolverhampton W	56	Leeds U	54	Stoke C	52
1932–33f	Stoke C	56	Tottenham H	55	Fulham	50
1933–34f	Grimsby T	59	Preston NE	52	Bolton W*	51
1934–35f	Brentford	61	Bolton W*	56	West Ham U	56
1935–36f	Manchester U	56	Charlton Ath	55	Sheffield U*	52
1936–37f	Leicester C	56	Blackpool	55	Bury	52
1937–38f	Aston Villa	57	Manchester U*	53	Sheffield U	53
1938–39f	Blackburn R	55	Sheffield U	54	Sheffield W	53
1946–47f	Manchester C	62	Burnley	58	Birmingham C	55
1947–48f	Birmingham C	59	Newcastle U	56	Southampton	52
1948–49f	Fulham	57	WBA	56	Southampton	55
1949–50f	Tottenham H	61	Sheffield W*	52	Sheffield U*	52
1950–51f	Preston NE	57	Manchester C	52	Cardiff C	50
1951–52f	Sheffield W	53	Cardiff C*	51	Birmingham C	51
1952–53f	Sheffield U	60	Huddersfield T	58	Luton T	52
1953–54f	Leicester C*	56	Everton	56	Blackburn R	55
1954–55f	Birmingham C*	54	Luton T*	54	Rotherham U	54
1955–56f	Sheffield W	55	Leeds U	52	Liverpool*	48
1956–57f	Leicester C	61	Nottingham F	54	Liverpool	53
1957–58f	West Ham U	57	Blackburn R	56	Charlton Ath	55
1958–59f	Sheffield W	62	Fulham	60	Sheffield U*	53
1959–60f	Aston Villa	59	Cardiff C	58	Liverpool*	50
1960–61f	Ipswich T	59	Sheffield U	58	Liverpool	52
1961–62f	Liverpool	62	Leyton Orient	54	Sunderland	53
1962–63f	Stoke C	53	Chelsea*	52	Sunderland	52
1963–64f	Leeds U	63	Sunderland	61	Preston NE	56
1964–65f	Newcastle U	57	Northampton T	56	Bolton W	50
1965–66f	Manchester C	59	Southampton	54	Coventry C	53
1966–67f	Coventry C	59	Wolverhampton W	58	Carlisle U	52
1967–68f	Ipswich T	59	QPR*	58	Blackpool	58
1968–69f	Derby Co	63	Crystal Palace	56	Charlton Ath	50
1969–70f	Huddersfield T	60	Blackpool	53	Leicester C	51
1970–71f	Leicester C	59	Sheffield U	56	Cardiff C*	53
1971–72f	Norwich C	57	Birmingham C	56	Millwall	55
1972–73f	Burnley	62	QPR	61	Aston Villa	50

	First	Pts	Second	Pts	Third	Pts
1973–74f	Middlesbrough	65	Luton T	50	Carlisle U	49
1974–75f	Manchester U	61	Aston Villa	58	Norwich C	53
1975–76f	Sunderland	56	Bristol C*	53	WBA	53
1976–77f	Wolverhampton W	57	Chelsea	55	Nottingham F	52
1977–78f	Bolton W	58	Southampton	57	Tottenham H*	56
1978–79f	Crystal Palace	57	Brighton & HA*	56	Stoke C	56
1979–80f	Leicester C	55	Sunderland	54	Birmingham C*	53
1980–81f	West Ham U	66	Notts Co	53	Swansea C*	50
1981–82g	Luton T	88	Watford	80	Norwich C	71
1982–83g	QPR	85	Wolverhampton W	75	Leicester C	70
1983–84g	Chelsea*	88	Sheffield W	88	Newcastle U	80
1984–85g	Oxford U	84	Birmingham C	82	Manchester C	74
1985–86g	Norwich C	84	Charlton Ath	77	Wimbledon	76
1986–87g	Derby Co	84	Portsmouth	78	Oldham Ath††	75
1987–88h	Millwall	82	Aston Villa*	78	Middlesbrough	78
1988–89k	Chelsea	99	Manchester C	82	Crystal Palace	81
1989–90k	Leeds U*	85	Sheffield U	85	Newcastle U††	80
1990–91k	Oldham Ath	88	West Ham U	87	Sheffield W	82
1991–92k	Ipswich T	84	Middlesbrough	80	Derby Co	78

No official competition during 1915–19 and 1939–46; Regional Leagues operating.
* Won or placed on goal average (ratio)/goal difference.
†† Not promoted after play-offs.

DIVISION 3 to 1991–92
Maximum points: 92; 138 from 1981–82.

1958–59	Plymouth Arg	62	Hull C	61	Brentford*	57
1959–60	Southampton	61	Norwich C	59	Shrewsbury T*	52
1960–61	Bury	68	Walsall	62	QPR	60
1961–62	Portsmouth	65	Grimsby T	62	Bournemouth*	59
1962–63	Northampton T	62	Swindon T	58	Port Vale	54
1963–64	Coventry C*	60	Crystal Palace	60	Watford	58
1964–65	Carlisle U	60	Bristol C*	59	Mansfield T	59
1965–66	Hull C	69	Millwall	65	QPR	57
1966–67	QPR	67	Middlesbrough	55	Watford	54
1967–68	Oxford U	57	Bury	56	Shrewsbury T	55
1968–69	Watford*	64	Swindon T	64	Luton T	61
1969–70	Orient	62	Luton T	60	Bristol R	56
1970–71	Preston NE	61	Fulham	60	Halifax T	56
1971–72	Aston Villa	70	Brighton & HA	65	Bournemouth*	62
1972–73	Bolton W	61	Notts Co	57	Blackburn R	55
1973–74	Oldham Ath	62	Bristol R*	61	York C	61
1974–75	Blackburn R	60	Plymouth Arg	59	Charlton Ath	55
1975–76	Hereford U	63	Cardiff C	57	Millwall	56
1976–77	Mansfield T	64	Brighton & HA	61	Crystal Palace*	59
1977–78	Wrexham	61	Cambridge U	58	Preston NE*	56
1978–79	Shrewsbury T	61	Watford*	60	Swansea C	60
1979–80	Grimsby T	62	Blackburn R	59	Sheffield W	58
1980–81	Rotherham U	61	Barnsley*	59	Charlton Ath	59
1981–82	Burnley*	80	Carlisle U	80	Fulham	78
1982–83	Portsmouth	91	Cardiff C	86	Huddersfield T	82
1983–84	Oxford U	95	Wimbledon	87	Sheffield U*	83
1984–85	Bradford C	94	Millwall	90	Hull C	87
1985–86	Reading	94	Plymouth Arg	87	Derby Co	84
1986–87	Bournemouth	97	Middlesbrough	94	Swindon T	87

	First	Pts	Second	Pts	Third	Pts
1987–88	Sunderland	93	Brighton & HA	84	Walsall	82
1988–89	Wolverhampton W	92	Sheffield U*	84	Port Vale	84
1989–90	Bristol R	93	Bristol C	91	Notts Co	87
1990–91	Cambridge U	86	Southend U	85	Grimsby T*	83
1991–92	Brentford	82	Birmingham C	81	Huddersfield T	78

* Won or placed on goal average (ratio)/goal difference.

DIVISION 4 (1958–1992)
Maximum points: 92; 138 from 1981–82.

	First	Pts	Second	Pts	Third	Pts
1958–59	Port Vale	64	Coventry C*	60	York C	60
1959–60	Walsall	65	Notts Co*	60	Torquay U	60
1960–61	Peterborough U	66	Crystal Palace	64	Northampton T*	60
1961–62†	Millwall	56	Colchester U	55	Wrexham	53
1962–63	Brentford	62	Oldham Ath*	59	Crewe Alex	59
1963–64	Gillingham*	60	Carlisle U	60	Workington	59
1964–65	Brighton & HA	63	Millwall*	62	York C	62
1965–66	Doncaster R*	59	Darlington	59	Torquay U	58
1966–67	Stockport Co	64	Southport*	59	Barrow	59
1967–68	Luton T	66	Barnsley	61	Hartlepools U	60
1968–69	Doncaster R	59	Halifax T	57	Rochdale*	56
1969–70	Chesterfield	64	Wrexham	61	Swansea C	60
1970–71	Notts Co	69	Bournemouth	60	Oldham Ath	59
1971–72	Grimsby T	63	Southend U	60	Brentford	59
1972–73	Southport	62	Hereford U	58	Cambridge U	57
1973–74	Peterborough U	65	Gillingham	62	Colchester U	60
1974–75	Mansfield T	68	Shrewsbury T	62	Rotherham U	59
1975–76	Lincoln C	74	Northampton T	68	Reading	60
1976–77	Cambridge U	65	Exeter C	62	Colchester U*	59
1977–78	Watford	71	Southend U	60	Swansea C*	56
1978–79	Reading	65	Grimsby T*	61	Wimbledon*	61
1979–80	Huddersfield T	66	Walsall	64	Newport Co	61
1980–81	Southend U	67	Lincoln C	65	Doncaster R	56
1981–82	Sheffield U	96	Bradford C*	91	Wigan Ath	91
1982–83	Wimbledon	98	Hull C	90	Port Vale	88
1983–84	York C	101	Doncaster R	85	Reading*	82
1984–85	Chesterfield	91	Blackpool	86	Darlington	85
1985–86	Swindon T	102	Chester C	84	Mansfield T	81
1986–87	Northampton T	99	Preston NE	90	Southend U	80
1987–88	Wolverhampton W	90	Cardiff C	85	Bolton W	78
1988–89	Rotherham U	82	Tranmere R	80	Crewe Alex	78
1989–90	Exeter C	89	Grimsby T	79	Southend U	75
1990–91	Darlington	83	Stockport Co*	82	Hartlepool U	82
1991–92§	Burnley	83	Rotherham U*	77	Mansfield T	77

* Won or placed on goal average (ratio)/goal difference.
†Maximum points: 88 owing to Accrington Stanley's resignation. ††Not promoted after play-offs.
§Maximum points: 126 owing to Aldershot being expelled.

DIVISION 3—SOUTH (1920–1958)
1920–21 Season as Division 3.
Maximum points: a 84; b 92.

	First	Pts	Second	Pts	Third	Pts
1920–21a	Crystal Palace	59	Southampton	54	QPR	53
1921–22a	Southampton*	61	Plymouth Arg	61	Portsmouth	53
1922–23a	Bristol C	59	Plymouth Arg*	53	Swansea T	53

130

	First	Pts	Second	Pts	Third	Pts
1923–24a	Portsmouth	59	Plymouth Arg	55	Millwall	54
1924–25a	Swansea T	57	Plymouth Arg	56	Bristol C	53
1925–26a	Reading	57	Plymouth Arg	56	Millwall	53
1926–27a	Bristol C	62	Plymouth Arg	60	Millwall	56
1927–28a	Millwall	65	Northampton T	55	Plymouth Arg	53
1928–29a	Charlton Ath*	54	Crystal Palace	54	Northampton T*	52
1929–30a	Plymouth Arg	68	Brentford	61	QPR	51
1930–31a	Notts Co	59	Crystal Palace	51	Brentford	50
1931–32a	Fulham	57	Reading	55	Southend U	53
1932–33a	Brentford	62	Exeter C	58	Norwich C	57
1933–34a	Norwich C	61	Coventry C*	54	Reading*	54
1934–35a	Charlton Ath	61	Reading	53	Coventry C	51
1935–36a	Coventry C	57	Luton T	56	Reading	54
1936–37a	Luton T	58	Notts Co	56	Brighton & HA	53
1937–38a	Millwall	56	Bristol C	55	QPR*	53
1938–39a	Newport Co	55	Crystal Palace	52	Brighton & HA	49
1939–46	Competition cancelled owing to war.					
1946–47a	Cardiff C	66	QPR	57	Bristol C	51
1947–48a	QPR	61	Bournemouth	57	Walsall	51
1948–49a	Swansea T	62	Reading	55	Bournemouth	52
1949–50a	Notts Co	58	Northampton T*	51	Southend U	51
1950–51b	Nottingham F	70	Norwich C	64	Reading*	57
1951–52b	Plymouth Arg	66	Reading*	61	Norwich C	61
1952–53b	Bristol R	64	Millwall*	62	Northampton T	62
1953–54b	Ipswich T	64	Brighton & HA	61	Bristol C	56
1954–55b	Bristol C	70	Leyton Orient	61	Southampton	59
1955–56b	Leyton Orient	66	Brighton & HA	65	Ipswich T	64
1956–57b	Ipswich T*	59	Torquay U	59	Colchester U	58
1957–58b	Brighton & HA	60	Brentford*	58	Plymouth Arg	58

* Won or placed on goal average (ratio).

DIVISION 3—NORTH (1921–1958)

Maximum points: a 76; b 84; c 80; d 92.

	First	Pts	Second	Pts	Third	Pts
1921–22a	Stockport Co	56	Darlington*	50	Grimsby T	50
1922–23a	Nelson	51	Bradford PA	47	Walsall	46
1923–24b	Wolverhampton W	63	Rochdale	62	Chesterfield	54
1924–25b	Darlington	58	Nelson*	53	New Brighton	53
1925–26b	Grimsby T	61	Bradford PA	60	Rochdale	59
1926–27b	Stoke C	63	Rochdale	58	Bradford PA	55
1927–28b	Bradford PA	63	Lincoln C	55	Stockport Co	54
1928–29b	Bradford C	63	Stockport Co	62	Wrexham	52
1929–30b	Port Vale	67	Stockport Co	63	Darlington*	50
1930–31b	Chesterfield	58	Lincoln C	57	Wrexham*	54
1931–32c	Lincoln C*	57	Gateshead	57	Chester	50
1932–33b	Hull C	59	Wrexham	57	Stockport Co	54
1933–34b	Barnsley	62	Chesterfield	61	Stockport Co	59
1934–35b	Doncaster R	57	Halifax T	55	Chester	54
1935–36b	Chesterfield	60	Chester*	55	Tranmere R	55
1936–37b	Stockport Co	60	Lincoln C	57	Chester	53
1937–38b	Tranmere R	56	Doncaster R	54	Hull C	53
1938–39b	Barnsley	67	Doncaster R	56	Bradford C	52
1939–46	Competition cancelled owing to war.					
1946–47b	Doncaster R	72	Rotherham U	60	Chester	56
1947–48b	Lincoln C	60	Rotherham U	59	Wrexham	50

	First	*Pts*	*Second*	*Pts*	*Third*	*Pts*
1948–49*b*	Hull C	65	Rotherham U	62	Doncaster R	50
1949–50*b*	Doncaster R	55	Gateshead	53	Rochdale*	51
1950–51*d*	Rotherham U	71	Mansfield T	64	Carlisle U	62
1951–52*d*	Lincoln C	69	Grimsby T	66	Stockport Co	59
1952–53*d*	Oldham Ath	59	Port Vale	58	Wrexham	56
1953–54*d*	Port Vale	69	Barnsley	58	Scunthorpe U	57
1954–55*d*	Barnsley	65	Accrington S	61	Scunthorpe U*	58
1955–56*d*	Grimsby T	68	Derby Co	63	Accrington S	59
1956–57*d*	Derby Co	63	Hartlepools U	59	Accrington S*	58
1957–58*d*	Scunthorpe U	66	Accrington S	59	Bradford C	57

* *Won or placed on goal average (ratio).*

PROMOTED AFTER PLAY-OFFS

(Not accounted for in previous section)

1986–87 Aldershot to Division 3.

1987–88 Swansea C to Division 3.

1988–89 Leyton Orient to Division 3.

1989–90 Cambridge U to Division 3; Notts Co to Division 2; Sunderland to Division 1.

1990–91 Notts Co to Division 1; Tranmere R to Division 2; Torquay U to Division 3.

1991–92 Blackburn R to Premier League; Peterborough U to Division 1.

1992–93 Swindon T to Premier League; WBA to Division 1; York C to Division 2.

1993–94 Leicester C to Premier League; Burnley to Division 1; Wycombe W to Division 2.

1994–95 Huddersfield T to Division 1.

1995–96 Leicester C to Premier League; Bradford C to Division 1; Plymouth Arg to Division 2.

1996–97 Crystal Palace to Premier League; Crewe Alex to Division 1; Northampton T to Division 2.

1997–98 Charlton Ath to Premier League; Colchester U to Division 2.

1998–99 Watford to Premier League; Scunthorpe to Division 2.

1999–00 Peterborough U to Division 2.

2000–01 Walsall to Division 1; Blackpool to Division 2.

2001–02 Birmingham C to Premier League; Stoke C to Division 1; Cheltenham T to Division 2.

2002–03 Wolverhampton W to Premier League; Cardiff C to Division 1; Bournemouth to Division 2.

2003–04 Crystal Palace to Premier League; Brighton & HA to Division 1; Huddersfield T to Division 2.

2004–05 West Ham U to Premier League; Sheffield W to Football League Championship, Southend U to Football League Championship 1.

2005–06 Watford to Premier League; Barnsley to Football League Championship; Cheltenham T to Football League Championship 1.

2006–07 Derby Co to Premier League; Blackpool to Football League Championship; Bristol R to Football League Championship 1.

2007–08 Hull C to Premier League; Doncaster R to Football League Championship; Stockport Co to Football League Championship 1.

2008–09 Burnley to Premier League; Scunthorpe U to Championship; Gillingham to Championship 1.

RELEGATED CLUBS

FA PREMIER LEAGUE TO DIVISION 1

1992–93	Crystal Palace, Middlesbrough, Nottingham F
1993–94	Sheffield U, Oldham Ath, Swindon T
1994–95	Crystal Palace, Norwich C, Leicester C, Ipswich T
1995–96	Manchester C, QPR, Bolton W
1996–97	Sunderland, Middlesbrough, Nottingham F
1997–98	Bolton W, Barnsley, Crystal Palace
1998–99	Charlton Ath, Blackburn R, Nottingham F
1999–90	Wimbledon, Sheffield W, Watford
2000–01	Manchester C, Coventry C, Bradford C
2001–02	Ipswich T, Derby Co, Leicester C
2002–03	West Ham U, WBA, Sunderland
2003–04	Leicester C, Leeds U, Wolverhampton W

FA PREMIER LEAGUE TO FOOTBALL LEAGUE CHAMPIONSHIP

2004–05	Crystal Palace, Norwich C, Southampton
2005–06	Birmingham C, WBA, Sunderland
2006–07	Sheffield U, Charlton Ath, Watford
2007–08	Reading, Birmingham C, Derby Co
2008–09	Newcastle U, Middlesbrough, WBA

DIVISION 1 TO DIVISION 2

1898–99	Bolton W and Sheffield W	1931–32	Grimsby T and West Ham U
1899–1900	Burnley and Glossop	1932–33	Bolton W and Blackpool
1900–01	Preston NE and WBA	1933–34	Newcastle U and Sheffield U
1901–02	Small Heath and Manchester C	1934–35	Leicester C and Tottenham H
1902–03	Grimsby T and Bolton W	1935–36	Aston Villa and Blackburn R
1903–04	Liverpool and WBA	1936–37	Manchester U and Sheffield W
1904–05	League extended. Bury and Notts Co, two bottom clubs in First Division, re-elected.	1937–38	Manchester C and WBA
		1938–39	Birmingham C and Leicester C
		1946–47	Brentford and Leeds U
1905–06	Nottingham F and Wolverhampton W	1947–48	Blackburn R and Grimsby T
		1948–49	Preston NE and Sheffield U
1906–07	Derby Co and Stoke C	1949–50	Manchester C and Birmingham C
1907–08	Bolton W and Birmingham C	1950–51	Sheffield W and Everton
1908–09	Manchester C and Leicester Fosse	1951–52	Huddersfield T and Fulham
1909–10	Bolton W and Chelsea	1952–53	Stoke C and Derby Co
1910–11	Bristol C and Nottingham F	1953–54	Middlesbrough and Liverpool
1911–12	Preston NE and Bury	1954–55	Leicester C and Sheffield W
1912–13	Notts Co and Woolwich Arsenal	1955–56	Huddersfield T and Sheffield U
1913–14	Preston NE and Derby Co	1956–57	Charlton Ath and Cardiff C
1914–15	Tottenham H and Chelsea*	1957–58	Sheffield W and Sunderland
1919–20	Notts Co and Sheffield W	1958–59	Portsmouth and Aston Villa
1920–21	Derby Co and Bradford PA	1959–60	Luton T and Leeds U
1921–22	Bradford C and Manchester U	1960–61	Preston NE and Newcastle U
1922–23	Stoke C and Oldham Ath	1961–62	Chelsea and Cardiff C
1923–24	Chelsea and Middlesbrough	1962–63	Manchester C and Leyton Orient
1924–25	Preston NE and Nottingham F	1963–64	Bolton W and Ipswich T
1925–26	Manchester C and Notts Co	1964–65	Wolverhampton W and Birmingham C
1926–27	Leeds U and WBA		
1927–28	Tottenham H and Middlesbrough	1965–66	Northampton T and Blackburn R
1928–29	Bury and Cardiff C	1966–67	Aston Villa and Blackpool
1929–30	Burnley and Everton	1967–68	Fulham and Sheffield U
1930–31	Leeds U and Manchester U	1968–69	Leicester C and QPR

1969–70	Sunderland and Sheffield W	1987–88	Chelsea**, Portsmouth, Watford, Oxford U
1970–71	Burnley and Blackpool		
1971–72	Huddersfield T and Nottingham F	1988–89	Middlesbrough, West Ham U, Newcastle U
1972–73	Crystal Palace and WBA		
1973–74	Southampton, Manchester U, Norwich C	1989–90	Sheffield W, Charlton Ath, Millwall
1974–75	Luton T, Chelsea, Carlisle U	1990–91	Sunderland and Derby Co
1975–76	Wolverhampton W, Burnley, Sheffield U	1991–92	Luton T, Notts Co, West Ham U
		1992–93	Brentford, Cambridge U, Bristol R
1976–77	Sunderland, Stoke C, Tottenham H	1993–94	Birmingham C, Oxford U, Peterborough U
1977–78	West Ham U, Newcastle U, Leicester C	1994–95	Swindon T, Burnley, Bristol C, Notts Co
1978–79	QPR, Birmingham C, Chelsea		
1979–80	Bristol C, Derby Co, Bolton W	1995–96	Millwall, Watford, Luton T
1980–81	Norwich C, Leicester C, Crystal Palace	1996–97	Grimsby T, Oldham Ath, Southend U
1981–82	Leeds U, Wolverhampton W, Middlesbrough	1997–98	Manchester C, Stoke C, Reading
		1998–99	Bury, Oxford U, Bristol C
1982–83	Manchester C, Swansea C, Brighton & HA	1999–00	Walsall, Port Vale, Swindon T
		2000–01	Huddersfield T, QPR, Tranmere R
1983–84	Birmingham C, Notts Co, Wolverhampton W	2001–02	Crewe Alex, Barnsley, Stockport Co
1984–85	Norwich C, Sunderland, Stoke C		
1985–86	Ipswich T, Birmingham C, WBA	2002–03	Sheffield W, Brighton & HA, Grimsby T
1986–87	Leicester C, Manchester C, Aston Villa	2003–04	Walsall, Bradford C, Wimbledon

**Relegated after play-offs.*
Subsequently re-elected to Division 1 when League was extended after the War.

FOOTBALL LEAGUE CHAMPIONSHIP
TO FOOTBALL LEAGUE CHAMPIONSHIP 1

2004–05	Gillingham, Nottingham F, Rotherham U
2005–06	Crewe Alex, Millwall, Brighton & HA
2006–07	Southend U, Luton T, Leeds U
2007–08	Leicester C, Scunthorpe U, Colchester U
2008–09	Norwich C, Southampton, Charlton Ath

DIVISION 2 TO DIVISION 3

1920–21	Stockport Co	1936–37	Doncaster R and Bradford C
1921–22	Bradford PA and Bristol C	1937–38	Barnsley and Stockport Co
1922–23	Rotherham Co and Wolverhampton W	1938–39	Norwich C and Tranmere R
		1946–47	Swansea T and Newport Co
1923–24	Nelson and Bristol C	1947–48	Doncaster R and Millwall
1924–25	Crystal Palace and Coventry C	1948–49	Nottingham F and Lincoln C
1925–26	Stoke C and Stockport Co	1949–50	Plymouth Arg and Bradford PA
1926–27	Darlington and Bradford C	1950–51	Grimsby T and Chesterfield
1927–28	Fulham and South Shields	1951–52	Coventry C and QPR
1928–29	Port Vale and Clapton Orient	1952–53	Southampton and Barnsley
1929–30	Hull C and Notts Co	1953–54	Brentford and Oldham Ath
1930–31	Reading and Cardiff C	1954–55	Ipswich T and Derby Co
1931–32	Barnsley and Bristol C	1955–56	Plymouth Arg and Hull C
1932–33	Chesterfield and Charlton Ath	1956–57	Port Vale and Bury
1933–34	Millwall and Lincoln C	1957–58	Doncaster R and Notts Co
1934–35	Oldham Ath and Notts Co	1958–59	Barnsley and Grimsby T
1935–36	Port Vale and Hull C	1959–60	Bristol C and Hull C

1960–61 Lincoln C and Portsmouth	1987–88 Huddersfield T, Reading, Sheffield U**
1961–62 Brighton & HA and Bristol R	1988–89 Shrewsbury T, Birmingham C, Walsall
1962–63 Walsall and Luton T	
1963–64 Grimsby T and Scunthorpe U	1989–90 Bournemouth, Bradford C, Stoke C
1964–65 Swindon T and Swansea T	
1965–66 Middlesbrough and Leyton Orient	1990–91 WBA and Hull C
1966–67 Northampton T and Bury	1991–92 Plymouth Arg, Brighton & HA, Port Vale
1967–68 Plymouth Arg and Rotherham U	
1968–69 Fulham and Bury	1992–93 Preston NE, Mansfield T, Wigan Ath, Chester C
1969–70 Preston NE and Aston Villa	
1970–71 Blackburn R and Bolton W	1993–94 Fulham, Exeter C, Hartlepool U, Barnet
1971–72 Charlton Ath and Watford	
1972–73 Huddersfield T and Brighton & HA	1994–95 Cambridge U, Plymouth Arg, Cardiff C, Chester C, Leyton Orient
1973–74 Crystal Palace, Preston NE, Swindon T	
	1995–96 Carlisle U, Swansea C, Brighton & HA, Hull C
1974–75 Millwall, Cardiff C, Sheffield W	
1975–76 Oxford U, York C, Portsmouth	1996–97 Peterborough U, Shrewsbury T, Rotherham U, Notts Co
1976–77 Carlisle U, Plymouth Arg, Hereford U	
	1997–98 Brentford, Plymouth Arg, Carlisle U, Southend U
1977–78 Blackpool, Mansfield T, Hull C	
1978–79 Sheffield U, Millwall, Blackburn R	1998–99 York C, Northampton T, Lincoln C, Macclesfield T
1979–80 Fulham, Burnley, Charlton Ath	1999–00 Cardiff C, Blackpool, Scunthorpe U, Chesterfield
1980–81 Preston NE, Bristol C, Bristol R	
1981–82 Cardiff C, Wrexham, Orient	2000–01 Bristol R, Luton T, Swansea C, Oxford U
1982–83 Rotherham U, Burnley, Bolton W	
1983–84 Derby Co, Swansea C, Cambridge U	2001–02 Bournemouth, Bury, Wrexham, Cambridge U
	2002–03 Cheltenham T, Huddersfield T, Mansfield T, Northampton T
1984–85 Notts Co, Cardiff C, Wolverhampton W	
1985–86 Carlisle U, Middlesbrough, Fulham	2003–04 Grimsby T, Rushden & D, Notts Co, Wycombe W
1986–87 Sunderland**, Grimsby T, Brighton & HA	

FOOTBALL LEAGUE CHAMPIONSHIP 1
TO FOOTBALL LEAGUE CHAMPIONSHIP 2

2004–05 Torquay U, Wrexham, Peterborough U, Stockport Co
2005–06 Hartlepool U, Milton Keynes D, Swindon T, Walsall
2006–07 Chesterfield, Bradford C, Rotherham U, Brentford
2007–08 Bournemouth, Gillingham, Port Vale, Luton T
2008–09 Northampton T, Crewe Alex, Cheltenham T, Hereford U

DIVISION 3 TO DIVISION 4

1958–59 Rochdale, Notts Co, Doncaster R, Stockport Co	1964–65 Luton T, Port Vale, Colchester U, Barnsley
1959–60 Accrington S, Wrexham, Mansfield T, York C	1965–66 Southend U, Exeter C, Brentford, York C
1960–61 Chesterfield, Colchester U, Bradford C, Tranmere R	1966–67 Doncaster R, Workington, Darlington, Swansea T
1961–62 Newport Co, Brentford, Lincoln C, Torquay U	1967–68 Scunthorpe U, Colchester U, Grimsby T, Peterborough U (demoted)
1962–63 Bradford PA, Brighton & HA, Carlisle U, Halifax T	
	1968–69 Oldham Ath, Crewe Alex, Hartlepool, Northampton T
1963–64 Millwall, Crewe Alex, Wrexham, Notts Co	

1969–70	Bournemouth, Southport, Barrow, Stockport Co
1970–71	Reading, Bury, Doncaster R, Gillingham
1971–72	Mansfield T, Barnsley, Torquay U, Bradford C
1972–73	Rotherham U, Brentford, Swansea C, Scunthorpe U
1973–74	Cambridge U, Shrewsbury T, Southport, Rochdale
1974–75	Bournemouth, Tranmere R, Watford, Huddersfield T
1975–76	Aldershot, Colchester U, Southend U, Halifax T
1976–77	Reading, Northampton T, Grimsby T, York C
1977–78	Port Vale, Bradford C, Hereford U, Portsmouth
1978–79	Peterborough U, Walsall, Tranmere R, Lincoln C
1979–80	Bury, Southend U, Mansfield T, Wimbledon
1980–81	Sheffield U, Colchester U, Blackpool, Hull C
1981–82	Wimbledon, Swindon T, Bristol C, Chester
1982–83	Reading, Wrexham, Doncaster R, Chesterfield
1983–84	Scunthorpe U, Southend U, Port Vale, Exeter C
1984–85	Burnley, Orient, Preston NE, Cambridge U
1985–86	Lincoln C, Cardiff C, Wolverhampton W, Swansea C
1986–87	Bolton W**, Carlisle U, Darlington, Newport Co
1987–88	Doncaster R, York C, Grimsby T, Rotherham U**
1988–89	Southend U, Chesterfield, Gillingham, Aldershot
1989–90	Cardiff C, Northampton T, Blackpool, Walsall
1990–91	Crewe Alex, Rotherham U, Mansfield T
1991–92	Bury, Shrewsbury T, Torquay U, Darlington

*Relegated after play-offs.

LEAGUE STATUS FROM 1986–1987

	RELEGATED FROM LEAGUE	PROMOTED TO LEAGUE
1986–87	Lincoln C	Scarborough
1987–88	Newport Co	Lincoln C
1988–89	Darlington	Maidstone U
1989–90	Colchester U	Darlington
1990–91	—	Barnet
1991–92	—	Colchester U
1992–93	Halifax T	Wycombe W
1993–94	—	—
1994–95	—	—
1995–96	—	—
1996–97	Hereford U	Macclesfield T
1997–98	Doncaster R	Halifax T
1998–99	Scarborough	Cheltenham T
1999–2000	Chester C	Kidderminster H
2000–01	Barnet	Rushden & D
2001–02	Halifax T	Boston U
2002–03	Shrewsbury T, Exeter C	Yeovil T, Doncaster R
2003–04	Carlisle U, York C	Chester C, Shrewsbury T
2004–05	Kidderminster H, Cambridge U	Barnet, Carlisle U
2005–06	Oxford U, Rushden & D	Accrington S, Hereford U
2006–07	Boston U, Torquay U	Dagenham & R, Morecambe
2007–08	Mansfield T, Wrexham	Aldershot T, Exeter C
2008–09	Chester C, Luton T	Burton Alb, Torquay U

LEAGUE TITLE WINS

FA PREMIER LEAGUE – Manchester U 11, Arsenal 3, Chelsea 2, Blackburn R 1.

FOOTBALL LEAGUE CHAMPIONSHIP – Sunderland 2, Reading 1, WBA 1, Wolverhampton W 1.

LEAGUE DIVISION 1 – Liverpool 18, Arsenal 10, Everton 9, Sunderland 8, Aston Villa 7, Manchester U 7, Newcastle U 5, Sheffield W 4. Huddersfield T 3, Leeds U 3, Manchester C 3, Portsmouth 3, Wolverhampton W 3, Blackburn R 2, Burnley 2, Derby Co 2, Nottingham F 2, Preston NE 2, Tottenham H 2; Bolton W, Charlton Ath, Chelsea, Crystal Palace, Fulham, Ipswich T, Middlesbrough, Norwich C, Sheffield U, WBA 1 each.

FOOTBALL LEAGUE CHAMPIONSHIP 1 – Leicester C 1, Luton T 1, Scunthorpe U 1, Southend U 1, Swansea C 1.

LEAGUE DIVISION 2 – Leicester C 6, Manchester C 6, Birmingham C (one as Small Heath) 5, Sheffield W 5, Derby Co 4, Liverpool 4, Preston NE 4, Ipswich T 3, Leeds U 3, Middlesbrough 3, Notts Co 3, Stoke C 3, Aston Villa 2, Bolton W 2, Burnley 2, Bury 2, Chelsea 2, Fulham 2, Grimsby T 2, Manchester U 2, Millwall 2, Norwich C 2, Nottingham F 2, Tottenham H 2, WBA 2, West Ham U 2, Wolverhampton W 2; Blackburn R, Blackpool, Bradford C, Brentford, Brighton & HA, Bristol C, Coventry C, Crystal Palace, Everton, Huddersfield T, Luton T, Newcastle U, Plymouth Arg, QPR, Oldham Ath, Oxford U, Reading, Sheffield U, Sunderland, Swindon T, Watford, Wigan Ath 1 each.

FOOTBALL LEAGUE CHAMPIONSHIP 2 – Brentford 1, Carlisle U 1, Milton Keynes D 1, Walsall 1, Yeovil T 1.

LEAGUE DIVISION 3 – Brentford 2, Carlisle U 2, Oxford U 2, Plymouth Arg 2, Portsmouth 2, Preston NE 2, Shrewsbury T 2; Aston Villa, Blackburn R, Bolton W, Bournemouth, Bradford C, Brighton & HA, Bristol R, Burnley, Bury, Cambridge U, Cardiff C, Coventry C, Doncaster R, Grimsby T, Hereford U, Hull C, Leyton Orient, Mansfield T, Northampton T, Notts Co, Oldham Ath, QPR, Reading, Rotherham U, Rushden & D, Southampton, Sunderland, Swansea C, Watford, Wigan Ath, Wolverhampton W, Wrexham 1 each.

LEAGUE DIVISION 4 – Chesterfield 2, Doncaster R 2, Peterborough U 2; Brentford, Brighton & HA, Burnley, Cambridge U, Darlington, Exeter C, Gillingham, Grimsby T, Huddersfield T, Lincoln C, Luton T, Mansfield T, Millwall, Northampton T, Notts Co, Port Vale, Reading, Rotherham U, Sheffield U, Southend U, Southport, Stockport Co, Swindon T, Walsall, Watford, Wimbledon, Wolverhampton W, York C 1 each.

DIVISION 3 (South) – Bristol C 3, Charlton Ath 2, Ipswich T 2, Millwall 2, Notts Co 2, Plymouth Arg 2, Swansea T 2; Brentford, Brighton & HA, Bristol R, Cardiff C, Coventry C, Crystal Palace, Fulham, Leyton Orient, Luton T, Newport Co, Norwich C, Nottingham F, Portsmouth, QPR, Reading, Southampton 1 each.

DIVISION 3 (North) – Barnsley 3, Doncaster R 3, Lincoln C 3, Chesterfield 2, Grimsby T 2, Hull C 2, Port Vale 2, Stockport Co 2; Bradford C, Bradford PA, Darlington, Derby Co, Nelson, Oldham Ath, Rotherham U, Scunthorpe U, Stoke C, Tranmere R, Wolverhampton W 1 each.

FOOTBALL LEAGUE PLAY-OFFS 2008–2009

■ *Denotes player sent off.*

CHAMPIONSHIP FIRST LEG

Preston NE	(1) 1	Sheffield U	(0) 1
Burnley	(0) 1	Reading	(0) 0

CHAMPIONSHIP SECOND LEG

Sheffield U	(0) 1	Preston NE	(0) 0
Reading	(0) 0	Burnley	(0) 2

CHAMPIONSHIP FINAL Sunday, 24 May 2009 *(at Wembley)*   80,518

Burnley (1) 1 *(Elliott 13)*

Sheffield U (0) 0

Burnley: Jensen; Duff, Kalvenes, McCann (Gudjonsson), Caldwell, Carlisle, Alexander, Thompson (Rodriguez), Blake (Eagles), Paterson, Elliott.
Sheffield U: Kenny; Walker, Naughton, Montgomery, Morgan, Kilgallon, Halford, Cotterill (Ward■), Beattie, Howard (Lupoli), Quinn (Hendrie).
Referee: M. Dean (Wirral).

LEAGUE 1 FIRST LEG

Scunthorpe U	(1) 1	Milton Keynes D	(1) 1
Millwall	(0) 1	Leeds U	(0) 0

LEAGUE 1 SECOND LEG

Leeds U	(0) 1	Millwall	(0) 1
Milton Keynes D	(0) 0	Scunthorpe U	(0) 0

(aet; Scunthorpe U won 7-6 on penalties.)

LEAGUE 1 FINAL Sunday, 24 May 2009 *(at Wembley)*   59,661

Millwall (2) 2 *(Alexander 37, 39)*

Scunthorpe U (1) 3 *(Sparrow 6, 70, Woolford 85)*

Millwall: Forde; Dunne, Craig, Bolder, Whitbread, Frampton (Robinson P), Grabban (Hackett), Abdou (Laird), Alexander, Harris, Martin.
Scunthorpe U: Murphy; Byrne, Morris, McCann, Mirfin, Crosby, Sparrow, Togwell (Trotter), Hayes, Hooper (Forte), Woolford.
Referee: M. Oliver (Northumberland).

LEAGUE 2 FIRST LEG

Rochdale	(0) 0	Gillingham	(0) 0
Shrewsbury T	(0) 0	Bury	(0) 1

LEAGUE 2 SECOND LEG

Bury	(0) 0	Shrewsbury T	(0) 1

(aet; Shrewsbury T won 4-3 on penalties.)

Gillingham	(1) 2	Rochdale	(1) 1

LEAGUE 2 FINAL Saturday, 23 May 2009 *(at Wembley)*   53,706

Gillingham (0) 1 *(Jackson 90)*

Shrewsbury T (0) 0

Gillingham: Royce; Fuller, Nutter, Weston, King, Richards, Wright, Barcham, Jackson, Oli, Lewis.
Shrewsbury T: Daniels; Moss, Ashton, Davies, Coughlan, Langmead, Humphrey (Ashikodi), Murray (Worrall), Chadwick (Riza), Holt, McIntyre.
Referee: C. Oliver (Northumberland).

LEAGUE ATTENDANCES 2008–2009

FA BARCLAYCARD PREMIERSHIP ATTENDANCES

	Average Gate			Season 2008–09	
	2007–08	2008–09	+/–%	Highest	Lowest
Arsenal	60,070	60,040	–0.05	60,109	59,317
Aston Villa	40,029	39,812	–0.54	42,585	35,134
Blackburn Rovers	23,944	23,479	–1.94	28,389	17,606
Bolton Wanderers	20,901	22,486	+7.58	26,021	19,884
Chelsea	41,397	41,589	+0.46	43,417	40,290
Everton	36,955	35,667	–3.49	39,574	31,063
Fulham	23,774	24,344	+2.40	25,661	22,259
Hull City	18,025	24,816	+37.68	24,945	24,282
Liverpool	43,532	43,611	+0.18	44,424	41,169
Manchester City	42,126	42,899	+1.83	47,331	36,635
Manchester United	75,691	75,304	–0.51	75,569	73,917
Middlesbrough	26,708	28,429	+6.44	33,767	24,020
Newcastle United	51,321	48,750	–5.01	52,114	44,567
Portsmouth	19,914	19,830	–0.42	20,540	18,111
Stoke City	16,823	26,960	+60.26	27,500	25,287
Sunderland	43,344	40,168	–7.33	47,936	35,222
Tottenham Hotspur	35,967	35,929	–0.11	36,183	35,507
West Bromwich Albion	22,311	25,828	+15.76	26,344	24,741
West Ham United	34,601	33,701	–2.60	34,958	30,842
Wigan Athletic	19,046	18,350	–3.65	22,954	14,169

FOOTBALL LEAGUE CHAMPIONSHIP ATTENDANCES

	Average Gate			Season 2008–09	
	2007–08	2008–09	+/–%	Highest	Lowest
Barnsley	11,425	13,189	+15.4	19,681	10,678
Birmingham City	26,181	19,090	–27.1	25,935	15,330
Blackpool	8,861	7,843	–11.5	9,643	6,648
Bristol City	16,276	16,816	+3.3	18,456	15,304
Burnley	12,365	13,082	+5.8	18,005	10,032
Cardiff City	13,939	18,044	+29.4	20,156	15,902
Charlton Athletic	23,191	20,894	–9.9	24,553	19,215
Coventry City	19,123	17,451	–8.7	22,637	14,621
Crystal Palace	16,031	15,220	–5.1	22,824	12,847
Derby County	32,432	29,440	–9.2	33,079	25,534
Doncaster Rovers	7,978	11,964	+50.0	14,823	9,534
Ipswich Town	21,935	20,961	–4.4	28,274	17,749
Norwich City	24,527	24,543	+0.1	25,487	23,225
Nottingham Forest	19,964	22,299	+11.7	29,140	17,568
Plymouth Argyle	13,000	11,533	–11.3	15,197	9,203
Preston North End	12,647	13,426	+6.2	21,273	10,558
Queens Park Rangers	13,959	14,090	+0.9	17,120	12,286
Reading	23,585	19,942	–15.4	24,011	16,514
Sheffield United	25,631	26,023	+1.5	30,786	23,045
Sheffield Wednesday	21,418	21,542	+0.6	30,658	14,792
Southampton	21,254	17,858	–16.0	27,228	13,257
Swansea City	13,520	15,195	+12.4	18,053	11,442
Watford	16,876	14,858	–12.0	16,386	13,193
Wolverhampton Wanderers	23,499	24,153	+2.8	28,252	21,326

Premiership and Football League attendance averages and highest crowd figures for 2008–09 are unofficial.

FOOTBALL LEAGUE CHAMPIONSHIP 1 ATTENDANCES

	Average Gate			Season 2008–09	
	2007–08	2008–09	+/–%	Highest	Lowest
Brighton & Hove Albion	5,937	6,092	+2.6	8,618	5,035
Bristol Rovers	6,850	7,171	+4.7	10,293	5,870
Carlisle United	7,835	6,268	–20.0	12,148	4,223
Cheltenham Town	4,310	3,854	–10.6	5,726	2,845
Colchester United	5,509	5,084	–7.7	9,559	3,179
Crewe Alexandra	4,932	4,537	–8.0	7,138	3,432
Hartlepool United	4,507	3,835	–14.9	6,402	3,033
Hereford United	3,421	3,270	–4.4	6,120	2,033
Huddersfield Town	9,391	13,298	+41.6	20,928	9,294
Leeds United	26,543	23,815	–10.3	34,214	18,847
Leicester City	23,509	20,253	–13.9	30,542	16,378
Leyton Orient	5,210	4,692	–9.9	6,951	3,381
Millwall	8,691	8,940	+2.9	13,261	6,685
Milton Keynes Dons	9,456	10,551	+11.6	17,717	6,931
Northampton Town	5,409	5,200	–3.9	7,028	4,402
Oldham Athletic	5,326	5,636	+5.8	8,901	3,745
Peterborough United	5,995	7,599	+26.8	14,110	4,876
Scunthorpe United	6,434	4,998	–22.3	8,315	3,423
Southend United	8,173	7,850	–4.0	10,241	6,028
Stockport County	5,643	6,130	+8.6	10,273	4,790
Swindon Town	7,170	7,499	+4.6	13,001	6,002
Tranmere Rovers	6,504	5,820	–10.5	8,700	4,535
Walsall	5,620	4,572	–18.6	8,920	3,549
Yeovil Town	5,468	4,423	–19.1	6,580	3,275

FOOTBALL LEAGUE CHAMPIONSHIP 2 ATTENDANCES

	Average Gate			Season 2008–09	
	2007–08	2008–09	+/–%	Highest	Lowest
Accrington Stanley	1,634	1,414	–13.5	3,012	1,033
Aldershot Town	3,031	3,276	+8.1	5,023	2,090
Barnet	2,147	2,153	+0.3	3,133	1,332
AFC Bournemouth	5,504	4,931	–10.4	9,008	3,068
Bradford City	13,569	12,704	–7.0	14,038	11,908
Brentford	4,469	5,707	+27.7	10,642	3,733
Bury	2,601	3,342	+28.5	7,589	2,068
Chester City	2,479	1,972	–20.5	3,349	1,235
Chesterfield	4,103	3,449	–15.9	4,951	2,451
Dagenham & Redbridge	2,007	2,048	+2.0	4,791	1,302
Darlington	3,818	2,932	–23.2	3,868	2,180
Exeter City	3,705	4,939	+33.3	8,544	2,839
Gillingham	6,077	5,307	–12.7	8,360	4,029
Grimsby Town	4,115	4,475	+8.7	7,095	2,644
Lincoln City	4,078	3,940	–3.4	6,156	2,478
Luton Town	6,492	6,019	–7.3	7,149	5,248
Macclesfield Town	2,298	1,898	–17.4	2,556	1,182
Morecambe	2,812	2,153	–23.4	4,546	1,253
Notts County	4,732	4,446	–6.0	6,686	2,886
Port Vale	4,417	5,522	+25.0	7,273	4,090
Rochdale	3,057	3,222	+5.4	5,500	2,162
Rotherham United	4,201	3,587	–14.6	6,184	2,078
Shrewsbury Town	5,659	5,664	+0.1	7,162	4,134
Wycombe Wanderers	4,747	5,109	+7.6	9,625	3,713

TRANSFERS 2008–2009

	From	To
JUNE 2008		
24 Carden, Paul A.	Accrington Stanley	Cambridge United
30 Duguid, Karl	Colchester United	Plymouth Argyle
27 Hoolahan, Wesley	Blackpool	Norwich City
6 Hughes, Jeffrey	Crystal Palace	Bristol Rovers
24 Hume, Iain	Leicester City	Barnsley
24 Legzdins, Adam R.	Birmingham City	Crewe Alexandra
3 Lockwood, Matthew D.	Nottingham Forest	Colchester United
18 McAuley, Gareth	Leicester City	Ipswich Town
12 McCarthy, Patrick	Charlton Athletic	Crystal Palace
4 Moore, Luke	Aston Villa	West Bromwich Albion
2 Muamba, Fabrice	Birmingham City	Bolton Wanderers
27 Paterson, Martin	Scunthorpe United	Burnley
29 Perry, Christopher J.	Luton Town	Southampton
10 Ramsey, Aaron J.	Cardiff City	Arsenal
4 Stockdale, David A.	Darlington	Fulham
28 Vokes, Samuel M.	AFC Bournemouth	Wolverhampton Wanderers
18 Westwood, Keiren	Carlisle United	Coventry City
16 Wood, Samuel J.	Bromley	Brentford
30 Zola, Calvin	Tranmere Rovers	Crewe Alexandra
JULY 2008		
18 Andrew, Calvin H.	Luton Town	Crystal Palace
30 Ashton, Nathan	Fulham	Wycombe Wanderers
25 Baker, Carl P.	Morecambe	Stockport County
23 Bell, David A.	Luton Town	Norwich City
8 Bent, Marcus N.	Charlton Athletic	Birmingham City
31 Bentley, David M.	Blackburn Rovers	Tottenham Hotspur
17 Boateng, George	Middlesbrough	Hull City
1 Carle, Nicholas A.	Bristol City	Crystal Palace
18 Carson, Scott P.	Liverpool	West Bromwich Albion
29 Cattermole, Lee B.	Middlesbrough	Wigan Athletic
28 Chimbonda, Pascal	Tottenham Hotspur	Sunderland
31 Cotterill, David	Wigan Athletic	Sheffield United
11 Craig, Tony A.	Crystal Palace	Millwall
14 Cresswell, Ryan	Sheffield United	Bury
11 Crouch, Peter J.	Liverpool	Portsmouth
3 Davies, Curtis E.	West Bromwich Albion	Aston Villa
25 Diagouraga, Toumani	Watford	Hereford United
1 Dickinson, Liam	Stockport County	Derby County
29 Diouf, El Hadji O.	Bolton Wanderers	Sunderland
22 Dodds, Louis	Leicester City	Port Vale
11 Duffy, Darryl A.	Swansea City	Bristol Rovers
2 Eastwood, Freddy	Wolverhampton Wanderers	Coventry City
24 Elding, Anthony L.	Leeds United	Crewe Alexandra
2 Fagan, Craig	Derby County	Hull City
18 Forecast, Tommy S.	Tottenham Hotspur	Southampton
8 Friedel, Bradley H.	Blackburn Rovers	Aston Villa
25 Garner, Joseph A.	Carlisle United	Nottingham Forest
1 Gillespie, Steven	Cheltenham Town	Colchester United
1 Grant, Joel V.	Aldershot Town	Crewe Alexandra
24 Guthrie, Danny S.	Liverpool	Newcastle United
22 Halmosi, Peter	Plymouth Argyle	Hull City
24 Henderson, Darius A.	Watford	Sheffield United
18 Hooper, Gary	Southend United	Scunthorpe United
11 Hulse, Robert W.	Sheffield United	Derby County
15 Iwelumo, Chris	Charlton Athletic	Wolverhampton Wanderers
17 Jean-Baptiste, Alex	Mansfield Town	Blackpool
29 Jones, David F.L.	Derby County	Wolverhampton Wanderers
24 Kapo, Narcisse O.	Birmingham City	Wigan Athletic
29 Keane, Robert D.	Tottenham Hotspur	Liverpool
8 Kitson, David	Reading	Stoke City
21 Lisbie, Kevin	Colchester United	Ipswich Town
9 MacDonald, Charles L.	Southend United	Brentford

141

7 Martin, Joseph J.	Tottenham Hotspur	Blackpool
4 Martin, Russell K.A.	Wycombe Wanderers	Peterborough United
4 Moore, Darren M.	Derby County	Barnsley
9 Morgan, Marvin	Woking	Aldershot Town
3 Morrison, Michael B.	Cambridge United	Leicester City
29 Olofinjana, Seyi G.	Wolverhampton Wanderers	Stoke City
18 Pantsil, John	West Ham United	Fulham
11 Perkins, David	Rochdale	Colchester United
4 Puncheon, Jason D.I.	Barnet	Plymouth Argyle
29 Roberts, Gary M.	Ipswich Town	Huddersfield Town
28 Robinson, Paul W.	Tottenham Hotspur	Blackburn Rovers
8 Shaw, Jon S.	FC Halifax Town	Rochdale
10 Sidwell, Steven J.	Chelsea	Aston Villa
2 Stearman, Richard	Leicester City	Wolverhampton Wanderers
18 Stefanovic, Dejan	Fulham	Norwich City
28 Tainio, Teemu	Tottenham Hotspur	Sunderland
22 Thomas, Simon	Boreham Wood	Crystal Palace
14 Torres, Sergio R.	Wycombe Wanderers	Peterborough United
17 Warner, Anthony R.	Fulham	Hull City
7 Williams, Gavin J.	Ipswich Town	Bristol City
1 Williams, Marvin T.	Yeovil Town	Brentford
21 Wright, Richard I.	West Ham United	Ipswich Town
16 Zamora, Robert L.	West Ham United	Fulham

TEMPORARY TRANSFERS

2 Anderson, Paul – Liverpool – Nottingham Forest; 25 Antwi–Birago, Godwin – Liverpool – Tranmere Rovers; 22 Bailey, Matthew – Wolverhampton Wanderers – Burton Albion; 22 Beardsley, Jason C. – Derby County – Notts County; 29 Bennett, Elliott – Wolverhampton Wanderers – Bury; 8 Bertrand, Ryan D. – Chelsea – Norwich City; 24 Brandy, Febian E. – Manchester United – Swansea City; 25 Bridges, Michael – Hull City – Carlisle United; 1 Charles, Wesley D.D. – Brentford – Ebbsfleet United; 28 Clarke, Andre N.J.E. – Blackburn Rovers – Accrington Stanley; 22 Cole, Jake S. – Queens Park Rangers – Oxford United; 18 Constable, James A. – Shrewsbury Town – Oxford United; 23 Davies, Scott – Reading – Aldershot Town; 4 Dawkins, Simon J. – Tottenham Hotspur – Leyton Orient; 28 Gall, Kevin A. – Carlisle United – Lincoln City; 31 Gardner, Anthony – Tottenham Hotspur – Hull City; 10 Gilbert, Kerrea K. – Arsenal – Leicester City; 29 Grocott, Marc D. – Stoke City – Alfreton Town; 26 Guy, Jamie – Colchester United – Oxford United; 17 Haldane, Lewis O. – Bristol Rovers – Oxford United; 3 Halford, Gregory – Sunderland – Sheffield United; 1 Hamer, Ben – Reading – Brentford; 26 Hammill, Adam J. – Liverpool – Blackpool; 25 Hobbs, Jack – Liverpool – Leicester City; 22 Howe, Jermaine R. – Peterborough United – Morecambe; 11 Kabba, Steven – Watford – Blackpool; 14 Livermore, Jake – Tottenham Hotspur – Crewe Alexandra; 5 Mills, Leigh – Tottenham Hotspur – Brentford; 10 Morgan, Paul M.T. – Bury – Macclesfield Town; 18 Omozusi, Elliott – Fulham – Norwich City; 25 Phillips, James P. – Stoke City – Alfreton Town; 31 Poke, Michael H. – Southampton – Torquay United; 19 Randolph, Darren E. – Charlton Athletic – Hereford United; 31 Rehman, Zeshan – Queens Park Rangers – Blackpool; 21 Richards, Matthew – Ipswich Town – Brighton & Hove Albion; 1 Sahar, Ben – Chelsea – Portsmouth; 5 Smith, James D. – Chelsea – Sheffield Wednesday; 24 Starosta, Ben M. – Sheffield United – Aldershot Town; 4 Taylor, Paul T. – Vauxhall Motors – Chester City; 23 Thorley, Thomas R. – Stoke City – Stafford Rangers; 30 Threlfall, Robert R. – Liverpool – Hereford United; 29 Walker, Richard M. – Bristol Rovers – Shrewsbury Town

AUGUST 2008

4 Ameobi, Oluwatomiwo	Leeds United	Doncaster Rovers
28 Andrews, Keith J.	Milton Keynes Dons	Blackburn Rovers
26 Armstrong, Christopher	Sheffield United	Reading
14 Bailey, Nicholas F.	Southend United	Charlton Athletic
19 Barker, Christopher A.	Queens Park Rangers	Plymouth Argyle
4 Ben–Haim, Tal	Chelsea	Manchester City
8 Betsy, Kevin	Bristol City	Southend United
5 Bothroyd, Jay	Wolverhampton Wanderers	Cardiff City
8 Canham, Sean	Team Bath	Notts County
5 Chambers, James	Leicester City	Doncaster Rovers
29 Connell, Alan J.	Brentford	AFC Bournemouth
22 Craney, Ian T.W.	Accrington Stanley	Huddersfield Town
5 Davies, Andrew	Southampton	Stoke City
19 Diagne Faye, Abdoulaye	Newcastle United	Stoke City
6 Eagles, Christopher M.	Manchester United	Burnley

7 Edwards, Robert O.	Wolverhampton Wanderers	Blackpool
15 Faye, Amdy M.	Charlton Athletic	Stoke City
8 Fenton, Nicholas L.	Grimsby Town	Rotherham United
27 Ferdinand, Anton J.	West Ham United	Sunderland
21 Gardner, Anthony	Tottenham Hotspur	Hull City
1 Gorkss, Kaspars	Blackpool	Queens Park Rangers
27 Green, Dominic A.	Dagenham & Redbridge	Peterborough United
8 Guyett, Scott B.	Yeovil Town	Bournemouth
19 Gyepes, Gabor	Northampton Town	Cardiff City
21 Healy, David J.	Fulham	Sunderland
21 Hoyte, Justin R.	Arsenal	Middlesbrough
30 Jalal, Shwan S.	Peterborough United	AFC Bournemouth
7 Johnson, Andrew	Everton	Fulham
12 Kaboul, Younes	Tottenham Hotspur	Portsmouth
22 Keogh, Richard J.	Bristol City	Carlisle United
1 Malbranque, Steed	Tottenham Hotspur	Sunderland
15 Marshall, Mark	Eastleigh	Swindon Town
8 Maynard, Nicholas D.	Crewe Alexandra	Bristol City
10 Meite, Abdoulaye	Bolton Wanderers	West Bromwich Albion
1 Mills, Matthew C.	Manchester City	Doncaster Rovers
29 Milner, James P.	Newcastle United	Aston Villa
13 Mirfin, David	Huddersfield Town	Scunthorpe United
14 Noone, Craig	Southport	Plymouth Argyle
20 Osei-Kuffour, Jonathan	AFC Bournemouth	Bristol Rovers
30 Pulis, Anthony J.	Stoke City	Southampton
15 Rigby, Lloyd J.	Vauxhall Motors	Stockport County
8 Shittu, Daniel O.	Watford	Bolton Wanderers
8 Shorey, Nicholas	Reading	Aston Villa
21 Silvestre, Mikael S.	Manchester United	Arsenal
29 Sonko, Ibrahima	Reading	Stoke City
1 Sorensen, Thomas	Aston Villa	Stoke City
20 Thomas, Jerome W.	Charlton Athletic	Portsmouth
15 Togwell, Samuel J.	Barnsley	Scunthorpe United
7 Walton, Simon W.	Queens Park Rangers	Plymouth Argyle
29 Weston, Curtis J.	Leeds United	Gillingham
14 Walford, Martyn P.	York City	Scunthorpe United
1 Williams, Ashley E.	Stockport County	Swansea City
29 Wright-Phillips, Shaun C.	Chelsea	Manchester City
8 Young, Luke P.	Middlesbrough	Aston Villa

TEMPORARY TRANSFERS

8 Aluko, Sone – Birmingham City – Blackpool; 27 Anderson, Russell – Sunderland – Burnley; 15 Araba, Hakeem A.C. – Dagenham & Redbridge – Thurrock – ; 8 Archibald–Henville, Troy – Tottenham Hotspur – Norwich City; 7 Artus, Frankie – Bristol City – Brentford; 5 Ashikodi, Moses – Watford – Hereford United; 22 Ashworth, Luke A. – Wigan Athletic – Leyton Orient; 22 Bailey, Matthew – Wolverhampton Wanderers – Burton Albion; 13 Baker, Lee – West Bromwich Albion – Kidderminster Harriers; 19 Barazite, Nacer – Arsenal – Derby County; 9 Barker, Christopher A. – Queens Park Rangers – Plymouth Argyle; 22 Bayliss, Ashton P. – Blackpool – Fleetwood Town; 21 Beardsley, Jason C. – Derby County – Notts County; 7 Begovic, Asmir – Portsmouth – Yeovil Town; 28 Bellamy, Adrian R. – Bradford City – Salford City; 8 Bennett, Alan J. – Reading – Brentford; 22 Black, Paul – Oldham Athletic – Barrow; 9 Bouazza, Hameur – Fulham – Charlton Athletic; 15 Boyce, Andrew T. – Doncaster Rovers – Worksop Town; 2 Brown, Simon J. – Brentford – Darlington; 5 Camara, Mohamed – Derby County – Blackpool; 8 Cathcart, Craig G. – Manchester United – Plymouth Argyle; 28 Church, Simon R. – Reading – Wycombe Wanderers; 28 Clarke, William C. – Ipswich Town – Darlington; 15 Clough, Charlie – Bristol Rovers – Mangotsfield United; 1 Collins, Lee H. – Wolverhampton Wanderers – Port Vale; 6 Cook, Lee – Fulham – Queens Park Rangers; 21 Cork, Jack F.P. – Chelsea – Southampton; 4 Cummings, Shaun M. – Chelsea – Milton Keynes Dons; 26 Daniels, Charlie – Tottenham Hotspur – Gillingham; 13 Daniels, Luke – West Bromwich Albion – Shrewsbury Town; 26 Dayton, James F. – Crystal Palace – Yeovil Town; 15 Dean, Harle J. – Dagenham & Redbridge – Dagenham & Redbridge; 19 Dickinson, Liam – Derby County – Huddersfield Town; 15 Erskine, Emmanuel J. – Dagenham & Redbridge – Redbridge; 15 Evans, Scott – Swansea City – Port Talbot Town; 29 Fogden, Wesley K. – Brighton & Hove Albion – Dorchester Town; 5 Fraser, James – Bristol Rovers – Lewes; 29 Gallagher, Paul – Blackburn Rovers – Plymouth Argyle; 11 Gamble, Patrick J. – Nottingham Forest – Mansfield Town; 8 Gargan, Sam J. – Brighton & Hove Albion – Havant & Waterlooville; 8 Gatting, Joe

143

S. – Brighton & Hove Albion – Bognor Regis Town; 8 Gleeson, Stephen M. – Wolverhampton Wanderers – Stockport County; 15 Graves, Kyle N. – Swansea City – Neath; 14 Groves, Matt – Bristol Rovers – Tiverton Town; 8 Harding, Daniel A. – Ipswich Town – Southend United; 12 Hardman, Lewis – Darlington – Sunderland Nissan; 22 Harris, Harry – Walsall – Chasetown; 27 Hatch, Liam M.A. – Peterborough United – Darlington; 14 Hayles, Barrington – Leicester City – Cheltenham Town; 8 Henry, Rhys E. – Southend United – Thurrock; 5 Heslop, Simon – Barnsley – Grimsby Town; 1 Jalal, Shwan S. – Peterborough United – AFC Bournemouth; 26 Johnson, Edward – Fulham – Cardiff City; 20 Jones, Christopher T. – Swansea City – Cambridge United; 8 Kandol, Tresor O. – Leeds United – Millwall; 14 King, Marlon F. – Wigan Athletic – Hull City; 8 Klein–Davies, Joshua – Bristol Rovers – Luton Town; 5 Koroma, Omar A. – Portsmouth – Norwich City; 7 Krysiak, Artur L. – Birmingham City – York City; 29 Lee, Alan D. – Ipswich Town – Crystal Palace; 22 Lindfield, Craig A. – Liverpool – AFC Bournemouth; 22 Little, Mark D. – Wolverhampton Wanderers – Northampton Town; 20 Logan, Conrad – Leicester City – Luton Town; 22 Louis, Kane T. – Brighton & Hove Albion – Burgess Hill Town; 13 Mahdi, Adam – Bristol Rovers – Cirencester Town; 7 Martin, Christopher – Norwich City – Luton Town; 7 Martin, David E. – Liverpool – Leicester City; 27 Martin, Lee R. – Manchester United – Nottingham Forest; 12 Martin, Neil J. – Exeter City – Hayes & Yeading United; 18 McDonald, Clayton – Manchester City – Macclesfield Town; 21 McMahon – Anthony – Middlesbrough – Sheffield Wednesday; 26 Mills, Leigh – Tottenham Hotspur – Gillingham; 29 Mitchell, Paul A. – Milton Keynes Dons – Barnet; 8 Moncur, Thomas J. – Fulham – Bradford City; 29 Moore, Karl – Manchester City – Millwall; 28 Morgan, Dean – Luton Town – Leyton Orient; 30 Morgan, Kerry D. – Swansea City – Neath; 15 Morrison, Stefan – Swansea City – Port Talbot Town; 15 Myrie–Williams, Jennison – Bristol City – Cheltenham Town; 22 Nelthorpe, Craig R. – Doncaster Rovers – Gateshead; 30 Parkin, Jonathan – Stoke City – Preston North End; 19 Pearce, Krystian M.V. – Birmingham City – Scunthorpe United; 27 Pekhart, Tomas – Tottenham Hotspur – Southampton; 21 Pidgeley, Leonard J. – Millwall – Woking; 7 Plummer, Tristan D. – Bristol City – Luton Town; 1 Potter, Alfie – Peterborough United – Kettering Town; 7 Puddy, Willem J.S. – Cheltenham Town – Tamworth; 14 Pugh, Andrew J. – Gillingham – Folkestone Invicta; 15 Rasiak, Grzegorz – Southampton – Watford; 8 Reay, Shaun – Darlington – Harrogate Town; 8 Rigby, Lloyd J. – Vauxhall Motors – Stockport County; 8 Rigters, Maceo – Blackburn Rovers – Barnsley; 22 Roberts, Gary S. – Crewe Alexandra – Yeovil Town; 21 Robson–Kanu, Thomas H. – Reading – Southend United; 12 Sappleton, Reneil – Leicester City – AFC Bournemouth; 18 Sawyer, Lee T. – Chelsea – Southend United; 14 Scott, Mark J. – Swindon Town – Thatcham Town; 29 Shotton, Ryan – Stoke City – Tranmere Rovers; 5 Simpson, Daniel P. – Manchester United – Blackburn Rovers; 21 Sinclair, Dean M. – Charlton Athletic – Cheltenham Town; 7 Spillane, Michael – Norwich City – Luton Town; 1 Spring, Matthew – Luton Town – Sheffield United; 21 Starosta, Ben M. – Sheffield United – Aldershot Town; 29 Taiwo, Thomas – Chelsea – Port Vale; 15 Teale, Gary – Derby County – Barnsley; 15 Thomas, Aswad – Charlton Athletic – Barnet; 15 Thomas, Jerome W. – Charlton Athletic – Portsmouth; 21 Thorley, Thomas R. – Stoke City – Stafford Rangers; 20 Thurgood, Stuart A. – Gillingham – Grays Athletic; 6 Todd, Simon – Darlington – Blyth Spartans; 21 Traore, Armand – Arsenal – Portsmouth; 29 Vipond, Shaun – Carlisle United – Workington; 28 Volz, Moritz – Fulham – Ipswich Town; 21 Wagstaff, Scott A. – Charlton Athletic – AFC Bournemouth; 13 Walker, Lance D. – Tooting & Mitcham United; 1 Wallace, Ross – Sunderland – Preston North End; 21 Ward, Joel E.P. – Portsmouth – AFC Bournemouth; 7 Warlow, Owain J. – Swansea City – Lincoln City – Kettering Town; 6 Weston, Curtis J. – Leeds United – Gillingham; 7 Wilson, James S. – Bristol City – Brentford; 22 Worrall, David – West Bromwich Albion – Accrington Stanley; 28 Yates, Adam P. – Morecambe – Burton Albion

SEPTEMBER 2008

1 Akinde, John	Ebbsfleet United	Bristol City
1 Berbatov, Dimitar	Tottenham Hotspur	Manchester United
1 Brayford, John R.	Burton Albion	Crewe Alexandra
1 Bunn, Mark	Northampton Town	Blackburn Rovers
1 Corluka, Vedran	Manchester City	Tottenham Hotspur
1 Elliott, Stephen W.	Wolverhampton Wanderers	Preston North End
1 Etuhu, Dixon P.	Sunderland	Fulham
1 Friend, George	Exeter City	Wolverhampton Wanderers
1 Harrold, Matthew	Southend United	Wycombe Wanderers
1 Higginbotham, Daniel J.	Sunderland	Stoke City
1 Hill, Matthew C.	Preston North End	Wolverhampton Wanderers
1 Lee, Alan D.	Ipswich Town	Crystal Palace
1 McCartney, George	West Ham United	Sunderland
1 Nash, Carlo J.	Wigan Athletic	Everton
1 Owusu, Lloyd	Yeovil Town	Cheltenham Town

1 Parkin, Jonathan	Stoke City	Preston North End
1 Saha, Louis	Manchester United	Everton
1 Shackell, Jason	Norwich City	Wolverhampton Wanderers
1 Soares, Thomas J.	Crystal Palace	Stoke City
15 Stead, Jonathan	Sheffield United	Ipswich Town
1 Thompson, Steven H.	Cardiff City	Burnley
1 Tonge, Michael W.	Sheffield United	Stoke City

TEMPORARY TRANSFERS

1 Alaile, Michael – Dagenham & Redbridge – Fisher Athletic; 25 Ameobi, Oluwatomiwo – Doncaster Rovers – Grimsby Town; 11 Anyinsah, Joseph G. – Preston North End – Brighton & Hove Albion; 12 Arestidou, Andreas J. – Blackburn Rovers – Nantwich Town; 9 Artus, Frankie – Bristol City – Brentford; 27 Ashworth, Luke A. – Wigan Athletic – Leyton Orient; 1 Baker, Lee – West Bromwich Albion – Kidderminster Harriers; 25 Barcham, Andrew – Tottenham Hotspur – Gillingham; 26 Bayliss, Ashton P. – Blackpool – Fleetwood Town; 26 Beattie, Craig – West Bromwich Albion – Crystal Palace; 23 Beavan, George D. – Luton Town – Salisbury City; 1 Bennett, Alan J. – Reading – Brentford; 23 Bevan, David – Aston Villa – Tamworth; 25 Bevan, Scott A. – Shrewsbury Town – Torquay United; 5 Blackmore, David – West Ham United – Thurrock; 18 Boden, Luke – Sheffield Wednesday – Chesterfield; 1 Bore, Peter – Grimsby Town – York City; 25 Borrowdale, Gary I. – Coventry City – Colchester United; 16 Botham, Calum – Wycombe Wanderers – Basingstoke Town; 19 Bradley, Jason – Darlington – Buxton; 18 Brown, Lee J. – Queens Park Rangers – AFC Hornchurch; 19 Bryant, Mitchell J. – Reading – Basingstoke Town; 19 Button, David R. – Tottenham Hotspur – Grays Athletic; 9 Camara, Mohamed – Derby County – Blackpool; 1 Campbell, Fraizer L. – Manchester United – Tottenham Hotspur; 1 Carr, Michael A. – Morecambe – Northwich Victoria; 16 Cartman, Nathan – Leeds United – Harrogate Railway; 30 Charge, Daniel – Dagenham & Redbridge – Potters Bar Town; 1 Christophe, Jean F. – Portsmouth – Southend United; 18 Clohessy, Seán D. – Gillingham – Salisbury City; 15 Clough, Charlie – Bristol Rovers – Mangotsfield United; 18 Cook, Anthony L.E. – Dagenham & Redbridge – Concord Rangers; 1 Cranie, Martin J. – Portsmouth – Charlton Athletic; 18 Diallo, Drissa – Milton Keynes Dons – Cheltenham Town; 19 Dickinson, Liam – Derby County – Huddersfield Town; 24 Dixon, Jonathan J. – Brighton & Hove Albion – Grays Athletic; 26 Dyer, Nathan A.J. – Southampton – Sheffield United; 26 Easter, Jermaine – Plymouth Argyle – Millwall; 19 Ennis, Paul – Stockport County – Salford City; 25 Federici, Adam – Reading – Southend United; 12 Fielding, Francis D. – Blackburn Rovers – Northampton Town; 26 Fleetwood, Stuart K. – Charlton Athletic – Cheltenham Town; 4 Fraser, James – Bristol Rovers – Tiverton Town; 1 Gallagher, Paul – Blackburn Rovers – Plymouth Argyle; 19 Gardner, Scott A. – Leeds United – Farsley Celtic; 23 Gargan, Sam J. – Brighton & Hove Albion – Lewes; 19 Gornell, Terence – Tranmere Rovers – Accrington Stanley; 1 Gray, Julian R. – Coventry City – Fulham; 9 Griffiths, Rostyn J. – Blackburn Rovers – Accrington Stanley; 12 Grocott, Marc D. – Stoke City – Solihull Moors; 1 Grounds, Jonathan M. – Middlesbrough – Norwich City; 26 Hardman, Lewis – Darlington – Bishop Auckland; 22 Harris, Harry – Walsall – Chasetown; 12 Hawley, Karl L. – Preston North End – Northampton Town; 11 Hayles, Barrington – Leicester City – Cheltenham Town; 12 Henry, Rhys E. – Southend United – Harlow Town; 22 Holmes, Peter J. – Rotherham United – York City; 11 Hotchkiss, Oliver – Leeds United – Garforth Town; 9 Howard, Charlie S. – Gillingham – Dulwich Hamlet; 1 Illugason, Viktor U. – Reading – Eastbourne Borough; 12 Jeffery, Jack C. – West Ham United – Leyton Orient; 8 Kalipha, Kayan – Dagenham & Redbridge – Hendon; 25 Kamara, Malvin G. – Huddersfield Town – Grimsby Town; 1 Killock, Shane – Huddersfield Town – Harrogate Town; 5 Kite, Alex – Bristol Rovers – Oxford City; 9 Lamplough, Joe – Hull City – North Ferriby United; 30 Lawrence, Dennis W. – Swansea City – Crewe Alexandra; 21 Little, Mark D. – Wolverhampton Wanderers – Northampton Town; 2 Liversedge, Nicholas – Darlington – Whitby Town; 1 Lokando, Peggy – Southend United – Dagenham & Redbridge; 23 Louis, Kane T. – Brighton & Hove Albion – Burgess Hill Town; 25 Lynch, Joel J. – Brighton & Hove Albion – Nottingham Forest; 26 MacKenzie, Neal – Notts County – Kidderminster Harriers; 19 Mahdi, Adam – Bristol Rovers – Clevedon Town; 23 Martin, Alan – Leeds United – Barrow; 11 Mayo, Kerry – Brighton & Hove Albion – Lewes; 11 McDermott, Donal J. – Manchester City – Milton Keynes Dons; 29 McEveley, James – Derby County – Preston North End; 19 McMahon, Anthony – Middlesbrough – Sheffield Wednesday; 1 McShane, Paul D. – Sunderland – Hull City; 19 Minto–St Aimie, Kieron L.J. – Barnet – Grays Athletic; 24 Montrose, Louis – Wigan Athletic – Cheltenham Town; 15 Murray, Scott G. – Bristol City – Cheltenham Town; 19 Myrie–Williams, Jennison – Bristol City – Carlisle United; 25 N'Gotty, Bruno – Leicester City – Hereford United; 1 Osborne, Karleigh A.J. – Brentford – Oxford United; 2 Ovington, Christopher – Leeds United – Guiseley; 19 Panther, Emmanuel – Exeter City – Rushden & Diamonds; 24 Payne, Joshua – West Ham United – Cheltenham Town; 1 Pearce, Krystian M.V. – Birmingham City – Scunthorpe United; 19 Pearson, Andrew C. –

Brighton & Hove Albion – Worthing; 11 Phillips, James P. – Stoke City – Stafford Rangers; 22 Pidgeley, Leonard J. – Millwall – Woking; 8 Plummer, Tristan D. – Bristol City – Luton Town; 11 Primus, Linvoy S. – Portsmouth – Charlton Athletic; 12 Pugh, Marc – Shrewsbury Town – Luton Town; 19 Redmond, Shane P. – Nottingham Forest – Eastwood Town; 12 Rhodes, Jordan L. – Ipswich Town – Rochdale; 19 Rigg, Sean M. – Bristol Rovers – Grays Athletic; 25 Ritchie, Matthew T. – Portsmouth – Dagenham & Redbridge; 26 Robertson, Jordan – Sheffield United – Southampton; 23 Robson–Kanu, Thomas H. – Reading – Southend United; 5 Rouse, Domaine – Bury – Droylsden; 3 Sak, Erwin P. – Cardiff City – Newport County; 19 Sharpe, Thomas R. – Nottingham Forest – Stalybridge Celtic; 30 Shotton, Ryan – Stoke City – Tranmere Rovers; 12 Shulton, Scott – Wycombe Wanderers – Basingstoke Town; 1 Sibierski, Antoine – Wigan Athletic – Norwich City; 9 Smith, Daniel – Plymouth Argyle – Morecambe; 26 Sodje, Samuel – Reading – Watford; 9 Southall, Leslie N. – Gillingham – Dover Athletic; 1 Stead, Jonathan – Sheffield United – Ipswich Town; 26 Sturrock, Blair D. – Swindon Town – AFC Bournemouth; 19 Swallow, Ben – Bristol Rovers – Taunton Town; 26 Thomas, Aswad – Charlton Athletic – Lewes; 26 Thornton, Kevin – Coventry City – Brighton & Hove Albion; 12 Thornton, Sean – Leyton Orient – Shrewsbury Town; 19 Thurlbourne, Luke D. – Southend United – St Albans City; 8 Todd, Simon – Darlington – Blyth Spartans; 19 Trotter, Liam – Ipswich Town – Grimsby Town; 30 Tyler, Mark R. – Peterborough United – Watford; 1 Upson, Edward J. – Ipswich Town – Stevenage Borough; 1 Vidal, Javan – Manchester City – Grimsby Town; 18 Vipond, Shaun – Carlisle United – Workington; 30 Ward, Darren P. – Wolverhampton Wanderers – Watford; 22 White, Joe – Bristol Rovers – Chippenham Town; 11 Wilkinson, David M. – Crystal Palace – Truro City; 29 Wilkinson, Ross – Leeds United – Ossett Albion; 1 Williams, Andrew – Bristol Rovers – Hereford United; 5 Wilson, James S. – Bristol City – Brentford; 1 Wordsworth, Daniel – Carlisle United – Kendal Town; 18 Worley, Harry J. – Leicester City – Luton Town; 19 Wright, Joshua W. – Charlton Athletic – Brentford; 11 Zakuani, Gabriel A. – Fulham – Peterborough United

OCTOBER 2008

28 Antonio, Michael	Tooting & Mitcham United	Reading
16 Braham–Barrett, Craig	Welling United	Peterborough United
22 Reay, Shaun	Darlington	Blyth Spartans
30 Roberts, Gary S.	Crewe Alexandra	Yeovil Town

TEMPORARY TRANSFERS

28 Ahmed, Adnan – Tranmere Rovers – Mansfield Town; 21 Alaile, Michael O. – Dagenham & Redbridge – Bishop's Stortford; 16 Alnwick, Ben – Tottenham Hotspur – Carlisle United; 24 Annerson, James – Sheffield United – Rotherham United; 13 Anyinsah, Joseph G. – Preston North End – Brighton & Hove Albion; 31 Atkins, Ross M. – Derby County – Southport; 31 Atkinson, Robert – Barnsley – Grimsby Town; 26 Barcham, Andrew – Tottenham Hotspur – Gillingham; 3 Barker, Richard I. – Hartlepool United – Rotherham United; 29 Beattie, Craig – West Bromwich Albion – Crystal Palace; 27 Bevan, David – Aston Villa – Tamworth; 26 Bevan, Scott A. – Shrewsbury Town – Torquay United; 6 Blackmore, David – West Ham United – Thurrock; 31 Bowditch, Dean – Ipswich Town – Brentford; 17 Bowes, Gary – Millwall – Ebbsfleet United; 31 Brammer, David – Millwall – Port Vale; 27 Brown, Wayne L. – Hull City – Preston North End; 22 Bryant, Mitchell J. – Reading – Basingstoke Town; 24 Button, David R. – Tottenham Hotspur – Grays Athletic; 17 Buxton, Lewis E. – Stoke City – Sheffield Wednesday; 17 Cahill, Thomas – Rotherham United – Ilkeston Town; 17 Camara, Mohamed – Derby County – Blackpool; 20 Camp, Lee M.J. – Queens Park Rangers – Nottingham Forest; 3 Cartman, Nathan – Leeds United – Harrogate Railway; 1 Chadwick, Luke H. – Norwich City – Milton Keynes Dons; 3 Chanot, Maxine – Sheffield United – Mansfield Town; 3 Charles, Elliott G. – Barnet – Farnborough; 17 Charnock, Kieran J. – Peterborough United – Accrington Stanley; 10 Christophe, Jean F. – Portsmouth – Southend United; 20 Church, Simon R. – Reading – Wycombe Wanderers; 23 Clarke, Tom – Huddersfield Town – Bradford City; 20 Clohessy, Sean D. – Gillingham – Salisbury City; 9 Compton, Jack L.P. – Brighton & Hove Albion – Lewes; 27 Cook, Anthony L.E. – Dagenham & Redbridge – Carshalton Athletic; 27 Craddock, Thomas – Middlesbrough – Luton Town; 2 Daniel, Colin – Crewe Alexandra – FC Halifax Town; 31 Davies, Craig M. – Oldham Athletic – Stockport County; 29 Dayton, James F. – Crystal Palace – Crawley Town; 16 Diallo, Drissa – Milton Keynes Dons – Cheltenham Town; 22 Dickinson, Liam – Derby County – Huddersfield Town; 27 Dunne, James W. – Arsenal – Nottingham Forest; 29 Easter, Jermaine – Plymouth Argyle – Millwall; 2 Edwards, Carlos – Sunderland – Wolverhampton Wanderers; 10 Evans, Raphael M. – Rochdale – Bradford Park Avenue; 23 Federici, Adam – Reading – Southend United; 31 Fleetwood, Stuart K. – Charlton Athletic – Brighton & Hove Albion; 17 Fletcher, Carl N. – Crystal Palace – Nottingham Forest; 9 Fojut, Jaroslaw – Bolton Wanderers – Stockport County; 31 Foran, Richard – Southend United – Darlington; 1 Forster, Fraser – Newcastle United – Stockport County; 10 Fraser, James – Bristol Rovers – Tiverton Town; 20 Garner, Scott – Leicester City – Ilkeston Town; 1 Gill, Jeremy M. – Cheltenham Town – Forest Green Rovers; 20 Gornell,

Terence – Tranmere Rovers – Accrington Stanley; 8 Griffiths, Rostyn J. – Blackburn Rovers – Accrington Stanley; 24 Grocott, Marc D. – Stoke City – Stafford Rangers; 28 Hardman, Lewis – Darlington – Bishop Auckland; 21 Hart, Daniel – Barnet – Thurrock; 17 Hateley, Thomas N. – Reading – Basingstoke Town; 15 Horley, Karl L. – Preston North End – Northampton Town; 20 Hayes, Jonathan – Leicester City – Cheltenham Town; 17 Higginbotham, Kallum – Rochdale – Accrington Stanley; 31 Hinshelwood, Adam – Brighton & Hove Albion – Lewis; 10 Hotchkiss, Oliver – Leeds United – Garforth Town; 3 Howard, Ryan R.W. – Barnsley – Sheffield United; 30 Howard, Charlie S. – Gillingham – Thurrock; 7 Ireland, Daniel – Coventry City – Nuneaton Town; 24 John, Stern – Southampton – Bristol City; 28 Johnson, Bradley – Leeds United – Brighton & Hove Albion; 3 Jones, Daniel J. – Wolverhampton Wanderers – Oldham Athletic; 17 Jones, Stephen G. – Burnley – Huddersfield Town; 30 Kamudimba Kalala, Jean P. – Oldham Athletic – Grimsby Town; 9 Kane, Anthony M. – Blackburn Rovers – Stockport County; 10 Kavanagh, Graham A. – Sunderland – Carlisle United; 17 Kay, Matthew – Blackpool – Fleetwood Town; 24 Kiely, Christopher M. – Gillingham – Potters Bar Town; Konstantopoulos, Dimitrios – Coventry City – Swansea City; 1 Kyle, Kevin – Coventry City – Hartlepool United; 10 Lambert, Kyle – Rochdale – Bradford Park Avenue; 27 Law, Nicholas – Sheffield United – Bradford City; 10 Ledgister, Aaron T. – Cheltenham Town – Chippenham Town; 2 Lita, Leroy – Reading – Norwich City; 1 Liversedge, Nicholas – Darlington – Whitby Town; 31 Lynch, Joel J. – Brighton & Hove Albion – Nottingham Forest; 27 Mancienne, Michael I. – Chelsea – Wolverhampton Wanderers; 23 Martin, Alan – Leeds United – Barrow; 31 Martis, Shelton – West Bromwich Albion – Doncaster Rovers; 23 McCarthy, Alex S. – Reading – Team Bath; 8 McCrory, Damien P. – Plymouth Argyle – Port Vale; 24 McGivern, Ryan – Manchester City – Morecambe; 28 McGleish, Scott – Wycombe Wanderers – Northampton Town; 17 Meredith, James G. – Shrewsbury Town – AFC Telford United; 24 Miller, Ashley – West Ham United – Bishop's Stortford; 17 Molesley, Mark C. – Grays Athletic – AFC Bournemouth; 24 Moloney, Brendan A. – Nottingham Forest – Rushden & Diamonds; 17 Montague, Ross P. – Brentford – Basingstoke Town; 28 Montrose, Lewis – Wigan Athletic – Cheltenham Town; 30 Moses-Garvey, Aaron – Birmingham City – Hinckley United; 16 Moussa, Franck N. – Southend United – Wycombe Wanderers; 13 Murray, Scott G. – Bristol City – Cheltenham Town; 20 Myrie-Williams, Jennison – Bristol City – Carlisle United; 31 Neal, Lewis – Preston North End – Notts County; 17 Newsham, Marc – Rotherham United – Gainsborough Trinity; 27 N'Gotty, Bruno – Leicester City – Hereford United; 7 Nolan, Edward W. – Blackburn Rovers – Preston North End; 17 O'Grady, Christopher – Oldham Athletic – Bury; 14 Ormerod, Brett R. – Preston North End – Oldham Athletic; 10 Osborne, Karleigh A.J. – Brentford – Eastbourne Borough; 1 Ovington, Christopher – Leeds United – Guiseley; 17 Owen, Gareth J. – Stockport County – Yeovil Town; 23 Parkin, Sam – Luton Town – Leyton Orient; 28 Payne, Joshua – West Ham United – Cheltenham Town; 30 Pearce, Alex – Reading – Southampton; 23 Pentney, Carl – Leicester City – Woking; 12 Phillips, James P. – Stoke City – Stafford Rangers; 27 Price, Lewis P. – Derby County – Milton Keynes Dons; 17 Primus, Linvoy S. – Portsmouth – Charlton Athletic; 24 Puncheon, Jason D.I. – Plymouth Argyle – Milton Keynes Dons; 21 Quashie, Nigel F. – West Ham United – Birmingham City; 9 Rankine, Michael – Rushden & Diamonds – AFC Bournemouth; 22 Redmond, Shane P. – Nottingham Forest – Eastwood Town; 17 Rendell, Scott – Peterborough United – Yeovil Town; 26 Ritchie, Matthew T. – Portsmouth – Dagenham & Redbridge; 16 Roberts, Dale – Nottingham Forest – Rushden & Diamonds; 27 Robson-Kanu, Thomas H. – Reading – Southend United; 8 Rouse, Domaine – Bury – Droylsden; 17 Rowe-Turner, Lathaniel – Leicester City – Cheltenham Town; 10 Royce, Daniel R. – Brighton & Hove Albion – Havant & Waterlooville; 3 Savage, Robert W. – Derby County – Brighton & Hove Albion; 22 Sharpe, Thomas R. – Nottingham Forest – Stalybridge Celtic; 31 Shotton, Ryan – Stoke City – Tranmere Rovers; 17 Sigurdsson, Gylfi T. – Reading – Shrewsbury Town; 31 Simmons, Paris M. – Derby County – Burton Albion; 17 Sinclair, Emile A. – Nottingham Forest – Mansfield Town; 20 Singh, Jasbir – Shrewsbury Town – Hinckley United; 16 Slater, Christopher J. – Port Vale – Chasetown; 3 Smith, Ryan C.M. – Millwall – Southampton; 17 Spence, Daniel M. – Reading – Woking; 17 Stokes, Anthony – Sunderland – Sheffield United; 31 Tabiri, Joe O. – Barnet – Lewes; 7 Taylforth, Sean J. – Bradford City – Guiseley; 6 Taylor, Lyle – Millwall – Eastbourne Borough; 31 Thomas, Aswad – Charlton Athletic – Lewes; 6 Thomas, Simon – Crystal Palace – Grays Athletic; 27 Thomas, Taylor J. – Gillingham – Folkestone Invicta; 17 Thompson, John – Oldham Athletic – Notts County; 9 Thompson, Joshua J. – Crewe Alexandra – Leek Town; 31 Thorley, Thomas R. – Stoke City – Burscough; 20 Thurlbourne, Luke D. – Southend United – St Albans City; 3 Todd, Andrew J. – Rotherham United – Eastwood Town; 20 Townsend, Michael J. – Cheltenham Town – Barnet; 20 Trotter, Liam – Ipswich Town – Grimsby Town; 29 Tyler, Mark R. – Peterborough United – Watford; 14 Vipond, Shaun – Carlisle United – Workington; 8 Walder, Daniel A.D. – Gillingham – Ramsgate; 29 Ward, Darren P. – Wolverhampton Wanderers – Watford; 13 Waterfall, Luke M. – Tranmere Rovers – Altrincham; 17 Wedgbury, Sam – Sheffield United – Mansfield Town; 28 Welsh, John J. – Hull City – Carlisle United; 2 Wesolowski, James – Leicester City –

Cheltenham Town; 24 Westlake, Ian J. – Leeds United – Cheltenham Town; 23 White, Joe –
Bristol Rovers – Chippenham Town; 30 Wilkinson, Ross – Leeds United – Garforth Town; 14
Wills, Kane J. – Brighton & Hove Albion – Bognor Regis Town; 13 Winn, Peter H. –
Scunthorpe United – Northwich Victoria; 2 Wordsworth, Daniel – Carlisle United – Kendal
Town; 20 Worley, Harry J. – Leicester City – Luton Town

NOVEMBER 2008

3 Roberts, Gary   Crewe Alexandra   Yeovil Town

TEMPORARY TRANSFERS

27 Ademeno, Charles – Southend United – Salisbury City; 27 Ahmed, Adnan – Tranmere
Rovers – Mansfield Town; 21 Ainsworth, Lionel – Watford – Hereford United; 11 Ambrose,
Darren – Charlton Athletic – Ipswich Town; 14 Antwi, William – Wycombe Wanderers –
Northwich Victoria; 20 Anyinsah, Joseph G. – Preston North End – Brighton & Hove Albion;
12 Araba, Hakeem A.C. – Dagenham & Redbridge – Redbridge; 21 Armstrong, Steven C. –
Cheltenham Town – Burton Albion; 28 Arter, Harry N. – Charlton Athletic – Staines Town; 4
Arthur, Christopher A. – Queens Park Rangers – Kettering Town; 13 Balanta, Angelo –
Queens Park Rangers – Wycombe Wanderers; 26 Barcham, Andrew – Tottenham Hotspur –
Gillingham; 27 Barnes, Ashley L. – Plymouth Argyle – Eastbourne Borough; 27 Bennett, Dale
O. – Watford – Kettering Town; 27 Bevan, Scott A. – Shrewsbury Town – Torquay United; 5
Bignall, Nicholas C. – Reading – Northampton Town; 27 Birchall, Christopher – Coventry City
– Carlisle United; 27 Blundell, Gregg – Darlington – Accrington Stanley; 7 Boden, Luke –
Sheffield Wednesday – Rushden & Diamonds; 21 Bolasie, Yannick – Plymouth Argyle –
Rushden & Diamonds; 8 Bolder, Adam P. – Queens Park Rangers – Millwall; 26 Borrowdale,
Gary I. – Coventry City – Queens Park Rangers; 13 Bradley, Jason – Darlington – Blyth
Spartans; 27 Bridcutt, Liam R. – Chelsea – Watford; 27 Brooker, Stephen M.L. – Bristol City –
Doncaster Rovers; 26 Brown, Jonathan D. – Cardiff City – Wrexham; 21 Brown, Scott –
Cheltenham Town – Port Vale; 18 Bryant, Mitchell J. – Reading – Basingstoke Town; 27
Burton, Deon J. – Sheffield Wednesday – Charlton Athletic; 25 Button, David R. – Tottenham
Hotspur – Grays Athletic; 14 Byfield, Darren – Doncaster Rovers – Oldham Athletic; 14
Byrne, Michael A. – Southampton – Bognor Regis Town; 7 Cahill, Thomas – Rotherham
United – Ilkeston Town; 12 Carlton, Daniel A. – Carlisle United – Morecambe; 4 Chanot,
Maxime – Sheffield United – Mansfield Town; 14 Charge, Daniel – Dagenham & Redbridge –
Hitchen Town; 16 Charnock, Kieran J. – Peterborough United – Accrington Stanley; 10
Christon, Lewis – Wycombe Wanderers – Oxford City; 11 Christophe, Jean F. – Portsmouth –
Southend United; 27 Clarke, Tom – Huddersfield Town – Bradford City; 17 Craddock, Thomas
– Middlesbrough – Luton Town; 19 Crofts, Andrew L. – Gillingham – Peterborough United; 27
Cureton, Jamie – Norwich City – Barnsley; 27 Davies, Mark N. – Wolverhampton Wanderers –
Leicester City; 14 Dean, Harle J. – Dagenham & Redbridge – Redbridge; 28 Dean, Harle J. –
Dagenham & Redbridge – Bishop's Stortford; 14 Dennis, Kristian – Macclesfield Town –
Ashton United; 27 Denton, Thomas – Huddersfield Town – Woking; 27 Dickinson, Liam –
Derby County – Blackpool; 27 Dobson, Craig G. – Milton Keynes Dons – Wycombe
Wanderers; 20 Easter, Jermaine – Plymouth Argyle – Colchester United; 27 Eastwood, Simon
– Huddersfield Town – Woking; 25 Erskine, Emmanuel J. – Dagenham & Redbridge –
Margate; 28 Evans, Thomas L.J. – Swindon Town – Truro City; 14 Fairhurst, Nathan S. –
Preston North End – Wrexham; 26 Feeney, Liam – Salisbury City – Southend United; 27 Flynn,
Michael J. – Huddersfield Town – Darlington; 14 Forshaw, Jamie D. – Southend United –
Bishop's Stortford; 13 Forte, Jonathan – Scunthorpe United – Notts County; 5 Fortune,
Clayton A. – Darlington – Rushden & Diamonds; 10 Fraser, James – Bristol Rovers – Tiverton
Town; 14 Gallen, Kevin A. – Milton Keynes Dons – Luton Town; 14 Gargan, Sam J. – Brighton
& Hove Albion – Lewes; 21 Gilks, Matthew – Blackpool – Shrewsbury Town; 24 Gillespie,
Keith R. – Sheffield United – Charlton Athletic; 17 Gornell, Terence – Tranmere Rovers –
Accrington Stanley; 26 Goulding, Jeff – AFC Bournemouth – Eastbourne Borough; 27
Gowling, Joshua – Carlisle United – Hereford United; 14 Green, Stuart – Blackpool – Crewe
Alexandra; 10 Griffiths, Rostyn J. – Blackburn Rovers – Accrington Stanley; 24 Hammond,
James – Colchester United – Fisher Athletic; 27 Hanson, Mitchell G.B. – Derby County –
Notts County; 21 Hart, Daniel – Barnet – Thurrock; 18 Hateley, Thomas N. – Reading –
Basingstoke Town; 21 Hayes, Jonathan – Leicester City – Cheltenham Town; 27 Hayles,
Barrington – Leicester City – Cheltenham Town; 26 Helguson, Heidar – Bolton Wanderers –
Queens Park Rangers; 14 Hendrie, Lee A. – Sheffield United – Blackpool; 27 Higgs, Shane P. –
Cheltenham Town – Wolverhampton Wanderers; 20 Hill, Rory D. – Gillingham – Salisbury
City; 13 Hills, Lee M. – Crystal Palace – Colchester United; 3 Hirst, Christopher – Macclesfield
Town – Mossley; 11 Hotchkiss, Oliver – Leeds United – Garforth Town; 27 Howell, Dean G. –
Aldershot Town – Bury; 3 Hunt, Nicholas B. – Bolton Wanderers – Birmingham City; 29
Jameson, Aaron T. – Sheffield Wednesday – Gainsborough Trinity; 24 Johnson, John –
Middlesbrough – Tranmere Rovers; 3 Jones, Daniel J. – Wolverhampton Wanderers – Oldham
Athletic; 27 Jones, Stephen G. – Burnley – Bradford City; 27 Joyce, Luke – Carlisle United –

148

Barrow; 21 Kalipha, Kayan – Dagenham & Redbridge – Concord Rangers; 28 Kavanagh, Conor M. – Blackburn Rovers – Clitheroe; 7 Kavanagh, Graham A. – Sunderland – Carlisle United; 22 Kay, Matthew – Blackpool – Fleetwood Town; 10 Kite, Alex – Bristol Rovers – Chippenham Town; 21 Krul, Tim – Newcastle United – Carlisle United; 13 Kyle, Kevin – Coventry City – Hartlepool United; 27 Law, Nicholas – Sheffield United – Bradford City; 14 Leitch–Smith, A-Jay – Crewe Alexandra – FC Halifax Town; 14 Liddle, Michael – Sunderland – Carlisle United; 4 Lita, Leroy – Reading – Norwich City; 3 Liversedge, Nicholas – Darlington – Whitby Town; 28 Liversidge, Sam – Sheffield Wednesday – Buxton; 14 Low, Joshua D. – Cheltenham Town – Forest Green Rovers; 20 Lunt, Kenny V. – Sheffield Wednesday – Crewe Alexandra; 27 MacKenzie, Neil – Notts County – Port Vale; 27 Magunda, Joseph – Leicester City – Woking; 22 Mahon, Craig D. – Wigan Athletic – Accrington Stanley; 27 Martin, Alan – Leeds United – Barrow; 21 Masters, Clark J. – Southend United – Welling United; 5 McCollin, Andre – Yeovil Town – Grays Athletic; 10 McCrory, Damien P. – Plymouth Argyle – Port Vale; 14 McCubbin, Martin K. – Blackburn Rovers – Vauxhall Motors; 27 McEveley, James – Derby County – Charlton Athletic; 24 McEvilly, Lee – Cambridge United – Rochdale; 26 McGleish, Scott – Wycombe Wanderers – Northampton Town; 3 McMahon, Anthony – Middlesbrough – Sheffield Wednesday; 13 Meredith, James G. – Shrewsbury Town – AFC Telford United; 21 Milsom, Robert S. – Fulham – Southend United; 27 Minto–St Aimie, Kieron L.J. – Barnet – Stevenage Borough; 13 Montague, Ross P. – Brentford – Basingstoke Town; 18 Moussa, Franck N. – Southend United – Wycombe Wanderers; 11 Murray, Matthew W. – Wolverhampton Wanderers – Hereford United; 13 N'Gala, Bondz – West Ham United – Milton Keynes Dons; 6 Noel–Williams, Gifton R.E. – Millwall – Yeovil Town; 27 Odhiambo, Eric – Leicester City – Brentford; 13 Ogogo, Abumere T. – Arsenal – Barnet; 25 Owen, Gareth J. – Stockport County – Port Vale; 27 Parkes, Jordan – Watford – Stevenage Borough; 28 Patterson, Marlon – Dagenham & Redbridge – Bishop's Stortford; 24 Payne, Joshua – West Ham United – Cheltenham Town; 6 Proudlock, Adam D. – Darlington – Grimsby Town; 24 Puncheon, Jason D.I. – Plymouth Argyle – Milton Keynes Dons; 24 Quashie, Nigel F. – West Ham United – Birmingham City; 17 Redmond, Shane P. – Nottingham Forest – Eastwood Town; 27 Reid, Kyel – West Ham United – Blackpool; 18 Rendell, Scott – Peterborough United – Cambridge United; 25 Ritchie, Matthew T. – Portsmouth – Dagenham & Redbridge; 27 Robinson, Kurt – Ipswich Town – Northampton Town; 24 Rodgers, Luke J. – Port Vale – Yeovil Town; 14 Rose, Romone A. – Queens Park Rangers – Histon; 10 Rouse, Domaine – Bury – Droylsden; 14 Sandell, Andrew C. – Salisbury City – Aldershot Town; 27 Scannell, Damian – Southend United – Brentford; 15 Sharpe, Thomas R. – Nottingham Forest – Stalybridge Celtic; 25 Shulton, Scott – Wycombe Wanderers – Hendon; 19 Sinclair, Emile A. – Nottingham Forest – Mansfield Town; 27 Slusarski, Bartosz – West Bromwich Albion – Sheffield Wednesday; 21 Smith, Andrew G. – Accrington Stanley – Clitheroe; 27 Smith, Daniel – Plymouth Argyle – Eastbourne Borough; 17 Spence, Daniel M. – Reading – Woking; 25 Spence, Jordan J. – West Ham United – Leyton Orient; 27 Stack, Graham – Plymouth Argyle – Blackpool; 27 Stanislas, Junior – West Ham United – Southend United; 21 Stockdale, David A. – Fulham – Rotherham United; 21 Swallow, Ben – Bristol Rovers – Bridgwater Town; 14 Symes, Michael – Shrewsbury Town – AFC Bournemouth; 4 Taylor, Lyle – Millwall – Eastbourne Borough; 28 Thomas, Taylor J. – Gillingham – Folkestone Invicta; 27 Thomas, Wesley – Dagenham & Redbridge – Grays Athletic; 6 Thompson, John – Oldham Athletic – Notts County; 9 Thompson, Joshua J. – Crewe Alexandra – Leek Town; 7 Thornton, Kevin – Coventry City – Brighton & Hove Albion; 16 Thurlbourne, Luke D. – Southend United – St Albans City; 27 Tierney, Marc – Shrewsbury Town – Colchester United; 25 Todd, Andrew J.J. – Derby County – Northampton Town; 27 Tomkins, James O.C. – West Ham United – Derby County; 24 Townsend, Michael J. – Cheltenham Town – Barnet; 27 Trotter, Liam – Ipswich Town – Grimsby Town; 21 Tubbs, Matthew S. – Salisbury City – AFC Bournemouth; 7 Turley, Jamie – Wycombe Wanderers – Hendon; 27 Varney, Luke I. – Charlton Athletic – Derby County; 17 Waghorn, Martyn – Sunderland – Charlton Athletic; 7 Wagstaff, Scott A. – Charlton Athletic – Northwich Victoria; 27 Walker, James B. – West Ham United – Colchester United; 13 Walker, Kyle – Sheffield United – Northampton Town; 27 Weale, Christopher – Bristol City – Hereford United; 27 Wedderburn, Nathaniel C. – Stoke City – Notts County; 27 Westwood, Ashley R. – Crewe Alexandra – Nantwich Town; 7 Whaley, Simon – Preston North End – Barnsley; 13 White, Jamie A. – Southampton – Shrewsbury Town; 28 White, Joe – Bristol Rovers – Chippenham Town; 28 White, Shane L. – Plymouth Argyle – Truro City; 7 Wilcox, Joe T. – Scunthorpe United – Rushden & Diamonds; 7 Williams, Peter D. – Wolverhampton Wanderers – Kettering Town; 3 Williams, Sam – Aston Villa – Colchester United; 20 Wilson, Mark A. – Doncaster Rovers – Tranmere Rovers; 12 Winn, Peter H. – Scunthorpe United – Northwich Victoria; 5 Wordsworth, Daniel – Carlisle United – Kendal Town; 14 Wynter, Thomas L. – Gillingham – Ramsgate; 7 Yussuf, Rashid O. – Charlton Athletic – Northwich Victoria; 27 Zieler, Ron R. – Manchester United – Northampton Town

DECEMBER 2008 TEMPORARY TRANSFERS

5 Ademola, Moses – Brentford – Welling United; 22 Ainsworth, Lionel – Watford – Hereford United; 5 Alaile, Michael O. – Dagenham & Redbridge – Witham Town; 9 Andersen, Mikkel – Reading – Brentford; 9 Annerson, James – Sheffield United – Mansfield Town; 13 Antwi, William – Wycombe Wanderers – Northwich Victoria; 29 Arter, Harry N. – Charlton Athletic – Staines Town; 19 Balanta, Angelo – Queens Park Rangers – Wycombe Wanderers; 23 Bateson, Jonathan A. – Blackburn Rovers – Buxton; 7 Bolder, Adam P. – Queens Park Rangers – Millwall; 24 Botham, Calum – Wycombe Wanderers – Hayes & Yeading United; 12 Bowes, Gary – Millwall – Croydon; 1 Brammer, David – Millwall – Port Vale; 31 Bridcutt, Liam R. – Chelsea – Watford; 16 Byfield, Darren – Doncaster Rovers – Oldham Athletic; 14 Byrne, Michael A. – Southampton – Bognor Regis Town; 8 Cahill, Thomas – Rotherham United – Ilkeston Town; 12 Campion – Darren – Carlisle United – Workington; 14 Carlton, Daniel A. – Carlisle United – Morecambe; 19 Cartman, Nathan – Leeds United – Harrogate Town; 5 Clements, Christopher L. – Crewe Alexandra – Leigh Genesis; 5 Cook, Anthony L.E. – Dagenham & Redbridge – Concord Rangers; 21 Craddock, Thomas – Middlesbrough – Luton Town; 12 Ellams, Darrell – Wycombe Wanderers – Hitchin Town; 8 Fleetwood, Stuart K. – Charlton Athletic – Brighton & Hove Albion; 1 Foran, Richard – Southend United – Darlington; 11 Fraser, James – Bristol Rovers – Bognor Regis Town; 18 Garner, Scott – Leicester City – Ilkeston Town; 12 Groves, Matt – Bristol Rovers – Mangotsfield United; 22 Hammond, James – Colchester United – Fisher Athletic; 19 Harwood, Liam R. – Bristol Rovers – Margate; 22 Hayes, Jonathan – Leicester City – Cheltenham Town; 1 Hinshelwood, Adam – Brighton & Hove Albion – Lewes; 5 Hirst, Christopher – Macclesfield Town – Mossley; 4 Howard, Charlie S. – Gillingham – Thurrock; 8 Hunt, Nicholas B. – Bolton Wanderers – Birmingham City; 11 Ireland, Daniel – Coventry City – Halesowen Town; 12 Jones, Craig N. – Hereford United – Redditch United; 23 Kalipha, Kayan – Dagenham & Redbridge – Concord Rangers; 16 Kavanagh, Graham A. – Sunderland – Carlisle United; 11 Kazmierczak, Przemyslaw – Darlington – Whitby Town; 10 Kite, Alex – Bristol Rovers – Chippenham Town; 23 Krul, Tim – Newcastle United – Carlisle United; 13 Leitch-Smith, A–Jay – Crewe Alexandra – FC Halifax Town; 8 Lita, Leroy – Reading – Norwich City; 24 Louis, Kane T. – Brighton & Hove Albion – Whitehawk; 9 Melbourne, Alex J. – Wolverhampton Wanderers – Tamworth; 8 Meredith, James G. – Shrewsbury – AFC Telford United; 19 Millar, Christian – Macclesfield Town – Stafford Rangers; 5 Newsham, Marc – Rotherham United – Sheffield; 8 Noel–Williams, Gifton R.E. – Millwall – Yeovil Town; 16 Agogo, Abumere T. – Arsenal – Barnet; 12 Parrinello, Tom – Bristol Rovers – Weston–Super–Mare; 29 Quashie, Nigel F. – West Ham United – Birmingham City; 1 Simmons, Paris M. – Derby County – Burton Albion; 18 Sinclair, Emile A. – Nottingham Forest – Mansfield Town; 2 Stockdale, David A. – Fulham – Rotherham United; 3 Tabiri, Joe O. – Barnet – Lewes; 12 Taylor, Lyle – Millwall – Croydon Athletic; 21 Townsend, Michael J. – Cheltenham Town – Barnet; 12 Turley, Jamie – Wycombe Wanderers – Hendon; 16 Waghorn, Martyn – Sunderland – Charlton Athletic; 22 Walker, Kyle – Sheffield United – Northampton Town; 16 White, Jamie A. – Southampton – Shrewsbury Town; 8 Wilkinson, David M. – Crystal Palace – Dover Athletic; 1 Wilkinson, Ross – Leeds United – Garforth Town; 17 Wynter, Thomas L. – Gillingham – Ramsgate; 2 Yussuf, Rashid O. – Charlton Athletic – Northwich Victoria

JANUARY 2009

26 Ainsworth, Lionel	Watford	Huddersfield Town
12 Anyinsah, Joseph G.	Preston North End	Carlisle United
14 Ashworth, Luke A.	Wigan Athletic	Leyton Orient
20 Atkinson, Robert	Barnsley	Grimsby Town
8 Baker, Lee	West Bromwich Albion	Kidderminster Harriers
2 Barcham, Andrew	Tottenham Hotspur	Gillingham
1 Barker, Richard I.	Hartlepool United	Rotherham United
13 Beattie, James S.	Sheffield United	Stoke City
30 Bell, David A.	Norwich City	Coventry City
20 Bellamy, Craig D.	West Ham United	Manchester City
1 Bevan, Scott A.	Shrewsbury Town	Torquay United
12 Blackman, Nicholas	Macclesfield Town	Blackburn Rovers
1 Borrowdale, Gary I.	Coventry City	Queens Park Rangers
7 Bridge, Wayne M.	Chelsea	Manchester City
29 Brooker, Stephen M.L.	Bristol City	Doncaster Rovers
23 Bullard, James R.	Fulham	Hull City
1 Burton, Deon J.	Sheffield Wednesday	Charlton Athletic
26 Buxton, Lewis E.	Stoke City	Sheffield Wednesday
1 Chadwick, Luke H.	Norwich City	Milton Keynes Dons
28 Chimbonda, Pascal	Sunderland	Tottenham Hotspur

1 Christophe, Jean F.	Portsmouth	Southend United
16 Collins, Lee H.	Wolverhampton Wanderers	Port Vale
8 Cook, Lee	Fulham	Queens Park Rangers
30 Craddock, Thomas	Middlesbrough	Luton Town
26 Cudicini, Carlo	Chelsea	Tottenham Hotspur
9 Daniels, Charlie	Tottenham Hotspur	Leyton Orient
26 Davies, Mark N.	Wolverhampton Wanderers	Bolton Wanderers
9 De Laet, Ritchie R.A.	Stoke City	Manchester United
9 Defoe, Jermaine C.	Portsmouth	Tottenham Hotspur
2 Diallo, Drissa	Milton Keynes Dons	Cheltenham Town
8 Etherington, Matthew	West Ham United	Stoke City
8 Garner, Scott	Leicester City	Mansfield Town
9 Gritton, Martin	Macclesfield Town	Chesterfield
26 Hackney, Simon	Carlisle United	Colchester United
1 Helguson, Heidar	Bolton Wanderers	Queens Park Rangers
23 Heskey, Emile I.	Wigan Athletic	Aston Villa
2 Howard, Brian R.W.	Barnsley	Sheffield United
16 Kilbane, Kevin	Wigan Athletic	Hull City
16 Lee, Jason	Mansfield Town	Kettering Town
15 Miller, Liam W.	Sunderland	Queens Park Rangers
2 Moncur, Thomas J.	Fulham	Wycombe Wanderers
1 Montgomery, Graeme	Wealdstone	Dagenham & Redbridge
26 Mullins, Hayden I.	West Ham United	Portsmouth
1 Nolan, Edward W.	Blackburn Rovers	Preston North End
30 Nolan, Kevin A.J.	Bolton Wanderers	Newcastle United
30 Oliver, Luke	Stevenage Borough	Wycombe Wanderers
26 Pilkington, Anthony	Stockport County	Huddersfield Town
8 Proudlock, Adam D.	Darlington	Grimsby Town
2 Roberts, Dale	Nottingham Forest	Rushden & Diamonds
2 Routledge, Wayne N.A.	Aston Villa	Queens Park Rangers
2 Sandell, Andrew C.	Salisbury City	Aldershot Town
1 Smith, Ryan C.M.	Millwall	Southampton
16 Spring, Matthew	Luton Town	Charlton Athletic
19 Tabb, Jay A.	Coventry City	Reading
2 Tierney, Marc	Shrewsbury Town	Colchester United
1 Varney, Luke I.	Charlton Athletic	Derby County
12 Wallace, Ross	Sunderland	Preston North End
20 Ward, Jamie J.	Chesterfield	Sheffield United
26 Watson, Ben	Crystal Palace	Wigan Athletic
29 Wright, Ben	Hampton & Richmond Borough	Peterborough United
1 Zakuani, Gabriel A.	Fulham	Peterborough United

TEMPORARY TRANSFERS

19 Adams, Nicholas – Leicester City – Rochdale; 5 Ademola, Moses – Brentford – Welling United; 29 Ahmed, Adnan – Tranmere Rovers – Port Vale; 4 Alaile, Michael O. – Dagenham & Redbridge – Witham Town; 16 Alberto, Mateus C. – Manchester United – Hull City; 15 Ameobi, Oluwatomiwo – Doncaster Rovers – Mansfield Town; 30 Anane, Richard – Bury – Workington; 30 Andrew, Calvin H. – Crystal Palace – Brighton & Hove Albion; 9 Antonio, Michael – Reading – Tooting & Mitcham United; 9 Anyinsah, Joseph G. – Preston North End – Carlisle United; 2 Araba, Hakeem A.C. – Dagenham & Redbridge – Redbridge; 20 Archibald–Henville, Troy – Tottenham Hotspur – Exeter City; 27 Artus, Frankie – Bristol City – Kettering Town; 9 Atkinson, Robert – Barnsley – Grimsby Town; 1 Barazite, Nacer – Arsenal – Derby County; 5 Barnes, Ashley L. – Plymouth Argyle – Eastbourne Borough; 27 Beavan, George D. – Luton Town – Grays Athletic; 2 Bennett, Alan J. – Reading – Brentford; 2 Bennett, Dale O. – Watford – Kettering Town; 27 Bennett, Elliott – Wolverhampton Wanderers – Bury; 1 Bertrand, Ryan D. – Chelsea – Norwich City; 23 Beswick, Ryan – Leicester City – Redditch United; 15 Bignall, Nicholas C. – Reading – Cheltenham Town; 5 Bolasie, Yannick – Plymouth Argyle – Rushden & Diamonds; 22 Bolasie, Yannick – Plymouth Argyle – Barnet; 9 Bouazza, Hameur – Fulham – Birmingham City; 26 Bower, Mark – Bradford City – Luton Town; 9 Bowyer, Lee D. – West Ham United – Birmingham City; 1 Boyce, Andrew T. – Doncaster Rovers – Worksop Town; 23 Bozanic, Oliver J. – Reading – Woking; 9 Braham-Barrett, Craig – Peterborough United – Kettering Town; 16 Broadbent, Daniel – Huddersfield Town – Rushden & Diamonds; 13 Bromby, Leigh – Watford – Sheffield United; 26 Broomes, Marlon C. – Blackpool – Crewe Alexandra; 29 Brown, Wayne L. – Hull City – Leicester City; 1 Butcher, Lee A. – Tottenham Hotspur – Grays Athletic; 16 Button, David R. – Tottenham Hotspur – AFC Bournemouth; 11 Cahill, Thomas – Rotherham United – Ilkeston Town; 8 Campbell, Dudley J. – Leicester City –

Blackpool; 23 Carew, Ashley – Barnet – Eastleigh; 14 Carlton, David A. – Carlisle United – Darlington; 28 Carney, David – Sheffield United – Norwich City; 8 Casement, Christopher – Ipswich Town – Wycombe Wanderers; 1 Cathcart, Craig G. – Manchester United – Plymouth Argyle; 8 Chalmers, Lewis – Aldershot Town – Crawley Town; 2 Chapman, Adam – Sheffield United – Oxford United; 16 Charge, Daniel – Dagenham & Redbridge – St Albans City; 9 Charles, Elliott G. – Barnet – Lewes; 5 Charnock, Kieran J. – Peterborough United – Accrington Stanley; 23 Clarke, William C. – Ipswich Town – Northampton Town; 16 Cleverley, Thomas W. – Manchester United – Leicester City; 1 Clohessy, Sean D. – Gillingham – Salisbury City; 16 Convey, Matthew T. – Bradford City – Salford City; 2 Cork, Jack F.P. – Chelsea – Watford; 22 Cox, Lee – Leicester City – Yeovil Town; 16 Crooks, Leon E.G. – Wycombe Wanderers – Ebbsfleet United; 5 Cummings, Shaun M. – Chelsea – Milton Keynes Dons; 1 Curtis, Wayne J. – Morecambe – Barrow; 4 Daniels, Luke – West Bromwich Albion – Shrewsbury Town; 9 Davies, Mark N. – Wolverhampton Wanderers – Leicester City; 30 Dean, Harle J. – Dagenham & Redbridge – Bishop's Stortford; 5 Denton, Thomas – Huddersfield Town – Woking; 29 Dervite, Dorian – Tottenham Hotspur – Southend United; 15 Dickinson, Carl – Stoke City – Leeds United; 30 Diouf, El Hadji O. – Sunderland – Blackburn Rovers; 9 Dixon, Jonathan J. – Brighton & Hove Albion – Eastleigh; 30 Dorney, Jack – Bury – Workington; 5 Eastwood, Simon – Huddersfield Town – Woking; 29 Edwards, Preston M. – Millwall – Dover Athletic; 5 Elding, Anthony L. – Crewe Alexandra – Lincoln City; 13 Ellams, Darrell – Wycombe Wanderers – Hitchin Town; 8 Elliott, Stuart – Doncaster Rovers – Grimsby Town; 27 Elliott, Thomas J. – Leeds United – Macclesfield Town; 23 Erskine, Emmanuel J. – Dagenham & Redbridge – Sutton United; 30 Fairhurst, Waide S. – Doncaster Rovers – Solihull Moors; 6 Fielding, Francis D. – Blackburn Rovers – Rochdale; 11 Fleetwood, Stuart K. – Charlton Athletic – Brighton & Hove Albion; 30 Fonte, Rui P. – Arsenal – Crystal Palace; 15 Fraser, James – Bristol Rovers – Bognor Regis Town; 2 Furlong, Paul A. – Southend United – Barnet; 2 Gallen, Kevin A. – Milton Keynes Dons – Luton Town; 3 Gargan, Sam J. – Brighton & Hove Albion – Eastbourne Borough; 15 Gerken, Dean J. – Colchester United – Darlington; 2 Gill, Jeremy M. – Cheltenham Town – Forest Green Rovers; 15 Gobern, Lewis T. – Wolverhampton Wanderers – Colchester United; 19 Golbourne, Julio S. – Reading – Oldham Athletic; 25 Gowling, Joshua – Carlisle United – Hereford United; 1 Graham, Richard S. – Dagenham & Redbridge – Kettering Town; 1 Gray, David P. – Manchester United – Plymouth Argyle; 9 Gray, Michael – Wolverhampton Wanderers – Sheffield Wednesday; 26 Greer, Gordon – Doncaster Rovers – Swindon Town; 7 Grounds, Jonathan M. – Middlesbrough – Norwich City; 16 Groves, Matt – Bristol Rovers – Mangotsfield United; 23 Hadfield, Jordan – Macclesfield Town – Altricham; 30 Harding, Daniel A. – Ipswich Town – Reading; 30 Hart, Daniel – Barnet – Thurrock; 18 Harwood, Liam R. – Bristol Rovers – Margate; 8 Hatch, Liam M.A. – Peterborough United – Darlington; 2 Hateley, Thomas N. – Reading – Basingstoke Town; 28 Henderson, Jordan – Sunderland – Coventry City; 16 Henderson, Liam – Watford – Hartlepool United; 5 Hewson, Sam – Manchester United – Hereford United; 23 Higginbotham, Kallum – Rochdale – Accrington Stanley; 29 Higgs, Shane P. – Cheltenham Town – Wolverhampton Wanderers; 3 Hines, Sebastian T. – Middlesbrough – Derby County; 9 Hirst, Christopher – Macclesfield Town – Mossley; 6 Holness, Marcus L. – Rochdale – Barrow; 30 Howard, Charlie S. – Gillingham – Thurrock; 1 Hoyte, Gavin A. – Arsenal – Watford; 2 John, Stern – Southampton – Bristol City; 8 Jones, Stephen G. – Burnley – Bradford City; 29 Judge, Alan C. – Blackburn Rovers – Plymouth Argyle; 30 Kalipha, Kayan – Dagenham & Redbridge – Boreham Wood; 9 Kamudimba Kalala, Jean P. – Oldham Athletic – Grimsby Town; 30 Kandol, Tresor O. – Leeds United – Charlton Athletic; 30 Kiely, Christopher M. – Gillingham – Bromsgrove Rovers; 2 Killock, Shane – Huddersfield Town – Oxford United; 8 King, Gary I. – Lincoln City – Boston United; 26 King, Marlon F. – Wigan Athletic – Middlesbrough; 29 Kissock, John P. – Everton – Accrington Stanley; 11 Kite, Alex – Bristol Rovers – Chippenham Town; 1 Klein–Davies, Joshua – Bristol Rovers – Lewes; 2 Labadie, Joss – West Bromwich Albion – Shrewsbury Town; 31 Lansbury, Henri G. – Arsenal – Scunthorpe United; 6 Law, Nicholas – Sheffield United – Bradford City; 27 Letheren, Kyle – Barnsley – Doncaster Rovers; 6 Liddle, Michael – Sunderland – Carlisle United; 20 Lillis, Joshua M. – Scunthorpe United – Notts County; 27 Lindfield, Craig A. – Liverpool – Accrington Stanley; 16 Liversedge, Nicholas – Darlington – Whitby Town; 13 Logan, Conrad – Leicester City – Luton Town; 4 Lunt, Kenny V. – Sheffield Wednesday – Crewe Alexandra; 1 Lynch, Joel J. – Brighton & Hove Albion – Nottingham Forest; 29 Magnay, Carl R.J. – Chelsea – Milton Keynes Dons; 9 Mahdi, Adam – Bristol Rovers – Godalming Town; 29 Marshall, Paul A. – Manchester City – Blackpool; 1 Martin, Alan – Leeds United – Barrow; 12 Martin, David E. – Liverpool – Leicester City; 23 McKerr, Michael – Birmingham City – Redditch United; 15 McLeod, Izale M. – Charlton Athletic – Millwall; 13 McPike, James – Birmingham City – Solihull Moors; 9 Meredith, James G. – Shrewsbury Town – AFC Telford United; 23 Mido, Middlesbrough – Wigan Athletic; 19 Millar, Christian – Macclesfield Town – Stafford Rangers; 9 Minto–St Aimie, Kieron L.J. – Barnet – Lewes; 5 Montrose, Lewis – Wigan Athletic – Cheltenham Town; 6 Mooney, David – Liverpool – Stockport County; 6 Murty, Graeme S. – Reading – Charlton Athletic; 23 Myrie–Williams, Jennison – Bristol City – Hereford United; 30 Nardiello, Daniel A. – Blackpool – Hartlepool

152

United; 14 Naylor, Richard A. – Ipswich Town – Leeds United; 26 Nemeth, Krisztian – Liverpool – Blackpool; 7 Newsham, Marc – Rotherham United – Ilkeston Town; 13 O'Brien, James – Birmingham City – Solihull Moors; 9 O'Donovan, Roy – Sunderland – Blackpool; 21 Ogogo, Abumere T. – Arsenal – Barnet; 2 O'Grady, Christopher – Oldham Athletic – Bradford City; 8 Owens, Graeme A. – Middlesbrough – Blackpool; 23 Palacios, Wilson R.S. – Wigan Athletic – Tottenham Hotspur; 27 Palmer, Aiden – Leighton Orient – Dagenham & Redbridge; 15 Parinello, Tomasso – Bristol Rovers – Weston–Super–Mare; 12 Parkin, Sam – Luton Town – Leyton Orient; 5 Pearce, Krystian M.V. – Birmingham City – Scunthorpe United; 2 Pearson, Andrew C. – Brighton & Hove Albion – Lewes; 21 Pennant, Jermaine – Liverpool – Portsmouth; 23 Peters, Jaime B. – Ipswich Town – Gillingham; 8 Picken, Philip J. – Chesterfield – Notts County; 2 Plummer, Tristan D. – Bristol City – Torquay United; 1 Potter, Alfie – Peterborough United – Kettering United; 15 Potter, Darren M. – Wolverhampton Wanderers – Sheffield Wednesday; 27 Prijovic, Aleksander – Derby County – Yeovil Town; 23 Pugh, Andrew J. – Gillingham – Grays Athletic; 12 Puncheon, Jason D.I. – Plymouth Argyle – Milton Keynes Dons; 22 Quashie, Nigel F. – West Ham United – Wolverhampton Wanderers; 2 Redmond, Shane P. – Nottingham Forest – Eastwood Town; 12 Reece, Charlie – Bristol Rovers – Solihull Moors; 15 Reid, Kyel – West Ham United – Wolverhampton Wanderers; 19 Rendell, Scott – Peterborough United – Cambridge United; 23 Rhodes, Jordan L. – Ipswich Town – Brentford; 2 Ritchie, Matthew T. – Portsmouth – Dagenham & Redbridge; 8 Robinson, Kurt – Ipswich Town – Rushden & Diamonds; 29 Robinson, Theo – Watford – Southend United; 26 Robson–Kanu, Thomas H. – Reading – Swindon Town; 30 Rochester, Kraig – Dagenham & Redbridge – Dulwich Hamlet; 23 Rodgers, Paul L.H. – Arsenal – Northampton Town; 29 Ruddy, John T.G. – Everton – Crewe Alexandra; 1 Sappleton, Reneil – Leicester City – Oxford United; 26 Sawyer, Lee T. – Chelsea – Coventry City; 6 Sharry, Luke I. – Bradford City – Barrow; 8 Shaw, Jon S. – Rochdale – Crawley Town; 16 Shotton, Ryan – Stoke City – Tranmere Rovers; 1 Simpson, Jay–Alistaire F. – Arsenal – West Bromwich Albion; 8 Sinclair, Dean M. – Charlton Athletic – Grimsby Town; 15 Sinclair, Emile A. – Nottingham Forest – Macclesfield Town; 6 Sinclair, Scott A. – Chelsea – Birmingham City; 23 Singh, Jasbir – Shrewsbury Town – Sutton Coldfield Town; 30 Smith, Andrew G. – Accrington Stanley – Clitheroe; 5 Smith, Daniel – Plymouth Argyle – Eastbourne Borough; 15 Soares, Thomas J. – Stoke City – Charlton Athletic; 24 Spence, Daniel M. – Reading – Salisbury City; 23 Spence, Jordan J. – West Ham United – Leyton Orient; 9 Spring, Matthew – Luton Town – Charlton Athletic; 23 Steer, Rene A. – Arsenal – Gillingham; 30 Tabiri, Joe O. – Barnet – Grays Athletic; 27 Talbot, Andrew – Luton Town – Chesterfield; 9 Taylor, Lyle – Millwall – Croydon Athletic; 26 Thomas, Wesley – Dagenham & Redbridge – Grays Athletic; 15 Thomson, Jake S. – Southampton – AFC Bournemouth; 30 Thorley, Thomas R. – Stoke City – Stafford Rangers; 3 Threlfall, Robert R. – Liverpool – Stockport County; 16 Till, Peter – Grimsby Town – Chesterfield; 3 Todd, Andrew J. – Rotherham United – Eastwood Town; 2 Todd, Simon – Darlington – Blyth Spartans; 9 Trundle, Lee C. – Bristol City – Leeds United; 9 Tyler, Mark R. – Peterborough United – Bury; 10 Walker, James B. – West Ham United – Colchester United; 23·Walker, Lauris D. – Millwall – Harrow Borough; 30 Ward, Darren P. – Wolverhampton Wanderers – Charlton Athletic; 15 Wasiu, Sunday A. – Colchester United – Luton Town; 9 Wedderburn, Nathaniel C. – Stoke City – Notts County; 5 Westwood, Christopher J. – Peterborough United – Cheltenham Town; 16 White, Joe – Bristol Rovers – Yate Town; 29 Widdowson, Joseph – West Ham United – Grimsby Town; 16 Wiggins, Rhys – Crystal Palace – AFC Bournemouth; 27 Wilkinson, David M. – Crystal Palace – Welling United; 6 Williams, Andrew – Bristol Rovers – Hereford United; 30 Williams, Rhys – Middlesbrough – Burnley; 30 Williams, Sam – Aston Villa – Walsall; 9 Wills, Kane J. – Brighton & Hove Albion – Bognor Regis Town; 21 Windass, Dean – Hull City – Oldham Athletic; 2 Winfield, David – Aldershot Town – Salisbury City; 30 Worthington, Jonathan – Huddersfield Town – Yeovil Town; 15 Wynter, Thomas L. – Gillingham – Ramsgate; 6 Yates, Jamie – Rotherham United – Burton Albion; 5 Zieler, Ron R. – Manchester United – Northampton Town

FEBRUARY 2009

2 Clarke, Andre N.J.E.(Jamie)	Blackburn Rovers	Rotherham United
2 Davies, Craig M.	Oldham Athletic	Brighton & Hove Albion
23 Dawson, Craig	Radcliffe Borough	Rochdale
2 Dunfield, Terry B.	Macclesfield Town	Shrewsbury Town
2 Given, Shay J.J.	Newcastle United	Manchester City
2 Gray, Julian R.	Coventry City	Fulham
2 Gray, Michael	Wolverhampton Wanderers	Sheffield Wednesday
2 Keane, Robert D.	Liverpool	Tottenham Hotspur
2 McConville, Sean	Skelmersdale United	Accrington Stanley
2 McDonald, Cody D.J.	Dartford	Norwich City
2 McNulty, Jimmy	Stockport County	Brighton & Hove Albion
2 N'Zogbia, Charles	Newcastle United	Wigan Athletic

2 Pittman, Jon P.   Crawley Town   Wycombe Wanderers
2 Taylor, Ryan A.   Wigan Athletic   Newcastle United

TEMPORARY TRANSFERS

19 Adams, Nicholas – Leicester City – Rochdale; 2 Ademeno, Charles – Southend United – Salisbury City; 17 Ademola, Moses – Brentford – Welling United; 6 Alaile, Michael O. – Dagenham & Redbridge – Billericay Town; 2 Alves, de Assis Silva Joao (Joe) – Manchester City – Everton; 20 Anderson, Joe – Fulham – Woking; 19 Antonio, Michael – Reading – Tooting & Mitcham United; 19 Antonio, Michael – Reading – Cheltenham Town; 17 Antwi-Birago, Godwin – Liverpool – Hereford United; 27 Appiah, Kwesi – Peterborough United – Weymouth; 2 Archibald-Henville, Troy – Tottenham Hotspur – Exeter City; 27 Arthur, Christopher A. – Queens Park Rangers – Rushden & Diamonds; 2 Barnes, Giles G. – Derby County – Fulham; 20 Beattie, Craig – West Bromwich Albion – Sheffield United; 19 Beavon, Stuart – Weymouth – Wycombe Wanderers; 2 Ben-Haim, Tal – Manchester City – Sunderland; 2 Bennett, Elliott – Wolverhampton Wanderers – Bury; 24 Beswick, Ryan A. – Leicester City – Redditch United; 19 Bignall, Nicholas C. – Reading – Cheltenham Town; 27 Bozanic, Oliver J. – Reading – Woking; 2 Brandy, Febian E. – Manchester United – Hereford United; 19 Broadbent, Daniel – Huddersfield Town – Gateshead; 13 Budtz, Jan – Hartlepool United – Oldham Athletic; 2 Camara, Henri – Wigan Athletic – Stoke City; 23 Carew, Ashley – Barnet – Eastleigh; 28 Cartman, Nathan – Leeds United – Curzon Ashton; 12 Casement, Christopher – Ipswich Town – Wycombe Wanderers; 8 Chalmers, Lewis – Aldershot Town – Crawley Town; 2 Chester, James G. – Manchester United – Peterborough United; 17 Church, Simon R. – Reading – Leyton Orient; 17 Cook, Andrew E. – Carlisle United – Workington; 19 Crooks, Leon E.G. – Wycombe Wanderers – Ebbsfleet United; 2 Davenport, Callum R.P. – West Ham United – Sunderland; 13 Davies, Andrew – Stoke City – Preston North End; 2 Davis, Claude – Derby County – Crystal Palace; 23 Dinning, Anthony – Chester City – Grays Athletic; 18 Dixon, Jonathan J. – Brighton & Hove Albion – Eastleigh; 20 D'Laryea, Nathan A. – Rochdale – Farsley Celtic; 23 Duffy, Mark – Southport – Morecambe; 2 Eastwood, Simon – Huddersfield Town – Woking; 19 Ebsworth, Darren – Millwall – Sutton United; 9 Elliott, Stuart – Doncaster Rovers – Grimsby Town; 10 Elvins, Robert – Aldershot Town – Woking; 2 Fielding, Francis D. – Blackburn Rovers – Rochdale; 14 Fitzgerald, Robert O. – Yeovil Town – Enfield Town; 20 Fletcher, Carl N. – Crystal Palace – Plymouth Argyle; 2 Forbes, Adrian E. – Millwall – Grimsby Town; 16 Forte, Jonathan – Scunthorpe United – Notts County; 25 Fraser-Allen, Kyle – Tottenham Hotspur – Macclesfield Town; 10 Frecklington, Lee – Lincoln City – Peterborough United; 2 Furlong, Paul A. – Southend United – Barnet; 24 Gall, Kevin A. – Carlisle United – Port Vale; 15 Gerken, Dean J. – Colchester United – Darlington; 2 Gobern, Lewis T. – Wolverhampton Wanderers – Colchester United; 15 Groves, Matt – Bristol Rovers – Mangotsfield United; 2 Gulacsi, Peter – Liverpool – Hereford United; 19 Guy, Lewis B. – Doncaster Rovers – Hartlepool United; 2 Hammill, Adam J. – Liverpool – Barnsley; 13 Harvey, Neil – Macclesfield Town – Retford United; 23 Hemmings, Ashley J. – Wolverhampton Wanderers – Cheltenham Town; 27 Henderson, Wayne – Preston North End – Grimsby Town; 12 Henry, James – Reading – Millwall; 20 Henry, Rhys D. – Southend United – Lewes; 13 Hines, Sebastian T. – Middlesbrough – Oldham Athletic; 6 Holness, Marcus L. – Rochdale – Barrow; 20 Hotchkiss, Oliver – Leeds United – Farsley Celtic; 23 Jameson, Arron T. – Sheffield Wednesday – Ilkeston Town; 2 Jones, Daniel J. – Wolverhampton Wanderers – Oldham Athletic; 2 Jones, Stephen G. – Burnley – Bradford City; 13 Jutkiewicz, Lukas I.P. – Everton – Huddersfield Town; 26 Kabba, Steven – Watford – Oldham Athletic; 10 Kane, Anthony M. – Blackburn Rovers – Carlisle United; 2 Kelly, Stephen M. – Birmingham City – Stoke City; 13 King, Gary I. – Lincoln City – Boston United; 27 Kite, Alexandrous – Bristol Rovers – Weston-Super-Mare; 3 Klein-Davies, Joshua – Bristol Rovers – Lewes; 2 Leijer, Adrian – Fulham – Norwich City; 27 Letheren, Kyle – Barnsley – Doncaster Rovers; 2 Liddle, Michael – Sunderland – Carlisle United; 2 Lindegaard, Andrew R. – Cheltenham Town – Aldershot Town; 13 Lindie, James – Southend United – Grays Athletic; 2 Lockwood, Matthew D. – Colchester United – Barnet; 2 Loft, Douglas J. – Brighton & Hove Albion – Dagenham & Redbridge; 2 McCarthy, Alex S. – Reading – Aldershot Town; 2 McDonald, Clayton – Manchester City – Chesterfield; 12 McGleish, Scott – Wycombe Wanderers – Leyton Orient; 18 McPike, James – Birmingham City – Solihull Moors; 19 Millar, Christian – Macclesfield Town – Stafford Rangers; 23 Mills, Joseph N. – Southampton – Scunthorpe United; 2 Mifsud, Michael – Coventry City – Barnsley; 26 Montrose, Lewis – Wigan Athletic – Chesterfield; 1 Morgan, Dean – Luton Town – Leyton Orient; 3 Murty, Graeme S. – Reading – Charlton Athletic; 2 Novak, Lee – Huddersfield Town – Gateshead; 26 Odejayi, Olukayode – Barnsley – Scunthorpe United; 2 O'Grady, Christopher – Oldham Athletic – Stockport County; 24 O'Toole, John-Joe – Watford – Sheffield United; 20 Ovington, Christopher – Leeds United – Farsley Celtic; 11 Owens, Graeme A. – Middlesbrough – Blackpool; 13 Pearson, Andrew C. – Brighton & Hove Albion – Bognor Regis Town; 20 Pericard, Vincent D.P. – Stoke City – Millwall; 2 Picken, Philip J. – Chesterfield – Notts County; 2 Potter, Luke A. – Barnsley – Kettering Town; 2 Price, Lewis P. – Derby County – Luton Town; 23 Pugh, Andrew J. –

Gillingham – Grays Athletic; 9 Reason, Jai M. – Ipswich Town – Cambridge United; 10 Robinson, Jake D. – Brighton & Hove Albion – Aldershot Town; 2 Robinson, Kurt – Ipswich Town – Rushden & Diamonds; 26 Robson–Kanu, Thomas H. – Reading – Swindon Town; 2 Rodgers, Paul L.H. – Arsenal – Northampton Town; 23 Rowe–Turner, Lathaniel – Leicester City – Redditch United; 26 Russell, Alexander J. – Cheltenham Town – Exeter City; 10 Shackell, Jason – Wolverhampton Wanderers – Norwich City; 12 Sharry, Liam I. – Bradford City – Barrow; 6 Shields, Solomon – Leyton Orient – St Albans City; 27 Sigurdsson, Gylfi T. – Reading – Crewe Alexandra; 9 Sinclair, Dean M. – Charlton Athletic – Grimsby Town; 27 Sinclair, Emile A. – Nottingham Forest – Macclesfield Town; 2 Sinclair, Scott A. – Chelsea – Birmingham City; 2 Smith, Daniel – Plymouth Argyle – Eastbourne Borough; 2 Smith, James D. – Chelsea – Leyton Orient; 20 Soares, Thomas J. – Stoke City – Charlton Athletic; 16 St Louis–Hamilton, Danzelle D. – Stoke City – Bristol Rovers; 23 Steer, Rene A. – Arsenal – Gillingham; 20 Swallow, Ben – Bristol Rovers – Chippenham Town; 21 Taylor, Lyle – Millwall – Croydon Athletic; 13 Thomas, Simon – Crystal Palace – Rotherham United; 20 Thomas, Taylor J. – Gillingham – Halesowen Town; 2 Till, Peter – Grimsby Town – Chesterfield; 2 Timotian–Samarani, Andranik – Fulham – Barnsley; 13 Traore, Djimi – Portsmouth – Birmingham City; 23 Trotter, Liam – Ipswich Town – Scunthorpe United; 10 Trundle, Lee C. – Bristol City – Leeds United; 8 Tyler, Mark R. – Peterborough United – Bury; 6 Tymon, Matthew R. – Hartlepool United – Newcastle Blue Star; 8 Walker, James B. – West Ham United – Colchester United; 27 Webb, Jonathan – Leeds United – Newcastle Blue Star; 9 Wedderburn, Nathaniel C. – Stoke City – Notts County; 2 Westwood, Christopher J. – Peterborough United – Cheltenham Town; 15 White, Joe – Bristol Rovers – Yate Town; 2 Wiggins, Rhoys – Crystal Palace – AFC Bournemouth; 2 Wilson, Jared A. – Birmingham City – Chesterfield; 26 Winn, Peter H. – Scunthorpe United – Barrow; 2 Yates, Jamie – Rotherham United – Burton Albion; 1 Zieler, Ron R. – Manchester United – Northampton Town

MARCH 2009

2 Diouf, El Hadji	Sunderland	Blackburn Rovers
10 Palacios, Wilson	Wigan Athletic	Tottenham Hotspur

Both players transferred in January, not registered until March.

TEMPORARY TRANSFERS

2 Ahmed, Adnan – Tranmere Rovers – Port Vale; 26 Ainge, Simon – Bradford City – Cambridge City; 26 Ajdarevic, Astrit – Liverpool – Leicester City; 12 Akinde, John – Bristol City – Wycombe Wanderers; 26 Akurang, Cliff – Barnet – Weymouth; 9 Alaile, Michael – Dagenham & Redbridge – Billericay Town; 26 Anane, Richard – Bury – Fleetwood Town; 6 Andersen, Mikkel – Reading – Brighton & Hove Albion; 26 Anderson, Joe – Fulham – Woking; 19 Antonio, Michael – Reading – Cheltenham Town; 6 Arter, Harry – Charlton Athletic – Welling United; 23 Artus, Frankie – Bristol City – Cheltenham Town; 20 Askham, Lee – Chesterfield – Garforth Town; 26 Atkins, Ross M. – Derby County – Southport; 3 Bangura, Alhassan – Watford – Brighton & Hove Albion; 13 Bannan, Barry – Aston Villa – Derby County; 24 Bayliss, Ashton P. – Blackpool – Burscough; 26 Beattie, Craig – West Bromwich Albion – Sheffield United; 2 Beavan, George D. – Luton Town – Grays Athletic; 26 Bennett, James R. – Hull City – Lincoln City; 26 Berchiche, Yuri – Tottenham Hotspur – Cheltenham Town; 27 Beswick, Ryan – Leicester City – Redditch United; 17 Bialkowski, Bartosz – Southampton – Ipswich Town; 16 Bignall, Nicholas C. – Reading – Cheltenham Town; 2 Blackman, Nicholas – Blackburn Rovers – Blackpool; 26 Blackstock, Dexter A.T. – Queens Park Rangers – Nottingham Forest; 30 Bolasie, Yannick – Plymouth Argyle – Barnet; 6 Borrowdale, Gary I. – Queens Park Rangers – Brighton & Hove Albion; 2 Bower, Mark – Bradford City – Luton Town; 8 Brandy, Febian E. – Manchester United – Hereford United; 24 Broadbent, Daniel – Huddersfield Town – Harrogate Town; 13 Broomes, Marlon C. – Blackpool – Crewe Alexandra; 20 Burns, Robbie L. – Leicester City – Tranmere Rovers; 10 Butcher, Lee A. – Tottenham Hotspur – St Albans City; 2 Butterfield, Daniel – Crystal Palace – Charlton Athletic; 6 Button, David R. – Tottenham Hotspur – Luton Town; 13 Byrne, Mark – Nottingham Forest – Burton Albion; 26 Cartman, Nathan – Leeds United – Curzon Ashton; 12 Casement, Christopher – Ipswich Town – Wycombe Wanderers; 9 Charles, Elliott G. – Barnet – Hemel Hempstead Town; 26 Charles, Ryan A. – Luton Town – Kettering Town; 22 Church, Simon R. – Reading – Leyton Orient; 21 Clarke, William C. – Ipswich Town – Brentford; 9 Clements, Christopher L. – Crewe Alexandra – Stafford Rangers; 10 Codman, Daniel – Huddersfield Town – Wakefield; 6 Cole, Jake S. – Queens Park Rangers – Barnet; 20 Conlon, Barry J. – Bradford City – Grimsby Town; 20 Constantine, Leon – Northampton Town – Cheltenham Town; 23 Cook, Andrew E. – Carlisle United – Workington; 20 Crooks, Leon E.G. – Wycombe Wanderers – Ebbsfleet United; 13 Cumbers, Luis – Gillingham – Ebbsfleet United; 24 Daniel, Colin – Crewe Alexandra – Macclesfield Town; 8 Danville, Luke A. – Crewe Alexandra – Curzon Ashton; 4 Davis, Claude – Derby County – Crystal Palace; 5 Dawson, Craig – Rochdale – Radcliffe Borough; 19 Dean, Harle J. – Dagenham & Redbridge – Thurrock; 6 Denton, Thomas – Huddersfield Town – Wakefield; 26 Dicker, Gary – Stockport County – Brighton & Hove Albion; 13 Dickinson, Liam – Derby County – Leeds United; 26

Dinning, Anthony – Chester City – Gateshead; 26 Dixon, Jonathan J. – Brighton & Hove Albion – Eastleigh; 24 D'Laryea, Nathan A. – Rochdale – Farsley Celtic; 13 Doe, Scott M. – Kettering Town – Dagenham & Redbridge; 26 Dorney, Jack – Bury – Leigh Genesis; 13 Giovani D. – Tottenham Hotspur – Ipswich Town; 26 Dudley, Mark – Derby County – Tamworth; 23 Ebbsworth, Darren – Millwall – Sutton United; 1 Edwards, Preston M. – Millwall – Dover Athletic; 17 Erskine, Emmanuel J. – Dagenham & Redbridge – Dorchester Town; 9 Eustace, John M. – Watford – Derby County; 27 Evans, Thomas L.J. – Swindon Town – Weston-Super-Mare; 23 Ferreira, Fabio M. – Chelsea – Oldham Athletic; 26 Flahavan, Darryl J. – Crystal Palace – Leeds United; 18 Fleetwood, Stuart K. – Charlton Athletic – Exeter City; 23 Fletcher, Carl N. – Crystal Palace – Plymouth Argyle; 24 Forte, Jonathan – Scunthorpe United – Notts County; 13 Gargan, Sam J. – Brighton & Hove Albion – Eastbourne Borough; 6 Gazet Du Chattelier, Ryan – Portsmouth – Bognor Regis Town; 25 Gleeson, Stephen M. – Wolverhampton Wanderers – Milton Keynes Dons; 27 Green, Darren – Stockport County – Farsley Celtic; 30 Green, Michael J. – Bristol Rovers – Clevedon Town; 12 Gunter, Christopher R. – Tottenham Hotspur – Nottingham Forest; 3 Guy, Jamie – Colchester United – Dagenham & Redbridge; 23 Harewood, Marlon A. – Aston Villa – Wolverhampton Wanderers; 9 Harvey, Daniel J. – Southend United – Tiptree United; 20 Harwood, Liam R. – Bristol Rovers – Carshalton Athletic; 20 Hawley, Karl L. – Preston North End – Colchester United; 3 Heath, Matthew P. – Colchester United – Brighton & Hove Albion; 28 Henderson, Wayne – Preston North End – Grimsby Town; 15 Henry, James – Reading – Millwall; 26 Hodgkiss, Jared – West Bromwich Albion – Northampton Town; 25 Hotchkiss, Oliver – Leeds United – Mansfield Town; 6 Hudson–Odoi, Bradley – Hereford United – Grays Athletic; 26 Hughes, Lee – Oldham Athletic – Blackpool; 3 Hutchins, Daniel – Tottenham Hotspur – Yeovil Town; 26 Hutton, David – Tottenham Hotspur – Cheltenham Town; 4 Hyde, Jake M. – Swindon Town – Weymouth; 3 Jeffery, Jack C. – West Ham United – Eastbourne Borough; 23 Jevons, Phillip – Huddersfield Town – Bury; 12 Joyce, Luke – Carlisle United – Northwich Victoria; 19 Kalipha, Kayan – Dagenham & Redbridge – Boreham Wood; 20 Kay, Adam B. – Burnley – Accrington Stanley; 26 Kelly, Martin R. – Liverpool – Huddersfield Town; 10 Kitson, David – Stoke City – Reading; 13 Klein–Davies, Joshua – Bristol Rovers – Bath City; 26 Lansbury, Henri G. – Arsenal – Scunthorpe United; 19 Lee, Alan D. – Crystal Palace – Norwich City; 26 Legzdins, Adam R. – Crewe Alexandra – Weymouth; 5 Leitch–Smith, A–Jay – Crewe Alexandra – Newcastle Town; 3 Lindgaard, Andrew R. – Cheltenham Town – Aldershot Town; 9 Little, Glen M. – Portsmouth – Reading; 26 Livermore, David – Brighton & Hove Albion – Luton Town; 6 Lockwood, Matthew D. – Colchester United – Barnet; 28 Logan, Conrad – Leicester City – Stockport County; 26 Lua Lua, Kazenga – Newcastle United – Doncaster Rovers; 20 Madine, Gary L. – Carlisle United – Rochdale; 9 Magnay, Carl R.J. – Chelsea – Northampton Town; 25 Maguire, Danny – Queens Park Rangers – Yeovil Town; 17 Mahon, Alan – Burnley – Blackpool; 6 Marshall, Paul A. – Manchester City – Port Vale; 5 Mayor, Danny – Preston North End – Tranmere Rovers; 19 McEvilly, Lee – Rochdale – Barrow; 20 McPike, James – Birmingham City – Solihull Moors; 5 McSheffrey, Gary – Birmingham City – Nottingham Forest; 23 Medley, Luke – Barnet – Havant & Waterlooville; 26 Mendes, Junior A. – Aldershot Town – Stevenage Borough; 24 Mills, Joseph N. – Southampton – Scunthorpe United; 27 Mitchley, Daniel – Blackpool – Southport; 6 Mooney, David – Reading – Norwich City; 26 Morris, Ian – Scunthorpe United – Carlisle United; 20 Morris, Samuel P. – Swindon Town – Swindon Supermarine; 20 Mullin, Paul – Accrington Stanley – Bradford City; 26 Myrie–Williams, Jennison – Bristol City – Hereford United; 26 Newbold, Adam C. – Nottingham Forest – Stalybridge Celtic; 25 Newey, Thomas – Grimsby Town – Rochdale; 25 Noble, David J. – Bristol City – Yeovil Town; 19 Obika, Jonathan – Tottenham Hotspur – Yeovil Town; 6 O'Connor, Michael – Crewe Alexandra – Lincoln City; 2 Osbourne, Isaiah – Aston Villa – Nottingham Forest; 26 Osman, Ben F. – Exeter City – Salisbury City; 26 Osman, Toby – Exeter City – Salisbury City; 12 Owens, Graeme A. – Middlesbrough – Blackpool; 2 Owusu, Lloyd – Cheltenham Town – Brighton & Hove Albion; 2 Parker, Keigan – Huddersfield Town – Hartlepool United; 16 Pearson, Andrew C. – Brighton & Hove Albion – Bognor Regis Town; 6 Pembleton, Martin J. – Lincoln City – Lincoln United; 6 Perry, Kyle – Port Vale – Northwich Victoria; 26 Price, Jason – Doncaster Rovers – Millwall; 28 Priest, Richard M. – Dagenham & Redbridge – Witham Town; 20 Prijovic, Aleksander – Derby County – Northampton Town; 24 Pugh, Andrew J. – Gillingham – Grays Athletic; 25 Pugh, Marc – Shrewsbury Town – Hereford United; 10 Reason, Jai M. – Ipswich Town – Cambridge United; 5 Renton, Kris – Norwich City – Kings Lynn; 13 Reynolds, Callum F. – Portsmouth – Basingstoke Town; 12 Rhodes, Alexander – Rotherham United – Woking; 26 Richards, Matthew W. – Wycombe Wanderers – Notts County; 26 Robson–Kanu, Thomas H. – Reading – Swindon Town; 6 Rocha Fonte, Rui – Arsenal – Crystal Palace; 24 Rose, Daniel – Tottenham Hotspur – Watford; 26 Rouse, Domaine – Bury – Fleetwood Town; 27 Rowe–Turner, Lathaniel – Leicester City – Redditch United; 1 Ruddy, John T.G. – Everton – Crewe Alexandra; 19 Sappleton, Reneil – Leicester City – AFC Telford United; 19 Sawyer, Lee T. – Chelsea – Wycombe Wanderers; 23 Sheehan, Alan – Leeds United – Crewe Alexandra; 6 Shields,

Solomon – Leyton Orient – St Albans City; 6 Shroot, Robin – Birmingham City – Walsall; 25 Sigurdsson, Gylfi T. – Reading – Crewe Alexandra; 9 Simmons, Paris M. – Derby County – Lincoln City; 26 Sinclair, Frank M. – Lincoln City – Wycombe Wanderers; 26 Skarz, Joe – Huddersfield Town – Hartlepool United; 13 Small, Wade K. – Sheffield Wednesday – Blackpool; 3 Smith, Andrew G. – Accrington Stanley – Clitheroe; 26 Sodje, Samuel – Reading – Leeds United; 20 Spencer, Damian M. – Cheltenham Town – Brentford; 18 St Louis–Hamilton, Danzelle D. – Stoke City – Bristol Rovers; 26 Stack, Graham – Plymouth Argyle – Wolverhampton Wanderers; 11 Stech, Marek – West Ham United – Wycombe Wanderers; 23 Steer, Rene A. – Arsenal – Gillingham; 2 Stockdale, David A. – Fulham – Leicester City; 2 Stokes, Anthony – Sunderland – Crystal Palace; 26 Sturrock, Blair D. – Swindon Town – Torquay United; 18 Supple, Shane – Ipswich Town – Oldham Athletic; 27 Swallow, Ben – Bristol Rovers – Mangotsfield United; 20 Sweeney, Peter – Leeds United – Grimsby Town; 20 Symes, Michael – Shrewsbury Town – Accrington Stanley; 13 Taarabt, Adel – Tottenham Hotspur – Queens Park Rangers; 26 Tait, Richard – Nottingham Forest – Tamworth; 2 Taylor, Gareth K. – Doncaster Rovers – Carlisle United; 13 Taylor, Stuart J. – Aston Villa – Cardiff City; 26 Thompson, Joshua J. – Crewe Alexandra – Cammell Laird; 21 Townsend, Andros – Tottenham Hotspur – Yeovil Town; 19 Trotman, Neal – Preston North End – Colchester United; 24 Trotter, Liam – Ipswich Town – Scunthorpe United; 19 Turner, Iain R. – Everton – Nottingham Forest; 8 Tymon, Matthew R. – Hartlepool United – Newcastle Blue Star; 20 Varney, Luke I. – Derby County – Sheffield Wednesday; 20 Vernon, Scott M. – Colchester United – Northampton Town; 19 Vincent, Ashley D. – Cheltenham Town – Colchester United; 26 Walton, Simon W. – Plymouth Argyle – Blackpool; 2 Ward, Darren – Sunderland – Wolverhampton Wanderers; 13 Warner, Anthony R. – Hull City – Leicester City; 26 Watts, Adam – Fulham – Northampton Town; 16 Weale, Christopher – Bristol City – Yeovil Town; 25 Webb, Jonathan – Leeds United – Newcastle Blue Star; 26 Welsh, John J. – Hull City – Bury; 19 Westlake, Ian J. – Cheltenham Town – Oldham Athletic; 18 White, Joe – Bristol Rovers – Yate Town; 26 Wilkinson, Alistair B. – York City – Altrincham; 9 Williams, Sam – Aston Villa – Brentford; 26 Williamson, Lee – Watford – Preston North End; 4 Worrall, David – West Bromwich Albion – Shrewsbury Town; 6 Worthington, Jonathan – Huddersfield Town – Yeovil Town; 20 Wright, Ben – Peterborough United – Kettering Town; 24 Wright, Joshua W. – Charlton Atletic – Gillingham; 26 Young, Martin – Hartlepool United – Kendal Town; 26 Yussuf, Rashid O. – Charlton Athletic – Ebbsfleet United

APRIL 2009

| 28 Constable, James A. | Shrewsbury Town | Oxford United |

TEMPORARY TRANSFERS
17 Butcher, Lee A. – Tottenham Hotspur – Grays Athletic; 17 Button, David R. – Tottenham Hotspur – Dagenham & Redbridge; 9 Convey, Matthew T. – Bradford City – Guiseley; 2 Elding, Anthony L. – Crewe Alexandra – Lincoln City; 4 Kite, Alexandrous – Bristol Rovers – Weston–Super–Mare; 17 Martin, Richard W. – Manchester City – Burton Albion; 23 Spencer, James M. – Rochdale – Chester City

MAY 2009

14 Duffy, Mark	Southport	Morecambe
14 Frecklington, Lee	Lincoln City	Peterborough United
1 Hobbs, Jack	Liverpool	Leicester City
16 Morison, Steve	Stevenage Borough	Millwall
12 Rowe, Thomas	Stockport County	Peterborough United
29 Vincent, Ashley D.	Cheltenham Town	Colchester United

TEMPORARY TRANSFERS
4 Fielding, Francis C. – Blackburn Rovers – Rochdale; 4 Newey, Thomas – Grimsby Town – Rochdale; 1 Price, Jason – Doncaster Rovers – Millwall; 6 Williamson, Lee – Watford – Preston North End; 6 Worrall, David – West Bromwich Albion – Shrewsbury Town; 5 Wright, Joshua W. – Charlton Athletic – Gillingham

FOREIGN TRANSFERS 2008–2009

JUNE 2008	From	To
5 Bednar, Roman	Hearts	West Bromwich Albion
9 Bosingwa, Jose	Porto	Chelsea
30 Deco	Barcelona	Chelsea
10 Giovani	Barcelona	Tottenham Hotspur

JULY 2008		
1 Bassong, Sebastien	Metz	Newcastle United
31 Behrami, Valon	Lazio	West Ham United
30 Bischoff, Amaury	Werder Bremen	Arsenal

28 Cavalieri, Diego	Palmeiras	Liverpool
21 Cech, Marek	Porto	West Bromwich Albion
18 Digard, Didier	Paris St Germain	Middlesbrough
21 Dossena, Andrea	Udinese	Liverpool
11 Elmander, Johan	Toulouse	Bolton Wanderers
21 Emnes, Marvin	Sparta Rotterdam	Middlesbrough
22 Gomes, Heurelho	PSV Eindhoven	Tottenham Hotspur
2 Gutierrez, Jonas	Mallorca	Newcastle United
11 Jo	CSKA Moscow	Manchester City
4 Kallio, Toni	Young Boys	Fulham
14 Kim	Seongnam	West Bromwich Albion
3 Modric, Luka	Dinamo Zagreb	Tottenham Hotspur
28 Mustapha, Riga	Levante	Bolton Wanderers
24 Nasri, Samir	Marseille	Arsenal
30 N'Gog, David	Paris St Germain	Liverpool
30 Stoor, Fredrik	Rosenborg	Fulham
22 Zaki, Amr	Zamalek	Wigan Athletic
3 Zuiverloon, Gianni	Heerenveen	West Bromwich Albion

AUGUST 2008

22 Borja Valero	Mallorca	West Bromwich Albion
29 Castillo, Segundo	Red Star Belgrade	Everton
30 Coloccini, Fabricio	La Coruna	Newcastle United
12 Cuellar, Carlos	Rangers	Aston Villa
31 Donk, Ryan	AZ	West Bromwich Albion
1 Guzan, Brad	Chivas USA	Aston Villa
28 Jacobsen, Lars	Nuremberg	Everton
22 Kompany, Vincent	Hamburg	Manchester City
31 Olsson, Jonas	NEC Nijmegen	West Bromwich Albion
29 Smolarek, Ebi	Santander	Bolton Wanderers
2 Villanueva, Carlos	Audax Italiano	Blackburn Rovers
31 Zabaleta, Pablo	Espanyol	Manchester City
31 Zayatte, Kamil	Young Boys	Hull City

(Then signed for £3,360,000.)

SEPTEMBER 2008

1 Belhadj Nadir	Lens	Portsmouth
1 Fellaini, Marouane	Standard Liege	Everton
1 Gonzalez, Ignacio	Valencia	Newcastle United
1 Ilunga, Herita	Toulouse	West Ham United
1 Pavlyuchenko, Roman	Spartak Moscow	Tottenham Hotspur
1 Riera, Albert	Espanyol	Liverpool
1 Robinho	Real Madrid	Manchester City
1 Xisco	La Coruna	Newcastle United

JANUARY 2009

21 De Jong, Nigel	Hamburg	Manchester City
8 De Laet, Ritchie	Stoke City	Manchester United

(Loan spell with Wrexham (Blue Square Premier).)

15 Fortune, Marc-Antoine	Nancy	West Bromwich Albion
14 Givet, Gael	Marseille	Blackburn Rovers
30 Kovac, Radoslav	Spartak Moscow	West Ham United
23 Lovenkrands, Peter	Schalke	Newcastle United
16 Makukla, Ariza	Benfica	Bolton Wanderers
26 Nsereko, Savio	Brescia	West Ham United
5 Puygrenier, Sebastien	Zenit	Bolton Wanderers
6 Rodallega, Hugo	Necaxa	Wigan Athletic
2 Tosic, Zoran	Partizan Belgrade	Manchester United

(Combined fee with Adem Ljajic.)

FEBRUARY 2009

3 Arshavin, Andrei	Zenit	Arsenal
2 Basinas, Angelos	AEK Athens	Portsmouth
2 Gekas, Theofanis	Leverkusen	Portsmouth
2 Menseguez, Juan Carlos	San Lorenzo	West Bromwich Albion
2 Mulumbu, Youssouf	Paris St Germain	West Bromwich Albion
2 Quaresma, Ricardo	Internazionale	Chelsea

MARCH 2009

9 Cho, Won Hee	Monaco	Wigan Athletic

FA CUP REVIEW 2008–2009

If any of the spectators at Wembley on 30 May were not alive to the events immediately following the kick-off, they would have missed the first goal. The match began with a record and ended with one, too. As it was the 25 second effort by Louis Saha of Everton was the fastest for an FA Cup final. Naturally Chelsea had barely entered the action and it took a while before they levelled matters with a Didier Drogba header. After that the game swung in favour of the London team and a real blaster from Frank Lampard provided the winning goal. No consolation for Everton as it was their eighth such loss in the final, an unwelcome record.

Naturally the competition is marathon-like and starts way back in September with the minnows, the strongest of which survive to the first round proper in November. Friday night has become the starting point and Leeds and Northampton played out a draw. The following day it was not long before the shock waves reverberated. Blyth Spartans with a proud record of their own in the FA Cup shot out Shrewsbury, Curzon Ashton took out newly restored Football League club Exeter and Blue Square Histon clipped Swindon's aspirations. There were replays, too, for AFC Telford United against Southend, Grays v Carlisle, Droylsden v Darlington, Kettering v Lincoln, Altrincham v Luton. The pairings had also given non-league clubs a real stake in the second round.

Droylsden prevailed as did Kettering away and Grays were winning before their lights failed and they were beaten in the rearranged tie. The second round carried on with surprises. Barrow edged out League Two high fliers Brentford, Eastwood Town dealt similarly with Wycombe, Forest Green put Rochdale out and Histon even took care of Leeds. Droylsden were even leading at Chesterfield when fog called a halt. Blyth earned another go against Bournemouth as did Kettering with Notts County. Both won! Trying again, Droylsden got a draw, too, before floodlights failed when they were losing. Another attempt, this time Droylsden were successful only to be thrown out for fielding an ineligible player!

Sorting it out before the big boys in round three there remained half a dozen non-league teams and one guaranteed for the fourth round. Naturally there were bigger casualties, none more so than Manchester City beaten 3-0 at home by Nottingham Forest. Torquay ousted Blackpool. Chelsea were held at the Bridge by Southend, Peterborough earned another stab at West Bromwich. Forest Green pushed Derby all the way. Kettering had the better of Eastwood. Frozen pitches were causing postponements, too. But both Chelsea and Albion won their replays. Everton won first time at Macclesfield.

The fourth round settled everything down a little, though Swansea won at Portsmouth. Kettering went out to Fulham, Torquay at home to Coventry. Manchester United finished off Tottenham, but Burnley earned another chance away to West Bromwich and Doncaster held Villa. Cardiff had on their Sunday best to draw with Arsenal and the Merseyside derby finished level at Anfield. Burnley proved too good for Albion, Everton won in extra time but Villa saw off Doncaster and Arsenal took four goals from Cardiff.

Premier League teams came out of the fifth round draw quite well. Even so Coventry drew at Blackburn, Sheffield United held Hull as did Swansea with Fulham. A Nicolas Anelka treble finished Watford for Chelsea and West Ham and Middlesbrough had to replay. Derby were beaten 4-1 by Manchester United, Everton beat Villa 3-1. Coventry upset Blackburn second time, Swansea and Sheffield United both failed. Boro won their tie with the Hammers. In the delayed match Arsenal defeated Burnley 3-0.

Quarter-finals and Everton beat Middlesbrough 2-1, Chelsea were successful 2-0 at Coventry and Manchester United scored four without reply at Fulham. Playing catch-up Arsenal edged Hull 2-1.

Wembley's semi-finals on successive days had a north-south divide. The all-London affair saw Arsenal take the lead against Chelsea before losing 2-1, while on the Sunday Everton and Manchester United finished goalless after extra time before Everton prevailed in the shoot-out.

THE FA CUP 2008–2009

FIRST ROUND

Leeds U	(1) 1	Northampton T	(1) 1
AFC Telford	(0) 2	Southend U	(1) 2
Accrington S	(0) 0	Tranmere R	(0) 0
Aldershot T	(0) 1	Rotherham U	(0) 1
Alfreton T	(1) 4	Bury T	(2) 2
Barnet	(0) 1	Rochdale	(0) 1
Blyth Spartans	(2) 3	Shrewsbury T	(0) 1
Bournemouth	(0) 1	Bristol R	(0) 0
Brighton & HA	(2) 3	Hartlepool U	(0) 3
Bury	(0) 0	Gillingham	(0) 1
Carlisle U	(0) 1	Grays Ath	(0) 1
Cheltenham T	(2) 2	Oldham Ath	(0) 2
Chester C	(0) 0	Millwall	(0) 3
Chesterfield	(1) 3	Mansfield T	(0) 1
Colchester U	(0) 0	Leyton Orient	(0) 1
Crewe Alex	(1) 1	Ebbsfleet U	(0) 0
Curzon Ashton	(1) 3	Exeter C	(0) 2
Darlington	(0) 0	Droylsden	(0) 0
Eastbourne B	(0) 0	Barrow	(0) 0
Eastwood T	(0) 2	Brackley	(1) 1
Harlow T	(0) 0	Macclesfield T	(0) 2
Hereford U	(0) 0	Dagenham & R	(0) 0
Histon	(0) 1	Swindon T	(0) 0
Huddersfield T	(1) 3	Port Vale	(1) 4
Kettering T	(0) 1	Lincoln C	(0) 1
Kidderminster H	(1) 1	Cambridge U	(0) 0
Leicester C	(1) 3	Stevenage B	(0) 0
Leiston	(0) 0	Fleetwood T	(0) 0
Luton T	(0) 0	Altrincham	(0) 0
Milton Keynes D	(1) 1	Bradford C	(1) 2
Morecambe	(1) 2	Grimsby T	(0) 1
Oxford U	(0) 0	Dorchester T	(0) 0
Sutton U	(0) 0	Notts Co	(0) 1
Torquay U	(1) 2	Evesham U	(0) 0
Walsall	(1) 1	Scunthorpe U	(1) 3
Yeovil T	(0) 1	Stockport Co	(1) 1
AFC Hornchurch	(0) 0	Peterborough U	(0) 1
Havant & W	(0) 1	Brentford	(1) 3
Team Bath	(0) 0	Forest Green R	(0) 1
AFC Wimbledon	(0) 1	Wycombe W	(2) 4

FIRST ROUND REPLAYS

Tranmere R	(0) 1	Accrington S	(0) 0
Northampton T	(1) 2	Leeds U	(4) 5
Altrincham	(0) 0	Luton T	(0) 0
(aet; Luton T won 4-2 on penalties.)			
Barrow	(1) 4	Eastbourne B	(0) 0
Dagenham & R	(2) 2	Hereford U	(1) 1
Dorchester T	(1) 1	Oxford U	(0) 3
(aet.)			
Droylsden	(1) 1	Darlington	(0) 0
Fleetwood T	(0) 2	Leiston	(0) 0
Hartlepool U	(0) 2	Brighton & HA	(1) 1
Lincoln C	(0) 1	Kettering T	(0) 2
Oldham Ath	(0) 0	Cheltenham T	(1) 1

Rochdale	(0) 3	Barnet	(2) 2

(aet.)

Rotherham U	(0) 0	Aldershot T	(1) 3
Southend U	(0) 2	AFC Telford U	(0) 0
Stockport Co	(3) 5	Yeovil T	(0) 0
Grays Ath	(0) 0	Carlisle U	(1) 2

SECOND ROUND

Barrow	(1) 2	Brentford	(0) 1
Port Vale	(0) 1	Macclesfield T	(1) 3
Bournemouth	(0) 0	Blyth Spartans	(0) 0
Bradford C	(0) 1	Leyton Orient	(1) 2
Chesterfield	(0) 0	Droylsden	(1) 1

(Abandoned half time; fog.)

Eastwood T	(1) 2	Wycombe W	(0) 0
Fleetwood T	(1) 2	Hartlepool U	(1) 3
Forest Green R	(1) 2	Rochdale	(0) 0
Gillingham	(0) 0	Stockport Co	(0) 0
Kidderminster H	(1) 2	Curzon Ashton	(0) 0
Leicester C	(2) 3	Dagenham & R	(2) 2
Millwall	(1) 3	Aldershot T	(0) 0
Morecambe	(1) 1	Cheltenham T	(0) 1

(Abandoned 65 minutes; fog.)

Peterborough U	(0) 0	Tranmere R	(0) 0
Scunthorpe U	(1) 4	Alfreton T	(0) 0
Southend U	(1) 3	Luton T	(0) 1
Torquay U	(1) 2	Oxford U	(0) 0
Histon	(1) 1	Leeds U	(0) 0
Notts Co	(1) 1	Kettering T	(1) 1
Morecambe	(2) 2	Cheltenham T	(2) 3
Carlisle U	(0) 0	Crewe Alex	(2) 2
Chesterfield	(1) 2	Droylsden	(0) 2

SECOND ROUND REPLAYS

Stockport Co	(1) 1	Gillingham	(2) 2
Tranmere R	(0) 1	Peterborough U	(0) 2

(aet.)

Kettering T	(0) 2	Notts Co	(1) 1
Blyth Spartans	(0) 1	Bournemouth	(0) 0
Droylsden	(0) 0	Chesterfield	(1) 2

(abandoned 72 minutes; floodlight failure.)

Droylsden	(1) 2	Chesterfield	(1) 1

(Droylsden removed from the Cup for fielding a suspended player.)

THIRD ROUND

Tottenham H	(0) 3	Wigan Ath	(0) 1
Arsenal	(0) 3	Plymouth Arg	(0) 1
Cardiff C	(0) 2	Reading	(0) 0
Charlton Ath	(1) 1	Norwich C	(0) 0
Chelsea	(1) 1	Southend U	(0) 1
Coventry C	(0) 2	Kidderminster H	(0) 0
Forest Green R	(2) 3	Derby Co	(2) 4
Hartlepool U	(0) 2	Stoke C	(0) 0
Hull C	(0) 0	Newcastle U	(0) 0
Ipswich T	(0) 3	Chesterfield	(0) 0
Kettering T	(1) 2	Eastwood T	(0) 1
Leicester C	(0) 0	Crystal Palace	(0) 0
Macclesfield T	(0) 0	Everton	(1) 1
Manchester C	(0) 0	Nottingham F	(2) 3

161

Middlesbrough	(1) 2	Barrow	(0) 1
Millwall	(2) 2	Crewe Alex	(1) 2
Portsmouth	(0) 0	Bristol C	(0) 0
Preston NE	(0) 0	Liverpool	(1) 2
QPR	(0) 0	Burnley	(0) 0
Sheffield W	(1) 1	Fulham	(1) 2
Sunderland	(0) 2	Bolton W	(0) 1
Torquay U	(1) 1	Blackpool	(0) 0
WBA	(0) 1	Peterborough U	(0) 1
Watford	(0) 1	Scunthorpe U	(0) 0
West Ham U	(2) 3	Barnsley	(0) 0
Gillingham	(0) 1	Aston Villa	(1) 2
Southampton	(0) 0	Manchester U	(1) 3
Blyth Spartans	(0) 0	Blackburn R	(0) 1
Birmingham C	(0) 0	Wolverhampton W	(1) 2
Cheltenham T	(0) 0	Doncaster R	(0) 0
Histon	(0) 1	Swansea C	(2) 2
Leyton Orient	(1) 1	Sheffield U	(0) 4

THIRD ROUND REPLAYS

Bristol C	(0) 0	Portsmouth	(1) 2
Burnley	(0) 2	QPR	(0) 1
(aet.)			
Crewe Alex	(1) 2	Millwall	(1) 3
Norwich C	(0) 0	Charlton Ath	(1) 1
Peterborough U	(0) 0	WBA	(2) 2
Crystal Palace	(1) 2	Leicester C	(0) 1
Newcastle U	(0) 0	Hull C	(0) 1
Southend U	(1) 1	Chelsea	(1) 4
Doncaster R	(2) 3	Cheltenham T	(0) 0

FOURTH ROUND

Derby Co	(1) 1	Nottingham F	(0) 1
Chelsea	(1) 3	Ipswich T	(1) 1
Doncaster R	(0) 0	Aston Villa	(0) 0
Hartlepool U	(0) 0	West Ham U	(2) 2
Hull C	(1) 2	Millwall	(0) 0
Kettering T	(1) 2	Fulham	(1) 4
Manchester U	(2) 2	Tottenham H	(1) 1
Portsmouth	(0) 0	Swansea C	(2) 2
Sheffield U	(1) 2	Charlton Ath	(0) 1
Sunderland	(0) 0	Blackburn R	(0) 0
Torquay U	(0) 0	Coventry C	(0) 1
WBA	(2) 2	Burnley	(1) 2
Watford	(2) 4	Crystal Palace	(0) 3
Wolverhampton W	(0) 1	Middlesbrough	(1) 2
Cardiff C	(0) 0	Arsenal	(0) 0
Liverpool	(0) 1	Everton	(1) 1

FOURTH ROUND REPLAYS

Burnley	(1) 3	WBA	(0) 1
Aston Villa	(2) 3	Doncaster R	(1) 1
Blackburn R	(1) 2	Sunderland	(1) 1
(aet.)			
Everton	(0) 1	Liverpool	(0) 0
(aet.)			
Nottingham F	(2) 2	Derby Co	(1) 3
Arsenal	(2) 4	Cardiff C	(0) 0

FIFTH ROUND

Blackburn R	(1) 2	Coventry C	(0) 2
Sheffield U	(1) 1	Hull C	(1) 1
Swansea C	(0) 1	Fulham	(1) 1
Watford	(0) 1	Chelsea	(0) 3
West Ham U	(0) 1	Middlesbrough	(1) 1
Derby Co	(0) 1	Manchester U	(2) 4
Everton	(2) 3	Aston Villa	(1) 1
Arsenal	(1) 3	Burnley	(0) 0

FIFTH ROUND REPLAYS

Coventry City	(0) 1	Blackburn R	(0) 0
Fulham	(0) 2	Swansea C	(0) 1
Middlesbrough	(2) 2	West Ham U	(0) 0
Hull C	(1) 2	Sheffield U	(1) 1

SIXTH ROUND

Coventry C	(0) 0	Chelsea	(1) 2
Fulham	(0) 0	Manchester U	(2) 4
Everton	(0) 2	Middlesbrough	(1) 1
Arsenal	(0) 2	Hull C	(1) 1

SEMI-FINALS

| Arsenal | (1) 1 | Chelsea | (1) 2 |
| Manchester U | (0) 0 | Everton | (0) 0 |

*(aet; Everton won 4-2 on penalties: Cahill missed; Berbatov saved; Baines scored;
Ferdinand saved; Neville scored; Vidic scored; Vaughan scored; Anderson scored;
Jagielka scored.)*

THE FA CUP FINAL

(Saturday, 30 May 2009 at Wembley Stadium, attendance 89,391)

Chelsea (1) 2   Everton (1) 1

Chelsea: Cech; Bosingwa, Cole A, Mikel, Terry, Alex, Essien (Ballack), Lampard,
Anelka, Drogba, Malouda.
Scorers: Drogba 21, Lampard 72.

Everton: Howard; Hibbert (Jacobsen), Baines, Yobo, Lescott, Neville, Osman
(Gosling), Fellani, Saha (Vaughan), Cahill, Pienaar.
Scorer: Saha 1.

Referee: H. Webb (South Yorkshire).

PAST FA CUP FINALS

Details of one goalscorer is not available in 1878.

1872	The Wanderers ....1 *Betts*	Royal Engineers 0		
1873	The Wanderers ....2 *Kinnaird, Wollaston*	Oxford University 0		
1874	Oxford University............2 *Mackarness, Patton*	Royal Engineers 0		
1875	Royal Engineers ....1 *Renny-Tailyour*	Old Etonians ....1* *Bonsor*		
Replay	Royal Engineers ....2 *Renny-Tailyour, Stafford*	Old Etonians 0		
1876	The Wanderers ....1 *Edwards*	Old Etonians ....1* *Bonsor*		
Replay	The Wanderers ....3 *Wollaston, Hughes 2*	Old Etonians 0		
1877	The Wanderers ....2 *Lindsay, Kenrick*	Oxford University ....1* *Kinnaird (og)*		
1878	The Wanderers ....3 *Kenrick 2, Kinnaird*	Royal Engineers ....1 *Unknown*		
1879	Old Etonians ....1 *Clerke*	Clapham Rovers 0		
1880	Clapham Rovers ....1 *Lloyd-Jones*	Oxford University 0		
1881	Old Carthusians ....3 *Wyngard, Parry, Todd*	Old Etonians 0		
1882	Old Etonians ....1 *Anderson*	Blackburn Rovers............0		
1883	Blackburn Olympic ....2 *Costley, Matthews*	Old Etonians ....1* *Goodhart*		
1884	Blackburn Rovers............2 *Sowerbutts, Forrest*	Queen's Park, Glasgow ....1 *Christie*		
1885	Blackburn Rovers............2 *Forrest, Brown*	Queen's Park, Glasgow 0		
1886	Blackburn Rovers............0	West Bromwich Albion 0		
Replay	Blackburn Rovers............2 *Brown, Sowerbutts*	West Bromwich Albion 0		
1887	Aston Villa ....2 *Hunter, Hodgetts*	West Bromwich Albion 0		
1888	West Bromwich Albion ....2 *Woodhall, Bayliss*	Preston NE ....1 *Dewhurst*		
1889	Preston NE ....3 *Dewhurst, J. Ross, Thompson*	Wolverhampton W 0		
1890	Blackburn Rovers............6 *Walton, John Southworth, Lofthouse, Townley 3*	Sheffield W ....1 *Bennett*		
1891	Blackburn Rovers............3 *Dewar, John Southworth, Townley*	Notts Co............1 *Oswald*		
1892	West Bromwich Albion ....3 *Geddes, Nicholls, Reynolds*	Aston Villa 0		
1893	Wolverhampton W ....1 *Allen*	Everton 0		

1894	Notts Co 4	Bolton W 1	
	Watson, Logan 3	*Cassidy*	
1895	Aston Villa 1	West Bromwich Albion 0	
	J. Devey		
1896	Sheffield W 2	Wolverhampton W 1	
	Spiksley 2	*Black*	
1897	Aston Villa 3	Everton 2	
	Campbell, Wheldon,	*Boyle, Bell*	
	Crabtree		
1898	Nottingham F 3	Derby Co 1	
	Cape 2, McPherson	*Bloomer*	
1899	Sheffield U 4	Derby Co 1	
	Bennett, Beers, Almond,	*Boag*	
	Priest		
1900	Bury 4	Southampton 0	
	McLuckie 2, Wood, Plant		
1901	Tottenham H 2	Sheffield U 2	
	Brown 2	*Bennett, Priest*	
Replay	Tottenham H 3	Sheffield U 1	
	Cameron, Smith, Brown	*Priest*	
1902	Sheffield U 1	Southampton 1	
	Common	*Wood*	
Replay	Sheffield U 2	Southampton 1	
	Hedley, Barnes	*Brown*	
1903	Bury 6	Derby Co 0	
	Ross, Sagar, Leeming 2,		
	Wood, Plant		
1904	Manchester C 1	Bolton W 0	
	Meredith		
1905	Aston Villa 2	Newcastle U 0	
	Hampton 2		
1906	Everton 1	Newcastle U 0	
	Young		
1907	Sheffield W 2	Everton 1	
	Stewart, Simpson	*Sharp*	
1908	Wolverhampton W 3	Newcastle U 1	
	Hunt, Hedley, Harrison	*Howey*	
1909	Manchester U 1	Bristol C....................0	
	A. Turnbull		
1910	Newcastle U 1	Barnsley....................1	
	Rutherford	*Tufnell*	
Replay	Newcastle U 2	Barnsley....................0	
	Shepherd 2 (1 pen)		
1911	Bradford C..................0	Newcastle U 0	
Replay	Bradford C..................1	Newcastle U 0	
	Speirs		
1912	Barnsley....................0	West Bromwich Albion 0	
Replay	Barnsley....................1	West Bromwich Albion 0*	
	Tufnell		
1913	Aston Villa 1	Sunderland 0	
	Barber		
1914	Burnley 1	Liverpool 0	
	Freeman		
1915	Sheffield U 3	Chelsea 0	
	Simmons, Masterman, Kitchen		

1920	Aston Villa 1	Huddersfield T 0*
	Kirton	
1921	Tottenham H 1	Wolverhampton W 0
	Dimmock	
1922	Huddersfield T 1	Preston NE 0
	Smith (pen)	
1923	Bolton W 2	West Ham U 0
	Jack, J.R. Smith	
1924	Newcastle U 2	Aston Villa 0
	Harris, Seymour	
1925	Sheffield U 1	Cardiff C 0
	Tunstall	
1926	Bolton W 1	Manchester C 0
	Jack	
1927	Cardiff C 1	Arsenal 0
	Ferguson	
1928	Blackburn Rovers................3	Huddersfield T 1
	Roscamp 2, McLean	*A. Jackson*
1929	Bolton W 2	Portsmouth 0
	Butler, Blackmore	
1930	Arsenal 2	Huddersfield T 0
	James, Lambert	
1931	West Bromwich Albion 2	Birmingham 1
	W.G. Richardson 2	*Bradford*
1932	Newcastle U 2	Arsenal 1
	Allen 2	*John*
1933	Everton 3	Manchester C 0
	Stein, Dean, Dunn	
1934	Manchester C 2	Portsmouth 1
	Tilson 2	*Rutherford*
1935	Sheffield W 4	West Bromwich Albion 2
	Rimmer 2, Palethorpe,	*Boyes, Sandford*
	Hooper	
1936	Arsenal 1	Sheffield U 0
	Drake	
1937	Sunderland 3	Preston NE 1
	Gurney, Carter, Burbanks	*F. O'Donnell*
1938	Preston NE 1	Huddersfield T 0*
	Mutch (pen)	
1939	Portsmouth 4	Wolverhampton W 1
	Parker 2, Barlow,	*Dorsett*
	Anderson	
1946	Derby Co 4	Charlton Ath...............................1*
	H. Turner (og), Doherty,	*H. Turner*
	Stamps 2	
1947	Charlton Ath 1	Burnley 0*
	Duffy	
1948	Manchester U 4	Blackpool 2
	Rowley 2, Pearson,	*Shimwell (pen), Mortensen*
	Anderson	
1949	Wolverhampton W 3	Leicester C 1
	Pye 2, Smyth,	*Griffiths*
1950	Arsenal 2	Liverpool 0
	Lewis 2	

1951	Newcastle U 2	Blackpool 0
	Milburn 2	
1952	Newcastle U 1	Arsenal 0
	G. Robledo	
1953	Blackpool...................................4	Bolton W 3
	Mortensen 3, Perry	*Lofthouse, Moir, Bell*
1954	West Bromwich Albion 3	Preston NE 2
	Allen 2 (1 pen), Griffin	*Morrison, Wayman*
1955	Newcastle U 3	Manchester C 1
	Milburn, Mitchell,	*Johnstone*
	Hannah	
1956	Manchester C 3	Birmingham C 1
	Hayes, Dyson, Johnstone	*Kinsey*
1957	Aston Villa 2	Manchester U 1
	McParland 2	*T. Taylor*
1958	Bolton W 2	Manchester U 0
	Lofthouse 2	
1959	Nottingham F 2	Luton T 1
	Dwight, Wilson	*Pacey*
1960	Wolverhampton W 3	Blackburn Rovers......................................0
	McGrath (og), Deeley 2	
1961	Tottenham H..............................2	Leicester C 0
	Smith, Dyson	
1962	Tottenham H..............................3	Burnley 1
	Greaves, Smith,	*Robson*
	Blanchflower (pen)	
1963	Manchester U 3	Leicester C 1
	Herd 2, Law	*Keyworth*
1964	West Ham U...............................3	Preston NE 2
	Sissons, Hurst, Boyce	*Holden, Dawson*
1965	Liverpool 2	Leeds U 1*
	Hunt, St John	*Bremner*
1966	Everton 3	Sheffield W 2
	Trebilcock 2, Temple	*McCalliog, Ford*
1967	Tottenham H..............................2	Chelsea 1
	Robertson, Saul	*Tambling*
1968	West Browmich Albion 1	Everton..0*
	Astle	
1969	Manchester C 1	Leicester C 0
	Young	
1970	Chelsea.....................................2	Leeds U 2*
	Houseman, Hutchinson	*Charlton, Jones*
Replay	Chelsea.....................................2	Leeds U 1*
	Osgood, Webb	*Jones*
1971	Arsenal.....................................2	Liverpool 1*
	Kelly, George	*Heighway*
1972	Leeds U 1	Arsenal 0
	Clarke	
1973	Sunderland 1	Leeds U 0
	Porterfield	
1974	Liverpool 3	Newcastle 0
	Keegan 2, Heighway	
1975	West Ham U...............................2	Fulham...0
	A. Taylor 2	

1976	Southampton	1	Manchester U	0
	Stokes			
1977	Manchester U	2	Liverpool	1
	Pearson, J. Greenhoff		*Case*	
1978	Ipswich T	1	Arsenal	0
	Osborne			
1979	Arsenal	3	Manchester U	2
	Talbot, Stapleton, Sunderland		*McQueen, McIlroy*	
1980	West Ham U	1	Arsenal	0
	Brooking			
1981	Tottenham H	1	Manchester C	1*
	Hutchison (og)		*Hutchison*	
Replay	Tottenham H	3	Manchester C	2
	Villa 2, Crooks		*MacKenzie, Reeves (pen)*	
1982	Tottenham H	1	QPR	1*
	Hoddle		*Fenwick*	
Replay	Tottenham H	1	QPR	0
	Hoddle (pen)			
1983	Manchester U	2	Brighton & HA	2*
	Stapleton, Wilkins		*Smith, Stevens*	
Replay	Manchester U	4	Brighton & HA	0
	Robson 2, Whiteside, Muhren (pen)			
1984	Everton	2	Watford	0
	Sharp, Gray			
1985	Manchester U	1	Everton	0*
	Whiteside			
1986	Liverpool	3	Everton	1
	Rush 2, Johnston		*Lineker*	
1987	Coventry C	3	Tottenham H	2*
	Bennett, Houchen, Mabbutt (og)		*C. Allen, Kilcline (og)*	
1988	Wimbledon	1	Liverpool	0
	Sanchez			
1989	Liverpool	3	Everton	2*
	Aldridge, Rush 2		*McCall 2*	
1990	Manchester U	3	Crystal Palace	3*
	Robson, Hughes 2		*O'Reilly, Wright 2*	
Replay	Manchester U	1	Crystal Palace	0
	Martin			
1991	Tottenham H	2	Nottingham F	1*
	Stewart, Walker (og)		*Pearce*	
1992	Liverpool	2	Sunderland	0
	Thomas, Rush			
1993	Arsenal	1	Sheffield W	1*
	Wright		*Hirst*	
Replay	Arsenal	2	Sheffield W	1*
	Wright, Linighan		*Waddle*	
1994	Manchester U	4	Chelsea	0
	Cantona 2 (2 pens), Hughes, McClair			
1995	Everton	1	Manchester U	0
	Rideout			
1996	Manchester U	1	Liverpool	0
	Cantona			

1997	Chelsea.................................2	Middlesbrough.............................0
	Di Matteo, Newton	
1998	Arsenal.................................2	Newcastle U 0
	Overmars, Anelka	
1999	Manchester U.......................2	Newcastle U 0
	Sheringham, Scholes	
2000	Chelsea.................................1	Aston Villa 0
	Di Matteo	
2001	Liverpool 2	Arsenal 1
	Owen 2	*Ljungberg*
2002	Arsenal.................................2	Chelsea 0
	Parlour, Ljungberg	
2003	Arsenal.................................1	Southampton..............................0
	Pires	
2004	Manchester U.......................3	Millwall.......................................0
	Ronaldo, Van Nistelrooy 2 (1 pen)	
2005	Arsenal.................................0	Manchester U 0*
	Arsenal won 5-4 on penalties	
2006	Liverpool 3	West Ham U 3*
	Cisse, Gerrard 2	*Carragher (og), Ashton, Konchesky*
	Liverpool won 3-1 on penalties	
2007	Chelsea.................................1	Manchester U 0*
	Drogba	
2008	Portsmouth 1	Cardiff C 0
	Kanu	
2009	Chelsea.................................2	Everton 1
	Drogba, Lampard	*Saha*

*After extra time

FA CUP ATTENDANCES 1969–2009

	Total	No. of matches	Average per match		Total	No. of matches	Average per match
2008–09	2,131,669	163	13,078	1988–89	1,966,318	164	12,173
2007–08	2,011,320	152	13,232	1987–88	2,050,585	155	13,229
2006–07	2,218,846	158	14,043	1986–87	1,877,400	165	11,378
2005–06	1,966,638	160	12,291	1985–86	1,971,951	168	11,738
2004–05	1,999,752	146	13,697	1984–85	1,909,359	157	12,162
2003–04	1,870,103	149	12,551	1983–84	1,941,400	166	11,695
2002–03	1,850,326	150	12,336	1982–83	2,209,625	154	14,348
2001–02	1,809,093	148	12,224	1981–82	1,840,955	160	11,506
2000–01	1,804,535	151	11,951	1980–81	2,756,800	169	16,312
1999–2000	1,700,913	158	10,765	1979–80	2,661,416	163	16,328
1998–99	2,107,947	155	13,599	1978–79	2,604,002	166	15,687
1997–98	2,125,696	165	12,883	1977–78	2,594,578	160	16,216
1996–97	1,843,998	151	12,211	1976–77	2,982,102	174	17,139
1995–96	2,046,199	167	12,252	1975–76	2,759,941	161	17,142
1994–95	2,015,249	161	12,517	1974–75	2,968,903	172	17,261
1993–94	1,965,146	159	12,359	1973–74	2,779,952	167	16,646
1992–93	2,047,670	161	12,718	1972–73	2,928,975	160	18,306
1991–92	1,935,340	160	12,095	1971–72	3,158,562	160	19,741
1990–91	2,038,518	162	12,583	1970–71	3,220,432	162	19,879
1989–90	2,190,463	170	12,885	1969–70	3,026,765	170	17,805

SUMMARY OF FA CUP WINNERS SINCE 1872

Manchester United	11
Arsenal	10
Tottenham Hotspur	8
Aston Villa	7
Liverpool	7
Blackburn Rovers	6
Newcastle United	6
Chelsea	5
Everton	5
The Wanderers	5
West Bromwich Albion	5
Bolton Wanderers	4
Manchester City	4
Sheffield United	4
Wolverhampton Wanderers	4
Sheffield Wednesday	3
West Ham United	3
Bury	2
Nottingham Forest	2
Old Etonians	2
Portsmouth	2
Preston North End	2
Sunderland	2
Barnsley	1
Blackburn Olympic	1
Blackpool	1
Bradford City	1
Burnley	1
Cardiff City	1
Charlton Athletic	1
Clapham Rovers	1
Coventry City	1
Derby County	1
Huddersfield Town	1
Ipswich Town	1
Leeds United	1
Notts County	1
Old Carthusians	1
Oxford University	1
Royal Engineers	1
Southampton	1
Wimbledon	1

APPEARANCES IN FA CUP FINAL

Manchester United	18
Arsenal	17
Everton	13
Liverpool	13
Newcastle United	13
Aston Villa	10
West Bromwich Albion	10
Tottenham Hotspur	9
Chelsea	9
Blackburn Rovers	8
Manchester City	8
Wolverhampton Wanderers	8
Bolton Wanderers	7
Preston North End	7
Old Etonians	6
Sheffield United	6
Sheffield Wednesday	6
Huddersfield Town	5
The Wanderers	5
West Ham United	5
Derby County	4
Leeds United	4
Leicester City	4
Oxford University	4
Portsmouth	4
Royal Engineers	4
Southampton	4
Sunderland	4
Blackpool	3
Burnley	3
Cardiff City	3
Nottingham Forest	3
Barnsley	2
Birmingham City	2
Bury	2
Charlton Athletic	2
Clapham Rovers	2
Notts County	2
Queen's Park (Glasgow)	2
Blackburn Olympic	1
Bradford City	1
Brighton & Hove Albion	1
Bristol City	1
Coventry City	1
Crystal Palace	1
Fulham	1
Ipswich Town	1
Luton Town	1
Middlesbrough	1
Millwall	1
Old Carthusians	1
Queen's Park Rangers	1
Watford	1
Wimbledon	1

CARLING CUP REVIEW 2008–2009

A quiet opening to the campaign back in August was a long way from a largely disappointing finale in March which went to the unsatisfactory method of a shoot-out to provide a winner, Manchester United having failed to beat Portsmouth in a goalless draw before becoming the masters of the spot kick lottery 4-1. Yet that initial first round had managed to restrict such nonsense to two matches.

The Lancastrian derby between Rochdale and Oldham – also goalless – was won by the Latics, while the Yorkshire equivalent involving Sheffield Wednesday and Rotherham United had gone to the Millers after a 2-2 draw. Leeds had led the goal-scoring parade proper with a 5-2 win at Chester City, with Jermaine Beckford scoring a hat trick. Nathan Ellington of Derby County was another treble shooter in beating Lincoln City.

In came the Premier teams who had no involvement in Europe affairs with their arrival the usual splattering of cup upsets, even allowing for the varying interest placed on the competition by such clubs. Bolton Wanderers were beaten at home by Northampton Town and West Bromwich Albion were the losers at Hartlepool United. Conversely there were some high scores with Middlesbrough putting Yeovil in their place 5-1 and Reading taken a similar line with Luton Town.

Four goals each were scored by Blackburn, Leeds, Queens Park Rangers (Ledesma hat trick) and West Ham United. Thankfully, too, just two wretched penalty-kick answers – Rotherham having decided it as the way forward again by beating Wolves, while Brighton caused something of a sensation in a delayed tie by ousting Manchester City from the competition.

Those with European commitments entered the third round, though City had had to endure defeat a round earlier of course. Arsenal's youngsters made swift work of Sheffield United, Carlos Vela grabbing three of their six goals! Burnley took out Fulham and Queens Park Rangers surprised Villa at Villa Park. Manchester United beat Middlesbrough 3-1, Tottenham Hotspur edged out Newcastle United at St James' Park, but Sunderland needed a shoot-out to dispose of Northampton. There was just one other last minute decision – Stoke City beating Reading after a 2-2 draw. Chelsea and Wigan Athletic both scored four goals away from home.

Brighton's tie in the round against Derby County was not played until early November, but they were well beaten 4-1 at home with Emanuel Villa scoring three times. The Rams had just a week to get organised for the fourth round and a visit from Leeds United. This time they were restricted to two goals, Villa and Ellington the previous hat trick marksmen, just one each.

Spurs proved the leading contestants in the round with a fine 4-2 win over Liverpool in contrast to Manchester United who looked to Carlos Tevez and his late penalty kick to remove Queens Park Rangers. Burnley produced the shock, but having held Chelsea at the Bridge, won on penalty kicks. An own goal helped Blackburn win at Sunderland, Stoke ended Rotherham's useful run and Watford won at Swansea City. Three goals from Arsène Wenger's second stringers put out Wigan.

So to the quarter-finals and not content with their victory at Chelsea, Burnley went on to compound it all by beating Arsenal at Turf Moor. This just about took first place in the honours because Manchester United won an enthralling 5-3 match with Blackburn. Tevez was again the main man scoring either three or four goals in the process. Spurs gave Watford a goal start before winning and Ellington saved the tie with Stoke entering extra time with an injury-time penalty for Derby.

Sadly for them, Burnley came unstuck at Tottenham in the first leg semi-final losing 4-1, while Derby were edging Manchester United by 1-0. The return games produced a remarkable recovery from Burnley who had they been able to call upon away goals counting double would have given them the tie. Spurs saved themselves with two extra time strikes. United made sure 4-2.

The Johnstone's Paint Trophy was a triumph for Luton Town after their reduced-points handicap in the League. They accounted for Scunthorpe United who ironically started the 2009–10 season three divisions higher!

CARLING CUP 2008–2009

FIRST ROUND

Bournemouth	(1) 1	Cardiff C	(2) 2	
Brighton & HA	(4) 4	Barnet	(0) 0	
Bristol C	(0) 2	Peterborough U	(1) 1	
Bury	(0) 0	Burnley	(1) 2	
Charlton Ath	(0) 0	Yeovil T	(1) 1	
Chester C	(1) 2	Leeds U	(5) 5	
Crewe Alex	(2) 2	Barnsley	(0) 0	
Crystal Palace	(1) 2	Hereford U	(1) 1	
Dagenham & R	(0) 1	Reading	(1) 2	
Derby Co	(0) 3	Lincoln C	(0) 1	
(aet.)				
Exeter C	(0) 1	Southampton	(1) 3	
Gillingham	(0) 0	Colchester U	(1) 1	
Grimsby T	(1) 2	Tranmere R	(0) 0	
Hartlepool U	(0) 3	Scunthorpe U	(0) 0	
Huddersfield T	(0) 4	Bradford C	(0) 0	
Ipswich T	(3) 4	Leyton Orient	(0) 1	
Leicester C	(1) 1	Stockport Co	(0) 0	
Luton T	(1) 2	Plymouth Arg	(0) 0	
Macclesfield T	(1) 2	Blackpool	(0) 0	
Millwall	(0) 0	Northampton T	(1) 1	
Milton Keynes D	(1) 1	Norwich C	(0) 0	
Notts Co	(0) 1	Doncaster R	(0) 0	
(aet.)				
Preston NE	(1) 2	Chesterfield	(0) 0	
Rochdale	(0) 0	Oldham Ath	(0) 0	
(aet; Oldham Ath won 4-1 on penalties.)				
Sheffield W	(1) 2	Rotherham U	(1) 2	
(aet; Rotherham U won 5-3 on penalties.)				
Shrewsbury T	(0) 0	Carlisle U	(1) 1	
Southend U	(0) 0	Cheltenham T	(0) 1	
(aet.)				
Swansea C	(1) 2	Brentford	(0) 0	
Swindon T	(2) 2	QPR	(1) 3	
Walsall	(1) 1	Darlington	(1) 2	
Watford	(0) 1	Bristol R	(0) 0	
Wolverhampton W	(0) 3	Accrington S	(1) 2	
(aet.)				
Coventry C	(1) 3	Aldershot T	(1) 1	
Nottingham F	(1) 4	Morecambe	(0) 0	
Sheffield U	(1) 3	Port Vale	(0) 1	
Wycombe W	(0) 0	Birmingham C	(1) 4	

SECOND ROUND

Bolton W	(0) 1	Northampton T	(2) 2	
Brighton & HA	(0) 2	Manchester C	(0) 2	
(aet; Brighton & HA won 5-3 on penalties.)				
Burnley	(1) 3	Oldham Ath	(0) 0	

172

Cardiff C	(1) 2	Milton Keynes D	(0) 1
Cheltenham T	(0) 2	Stoke C	(0) 3
Coventry C	(1) 2	Newcastle U	(2) 3
Crewe Alex	(1) 2	Bristol C	(0) 1
Hartlepool U	(0) 3	WBA	(0) 1
(aet.)			
Ipswich T	(1) 2	Colchester U	(0) 1
Leeds U	(2) 4	Crystal Palace	(0) 0
Middlesbrough	(3) 5	Yeovil T	(1) 1
Preston NE	(0) 0	Derby Co	(1) 1
QPR	(0) 4	Carlisle U	(0) 0
Reading	(2) 5	Luton T	(0) 1
Rotherham U	(0) 0	Wolverhampton W	(0) 0
(aet; Rotherham U won 4-3 on penalties.)			
Southampton	(1) 2	Birmingham C	(0) 0
Swansea C	(0) 2	Hull C	(1) 1
(aet.)			
Watford	(1) 2	Darlington	(0) 1
(aet.)			
Wigan Ath	(1) 4	Notts Co	(0) 0
Blackburn R	(3) 4	Grimsby T	(1) 1
Fulham	(1) 3	Leicester C	(0) 2
Huddersfield T	(1) 1	Sheffield U	(0) 2
Nottingham F	(0) 1	Sunderland	(0) 2
(aet.)			
West Ham U	(0) 4	Macclesfield T	(1) 1
(aet.)			

THIRD ROUND

Arsenal	(3) 6	Sheffield U	(0) 0
Aston Villa	(0) 0	QPR	(0) 1
Blackburn R	(1) 1	Everton	(0) 0
Brighton & HA	(1) 1	Derby Co	(2) 4
Burnley	(0) 1	Fulham	(0) 0
Ipswich T	(0) 1	Wigan Ath	(0) 4
Leeds U	(1) 3	Hartlepool U	(2) 2
Liverpool	(1) 2	Crewe Alex	(1) 1
Manchester U	(1) 3	Middlesbrough	(0) 1
Newcastle U	(0) 1	Tottenham H	(0) 2
Portsmouth	(0) 0	Chelsea	(2) 4
Rotherham U	(1) 3	Southampton	(0) 1
Stoke C	(1) 2	Reading	(1) 2
(aet; Stoke C won 4-3 on penalties.)			
Sunderland	(0) 2	Northampton T	(1) 2
(aet; Sunderland won 4-3 on penalties.)			
Swansea C	(0) 1	Cardiff C	(0) 0
Watford	(0) 1	West Ham U	(0) 0

FOURTH ROUND

Arsenal	(1) 3	Wigan Ath	(0) 0
Derby Co	(2) 2	Leeds U	(1) 1
Manchester U	(0) 1	QPR	(0) 0

173

Stoke C	(1) 2	Rotherham U	(0) 0
Swansea C	(0) 0	Watford	(1) 1
Chelsea	(1) 1	Burnley	(0) 1

(aet; Burnley won 5-4 on penalties.)

| Sunderland | (0) 1 | Blackburn R | (0) 2 |
| Tottenham H | (3) 4 | Liverpool | (0) 2 |

QUARTER-FINALS

Burnley	(1) 2	Arsenal	(0) 0
Stoke C	(0) 0	Derby Co	(0) 1
Manchester United	(2) 5	Blackburn R	(0) 3
Watford	(1) 1	Tottenham H	(1) 2

SEMI-FINAL FIRST LEG

| Tottenham H | (0) 4 | Burnley | (1) 1 |
| Derby Co | (1) 1 | Manchester U | (0) 0 |

SEMI-FINAL SECOND LEG

| Manchester U | (3) 4 | Derby Co | (0) 2 |
| Burnley | (1) 3 | Tottenham H | (0) 2 |

(aet.)

CARLING CUP FINAL

Sunday, 1 March 2009

Manchester U (0) 0   Tottenham H (0) 0

(aet.)

(at Wembley Stadium, attendance 88,217)

Manchester U: Foster; O'Shea (Vidic), Evra, Gibson (Giggs), Ferdinand, Evans, Ronaldo, Scholes, Welbeck (Anderson), Tevez, Nani.

Tottenham H: Gomes; Corluka, Assou-Ekotto, Zokora, Dawson, King, Lennon (Bentley), Jenas (Bale), Pavlyuchenko (O'Hara), Bent, Modric.

aet; Manchester U won 4-1 on penalties: Giggs scored; O'Hara saved; Tevez scored; Corluka scored; Ronaldo scored; Bentley missed; Anderson scored.

Referee: C. Foy (Merseyside).

PAST LEAGUE CUP FINALS

Played as two legs up to 1966

1961	Rotherham U 2	Aston Villa 0
	Webster, Kirkman	
	Aston Villa 3	Rotherham U 0*
	O'Neill, Burrows, McParland	
1962	Rochdale 0	Norwich C 3
	Lythgoe 2, Punton	
	Norwich C 1	Rochdale 0
	Hill	
1963	Birmingham C 3	Aston Villa 1
	Leek 2, Bloomfield	*Thomson*
	Aston Villa 0	Birmingham C 0
1964	Stoke C 1	Leicester C 1
	Bebbington	*Gibson*
	Leicester C 3	Stoke C 2
	Stringfellow, Gibson, Riley	*Viollet, Kinnell*
1965	Chelsea 3	Leicester C 2
	Tambling, Venables (pen), McCreadie	*Appleton, Goodfellow*
	Leicester C 0	Chelsea 0
1966	West Ham U 2	WBA 1
	Moore, Byrne	*Astle*
	WBA 4	West Ham U 1
	Kaye, Brown, Clark, Williams	*Peters*
1967	QPR 3	WBA 2
	Morgan R, Marsh, Lazarus	*Clark C 2*
1968	Leeds U 1	Arsenal 0
	Cooper	
1969	Swindon T 3	Arsenal 1*
	Smart, Rogers 2	*Gould*
1970	Manchester C 2	WBA 1*
	Doyle, Pardoe	*Astle*
1971	Tottenham H 2	Aston Villa 0
	Chivers 2	
1972	Chelsea 1	Stoke C 2
	Osgood	*Conroy, Eastham*
1973	Tottenham H 1	Norwich C 0
	Coates	
1974	Wolverhampton W 2	Manchester C 1
	Hibbitt, Richards	*Bell*
1975	Aston Villa 1	Norwich C 0
	Graydon	
1976	Manchester C 2	Newcastle U 1
	Barnes, Tueart	*Gowling*
1977	Aston Villa 0	Everton 0
Replay	Aston Villa 1	Everton 1*
	Kenyon (og)	*Latchford*

Replay	Aston Villa 3	Everton 2*	
	Little 2, Nicholl	*Latchford, Lyons*	
1978	Nottingham F 0	Liverpool 0*	
Replay	Nottingham F 1	Liverpool 0	
	Robertson (pen)		
1979	Nottingham F 3	Southampton 2	
	Birtles 2, Woodcock	*Peach, Holmes*	
1980	Wolverhampton W 1	Nottingham F 0	
	Gray		
1981	Liverpool 1	West Ham U........................1*	
	Kennedy A	*Stewart (pen)*	
Replay	Liverpool 2	West Ham U........................1	
	Dalglish, Hansen	*Goddard*	
1982	Liverpool 3	Tottenham H.......................1*	
	Whelan 2, Rush	*Archibald*	
1983	Liverpool 2	Manchester U......................1*	
	Kennedy A, Whelan	*Whiteside*	
1984	Liverpool 0	Everton 0*	
Replay	Liverpool 1	Everton 0	
	Souness		
1985	Norwich C..........................1	Sunderland 0	
	Chisholm (og)		
1986	Oxford U............................3	QPR....................................0	
	Hebberd, Houghton, Charles		
1987	Arsenal...............................2	Liverpool 1	
	Nicholas 2	*Rush*	
1988	Luton T...............................3	Arsenal...............................2	
	Stein B 2, Wilson	*Hayes, Smith*	
1989	Nottingham F 3	Luton T 1	
	Clough 2, Webb	*Harford*	
1990	Nottingham F 1	Oldham Ath 0	
	Jemson		
1991	Sheffield W 1	Manchester U......................0	
	Sheridan		
1992	Manchester U......................1	Nottingham F 0	
	McClair		
1993	Arsenal...............................2	Sheffield W 1	
	Merson, Morrow	*Harkes*	
1994	Aston Villa 3	Manchester U......................1	
	Atkinson, Saunders 2 (1 pen)	*Hughes*	
1995	Liverpool 2	Bolton W 1	
	McManaman 2	*Thompson*	
1996	Aston Villa 3	Leeds U...............................0	
	Milosevic, Taylor, Yorke		
1997	Leicester C..........................1	Middlesbrough 1*	
	Heskey	*Ravanelli*	
Replay	Leicester C..........................1	Middlesbrough 0*	
	Claridge		
1998	Chelsea...............................2	Middlesbrough 0*	
	Sinclair, Di Matteo		

1999	Tottenham H	1	Leicester C	0
	Nielsen			
2000	Leicester C	2	Tranmere R	1
	Elliott 2		*Kelly*	
2001	Liverpool	1	Birmingham C	1
	Fowler		*Purse (pen)*	

Liverpool won 5-4 on penalties.

2002	Blackburn	2	Tottenham H	1
	Jansen, Cole		*Ziege*	
2003	Liverpool	2	Manchester U	0
	Gerrard, Owen			
2004	Middlesbrough	2	Bolton W	1
	Job, Zenden (pen)		*Davies*	
2005	Chelsea	3	Liverpool	2*
	Gerrard (og), Drogba, Kezman		*Riise, Nunez*	
2006	Manchester U	4	Wigan Ath	0
	Rooney 2, Saha, Ronaldo			
2007	Chelsea	2	Arsenal	1
	Drogba 2		*Walcott*	
2008	Tottenham H	2	Chelsea	1*
	Berbatov, Woodgate		*Drogba*	
2009	Manchester U	0	Tottenham H	0*

Manchester U won 4-1 on penalties.

*After extra time

LEAGUE CUP ATTENDANCES 1960–2009

	Total	No. of matches	Average per match		Total	No. of matches	Average per match
2008–09	1,329,753	93	14,298	1983–84	1,900,491	168	11,312
2007–08	1,332,841	94	14,179	1982–83	1,679,756	160	10,498
2006–07	1,098,403	93	11,811	1981–82	1,880,682	161	11,681
2005–06	1,072,362	93	11,531	1980–81	2,051,576	161	12,743
2004–05	1,313,693	93	14,216	1979–80	2,322,866	169	13,745
2003–04	1,267,729	93	13,631	1978–79	1,825,643	139	13,134
2002–03	1,242,478	92	13,505	1977–78	2,038,295	148	13,772
2001–02	1,076,390	93	11,574	1976–77	2,236,636	147	15,215
2000–01	1,501,304	154	9,749	1975–76	1,841,735	140	13,155
1999–2000	1,354,233	153	8,851	1974–75	1,901,094	127	14,969
1998–99	1,555,856	153	10,169	1973–74	1,722,629	132	13,050
1997–98	1,484,297	153	9,701	1972–73	1,935,474	120	16,129
1996–97	1,529,321	163	9,382	1971–72	2,397,154	123	19,489
1995–96	1,776,060	162	10,963	1970–71	2,035,315	116	17,546
1994–95	1,530,478	157	9,748	1969–70	2,299,819	122	18,851
1993–94	1,744,120	163	10,700	1968–69	2,064,647	118	17,497
1992–93	1,558,031	161	9,677	1967–68	1,671,326	110	15,194
1991–92	1,622,337	164	9,892	1966–67	1,394,553	118	11,818
1990–91	1,675,496	159	10,538	1965–66	1,205,876	106	11,376
1989–90	1,836,916	168	10,934	1964–65	962,802	98	9,825
1988–89	1,552,780	162	9,585	1963–64	945,265	104	9,089
1987–88	1,539,253	158	9,742	1962–63	1,029,893	102	10,097
1986–87	1,531,498	157	9,755	1961–62	1,030,534	104	9,909
1985–86	1,579,916	163	9,693	1960–61	1,204,580	112	10,755
1984–85	1,876,429	167	11,236				

JOHNSTONE'S PAINT TROPHY 2008–2009

NORTHERN SECTION FIRST ROUND

Chesterfield	(1) 2	Grimsby T	(1) 2
(Grimsby T won 4-1 on penalties.)			
Crewe Alex	(3) 3	Macclesfield T	(0) 0
Hartlepool U	(0) 0	Leicester C	(0) 3
Leeds U	(2) 2	Bradford C	(0) 1
Oldham Ath	(0) 1	Morecambe	(0) 1
(Morecambe won 5-4 on penalties.)			
Scunthorpe U	(0) 2	Notts Co	(1) 1
Stockport Co	(1) 1	Port Vale	(0) 0
Tranmere R	(0) 1	Accrington S	(0) 0

SOUTHERN SECTION FIRST ROUND

Aldershot T	(1) 2	Swindon T	(1) 2
(Swindon T won 7-6 on penalties.)			
Bournemouth	(1) 3	Bristol R	(0) 0
Brentford	(2) 2	Yeovil T	(1) 2
(Brentford won 4-2 on penalties.)			
Dagenham & R	(3) 4	Barnet	(2) 2
Exeter C	(1) 1	Shrewsbury T	(1) 2
Millwall	(0) 0	Colchester U	(1) 1
Northampton T	(0) 0	Brighton & HA	(0) 1
Southend U	(2) 2	Leyton Orient	(2) 4

NORTHERN SECTION SECOND ROUND

Bury	(0) 1	Stockport Co	(0) 0
Chester C	(0) 1	Morecambe	(1) 1
(Morecambe won 3-1 on penalties.)			
Darlington	(1) 1	Huddersfield T	(0) 0
Leicester C	(0) 0	Lincoln C	(0) 0
(Leicester C won 3-1 on penalties.)			
Rochdale	(2) 2	Carlisle U	(1) 2
(Rochdale won 4-3 on penalties.)			
Rotherham U	(2) 4	Leeds U	(1) 2
Scunthorpe U	(2) 2	Grimsby T	(0) 1
Tranmere R	(0) 1	Crewe Alex	(0) 0

SOUTHERN SECTION SECOND ROUND

Brighton & HA	(2) 2	Leyton Orient	(1) 2
(Brighton & HA won 5-4 on penalties.)			
Cheltenham T	(1) 1	Walsall	(0) 2
Gillingham	(0) 0	Colchester U	(1) 2
Hereford U	(1) 1	Swindon T	(1) 2
Luton T	(1) 2	Brentford	(2) 2
(Luton T won 4-3 on penalties.)			
Milton Keynes D	(0) 0	Bournemouth	(0) 1
Peterborough U	(0) 0	Dagenham & R	(0) 1
Wycombe W	(0) 0	Shrewsbury T	(3) 7

NORTHERN SECTION QUARTER-FINALS

Darlington	(0) 1	Bury	(0) 0
Rotherham U	(1) 2	Leicester C	(0) 0
Scunthorpe U	(0) 1	Rochdale	(0) 0
Tranmere R	(1) 1	Morecambe	(0) 0

SOUTHERN SECTION QUARTER-FINALS

Brighton & HA	(1) 2	Swindon T	(0) 0
Bournemouth	(0) 0	Colchester U	(1) 1
Shrewsbury T	(3) 5	Dagenham & R	(0) 0
Walsall	(0) 0	Luton T	(0) 1

NORTHERN SECTION SEMI-FINALS

Rotherham U	(0) 1	Darlington	(1) 1

(Rotherham U won 4-2 on penalties.)

Scunthorpe U	(1) 2	Tranmere R	(0) 1

SOUTHERN SECTION SEMI-FINALS

Luton T	(1) 1	Colchester U	(0) 0
Shrewsbury T	(0) 0	Brighton & HA	(0) 0

(Brighton & HA won 5-4 on penalties.)

NORTHERN SECTION FINAL FIRST LEG

Scunthorpe U	(0) 2	Rotherham U	(0) 0

NORTHERN SECTION FINAL SECOND LEG

Rotherham U	(0) 0	Scunthorpe U	(0) 1

SOUTHERN SECTION FINAL FIRST LEG

Brighton & HA	(0) 0	Luton T	(0) 0

SOUTHERN SECTION FINAL SECOND LEG

Luton T	(1) 1	Brighton & HA	(1) 1

(Luton T won 4-3 on penalties.)

JOHNSTONE'S PAINT TROPHY FINAL

Sunday, 5 April 2009

(at Wembley Stadium, attendance 55,378)

Luton T (1) 3   Scunthorpe U (1) 2

(aet.)

Luton T: Brill; Asafu-Adjaye, Emanuel, Keane, Pilkington, Spillane, Nicholls, Hall, Martin, Craddock (Gnakpa), Jarvis (Parkin).

Scorers: Martin 32, Craddock 70, Gnakpa 95.

Scunthorpe U: Murphy; Byrne, Williams, McCann, Mirfin, Pearce (Wright), Lansbury, Sparrow (Woolford), Hayes, Hooper, Hurst (Togwell).

Scorers: Hooper 14, McCann 88.

Referee: P. Crossley.

FA CHARITY SHIELD WINNERS 1908–2008

1908	Manchester U v QPR	
	4-0 after 1-1 draw	
1909	Newcastle U v Northampton T	2-0
1910	Brighton v Aston Villa	1-0
1911	Manchester U v Swindon T	8-4
1912	Blackburn R v QPR	2-1
1913	Professionals v Amateurs	7-2
1920	Tottenham H v Burnley	2-0
1921	Huddersfield T v Liverpool	1-0
1922	Not played	
1923	Professionals v Amateurs	2-0
1924	Professionals v Amateurs	3-1
1925	Amateurs v Professionals	6-1
1926	Amateurs v Professionals	6-3
1927	Cardiff C v Corinthians	2-1
1928	Everton v Blackburn R	2-1
1929	Professionals v Amateurs	3-0
1930	Arsenal v Sheffield W	2-1
1931	Arsenal v WBA	1-0
1932	Everton v Newcastle U	5-3
1933	Arsenal v Everton	3-0
1934	Arsenal v Manchester C	4-0
1935	Sheffield W v Arsenal	1-0
1936	Sunderland v Arsenal	2-1
1937	Manchester C v Sunderland	2-0
1938	Arsenal v Preston NE	2-1
1948	Arsenal v Manchester U	4-3
1949	Portsmouth v Wolverhampton W	1-1*
1950	World Cup Team v	4-2
	Canadian Touring Team	
1951	Tottenham H v Newcastle U	2-1
1952	Manchester U v Newcastle U	4-2
1953	Arsenal v Blackpool	3-1
1954	Wolverhampton W v WBA	4-4*
1955	Chelsea v Newcastle U	3-0
1956	Manchester U v Manchester C	1-0
1957	Manchester U v Aston Villa	4-0
1958	Bolton W v Wolverhampton W	4-1
1959	Wolverhampton W v	3-1
	Nottingham F	
1960	Burnley v Wolverhampton W	2-2*
1961	Tottenham H v FA XI	3-2
1962	Tottenham H v Ipswich T	5-1
1963	Everton v Manchester U	4-0
1964	Liverpool v West Ham U	2-2*

1965	Manchester U v Liverpool	2-2*
1966	Liverpool v Everton	1-0
1967	Manchester U v Tottenham H	3-3*
1968	Manchester C v WBA	6-1
1969	Leeds U v Manchester C	2-1
1970	Everton v Chelsea	2-1
1971	Leicester C v Liverpool	1-0
1972	Manchester C v Aston Villa	1-0
1973	Burnley v Manchester C	1-0
1974	Liverpool† v Leeds U	1-1
1975	Derby Co v West Ham U	2-0
1976	Liverpool v Southampton	1-0
1977	Liverpool v Manchester U	0-0*
1978	Nottingham F v Ipswich T	5-0
1979	Liverpool v Arsenal	3-1
1980	Liverpool v West Ham U	1-0
1981	Aston Villa v Tottenham H	2-2*
1982	Liverpool v Tottenham H	1-0
1983	Manchester U v Liverpool	2-0
1984	Everton v Liverpool	1-0
1985	Everton v Manchester U	2-0
1986	Everton v Liverpool	1-1*
1987	Everton v Coventry C	1-0
1988	Liverpool v Wimbledon	2-1
1989	Liverpool v Arsenal	1-0
1990	Liverpool v Manchester U	1-1*
1991	Arsenal v Tottenham H	0-0*
1992	Leeds U v Liverpool	4-3
1993	Manchester U† v Arsenal	1-1
1994	Manchester U v Blackburn R	2-0
1995	Everton v Blackburn R	1-0
1996	Manchester U v Newcastle U	4-0
1997	Manchester U† v Chelsea	1-1
1998	Arsenal v Manchester U	3-0
1999	Arsenal v Manchester U	2-1
2000	Chelsea v Manchester U	2-0
2001	Liverpool v Manchester U	2-1
2002	Arsenal v Liverpool	1-0
2003	Manchester U† v Arsenal	1-1
2004	Arsenal v Manchester U	3-1
2005	Chelsea v Arsenal	2-1
2006	Liverpool v Chelsea	2-1
2007	Manchester U† v Chelsea	1-1
2008	Manchester U† v Portsmouth	0-0

*Each club retained shield for six months. †Won on penalties.

THE FA COMMUNITY SHIELD 2008

Manchester United (0) 0, Portsmouth (0) 0

aet; Manchester U won 3-1 on penalties.

At Wembley Stadium, 10 August 2008, attendance 84,808

Manchester United: Van der Sar; Neville (Brown), Evra, O'Shea (Carrick), Ferdinand, Vidic, Fletcher, Scholes, Giggs, Tevez, Nani (Campbell).

Portsmouth: James; Johnson, Hreidarsson (Lauren), Diarra, Campbell, Distin, Pedro Mendes (Mvemba), Diop, Crouch, Defoe, Kranjcar (Utaka).

Referee: P. Walton (Northants).

SCOTTISH LEAGUE REVIEW 2008–2009

In too many seasons since the cut was introduced into the Scottish Premier League the number of outstanding issues have been minimal with five matches remaining. Not so in 2008–09 where Rangers were trailing Celtic by just one point, three of the other top six were in with a chance of European entry and just six points separated the bottom five!

With a breather for the Homecoming Scottish Cup semi-finals the struggles were renewed with Celtic dealing a blow to Aberdeen's continental plans at Pittodrie as well as giving themselves a further boost over Rangers. At the other end of the table, Falkirk's position improved with a 2-1 win over Motherwell. The next day Rangers kept in touch beating Hearts whose third place was anything but secure.

Dundee United lost an opportunity of catching up with Hearts who were losers in the Edinburgh derby, by being held by the Dons. Then there was the last Auld Firm clash of the season at Ibrox and a precious single goal victory for Rangers to put themselves two points in front, a situation at the head of affairs they had not enjoyed in a serious sense since September.

With Falkirk earning a point at Kilmarnock and St Mirren losing to Motherwell, the Bairns had clawed back to within two points of the Buddies. With Rangers inactive, Celtic recaptured the leadership against Dundee United, who once more lost out on chasing Hearts who had managed a goalless draw at Aberdeen.

Enter Hibernian, in no position to improve their own prospects, but taking a point off Rangers. In the cellar region, Falkirk swapped places with St Mirren at last with a narrow victory at Hamilton while St Mirren was losing at Kilmarnock. Yet just when it seemed their situation was looking more comfortable, Falkirk was beaten at home by St Mirren!

During this period, Inverness Caley were slipping along with newcomers Hamilton. Ironically these two clubs had been the first two table-toppers of the season! Rangers edged out Aberdeen to lead by three points, Celtic having a game in hand. Meanwhile Hearts had put Dundee United out of their misery. Again the Hi-Bees proved the king makers, this time preventing Celtic from winning at Easter Road. Rangers had a two point lead with a game to go.

Depending on individual results four teams were threatened by relegation. The last weekend settled the drama. Hamilton were saved with a win at St Mirren, who in turn survived by Falkirk relegating Caley! Kilmarnock at one stage drawn into the danger zone won their last three – their best run all season. The following day Rangers needed a win at Dundee, a draw or defeat would give Celtic the title again provided they beat Hearts.

Rangers ran out easy 3-0 winners to take their 52nd championship denying Dundee United a European spot as Aberdeen snatched it by defeating Hibs while Celtic were held by Hearts. Celtic had won the CIS Insurance Cup beating Rangers 2-0, but Rangers took the Scottish Cup beating Falkirk 1-0. Gordon Strachan resigned after Celtic's championship loss.

Again there has been speculation about a Second Division for the SPL. Another rumour concerned Rangers and Celtic being linked with a Second Division in the FA Premier League!

Promoted to the SPL is St Johnstone, who began quietly but established a useful lead and had a lengthy unbeaten run in the middle of the season to take the Irn-Bru Championship. Dundee had flattered early on, Livingston shortly afterwards. Queen of the South had made similar moves in front, but the Saints had put a firm hand on events by early November.

Clyde were relegated to Division Two, Airdrie United, who had beaten Ross County on penalties in the Scottish League Challenge Cup Final after a 2-2 draw, were beaten in the play-offs by Ayr United, runners-up to Division Two leaders Raith Rovers. In Division Three, Dumbarton had timed their run perfectly to head off Cowdenbeath who lost out in the play-off final on penalties against Stenhousemuir, early favourites for promotion.

Queen's Park beaten in the play-offs and Stranraer threatened by extinction at one time went down to Division Three.

SCOTTISH LEAGUE TABLES 2008–2009

		Home					Away					Total						
Premier League	P	W	D	L	F	A	W	D	L	F	A	W	D	L	F	A	GD	Pts
1 Rangers	38	15	2	2	44	15	11	6	2	33	13	26	8	4	77	28	49	86
2 Celtic	38	14	4	1	48	13	10	6	3	32	20	24	10	4	80	33	47	82
3 Hearts	38	11	5	3	28	18	5	6	8	12	19	16	11	11	40	37	3	59
4 Aberdeen	38	9	5	5	22	17	5	6	8	19	23	14	11	13	41	40	1	53
5 Dundee U	38	7	8	4	25	24	6	6	7	22	26	13	14	11	47	50	-3	53
6 Hibernian	38	6	7	6	23	23	5	7	7	19	23	11	14	13	42	46	-4	47
7 Motherwell	38	7	6	6	24	27	6	3	10	22	24	13	9	16	46	51	-5	48
8 Kilmarnock	38	7	3	9	18	22	5	5	9	20	26	12	8	18	38	48	-10	44
9 Hamilton A	38	7	2	10	18	20	6	3	10	12	33	13	5	20	30	53	-23	44
10 Falkirk	38	6	4	9	19	20	3	7	9	18	32	9	11	18	37	52	-15	38
11 St Mirren	38	3	8	8	14	21	6	2	11	19	31	9	10	19	33	52	-19	37
12 Inverness CT	38	4	5	10	18	27	6	2	11	19	31	10	7	21	37	58	-21	37

		Home					Away					Total						
First Division	P	W	D	L	F	A	W	D	L	F	A	W	D	L	F	A	GD	Pts
1 St Johnstone	36	10	5	3	26	13	7	9	2	29	22	17	14	5	55	35	20	65
2 Partick Th	36	9	3	6	20	14	4	7	7	19	24	13	10	13	39	38	1	49
3 Dunfermline Ath	36	8	5	5	20	24	6	4	8	32	20	14	9	13	52	44	8	51
4 Dundee	36	8	5	5	22	14	5	6	7	11	18	13	11	12	33	32	1	50
5 Queen of the S	36	6	6	6	37	28	5	7	6	20	22	11	13	12	57	50	7	46
6 Morton	36	8	7	3	23	14	4	4	10	17	26	12	11	13	40	40	0	47
7 Livingston	36	8	3	7	29	25	5	5	8	27	33	13	8	15	56	58	-2	47
8 Ross Co	36	6	6	6	22	22	7	2	9	20	24	13	8	15	42	46	-4	47
9 Airdrie U	36	7	5	6	20	19	5	1	12	9	24	12	6	18	29	43	-14	42
10 Clyde	36	6	5	7	24	28	4	4	10	17	30	10	9	17	41	58	-17	39

		Home					Away					Total						
Second Division	P	W	D	L	F	A	W	D	L	F	A	W	D	L	F	A	GD	Pts
1 Raith R	36	11	6	1	33	16	11	4	3	27	11	22	10	4	60	27	33	76
2 Ayr U	36	11	7	0	38	16	11	1	6	33	22	22	8	6	71	38	33	74
3 Brechin C	36	12	2	4	27	18	6	6	6	24	27	18	8	10	51	45	6	62
4 Peterhead	36	9	5	4	32	16	6	6	6	22	23	15	11	10	54	39	15	56
5 Stirling Alb	36	7	5	6	26	23	7	6	5	33	26	14	11	11	59	49	10	53
6 East Fife	36	6	2	10	19	24	7	3	8	20	20	13	5	18	39	44	-5	44
7 Arbroath	36	6	3	9	22	23	5	5	8	23	23	11	8	17	45	46	-1	44
8 Alloa Ath	36	6	3	9	22	23	5	5	8	25	36	11	8	17	47	59	-12	41
9 Queen's Park	36	4	6	8	17	22	3	6	9	18	32	7	12	17	35	54	-19	33
10 Stranraer	36	1	4	13	14	48	2	3	13	17	42	3	7	26	31	90	-59	16

		Home					Away					Total						
Third Division	P	W	D	L	F	A	W	D	L	F	A	W	D	L	F	A	GD	Pts
1 Dumbarton	36	11	5	2	38	13	8	5	5	27	23	19	10	7	65	36	29	67
2 Cowdenbeath	36	11	5	2	27	15	7	4	7	21	19	18	9	9	48	34	14	63
3 East Stirling	36	10	1	7	30	29	9	3	6	27	21	19	4	13	57	50	7	61
4 Stenhousemuir	36	8	5	5	32	19	8	3	7	23	27	16	8	12	55	46	9	56
5 Montrose	36	8	3	7	23	24	8	3	7	24	24	16	6	14	47	48	-1	54
6 Forfar Ath	36	6	5	7	26	28	8	4	6	27	23	14	9	13	53	51	2	51
7 Annan Ath	36	6	3	9	24	22	8	5	5	32	23	14	8	14	56	45	11	50
8 Albion R	36	6	2	10	18	25	5	4	9	19	35	11	6	19	37	60	-23	39
9 Berwick R	36	6	4	8	24	29	4	3	11	22	32	10	7	19	46	61	-15	37
10 Elgin C	36	5	2	11	16	32	2	3	13	15	47	7	5	24	31	79	-48	26

CLYDESDALE BANK SCOTTISH PREMIER LEAGUE RESULTS 2008–2009

	Aberdeen	Celtic	Dundee U	Falkirk	Hamilton A	Hearts	Hibernian	Inverness CT	Kilmarnock	Motherwell	Rangers	St Mirren
Aberdeen	—	4-2 *1-3*	0-1 2-2	2-1	1-2 1-0	1-0 *0-0*	1-2 *2-1*	0-2 1-0	1-0 0-0	2-0	1-1 0-0	2-0
Celtic	3-2	—	2-2 *2-1*	3-0	1-0	1-1 0-0	4-2	1-0	0-0	2-0	2-4	1-0
Dundee U	2-0	1-1	—	4-0	4-0	0-1	2-0	1-0	3-0	0-4	0-0	7-0
Falkirk	2-1 *1-1*	2-2	0-0	—	4-1	3-0	0-1	2-1	0-2	1-0 *2-1*	2-2 0-3	3-2
Hamilton A	0-1	0-3	3-1	*0-1*	—	1-2 2-0	0-1	4-0	1-0 *2-1*	2-0 0-3	0-1	1-2 *0-2*
Hearts	1-0	1-2	0-1	— *1-1*	4-1 1-0	—	0-1 0-0	1-0	1-2	2-0 *0-3*	1-3	1-2
Hibernian	2-0	2-0 *0-0*	0-0	2-0	1-0	1-1 *0-1*	—	1-0 3-2	3-1 2-4	2-1 1-1	2-1 *1-1*	0-0
Inverness CT	0-3	1-2	1-3	0-1 *1-1*	0-1 1-1	1-1 1-0	1-1 2-0	—	3-1 1-0	1-2 1-0	0-3 2-3	1-2 *2-1*
Kilmarnock	1-2	1-3	2-0	1-2 3-0	2-0 1-0	0-1	2-1 1-1	3-2 2-2	—	1-0 0-0	0-4	0-1
Motherwell	0-1 1-1	2-4	1-1	3-2 3-1	2-0 7-1	1-0 2-2	1-4	5-0 0-1	2-1 *1-2*	—	0-0	2-1 3-1
Rangers	2-0 *2-1*	0-1 *1-0*	3-3 2-0	1-0	1-0 *0-1*	2-0 2-2	0-0	2-0 *1-2*	0-0	2-1 3-1	—	2-1 0-2 2-1
St Mirren	1-1	1-3	0-2	1-1 2-2	1-0 *0-1*	0-0 1-1	1-2	2-0 *1-2*	1-1	1-0 1-2	1-0 1-2	—

IRN BRU SCOTTISH LEAGUE—DIVISION ONE RESULTS 2008–2009

	Airdrie U	Clyde	Dundee	Dunfermline Ath	Livingston	Morton	Partick Th	Queen of the S	Ross Co	St Johnstone
Airdrie U	—	0-2	0-0	1-3	0-0	5-0	0-1	2-0	0-2	1-1
Clyde	1-0	—	1-0	1-1	4-4	1-1	0-1	0-2	1-0	0-4
Dundee	3-0	1-0	—	0-2	2-1	1-1	1-1	0-2	2-2	2-2
Dunfermline Ath	1-1	2-1	2-0	—	0-3	2-4	4-0	1-1	2-0	1-3
Livingston	0-0	4-4	0-1	1-4	—	0-0	0-0	2-3	1-2	1-1
Morton	1-2	1-1	1-1	0-0	4-1	—	1-0	2-1	2-0	0-1
Partick Th	1-1	1-0	1-2	2-3	1-2	2-1	—	0-2	3-1	1-2
Queen of the S	0-0	7-1	0-1	4-2	2-2	1-0	3-1	—	4-2	1-3
Ross Co	2-0	0-0	2-0	1-1	6-1	0-2	2-4	2-2	—	0-1
St Johnstone	3-0	2-3	0-0	2-1	3-3	2-1	0-1	0-2	2-1	—

IRN BRU SCOTTISH LEAGUE—DIVISION TWO RESULTS 2008–2009

	Alloa Ath	Arbroath	Ayr U	Brechin C	East Fife	Peterhead	Queen's Park	Raith R	Stirling Alb	Stranraer
Alloa Ath		2-1	0-2	2-1	0-3	1-0	1-3	1-1	4-3	5-1
Arbroath	4-1		3-2	3-2	0-1	1-2	0-0	0-0	2-3	2-2
Ayr U	1-0	2-1		1-2	0-1	4-0	1-1	0-2	1-2	1-0
Brechin C	3-0	2-1	1-3		4-2	2-2	3-0	0-0	1-1	2-0
East Fife	1-1	2-1	0-1	1-1		0-0	2-1	2-2	3-1	5-0
Peterhead	1-0	3-1	0-1	4-2	2-0		2-1	0-4	2-1	2-1
Queen's Park	0-2	0-1	1-0	0-0	2-1	2-2		0-2	1-2	1-2
Raith R	1-0	3-2	3-0	2-1	2-1	1-1	4-2		0-1	4-0
Stirling Alb	2-2	0-0	0-1	5-1	0-1	0-2	4-1	1-2		4-0
Stranraer	1-2	1-1	3-0	1-1	2-0	0-3	0-3	1-2	1-0	

IRN BRU SCOTTISH LEAGUE—DIVISION THREE RESULTS 2008–2009

	Albion R	Annan Ath	Berwick R	Cowdenbeath	Dumbarton	East Stirling	Elgin C	Forfar Ath	Montrose	Stenhousemuir
Albion R	—	0-1	2-0	3-1	1-3	0-2	2-1	1-3	0-1	1-2
Annan Ath	2-4	—	1-2	0-0	1-1	0-2	0-3	2-0	0-1	1-1
Berwick R	0-3	3-0	—	3-1	1-3	4-0	5-0	1-0	1-2	3-2
Cowdenbeath	1-1	1-1	2-3	—	1-2	2-1	1-1	1-0	2-1	1-2
Dumbarton	2-1	1-4	2-0	2-1	—	0-0	4-1	0-0	3-2	1-0
East Stirling	1-1	0-2	1-0	1-1	5-2	—	2-0	4-0	1-1	0-3
Elgin C	1-0	0-3	0-2	0-1	3-1	1-4	—	0-3	1-1	0-2
Forfar Ath	0-0	2-1	2-0	1-1	0-2	0-2	1-0	—	5-0	4-4
Montrose	1-2	1-1	1-1	1-0	1-2	3-0	1-0	1-3	—	5-3
Stenhousemuir	2-0	1-0	0-1	1-0	0-2	1-4	4-2	0-1	2-1	—

ABERDEEN PREMIER LEAGUE

Ground: Pittodrie Stadium, Aberdeen AB24 5QH (01224) 650400
Ground capacity: 21,421 (all seated). **Colours:** All red.
Manager: Mark McGhee.
League Appearances: Aluko S 28(4); Bossu B (1); Considine A 17(3); De Visscher J 6(5); Diamond Z 26(2); Duff S 9(10); Foster R 30(4); Hodgkiss J 6(1); Kerr M 31(1); Langfield J 38; Mackie D 25(4); Maguire C 13(18); Mair L 21(3); McDonald G 24(4); Miller L 34; Mulgrew C 32(3); Paton M (4); Pawlett P 2(3); Severin S 37; Smith J 9(3); Stewart S (1); Vidal J 9(4); Wright T 4(11); Young D 17(5).
Goals – League (41): Miller 10 (3 pens), Mackie 6, McDonald 5, Mulgrew 5, Diamond 4, Maguire 3, Aluko 2, Considine 1, Duff 1, Paton 1, Severin 1, Wright 1, Young 1.
Scottish Cup (8): Aluko 2, Maguire 2, Miller 1, Vidal 1, Wright 1, own goal 1.
CIS Cup (3): McDonald 1, Maguire 1, Miller 1 (pen).
Honours – Division 1: Champions – 1954–55. **Premier Division:** Champions – 1979–80, 1983–84, 1984–85. **Scottish Cup winners** 1947, 1970, 1982, 1983, 1984, 1986, 1990. **League Cup winners** 1956, 1977, 1986, 1990, 1996. **European Cup-Winners' Cup winners** 1983.

AIRDRIE UNITED DIV. 2

Ground: Shyberry Excelsior Stadium, Airdrie ML6 8QZ (01236) 622000
Postal address: 60 St Enoch Square, Glasgow G1 4AG.
Ground capacity: 10,000 (all seated). **Colours:** White shirts with red diamond, red shorts, red stockings.
Manager: Kenny Black.
League Appearances: Bain J 1; Baird J 9(3); Brown M 2(9); Cardle J 21(3); Di Giacomo P 30(3); Donnaghy K (1); Donnelly B 31(1); Floan L 1; Hazley M 17(2); Hollis L 3; Keast F 1; Lovering P 10(1); Lynch S 24(9); Maguire S 3(8); McCabe P 1; McCluskey S (1); McDonald K 27(5); McDougall S 20(10); McKenna S 35; McLachlan W 18; McLaughlin S 28(6); Nixon D 28(4); Noble S 3(13); Robertson S 33; Smith Darran 1; Smith Darren 14(7); Smith L 1; Smyth M 32; Taylor D 1; Watt K 1(5).
Goals – League (29): Lynch 10 (1 pen), Di Giacomo 5, McLaughlin 4, Baird 2, Nixon 2, Smyth 2, Cardle 1, Maguire 1, McKenna 1, Smith Darren 1.
Scottish Cup (6): Lynch 3, Cardle 1, Di Giacomo 1, McLaughlin 1 (pen).
CIS Cup (0).
Challenge Cup (10): Di Giacomo 4, Cardle 1, Lynch 1, McKenna 1, Noble 1, Smith 1, own goal 1.
Play-Offs (6): Baird 3, Di Giacomo 1, McLaughlin 1, Smyth 1.
Honours – Second Division: Champions – 2003–04. **League Challenge Cup winners** 2008–09.

ALBION ROVERS DIV. 3

Ground: Cliffhill Stadium, Main Street, Coatbridge ML5 3RB (01236) 606334
Ground capacity: 1249 (seated: 489). **Colours:** Red and yellow striped shirts, red shorts with yellow flashes, yellow stockings.
Manager: Paul Martin.
League Appearances: Adam C 18(1); Adreoni M 8(8); Archdeacon M 3(7); Barr B 31(1); Benton A 20; Canning S 7; Casey M 1; Coyne T 7(6); Crozier B 8(13); Donnelly C 31; Eaglesham G 1(5); Ewings J 19; Ferry D 17(8); Fleming S 16(1); Harris R 17(5); Harty I 15; Hughes C 3(1); Lumsden T 9; Martin W 2(1); McCluskey C 7; McCusker M 3; McGoldrick M 6(3); McGowan M 33; McKenna G (3); McKeown S 17; Pollock M 19(14); Reid A 32; Scott D 10(1); Smith B 2(1); Walker P 5(1); Walker R 24(3); Watt K 3(1); Wright B 2(2).

187

Goals – League (39): Barr 11, Walker P 6 (1 pen), Harty 5 (2 pens), Donnelly 3, Harris 3, Watt 3, Adam 2, Adreoni 1, Benton 1, Crozier 1, McCusker 1, McKeown 1, Pollock 1.
Scottish Cup (3): Barr 1, Coyne 1, Harris 1.
Challenge Cup (3): Barr 1, Donnelly 1 (pen), Martin 1.
Honours – Division II: Champions – 1933–34. **Second Division:** Champions 1988–89.

ALLOA ATHLETIC DIV. 2

Ground: Recreation Park, Alloa FK10 1RY (01259) 722695
Ground capacity: 3100. **Colours:** Black shirts with gold hoops on front, black shorts, black stockings.
Manager: Allan Maitland.
League Appearances: Barker S (4); Brown G 8(3); Buist S 27; Campbell I 30; Carrigan B 6(3); Carroll G 4(2); Ferguson A 8(4); Ferguson B 30(1); Ferguson M 1; Forrest F 9(1); Grant J 24(4); Hay J 1(3); Hill D 30(2); Jellema R 35; Kelly F (6); Kerr H (2); MacAulay K 21(9); McCafferty M 4; McClune D 23(3); McKeown S 9(4); Noble S 14; O'Neill M (1); Scott A 24(6); Scullion P 21(9); Spence G 6(12); Stevenson J 13(3); Townsley C 31; White M 1; Wilson D 16(5).
Goals – League (47): Scott 7 (2 pens), MacAulay 5, Ferguson B 4 (1 pen), Noble 4, Spence 4, Ferguson A 3, Wilson 3, Brown 2, Campbell 2, Carrigan 2 (2 pens), Forrest 2, Grant 2, Stevenson 2, Buist 1, Hill 1, McClune 1, Scullion 1, Townsley 1.
Scottish Cup (3): Ferguson B 2, Scott 1 (pen).
CIS Cup (0).
Challenge Cup (2): Stevenson 1, Townsley 1.
Honours – Division II: Champions – 1921–22. **Third Division:** Champions – 1997–98.
League Challenge Cup winners 1999–2000.

ANNAN ATHLETIC DIV. 3

Ground: Galabank, North Street, Annan DG12 5DQ (01461) 204108
Ground capacity: 3000 (426 seated). **Colours:** Black and gold striped shirts, black shorts, black stockings.
Manager: Harry Cairney.
League Appearances: Adamson R 10(18); Anson S 3; Archibald S 7(4); Batey J (1); Bell G 26(3); Brown G 13; Calder D 2(1); Cameron H 2(2); Campbell R 7(4); Cuseck L 2(1); Dunbar J 24(4); Gilfillan B 6; Grainger I 3(1); Hill S 7; Hoolickin L 26; Inglis A 18(2); Jack M 33; Jardine C 14(3); Johnstone D 12(4); Kassim A (1); McBeth J 15(1); Muirhead A 9(2); Neilson K 32; Parker G (1); Sloan S 34; Storey P 7(11); Summersgill C 34; Townsley D 27; Walker L (5); Watson P 23(2).
Goals – League (56): Jack 15 (8 pens), Bell 8, Neilson 6, Storey 6, Dunbar 5, Hoolickin 3, Anson 2, Johnstone 2, Sloan 2, Adamson 1, Archibald 1, Inglis 1, McBeth 1, Townsley 1, Watson 1, own goal 1.
Scottish Cup (1): Neilson 1.
Challenge Cup (0).
Honours – None.

ARBROATH DIV. 2

Ground: Gayfield Park, Arbroath DD11 1QB (01241) 872157
Ground capacity: 8488. **Colours:** Maroon shirts with white trim, maroon shorts, maroon stockings.
Manager: John McGlashan.
League Appearances: Bishop J 24(1); Black R 18(4); Cameron C 3; Campbell A 8; Dobbins I 15; Dorris S 6; Forsyth C 26; Fraser J 10(2); Gates S 12(11); Gibson K 8; Hill D 35; Lunan P 25; Masson T 1(11); McCulloch M 11; McGowan D 10(4);

McMullan K 26(5); Morrison S 1; Raeside R 31; Rattray A 15; Reilly A 1(7); Rennie S 30(4); Ross R 9(6); Scott B 16(5); Sellars B 31; Simpson S 1(3); Smith N 1(3); Tosh P 3(9); Watson P 4(3); Weir S 15(9); Wright K (3).

Goals – League (44): Scott 6, Sellars 6, Ross 5, Weir 5 (2 pens), McGowan 3, Raeside 3 (2 pens), Dorris 2, Forsyth 2, Gates 2, McMullan 2, Bishop 1, Dobbins 1, Masson 1, Rattray 1, Reilly 1, Rennie 1, own goals 2.

Scottish Cup (0).

CIS Cup (2): Sellars 1 (pen), Tosh 1.

Challenge Cup (1): Scott 1.

Honours – Nil.

AYR UNITED   DIV. 1

Ground: Somerset Park, Ayr KA8 9NB (01292) 263435
Ground capacity: 10,185 (1549 seated). **Colours:** White shirts with black hoops, white shorts with black flashes, black stockings.
Manager: Brian Reid.
League Appearances: Agnew S 7(10); Aitken C 27(2); Borris R 25(3); Campbell M 28; Connolly K 13(5); Dempsie A 31(1); Easton W 25(4); Fisher I 1(1); Gillies D (1); Gormley D 17(19); Grindlay S 36; Henderson M 1(1); James K 5; Keenan D 33(1); McGowan N 24(3); Prunty B 29(2); Roberts M 12(2); Stevenson R 32(2); Walker S 33(1); Weaver P 1(4); Williams A 16(17); Woodburn A 1(5).
Goals – League (71): Prunty 15, Stevenson 10 (1 pen), Gormley 9, Williams 7, Aitken 5 (2 pens), Roberts 5, Connolly 4, Easton 4, Agnew 3, Borris 3, Campbell 1, Keenan 1, McGowan 1, Walker 1, own goals 2.
Scottish Cup (7): Prunty 2, Williams 2, Gormley 1, Keenan 1, McGowan 1.
CIS Cup (0).
Play-Offs (8): Aitken 3 (1 pen), Baird 2, Connelly 1, Prunty 1, Stevenson 1.
Honours – Division II: Champions – 1911–12, 1912–13, 1927–28, 1936–37, 1958–59, 1965–66. **Second Division:** Champions – 1987–88, 1996–97.

BERWICK RANGERS   DIV. 3

Ground: Shielfield Park, Berwick-on-Tweed TD15 2EF (01289) 307424
Ground capacity: 4131. **Colours:** Black shirt with broad gold vertical stripes, black shorts, black stockings.
Manager: Alan McGonigal.
League Appearances: Anderson Chris 1(14); Anderson Craig 6(5); Barclay J 13; Bonar S 24(3); Callaghan S 28(3); Dillon J 28; Ewart J 35; Forrest F 10(2); Fraser S 5(2); Grant D (7); Greenhill D 23(10); Greenhill G 8(1); Gribben D 31(3); Guy G 20(1); Hampshire S 6(1); Horn R 24(3); Howat A 1(2); Kiczynski S 3; Lennox T 13(3); Lister J 9; Little I 6(11); Lunn M 2; McGurk R 21; McLaren F 34; McLean A 2(1); McMahon P 13(3); McMenamin C 22(2); Mearns E 6(4); Robertson D 2.
Goals – League (46): Gribben 14 (2 pens), McLaren 8, Callaghan 4, Ewart 4, Dillon 3 (2 pens), McMenamin 3, Anderson Craig 1, Bonar 1, Forrest 1, Guy 1, Horn 1, Howat 1, Lister 1, own goals 3.
Scottish Cup (1): Gribben 1.
Challenge Cup (1): Little 1.
Honours – Second Division: Champions – 1978–79. **Third Division:** Champions – 2006–07.

BRECHIN CITY   DIV. 2

Ground: Glebe Park, Brechin DD9 6BJ (01356) 622856
Ground capacity: 3960. **Colours:** Red with white trim.
Manager: Jim Duffy.

League Appearances: Baird J 5(5); Byers K 27(3); Canning S 5(7); Diack I 8(4); Dyer W 35; Ettien S 8(6); Fusco G 15(4); Harvey R (3); Janczyk N 30(1); King C 26(9); McAllister R 13(2); Murie D 12(6); Nelson A 1(6); Nelson J 36; Nimmo I 27(6); Paton M 7(1); Seeley J 17(1); Smith B 14; Smith C (5); Smith D 21(6); Twigg G 23; Walker R 28(7); Ward J 20(1); White D 18.
Goals – League (51): Twigg 12 (1 pen), Byers 7, McAllister 5, Diack 4, Ettien 4, King 4, Smith D 4, Nimmo 3, Smith C 2, Dyer 1, Janczyk 1, Paton 1, Walker 1, White 1, own goal 1.
Scottish Cup (4): Diack 3 (1 pen), Janczyk 1.
Challenge Cup (0).
Play-Offs (2): McAllister 2 (1 pen).
Honours – Second Division: Champions – 1982–83, 1989–90, 2004–05. **Third Division:** Champions – 2001–02. **C Division:** Champions – 1953–54.

CELTIC   PREMIER LEAGUE

Ground: Celtic Park, Glasgow G40 3RE (0871) 226 1888
Ground capacity: 60,355 (all seated). **Colours:** Emerald green and white hooped shirts, white shorts with emerald green trim, whie stockings.
Manager: Tony Mowbray.
League Appearances: Boruc A 34; Brown M 4; Brown S 36; Caddis P (5); Caldwell G 36; Conroy R (1); Crosas M 14(4); Donati M 2(2); Flood W 2(3); Hartley P 20(5); Hinkel A 32; Hutchinson B 3; Killen C (1); Loovens G 13(4); Maloney S 14(6); McCourt P (4); McDonald S 33(1); McGeady A 21(8); McManus S 31; Mizuno K 2(8); Nakamura S 30(2); Naylor L 19(4); O'Dea D 7(3); Robson B 13(4); Samaras G 19(12); Sheridan C 6(6); Vennegoor J 15(10); Wilson M 15(3).
Goals – League (80): McDonald 16, Samaras 15 (1 pen), Nakamura 8 (1 pen), Vennegoor 6, Brown S 5, Maloney 4, McManus 4, Sheridan 4, Hartley 3, Loovens 3, McGeady 3, Caldwell 2, Crosas 1, Mizuno 1, Naylor 1, O'Dea 1, Robson 1 (pen), own goals 2.
Scottish Cup (4): Brown S 1, Caldwell 1, McDonald 1, McGeady 1.
CIS Cup (9): McGeady 2 (1 pen), Samaras 2 (1 pen), Brown S 1, Loovens 1, McDonald 1, Nakamura 1, O'Dea 1.
Champions League (4): Maloney 1, McDonald 1, McGeady 1, Robson 1.
Honours – Division I: Champions – 1892–93, 1893–94, 1895–96, 1897–98, 1904–05, 1905–06, 1906–07, 1907–08, 1908–09, 1909–10, 1913–14, 1914–15, 1915–16, 1916–17, 1918–19, 1921–22, 1925–26, 1935–36, 1937–38, 1953–54, 1965–66, 1966–67, 1967–68, 1968–69, 1969–70, 1970–71, 1971–72, 1972–73, 1973–74. **Premier Division:** Champions – 1976–77, 1978–79, 1980–81, 1981–82, 1985–86, 1987–88, 1997–98. **Premier League:** 2000–01, 2001–02, 2003–04, 2005–06, 2006–07, 2007–08. **Scottish Cup winners** 1892, 1899, 1900, 1904, 1907, 1908, 1911, 1912, 1914, 1923, 1925, 1927, 1931, 1933, 1937, 1951, 1954, 1965, 1967, 1969, 1971, 1972, 1974, 1975, 1977, 1980, 1985, 1988, 1989, 1995, 2001, 2004, 2005, 2007. **League Cup winners** 1957, 1958, 1966, 1967, 1968, 1969, 1970, 1975, 1983, 1998, 2000, 2001, 2004, 2006, 2009. **European Cup winners** 1967.

CLYDE   DIV. 2

Ground: Broadwood Stadium, Cumbernauld G68 9NE (01236) 451511
Ground capacity: 8200. **Colours:** White shirts with red flashes, black shorts with red flashes, red stockings with white hoops.
Manager: John Brown.
League Appearances: Brown M 24(2); Cherrie P 5(1); Clarke P 28(1); Emslie P 9; Gemmill S 23(7); Gibson B 30; Higgins C 30(2); Hutton D 31; Kettlewell S 26; Lithgow A 22; Lowing A 17; MacLennan Roddy (3); MacLennan Ruari 16(13); McCusker M (1); McGowan D (1); McGregor N 7; McKay D 14(16); McLaren W 24; McLaughlin G ; McSwegan G 2(14); Murch J (1); O'Reilly C (3); Ohnesorge M

10; Stevenson T 9(2); Tade G 11(2); Trouten A 15(12); Waddell R 24(4); Wilson M 14(5); Winters R 4(2).
Goals – League (41): Clarke 11 (2 pens), MacLennan Ruari 6, McLaren 6, Trouten 4 (1 pen), Waddell 4, Gemmill 2, Higgins 2, Brown 1, Lithgow 1, McKay 1, McSwegan 1, own goals 2.
Scottish Cup (2): Clarke 1 (pen), McKay 1.
CIS Cup (1): Clarke 1.
Challenge Cup (4): Trouten 2 (1 pen), Clarke 1, Gibson 1.
Honours – Division II: Champions – 1904–05, 1951–52, 1956–57, 1961–62, 1972–73. **Second Division:** Champions – 1977–78, 1981–82, 1992–93, 1999–2000. **Scottish Cup winners** 1939, 1955, 1958. **League Challenge Cup winners** 2006–07.

COWDENBEATH   DIV. 3

Ground: Central Park, Cowdenbeath KY4 9EY (01383) 610166
Ground capacity: 5268. **Colours:** Royal blue shirts, royal blue shorts, royal blue stockings.
Manager: Brian Welsh.
League Appearances: Adamson K 21(4); Armstrong J 31; Baxter M 24(2); Brown G 8(9); Cennerazzo G 1; Dempster J 17(9); Droudge D 3(1); Fairbairn B 20(8); Ferguson J 1(1); Fleming D 19(5); Forbes M (1); Gallacher S 7; Gemmell J 25(6); Hay D 29; Hodge S 12; Lennon D (1); Linton S 5(4); MacKay D 21(1); Mbu J 18(1); McGregor D 34; McQuade P 20(3); O'Neil J (1); Ramsay M 26(6); Reid J 1; Robertson J 3(6); Ross G 2(2); Shields J 20(2); Stein J 10(9); Tomana M 18(9); Wallace D (1); Young C (1).
Goals – League (48): Gemmell 12, McQuade 9, Dempster 6, Armstrong 5, Fairbairn 5, Adamson 2, Ferguson 2, Stein 2, Brown 1, MacKay 1, McGregor 1, Ramsay 1, Tomana 1.
Scottish Cup (1): McQuade 1.
CIS Cup (1): Dempster 1.
Challenge Cup (6): Fairbairn 2, McQuade 2, Gemmell 1, McGregor 1.
Play-Offs (3): Dempster 1, Gemmell 1, Stein 1.
Honours – Division II: Champions – 1913–14, 1914–15, 1938–39. **Third Division:** Champions – 2005–06.

DUMBARTON   DIV. 2

Ground: Strathclyde Homes Stadium, Dumbarton G82 1JJ (01389) 762569/767864
Ground capacity: 2050. **Colours:** White shirts with black and amber, white shorts, white stockings.
Manager: Jim Chapman.
League Appearances: Boyle P 20; Brannan K (6); Brittain C 3; Canning M 10(10); Carcary D 25(8); Chisholm I 15(12); Clark R 30(1); Craig P 3; Cusack L 1(8); Dunlop M 21; Forbes R 15(3); Geggan A 23(2); Gordon B 36; Gourlay A (3); Gray D 2(5); Keegan P 12(9); Lennon G 32(2); Logan R 4(2); McAnespie K 2(2); McEwan D 22; McGeown M 14(1); McKillen R 2; McLaughlin D 16; McLeod P 19(5); McNiff M (1); McStay R 10(2); Moore M (6); Murray S 34(1); O'Byrne M 13; Taylor N (1); Tiernan F 2(2); Weir S 1; White M 1; Wilson G 8.
Goals – League (65): Clark 14 (4 pens), Carcary 11, McLaughlin 6, McLeod 6 (1 pen), Murray 4, Boyle 3, Gordon 3, Keegan 3, Chisholm 2, Brannan 1, Craig 1, Cusack 1, Forbes 1, Lennon 1, Logan 1, Moore 1, Tiernan 1, own goals 5.
Scottish Cup (4): Carcary 2, Chisholm 1, Gordon 1.
CIS Cup (0).
Challenge Cup (2): Carcary 1, Clark 1.
Honours – Division I: Champions – 1890–91 (Shared), 1891–92. **Division II:** Champions – 1910–11, 1971–72. **Second Division:** Champions – 1991–92. **Third Division:** Champions – 2008–09. **Scottish Cup winners** 1883.

DUNDEE   DIV. 1

Ground: Dens Park, Dundee DD3 7JY (01382) 889966
Ground capacity: 11,760 (all seated). **Colours:** Navy blue shirts, white shorts, navy blue stockings.
Manager: Jocky Scott.
League Appearances: Antoine-Curier M 29(3); Benedictus K 10(1); Cameron C 7(2); Cowan D 15(3); Daquin F 16(3); Davidson R 6(6); Deasley B 9(4); Dodds R 4; Douglas R 36; Efrem G 8; Forsyth C (1); Gilhaney M 13(6); Lauchlan J 15(1); MacKenzie G 17(2); Malone E 35; McHale P 21(2); McKeown C 19(2); McMenamin C 24(5); Mearns E 1(2); O'Brien D 18(6); Paton E 31; Pozniak C 23(3); Roy L (1); Shinnie A 19(1); Williams D 16(4); Young D 4(3).
Goals – League (33): Antoine-Curier 14 (2 pens), McMenamin 7, Paton 4, Efrem 2, Young 2, Deasley 1, Malone 1, Pozniak 1, Shinnie 1.
Scottish Cup (1): McMenamin 1.
CIS Cup (1): McHale 1.
Challenge Cup (1): Antoine-Curier 1.
Honours – Division I: Champions – 1961–62. **First Division:** Champions – 1978–79, 1991–92, 1997–98. **Division II:** Champions – 1946–47. **Scottish Cup winners** 1910. **League Cup winners** 1952, 1953, 1974. **B&Q (Centenary) Cup winners** 1991.

DUNDEE UNITED   PREMIER LEAGUE

Ground: Tannadice Park, Dundee DD3 7JW (01382) 833166
Ground capacity: 14,223. **Colours:** Tangerine shirts, tangerine shorts, tangerine stockings.
Manager: Craig Levein.
League Appearances: Buaben P 20(2); Caddis P 10(1); Conway C 28(8); Daly J 16(7); Dillon S 18(1); Dixon P 28(1); Dods D 19; Feeney W 18(5); Flood W 20; Gomis M 36(1); Goodwillie D 3(13); Grainger D 9; Kenneth G 22(3); Kovacevic M 17; O'Donovan R 7(4); Robertson D 12(7); Robertson S 22(1); Sandaza F 23(8); Shala A 3(5); Swanson D 7(23); Wesolowski J 7(1); Wilkie L 35; Zaluska L 38.
Goals – League (47): Sandaza 10 (2 pens), Feeney 6 (1 pen), Conway 5 (1 pen), Daly 5 (1 pen), Wilkie 5, Goodwillie 3, Robertson D 3, Robertson S 3, Buaben 1, Dixon 1, Dods 1, Kenneth 1, O'Donovan 1, own goals 2.
Scottish Cup (5): Buaben 1, Daly 1, Dods 1, Grainger 1, Russell 1 (pen).
CIS Cup (8): Daly 3, Goodwillie 3, Robertson S 2.
Honours – Premier Division: Champions – 1982–83. **Division II:** Champions – 1924–25, 1928–29. **Scottish Cup winners** 1994. **League Cup winners** 1980, 1981.

DUNFERMLINE ATHLETIC   DIV. 1

Ground: East End Park, Dunfermline KY12 7RB (01383) 724295
Ground capacity: 11,780. **Colours:** Black and white striped shirts, white shorts, black stockings.
Manager: Jim McIntyre.
League Appearances: Bamba S 1; Bayne G 32; Bell S 19(5); Burke A 29(3); Campbell R (3); Gallacher P 36; Glass S 26; Graham D 14(1); Harper K 12(2); Holmes G 4(3); Kirk A 27(5); Loy R 6(12); McCann A 30(2); McIntyre J 2(2); Mole J 3(7); Muirhead S 8(11); Phinn N 33(2); Ross G 10(6); Shields G 27(1); Thomson S 21(6); Wiles S 2(7); Williamson I 2(7); Willis P (3); Wilson S 29; Woods C 25(5).
Goals – League (52): Kirk 15 (2 pens), Phinn 8, Bayne 6, Woods 5, Bell 3, Loy 3, Glass 2 (1 pen), Graham 2, Burke 1, Campbell 1, Harper 1, Ross 1, Shields 1, Thomson 1, Williamson 1, Wilson 1.
Scottish Cup (5): Bayne 2, Phinn 2, Holmes 1.
CIS Cup (3): Bayne 1, Kirk 1, Wiles 1.

Challenge Cup (3): Burke 1, Phinn 1, Williamson 1.
Honours – First Division: Champions – 1988–89, 1995–96. **Division II:** Champions – 1925–26. **Second Division:** Champions – 1985–86. **Scottish Cup winners** 1961, 1968.

EAST FIFE   DIV. 2

Ground: Bayview Park, Methil, Fife KY8 3RW (01333) 426323
Ground capacity: 2000 (all seated). **Colours:** Gold and black shirts, black shorts, black stockings.
Manager: Stevie Crawford.
League Appearances: Blackadder R (1); Brown M 13; Cameron D 36; Campbell R 5(5); Cargill S (4); Crawford S 22(5); Fagan S 18(5); Fotheringham K 23(1); Gordon K (2); Linn B 32(2); Makel L 7(1); McCulloch W 23; McDonald G 23(1); McManus P 30(3); McRae J (1); Muir D 14(5); Nugent P 19(2); O'Reilly C (11); Sheerin J (4); Shields D 7(2); Smart J 28; Stanik G 11(2); Stewart P 21(9); Templeman C 25(8); Thomson D (1); Tweed S 16; Walker P (1); Young L 22(10).
Goals – League (39): McManus 12 (5 pens), Linn 6 (2 pens), McDonald 5, Templeman 4, Crawford 3, Fotheringham 3, Cameron 2, Makel 1, Tweed 1, Young 1, own goal 1.
Scottish Cup (3): Crawford 1, Linn 1, O'Reilly 1.
Challenge Cup (1): Templeman 1.
Honours – Division II: Champions – 1947–48. **Third Division:** Champions – 2007–08. **Scottish Cup winners** 1938. **League Cup winners** 1948, 1950, 1954.

EAST STIRLINGSHIRE   DIV. 3

Ground: Firs Park, Falkirk FK2 7AY (01324) 623583
Ground capacity: 1880. **Colours:** Black shirts, black shorts, black stockings.
Manager: Jim McInally.
League Appearances: Anderson S 16(10); Barclay J 11; Bolochoweckyj M 33; Camara K 1; Corr B 1; Cramb C 15(6); Donaldson C 26(4); Dunn D 18(15); Elliot J (1); Forrest E 25(1); Gibson J 2(1); Graham B 29(4); Hay P 31(1); Hillcoat J 3; Kelly G 14(11); King D 7; Krivokapic B 1(1); McKenzie M 1(33); Mitchell G 2; Moffat G (1); Newman J (1); Nicholls D 4; O'Hara G 1; O'Neill J 1(1); Oates S 2; Paige S (1); Peat M 16; Peters M 2; Richardson D 19(6); Rodgers A 28(2); Stevenson J 13; Thornton D 1(2); Tully C 27; Ure D 31(1); Weaver P 15.
Goals – League (57): Graham 15, Rodgers 14 (2 pens), Cramb 9 (3 pens), Bolochoweckyj 4, Stevenson 4, Donaldson 3, Dunn 2, McKenzie 2, Forrest 1, Hay 1, Richardson 1, own goal 1.
Scottish Cup (2): Forrest 1, Graham 1.
Challenge Cup (0).
Play-Offs (2): Graham 1, Rodgers 1.
Honours – Division II: Champions – 1931–32. **C Division:** Champions – 1947–48.

ELGIN CITY   DIV. 3

Ground: Borough Briggs, Elgin IV30 1AP (01343) 551114
Ground capacity: 3927 (478 seated). **Colours:** Black and white striped shirts, black shorts, white stockings.
Manager: Ross Jack.
League Appearances: Allan D 1(7); Archibald L (1); Cameron B 4(10); Campbell C 29; Charlesworth C (1); Craig D 8; Craig D 9(6); Crooks J 26(7); Edwards S 5(2); Gilbert K 9; Gillespie D 16(1); Hind D 10(3); Jack Z 6(5); Kaczan P 27(1); Keogh L 5; Kerr G 13(1); Lindsay A (1); Low T 2(4); MacDonald A 30(1); MacKay S 23(3); Malin J 2; McKenzie G 2(7); McNulty A 19; McPhee D 2(2); Munro G 7;

Nicolson M 33; Niven D 17(2); Nixon D 1; O'Donoghue R 33; Ramsay D (3); Ridgers A 15(3); Shallicker D 22(7); Smith D (1); Tweegie G (1); Wright K 20(3).
Goals – League (31): Shallicker 7 (3 pens), Wright 6, Campbell 4, MacKay 4 (1 pen), Crooks 2, Kerr 2, Nicolson 2, Kaczan 1, MacDonald 1, O'Donoghue 1, own goal 1.
Scottish Cup (5): Wright 2, Kaczan 1, Mackay 1 (pen), Nicolson 1.
Challenge Cup (0).
Honours – Nil.

FALKIRK   PREMIER LEAGUE

Ground: Brockville Park, Falkirk FK1 5AX (01324) 624121
Ground capacity: 6123. **Colours:** Navy blue shirts with white seams, navy shorts, navy stockings with two white hoops.
Manager: Eddie May.
League Appearances: Aafjes G 10(7); Arfield S 35(2); Arnau 14(3); Barr D 35; Barrett G 9(6); Bullen L 29(3); Cregg P 16(7); Dani Mallo 15; Finnigan C 10(4); Flinders S 8; Higdon M 27(7); Holden D 16(3); Latapy R 2(1); Lovell S 25(3); Lynch S (2); McBride K 25(3); McCaffrey D 1(1); McCann N 22(2); McNamara J 29; Mitchell C 3(6); Moffat K (4); O'Brien B 30(2); Olejnik R 15; Pressley S 15(1); Robertson D (4); Scobbie T 18(2); Stewart J 4; Stewart M 5(15).
Goals – League (37): Lovell 8, Arfield 7 (4 pens), Higdon 7, Finnigan 4, Barr 2, Barrett 2, Stewart M 2, Holden 1, McCann 1, O'Brien 1, Scobbie 1, own goal 1.
Scottish Cup (8): Arfield 3 (2 pens), Barrett 2, Finnigan 1 (pen), Lovell 1, Scobbie 1.
CIS Cup (6): McCann 2, Higdon 1, Lovell 1, Stewart M 1, Stewart J 1 (pen).
Honours – Division II: Champions – 1935–36, 1969–70, 1974–75. **First Division:** Champions – 1990–91, 1993–94, 2002–03, 2004–05. **Second Division:** Champions – 1979–80. **Scottish Cup winners** 1913, 1957. **B&Q Cup winners** 1994. **League Challenge Cup winners** 1998, 2005.

FORFAR ATHLETIC   DIV. 3

Ground: Station Park, Forfar, Angus (01307) 463576
Ground capacity: 4602. **Colours:** Sky blue shirts with navy stripes, navy blue shorts, navy blue stockings.
Manager: Dick Campbell.
League Appearances: Brady D 30; Brown A 32; Cairns S 12; Campbell R 24(7); Derden S 1; Divine A 14(1); Donachie B 6(6); Duell B (3); Dunn D 10(1); Ferguson S 4; Fotheringham M 22(10); Gibson G 26(3); Gibson J 4; Gordon K 24(5); Keogh P 2; Kilgannon S 7(9); Lilley D 23(3); Manson S (4); McGuigan M (1); McLeish K 11(7); McNally S 20(7); Russell J 25(1); Simpson S 3(7); Smith C 3(12); Smith E 14(5); Tod A 23; Tosh S 2; Tulloch S 33; Winter C 21(12).
Goals – League (53): Campbell 13 (3 pens), Russell 8, Gibson G 7, Gordon 5, Fotheringham 4, McLeish 3 (2 pens), Tulloch 3, Kilgannon 2 (1 pen), Lilley 2 (1 pen), Brady 1, Divine 1, Manson 1, McNally 1, Winter 1, own goal 1.
Scottish Cup (11): Gordon 3, Campbell 2, Gibson G 2, Dunn 1, Kilgannon 1, Tulloch 1, own goal 1.
Challenge Cup (2): Kilgannon 1 (pen), McLeish 1.
Honours – Second Division: Champions – 1983–84. **Third Division:** Champions – 1994–95.

HAMILTON ACADEMICAL   PREMIER LEAGUE

Ground: New Douglas Park, Cadzow Avenue, Hamilton ML3 0FT (01698) 368652
Ground capacity: 6078. **Colours:** Red and white hooped shirts, white shorts.
Manager: Billy Reid.

League Appearances: Akins L 4(7); Asamoah D 1(2); Canning M 29(1); Casement C (1); Cerny T 36; Corcoran M 3(10); Deuchar K 3(6); Easton B 35; Elebert D 14(3); Ettien S (6); Evans G 2(1); Gibson J 7(10); Graham D 11(5); Lyle D 8(13); McArthur J 36; McCarthy J 34(4); McClenahan T 20(3); McGowan P 11(3); McLaughlin M 27; McMillan J 3(1); Mensing S 33; Mills S 1; Murdoch S 2(2); Neil A 33; Offiong R 24(6); Quinn R (2); Sorsa S 2; Stevenson T 7; Swailes C 22(3); Taylor S (2); Thomas J 10(16).
Goals – League (30): McCarthy 6, Mensing 6 (3 pens), Offiong 6, Graham 2, McArthur 2, Canning 1, Corcoran 1, Easton 1, Gibson 1, Lyle 1, McGowan 1, Stevenson 1, own goal 1.
Scottish Cup (4): Swailes 3, Quinn 1.
CIS Cup (5): Ettien 1, Grady 1, Graham 1, Stevenson 1 (pen), Thomas 1.
Honours – First Division: Champions – 1985–86, 1987–88, 2007–08. **Division II:** Champions – 1903–04. **Division III:** Champions – 2000–01. **B&Q Cup winners** 1992, 1993.

HEART OF MIDLOTHIAN   PREMIER LEAGUE

Ground: Tynecastle Park, Gorgie Road, Edinburgh EH11 2NL (0871) 663 1874
Ground capacity: 17,402. **Colours:** Maroon shirts, white shorts, maroon stockings.
Manager: Csaba Laszlo.
League Appearances: Aguiar B 26; Balogh J 18(1); Banks S 1; Berra C 23; Cesnauskis D 2(11); Driver A 29; Elliot C 8(4); Glen G 2(6); Jonsson E 27(3); Karipidis C 34; Kello M 13; Kingston L 15(4); Ksanavicius A 4(5); MacDonald J 6(1); Makela J (4); Mikoliunas S 6(6); Mole J 8(6); Mrowiec A 6(4); Nade C 20(16); Nielson R 25(2); Novikovas A (1); Obua D 21(6); Palazuelos R 18(7); Stewart J (1); Stewart M 33(1); Templeton D 1(2); Thomson J 8(3); Tullberg M 2(5); Wallace L 34; Zaliukas M 28.
Goals – League (40): Aguiar 7, Driver 5, Stewart M 4 (1 pen), Jonsson 3 (1 pen), Kingston 3, Elliot 2, Karipidis 2, Mikoliunas 2, Nade 2, Obua 2, Palazuelos 2, Wallace 2, Zaliukas 2, Ksanavicius 1, Mole 1.
Scottish Cup (2): Glen 1, Nade 1.
CIS Cup (0).
Honours – Division I: Champions – 1894–95, 1896–97, 1957–58, 1959–60. **First Division:** Champions – 1979–80. **Scottish Cup winners** 1891, 1896, 1901, 1906, 1956, 1998, 2006. **League Cup winners** 1955, 1959, 1960, 1963.

HIBERNIAN   PREMIER LEAGUE

Ground: Easter Road Stadium, Edinburgh EH7 5QG (0131) 661 2159
Ground capacity: 17,400. **Colours:** Green shirts with white sleeves and collar, white shorts with green stripe, white stockings with green trim.
Manager: John Hughes.
League Appearances: Bamba S 29; Campbell R (2); Canning M 1; Chisholm R 10(9); Fletcher S 34; Hanlon P 6(1); Hogg C 31; Johansson J 5(4); Jones R 32; Keenan J 9(6); Ma-Kalambay Y 21; McCormack D 7(1); McNeil A 5(1); Morais F (2); Murray I 23(5); Nish C 27(4); O'Brien A 14(10); Pinau S (8); Rankin J 30(3); Riordan D 28(4); Rosa D 10(2); Shiels D 16(3); Stevenson L 26(3); Szamotulski G 12; Thicot S 15(5); Van Zanten D 26(3); Yantorno F 1(6); Zemmmama M (1).
Goals – League (42): Fletcher 12, Riordan 12 (2 pens), Nish 7, Jones 4, Rankin 3, Shiels 3 (2 pens), Hanlon 1.
Scottish Cup (0).
CIS Cup (3): Keenan 1, Pinao 1, Shiels 1.
Honours – Division I: Champions – 1902–03, 1947–48, 1950–51, 1951–52. **First Division:** Champions – 1980–81, 1998–99. **Division II:** Champions – 1893–94, 1894–95, 1932–33. **Scottish Cup winners** 1887, 1902. **League Cup winners** 1973, 1992, 2007.

INVERNESS CALEDONIAN THISTLE DIV. 1

Ground: Tulloch Caledonian Stadium, East Longman, Inverness IV1 1FF (01463) 715816
Ground capacity: 7780. **Colours:** Royal blue and red shirts, royal blue and red shorts, royal blue stockings.
Manager: Terry Butcher.
League Appearances: Barrowman A 14(16); Black I 34; Cowie D 21(1); Djebi-Zadi L 15(1); Duff J 7(5); Duncan R 24(3); Esson R 21; Foran R 15; Fraser M 17(1); Gathuessi T 1; Hastings R 22(3); Imrie D 33(5); Kerr G 10; McAllister R (3); McBain R 21(6); McGuire P 10(1); Mihadjuks P 12; Morais F 9(3); Munro G 34; Odhiambo E 3(5); Proctor D 25(1); Rooney A 10(20); Sutherland Z (3); Tokely R 36; Vigurs I 12(5); Wilson B 1(11); Wood G 11(7).
Goals – League (37): Rooney 5 (1 pen), Black 4 (1 pen), Imrie 4, Cowie 3, Foran 3, Morais 3, Barrowman 2 (1 pen), Munro 2, Tokely 2, Wood 2, Kerr 1, McBain 1, McGuire 1, Mihadjuks 1, Odhiambo 1, Proctor 1, own goal 1.
Scottish Cup (5): Morais 2, Mihadjuks 1, Rooney 1, Vigurs 1.
CIS Cup (4): Hastings 1, Imrie 1, Vigurs 1, Wood 1.
Honours – First Division: Champions – 2003–04. **Third Division:** Champions – 1996–97. **League Challenge Cup winners** 2004.

KILMARNOCK PREMIER LEAGUE

Ground: Rugby Park, Kilmarnock KA1 2DP (01563) 525184
Ground capacity: 18,128. **Colours:** Blue and white striped shirts, white shorts, white stockings.
Manager: Jim Jefferies.
League Appearances: Anson S (1); Bell C 1; Bryson C 31(2); Clancy T 12(1); Combe A 34; Corrigan M 1; Cox D (2); Fernandez D 28(4); Flannigan I 1(6); Ford S 27; Fowler J 23(3); Gibson W 10(12); Hamill J 28(5); Hay G 30; Invincibile D 21(4); Kyle K 11; Lilley D 20; Murray G 10; O'Leary R 1(2); Pascali M 31(1); Rascle D 3(2); Russell A 8(3); Sammon C 10(9); Simmonds D 4(15); Skelton G 20(7); Taouil M 30(4); Wright F 23(4).
Goals – League (38): Kyle 8, Invincibile 6, Hamill 5 (2 pens), Russell 3, Taouil 3 (1 pen), Bryson 2, Fernandez 2, Pascali 2, Ford 1, Gibson 1, Hay 1, Sammon 1, Simmonds 1, Skelton 1, Wright 1.
Scottish Cup (5): Ford 2, Bryson 1, Pascali 1, Taoul 1.
CIS Cup (7): Sammon 2, Bryson 1, Fernandez 1, Invincibile 1, Taoul 1 (pen), Wright 1.
Honours – Division I: Champions – 1964–65. **Division II:** Champions – 1897–98, 1898–99. **Scottish Cup winners** 1920, 1929, 1997.

LIVINGSTON DIV. 1

Ground: Almondvale Stadium, Alderton Road, Livingston EH54 7DN (01506) 417 000
Ground capacity: 10,005. **Colours:** Yellow shirts, black shorts, yellow stockings.
Head Coach: John Murphy.
League Appearances: Cave P 2(1); Cuenca J 2(6); Davidson M 29; De Vita R 2(5); Elliot C 13; Fox L 18(2); Giarrizzo F 2(2); Griffin D 17; Griffiths L 25(2); Halliday A 7(6); Hamill J 32(1); Innes C 30; Jacobs K 2(14); MacKay D 28; Malone C 8; Martini P 12(1); McDonald C 12(5); McKenzie R 24; McPake J 18; McPartland A 36; Millar G 13(10); One A 12(3); Quinn R 14(1); Sinclair D (1); Smith G 1(3); Talbot J 24(4); Thomas M 1(1); Torrance M 2(2); Winters D 10(4).

Goals – League (56): Griffiths 17 (2 pens), Elliot 11, Davidson 6, MacKay 3 (2 pens), McPartland 3, One 3, Winters 3, McPake 2, De Vita 1, Griffin 1, Halliday 1, Hamill 1, Innes 1, Quinn 1, Talbot 1, own goal 1.
Scottish Cup (1): Fox 1.
CIS Cup (2): Cuenca 1, Griffiths 1.
Challenge Cup (5): Griffiths 3, Hamil 1, McParland 1.
Honours – First Division: Champions – 2000–01. **Second Division:** Champions – 1986–87, 1998–99. **Third Division:** Champions – 1995–96. **League Cup winners** 2004.

MONTROSE   DIV. 3

Ground: Links Park, Montrose DD10 8QD (01674) 673200
Ground capacity: 3292. **Colours:** Royal blue shirts, royal blue shorts, royal blue stockings.
Manager: Steven Tweed.
League Appearances: Adams K (1); Anson S 9(1); Baird J 8; Black S 30(2); Bradley K 23(9); Buchan J 28; Bullock T 16; Cox D 10(1); Craig D 4; Crighton S 18; Cumming S 1(1); Davidson H 30; Doris S 5; Gardiner R (1); Gibson K 18(2); Gray N 1(1); Hannah D 1; Hegarty C 24(4); Hunter R 18(7); Kelly G 16; Leyden J (1); Maitland J 3(6); McCay R 2; McKenzie J 7; McLaughlan G 12(1); McLeod C 13(1); Milligan F 8(1); Nicol D 2(14); O'Reilly C 8; Peat M 3; Pope G 16; Russell M (2); Sinclair A 1; Smith C 7(3); Stark F 1; Stein J 1(2); Stewart P 14(17); Thomson S 11; Tweed S 15(1); Winton J (1); Worrell D 12(1); Wright K (1).
Goals – League (47): Hunter 9, Bradley 6, Anson 3, Davidson 3, O'Reilly 3, Baird 2, Black 2, Buchan 2, Cox 2, Gibson 2, Hegarty 2 (2 pens), McKenzie 2, Stewart 2, Tweed 2, McLeod 1, Nicol 1, Pope 1, Smith 1, own goal 1.
Scottish Cup (2): Davidson 1, Smith 1.
Challenge Cup (0).
Honours – Second Division: Champions – 1984–85.

MORTON   DIV. 1

Ground: Cappielow Park, Greenock (01475) 723571
Ground capacity: 11,612. **Colours:** Canary yellow shirts, canary yellow shorts, canary yellow stockings.
Manager: Davie Irons.
League Appearances: Cuthbert K 34; Finlayson K 27(5); Grady J 16(6); Greacen S 28; Harding R 7(1); Jenkins A 20(9); MacGregor D 10; Masterton S 21(7); McAlister J 35; McGuffie R 31(1); McManus A 18(1); Monti C 3(1); Newby J 3(1); Paartalu E 19(8); Reid A (1); Russell I 11(14); Shimmin D 21; Smith C 18(3); Stewart C 2(2); Wake B 18(14); Walker A 23(1); Weatherson P 31(3).
Goals – League (40): Wake 9, Weatherson 9, McGuffie 4 (2 pens), Jenkins 3, Masterton 3 (1 pen), Paartalu 3, Russell 3, Grady 2, Greacen 2, Monti 1, Newby 1.
Scottish Cup (1): Masterton 1.
CIS Cup (5): Russell 2 (1 pen), Harding 1, McAlister 1, Masterton 1.
Challenge Cup (6): McGuffie 3, Masterton 1, Wake 1, Weatherson 1.
Honours – First Division: Champions – 1977–78, 1983–84, 1986–87. **Division II:** Champions – 1949–50, 1963–64, 1966–67. **Second Division:** Champions – 1994–95, 2006–07. **Third Division:** Champions 2002–03. **Scottish Cup winners** 1922.

MOTHERWELL   PREMIER LEAGUE

Ground: Fir Park, Motherwell ML1 2QN (01698) 333333
Ground capacity: 13,742. **Colours:** Amber shirts with claret hoop and trim, amber shorts, amber stockings with claret trim.
Manager: Jim Gannon.

League Appearances: Clarkson D 30(3); Craigan S 22; Fitzpatrick M 14(9); Hammell S 37; Hughes S 35; Hutchinson S 1; Klimpl M 20(1); Krysiak A 1; Lasley K 24(4); Malcolm R 11(2); McGarry S 16(7); McHugh R (2); McLean B 12; Murphy J 11(19); O'Brien J 19(10); Porter C 21(1); Quinn P 33; Reynolds M 36; Saunders S 2(1); Sheridan C 9(4); Slane P (1); Smith D 1(15); Smith G 37; Sutton J 26(2).
Goals – League (46): Clarkson 14 (2 pens), Sutton 10, Porter 8, Malcolm 3, McLean 2, Murphy 2, Sheridan 2, Fitzpatrick 1, Hughes 1, Klimpl 1, O'Brien 1, Quinn 1.
Scottish Cup (4): Sutton 2, Clarkson 1, Hughes 1.
CIS Cup (1): Murphy 1.
UEFA Cup (0).
Honours – Division I: Champions – 1931–32. **First Division:** Champions – 1981–82, 1984–85. **Division II:** Champions – 1953–54, 1968–69. **Scottish Cup winners** 1952, 1991. **League Cup winners** 1951.

PARTICK THISTLE   DIV. 1

Ground: Firhill Stadium, Glasgow G20 7AL (0141) 579 1971
Ground capacity: 13,141. **Colours:** Red and yellow halves with black sleeves, black shorts, black stockings.
Manager: Ian McCall.
League Appearances: Akins L 6(3); Archibald A 19(1); Buchanan L 17(2); Chaplain S 13(17); Donnelly S 19(12); Doohlan K 15(1); Gray D 5(5); Harkins G 34; Kinniburgh W 14(4); Lennon S 5(4); Little R (1); Maxwell I 21(3); McKeown S 18(7); McKinlay K 12(17); McStay R 1(2); Paton P 32(3); Roberts M 6(9); Robertson J 28; Rowson D 35; Storey S 31(1); Tuffey J 36; Turner C 1(1); Twaddle M 28(2).
Goals – League (39): Harkins 9 (4 pens), Buchanan 6 (1 pen), Doohlan 5, Maxwell 3, McKeown 3, Paton 3, Chaplain 2, McKinlay 2, Akins 1, Donnelly 1, Gray 1, Robertson J 1, Rowson 1, own goal 1.
Scottish Cup (3): Buchanan 1, Chaplain 1, Harkins 1 (pen).
CIS Cup (3): Harkins 1 (pen), Maxwell 1, McKeown 1.
Challenge Cup (8): McKeown 2, Donnelly 1, Gray 1, Harkins 1, Roberts 1, Turner 1, Twaddle 1.
Honours – First Division: Champions – 1975–76, 2001–02. **Division II:** Champions – 1896–97, 1899–1900, 1970–71. **Second Division:** Champions 2000–01. **Scottish Cup winners** 1921. **League Cup winners** 1972.

PETERHEAD   DIV. 2

Ground: Balmoor Stadium, Peterhead AB42 1EU (01779) 478256
Ground capacity: 3250 (1000 seated). **Colours:** Royal blue shirts with navy sleeves, royal blue shorts, royal blue stockings.
Manager: Neil Cooper.
League Appearances: Anderson S 35(1); Bagshaw A 4(2); Bavidge M 32(1); Cowie D 2(5); Davidson L (1); Donald D 36; Duncan R (2); Flemming S 5(2); Gunn C 26(10); Jarvie P 11; Kozminski K 1(16); Kula M 25(1); MacDonald C 34; Mann B 17(4); McKay S 32(3); McVitie N 24; Moore D 32(1); Ross D 16(14); Sharp G 29(1); Skinner M 13(1); Smith S 22.
Goals – League (54): Bavidge 9 (1 pen), Sharp 9, Anderson 7 (1 pen), MacDonald 6, McKay 6, Ross 6, Gunn 4, Mann 2 (1 pen), Moore 2, Cowie 1, Kozminski 1, McVitie 1.
Scottish Cup (4): Bavidge 2, Anderson 1, Ross 1.
Challenge Cup (8): Gunn 4 (1 pen), Bavidge 2, Kozminski 1, own goal 1.
Play-Offs (1): McKay 1.
Honours – None.

QUEEN OF THE SOUTH   DIV. 1

Ground: Palmerston Park, Dumfries DG2 9BA (01387) 254853
Ground capacity: 7412 (seated: 3509). **Colours:** Royal blue shirts with white flashes, white shorts, royal blue stockings.
Manager: Gordon Chisholm.
League Appearances: Adams J 2(1); Aitken A 9(4); Arbuckle G 5(3); Barr C 22(2); Bell C 15; Burns P 28(1); Dobbie S 30(3); Halliwell B 4; Harris R 21; Kean S 19(12); Kinniburgh S 2; Lancaster M 15; MacFarlane N 26(7); McCann R 8(4); McGowan M 8(5); McLaughlan G 1; McQuilken J 24(10); O'Connor S 22(6); Parratt T 9; Reid C 12(3); Robertson S 5(5); Robinson L 17; Scally N 10(1); Simmons S 6(4); Sives C 10; Thomson J 22(2); Tosh S 26(3); Weatherston D 4(16); Wilson B 14(2).
Goals – League (57): Dobbie 23 (1 pen), Tosh 6 (3 pens), Burns 4 (1 pen), Weatherston 4, Wilson 4, Kean 3, Arbuckle 2, Harris 2, Lancaster 2, McQuilken 2, Barr 1, McCann 1, McGowan 1, O'Connor 1, Thomson 1.
Scottish Cup (2): Harris 1, Wilson 1.
CIS Cup (1): Kean 1.
Challenge Cup (7): Kean 3, O'Connor 3, Barr 1.
UEFA Cup (2): Harris 1, O'Connor 1.
Honours – Division II: Champions – 1950–51. **Second Division:** Champions – 2001–02. **League Challenge Cup winners** 2003.

QUEEN'S PARK   DIV. 3

Ground: Hampden Park, Glasgow G42 9BA (0141) 632 1275
Ground capacity: 52,000. **Colours:** Black and white shirts, white shorts, white stockings with black tops.
Coach: Gardner Spiers.
League Appearances: Agostini D 14(2); Baillie S (1); Barry D 1; Boslem A 3(4); Brough J 32(1); Cairney P 33; Capuano G (1); Coakley A 12(9); Cowie A 13; Crawford D 23; Douglas B 30; Dunlop R 17(10); Dunn R 2(5); Harkins P 27(3); Henry J 3(1); Holmes R 25(6); Little R 11; McGinn P (1); McGrady S 5(5); McGrogan A (7); Murray S 5(8); Neill J 20; Nicholas S 16(1); Odenewo S 10; Quinn T 22(1); Reilly S 6(1); Ronald P 4(7); Sinclair R 17; Ure M 24; Waters D 5; Watt I 16(13).
Goals – League (35): Cairney 8 (4 pens), Watt 6, Harkins 5, Coakley 3, Brough 2, Douglas 2, Holmes 2, Odenewo 2, Barry 1, Dunlop 1, Dunn 1, Nicholas 1, Quinn 1.
Scottish Cup (6): Cairney 2 (1 pen), Brough 1, Coakley 1, Holmes 1, Watt 1.
Challenge Cup (1): Henry 1.
Play-Offs (1): Harkins 1.
Honours – Second Division: Champions – 1980–81. **Third Division:** Champions – 1999–2000. **Scottish Cup winners** 1874, 1875, 1876, 1880, 1881, 1882, 1884, 1886, 1890, 1893.

RAITH ROVERS   DIV. 1

Ground: Stark's Park, Pratt Street, Kirkcaldy KY1 1SA (01592) 263514
Ground capacity: 10,104 (all seated). **Colours:** Navy with white shirts, navy shorts, navy stockings with white tops.
Manager: John McGlynn.
League Appearances: Andrews M 11; Armstrong D (1); Bryce L (12); Campbell M 31; Cook A 13(5); Davidson I 33; Dunbar J (3); Ellis L 28; Ferry M 27(8); Graham T (2); Guerrero J (1); Hislop S 3(8); Lumsden T 10(1); McGurn D 30; O'Connor G 6(1); Silvestro C 8(3); Simmons S 13(1); Sloan R 31(2); Smith K 25(3); Wales G 20(3); Walker A 24(8); Wardlaw G 4(16); Weir G 34(2); Williamson I 9(3); Wilson C 36.

Goals – League (60): Smith 18 (1 pen), Weir 9, Wales 8 (2 pens), Campbell 5, Ferry 5, Sloan 5, Hislop 2, Walker 2, Wardlaw 2, Davidson 1, Ellis 1, Williamson 1, Wilson 1.
Scottish Cup (1):Wales 1.
CIS Cup (1): Campbell 1.
Challenge Cup (1): Weir 1.
Honours – First Division: Champions – 1992–93, 1994–95. **Second Division:** Champions – 2002–03, 2008–09. **Division II:** Champions – 1907–08, 1909–10 (Shared), 1937–38, 1948–49. **League Cup winners** 1995.

RANGERS   PREMIER LEAGUE

Ground: Ibrox Stadium, Glasgow G51 2XD 0871 7021972
Ground capacity: 51,082. **Colours:** Royal blue shirts with red and white trim, white shorts with red and blue trim, black stockings with red tops.
Manager: Walter Smith.
League Appearances: Adam C 7(2); Alexander N 11; Beasley D 6(4); Bougherra M 31; Boyd K 33(2); Broadfoot K 27; Burke C (2); Cousin D 1(1); Dailly C 7(2); Darcheville J 4(4); Davis S 34; Edu M 11(1); Ferguson B 17(5); Fleck J 7(1); Lafferty K 11(14); Loy R (1); McCulloch L 10(2); McGregor A 27; Miller K 25(5); Naismith S 1(6); Niguez A (3); Novo N 7(22); Papac S 29; Pedro Mendes 35; Smith S 5; Thomson K 11; Velicka A 6(2); Weir D 36; Whittaker S 19(5).
Goals – League (77): Boyd 27 (7 pens), Miller 10, Davis 6, Lafferty 6, Novo 5, Velicka 4, Pedro Mendes 3, Edu 2, Ferguson 2, Weir 2, Whittaker 2, Bougherra 1, Cousin 1, Darcheville 1, Fleck 1 (pen), Papac 1, Thomson 1, own goals 2.
Scottish Cup (15): Miller 3, Lafferty 2, Niguez 2 (1 pen), Novo 2, Boyd 1, Davis 1, Papac 1, Velicka 1, Whittaker 1, own goal 1.
CIS Cup (7): Boyd 3, Novo 2, Lafferty 1, Pedro Mendes 1.
Champions League (1): Thomson 1.
Honours – Division I: Champions – 1890–91 (Shared), 1898–99, 1899–1900, 1900–01, 1901–02, 1910–11, 1911–12, 1912–13, 1917–18, 1919–20, 1920–21, 1922–23, 1923–24, 1924–25, 1926–27, 1927–28, 1928–29, 1929–30, 1930–31, 1932–33, 1933–34, 1934–35, 1936–37, 1938–39, 1946–47, 1948–49, 1949–50, 1952–53, 1955–56, 1956–57, 1958–59, 1960–61, 1962–63, 1963–64, 1974–75. **Premier Division:** Champions – 1975–76, 1977–78, 1986–87, 1988–89, 1989–90, 1990–91, 1991–92, 1992–93, 1993–94, 1994–95, 1995–96, 1996–97. **Premier League:** Champions – 1998–99, 1999–2000, 2002–03, 2004–05, 2008–09. **Scottish Cup winners** 1894, 1897, 1898, 1903, 1928, 1930, 1932, 1934, 1935, 1936, 1948, 1949, 1950, 1953, 1960, 1962, 1963, 1964, 1966, 1973, 1976, 1978, 1979, 1981, 1992, 1993, 1996, 1999, 2000, 2002, 2003, 2008, 2009. **League Cup winners** 1947, 1949, 1961, 1962, 1964, 1965, 1971, 1976, 1978, 1979, 1982, 1984, 1985, 1987, 1988, 1989, 1991, 1993, 1994, 1997, 1999, 2002, 2003, 2005, 2008. **European Cup-Winners' Cup winners** 1972.

ROSS COUNTY   DIV. 1

Ground: Victoria Park, Dingwall IV15 9QW (01349) 860860
Ground capacity: 6700. **Colours:** Navy blue with white flashes, navy shorts with white flashes, white stockings.
Manager: Derek Adam.
League Appearances: Boyd S 28; Brewster C 10; Brittain R 30; Bullock T 16; Corrigan M 10; Craig S 26(5); Daal D 16(12); Dowie A 28(1); Gardyne M 9(18); Golabek S 14(1); Hart R 24(9); Higgins S 23(8); Keddie A 25(4); Lawson P 18(2); Malin J 7(1); McCulloch M 35; Morrison S 7(8); Scott M 16(8); Shields D (1); Soutar D 13; Stewart J 3(6); Strachan A 12(12); Watt S 23(5); Winters D 3(3).
Goals – League (42): Craig 10 (1 pen), Higgins 10, Brittain 4, Brewster 3, Daal 3, Hart 3, McCulloch 3, Morrison 2, Dowie 1, Gardyne 1, Keddie 1, own goal 1.

Scottish Cup (4): Higgins 2, Brittain 1 (pen), Hart 1.
Challenge Cup (11): Craig 2, Daal 2, Higgins 2, Keddie 2, Dowie 1, Winters 1, own goal 1.
Honours – Second Division: Champions – 2007–08. **Third Division:** Champions – 1998–99. **League Challenge Cup winners** 2007.

ST JOHNSTONE   PREMIER LEAGUE

Ground: McDiarmid Park, Crieff Road, Perth PH1 2SJ (01738) 459090
Ground capacity: 10,673. **Colours:** Royal blue shirts with white trim, white shorts.
Manager: Derek Adams.
League Appearances: Anderson S 11(4); Barrett G 4(5); Byrne R 5; Craig L 31(3); Doris S 1(1); Gartland G 7; Hanlon P 2; Hardie M 20(4); Holmes D 22(13); Irvine G 34(1); Jackson A 5(5); James K 4; Lindsay J 1; MacDonald P 2(10); Main A 32; May S (1); McCaffrey S 25(1); McKoy N 2(3); McLean E 4; Millar C 30(4); Milne S 26(6); Moon K 12(10); Morgan A 2(2); Morris J 10(4); Reynolds S 1; Rutkiewicz K 34; Samuel C 20(8); Sheerin P 29(5); Smith D 3; Swankie G 17(10); Weatherston D (1).
Goals – League (55): Milne 14, Samuel 6, Craig 5 (4 pens), Holmes 5, Hardie 4, Swankie 4, McCaffrey 3, Rutkiewicz 3, Sheerin 3 (1 pen), Millar 2, Anderson 1, Barrett 1, Irvine 1, MacDonald 1, May 1, own goal 1.
Scottish Cup (0).
CIS Cup (1): Craig 1.
Challenge Cup (1): Samuel 1.
Honours – First Division: Champions – 1982–83, 1989–90, 1996–97, 2008–09. **Division II:** Champions – 1923–24, 1959–60, 1962–63. **League Challenge Cup winners** 2008.

ST MIRREN   PREMIER LEAGUE

Ground: St Mirren Park, Paisley PA3 2EJ (0141) 889 2558
Ground capacity: 10,476 (all seated). **Colours:** Black and white striped shirts, white shorts with black trim, white stockings with two black hoops.
Manager: Gus MacPherson.
League Appearances: Barron D 5(5); Brady G 31(3); Brighton T 1(4); Burns S (2); Camara M 10; Cuthbert S 28(1); Dargo C 12(15); Dorman A 32(4); Guerao T 2(1); Haining W 17(2); Hamilton J 13(11); Howard M 34; Mason G 20(3); McAusland M (4); McGinn S 17(12); Mehmet B 28(6); Miranda F 22; Murray H 28(2); O'Donnell S 3(5); Potter J 35; Robb S 11(4); Ross J 36; Smith C 4; Thomson S 12(2); Wyness D 17(14).
Goals – League (33): Dorman 10, Mehmet 7 (2 pens), Hamilton 3, Wyness 3, Brady 2, Dargo 2, Miranda 2, McGinn 1, O'Donnell 1, Ross 1, Thomson 1.
Scottish Cup (6): Hamilton 2 (1 pen), Mehmet 2 (1 pen), Dorman 1, Wyness 1.
CIS Cup (7): Mehmet 3, Dargo 1, Dorman 1, Mason 1, Robb 1.
Honours – First Division: Champions – 1976–77, 1999–2000, 2005–06. **Division II:** Champions – 1967–68. **Scottish Cup winners** 1926, 1959, 1987.
League Challenge Cup winners 2005–06.

STENHOUSEMUIR   DIV. 2

Ground: Ochilview Park, Stenhousemuir FK5 4QL (01324) 562992
Ground capacity: 3746. **Colours:** Maroon shirts with white flashes, white shorts, white stockings.
Manager: John Coughlin.
League Appearances: Bennett S 24; Brand A 25(5); Brazil A 8(2); Connolly S 1(2); Dalziel S 28(7); Desmond S 2(5); Diack I 13(1); Ferguson A 2(1); Ferguson S 16(1); Forde R 1; Gibson G (2); Hampshire S 8(6); Jack M (1); Love R 12(11);

Lyle W 28; McEwan C 3(3); McGroarty C 30; McLeod C 11; McManus S (1); Molloy C 12(1); Morgan A 4(3); Motion K 28(4); Ovenstone J 31; Rankin C 1; Reid A 7; Renton K 11; Shirra A 11(12); Smith J 24(1); Stirling A 1(3); Thom G 15(1); Thomson I 26(3); Tyrrell P 13(4).
Goals – League (55): Dalziel 14 (1 pen), Motion 12, Brand 5, Love 4, Diack 3, Ovenstone 3, Thom 3, Hampshire 2, McLeod 2, Smith 2, Thomson 2, Shirra 1, Stirling 1, own goal 1.
Scottish Cup (10): Dalziel 3, Motion 2, Desmond 1, Hampshire 1, Shirra 1, Thom 1, Thomson 1.
Challenge Cup (0).
Play-Offs (2): Dalziel 1 (pen), Love 1.
Honours – League Challenge Cup winners 1996.

STIRLING ALBION   DIV. 2

Ground: Forthbank Stadium, Springkerse Industrial Estate, Stirling FK7 7UJ (01786) 450399
Ground capacity: 3808. **Colours:** All red.
Manager: Allan Moore.
League Appearances: Andrew G 1; Boyle J 2(9); Christie S 19; Corr L 12(12); Devine S 20(3); Docherty M 22(7); Dunn R (5); Fagan S (1); Feaks K 2(1); Forsyth R 26(1); Gibb S 20; Graham A 24(1); Grehan M 30(3); Hamilton C 12(9); Harty I 12(1); Hogarth M 17(1); Lawrie A 25(1); Lowing D 20(1); McCord R 3(4); McKenna D 26(8); Molloy C 11; Mullen M 5(7); Murphy P 26(6); O'Neil J 30(1); Roycroft S 20; Taggart N 11(2); Waddell S (8).
Goals – League (59): Grehan 12, McKenna 12 (1 pen), O'Neil 7, Hamilton 4, Docherty 3, Harty 3 (1 pen), Mullen 3, Graham 2, Molloy 2, Murphy 2, Taggart 2, Corr 1, McCord 1, Roycroft 1, own goals 4.
Scottish Cup (2): Molloy 1, Murphy 1.
Challenge Cup (0).
Honours – Division II: Champions – 1952–53, 1957–58, 1960–61, 1964–65. **Second Division:** Champions – 1976–77, 1990–91, 1995–96.

STRANRAER   DIV. 3

Ground: Stair Park, Stranraer DG9 8BS (01776) 703271
Ground capacity: 5600. **Colours:** Royal blue shirts with white design, white shorts, royal blue stockings.
Manager: Keith Knox.
League Appearances: Aitken S 9(1); Anglade A (1); Black S 26; Bradley C (7); Campbell M (1); Cantley F 1(1); Connolly S 1(2); Cooksley R (4); Craig D 3; Creaney J 13(7); Crosthwaite D 9; Dobbins I 16; Dougan D 1; Frizzel C 26(6); Gibson A 26(2); Hogan D (1); Jones R 3(1); Kane J 36; Kiltie J (1); McBride M 23(2); McColm S 11(10); McConalogue S 28(6); McGrath P 5(2); McGregor S 1; McKinstry J 26(3); Miller I (1); Mitchell D 27(6); Moore M 6(2); Mullen M 11(7); Murdoch A (4); Mutch J 1(1); Nicoll K 21(1); Noble S 27(4); Paisley R 1(3); Ritchie J (1); Tade G 16; White A 10(2); Whorlow M 2(2); Wilson M 10(1).
Goals – League (31): Tade 7 (2 pens), McConalogue 6, Mitchell 5, Mullen 3, Frizzel 2, McBride 2 (1 pen), Dobbins 1, Kane 1, McColm 1, Moore 1, Nicoll 1, White 1.
Scottish Cup (0).
Challenge Cup (0).
Honours – Second Division: Champions – 1993–94, 1997–98. **Third Division:** Champions – 2003–04. **League Challenge Cup winners** 1997.

SCOTTISH LEAGUE HONOURS

*On goal average (ratio)/difference. †Held jointly after indecisive play-off.
‡Won on deciding match. ††Held jointly. ¶Two points deducted for fielding ineligible
player. Competition suspended 1940–45 during war; Regional Leagues operating.
‡‡Two points deducted for registration irregularities. §Not promoted after play-offs.

PREMIER LEAGUE

Maximum points: 108

	First	Pts	Second	Pts	Third	Pts
1998–99	Rangers	77	Celtic	71	St Johnstone	57
1999–00	Rangers	90	Celtic	69	Hearts	54

Maximum points: 114

	First	Pts	Second	Pts	Third	Pts
2000–01	Celtic	97	Rangers	82	Hibernian	66
2001–02	Celtic	103	Rangers	85	Livingston	58
2002–03	Rangers*	97	Celtic	97	Hearts	63
2003–04	Celtic	98	Rangers	81	Hearts	68
2004–05	Rangers	93	Celtic	92	Hibernian*	61
2005–06	Celtic	91	Hearts	74	Rangers	73
2006–07	Celtic	84	Rangers	72	Aberdeen	65
2007–08	Celtic	89	Rangers	86	Motherwell	60
2008–09	Rangers	86	Celtic	82	Hearts	59

PREMIER DIVISION

Maximum points: 72

	First	Pts	Second	Pts	Third	Pts
1975–76	Rangers	54	Celtic	48	Hibernian	43
1976–77	Celtic	55	Rangers	46	Aberdeen	43
1977–78	Rangers	55	Aberdeen	53	Dundee U	40
1978–79	Celtic	48	Rangers	45	Dundee U	44
1979–80	Aberdeen	48	Celtic	47	St Mirren	42
1980–81	Celtic	56	Aberdeen	49	Rangers*	44
1981–82	Celtic	55	Aberdeen	53	Rangers	43
1982–83	Dundee U	56	Celtic*	55	Aberdeen	55
1983–84	Aberdeen	57	Celtic	50	Dundee U	47
1984–85	Aberdeen	59	Celtic	52	Dundee U	47
1985–86	Celtic*	50	Hearts	50	Dundee U	47

Maximum points: 88

	First	Pts	Second	Pts	Third	Pts
1986–87	Rangers	69	Celtic	63	Dundee U	60
1987–88	Celtic	72	Hearts	62	Rangers	60

Maximum points: 72

	First	Pts	Second	Pts	Third	Pts
1988–89	Rangers	56	Aberdeen	50	Celtic	46
1989–90	Rangers	51	Aberdeen*	44	Hearts	44
1990–91	Rangers	55	Aberdeen	53	Celtic*	41

Maximum points: 88

	First	Pts	Second	Pts	Third	Pts
1991–92	Rangers	72	Hearts	63	Celtic	62
1992–93	Rangers	73	Aberdeen	64	Celtic	60
1993–94	Rangers	58	Aberdeen	55	Motherwell	54

Maximum points: 108

	First	Pts	Second	Pts	Third	Pts
1994–95	Rangers	69	Motherwell	54	Hibernian	53
1995–96	Rangers	87	Celtic	83	Aberdeen*	55
1996–97	Rangers	80	Celtic	75	Dundee U	60
1997–98	Celtic	74	Rangers	72	Hearts	67

DIVISION 1

Maximum points: 52

	First	Pts	Second	Pts	Third	Pts
1975–76	Partick Th	41	Kilmarnock	35	Montrose	30

	First	Pts	Second	Pts	Third	Pts
			Maximum points: 78			
1976–77	St Mirren	62	Clydebank	58	Dundee	51
1977–78	Morton*	58	Hearts	58	Dundee	57
1978–79	Dundee	55	Kilmarnock*	54	Clydebank	54
1979–80	Hearts	53	Airdrieonians	51	Ayr U*	44
1980–81	Hibernian	57	Dundee	52	St Johnstone	51
1981–82	Motherwell	61	Kilmarnock	51	Hearts	50
1982–83	St Johnstone	55	Hearts	54	Clydebank	50
1983–84	Morton	54	Dumbarton	51	Partick Th	46
1984–85	Motherwell	50	Clydebank	48	Falkirk	45
1985–86	Hamilton A	56	Falkirk	45	Kilmarnock	44
			Maximum points: 88			
1986–87	Morton	57	Dunfermline Ath	56	Dumbarton	53
1987–88	Hamilton A	56	Meadowbank Th	52	Clydebank	49
			Maximum points: 78			
1988–89	Dunfermline Ath	54	Falkirk	52	Clydebank	48
1989–90	St Johnstone	58	Airdrieonians	54	Clydebank	44
1990–91	Falkirk	54	Airdrieonians	53	Dundee	52
			Maximum points: 88			
1991–92	Dundee	58	Partick Th*	57	Hamilton A	57
1992–93	Raith R	65	Kilmarnock	54	Dunfermline Ath	52
1993–94	Falkirk	66	Dunfermline Ath	65	Airdrieonians	54
			Maximum points: 108			
1994–95	Raith R	69	Dunfermline Ath*	68	Dundee	68
1995–96	Dunfermline Ath	71	Dundee U*	67	Morton	67
1996–97	St Johnstone	80	Airdrieonians	60	Dundee*	58
1997–98	Dundee	70	Falkirk	65	Raith R*	60
1998–99	Hibernian	89	Falkirk	66	Ayr U	62
1999–00	St Mirren	76	Dunfermline Ath	71	Falkirk	68
2000–01	Livingston	76	Ayr U	69	Falkirk	56
2001–02	Partick Th	66	Airdrieonians	56	Ayr U	52
2002–03	Falkirk	81	Clyde	72	St Johnstone	67
2003–04	Inverness CT	70	Clyde	69	St Johnstone	57
2004–05	Falkirk	75	St Mirren*	60	Clyde	60
2005–06	St Mirren	76	St Johnstone	66	Hamilton A	59
2006–07	Gretna	66	St Johnstone	65	Dundee*	53
2007–08	Hamilton A	76	Dundee	69	St Johnstone	58
2008–09	St Johnstone	65	Partick Th	55	Dunfermline Ath	51

DIVISION 2

	First	Pts	Second	Pts	Third	Pts
			Maximum points: 52			
1975–76	Clydebank*	40	Raith R	40	Alloa Ath	35
			Maximum points: 78			
1976–77	Stirling A	55	Alloa Ath	51	Dunfermline Ath	50
1977–78	Clyde*	53	Raith R	53	Dunfermline Ath	48
1978–79	Berwick R	54	Dunfermline Ath	52	Falkirk	50
1979–80	Falkirk	50	East Stirling	49	Forfar Ath	46
1980–81	Queen's Park	50	Queen of the S	46	Cowdenbeath	45
1981–82	Clyde	59	Alloa Ath*	50	Arbroath	50
1982–83	Brechin C	55	Meadowbank Th	54	Arbroath	49
1983–84	Forfar Ath	63	East Fife	47	Berwick R	43
1984–85	Montrose	53	Alloa Ath	50	Dunfermline Ath	49
1985–86	Dunfermline Ath	57	Queen of the S	55	Meadowbank Th	49
1986–87	Meadowbank Th	55	Raith R*	52	Stirling A*	52
1987–88	Ayr U	61	St Johnstone	59	Queen's Park	51

	First	Pts	Second	Pts	Third	Pts
1988–89	Albion R	50	Alloa Ath	45	Brechin C	43
1989–90	Brechin C	49	Kilmarnock	48	Stirling A	47
1990–91	Stirling A	54	Montrose	46	Cowdenbeath	45
1991–92	Dumbarton	52	Cowdenbeath	51	Alloa Ath	50
1992–93	Clyde	54	Brechin C*	53	Stranraer	53
1993–94	Stranraer	56	Berwick R	48	Stenhousemuir*	47

Maximum points: 108

	First	Pts	Second	Pts	Third	Pts
1994–95	Morton	64	Dumbarton	60	Stirling A	58
1995–96	Stirling A	81	East Fife	67	Berwick R	60
1996–97	Ayr U	77	Hamilton A	74	Livingston	64
1997–98	Stranraer	61	Clydebank	60	Livingston	59
1998–99	Livingston	77	Inverness CT	72	Clyde	53
1999–00	Clyde	65	Alloa Ath	64	Ross County	62
2000–01	Partick Th	75	Arbroath	58	Berwick R*	54
2001–02	Queen of the S	67	Alloa Ath	59	Forfar Ath	53
2002–03	Raith R	59	Brechin C	55	Airdrie U	54
2003–04	Airdrie U	70	Hamilton A	62	Dumbarton	60
2004–05	Brechin C	72	Stranraer	63	Morton	62
2005–06	Gretna	88	Morton§	70	Peterhead*§	57
2006–07	Morton	77	Stirling A	69	Raith R§	62
2007–08	Ross Co	73	Airdrie U	66	Raith R§	60
2008–09	Raith R	76	Ayr U	74	Brechin C§	62

DIVISION 3
Maximum points: 108

	First	Pts	Second	Pts	Third	Pts
1994–95	Forfar Ath	80	Montrose	67	Ross Co	60
1995–96	Livingston	72	Brechin C	63	Caledonian T	57
1996–97	Inverness CT	76	Forfar Ath*	67	Ross Co	67
1997–98	Alloa Ath	76	Arbroath	68	Ross Co*	67
1998–99	Ross Co	77	Stenhousemuir	64	Brechin C	59
1999–00	Queen's Park	69	Berwick R	66	Forfar Ath	61
2000–01	Hamilton A*	76	Cowdenbeath	76	Brechin C	72
2001–02	Brechin C	73	Dumbarton	61	Albion R	59
2002–03	Morton	72	East Fife	71	Albion R	70
2003–04	Stranraer	79	Stirling A	77	Gretna	68
2004–05	Gretna	98	Peterhead	78	Cowdenbeath	51
2005–06	Cowdenbeath*	76	Berwick R§	76	Stenhousemuir§	73
2006–07	Berwick R	75	Arbroath§	70	Queen's Park	68
2007–08	East Fife	88	Stranraer	65	Montrose§	59
2008–09	Dumbarton	67	Cowdenbeath§	63	East Stirling§	61

DIVISION 1 to 1974–75
Maximum points: a 36; b 44; c 40; d 52; e 60; f 68; g 76; h 84.

	First	Pts	Second	Pts	Third	Pts
1890–91a	Dumbarton††	29	Rangers††	29	Celtic	21
1891–92b	Dumbarton	37	Celtic	35	Hearts	34
1892–93a	Celtic	29	Rangers	28	St Mirren	20
1893–94a	Celtic	29	Hearts	26	St Bernard's	23
1894–95a	Hearts	31	Celtic	26	Rangers	22
1895–96a	Celtic	30	Rangers	26	Hibernian	24
1896–97a	Hearts	28	Hibernian	26	Rangers	25
1897–98a	Celtic	33	Rangers	29	Hibernian	22
1898–99a	Rangers	36	Hearts	26	Celtic	24
1899–1900a	Rangers	32	Celtic	25	Hibernian	24
1900–01c	Rangers	35	Celtic	29	Hibernian	25
1901–02a	Rangers	28	Celtic	26	Hearts	22
1902–03b	Hibernian	37	Dundee	31	Rangers	29
1903–04d	Third Lanark	43	Hearts	39	Celtic*	38

	First	Pts	Second	Pts	Third	Pts
1904–05d	Celtic‡	41	Rangers	41	Third Lanark	35
1905–06e	Celtic	49	Hearts	43	Airdrieonians	38
1906–07f	Celtic	55	Dundee	48	Rangers	45
1907–08f	Celtic	55	Falkirk	51	Rangers	50
1908–09f	Celtic	51	Dundee	50	Clyde	48
1909–10f	Celtic	54	Falkirk	52	Rangers	46
1910–11f	Rangers	52	Aberdeen	48	Falkirk	44
1911–12f	Rangers	51	Celtic	45	Clyde	42
1912–13f	Rangers	53	Celtic	49	Hearts*	41
1913–14g	Celtic	65	Rangers	59	Hearts*	54
1914–15g	Celtic	65	Hearts	61	Rangers	50
1915–16g	Celtic	67	Rangers	56	Morton	51
1916–17g	Celtic	64	Morton	54	Rangers	53
1917–18f	Rangers	56	Celtic	55	Kilmarnock*	43
1918–19f	Celtic	58	Rangers	57	Morton	47
1919–20h	Rangers	71	Celtic	68	Motherwell	57
1920–21h	Rangers	76	Celtic	66	Hearts	50
1921–22h	Celtic	67	Rangers	66	Raith R	51
1922–23g	Rangers	55	Airdrieonians	50	Celtic	46
1923–24g	Rangers	59	Airdrieonians	50	Celtic	46
1924–25g	Rangers	60	Airdrieonians	57	Hibernian	52
1925–26g	Celtic	58	Airdrieonians*	50	Hearts	50
1926–27g	Rangers	56	Motherwell	51	Celtic	49
1927–28g	Rangers	60	Celtic*	55	Motherwell	55
1928–29g	Rangers	67	Celtic	51	Motherwell	50
1929–30g	Rangers	60	Motherwell	55	Aberdeen	53
1930–31g	Rangers	60	Celtic	58	Motherwell	56
1931–32g	Motherwell	66	Rangers	61	Celtic	48
1932–33g	Rangers	62	Motherwell	59	Hearts	50
1933–34g	Rangers	66	Motherwell	62	Celtic	47
1934–35g	Rangers	55	Celtic	52	Hearts	50
1935–36g	Celtic	66	Rangers*	61	Aberdeen	61
1936–37g	Rangers	61	Aberdeen	54	Celtic	52
1937–38g	Celtic	61	Hearts	58	Rangers	49
1938–39g	Rangers	59	Celtic	48	Aberdeen	46
1946–47e	Rangers	46	Hibernian	44	Aberdeen	39
1947–48e	Hibernian	48	Rangers	46	Partick Th	36
1948–49e	Rangers	46	Dundee	45	Hibernian	39
1949–50e	Rangers	50	Hibernian	49	Hearts	43
1950–51e	Hibernian	48	Rangers*	38	Dundee	38
1951–52e	Hibernian	45	Rangers	41	East Fife	37
1952–53e	Rangers*	43	Hibernian	43	East Fife	39
1953–54e	Celtic	43	Hearts	38	Partick Th	35
1954–55e	Aberdeen	49	Celtic	46	Rangers	41
1955–56f	Rangers	52	Aberdeen	46	Hearts*	45
1956–57f	Rangers	55	Hearts	53	Kilmarnock	42
1957–58f	Hearts	62	Rangers	49	Celtic	46
1958–59f	Rangers	50	Hearts	48	Motherwell	44
1959–60f	Hearts	54	Kilmarnock	50	Rangers*	42
1960–61f	Rangers	51	Kilmarnock	50	Third Lanark	42
1961–62f	Dundee	54	Rangers	51	Celtic	46
1962–63f	Rangers	57	Kilmarnock	48	Partick Th	46
1963–64f	Rangers	55	Kilmarnock	49	Celtic*	47
1964–65f	Kilmarnock*	50	Hearts	50	Dunfermline Ath	49
1965–66f	Celtic	57	Rangers	55	Kilmarnock	45
1966–67f	Celtic	58	Rangers	55	Clyde	46
1967–68f	Celtic	63	Rangers	61	Hibernian	45
1968–69f	Celtic	54	Rangers	49	DunfermlineAth	45
1969–70f	Celtic	57	Rangers	45	Hibernian	44

	First	Pts	Second	Pts	Third	Pts
1970–71f	Celtic	56	Aberdeen	54	St Johnstone	44
1971–72f	Celtic	60	Aberdeen	50	Rangers	44
1972–73f	Celtic	57	Rangers	56	Hibernian	45
1973–74f	Celtic	53	Hibernian	49	Rangers	48
1974–75f	Rangers	56	Hibernian	49	Celtic	45

DIVISION 2 to 1974–75

Maximum points: a 76; b 72; c 68; d 52; e 60; f 36; g 44.

	First	Pts	Second	Pts	Third	Pts
1893–94f	Hibernian	29	Cowlairs	27	Clyde	24
1894–95f	Hibernian	30	Motherwell	22	Port Glasgow	20
1895–96f	Abercorn	27	Leith Ath	23	Renton	21
1896–97f	Partick Th	31	Leith Ath	27	Kilmarnock*	21
1897–98f	Kilmarnock	29	Port Glasgow	25	Morton	22
1898–99f	Kilmarnock	32	Leith Ath	27	Port Glasgow	25
1899–1900f	Partick Th	29	Morton	28	Port Glasgow	20
1900–01f	St Bernard's	25	Airdrieonians	23	Abercorn	21
1901–02g	Port Glasgow	32	Partick Th	31	Motherwell	26
1902–03g	Airdrieonians	35	Motherwell	28	Ayr U*	27
1903–04g	Hamilton A	37	Clyde	29	Ayr U	28
1904–05g	Clyde	32	Falkirk	28	Hamilton A	27
1905–06g	Leith Ath	34	Clyde	31	Albion R	27
1906–07g	St Bernard's	32	Vale of Leven*	27	Arthurlie	27
1907–08g	Raith R	30	Dumbarton‡‡	27	Ayr U	27
1908–09g	Abercorn	31	Raith R*	28	Vale of Leven	28
1909–10g	Leith Ath‡	33	Raith R	33	St Bernard's	27
1910–11g	Dumbarton	31	Ayr U	27	Albion R	27
1911–12g	Ayr U	35	Abercorn	30	Dumbarton	27
1912–13d	Ayr U	34	Dunfermline Ath	33	East Stirling	32
1913–14g	Cowdenbeath	31	Albion R	27	Dunfermline Ath*	26
1914–15d	Cowdenbeath*	37	St Bernard's*	37	Leith Ath	37
1921–22a	Alloa Ath	60	Cowdenbeath	47	Armadale	45
1922–23a	Queen's Park	57	Clydebank ¶	50	St Johnstone ¶	45
1923–24a	St Johnstone	56	Cowdenbeath	55	Bathgate	44
1924–25a	Dundee U	50	Clydebank	48	Clyde	47
1925–26a	Dunfermline Ath	59	Clyde	53	Ayr U	52
1926–27a	Bo'ness	56	Raith R	49	Clydebank	45
1927–28a	Ayr U	54	Third Lanark	45	King's Park	44
1928–29b	Dundee U	51	Morton	50	Arbroath	47
1929–30a	Leith Ath*	57	East Fife	57	Albion R	54
1930–31a	Third Lanark	61	Dundee U	50	Dunfermline Ath	47
1931–32a	East Stirling	55	St Johnstone	55	Raith R*	46
1932–33c	Hibernian	54	Queen of the S	49	Dunfermline Ath	47
1933–34c	Albion R	45	Dunfermline Ath*	44	Arbroath	44
1934–35c	Third Lanark	52	Arbroath	50	St Bernard's	47
1935–36c	Falkirk	59	St Mirren	52	Morton	48
1936–37c	Ayr U	54	Morton	51	St Bernard's	48
1937–38c	Raith R	59	Albion R	48	Airdrieonians	47
1938–39c	Cowdenbeath	60	Alloa Ath*	48	East Fife	48
1946–47d	Dundee	45	Airdrieonians	42	East Fife	31
1947–48e	East Fife	53	Albion R	42	Hamilton A	40
1948–49e	Raith R*	42	Stirling A	42	Airdrieonians*	41
1949–50e	Morton	47	Airdrieonians	44	Dunfermline Ath*	36
1950–51e	Queen of the S*	45	Stirling A	45	Ayr U*	36
1951–52e	Clyde	44	Falkirk	43	Ayr U	39
1952–53e	Stirling A	44	Hamilton A	43	Queen's Park	37
1953–54e	Motherwell	45	Kilmarnock	42	Third Lanark*	36
1954–55e	Airdrieonians	46	Dunfermline Ath	42	Hamilton A	39
1955–56b	Queen's Park	54	Ayr U	51	St Johnstone	49

	First	Pts	Second	Pts	Third	Pts
1956–57b	Clyde	64	Third Lanark	51	Cowdenbeath	45
1957–58b	Stirling A	55	Dunfermline Ath	53	Arbroath	47
1958–59b	Ayr U	60	Arbroath	51	Stenhousemuir	46
1959–60b	St Johnstone	53	Dundee U	50	Queen of the S	49
1960–61b	Stirling A	55	Falkirk	54	Stenhousemuir	50
1961–62b	Clyde	54	Queen of the S	53	Morton	44
1962–63b	St Johnstone	55	East Stirling	49	Morton	48
1963–64b	Morton	67	Clyde	53	Arbroath	46
1964–65b	Stirling A	59	Hamilton A	50	Queen of the S	45
1965–66b	Ayr U	53	Airdrieonians	50	Queen of the S	47
1966–67a	Morton	69	Raith R	58	Arbroath	57
1967–68b	St Mirren	62	Arbroath	53	East Fife	49
1968–69b	Motherwell	64	Ayr U	53	East Fife*	48
1969–70b	Falkirk	56	Cowdenbeath	55	Queen of the S	50
1970–71b	Partick Th	56	East Fife	51	Arbroath	46
1971–72b	Dumbarton*	52	Arbroath	52	Stirling A	50
1972–73b	Clyde	56	Dumfermline Ath	52	Raith R*	47
1973–74b	Airdrieonians	60	Kilmarnock	58	Hamilton A	55
1974–75a	Falkirk	54	Queen of the S*	53	Montrose	53

Elected to Division 1: 1894 Clyde; 1895 Hibernian; 1896 Abercorn; 1897 Partick Th; 1899 Kilmarnock; 1900 Morton and Partick Th; 1902 Port Glasgow and Partick Th; 1903 Airdrieonians and Motherwell; 1905 Falkirk and Aberdeen; 1906 Clyde and Hamilton A; 1910 Raith R; 1913 Ayr U and Dumbarton.

SCOTTISH LEAGUE PLAY-OFFS 2008–2009

DIV 1 SEMI-FINALS FIRST LEG

Brechin C	(0) 0	Ayr U	(2) 2
Peterhead	(0) 0	Airdrie U	(1) 2

DIV 1 SEMI-FINALS SECOND LEG

Ayr U	(1) 3	Brechin C	(1) 2
Airdrie U	(0) 2	Peterhead	(1) 1

DIV 1 FINAL FIRST LEG

Ayr U	(0) 2	Airdrie U	(2) 2

DIV 1 FINAL SECOND LEG

Airdrie U	(0) 0	Ayr U	(1) 1

DIV 2 SEMI-FINALS FIRST LEG

East Stirling	(0) 1	Cowdenbeath	(2) 2
Stenhousemuir	(2) 2	Queen's Park	(1) 1

DIV 2 SEMI-FINALS SECOND LEG

Cowdenbeath	(0) 1	East Stirling	(1) 1
Queen's Park	(0) 0	Stenhousemuir	(0) 0

DIV 2 FINAL FIRST LEG

Cowdenbeath	(0) 0	Stenhousemuir	(0) 0

DIV 2 FINAL SECOND LEG

Stenhousemuir	(0) 0	Cowdenbeath	(0) 0

(aet; Stenhousemuir won 5-4 on penalties.)

RELEGATED CLUBS

From Premier League

1998–99 Dunfermline Ath	2004–05 Dundee
1999–00 *No relegated team*	2005–06 Livingston
2000–01 St Mirren	2006–07 Dunfermline Ath
2001–02 St Johnstone	2007–08 Gretna
2002–03 *No relegated team*	2008–09 Inverness CT
2003–04 Partick Th	

From Premier Division

1974–75 *No relegation due to League reorganisation*
1975–76 Dundee, St Johnstone
1976–77 Hearts, Kilmarnock
1977–78 Ayr U, Clydebank
1978–79 Hearts, Motherwell
1979–80 Dundee, Hibernian
1980–81 Kilmarnock, Hearts
1981–82 Partick Th, Airdrieonians
1982–83 Morton, Kilmarnock
1983–84 St Johnstone, Motherwell
1984–85 Dumbarton, Morton
1985–86 *No relegation due to League reorganisation*

1986–87 Clydebank, Hamilton A
1987–88 Falkirk, Dunfermline Ath, Morton
1988–89 Hamilton A
1989–90 Dundee
1990–91 None
1991–92 St Mirren, Dunfermline Ath
1992–93 Falkirk, Airdrieonians
1993–94 *See footnote, page 210*
1994–95 Dundee U
1995–96 Partick Th, Falkirk
1996–97 Raith R
1997–98 Hibernian

From Division 1

1974–75 *No relegation due to League reorganisation*
1975–76 Dunfermline Ath, Clyde
1976–77 Raith R, Falkirk
1977–78 Alloa Ath, East Fife
1978–79 Montrose, Queen of the S
1979–80 Arbroath, Clyde
1980–81 Stirling A, Berwick R
1981–82 East Stirling, Queen of the S
1982–83 Dunfermline Ath, Queen's Park
1983–84 Raith R, Alloa Ath
1984–85 Meadowbank Th, St Johnstone
1985–86 Ayr U, Alloa Ath
1986–87 Brechin C, Montrose
1987–88 East Fife, Dumbarton
1988–89 Kilmarnock, Queen of the S
1989–90 Albion R, Alloa Ath
1990–91 Clyde, Brechin C

1991–92 Montrose, Forfar Ath
1992–93 Meadowbank Th, Cowdenbeath
1993–94 *See footnote*
1994–95 Ayr U, Stranraer
1995–96 Hamilton A, Dumbarton
1996–97 Clydebank, East Fife
1997–98 Partick Th, Stirling A
1998–99 Hamilton A, Stranraer
1999–00 Clydebank
2000–01 Morton, Alloa Ath
2001–02 Raith R
2002–03 Alloa Ath, Arbroath
2003–04 Ayr U, Brechin C
2004–05 Partick Th, Raith R
2005–06 Stranraer, Brechin C
2006–07 Airdrie U, Ross Co
2007–08 Stirling A
2008–09 Clyde, Airdrie U

From Division 2

1994–95 Meadowbank Th, Brechin C
1995–96 Forfar Ath, Montrose
1996–97 Dumbarton, Berwick R
1997–98 Stenhousemuir, Brechin C
1998–99 East Fife, Forfar Ath
1999–00 Hamilton A**
2000–01 Queen's Park, Stirling A
2001–02 Morton

2002–03 Stranraer, Cowdenbeath
2003–04 East Fife, Stenhousemuir
2004–05 Arbroath, Berwick R
2005–06 Dumbarton
2006–07 Stranraer, Forfar Ath
2007–08 Cowdenbeath, Berwick R
2008–09 Stranraer, Queen's Park

209

From Division 1 1973–74

1921–22 *Queen's Park, Dumbarton, Clydebank	1950–51 Clyde, Falkirk
1922–23 Albion R, Alloa Ath	1951–52 Morton, Stirling A
1923–24 Clyde, Clydebank	1952–53 Motherwell, Third Lanark
1924–25 Third Lanark, Ayr U	1953–54 Airdrieonians, Hamilton A
1925–26 Raith R, Clydebank	1954–55 *No clubs relegated*
1926–27 Morton, Dundee U	1955–56 Stirling A, Clyde
1927–28 Dunfermline Ath, Bo'ness	1956–57 Dunfermline Ath, Ayr U
1928–29 Third Lanark, Raith R	1957–58 East Fife, Queen's Park
1929–30 St Johnstone, Dundee U	1958–59 Queen of the S, Falkirk
1930–31 Hibernian, East Fife	1959–60 Arbroath, Stirling A
1931–32 Dundee U, Leith Ath	1960–61 Ayr U, Clyde
1932–33 Morton, East Stirling	1961–62 St Johnstone, Stirling A
1933–34 Third Lanark, Cowdenbeath	1962–63 Clyde, Raith R
1934–35 St Mirren, Falkirk	1963–64 Queen of the S, East Stirling
1935–36 Airdrieonians, Ayr U	1964–65 Airdrieonians, Third Lanark
1936–37 Dunfermline Ath, Albion R	1965–66 Morton, Hamilton A
1937–38 Dundee, Morton	1966–67 St Mirren, Ayr U
1938–39 Queen's Park, Raith R	1967–68 Motherwell, Stirling A
1946–47 Kilmarnock, Hamilton A	1968–69 Falkirk, Arbroath
1947–48 Airdrieonians, Queen's Park	1969–70 Raith R, Partick Th
1948–49 Morton, Albion R	1970–71 St Mirren, Cowdenbeath
1949–50 Queen of the S, Stirling A	1971–72 Clyde, Dunfermline Ath
	1972–73 Kilmarnock, Airdrieonians
	1973–74 East Fife, Falkirk

*Season 1921–22 – only 1 club promoted, 3 clubs relegated.
**15 pts deducted for failing to field a team.*

Scottish League championship wins: Rangers 52, Celtic 41, Aberdeen 4, Hearts 4, Hibernian 4, Dumbarton 2, Dundee 1, Dundee U 1, Kilmarnock 1, Motherwell 1, Third Lanark 1.

The Scottish Football League was reconstructed into three divisions at the end of the 1974–75 season, so the usual relegation statistics do not apply. Further reorganization took place at the end of the 1985–86 season. From 1986–87, the Premier and First Division had 12 teams each. The Second Division remained at 14. From 1988–89, the Premier Division reverted to 10 teams, and the First Division to 14 teams but in 1991–92 the Premier and First Division reverted to 12. At the end of the 1997–98 season, the top nine clubs in Premier Division broke away from the Scottish League to form a new competition, the Scottish Premier League, with the club promoted from Division One. At the end of the 1999–2000 season two teams were added to the Scottish League. There was no relegation from the Premier League but two promoted from the First Division and three from each of the Second and Third Divisions. One team was relegated from the First Division and one from the Second Division, leaving 12 teams in each division. In season 2002–03, Falkirk were not promoted to the Premier League due to the failure of their ground to meet League standards. Inverness CT were promoted after a previous refusal in 2003–04 because of ground sharing. At the end of 2005–06 the Scottish League introduced play-offs for the team finishing second from the bottom of Division 1 against the winners of the second, third and fourth finishing teams in Division 2 and with a similar procedure for Division 2 and Division 3.

PAST SCOTTISH LEAGUE CUP FINALS

Season	Winner	Score	Runner-up	Score
1946–47	Rangers	4	Aberdeen	0
1947–48	East Fife	0 4	Falkirk	0* 1
1948–49	Rangers	2	Raith Rovers	0
1949–50	East Fife	3	Dunfermline	0
1950–51	Motherwell	3	Hibernian	0
1951–52	Dundee	3	Rangers	2
1952–53	Dundee	2	Kilmarnock	0
1953–54	East Fife	3	Partick Th	2
1954–55	Hearts	4	Motherwell	2
1955–56	Aberdeen	2	St Mirren	1
1956–57	Celtic	0 3	Partick Th	0 0
1957–58	Celtic	7	Rangers	1
1958–59	Hearts	5	Partick Th	1
1959–60	Hearts	2	Third Lanark	1
1960–61	Rangers	2	Kilmarnock	0
1961–62	Rangers	1 3	Hearts	1 1
1962–63	Hearts	1	Kilmarnock	0
1963–64	Rangers	5	Morton	0
1964–65	Rangers	2	Celtic	1
1965–66	Celtic	2	Rangers	1
1966–67	Celtic	1	Rangers	0
1967–68	Celtic	5	Dundee	3
1968–69	Celtic	6	Hibernian	2
1969–70	Celtic	1	St Johnstone	0
1970–71	Rangers	1	Celtic	0
1971–72	Partick Th	4	Celtic	1
1972–73	Hibernian	2	Celtic	1
1973–74	Dundee	1	Celtic	0
1974–75	Celtic	6	Hibernian	3
1975–76	Rangers	1	Celtic	0
1976–77	Aberdeen	2	Celtic	1
1977–78	Rangers	2	Celtic	1*
1978–79	Rangers	2	Aberdeen	1
1979–80	Aberdeen	0 0	Dundee U	0* 3
1980–81	Dundee	0	Dundee U	3
1981–82	Rangers	2	Dundee U	1
1982–83	Celtic	2	Rangers	1
1983–84	Rangers	3	Celtic	2
1984–85	Rangers	1	Dundee U	0
1985–86	Aberdeen	3	Hibernian	0
1986–87	Rangers	2	Celtic	1
1987–88	Rangers†	3	Aberdeen	3*
1988–89	Aberdeen	2	Rangers	3*
1989–90	Aberdeen	2	Rangers	1
1990–91	Rangers	2	Celtic	1
1991–92	Hibernian	2	Dunfermline Ath	0
1992–93	Rangers	2	Aberdeen	1*
1993–94	Rangers	2	Hibernian	1
1994–95	Raith R†	2	Celtic	2*

1995–96	Aberdeen	2	Dundee	0
1996–97	Rangers	4	Hearts	3
1997–98	Celtic	3	Dundee U	0
1998–99	Rangers	2	St Johnstone	1
1999–2000	Celtic	2	Aberdeen	0
2000–01	Celtic	3	Kilmarnock	0
2001–02	Rangers	4	Ayr U	0
2002–03	Rangers	2	Celtic	1
2003–04	Livingston	2	Hibernian	0
2004–05	Rangers	5	Motherwell	1
2005–06	Celtic	3	Dunfermline Ath	0
2006–07	Hibernian	5	Kilmarnock	1
2007–08	Rangers†	2	Dundee U	2*
2008–09	Celtic	2	Rangers	0*

†*Won on penalties *After extra time*

PAST LEAGUE CHALLENGE FINALS

1990–91	Dundee	3	Ayr U	2
1991–92	Hamilton A	1	Ayr U	0
1992–93	Hamilton A	3	Morton	2
1993–94	St Mirren	9	Falkirk	3
1994–95	Airdrieonians	3	Dundee	2
1995–96	Stenhousemuir	0	Dundee U	0
	(aet; Stenhousemuir won 5-4 on penalties.)			
1996–97	Stranraer	1	St Johnstone	0
1997–98	Falkirk	1	Qeeen of the South	0
1998–99	no competition			
1999–2000	Alloa Ath	4	Inverness CT	4
	(aet; Alloa Ath won 5-4 on penalties.)			
2000–01	Airdrieonians	2	Livingston	2
	(aet; Airdrieonians won 3-2 on penalties.)			
2001–02	Airdrieonians	2	Alloa Ath	1
2002–03	Queen of the S	2	Brechin C	0
2003–04	Inverness CT	2	Airdrie U	0
2004–05	Falkirk	2	Ross Co	1
2005–06	St Mirren	2	Hamilton A	1
2006–07	Ross Co	1	Clyde	1
	(aet; Ross Co won 5-4 on penalties.)			
2007–08	St Johnstone	3	Dunfermline Ath	2
2008–09	Airdrie	2	Ross Co	2
	(aet; Airdrie U won 3-2 on penalties.)			

CIS SCOTTISH LEAGUE CUP 2008–2009

After extra time.

FIRST ROUND

Albion R	(0) 0	Raith R	(0) 0
(aet; Raith R won 4-3 on penalties.)			
Alloa Ath	(0) 2	Elgin C	(0) 0
Clyde	(1) 4	Queen's Park	(0) 1
Dumbarton	(0) 1	Annan Ath	(0) 1
(aet; Dumbarton won 5-4 on penalties.)			
Montrose	(0) 0	Cowdenbeath	(1) 2
Partick Th	(1) 4	Forfar Ath	(1) 3*
Peterhead	(0) 0	Dunfermline Ath	(0) 2
Ross Co	(1) 2	Airdrie U	(1) 3*
Stenhousemuir	(1) 1	St Johnstone	(1) 5
Stranraer	(1) 3	Morton	(5) 6
Arbroath	(0) 3	Stirling Alb	(1) 2
Ayr U	(2) 2	Berwick R	(1) 1
East Fife	(0) 0	Brechin C	(1) 3
East Stirling	(0) 1	Livingston	(0) 2*

SECOND ROUND

Cowdenbeath	(0) 1	Dundee U	(2) 5
Dundee	(0) 1	Partick Th	(0) 2
Dunfermline Ath	(1) 1	Alloa Ath	(0) 0
Hamilton A	(1) 3	Clyde	(1) 1
Hibernian	(0) 3	Morton	(1) 4*
Livingston	(0) 2	St Johnstone	(0) 1*
Raith R	(0) 1	Falkirk	(2) 3
St Mirren	(3) 7	Dumbarton	(0) 0
Arbroath	(1) 2	Inverness CT	(1) 2
(aet; Inverness CT won 4-2 on penalties.)			
Ayr U	(0) 0	Aberdeen	(1) 1
Brechin C	(0) 0	Kilmarnock	(0) 2
Hearts	(0) 0	Airdrie U	(0) 0
(aet; Airdrie U won 4-3 on penalties.)			

THIRD ROUND

Celtic	(1) 4	Livingston	(0) 0
Dundee U	(2) 2	Airdrie U	(0) 0
Dunfermline Ath	(0) 2	St Mirren	(0) 0
Falkirk	(1) 2	Queen of the S	(0) 1
Morton	(1) 1	Inverness CT	(0) 2*
Kilmarnock	(4) 4	Aberdeen	(2) 2
Motherwell	(0) 1	Hamilton A	(0) 2*
Partick TH	(1) 1	Rangers	(1) 2

QUARTER-FINALS

Dundee U	(1) 1	Dunfermline Ath	(0) 0
Falkirk	(1) 1	Inverness CT	(0) 0
Rangers	(1) 2	Hamilton A	(0) 0
Kilmarnock	(0) 1	Celtic	(2) 3

SEMI-FINALS

Rangers	(2) 3	Falkirk	(0) 0
Celtic	(0) 0	Dundee U	(0) 0
(aet; Celtic won 11-10 on penalties.)			

FINAL

Rangers	(0) 0	Celtic	(0) 2*

ALBA LEAGUE CHALLENGE CUP 2008–2009

FIRST ROUND NORTH-EAST

Alloa Ath	(0) 2	Dundee	(0) 1
Arbroath	(1) 1	Forfar Ath	(0) 2
Brechin C	(0) 0	East Fife	(0) 1
Dunfermline Ath	(1) 3	Stirling Alb	(0) 0
Elgin C	(0) 0	Cowdenbeath	(1) 2
Peterhead	(2) 6	Montrose	(0) 0
Ross Co	(0) 2	St Johnstone	(0) 1

FIRST ROUND SOUTH-WEST

Airdrie U	(0) 3	Dumbarton	(2) 2
Berwick R	(0) 1	Queen of the S	(2) 5
Clyde	(0) 2	Annan Ath	(0) 0
Livingston	(1) 4	Stranraer	(0) 0
Partick Th	(2) 2	Queen's Park	(1) 1
Stenhousemuir	(0) 0	Albion R	(0) 1
East Stirling	(0) 2	Ayr U	(1) 1

SECOND ROUND

Alloa Ath	(0) 0	Clyde	(0) 2
Cowdenbeath	(1) 3	Albion R	(1) 2
Livingston	(0) 1	Forfar Ath	(0) 0
Partick Th	(0) 4	Peterhead	(1) 2
Raith R	(0) 1	Ross Co	(0) 2
East Fife	(0) 0	Airdrie U	(1) 2
East Stirling	(0) 0	Morton	(2) 3
Dunfermline Ath	(0) 0	Queen of the S	(1) 2

QUARTER-FINALS

Clyde	(0) 0	Ross Co	(1) 1
Cowdenbeath	(0) 1	Airdrie U	(0) 2
Livingston	(0) 0	Partick Th	(0) 2
Queen of the S	(0) 0	Morton	(0) 2

SEMI-FINALS

Partick Th	(0) 0	Airdrie U	(1) 1
Ross Co	(2) 4	Morton	(0) 1

FINAL

Airdrie U	(0) 2	Ross Co	(0) 2

(aet; Airdrie U won 3-2 on penalties.)

HOMECOMING SCOTTISH CUP 2008–2009

FIRST ROUND

Banks o'Dee	10	Fort William	0
Clachnacuddin	4	Burntisland Shipyard	0
Dalbeattie Star	5	Lossiemouth	1
Edinburgh City	2	Nairn County	0
Edinburgh Univ	1	Civil Service Strollers	2
Fraserburgh	6	Hawick Royal Albert	3
Glasgow Univ	0	Vale of Leithen	1
Golspie	0	Threave Rovers	3
Huntly	1	Girvan	0
Inverurie Loco Works	5	Deveronvale	2
Lochee United	3	Bathgate Thistle	1
Newton Stewart	1, 1	Brora Rangers	1, 2
Pollok	1, 0	Spartans	1, 1
Preston Ath	3	Gala Fairydean	1
Rothes	1	Buckie Thistle	3
Selkirk	1, 2	Coldstream	1, 2
(Selkirk won 3-2 on penalties.)			
St Cuthbert's	0	Wick Academy	3
Wigtown & B	2, 0	Forres Mechanics	2, 2

SECOND ROUND

East Stirling	4	Preston Ath	2
Berwick R	1	Albion R	2
Brora Rangers	1	Forfar Ath	2
Clachnacuddin	1	Crichton	0
Cove Rangers	1	Whitehill Welfare	0
Cowdenbeath	1	Elgin City	2
Dalbeattie Star	6	Selkirk	0
Edinburgh City	0, 4	Wick Academy	0, 1
Forres Mechanics	1, 1	Keith	1, 1
(Forres Mechanics won on penalties.)			
Fraserburgh	0	Dumbarton	1
Inverurie Loco Works	5	Banks o'Dee	1
Lochee United	3	Buckie Thistle	0
Montrose	2	Huntly	0
Stenhousemuir	5	Threave Rovers	0
Annan Athletic	1	Spartans	2
Civil Service Strollers	0	Vale of Leithen	1

THIRD ROUND

Airdrie U	(3) 3	Cove R	(0) 0
Albion R	(0) 1	Queen's Park	(1) 2
Clachnacuddin	(0) 0	Stenhousemuir	(2) 5
Clyde	(1) 2	Montrose	(0) 0
East Fife	(0) 2	Arbroath	(0) 0
East Stirling	(1) 2	Livingston	(1) 1
Peterhead	(0) 2	Morton	(1) 1
Raith R	(0) 0	Alloa A	(0) 0
Ross Co	(1) 2	Dumbarton	(0) 2
Stirling Alb	(0) 2	Partick Th	(2) 3
Elgin C	(0) 2	Spartans	(0) 1
(Tie replayed; Elgin City fielded ineligible player.)			
Elgin C	(0) 1	Spartans	(1) 2

215

Forres Mechanics	(1) 2	Dalbeattie Star	(1) 2
Edinburgh C	(0) 0	Brechin C	(3) 3
Inverurie Loco Works	(2) 4	Vale of Leithen	(0) 0
Forfar Ath	(0) 2	Stranraer	(0) 0
Lochee U	(0) 1	Ayr U	(0) 1

THIRD ROUND REPLAYS

Alloa Ath	(0) 2	Raith R	(0) 1
Dalbeattie Star	(1) 2	Forres Mechanics	(0) 4
(aet.)			
Dumbarton	(0) 1	Ross Co	(2) 2
Ayr U	(1) 3	Lochee U	(0) 1

FOURTH ROUND

Airdrie U	(2) 2	Spartans	(0) 1
Alloa Ath	(1) 1	Aberdeen	(1) 2
Ayr U	(1) 2	Kilmarnock	(1) 2
Celtic	(2) 2	Dundee	(1) 1
Dunfermline Ath	(1) 2	Clyde	(0) 0
Falkirk	(1) 4	Queen of the S	(1) 2
Inverness CT	(1) 3	Partick Th	(0) 0
Peterhead	(1) 2	Queen's Park	(2) 2
Ross Co	(0) 0	Hamilton A	(1) 1
Stenhousemuir	(0) 0	East Fife	(0) 1
East Stirling	(0) 0	Dundee U	(3) 4
Hibernian	(0) 0	Hearts	(1) 2
Brechin C	(0) 1	St Mirren	(1) 3
Forfar Ath	(5) 6	Forres Mechanics	(1) 1
St Johnstone	(0) 0	Rangers	(1) 2
Inverurie Loco Works	(0) 0	Motherwell	(1) 3

FOURTH ROUND REPLAYS

| Queen's Park | (0) 1 | Peterhead | (0) 0 |
| Kilmarnock | (0) 3 | Ayr U | (1) 1 |

FIFTH ROUND

Celtic	(2) 2	Queen's Park	(0) 1
Hamilton A	(0) 2	Dundee U	(1) 1
Hearts	(0) 0	Falkirk	(0) 1
Inverness CT	(1) 2	Kilmarnock	(0) 0
Motherwell	(0) 1	St Mirren	(1) 1
Aberdeen	(3) 5	East Fife	(0) 0
Airdrie U	(1) 1	Dunfermline Ath	(1) 2
Forfar Ath	(0) 0	Rangers	(1) 4

FIFTH ROUND REPLAY

| St Mirren | (0) 1 | Motherwell | (0) 0 |

SIXTH ROUND

Dunfermline Ath	(0) 1	Aberdeen	(0) 0
Inverness CT	(0) 0	Falkirk	(1) 1
St Mirren	(0) 1	Celtic	(0) 0
Rangers	(3) 5	Hamilton A	(1) 1

SIXTH ROUND REPLAY

| Aberdeen | (0) 0 | Dunfermline Ath | (0) 0 |
| *(aet; Dunfermline Ath won 4-2 on penalties.)* | | | |

SEMI-FINALS

| Rangers | (1) 3 | St Mirren | (0) 0 |
| Falkirk | (0) 2 | Dunfermline Ath | (0) 0 |

PAST SCOTTISH CUP FINALS

Year	Team 1	Score	Team 2	Score
1874	Queen's Park	2	Clydesdale	0
1875	Queen's Park	3	Renton	0
1876	Queen's Park	1 2	Third Lanark	1 0
1877	Vale of Leven	0 1 3	Rangers	0 1 2
1878	Vale of Leven	1	Third Lanark	0
1879	Vale of Leven	1	Rangers	1

Vale of Leven awarded cup, Rangers did not appear for replay

Year	Team 1	Score	Team 2	Score
1880	Queen's Park	3	Thornlibank	0
1881	Queen's Park	2 3	Dumbarton	1 1

Replayed because of protest

Year	Team 1	Score	Team 2	Score
1882	Queen's Park	2 4	Dumbarton	2 1
1883	Dumbarton	2 2	Vale of Leven	2 1

| 1884 | *Queen's Park awarded cup when Vale of Leven did not appear for the final* |

Year	Team 1	Score	Team 2	Score
1885	Renton	0 3	Vale of Leven	0 1
1886	Queen's Park	3	Renton	1
1887	Hibernian	2	Dumbarton	1
1888	Renton	6	Cambuslang	1
1889	Third Lanark	3 2	Celtic	0 1

Replayed because of protest

Year	Team 1	Score	Team 2	Score
1890	Queen's Park	1 2	Vale of Leven	1 1
1891	Hearts	1	Dumbarton	0
1892	Celtic	1 5	Queen's Park	0 1

Replayed because of protest

Year	Team 1	Score	Team 2	Score
1893	Queen's Park	2	Celtic	1
1894	Rangers	3	Celtic	1
1895	St Bernards	3	Renton	1
1896	Hearts	3	Hibernian	1
1897	Rangers	5	Dumbarton	1
1898	Rangers	2	Kilmarnock	0
1899	Celtic	2	Rangers	0
1900	Celtic	4	Queen's Park	3
1901	Hearts	4	Celtic	3
1902	Hibernian	1	Celtic	0
1903	Rangers	1 0 2	Hearts	1 0 0
1904	Celtic	3	Rangers	2
1905	Third Lanark	0 3	Rangers	0 1
1906	Hearts	1	Third Lanark	0
1907	Celtic	3	Hearts	0
1908	Celtic	5	St Mirren	1
1909	*After two drawn games between Celtic and Rangers, 2.2, 1.1, there was a riot and the cup was withheld*			
1910	Dundee	2 0 2	Clyde	2 0 1
1911	Celtic	0 2	Hamilton Acad	0 0
1912	Celtic	2	Clyde	0
1913	Falkirk	2	Raith R	0
1914	Celtic	0 4	Hibernian	0 1
1920	Kilmarnock	3	Albion R	2
1921	Partick Th	1	Rangers	0
1922	Morton	1	Rangers	0
1923	Celtic	1	Hibernian	0
1924	Airdrieonians	2	Hibernian	0
1925	Celtic	2	Dundee	1
1926	St Mirren	2	Celtic	0
1927	Celtic	3	East Fife	1

1928	Rangers	4	Celtic	0
1929	Kilmarnock	2	Rangers	0
1930	Rangers	0 2	Partick Th	0 1
1931	Celtic	2 4	Motherwell	2 2
1932	Rangers	1 3	Kilmarnock	1 0
1933	Celtic	1	Motherwell	0
1934	Rangers	5	St Mirren	0
1935	Rangers	2	Hamilton A	1
1936	Rangers	1	Third Lanark	0
1937	Celtic	2	Aberdeen	1
1938	East Fife	1 4	Kilmarnock	1 2
1939	Clyde	4	Motherwell	0
1947	Aberdeen	2	Hibernian	1
1948	Rangers	1 1	Morton	1 0
1949	Rangers	4	Clyde	1
1950	Rangers	3	East Fife	0
1951	Celtic	1	Motherwell	0
1952	Motherwell	4	Dundee	0
1953	Rangers	1 1	Aberdeen	1 0
1954	Celtic	2	Aberdeen	1
1955	Clyde	1 1	Celtic	1 0
1956	Hearts	3	Celtic	1
1957	Falkirk	1 2	Kilmarnock	1 1
1958	Clyde	1	Hibernian	0
1959	St Mirren	3	Aberdeen	1
1960	Rangers	2	Kilmarnock	0
1961	Dunfermline Ath	0 2	Celtic	0 0
1962	Rangers	2	St Mirren	0
1963	Rangers	1 3	Celtic	1 0
1964	Rangers	3	Dundee	1
1965	Celtic	3	Dunfermline Ath	2
1966	Rangers	0 1	Celtic	0 0
1967	Celtic	2	Aberdeen	0
1968	Dunfermline Ath	3	Hearts	1
1969	Celtic	4	Rangers	0
1970	Aberdeen	3	Celtic	1
1971	Celtic	1 2	Rangers	1 1
1972	Celtic	6	Hibernian	1
1973	Rangers	3	Celtic	2
1974	Celtic	3	Dundee U	0
1975	Celtic	3	Airdrieonians	1
1976	Rangers	3	Hearts	1
1977	Celtic	1	Rangers	0
1978	Rangers	2	Aberdeen	1
1979	Rangers	0 0 3	Hibernian	0 0 2
1980	Celtic	1	Rangers	0
1981	Rangers	0 4	Dundee U	0 1
1982	Aberdeen	4	Rangers	1 (aet)
1983	Aberdeen	1	Rangers	0 (aet)
1984	Aberdeen	2	Celtic	1 (aet)
1985	Celtic	2	Dundee U	1
1986	Aberdeen	3	Hearts	0
1987	St Mirren	1	Dundee U	0 (aet)
1988	Celtic	2	Dundee U	1
1989	Celtic	1	Rangers	0
1990	Aberdeen	0	Celtic	0

(aet; Aberdeen won 9-8 on penalties)

218

1991	Motherwell (aet.)	4	Dundee U	3
1992	Rangers	2	Airdrieonians	1
1993	Rangers	2	Aberdeen	1
1994	Dundee U	1	Rangers	0
1995	Celtic	1	Airdrieonians	0
1996	Rangers	5	Hearts	1
1997	Kilmarnock	1	Falkirk	0
1998	Hearts	2	Rangers	1
1999	Rangers	1	Celtic	0
2000	Rangers	4	Aberdeen	0
2001	Celtic	3	Hibernian	0
2002	Rangers	3	Celtic	2
2003	Rangers	1	Dundee	0
2004	Celtic	3	Dunfermline Ath	1
2005	Celtic	1	Dundee U	0
2006	Hearts (aet; Hearts won 4-2 on penalties)	1	Gretna	1
2007	Celtic	1	Dunfermline Ath	0
2008	Rangers	3	Queen of the S	2
2009	Rangers	1	Fakirk	0

SCOTS-ADS HIGHLAND LEAGUE 2008–2009

	P	W	D	L	F	A	GD	Pts
Cove Rangers	28	22	4	2	96	26	70	70
Deveronvale	28	18	7	3	78	31	47	61
Inverurie Loco Works	28	18	3	7	75	33	42	57
Keith	28	18	2	8	62	35	27	56
Wick Academy	28	16	3	9	54	46	8	51
Buckie Thistle	28	15	4	9	61	38	23	49
Fraserburgh	28	13	8	7	62	47	15	47
Huntly	28	14	4	10	50	43	7	46
Forres Mechanics	28	12	7	9	64	42	22	43
Nairn County	28	12	5	11	44	45	−1	41
Clachnacuddin	28	8	7	13	53	58	−5	31
Lossiemouth	28	7	4	17	31	55	−24	25
Rothes	28	2	4	22	24	80	−56	10
Brora Rangers	28	2	3	23	21	91	−70	9
Fort William	28	0	1	27	16	121	−105	1

IMAGE PRINTERS EAST OF SCOTLAND LEAGUE PREMIER DIVISION 2008–2009

	P	W	D	L	F	A	GD	Pts
Spartans	22	16	4	2	73	26	47	52
Dalbeattie Star	22	14	4	4	61	26	35	46
Lothian Thistle	22	11	3	8	46	26	20	36
Edinburgh University	22	9	7	6	37	18	19	34
Whitehill Welfare	22	8	8	6	38	28	10	32
Preston Athletic	22	9	5	8	36	31	5	32
Heriot–Watt University	22	9	3	10	33	31	2	30
Edinburgh City	22	8	5	9	45	34	11	29
Coldstream	22	8	4	10	29	30	−1	28
Selkirk	22	8	3	11	19	55	−36	27
Easthouses Lily MW	22	7	2	13	40	40	0	23
Peebles	22	1	0	21	12	124	−112	3

WELSH LEAGUE 2008–2009

PRINCIPALITY BUILDING SOCIETY WELSH PREMIER LEAGUE

			Home				Away					Total						
		P	W	D	L	F	A	W	D	L	F	A	W	D	L	F	A	GD	Pts
1	Rhyl	34	14	1	2	54	16	15	2	0	41	13	29	3	2	95	29	66	90
2	Llanelli	34	14	2	1	51	18	12	3	2	47	20	26	5	3	98	38	60	83
3	The New Saints	34	12	4	1	44	10	8	7	2	35	17	20	11	3	79	27	52	71
4	Carmarthen Town	34	10	3	4	27	17	9	2	6	25	30	19	5	10	52	47	5	62
5	Port Talbot Town	34	8	4	5	29	23	8	4	5	28	25	16	8	10	57	48	9	56
6	Bangor City	34	7	5	5	25	16	9	2	6	33	24	16	7	11	58	40	18	55
7	Haverfordwest Co	34	9	4	4	31	17	7	3	7	22	22	16	7	11	53	39	14	55
8	Aberystwyth Town	34	6	6	5	28	25	6	4	7	23	25	12	10	12	51	50	1	46
9	Connah's Quay N	34	7	2	8	31	29	5	3	9	18	36	12	5	17	49	65	−16	41
10	Newtown	34	7	4	6	29	24	3	6	8	17	30	10	10	14	46	54	−8	40
11	Welshpool Town	34	6	5	6	26	27	5	2	10	22	43	11	7	16	48	70	−22	40
12	Airbus UK	34	6	3	8	26	31	6	0	11	21	26	12	3	19	47	57	−10	39
13	NEWI Cefn Druids	34	5	2	10	29	35	4	5	8	28	39	9	7	18	57	74	−17	34
14	Neath Athletic	34	8	3	6	25	23	2	1	14	18	42	10	4	20	43	65	−22	34
15	Prestatyn Town	34	7	4	6	29	28	1	5	11	19	42	8	9	17	48	70	−22	33
16	Porthmadog	34	6	2	9	34	45	4	0	13	23	46	10	2	22	57	91	−34	32
17	Caersws	34	4	2	11	16	31	2	5	10	12	30	6	7	21	28	61	−33	25
18	Caernarfon Town*	34	3	3	11	14	35	2	5	10	18	38	5	8	21	32	73	−41	20

* 3 points deducted.

NORTHERN IRELAND LEAGUE 2008–2009

CARNEGIE IRISH PREMIER LEAGUE

			Home				Away					Total						
		P	W	D	L	F	A	W	D	L	F	A	W	D	L	F	A	GD	Pts
1	Glentoran	38	12	6	2	37	21	12	3	3	26	15	24	9	5	63	36	27	81
2	Linfield	38	11	4	3	28	12	13	4	3	41	16	24	8	6	69	28	41	80
3	Crusaders	38	9	6	4	31	24	7	8	4	32	21	16	14	8	63	45	18	62
4	Lisburn Distillery	38	8	4	6	30	21	7	7	6	23	20	15	11	12	53	41	12	56
5	Coleraine	38	9	4	7	28	28	6	2	10	18	23	15	6	17	46	51	−5	51
6	Cliftonville	38	6	9	4	24	21	6	5	8	28	27	12	14	12	52	48	4	50
7	Institute	38	8	5	6	26	21	4	5	10	20	34	12	10	16	46	55	−9	46
8	Newry City	38	6	6	8	21	28	5	5	8	26	29	11	11	16	47	57	−10	44
9	Glenavon	38	6	4	8	22	26	5	4	11	27	37	11	8	19	49	63	−14	41
10	Ballymena United	38	6	1	12	18	34	5	7	7	21	23	11	8	19	39	57	−18	41
11	Dungannon Swifts	38	4	5	10	21	35	4	7	8	28	35	8	12	18	49	70	−21	36
12	Bangor	38	5	6	8	25	36	4	3	12	17	31	9	9	20	42	67	−25	36

EUROPEAN REVIEW 2008–2009

Manchester United were unable to repeat their Champions League success and Chelsea just failed to make the final again, but it was not all negative for English clubs in Europe. Sadly in the final against Barcelona, United lacked their usual focus, certainly after the opening ten minutes when they might have actually taken the lead against Barcelona.

Sadly this was the only period in the entire match they looked comfortable. Ronaldo was active in these early stages and from a free-kick – not one of his best but good enough for Victor Valdes to spill the ball in front of him – the reaction was not accurate enough and Barcelona put under pressure hit the rebound away.

Enter Samuel Eto'o with his first touch setting himself up with a stab inside Van der Sar's near post and off the goalkeeper's hand. One down and Barcelona started to control the affair. It was not until the 70th minute that they were able to add to the scoreline but Xavi's perfect diagonal was majestically headed home by the mercurial Lionel Messi.

Of course the British and Irish contingent began their challenges in July long before even the FA Cup kicks off. The Irish had a mixed start, Drogheda going on, Linfield going out. Llanelli won its home leg against Ventspils but were well beaten away. However the shock of the second qualifying round was the departure of Rangers against Kaunas, joined by Drogheda.

Arsenal comfortably against Twente, Liverpool struggling with Standard Liege made it to the group stage. Meanwhile Manchester United had lost the Super Cup to Zenit. Chelsea finished second to Roma in Group A, unbeaten Liverpool and Manchester United topped Groups D and E respectively. In the latter section Celtic managed just one win – when already eliminated. Arsenal were runners-up in Group G. Knock-out time and all Italian opposition for the three English survivors. Chelsea edged out Juventus, United prevented Internazionale from scoring against them but Arsenal needed a shoot-out to take care of Roma.

A late leveller by Porto at Old Trafford was of concern to United in the quarter-final, but Arsenal drew at Villarreal. However Chelsea stunned Liverpool 3-1 at Anfield and Barcelona took four goals off Bayern Munich to emphasise their claim. In a classic second leg at the Bridge, Liverpool gave everything in a 4-4 draw, Arsenal eased through and Ronaldo scored early against Porto. Barcelona drew and were paired with Chelsea in the semi-final, but were held at home. United led Arsenal 1-0 then won 3-1 at the Emirates. Chelsea might have put Barcelona out leading against ten men, tactics failing them in injury time.

Shakhtar Donetsk beat Werder Bremen 2-1 after extra time in the UEFA Cup final. Intertoto winners Aston Villa lasted into the third round, Everton found Standard even more difficult than had Liverpool, but Manchester City who had a poor home record in the Premier League saved themselves from the first qualifying stage with better results on travel before eventually losing to Hamburg in the quarter-finals. Shakhtar accounted for Tottenham Hotspur in the third round and Portsmouth on their European debut went out at the group stage.

Cliftonville heavily beaten by FC Copenhagen, Bangor even more so by Midtjylland, Cork by Haka and Glentoran narrowly losing were the first qualifying casualties. But St Patrick's Athletic overcame Olimps Baku. Queen of the South flying the Scottish League flag gave a plucky performance against Nordsjaelland and St Pat's put out Elfsborg.

The first round proper had Motherwell on view but Nancy proved too tough and Hertha Berlin defeated St Pat's. This left Villa, Pompey, City and Spurs at the group stage. Manchester City topped their group, Spurs finished runners-up in their section, Villa third in another.

Thus only Manchester City survived to the last sixteen and after a fright by Aalborg were eliminated by Hamburg. The semi-final draw put the two Germans and two Ukranians together, Werder Bremen losing at home but going through on the away goals rule and Dynamo Kiev finding themselves losing to an 88th minute winner.

UEFA CHAMPIONS LEAGUE 2008–2009

■ *Denotes player sent off.* * Winner after extra time.*

FIRST QUALIFYING ROUND, FIRST LEG

Anorthosis	(0) 1	Pyunik		(0) 0
BATE Borisov	(0) 2	Valur		(0) 0
Dinamo Tirana	(0) 0	Modrica		(0) 2
F91 Dudelange	(0) 0	Domzale		(0) 1
Inter Baku	(0) 0	Rabotnicki		(0) 0
Llanelli	(1) 1	Ventspils		(0) 0
Murata	(0) 0	IFK Gothenberg		(3) 5
Santa Coloma	(0) 1	Kaunas		(3) 4
Tampere United	(1) 2	Buducnost		(0) 1
Valletta	(0) 0	Artmedia		(0) 2
Aktobe	(0) 1	Serif		(0) 0
Dinamo Tbilisi	(3) 3	Runavik		(0) 0
Drogheda United	(0) 2	Levadia		(1) 1
Linfield	(0) 0	Dinamo Zagreb		(1) 2

Tuesday, 15 July 2008

Llanelli (1) 1 *(Jones S 12)*

Ventspils (0) 0   942

Llanelli: Roberts; Corbisiero, Jones S, Jones M (Holland 66), Thomas, Mumford, Jones C (Pritchard 55), Legg, Evans (Williams 71), Bowen, Griffiths.
Ventspils: Vanins; Savcenkovs, Cilinsek, Dubenskiy, Zangaryeev, Kacanovs, Menteshashvili (Butriks 65), Zizilevs (Rugins 86), Tigirlas, Rimkus, Kolesnicenko (Kosmacovs 72).

Wednesday, 16 July 2008

Drogheda United (0) 2 *(Cahill 50, Kudozovic 68)*

Levadia (1) 1 *(Kink 23)*   2,135

Drogheda United: Connor; Kendrick, Gartland, Maher, Robinson, Hughes, Baker, Byrne, Keegan (Zayed 51), Cahill, Kudozovic.
Levadia: Kaalma; Kalimullin, Sisov, Lemsalu, Nahk, Malov, Petrenka (Marmor 82), Puri (Leitan 67), Teniste, Kink, Andrejev (Zelinski 90).

Linfield (0) 0

Dinamo Zagreb (1) 2 *(Mandzukic 19, Morales 90)*   2,900

Linfield: Mannus; Douglas, Murphy, Bailie, Lindsay (Burns 73), Gault, Hagan, McAreavey (Thompson 76), O'Kane, Mulgrew, Downey.
Dinamo Zagreb: Butina; Vrdoljak, Drpic, Etto, Chago (Badelj 57), Mikic (Sammir 46), Biscan, Morales, Balaban (Tadic 78), Mandzukic.

FIRST QUALIFYING ROUND, SECOND LEG

Kaunas	(2) 3	Santa Coloma	(1) 1
Rabotnicki	(0) 1	Inter Baku	(0) 1
Runavik	(1) 1	Dinamo Tbilisi	(0) 0
Serif	(0) 4	Aktobe	(0) 0
Ventspils	(2) 4	Llanelli	(0) 0
Artmedia	(1) 1	Valletta	(0) 0
Buducnost	(0) 1	Tampere United	(1) 1
Dinamo Zagreb	(1) 1	Linfield	(0) 1
Domzale	(0) 2	F91 Dudelange	(0) 0

IFK Gothenburg	(1) 4	Murata	(0) 0
Levadia	(0) 0	Drogheda U	(0) 1
Modrica	(0) 2	Dinamo Tirana	(0) 1
Pyunik	(0) 0	Anorthosis	(1) 2
Valur	(0) 0	BATE Borisov	(1) 1

Tuesday, 22 July 2008

Ventspils (2) 4 *(Kosmacovs 28, Rimkus 30, 75, Butriks 69)*

Llanelli (0) 0   2,000

Ventspils: Pavlovs; Soleicuks (Bespalovs 84), Savcenkovs, Dubenskiy, Kosmacovs, Zangaryeev, Kacanovs, Menteshashvili, Tigirlas, Rimkus (Tedov 77), Butriks (Rugins 82).
Llanelli: Roberts; Corbisiero, Jones S, Jones M, Thomas, Mumford (Pritchard 62), Holloway (Williams 55), Legg, Evans, Bowen (Jones C 79), Griffiths.

Wednesday, 23 July 2008

Dinamo Zagreb (1) 1 *(Mandzukic 3)*

Linfield (0) 1 *(Gault 53)*   2,835

Dinamo Zagreb: Butina; Vrdoljak, Drpic, Etto, Chago (Males 59), Mikic, Badelj, Biscan, Balaban, Mandzukic (Tadic 46), Suarez (Tomic 83).
Linfield: Mannus; Douglas, Murphy, Bailie, Lindsay (Ferguson 59), Gault, Hagan, McAreavey (Kearney 82), O'Kane, Mulgrew, Downey (Miskimmin 86).

Levadia (0) 0

Drogheda U (0) 1 *(Gartland 47)*   1,500

Levadia: Kaalma; Kalimullin, Sisov (Malov 70), Lemsalu, Leitan (Zelinski 60), Nahk, Petrenka■, Puri (Marmor 82), Teniste, Kink, Andrejev.
Drogheda U: Ewings; Kendrick, Gartland, Maher, Hughes, Baker, Byrne, Keegan, Cahill, Kudozovic (Ristila 90), Zayed (O'Brien 88).

SECOND QUALIFYING ROUND, FIRST LEG

Inter Baku	(0) 1	Partizan Belgrade	(1) 1
Brann	(0) 1	Ventspils	(0) 0
Drogheda United	(0) 1	Dynamo Kiev	(1) 2
Tampere United	(1) 1	Artmedia	(2) 3
Aalborg	(3) 5	Modrica	(0) 0
Anderlecht	(0) 1	BATE Borisov	(0) 2
Anorthosis	(1) 3	Rapid Vienna	(0) 0
Beitar Jerusalem	(0) 2	Wisla	(1) 1
Domzale	(0) 0	Dinamo Zagreb	(3) 3
Fenerbahce	(1) 2	MTK	(0) 0
IFK Gothenburg	(1) 1	Basle	(1) 1
Panathinaikos	(2) 3	Dinamo Tbilisi	(0) 0
Rangers	(0) 0	Kaunas	(0) 0
Serif	(0) 0	Sparta Prague	(0) 1

Tuesday, 29 July 2008

Drogheda United (0) 1 *(Hughes 47)*

Dynamo Kiev (1) 2 *(Mikhalik 23, Aliev 86)*   4,545

Drogheda United: Ewings; Kendrick, Gartland, Maher, Hughes, Baker (O'Brien 90), Byrne, Keegan (Shelley 70), Cahill, Kudozovic (Barrett 60), Zayed.
Dynamo Kiev: Shovskiy; Betao, Diakhate, Nesmachniy, Ghioane (Shatskikh 79), Vukojevic, Aliev, Mikhalik, Ninkovic, Bangoura (Kravets 59), Milevsky (El-Kaddouri 89).

Wednesday, 30 July 2008

Rangers (0) 0

Kaunas (0) 0   38,283

Rangers: McGregor; Broadfoot, Papac, Dailly (Novo 46), Weir, Whittaker, Thomson, Adam, Darcheville (Boyd 66), Miller (Velicka 74), McCulloch.
Kaunas: Kello; Radzius, Mrowiec, Mendy, Kancelskis, Zelmikas, Fridrikas, Pilibaitis (Cinikas 83), Luksa, Grigalevicius (Rimkevicius 68), Gaucho (Manchkhava 62).

SECOND QUALIFYING ROUND, SECOND LEG

Ventspils	(2) 2	Brann	(0) 1
Kaunas	(1) 2	Rangers	(1) 1
Dinamo Tbilisi	(0) 0	Panathinaikos	(0) 0
Artmedia	(3) 4	Tampere United	(0) 2
BATE Borisov	(1) 2	Anderlecht	(1) 2
Basle	(1) 4	IFK Gothenburg	(1) 2
Dinamo Zagreb	(1) 3	Domzale	(1) 2
Dynamo Kiev	(1) 2	Drogheda United	(1) 2
MTK	(0) 0	Fenerbahce	(1) 5
Modrica	(0) 1	Aalborg	(1) 2
Partizan Belgrade	(0) 2	Inter Baku	(0) 0
Rapid Vienna	(1) 3	Anorthosis	(1) 1
Sparta Prague	(1) 2	Serif	(0) 0
Wisla	(3) 5	Beitar Jerusalem	(0) 0

Tuesday, 5 August 2008

Kaunas (1) 2 *(Radzius 43, Pilibaitis 87)*

Rangers (1) 1 *(Thomson 33)*   5,250

Kaunas: Kello; Radzius, Mrowiec, Mendy, Manchkhava, Zelmikas, Baguzis (Grigalevicius 67), Pilibaitis, Luksa (Mamic 77), Rafael (Zubavicius 89), Cinikas.
Rangers: McGregor; Broadfoot, Papac, Dailly, Weir, Thomson, Whittaker, McCulloch, Novo (Boyd 88), Miller (Lafferty 89), Adam (Velicka 66).

Wednesday, 6 August 2008

Dynamo Kiev (1) 2 *(Aliev 13, Milevski 72 (pen))*

Drogheda United (1) 2 *(Robinson 42, Gartland 88)*   11,400

Dynamo Kiev: Lutsenko; Betao, Diakhate, Ghioane, Vukojevic, Aliev, Mikhalik, El-Kaddouri, Ninkovic (Morozyuk 83), Bangoura (Milevski 46), Kravets (Shatskikh 79).
Drogheda United: Ewings; Kendrick, Gartland, Shelley, Robinson, Hughes, Baker (Kudozovic 77), Byrne, Keegan, Cahill, Zayed (Thiam 77).

THIRD QUALIFYING ROUND, FIRST LEG

Fiorentina	(1) 2	Slavia Prague	(0) 0
Spartak Moscow	(1) 1	Dynamo Kiev	(2) 4
Aalborg	(0) 2	Kaunas	(0) 0
Anorthosis	(2) 3	Olympiakos	(0) 0
Barcelona	(2) 4	Wisla	(0) 0
Brann	(0) 0	Marseille	(1) 1
Galatasaray	(1) 2	Steaua	(2) 2
Guimaraes	(0) 0	Basle	(0) 0
Juventus	(3) 4	Artmedia	(0) 0
Levski	(0) 0	BATE Borisov	(0) 1
Partizan Belgrade	(2) 2	Fenerbahce	(1) 2

Schalke	(1) 1	Atletico Madrid	(0) 0
Shakhtar Donetsk	(2) 2	Dinamo Zagreb	(0) 0
Sparta Prague	(1) 1	Panathinaikos	(1) 2
Standard Liege	(0) 0	Liverpool	(0) 0
Twente	(0) 0	Arsenal	(0) 2

Wednesday, 13 August 2008

Standard Liege (0) 0

Liverpool (0) 0   26,000

Standard Liege: Aragon; Bonfim, Mikulic (Nicaise 90), Camozzato, Sarr, Dalmat, Defour, Fellaini, Witsel, Mbokani, De Camargo.
Liverpool: Reina; Arbeloa, Dossena, Xabi Alonso, Carragher, Agger, Kuyt (El Zhar 83), Plessis, Torres, Keane (Gerrard 67), Benayoun.

Twente (0) 0

Arsenal (0) 2 *(Gallas 63, Adebayor 82)*   26,000

Twente: Boschker; Wielaert, Braafheid, Douglas, Brama, Wilkshire, Tiote, Janssen (Heubach 90), Denneboom, Elia (Huysegems 86), Arnautovic (Gerritsen 90).
Arsenal: Almunia; Sagna, Clichy, Denilson, Djourou, Gallas, Eboue, Ramsey, Adebayor, Van Persie (Bendtner 88), Walcott (Randall 84).

THIRD QUALIFYING ROUND, SECOND LEG

Wisla	(0) 1	Barcelona	(0) 0
Artmedia	(1) 1	Juventus	(1) 1
Panathinaikos	(0) 1	Sparta Prague	(0) 0
BATE Borisov	(1) 1	Levski	(1) 1
Arsenal	(1) 4	Twente	(0) 0
Atletico Madrid	(1) 4	Schalke	(0) 0
Basle	(1) 2	Guimaraes	(1) 1
Dinamo Zagreb	(0) 1	Shakhtar Donetsk	(1) 3
Dynamo Kiev	(2) 4	Spartak Moscow	(0) 1
Fenerbahce	(1) 2	Partizan Belgrade	(0) 1
Kaunas	(0) 0	Aalborg	(0) 2
Liverpool*	(0) 1	Standard Liege	(0) 0
Marseille	(0) 2	Brann	(0) 1
Olympiakos	(0) 1	Anorthosis	(0) 0
Slavia Prague	(0) 0	Fiorentina	(0) 0
Steaua	(0) 1	Galatasaray	(0) 0

Wednesday, 27 August 2008

Arsenal (1) 4 *(Nasri 27, Gallas 52, Walcott 66, Bendtner 89)*

Twente (0) 0   59,583

Arsenal: Almunia; Sagna, Clichy, Denilson, Djourou, Gallas, Nasri (Eboue 46), Fabregas (Song Billong 68), Bendtner, Van Persie (Adebayor 65), Walcott.
Twente: Michailov; Wielaert, Braafheid (Rajkovic 87), Heubach (Wellenberg 46), Douglas, Brama, Tiote, Janssen, Denneboom, Huysegems, Elia.

Liverpool (0) 1 *(Kuyt 118)*

Standard Liege (0) 0   43,889

Liverpool: Reina; Arbeloa, Fabio Aurelio, Xabi Alonso, Carragher, Skrtel, Kuyt, Gerrard, Torres (Plessis 120), Keane (El Zhar 83), Benayoun (Babel 61).
Standard Liege: Aragon; Bonfim, Onyewu, Camozzato, Sarr, Dalmat (Jovanovic 86), Defour (Nicaise 118), Fellaini, Witsel, Mbokani, De Camargo (Toama 101).
(aet.)

GROUP A

Chelsea	(2) 4	Bordeaux	(0) 0
Roma	(1) 1	Cluj	(1) 2
Bordeaux	(1) 1	Roma	(0) 3
Cluj	(1) 1	Chelsea	(0) 0
Bordeaux	(0) 0	Cluj	(0) 0
Chelsea	(0) 1	Roma	(0) 0
Cluj	(0) 1	Bordeaux	(2) 2
Roma	(1) 1	Chelsea	(0) 1
Bordeaux	(1) 3	Chelsea	(0) 1
Cluj	(0) 1	Roma	(2) 3
Chelsea	(1) 1	Cluj	(0) 1
Roma	(1) 2	Bordeaux	(0) 0
	(0) 2		(0) 0

Tuesday, 16 September 2008

Chelsea (2) 4 *(Lampard 14, Cole J 30, Malouda 82, Anelka 90)*

Bordeaux (0) 0
39,635

Chelsea: Cech; Bosingwa, Cole A, Mikel, Terry, Ricardo Carvalho, Deco (Ballack 61), Lampard, Anelka, Cole J (Belletti 74), Malouda (Kalou 84).
Bordeaux: Rame; Jurietti, Placente, Diawara, Planus, Diarra, Fernando (Ducasse 74), Gourcuff, Wendel, Gouffran (Cavenaghi 66), Chamakh (Obertan 66).

Wednesday, 1 October 2008

Cluj (0) 0

Chelsea (0) 0
20,320

Cluj: Stancioiu; Hugo Alcantara, Muresan, Cadu, Galiassi, Trica (Didi 89), Culio, Dani, Pereira, Dubarbier, Kone Y.
Chelsea: Cech; Bosingwa, Bridge, Mikel, Terry, Alex, Ballack, Lampard, Drogba (Belletti 58), Kalou (Anelka 46), Malouda (Di Santo 74).

Wednesday, 22 October 2008

Chelsea (0) 1 *(Terry 77)*

Roma (0) 0
41,002

Chelsea: Cech; Bosingwa, Bridge, Mikel, Terry, Ricardo Carvalho, Deco, Lampard, Anelka (Paulo Ferreira 90), Kalou (Di Santo 77), Malouda (Belletti 46).
Roma: Doni; Panucci, Cicinho, Mexes, Aquilani (Perrotta 61), Taddei (Menez 81), De Rossi, Riise (Tonetto 82), Brighi, Vucinic, Totti.

Tuesday, 4 November 2008

Roma (1) 3 *(Panucci 34, Vucinic 48, 58)*

Chelsea (0) 1 *(Terry 75)*
35,038

Roma: Doni; Panucci, Cicinho, Juan, Mexes, Pizarro, De Rossi, Perrotta (Taddei 72), Brighi, Vucinic (Riise 88), Totti (Julio Baptista 62).
Chelsea: Cech; Bosingwa (Kalou 63), Bridge, Mikel, Terry, Alex, Deco■, Lampard, Anelka, Cole J (Drogba 46), Malouda (Belletti 46).

Wednesday, 26 November 2008

Bordeaux (0) 1 *(Diarra 82)*

Chelsea (0) 1 *(Anelka 59)*
32,486

Bordeaux: Valverde; Jurietti, Diawara, Chalme, Planus, Diarra, Fernando, Gourcuff, Wendel (Obertan 75), Gouffran (Cavenaghi 67), Chamakh.
Chelsea: Cech; Bosingwa, Cole A, Mikel, Terry, Ivanovic, Ballack, Lampard■, Anelka (Drogba 63), Cole J (Paulo Ferreira 85), Malouda.

226

Tuesday, 9 December 2008

Chelsea (1) 2 *(Kalou 39, Drogba 71)*

Cluj (0) 1 *(Kone Y 54)*   41,060

Chelsea: Cech; Bosingwa, Cole A, Mikel (Bridge 76), Terry, Alex, Deco, Kalou (Drogba 64), Anelka, Cole J (Belletti 74), Ballack.
Cluj: Nuno Claro; Panin, Muresan, Hugo Alcantara, Cadu, Trica (Peralta 72), Culio, Dani, Pereira, Dubarbier (Kone E 61), Kone Y.

Group A Final Table	P	W	D	L	F	A	Pts
Roma	6	4	0	2	12	6	12
Chelsea	6	3	2	1	9	5	11
Bordeaux	6	2	1	3	5	11	7
Cluj	6	1	1	4	5	9	4

GROUP B

Panathinaikos	(0) 0	Internazionale	(1) 2
Werder Bremen	(0) 0	Anorthosis	(0) 0
Anorthosis	(2) 3	Panathinaikos	(1) 1
Internazionale	(1) 1	Werder Bremen	(0) 1
Internazionale	(1) 1	Anorthosis	(0) 0
Panathinaikos	(1) 2	Werder Bremen	(1) 2
Anorthosis	(2) 3	Internazionale	(2) 3
Werder Bremen	(0) 0	Panathinaikos	(0) 3
Anorthosis	(0) 2	Werder Bremen	(0) 2
Internazionale	(0) 0	Panathinaikos	(0) 1
Panathinaikos	(0) 1	Anorthosis	(0) 0
Werder Bremen	(0) 2	Internazionale	(0) 1

Group B Final Table	P	W	D	L	F	A	Pts
Panathinaikos	6	3	1	2	8	7	10
Internazionale	6	2	2	2	8	7	8
Werder Bremen	6	1	4	1	7	9	7
Anorthosis	6	1	3	2	8	8	6

GROUP C

Barcelona	(1) 3	Sporting Lisbon	(0) 1
Basle	(0) 1	Shakhtar Donetsk	(2) 2
Shakhtar Donetsk	(1) 1	Barcelona	(0) 2
Sporting Lisbon	(0) 2	Basle	(0) 0
Basle	(0) 0	Barcelona	(3) 5
Shakhtar Donetsk	(0) 0	Sporting Lisbon	(0) 1
Barcelona	(0) 1	Basle	(0) 1
Sporting Lisbon	(0) 1	Shakhtar Donetsk	(0) 0
Shakhtar Donetsk	(1) 5	Basle	(0) 0
Sporting Lisbon	(0) 2	Barcelona	(2) 5
Barcelona	(0) 2	Shakhtar Donetsk	(1) 3
Basle	(0) 0	Sporting Lisbon	(1) 1

Group C Final Table	P	W	D	L	F	A	Pts
Barcelona	6	4	1	1	18	8	13
Sporting Lisbon	6	4	0	2	8	8	12
Shakhtar Donetsk	6	3	0	3	11	7	9
Basle	6	0	1	5	2	16	1

GROUP D

Marseille	(1) 1	Liverpool	(2) 2
PSV Eindhoven	(0) 0	Atletico Madrid	(2) 3
Atletico Madrid	(2) 2	Marseille	(1) 1
Liverpool	(2) 3	PSV Eindhoven	(1) 1
Atletico Madrid	(0) 1	Liverpool	(1) 1
PSV Eindhoven	(0) 2	Marseille	(0) 0
Liverpool	(0) 1	Atletico Madrid	(1) 1
Marseille	(1) 3	PSV Eindhoven	(0) 0
Atletico Madrid	(2) 2	PSV Eindhoven	(0) 1
(Behind closed doors.)			
Liverpool	(0) 1	Marseille	(0) 0
Marseille	(0) 0	Atletico Madrid	(0) 0
PSV Eindhoven	(1) 1	Liverpool	(1) 3

Tuesday, 16 September 2008

Marseille (1) 1 *(Cana 23)*

Liverpool (2) 2 *(Gerrard 26, 32 (pen))* 44,841

Marseille: Mandanda; Taiwo, Hilton, Zubar, Bonnart, Cheyrou, Cana, Ben Arfa (Ziani 57), M'Bami (Valbuena 41), Niang, Kone (Samassa 75).
Liverpool: Reina; Arbeloa, Dossena, Mascherano, Carragher, Skrtel, Lucas, Gerrard (Benayoun 69), Torres (Riera 65), Kuyt (Keane 86), Babel.

Wednesday, 1 October 2008

Liverpool (2) 3 *(Kuyt 4, Keane 34, Gerrard 76)*

PSV Eindhoven (0) 1 *(Koevermans 78)* 41,097

Liverpool: Reina; Arbeloa, Fabio Aurelio, Xabi Alonso, Carragher, Skrtel, Kuyt, Gerrard (Babel 81), Torres, Keane (Lucas 75), Riera (Benayoun 68).
PSV Eindhoven: Isaksson; Kromkamp, Salcido, Brechet (Pieters 46), Marcellis, Simons, Mendez (Dzsudzsak 76), Culina, Bakkal, Wuytens (Koevermans 60), Amrabat.

Wednesday, 22 October 2008

Atletico Madrid (0) 1 *(Simeo 83)*

Liverpool (1) 1 *(Keane 15)* 48,769

Atletico Madrid: Leo Franco; Seitaridis, Antonio Lopez, Perea, Dominguez, Luis Garcia (Aguero 46), Maniche, Simao, Camacho (Raul Garcia 73), Forlan, Sinama Pongolle (Miguel 75).
Liverpool: Reina; Arbeloa, Dossena, Xabi Alonso (Lucas 75), Carragher, Agger, Benayoun, Gerrard (Babel 61), Keane (Kuyt 53), Mascherano, Riera.

Tuesday, 4 November 2008

Liverpool (0) 1 *(Gerrard 90 (pen))*

Atletico Madrid (1) 1 *(Maxi Rodriguez 37)* 42,010

Liverpool: Reina; Arbeloa, Fabio Aurelio, Xabi Alonso, Carragher, Agger, Mascherano (Lucas 77), Gerrard, Kuyt, Keane (N'Gog 71), Riera (Babel 61).
Atletico Madrid: Leo Franco; Antonio Lopez, Pernia, Heitinga, Perea, Raul Garcia, Maxi Rodriguez, Paulo Assuncao, Maniche, Simao (Luis Garcia 89), Forlan (Aguero 70).

Wednesday, 26 November 2008

Liverpool (0) 1 *(Gerrard 22)*

Marseille (0) 0   42,010

Liverpool: Reina; Arbeloa, Fabio Aurelio (Dossena 46), Xabi Alonso, Carragher, Agger, Mascherano, Gerrard, Torres, Kuyt (Lucas 85), Riera (Benayoun 64).
Marseille: Mandanda; Taiwo, Hilton, Zubar, Bonnart (Samassa 89), Ziani, Cheyrou, Cana, Ben Arfa, Niang, Kone (Valbuena 78).

Tuesday, 9 December 2008

PSV Eindhoven (1) 1 *(Lazovic 35)*

Liverpool (1) 3 *(Babel 45, Riera 68, N'Gog 77)*   33,500

PSV Eindhoven: Isaksson; Salcido, Brechet, Marcellis, Simons, Mendez (Manco 80), Culina, Dzsudzsak, Bakkal (Nijland 83), Lazovic, Amrabat (Koevermans 72).
Liverpool: Cavalieri; Arbeloa (Darby 69), Dossena, Mascherano, Carragher (Kelly 82), Agger, Riera (Spearing 76), Lucas, N'Gog, Keane, Babel.

Group D Final Table	P	W	D	L	F	A	Pts
Liverpool	6	4	2	0	11	5	14
Atletico Madrid	6	3	3	0	9	4	12
Marseille	6	1	1	4	5	7	4
PSV Eindhoven	6	1	0	5	5	14	3

GROUP E

Celtic	(0) 0	Aalborg	(0) 0
Manchester United	(0) 0	Villarreal	(0) 0
Aalborg	(0) 0	Manchester United	(1) 3
Villarreal	(0) 1	Celtic	(0) 0
Manchester United	(1) 3	Celtic	(0) 0
Villarreal	(2) 6	Aalborg	(2) 3
Aalborg	(0) 2	Villarreal	(1) 2
Celtic	(1) 1	Manchester United	(0) 1
Aalborg	(0) 2	Celtic	(0) 1
Villarreal	(0) 0	Manchester United	(0) 0
Celtic	(2) 2	Villarreal	(0) 0
Manchester United	(1) 2	Aalborg	(2) 2

Wednesday, 17 September 2008

Celtic (0) 0

Aalborg (0) 0   58,754

Celtic: Boruc; Hinkel, Naylor, Brown S, Caldwell, McManus, Nakamura, Maloney (Vennegoor 72), McDonald (McGeady 63), Samaras, Robson.
Aalborg: Zaza; Jakobsen, Pedersen, Beauchamp■, Olfers, Johansson, Augustinussen, Risgard, Enevoldsen, Saganowski, Curth (Nielsen 86).

Manchester United (0) 0

Villarreal (0) 0   74,944

Manchester United: Van der Sar; Neville, Evra, Hargreaves (Anderson 62), Evans, Ferdinand, Park (Ronaldo 62), Fletcher, Rooney, Tevez (Giggs 81), Nani.
Villarreal: Diego Lopez; Gonzalo, Edmilson, Godin, Capdevila, Angel, Pires (Ibagaza 67), Cani (Cazorla 46), Matias Fernandez, Eguren, Guille Franco (Llorente 77).

Tuesday, 30 September 2008

Aalborg (0) 0

Manchester United (1) 3 *(Rooney 22, Berbatov 55, 79)*   10,346

Aalborg: Zaza; Pedersen, Beauchamp (Caca 38), Olfers, Bogelund, Johansson, Augustinussen, Risgard, Enevoldsen, Saganowski, Curth.
Manchester United: Van der Sar; Rafael (Brown 66), Evra, O'Shea, Ferdinand, Vidic, Ronaldo, Scholes (Giggs 16), Berbatov, Rooney (Tevez 59), Nani.

Villarreal (0) 1 *(Senna 67)*

Celtic (0) 0   21,515

Villarreal: Diego Lopez; Gonzalo, Godin, Capdevila, Angel, Pires (Bruno 83), Cazorla (Cani 90), Senna, Eguren, Llorente, Rossi (Ibagaza 77).
Celtic: Boruc; Wilson, Naylor, Hartley (Vennegoor 82), Caldwell, McManus, Nakamura (Robson 74), Brown S, Samaras, Maloney (McDonald 72), McGeady.

Tuesday, 21 October 2008

Manchester United (1) 3 *(Berbatov 30, 51, Rooney 77)*

Celtic (0) 0   74,655

Manchester United: Van der Sar; Neville (Brown 60), O'Shea, Anderson, Evans, Vidic, Ronaldo (Park 82), Fletcher, Berbatov (Tevez 60), Rooney, Nani.
Celtic: Boruc; Wilson, Naylor, Loovens, Caldwell, McManus, Nakamura (Hartley 61), Brown S, McDonald (Sheridan 77), Robson (Maloney 61), McGeady.

Wednesday, 5 November 2008

Celtic (1) 1 *(McDonald 13)*

Manchester United (0) 1 *(Giggs 83)*   58,903

Celtic: Boruc; Hinkel, Wilson, Hartley, Caldwell, McManus, Robson, Brown S, McDonald (Hutchinson 81), Sheridan (Donati 64), Maloney (O'Dea 75).
Manchester United: Foster; Rafael (Evra 65), O'Shea, Carrick, Ferdinand, Vidic, Nani (Berbatov 46), Fletcher, Ronaldo, Tevez (Rooney 69), Giggs.

Tuesday, 25 November 2008

Aalborg (0) 2 *(Caca 73, Caldwell 87 (og))*

Celtic (0) 1 *(Robson 53)*   10,096

Aalborg: Zaza; Jakobsen, Pedersen (Kristensen 81), Olfers, Bogelund, Johansson, Augustinussen, Caca, Risgard, Enevoldsen (Due 70), Curth (Saganowski 70).
Celtic: Boruc; Hinkel, Wilson (Maloney 90), Loovens, Caldwell, McManus, Nakamura, Brown S, McDonald, Samaras (Sheridan 69), Robson.

Villarreal (0) 0

Manchester United (0) 0   22,529

Villarreal: Diego Lopez; Gonzalo, Capdevila■, Javi Venta, Fuentes, Eguren, Pires (Matias Fernandez 65), Cazorla, Ibagaza, Senna (Bruno 46), Rossi (Guille Franco 78).
Manchester United: Kuszczak; O'Shea, Evra, Carrick (Tevez 86), Ferdinand, Evans, Ronaldo, Anderson, Rooney, Fletcher (Gibson 78), Nani (Park 84).

Wednesday, 10 December 2008

Celtic (2) 2 *(Maloney 14, McGeady 45)*

Villarreal (0) 0   58,104

Celtic: Boruc; Hinkel, Wilson (O'Dea 81), Hartley, Caldwell, McManus, Nakamura, Brown S, Samaras (McDonald 81), Maloney, McGeady (McGowen 74).
Villarreal: Viera; Gonzalo, Edmilson, Angel, Fuentes, Cani, Ibagaza (Cazorla 60), Matias Fernandez, Senna (Nihat 46), Bruno, Guille Franco■.

Manchester United (1) 2 *(Tevez 3, Rooney 52)*
Aalborg (2) 2 *(Jakobsen 31, Curth 45)*   74,382

Manchester United: Kuszczak; Neville (Rafael 77), O'Shea, Anderson, Ferdinand, Evans, Nani, Gibson (Park 46), Rooney, Tevez, Giggs (Scholes 46).
Aalborg: Zaza; Jakobsen, Pedersen (Sorensen 76), Olfers, Bogelund, Due (Kristensen 66), Augustinussen, Risgard, Enevoldsen, Saganowski, Curth (Caca 75).

Group E Final Table	P	W	D	L	F	A	Pts
Manchester United	6	2	4	0	9	3	10
Villarreal	6	2	3	1	9	7	9
Aalborg	6	1	3	2	9	14	6
Celtic	6	1	2	3	4	7	5

GROUP F

Lyon	(0) 2	Fiorentina	(2) 2
Steaua	(0) 0	Bayern Munich	(1) 1
Bayern Munich	(0) 1	Lyon	(1) 1
Fiorentina	(0) 0	Steaua	(0) 0
Bayern Munich	(2) 3	Fiorentina	(0) 0
Steaua	(3) 3	Lyon	(2) 5
Fiorentina	(1) 1	Bayern Munich	(0) 1
Lyon	(1) 2	Steaua	(0) 0
Bayern Munich	(0) 3	Steaua	(0) 0
Fiorentina	(1) 1	Lyon	(2) 2
Lyon	(0) 2	Bayern Munich	(3) 3
Steaua	(0) 0	Fiorentina	(0) 1

Group F Final Table	P	W	D	L	F	A	Pts
Bayern Munich	6	4	2	0	12	4	14
Lyon	6	3	2	1	14	10	11
Fiorentina	6	1	3	2	5	8	6
Steaua	6	0	1	5	3	12	1

GROUP G

Dynamo Kiev	(0) 1	Arsenal	(0) 1
Porto	(2) 3	Fenerbahce	(1) 1
Arsenal	(2) 4	Porto	(0) 0
Fenerbahce	(0) 0	Dynamo Kiev	(0) 0
Fenerbahce	(1) 2	Arsenal	(3) 5
Porto	(0) 0	Dynamo Kiev	(1) 1
Arsenal	(0) 0	Fenerbahce	(0) 0
Dynamo Kiev	(1) 1	Porto	(0) 2
Arsenal	(0) 1	Dynamo Kiev	(0) 0
Fenerbahce	(0) 1	Porto	(2) 2
Dynamo Kiev	(1) 1	Fenerbahce	(0) 0
Porto	(1) 2	Arsenal	(0) 0

Wednesday, 17 September 2008
Dynamo Kiev (0) 1 *(Bangoura 64 (pen))*
Arsenal (0) 1 *(Gallas 88)*   16,800

Dynamo Kiev: Bogush; Betao, Diakhate, Nesmachni, Vukojevic, Aliev, Eremenko, Mikhalik, Ninkovic, Ayila (Asatiani 90), Bangoura (Kravets 90).
Arsenal: Almunia; Sagna (Eboue 78), Clichy, Denilson, Toure, Gallas, Song Billong (Bendtner 70), Fabregas, Adebayor, Van Persie (Vela 84), Walcott.

231

Tuesday, 30 September 2008

Arsenal (2) 4 *(Van Persie 31, 48, Adebayor 40, 71 (pen))*

Porto (0) 0   59,623

Arsenal: Almunia; Sagna, Clichy, Denilson, Toure, Gallas, Nasri (Eboue 65), Fabregas, Adebayor, Van Persie (Bendtner 65), Walcott (Vela 72).
Porto: Helton; Bruno Alves, Nelson Benitez, Rolando, Sapunaru, Guarin, Rodriguez (Candeias 79), Raul Meireles (Hulk 64), Tomas Costa, Fernando (Gonzalez L 46), Lisandro.

Tuesday, 21 October 2008

Fenerbahce (1) 2 *(Silvestre 19 (og), Guiza 78)*

Arsenal (3) 5 *(Adebayor 10, Walcott 11, Diaby 22, Song Billong 49, Ramsey 90)*
                                                                                               42,619

Fenerbahce: Volkan; Lugano, Roberto Carlos, Edu Dracena, Ugur, Gokhan G (Burak 79), Alex, Selcuk, Maldonado (Ali Bilgin 52), Guiza, Semih.
Arsenal: Almunia; Song Billong, Clichy, Denilson, Eboue, Silvestre, Diaby (Ramsey 73), Fabregas, Adebayor (Vela 86), Walcott (Djourou 84), Nasri.

Wednesday, 5 November 2008

Arsenal (0) 0

Fenerbahce (0) 0   60,003

Arsenal: Fabianski; Toure, Clichy, Denilson, Djourou, Silvestre (Song Billong 82), Ramsey (Diaby 59), Fabregas, Bendtner (Vela 59), Van Persie, Nasri.
Fenerbahce: Volkan; Lugano, Roberto Carlos (Wederson 68), Edu Dracena, Ugur, Gokhan G, Kazim-Richards (Ali Bilgin 59), Selcuk, Maldonado (Josico 67), Guiza, Semih.

Tuesday, 25 November 2008

Arsenal (0) 1 *(Bendtner 85)*

Dynamo Kiev (0) 0   59,374

Arsenal: Almunia; Djourou, Clichy, Denilson, Djourou, Silvestre, Song Billong, Fabregas, Vela (Wilshere 76), Van Persie, Ramsey (Bendtner 68).
Dynamo Kiev: Bogush; Betao, Diakhate, Ghioane, Vukojevic, Aliev■, Eremenko, El-Kaddouri, Asatiani, Bangoura, Milevskiy.

Wednesday, 10 December 2008

Porto (1) 2 *(Bruno Alves 38, Lisandro 53)*

Arsenal (0) 0   37,602

Porto: Helton; Bruno Alves, Pedro Emanuel, Fucile, Rolando, Gonzalez L (Gonzalez M 78), Rodriguez (Tomas Costa 78), Raul Meireles, Fernando, Lisandro, Hulk (Guarin 88).
Arsenal: Almunia; Eboue, Djourou, Denilson, Silvestre, Gallas, Song Billong (Randall 78), Ramsey (Wilshere 59), Vela, Bendtner, Diaby (Gibbs 60).

Group G Final Table	P	W	D	L	F	A	Pts
Porto	6	4	0	2	9	8	12
Arsenal	6	3	2	1	11	5	11
Dynamo Kiev	6	2	2	2	4	4	8
Fenerbahce	6	0	2	4	4	11	2

GROUP H

Juventus	(0) 1	Zenit	(0) 0
Real Madrid	(1) 2	BATE Borisov	(0) 0
BATE Borisov	(2) 2	Juventus	(2) 2
Zenit	(1) 1	Real Madrid	(2) 2
Juventus	(1) 2	Real Madrid	(0) 1
Zenit	(0) 1	BATE Borisov	(0) 1
BATE Borisov	(0) 0	Zenit	(1) 2
Real Madrid	(0) 0	Juventus	(1) 2
BATE Borisov	(0) 0	Real Madrid	(1) 1
Zenit	(0) 0	Juventus	(0) 0
Juventus	(0) 0	BATE Borisov	(0) 0
Real Madrid	(1) 3	Zenit	(0) 0

Group H Final Table	P	W	D	L	F	A	Pts
Juventus	6	3	3	0	7	3	12
Real Madrid	6	4	0	2	9	5	12
Zenit	6	1	2	3	4	7	5
BATE Borisov	6	0	3	3	3	8	3

KNOCK-OUT ROUND, FIRST LEG

Arsenal	(1) 1	Roma	(0) 0

(aet; Arsenal won 7-6 on penalties.)

Atletico Madrid	(2) 2	Porto	(1) 2
Internazionale	(0) 0	Manchester United	(0) 0
Lyon	(1) 1	Barcelona	(0) 1
Chelsea	(1) 1	Juventus	(0) 0
Real Madrid	(0) 0	Liverpool	(0) 1
Sporting Lisbon	(0) 0	Bayern Munich	(1) 5
Villarreal	(0) 1	Panathinaikos	(0) 1

Tuesday, 24 February 2009

Arsenal (1) 1 *(Van Persie 36 (pen))*

Roma (0) 0   60,003

Arsenal: Almunia; Sagna, Clichy, Denilson, Toure, Gallas, Eboue (Ramsey 82), Diaby (Song Billong 62), Bendtner (Vela 67), Van Persie, Nasri.
Roma: Doni; Mexes, Motta, Loria (Diamoutene 70), Riise, Taddei, De Rossi, Julio Baptista (Vucinic 82), Perrotta, Brighi (Pizarro 57), Totti.

Internazionale (0) 0

Manchester United (0) 0   80,018

Internazionale: Julio Cesar; Zanetti, Maicon, Rivas (Cordoba 46), Chivu, Santon, Stankovic, Cambiasso, Ali Muntari (Cruz 77), Ibrahimovic, Adriano (Balotelli 77).
Manchester United: Van der Sar; O'Shea, Evra, Carrick, Ferdinand, Evans, Ronaldo, Fletcher, Berbatov, Giggs, Park (Rooney 83).

Wednesday, 25 February 2009

Chelsea (1) 1 *(Drogba 12)*

Juventus (0) 0   38,079

Chelsea: Cech; Bosingwa, Cole A, Mikel, Terry, Alex, Ballack (Mancienne 81), Lampard, Anelka, Drogba, Kalou (Malouda 72).
Juventus: Buffon; Chiellini, Mellberg, Molinaro, Legrottaglie, Nedved, Camoranesi (Marchionni 52), Sissoko (Trezeguet 86), Tiago (Marchisio 62), Amauri, Del Piero.

Real Madrid (0) 0

Liverpool (0) 1 *(Benayoun 82)* 71,579

Real Madrid: Casillas; Pepe, Sergio Ramos, Cannavaro, Marcelo (Guti 46), Heinze, Gago, Diarra, Raul, Robben, Higuain.
Liverpool: Reina; Arbeloa, Fabio Aurelio, Xabi Alonso, Carragher, Skrtel, Benayoun, Mascherano, Torres (Babel 62), Kuyt (Lucas 90), Riera (Gerrard 88).

KNOCK-OUT ROUND, SECOND LEG

Bayern Munich	(4) 7	Sporting Lisbon	(1) 1
Juventus	(1) 2	Chelsea	(1) 2
Liverpool	(2) 4	Real Madrid	(0) 0
Panathinaikos	(0) 1	Villarreal	(0) 2
Barcelona	(4) 5	Lyon	(1) 2
Manchester United	(1) 2	Internazionale	(0) 0
Porto	(0) 0	Atletico Madrid	(0) 0
Roma	(1) 1	Arsenal	(0) 0

Tuesday, 10 March 2009

Juventus (1) 2 *(Iaquinta 19, Del Piero 74 (pen))*

Chelsea (1) 2 *(Essien 45, Drogba 83)* 27,319

Juventus: Buffon; Chiellini■, Mellberg, Grygera, Molinaro, Nedved (Salihamidzic 13), Marchisio, Tiago, Iaquinta (Giovinco 61), Del Piero, Trezeguet (Amauri 79).
Chelsea: Cech; Bosingwa, Cole A, Mikel, Terry, Alex (Ricardo Carvalho 89), Essien (Belletti 66), Lampard, Anelka, Drogba, Ballack.

Liverpool (2) 4 *(Torres 16, Gerrard 28 (pen), 47, Dossena 88)*

Real Madrid (0) 0 42,550

Liverpool: Reina; Arbeloa, Fabio Aurelio, Xabi Alonso (Lucas 61), Carragher, Skrtel, Mascherano, Gerrard (Spearing 73), Torres (Dossena 84), Kuyt, Babel.
Real Madrid: Casillas; Pepe, Sergio Ramos, Cannavaro (Van der Vaart 64), Heinze, Diarra, Gago (Guti 77), Sneijder, Raul, Robben (Marcelo 46), Higuain.

Wednesday, 11 March 2009

Manchester United (1) 2 *(Vidic 4, Ronaldo 49)*

Internazionale (0) 0 74,769

Manchester United: Van der Sar; O'Shea, Evra, Carrick, Ferdinand, Vidic, Ronaldo, Scholes (Anderson 70), Berbatov, Rooney (Park 84), Giggs.
Internazionale: Julio Cesar; Cordoba, Zanetti, Maicon, Samuel, Santon, Stankovic (Adriano 58), Vieira (Ali Muntari 46), Cambiasso, Ibrahimovic, Balotelli (Figo 70).

Roma (1) 1 *(Juan 9)*

Arsenal (0) 0 62,383

Roma: Doni; Juan (Julio Baptista 28), Motta, Riise, Diamoutene, Pizarro, Taddei (Aquilani 90), Tonetto, Brighi (Montella 120), Vucinic, Totti.
Arsenal: Almunia; Sagna, Clichy, Denilson, Toure, Gallas, Eboue (Walcott 74), Diaby, Bendtner (Eduardo 85), Van Persie, Nasri.
aet; Arsenal won 7-6 on penalties: Eduardo saved; Pizarro scored; Van Persie scored; Vucinic saved; Walcott scored; Julio Baptista scored; Nasri scored; Montella scored; Denilson scored; Totti scored; Toure scored; Aquilani scored; Sagna scored; Riise scored; Diaby scored; Tonetto missed.

QUARTER-FINALS, FIRST LEG

Manchester United	(1) 2	Porto	(1) 2
Villarreal	(1) 1	Arsenal	(0) 1
Barcelona	(4) 4	Bayern Munich	(0) 0
Liverpool	(1) 1	Chelsea	(1) 3

Tuesday, 7 April 2009

Manchester United (1) 2 *(Rooney 15, Tevez 85)*

Porto (1) 2 *(Rodriguez 4, Gonzalez M 89)* 74,517

Manchester United: Van der Sar; O'Shea, Evra, Carrick, Evans (Neville 72), Vidic, Ronaldo, Scholes (Tevez 72), Rooney, Fletcher, Park (Giggs 59).
Porto: Helton; Bruno Alves, Rolando, Sapunaru, Cissokho, Gonzalez L, Rodriguez (Gonzalez M 79), Raul Meireles (Tomas Costa 79) (Madrid 90), Fernando, Lisandro, Hulk.

Villarreal (1) 1 *(Senna 10)*

Arsenal (0) 1 *(Adebayor 65)* 21,577

Villarreal: Diego Lopez; Gonzalo, Godin, Capdevila, Angel, Eguren, Cani (Matias Fernandez 46), Ibagaza (Guille Franco 78), Senna, Llorente (Pires 70), Rossi.
Arsenal: Almunia (Fabianski 27); Sagna, Clichy, Denilson, Toure, Gallas (Djourou 43), Song Billong, Fabregas, Adebayor, Walcott (Eboue 78), Nasri.

Wednesday, 8 April 2009

Liverpool (1) 1 *(Torres 6)*

Chelsea (1) 3 *(Ivanovic 39, 62, Drogba 67)* 42,543

Liverpool: Reina; Arbeloa, Fabio Aurelio (Dossena 75), Xabi Alonso, Carragher, Skrtel, Lucas (Babel 79), Gerrard, Torres, Kuyt, Riera (Benayoun 68).
Chelsea: Cech; Ivanovic, Cole A, Essien, Terry, Alex, Ballack, Lampard, Drogba (Anelka 80), Kalou, Malouda.

QUARTER-FINALS, SECOND LEG

Bayern Munich	(0) 1	Barcelona	(0) 1
Chelsea	(0) 4	Liverpool	(2) 4
Arsenal	(1) 3	Villarreal	(0) 0
Porto	(0) 0	Manchester United	(1) 1

Tuesday, 14 April 2009

Chelsea (0) 4 *(Drogba 51, Alex 57, Lampard 76, 89)*

Liverpool (2) 4 *(Fabio Aurelio 19, Xabi Alonso 28 (pen), Lucas 81, Kuyt 83)* 38,286

Chelsea: Cech; Ivanovic, Cole A, Essien, Alex, Ricardo Carvalho, Ballack, Lampard, Drogba (Di Santo 90), Kalou (Anelka 36), Malouda.
Liverpool: Reina; Arbeloa (Babel 85), Fabio Aurelio, Xabi Alonso, Carragher, Skrtel, Benayoun, Mascherano (Riera 70), Torres (N'Gog 80), Kuyt, Lucas.

Wednesday, 15 April 2009

Arsenal (1) 3 *(Walcott 11, Adebayor 60, Van Persie 69 (pen))*

Villarreal (0) 0 58,233

Arsenal: Fabianski; Eboue, Gibbs, Nasri, Toure, Silvestre, Song Billong, Fabregas, Adebayor (Bendtner 83), Van Persie (Diaby 77), Walcott (Denilson 77).
Villarreal: Diego Lopez; Gonzalo, Godin, Capdevila, Angel, Eguren*, Pires, Cani (Pablo 70), Fernandez (Nihat 64), Bruno (Ibagaza 64), Rossi.

Porto (0) 0

Manchester United (1) 1 *(Ronaldo 6)*   50,000

Porto: Helton; Bruno Alves, Rolando, Sapunaru (Tomas Costa 80), Cissokho, Gonzalez L (Gonzalez M 32), Rodriguez (Farias 64), Raul Meireles, Fernando, Lisandro, Hulk.
Manchester United: Van der Sar; O'Shea, Evra, Carrick, Ferdinand, Vidic, Ronaldo, Anderson (Scholes 78), Berbatov (Nani 68), Rooney, Giggs.

SEMI-FINALS, FIRST LEG

Barcelona	(0) 0	Chelsea		(0) 0
Manchester United	(1) 1	Arsenal		(0) 0

Tuesday, 28 April 2009

Barcelona (0) 0

Chelsea (0) 0   95,231

Barcelona: Victor Valdes; Pique, Marquez (Puyol 52), Dani Alves, Abidal, Xavi, Iniesta, Toure Yaya, Eto'o (Bojan 82), Messi, Henry (Hleb 87).
Chelsea: Cech; Ivanovic, Bosingwa, Mikel, Terry, Alex, Essien, Lampard (Belletti 71), Drogba, Ballack (Anelka 90), Malouda.

Wednesday, 29 April 2009

Manchester United (1) 1 *(O'Shea 17)*

Arsenal (0) 0   74,517

Manchester United: Van der Sar; O'Shea, Evra, Carrick, Ferdinand (Evans 88), Vidic, Ronaldo, Anderson (Berbatov 67), Rooney, Tevez (Giggs 67), Fletcher.
Arsenal: Almunia; Sagna, Gibbs, Diaby, Toure, Silvestre, Song Billong, Fabregas, Adebayor (Eduardo 83), Walcott (Bendtner 71), Nasri.

SEMI-FINALS, SECOND LEG

Arsenal	(0) 1	Manchester United	(2) 3
Chelsea	(1) 1	Barcelona	(0) 1

Tuesday, 5 May 2009

Arsenal (0) 1 *(Van Persie 76 (pen))*

Manchester United (2) 3 *(Park 8, Ronaldo 11, 61)*   59,867

Arsenal: Almunia; Sagna, Gibbs (Eboue 46), Song Billong, Djourou, Toure, Walcott (Bendtner 63), Fabregas, Adebayor, Van Persie (Vela 80), Nasri.
Manchester United: Van der Sar; O'Shea, Evra (Rafael 65), Carrick, Ferdinand, Vidic, Ronaldo, Fletcher■, Rooney (Berbatov 66), Anderson (Giggs 63), Park.

Wednesday, 6 May 2009

Chelsea (1) 1 *(Essien 9)*

Barcelona (0) 1 *(Iniesta 90)*   37,857

Chelsea: Cech; Bosingwa, Cole A, Essien, Terry, Alex, Ballack, Lampard, Anelka, Drogba (Belletti 72), Malouda.
Barcelona: Victor Valdes; Pique, Dani Alves, Abidal■, Xavi, Iniesta (Sylvinho 90), Keita, Toure Yaya, Busquets (Bojan 85), Messi, Eto'o (Gudjohnsen 90).

UEFA CHAMPIONS LEAGUE FINAL 2009

Wednesday, 27 May 2009

Manchester U (0) 0   Barcelona (1) 2 *(Eto'o 10, Messi 70)*

(in Rome, 62,467)

Manchester U: Van der Sar; O'Shea, Evra, Carrick, Ferdinand, Vidic, Park (Berbatov 66), Anderson (Tevez 46), Ronaldo, Rooney, Giggs (Scholes 75).

Barcelona: Victor Valdes; Puyol, Sylvinho, Busquets, Pique, Toure Yaya, Eto'o, Xavi, Henry (Keita 72), Messi, Iniesta (Pedrito 90).

Referee: Busacca (Switzerland).

UEFA CHAMPIONS LEAGUE 2009–2010

PARTICIPATING CLUBS FC Barcelona (ESP); Liverpool FC (ENG); Chelsea FC (ENG); Manchester United FC (ENG); Sevilla FC (ESP); AC Milan (ITA); FC Bayern München (GER); FC Internazionale Milano (ITA); Real Madrid CF (SPA); PFC CSKA Moskva (RUS); FC Porto (POR); AZ Alkmaar (NED); Juventus (ITA); Rangers FC (SCO); Olympique de Marseille (FRA); FC Dynamo Kyiv (UKR); FC Girondins de Bordeaux (FRA); Beşiktaş JK (TUR); VfL Wolfsburg (GER) ; R. Standard de Liège (BEL); FC Rubin Kazan (RUS); AFC Unirea Urziceni (ROU); Arsenal FC (ENG); Olympique Lyonnais (FRA); VfB Stuttgart (GER); ACF Fiorentina (ITA); Club Atlético de Madrid (SPA); FC Shakhtar Donetsk (UKR); Sporting Clube de Portugal (POR); Panathinaikos FC (GRE); Celtic FC (SCO); RSC Anderlecht (BEL); AC Sparta Praha (CZE); FC Dinamo 1948 Bucureşti (tbc) (ROU); FC Twente (NED); FC Dinamo Moskva (RUS); Sivasspor (TUR); Olympiacos CFP (GRE); SK Slavia Praha (CZE); FC Zürich (SUI); FC København (DEN); PFC Levski Sofia (BUL); FK Partizan (SRB); Maccabi Haifa FC (ISR); NK Dinamo Zagreb (CRO); Wisla Kraków (POL); FC BATE Borisov (BLR); FC Salzburg (AUS); Kalmar FF (SWE); APOEL FC (CYP); Stabæk IF (NOR); ŠK Slovan Bratislava (SVK); FK Ventspils (LVA); NK Maribor (SVN); FH Hafnarfjördur (ISL); FC International Turku (FIN); FK Ekranas (LTU); Bohemian FC (IRL); NK Zrinjski (BIH); Debreceni VSC (LTU); FC Sheriff (MDA); FC WIT Georgia (GEO); FK Makedonija GP Skopje (MKD); FK Bakı (AZE); FC Levdia Tallinn (EST); KF Tirana (ALB); FK Aktobe (KAZ); FC Pyunik (ARM); Rhyl FC (WAL); Glentoran FC (NIR); EB/Streymur (FRO); F91 Dudelange (LUX); FK Mogren (MNE); UE Sant Julià (AND); Hibernians FC (MLT); SP Tre Fiori (SMR.

INTERTOTO CUP 2008

FIRST ROUND, FIRST LEG
Mika 2, Tiraspol 2
Lisburn Distillery 2, TPS Turku 3
Etzella 0, Lokomotiv Tbilisi 0
Riga 1, Fylkir 2
Hibernians 0, Gorica 3
Neftchi 2, Nitra 0
Cracovia 1, Soligorsk 2
Rijeka 0, Renova 0
Celik 3, Grbalj 2
Bohemian 5, Rhyl 1
Besa 0, Ethnikos 0
Zhetysu 1, Honved 2
Ekranas 1, Trans 0
HB Torshavn 1, Elfsborg 4

FIRST ROUND, SECOND LEG
Elfsborg 0, HB Torshavn 0
Rhyl 2, Bohemian 4
Trans 0, Ekranas 3
Ethnikos 1, Besa 1
Renova 2, Rijeka 0
Tiraspol 0, Mika 0
Nitra 3, Neftchi 1
Lokomotiv Tbilisi 2, Etzella 2
Grbalj 2, Celik 1
Honved 4, Zhetysu 2
Gorica 0, Hibernians 0
Soligorsk 3, Cracovia 0
TPS Turku 3, Lisburn Distillery 1
Fylkir 0, Riga 2

SECOND ROUND, FIRST LEG
Saturn 7, Etzella 0
Grasshoppers 2, Besa 1
Grbalj 2, Sivasspor 2
Sturm Graz 2, Soligorsk 0
Teplice 1, Honved 3
Tiraspol 0, Tavriya 0
Chernomorets 1, Gorica 1
Beerschot 1, Neftchi 1
Hibernian 0, Elfsborg 2
Ekranas 0, Rosenborg 3
OFK Belgrade 1, Panionios 0
Riga 1, Bohemian 0
TPS Turku 1, Odense 2
Renova 1, Bnei Sachnin 2

SECOND ROUND, SECOND LEG
Elfsborg 2, Hibernian 0
Besa 0, Grasshoppers 3
Neftchi 1, Beerschot 1
Honved 0, Teplice 2
Bnei Sachnin 1, Renova 0

Gorica 0, Chernomorets 2
Bohemian 2, Riga 1
Rosenborg 4, Ekranas 0
Soligorsk 0, Sturm Graz 0
Panionios 3, OFK Belgrade 1
Etzella 1, Saturn 1
Tavriya 3, Tiraspol 1
Sivasspor 1, Grbalj 0
Odense 2, TPS Turku 0

THIRD ROUND, FIRST LEG
Bnei Sachnan 1, La Coruna 2
Panionios 0, Napoli 1
Sivasspor 0, Braga 2
Grasshoppers 3, Chernomorets 0
Saturn 1, Stuttgart 0
Neftchi 2, Vaslui 1
Rennes 1, Tavriya 0
Sturm Graz 0, Honved 0
NAC Breda 1, Rosenborg 0
Odense 2, Aston Villa 2
Elfsborg 1, Riga 0

THIRD ROUND, SECOND LEG
La Coruna 1, Bnei Sachnan 0
Napoli 1, Panionios 0
Braga 3, Sivasspor 0
Chernomorets 0, Grasshoppers 0
Stuttgart 3, Saturn 0
Vaslui 2, Neftchi 0
Tavriya 1, Rennes 0
Rennes won 10-9 on penalties.
Honved 1, Sturm Graz 2
Rosenborg 2, NAC Breda 0
Aston Villa 1, Odense 0
Riga 0, Elfsborg 0

Odense (1) 2 *(Sidwell 25 og, Christensen 90)*

Aston Villa (1) 2 *(Carew 7, Laursen 76)*   11,350

Aston Villa: Taylor; Gardner, Bouma, Reo-Coker, Knight, Laursen, Young, Sidwell (Routledge 82), Agbonlahor, Carew, Petrov.

Aston Villa (0) 1 *(Young 51)*
Odense (0) 0   31,423

Aston Villa: Taylor; Gardner, Bouma (Barry 14), Reo-Coker, Knight, Laursen, Young, Sidwell, Agbonlahor, Carew, Petrov.

UEFA CUP 2008–2009

■ *Denotes player sent off.*
* *Winner after extra time.* †*Winner after extra time and penalties*

FIRST QUALIFYING ROUND, FIRST LEG

Ararat	(0) 0	Bellinzona	(1) 1
Bangor City	(1) 1	Midtjylland	(2) 6
Brondby	(0) 1	B36	(0) 0
Chernomore	(0) 4	Sant Julia	(0) 0
Cliftonville	(0) 0	FC Copenhagen	(1) 4
Cork City	(0) 2	Haka	(1) 2
Dacia	(0) 1	Borac	(0) 1
Djurgaarden	(0) 0	Flora	(0) 0
EB/Streymur	(0) 0	Manchester City	(2) 2
Glentoran	(1) 1	Metalurgs Liepajas	(1) 1
Gyor	(0) 1	Zestafoni	(1) 1
Hafnarfjordur	(1) 3	Grevenmacher	(2) 2
Hajduk Split	(2) 4	Birkirkara	(0) 0
Hapoel Tel Aviv	(3) 3	Juvenes	(0) 0
Hertha Berlin	(5) 8	Otaci	(0) 1
Honka	(2) 3	IA Akranes	(0) 1
Ironi Kiryat	(1) 1	Mogren	(0) 1
Koper	(0) 1	Vllaznia	(2) 2
Legia	(0) 0	Gomel	(0) 0
Lenkoran	(0) 0	Lech	(0) 1
MTZ-Ripo	(0) 2	Zilina	(0) 2
Marsaxlokk	(0) 0	Slaven	(3) 4
Olimps Riga	(0) 0	St Patrick's Ath	(0) 1
Omonia	(1) 2	Milano	(0) 0
Pelister	(0) 0	Apoel	(0) 0
Racing	(0) 0	Kalmar	(1) 3
Salzburg	(4) 7	Banants	(0) 0
Shakter Karaganda	(0) 1	Debrecen	(0) 1
Siroki	(0) 0	Partizani	(0) 0
Spartak Trnava	(0) 2	WIT Georgia	(2) 2
Suduva	(0) 1	The New Saints	(0) 0
Tobol	(0) 1	FK Austria	(0) 0
VMK	(0) 0	Nordsjaelland	(1) 3
Vaduz	(1) 1	Zrinjski	(1) 2
Vetra	(0) 1	Viking	(0) 0
Vojvodina	(0) 1	Olimpik Baku	(0) 0
Zeta	(1) 1	Interblock	(0) 1

Thursday, 17 July 2008

Bangor City (1) 1 *(Davies 24)*

Midtjylland (2) 6 *(Florescu 19, Reid 40, Christensen 53, 58, 63, Thygesen 71)*   703

Bangor City: Smith; Swanick (Hoy 68), Beattie, Johnston, Brewerton, Sergeant, Limbert, Walsh (Fowler 68), Davies, Stott, Noon (Edwards 62).
Midtjylland: Heinze; Afriyie, Califf, Poulsen, Reid (Ipsa 76), Borring, Florescu, Thygesen, Salami, Olsen PF (Olsen D 60), Fagerberg (Christensen 48).

Cliftonville (0) 0

FC Copenhagen (1) 4 *(Norregaard 22, Junior 67, 82, Pospech 77)*   800

Cliftonville: Connolly; Fleming, Scannell R, Holland B, O'Hara, Smyth (Murphy 77), Donaghy, Catney, O'Connor (Patterson 82), Holland M, Scannell C (O'Neill 82).
FC Copenhagen: Christiansen; Pospech, Laursen, Wendt (Jensen N 61), Jorgensen, Norregaard, Kvist (Kristensen 69), Hutchinson, Sionko, Ailton (Junior 61), Nordstrand.

Cork City (0) 2 *(Mooney 64, Murray 67)*

Haka (1) 2 *(Mahlakaarto 17, Lehtinen 52)*   3,791

Cork City: Devine; Horgan, Murray, Sullivan, Danny Murphy, Gamble, Healy, Darren Murphy, Kearney, Behan, Mooney.
Haka: Doybnya; Kangaskorpi, Okkonen, Innanen (Minkenen 84), Kauppila, Manninen (Mattila 79), Mahlakaarto (Viljanen 66), Fowler, Parviainen, Lehtinen, Holopainen.

EB/Streymur (0) 0

Manchester City (2) 2 *(Petrov 9, Hamann 28)*   5,400

EB/Streymur: Torgard; Jacobsen (Brian Olsen 76), Foldgast (Davidsen 85), Clementsen, Djurhuus, Bardur Olsen, Hansen L, Bo, Hansen A, Niclasen, Samuelsen (Eliasen 76).
Manchester City: Hart; Onuoha, Ball, Dunne, Richards, Johnson, Ireland, Hamann (Gelson 73), Jo (Evans 73), Vassell, Petrov.

Glentoran (1) 1 *(Halliday 29)*

Metalurgs Liepajas (1) 1 *(Surnins 15)*   300

Glentoran: Morris; Nixon, Neill (Burrows 85), Leeman, Ward, Hill, McCabe, Fordyce (McGovern 78), Boyce (Fitzgerald 78), Halliday, Hamilton.
Metalurgs Liepajas: Spole; Klava, Zirnis, Antonio, Jemelins, Tamosauskas, Surnins, Solonicins, Miceika, Beniusis (Grebis 64), Karlsons.

Olimps Riga (0) 0

St Patrick's Ath (0) 1 *(Guy 76)*   1,000

Olimps Riga: Ikstens; Petrenko, Kandov, Junior, Kostjuks (Sinelnikovs 59), Zolotarjovs (Jakovlevs 66), Tarasovs, Perepechko (Mendez 78), Dubra, Shtolcers, Fertovs.
St Patrick's Ath: Barry Ryan; Kirby (Fitzpatrick 58), Fahey, Paisley, Quigley, Guy, Dempsey, Harris, Byrne, Lynch, O'Brien (Bobby Ryan 72).

Suduva (0) 1 *(Koziuberda 88)*

The New Saints (0) 0   2,500

Suduva: Vitkauskas; Skinderis, Mikuckis, Slavickas V, Koziuberda, Barevicius (Slavickas G 62), Bozinovski, Luksys (Urbsys 77), Lukjanovis, Leimonas, Radavicius.
The New Saints: Harrison; Baker, Courtney, Ruscoe (Toner 68), Wood, Holmes, Beck, Leah, Wilde (Whitfield 78), Hogan (Darlington 56), Taylor.

FIRST QUALIFYING ROUND, SECOND LEG

Nordsjaelland	(2) 5	VMK	(0) 0
Apoel	(0) 1	Pelister	(0) 0
B36	(0) 0	Brondby	(0) 2
Banants	(0) 0	Salzburg	(0) 3
Bellinzona	(3) 3	Ararat	(0) 1
Birkirkara	(0) 0	Hajduk Split	(2) 3
Borac	(1) 3	Dacia	(1) 1
Debrecen	(1) 1	Shakter Karaganda	(0) 0
FC Copenhagen	(3) 7	Cliftonville	(0) 0
FK Austria	(1) 2	Tobol	(0) 0
Flora	(0) 2	Djurgaarden	(1) 2
Gomel	(1) 1	Legia	(1) 4
Grevenmacher	(1) 1	Hafnarfjordur	(1) 5
Haka	(2) 4	Cork City	(0) 0
IA Akranes	(1) 2	Honka	(0) 1
Interblock	(0) 1	Zeta	(0) 0
Juvenes	(0) 0	Hapoel Tel Aviv	(2) 2

240

Kalmar	(3) 7	Racing	(0) 1
Lech	(1) 4	Lenkoran	(1) 1
Manchester City	(0) 2	EB/Streymur	(0) 0
(at Barnsley.)			
Metalurgs Liepajas	(1) 2	Glentoran	(0) 0
Midtjylland	(2) 4	Bangor City	(0) 0
Milano	(1) 1	Omonia	(0) 2
Mogren	(0) 0	Ironi Kiryat	(1) 3
Olimpik Baku	(0) 1	Vojvodina	(0) 1
Otaci	(0) 0	Hertha Berlin	(0) 0
Partizani	(1) 1	Siroki	(2) 3
Sant Julia	(0) 0	Chernomore	(3) 5
Slaven	(1) 4	Marsaxlokk	(0) 0
St Patrick's Ath	(1) 2	Olimps Riga	(0) 0
The New Saints	(0) 0	Suduva	(0) 1
Viking	(2) 2	Vetra	(0) 0
Vllaznia	(0) 0	Koper	(0) 0
WIT Georgia	(0) 1	Spartak Trnava	(0) 0
Zestafoni	(0) 1	Gyor	(0) 2
Zilina	(0) 1	MTZ-Ripo	(0) 0
Zrinjski	(2) 3	Vaduz	(0) 0

Thursday, 31 July 2008

FC Copenhagen (3) 7 *(Ailton 23, Junior 25, 60, Hutchinson 45, Kvist 46, Nordstrand 55 (pen), Kristensen 57)*

Cliftonville (0) 0   10,695

FC Copenhagen: Coe; Pospech (Jensen D 46), Janka, Wendt (Albrechtsen 71), Jensen N, Kristensen, Kvist, Nordstrand, Hutchinson (Norregaard 46), Ailton, Junior.
Cliftonville: Connolly; Scannell R, Holland B, O'Hara (McAlinden 69), Holland M, Hamill (Patterson 69), Scannell G, McMullan (Boyd 69), Donaghy, Catney, O'Connor.

Haka (2) 4 *(Mahlakaarto 10, Popovitch 15, Manninen 70, Minkenen 78)*

Cork City (0) 0   3,200

Haka: Dovbnya; Kangaskorpi, Viljanen (Minkenen 61), Okkonen, Kauppila, Manninen (Nikkila 85), Mahlakaarto, Fowler, Parviainen, Lehtinen (Mattila 52), Popovitch.
Cork City: Devine; Horgan, Murray, Lordan (Behan■ 46), Sullivan, Danny Murphy, Gamble, Healy, Darren Murphy, Kearney (Ryan 61), Mooney (O'Flynn 81).

Manchester City (0) 2 *(Petrov 48, Vassell 90)*

EB/Streymur (0) 0   7,334

Manchester City: Hart; Corluka, Ball, Dunne, Richards, Johnson, Gelson (Hamann 62), Sturridge (Evans 70), Elano, Vassell, Petrov (Etuhu 69).
EB/Streymur: Torgard; Jacobsen (Thomassen 77), Clementsen, Bo, Djurhuus, Bardur Olsen, Foldgast (Brian Olsen 55), Anghel, Samuelsen, Hansen Á (Balog 61), Niclasen.
(at Barnsley.)

Metalurgs Liepajas (1) 2 *(Karlsons 36, 86)*

Glentoran (0) 0   3,500

Metalurgs Liepajas: Krucs■; Klava, Zirnis, Antonio, Jemelins (Spole 7), Tamosauskas, Surnins, Solonicins (Kamess 89), Miceika, Beniusis (Grebis 61), Karlsons.
Glentoran: Morris; Nixon, Neill (Carson 80), Leeman, Ward, Hill (Burrows■ 73), McCabe■, Fordyce, Boyce (Fitzgerald 61), Halliday, Hamilton.

241

Midtjylland (2) 4 *(Nworuh 3, 34, Sivebaek 56, Babatunde 77)*

Bangor City (0) 0   4,069

Midtjylland: Raska; Kristensen J, Klimpl, Ipsa, Marcic, Olsen PF (Oliseh 46), Flinta, Akilu, Sivebaek (Gnanou 70), Babatunde, Nworuh (Thygesen 70).
Bangor City: Smith; Swanick, Beattie, Johnson, Brewerton, Seargeant, Limbert (Fowler 63), Walsh (Hoy 70), Davies, Noon, Edwards (Stott 57).

St Patrick's Ath (1) 2 *(Harris 41, Quigley 71 (pen))*

Olimps Riga (0) 0   3,000

St Patrick's Ath: Barry Ryan; Byrne, Lynch, Harris, Paisley, Dempsey, Fahey (O'Cearuill 90), O'Brien (Kirby 76), Quigley (Bobby Ryan 81), Fitzpatrick, Guy.
Olimps Riga: Ikstens; Junior, Petrenko, Kazura, Kandov (Sinelnikovs 64), Zolotarjovs, Fertovs, Jakovlev (Sputajs 61), Tarasovs, Perepecko (Turkovs 72), Zils.

The New Saints (0) 0

Suduva (0) 1 *(Lukjanovs 85)*   879

The New Saints: Harrison; Courtney, Baker (Carter 51), Taylor, Holmes, Ruscoe, Wilde, Beck, Wood, Toner (Darlington 65), Hogan.
Suduva: Vitkauskas; Skinderis, Mikuckis, Leimonas, Slavickas V, Bozinovski, Koziuberda, Barevicius (Jasaitis 64), Radavicius (Slavickas G 79), Luksys (Gardzijauskas 86), Lukjanovs.

SECOND QUALIFYING ROUND, FIRST LEG

AEK Athens	(0) 0	Omonia	(1) 1
Apoel	(1) 2	Red Star Belgrade	(1) 2
Aris Salonika	(0) 1	Slaven	(0) 0
Borac	(0) 1	Lokomotiv Sofia	(0) 0
Braga	(0) 1	Zrinjski	(0) 0
Djurgaarden	(1) 2	Rosenborg	(0) 1
Dnepr	(1) 3	Bellinzona	(0) 2
Elfsborg	(2) 2	St Patrick's Ath	(0) 2
FC Copenhagen	(1) 3	Lillestrom	(0) 1
Gent	(0) 2	Kalmar	(0) 1
Hafnarfjordur	(1) 1	Aston Villa	(3) 4
Haka	(0) 0	Brondby	(1) 4
Honka	(0) 0	Viking	(0) 0
Interblock	(0) 0	Hertha Berlin	(1) 2
La Coruna	(0) 0	Hajduk Split	(0) 2
Lech	(2) 6	Grasshoppers	(0) 0
Legia	(0) 1	FC Moscow	(0) 2
Litex	(0) 0	Ironi Kiryat	(0) 0
Maccabi Netanya	(1) 1	Chernomore	(1) 1
Manchester City	(0) 0	Midtjylland	(1) 1
Metalurgs Liepajas	(0) 0	Vaslui	(0) 2
Queen of the South	(1) 1	Nordsjaelland	(2) 2
Siroki	(0) 1	Besiktas	(2) 2
Slovan	(0) 1	Zilina	(1) 2
Stabaek	(1) 2	Rennes	(0) 1
Stuttgart	(2) 2	Gyor	(1) 1
Suduva	(1) 1	Salzburg	(1) 4
Vllaznia	(0) 0	Napoli	(1) 3
Vojvodina	(0) 0	Hapoel Tel Aviv	(0) 0
WIT Georgia		FK Austria	(0) 0
(Match not played; unrest in Georgia. Tie to be decided on second leg.)			
Young Boys	(1) 4	Debrecen	(1) 1
Zurich	(1) 1	Sturm Graz	(0) 1

Thursday, 14 August 2008

Elfsborg (2) 2 *(Ishizaki 24 (pen), Karlsson 29)*

St Patrick's Ath (0) 2 *(Quigley 57 (pen), Dempsey 82)*   3,918

Elfsborg: Wiland; Floren, Karlsson, Mobaeck, Lucic, Augustsson, Svensson A, Bajrami (Nordmark 79), Ishizaki, Nilsson, Berglund (Floren 71).
St Patrick's Ath: Barry Ryan; Lynch (Bobby Ryan 67), O'Cearuill, Harris, Gavin, Paisley, Fahey, Dempsey, Quigley, Murphy, Guy.

Hafnarfjordur (1) 1 *(Gudmundsson M 45)*

Aston Villa (3) 4 *(Barry 4, Young A 7, Agbonlahor 38, Laursen 64)*   2,200

Hafnarfjordur: Sigurdsson; Sverrisson B, Eriksson (Saevarsson 75), Siim, Nielsen, Valgardsson, Vidarsson D (Asgeirsson 63), Gudmundsson M, Gudmundsson T, Vilhjalmsson, Gudnason (Gardarsson 75).
Aston Villa: Friedel; Gardner, Shorey, Reo-Coker, Davies, Laursen, Petrov (Salifou 66), Agbonlahor (Delfouneso 76), Harewood, Barry, Young A (Routledge 71).

Manchester City (0) 0

Midtjylland (1) 1 *(Olsen D 15)*   17,200

Manchester City: Hart; Corluka, Richards, Dunne, Ben Haim, Johnson, Caicedo (Bojinov 64), Gelson, Sturridge, Elano (Etuhu 67), Petrov.
Midtjylland: Heinze; Afriyie, Califf, Poulsen, Reid, Borring, Florescu, Thygesen, Olsen D (Madsen 73), Salami (Flinta 84), Nworuh (Babatunde 55).

Queen of the South (1) 1 *(O'Connor 27)*

Nordsjaelland (2) 2 *(Kibebe 2, Bernier 32)*   4,406

Queen of the South: Halliwell; Reid (Harris 77), McQuilken, Barr, Thomson, MacFarlane (Adams 69), Tosh, Burns, Kean, O'Connor, Arbuckle (Dobbie 46).
Nordsjaelland: Hansen; Kibebe, Kildentoft, Lundberg, Richter, Karlsen, Bernier, Christensen (Nakajima-Farran 65), Petersen (Pode 70), Bernburg (Dahl 80), Fetai.

SECOND QUALIFYING ROUND, SECOND LEG

Lokomotiv Sofia	(1) 1	Borac	(1) 1
Nordsjaelland	(0) 2	Queen of the South	(1) 1
Aston Villa	(1) 1	Hafnarfjordur	(1) 1
Bellinzona	(1) 2	Dnepr	(1) 1
Besiktas	(1) 4	Siroki	(0) 0
Brondby	(2) 2	Haka	(0) 0
Chernomore	(1) 2	Maccabi Netanya	(0) 0
Debrecen	(1) 2	Young Boys	(1) 3
FC Moscow	(1) 2	Legia	(0) 0
FK Austria	(1) 2	WIT Georgia	(0) 0

(One match tie because of uncertain civil situation in Georgia.)

Grasshoppers	(0) 0	Lech	(0) 0
Gyor	(0) 1	Stuttgart	(2) 4
Hajduk Split	(0) 0	La Coruna	(1) 2
Hapoel Tel Aviv	(1) 3	Vojvodina	(0) 0
Hertha Berlin	(1) 1	Interblock	(0) 0
Ironi Kiryat	(1) 1	Litex	(1) 2
Kalmar	(1) 4	Gent	(0) 0
Lillestrom	(1) 2	FC Copenhagen	(2) 4
Midtjylland	(0) 0	Manchester City	(0) 1

(aet; Manchester City won 4-2 on penalties.)

Napoli	(1) 5	Vllaznia	(0) 0
Omonia	(1) 2	AEK Athens	(1) 2
Red Star Belgrade	(0) 3	Apoel*	(0) 3
Rennes	(1) 2	Stabaek	(0) 0
Rosenborg	(1) 5	Djurgaarden	(0) 0

Salzburg	(0) 0	Suduva	(0) 1
Slaven	(1) 2	Aris Salonika	(0) 0
St Patrick's Ath	(0) 2	Elfsborg	(0) 1
Sturm Graz	(1) 1	Zurich	(1) 1

(aet; Zurich won 4-2 on penalties.)

Vaslui	(3) 3	Metalurgs Liepajas	(0) 1
Viking	(1) 1	Honka	(1) 2
Zilina	(0) 2	Slovan	(0) 1
Zrinjski	(0) 0	Braga	(0) 2

Tuesday, 26 August 2008

Nordsjaelland (0) 2 *(Bernburg 85, 89)*

Queen of the South (1) 1 *(Harris 2)* 3,452

Nordsjaelland: Hansen; Kibebe, Kildentoft, Lundberg, Richter S, Karlsen (Dahl 46), Bernier, Christensen (Nielsen 86), Petersen (Fetai 68), Richter J, Bernburg.
Queen of the South: Bell; Reid, Barr, Thomson, Harris, MacFarlane (Robertson 79), Tosh, Burns, Adams (Dobbie 64), Kean (McQuilken 69), O'Connor.

Thursday, 28 August 2008

Aston Villa (1) 1 *(Gardner 27)*

Hafnarfjordur (1) 1 *(Bjornsson 30)* 25,000

Aston Villa: Friedel; Gardner, Salifou, Reo-Coker, Davies, Knight, Osbourne, Harewood, Agbonlahor (Delfouneso 62), Barry, Routledge.
Hafnarfjordur: Sigurdsson; Sverrisson B (Gardarsson 85), Siim, Nielsen, Valgardsson, Asgeirsson, Vidarsson D, Gudmundsson M, Gudmundsson T (Saevarsson 83), Vilhjalmsson, Bjornsson (Gudnason 58).

Midtjylland (0) 0

Manchester City (0) 1 *(Califf 90 (og))* 9,552

Midtjylland: Heinze; Afriyie, Califf, Poulsen, Reid, Borring, Florescu, Thygesen (Madsen 78), Olsen D (Christensen 88), Salami, Nworuh (Babatunde 66).
Manchester City: Hart; Corluka, Ball, Dunne, Ben Haim (Hamann 58), Richards, Ireland, Johnson, Jo (Evans 80), Elano (Sturridge 57), Petrov.
(aet; Manchester City won 4-2 on penalties.)

St Patrick's Ath (0) 2 *(Gavin 87, Fitzpatrick 90)*

Elfsborg (0) 1 *(Ishizaki 63)* 3,000

St Patrick's Ath: Barry Ryan; Byrne (O'Brien 82), Lynch, Gavin, Paisley, Fahey, Bobby Ryan (Kirby 74), Dempsey, O'Neill (Fitzpatrick 69), Quigley, Guy.
Elfsborg: Wiland; Floren, Karlsson, Mobaek, Lucic, Augustsson, Svensson A, Avdic (Berglund 59), Bajrami (Keene 65), Ishizaki (Kurbegovic 82), Nilsson.

FIRST ROUND, FIRST LEG

Apoel	(0) 1	Schalke	(3) 4
Hertha Berlin	(0) 2	St Patrick's Ath	(0) 0
Nordsjaelland	(0) 0	Olympiakos	(0) 2
AC Milan	(1) 3	Zurich	(0) 1
Banik Ostrava	(0) 0	Spartak Moscow	(0) 1
Bellinzona	(1) 3	Galatasaray	(1) 4
Besiktas	(0) 1	Metalist Kharkiv	(0) 0
Borac	(0) 1	Ajax	(2) 4
Borussia Dortmund	(0) 0	Udinese	(2) 2
Braga	(3) 4	Artmedia	(0) 0
Brann	(2) 2	La Coruna	(0) 0
Brondby	(0) 1	Rosenborg	(1) 2
Chernomore	(1) 1	Stuttgart	(0) 2

Dinamo Zagreb	(0) 0	Sparta Prague	(0) 0
Everton	(2) 2	Standard Liege	(2) 2
FC Moscow	(0) 1	FC Copenhagen	(1) 2
FK Austria	(0) 2	Lech	(0) 1
Feyenoord	(0) 0	Kalmar	(0) 1
Hamburg	(0) 0	Unirea	(0) 0
Hapoel Tel Aviv	(0) 1	St Etienne	(1) 2
Kyseri	(0) 1	Paris St Germain	(1) 2
Litex	(1) 1	Aston Villa	(1) 3
Maritimo	(0) 0	Valencia	(1) 1
NEC Nijmegen	(0) 1	Dinamo Bucharest	(0) 0
Nancy	(1) 1	Motherwell	(0) 0
Napoli	(2) 3	Benfica	(1) 2
Omonia	(0) 1	Manchester City	(0) 2
Portsmouth	(1) 2	Guimaraes	(0) 0
Rennes	(1) 2	Twente	(1) 1
Sampdoria	(3) 5	Kaunas	(0) 0
Santander	(0) 1	Honka	(0) 0
Setubal	(0) 1	Heerenveen	(0) 1
Sevilla	(1) 2	Salzburg	(0) 0
Slaven	(1) 1	CSKA Moscow	(0) 2
Slavia Prague	(0) 0	Vaslui	(0) 0
Timisoara	(1) 1	Partizan Belgrade	(1) 2
Tottenham Hotspur	(1) 2	Wisla	(1) 1
Wolfsburg	(1) 1	Rapid Bucharest	(0) 0
Young Boys	(1) 2	Club Brugge	(1) 2
Zilina	(0) 1	Levski	(0) 1

Tuesday, 16 September 2008

Hertha Berlin (0) 2 *(Nicu 50, Cicero 76)*

St Patrick's Ath (0) 0   13,045

Hertha Berlin: Drobny; Kaka, Friedrich, Simunic, Cicero, Dardai (Nicu 46), Stein, Piszczek, Kacar (Lustenberger 46), Pantelic (Domovchiyski 83), Voronin.
St Patrick's Ath: Barry Ryan; Byrne, Lynch, Harris, Gavin, Kirby (Bobby Ryan 63), Fahey, Dempsey (Bialek 90), O'Neill (Fitzpatrick 83), Quigley, Guy.

Thursday, 18 September 2008

Everton (2) 2 *(Yakubu 23, Castillo 38)*

Standard Liege (2) 2 *(Mbokani 8, Yobo 34 (og))*   28,312

Everton: Howard; Neville, Lescott, Yobo, Jagielka, Castillo, Osman, Anichebe (Vaughan 64), Yakubu, Cahill, Arteta.
Standard Liege: Aragon; Dante, Onyewu, Camozzato, Sarr, Dalmat, Defour, Witsel, Mbokani, De Camargo (Nicaise 86), Jovanovic.

Litex (1) 1 *(Popov 10)*

Aston Villa (1) 3 *(Reo-Coker 45, Barry 72 (pen), Petrov 90)*   7,000

Litex: Golubovic; Cambon■, Venkov■, Manolev, Nikolov, Berberovic, Wellington (Angelov 85), Dudu (Barthe 62), Sandrinho, Niflore (Acedo 74), Popov.
Aston Villa: Friedel; Young L, Shorey, Reo-Coker (Routledge 74), Laursen, Cuellar, Petrov, Gardner (Harewood 68), Agbonlahor, Barry (Salifou 78), Milner.

Nancy (1) 1 *(Berenguer 42)*

Motherwell (0) 0   16,094

Nancy: Bracigliano; Helder (Dia 56), Macaluso, Chretien, Calve, Ouaddou, Malonga (Fortune 56), Berenguer, Feret (N'Guemo 87), Brison, Zerka.
Motherwell: Smith G; Quinn, Hammell, Reynolds, Craigan, Malcolm (Smith D 67), Hughes, Fitzpatrick, Sutton (Porter 67), Clarkson (Murphy 82), Lasley.

Omonia (0) 1 *(Duro 49)*

Manchester City (0) 2 *(Jo 59, 72)* 15,907

Omonia: Georgallides; Ndikumana, Wenzel, Pletsch, Kaseke, Duro, Charalambous, Aguirre, Okkas (Clayton 81), Aloneftis (Niculescu 74), Christofi.

Manchester City: Hart; Zabaleta, Richards, Dunne, Garrido, Kompany (Gelson 84), Ireland, Robinho, Jo (Sturridge 76), Elano (Hamman 85), Wright-Phillips.

Portsmouth (1) 2 *(Diarra 39, Defoe 60)*

Guimaraes (0) 0 19,612

Portsmouth: James; Johnson, Traore A (Hreidarsson 90), Diarra, Campbell, Distin, Davis, Utaka (Diop 73), Crouch (Kanu 90), Defoe, Belhadj.

Guimaraes: Nilson; Arnolin, Danilo, Andrezinho, Mornha (Amaral 55), Wenio, Fajardo (Jean Coral 64), Moreno, Desmarets, Joao Alves, Roberto.

Tottenham Hotspur (1) 2 *(Bentley 33, Bent 73)*

Wisla (1) 1 *(Jirsak 34)* 35,751

Tottenham Hotspur: Gomes; Gunter (O'Hara 57), Bale, Zokora, Woodgate, King, Bentley, Jenas, Giovani (Assou-Ekotto 70), Bent, Lennon (Campbell 57).

Wisla: Pawelek; Singlar, Baszczynski, Diaz, Cleber, Sobolewski, Jirsak (Lobodzinski 61), Zienczuk, Cantoro, Boguski (Malecki 72), Pawel Brozek (Niedzielan 79).

FIRST ROUND, SECOND LEG

CSKA Moscow	(1) 1	Slaven	(0) 0
St Patrick's Ath	(0) 0	Hertha Berlin	(0) 0
Ajax	(0) 2	Borac	(0) 0
Artmedia	(0) 0	Braga	(2) 2
Aston Villa	(1) 1	Litex	(0) 1
Benfica	(0) 2	Napoli	(0) 0
Club Brugge	(2) 2	Young Boys	(0) 0
Dinamo Bucharest	(0) 0	NEC Nijmegen	(0) 0
FC Copenhagen	(0) 1	FC Moscow	(1) 1
Galatasaray	(1) 2	Bellinzona	(0) 1
Guimaraes	(2) 2	Portsmouth*	(0) 2
Heerenveen	(3) 5	Setubal	(0) 2
Honka	(0) 0	Santander	(1) 1
Kalmar	(0) 1	Feyenoord	(1) 2
Kaunas	(1) 1	Sampdoria	(0) 2
La Coruna	(1) 2	Brann	(0) 0
(aet; La Coruna won 3-2 on penalties.)			
Lech*	(1) 4	FK Austria	(0) 2
Levski	(0) 0	Zilina	(0) 1
Manchester City	(0) 2	Omonia	(0) 1
Metalist Kharkiv	(2) 4	Besiktas	(0) 1
Motherwell	(0) 0	Nancy	(2) 2
Olympiakos	(3) 5	Nordsjaelland	(0) 0
Paris St Germain	(0) 0	Kayseri	(0) 0
Partizan Belgrade	(0) 1	Timisoara	(0) 0
Rapid Bucharest	(0) 1	Wolfsburg	(1) 1
Rosenborg	(1) 3	Brondby	(2) 2
Salzburg	(0) 0	Sevilla	(1) 2
Schalke	(0) 1	Apoel	(1) 1
Sparta Prague	(2) 3	Dinamo Zagreb	(2) 3
Spartak Moscow	(1) 1	Banik Ostrava	(1) 1
St Etienne	(1) 2	Hapoel Tel Aviv	(0) 0
Standard Liege	(1) 2	Everton	(0) 1
Stuttgart	(0) 2	Chernomore	(0) 2
Twente	(0) 1	Rennes	(0) 0

Udinese	(0) 0	Borussia Dortmund	(1) 2

(aet; Udinese won 4-3 on penalties.)

Unirea	(0) 0	Hamburg	(1) 2
Valencia	(0) 2	Maritimo	(1) 1
Vaslui	(1) 1	Slavia Prague	(0) 1
Wisla	(0) 1	Tottenham Hotspur	(0) 1
Zurich	(0) 0	AC Milan	(0) 1

Tuesday, 30 September 2008

St Patrick's Ath (0) 0

Hertha Berlin (0) 0 3,021

St Patrick's Ath: Barry Ryan; Lynch■, Rogers, Harris, Gavin, Kirby (O'Brien 80), Fahey, Dempsey (O'Cearuill 90), Quigley, Fitzpatrick (Murphy 80), Guy.
Hertha Berlin: Drobny; Friedrich, Von Bergen, Simunic, Chahed, Cicero, Nicu, Piszczek (Stein 90), Lustenberger (Dardai 71), Raffael (Domovchiyski 65), Voronin.

Thursday, 2 October 2008

Aston Villa (1) 1 *(Harewood 27)*

Litex (0) 1 *(Niflore 53 (pen))* 27,230

Aston Villa: Friedel; Young L, Shorey, Cuellar, Knight, Salifou, Petrov, Young A (Osbourne 85), Harewood, Milner, Routledge.
Litex: Todorov; Barthe, Manolev, Nikolov, Zanev, Berberovic, Wellington (Angelov 78), Dudu (Tsvetanov 46), Sandrinho, Niflore, Popov (Du Bala 85).

Guimaraes (2) 2 *(Douglas 19, Joao Alves 32)*

Portsmouth (0) 2 *(Crouch 105, 111)* 12,000

Guimaraes: Nilson; Amaral (Fajardo 79), Arnolin, Danilo, Andrezinho, Wenio, Desmarets, Meireles, Joao Alves, Roberto (Carlitos 62) (Jean Coral 76), Douglas.
Portsmouth: James; Johnson, Pamarot, Diarra, Campbell, Distin, Davis (Mvuemba 73), Hughes (Belhadj 99), Crouch, Defoe (Kaboul 106), Traore A.
(aet.)

Manchester City (0) 2 *(Elano 48, Wright-Phillips 55)*

Omonia (0) 1 *(Alabi 78)* 25,304

Manchester City: Hart; Zabaleta, Garrido, Kompany (Hamann 66), Richards, Ben Haim, Wright-Phillips, Robinho (Petrov 70), Jo (Evans 67), Elano, Ireland.
Omonia: Georgallides; Ndikumana, Wenzel, Pletsch, Zlogar, Kaiafas (Alabi 46), Bangura (Clayton 59), Charalambous, Okkas, Aloneftis, Christofi (Cafu 82).

Motherwell (0) 0

Nancy (2) 2 *(Fortune 18, Gavanon 23)* 11,318

Motherwell: Smith G; Quinn, Hammell, Reynolds, Craigan (Smith D 75), Malcolm (Murphy 32), Lasley (Sutton 64), Hughes, Porter, Clarkson, McGarry.
Nancy: Bracigliano; Sami (Ouaddou 20), Andre Luiz, Macaluso, Chretien, Hadji, Brison, Gavanon (N'Guemo 66), N'Diaye, Zerka, Fortune (Berenguer 75).

Standard Liege (1) 2 *(Nicaise 23, Jovanovic 79 (pen))*

Everton (0) 1 *(Jagielka 67)* 27,406

Standard Liege: Aragon; Dante, Onyewu, Camozzato, Sarr, Dalmat, Defour, Nicaise, Witsel, Mbokani, Jovanovic.
Everton: Howard; Hibbert (Anichebe 63), Baines, Neville (Yobo 88), Jagielka, Lescott, Osman, Saha (Pienaar 70), Yakubu, Cahill, Arteta.

Wisla (0) 1 *(Pawel Brozek 83)*

Tottenham Hotspur (0) 1 *(Glowacki 58 (og))*   15,000

Wisla: Pawelek; Baszczynski, Glowacki, Diaz, Cleber, Sobolewski, Piotr Brozek, Jirsak (Lobodzinski 32), Cantoro (Zienczuk 66), Boguski (Marcelo 82), Pawel Brozek.

Tottenham Hotspur: Gomes; Gunter, Bale, Zokora, Woodgate, King, Lennon (Dawson 88), Modric (Huddlestone 77), Bent, Campbell (O'Hara 68), Jenas.

GROUP A

Schalke	(2) 3	Paris St Germain	(0) 1
Twente	(1) 1	Santander	(0) 0
Manchester City	(1) 3	Twente	(1) 2
Santander	(0) 1	Schalke	(0) 1
Paris St Germain	(2) 2	Santander	(1) 2
Schalke	(0) 0	Manchester City	(1) 2
Manchester City	(0) 0	Paris St Germain	(0) 0
Twente	(1) 2	Schalke	(0) 1
Paris St Germain	(2) 4	Twente	(0) 0
Santander	(2) 3	Manchester City	(0) 1

Thursday, 6 November 2008

Manchester City (1) 3 *(Wright-Phillips 6, Robinho 57, Mwaruwari 62)*

Twente (1) 2 *(Elia 17, Wielaert 65)*   21,247

Manchester City: Hart; Zabaleta, Richards, Gelson, Garrido, Dunne, Wright-Phillips, Robinho, Jo (Mwaruwari 59), Vassell (Elano 66), Ireland.

Twente: Boschker; Wielaert, Braafheid, Douglas, Brama (Wellenberg 64), Stam, Hersi, Tiote (Janssen 79), Nkufo, Elia, Arnautovic (Huysegems 31).

Thursday, 27 November 2008

Schalke (0) 0

Manchester City (1) 2 *(Mwaruwari 32, Ireland 67)*   54,142

Schalke: Neuer; Westermann, Bordon (Howedes 73), Rafinha, Pander, Rakitic (Asamoah 63), Jones, Engelaar, Farfan, Halil Altintop (Sanchez 80), Kuranyi.

Manchester City: Hart; Kompany, Garrido (Ball 46), Hamann, Richards, Dunne, Wright-Phillips, Vassell, Mwaruwari (Jo 84), Sturridge, Ireland.

Wednesday, 3 December 2008

Manchester City (0) 0

Paris St Germain (0) 0   25,626

Manchester City: Hart; Zabaleta, Garrido, Kompany, Ben Haim, Dunne, Ireland, Vassell (Hamann 76), Elano (Mwaruwari 49), Jo (Evans 65), Sturridge.

Paris St Germain: Landreau; Sakho, Bourillon, Traore, Camara, Makelele (Armand 59), Clement, Rothen, Luyindula, Pancrate (Giuly 69), Kezman (Hoarau 69).

Thursday, 18 December 2008

Santander (2) 3 *(Pereira 20, Serrano 30, Valera 54)*

Manchester City (0) 1 *(Caicedo 90)*   18,360

Santander: Coltorti; Garay, Cesar Navas, Marcano, Colsa (Lacen 77), Luccin, Valera, Tchite, Munitis, Serrano, Pereira (Juanjo 83).

Manchester City: Schmeichel; Zabaleta, Garrido, Gelson, Richards, Ben Haim, Hamann, Vassell, Evans (Caicedo 75), Robinho (Ireland 46), Elano (Kompany 60).

Group A Final Table	P	W	D	L	F	A	Pts
Manchester City	4	2	1	1	6	5	7
Twente	4	2	0	2	5	8	6
Paris St Germain	4	1	2	1	7	5	5
Santander	4	1	2	1	6	5	5
Schalke	4	1	1	2	5	6	4

GROUP B

Galatasaray	(1) 1	Olympiakos	(0) 0
Hertha Berlin	(0) 1	Benfica	(0) 1
Benfica	(0) 0	Galatasaray	(0) 2
Metalist Kharkiv	(0) 0	Hertha Berlin	(0) 0
Galatasaray	(0) 0	Metalist Kharkiv	(0) 1
Olympiakos	(4) 5	Benfica	(1) 1
Hertha Berlin	(0) 0	Galatasaray	(0) 1
Metalist Kharkiv	(0) 1	Olympiakos	(0) 0
Benfica	(0) 0	Metalist Kharkiv	(0) 1
Olympiakos	(0) 4	Hertha Berlin	(0) 0

Group B Final Table	P	W	D	L	F	A	Pts
Metalist Kharkiv	4	3	1	0	3	0	10
Galatasaray	4	3	0	1	4	1	9
Olympiakos	4	2	0	2	9	3	6
Hertha Berlin	4	0	2	2	1	6	2
Benfica	4	0	1	3	2	9	1

GROUP C

Partizan Belgrade	(1) 1	Sampdoria	(1) 2
Sevilla	(2) 2	Stuttgart	(0) 0
Standard Liege	(1) 1	Sevilla	(0) 0
Stuttgart	(0) 2	Partizan Belgrade	(0) 0
Partizan Belgrade	(0) 0	Standard Liege	(1) 1
Sampdoria	(1) 1	Stuttgart	(1) 1
Sevilla	(1) 3	Partizan Belgrade	(0) 0
Standard Liege	(3) 3	Sampdoria	(0) 0
Sampdoria	(0) 1	Sevilla	(0) 0
Stuttgart	(1) 3	Standard Liege	(0) 0

Group C Final Table	P	W	D	L	F	A	Pts
Standard Liege	4	3	0	1	5	3	9
Stuttgart	4	2	1	1	6	3	7
Sampdoria	4	2	1	1	4	5	7
Sevilla	4	2	0	2	5	2	6
Partizan Belgrade	4	0	0	4	1	8	0

GROUP D

Dinamo Zagreb	(1) 3	NEC Nijmegen	(1) 2
Udinese	(1) 2	Tottenham Hotspur	(0) 0
Spartak Moscow	(1) 1	Udinese	(1) 2
Tottenham Hotspur	(2) 4	Dinamo Zagreb	(0) 0
Dinamo Zagreb	(0) 0	Spartak Moscow	(0) 1
NEC Nijmegen	(0) 0	Tottenham Hotspur	(1) 1
Spartak Moscow	(1) 1	NEC Nijmegen	(0) 2
Udinese	(1) 2	Dinamo Zagreb	(0) 1
NEC Nijmegen	(0) 2	Udinese	(0) 0
Tottenham Hotspur	(0) 2	Spartak Moscow	(2) 2

Thursday, 23 October 2008

Udinese (1) 2 *(Di Natale 24 (pen), Pepe 86)*

Tottenham Hotspur (0) 0   22,000

Udinese: Handanovic; Domizzi, Coda, Motta, Lukovic (Pasquale 89), Isla, D'Agostino, Inler, Di Natale, Sanchez (Pepe 79), Quagliarella (Flores 86).
Tottenham Hotspur: Gomes; Hutton, Assou-Ekotto (Modric 46), Zokora, Woodgate (Giovani 63), King, Lennon, Jenas, O'Hara[■], Bent, Bale.

Thursday, 6 November 2008

Tottenham Hotspur (2) 4 *(Bent 30, 33, 70, Huddlestone 59)*

Dinamo Zagreb (0) 0   16,295

Tottenham Hotspur: Gomes; Hutton, Bale, Zokora, Woodgate (Gunter 85), Dawson, Lennon, Huddlestone, Bent, Modric (Campbell 75), Bentley (Bostock 79).
Dinamo Zagreb: Kelava; Ibanez, Lovren, Vrdoljak, Drpic (Etto 46), Hrgovic, Sammir (Morales 43), Mikic, Biscan, Balaban (Badelj 60), Manduzic.

Thursday, 27 November 2008

NEC Nijmegen (0) 0

Tottenham Hotspur (1) 1 *(O'Hara 14)*   12,500

NEC Nijmegen: Babos; Zomer, Wisgerhof, El-Akchaoui, Fernandez (Tshibamba 81), El Kabir, Davids, Schone, Sibum (Bouaouzan 65), Radomski (Kivuvu 46), Van Beukering.
Tottenham Hotspur: Gomes; Gunter, Bale, Zokora, Woodgate, Dawson, Bentley (Mason 90), Huddlestone, Campbell (Obika 83), Bent (Lennon 71), O'Hara.

Thursday, 18 December 2008

Tottenham Hotspur (0) 2 *(Modric 67, Huddlestone 74)*

Spartak Moscow (2) 2 *(Dzyuba 23, 33)*   28,906

Tottenham Hotspur: Gomes; Gunter, Bale, Huddlestone, Zokora, Dawson, Bentley, O'Hara, Campbell, Modric, Gilberto (Lennon 46).
Spartak Moscow: Pletikosa; Fathi, Jiranek, Rodriguez, Shishkin (Bazhenov 85), Covalciuc, Parshivlyuk, Maloyan (Zotov 73), Ryzhkov (Grigoriev 60), Saenko, Dzyuba.

Group D Final Table	P	W	D	L	F	A	Pts
Udinese	4	3	0	1	6	4	9
Tottenham Hotspur	4	2	1	1	7	4	7
NEC Nijmegen	4	2	0	2	6	5	6
Spartak Moscow	4	1	1	2	5	6	4
Dinamo Zagreb	4	1	0	3	4	9	3

GROUP E

Braga	(1) 3	Portsmouth	(0) 0
Heerenveen	(0) 1	AC Milan	(2) 3
AC Milan	(0) 1	Braga	(0) 0
Wolfsburg	(2) 5	Heerenveen	(1) 1
Braga	(1) 2	Wolfsburg	(1) 3
Portsmouth	(0) 2	AC Milan	(0) 2
Heerenveen	(1) 1	Braga	(1) 2
Wolfsburg	(2) 3	Portsmouth	(2) 2
AC Milan	(1) 2	Wolfsburg	(0) 2
Portsmouth	(2) 3	Heerenveen	(0) 0

Thursday, 23 October 2008

Braga (1) 3 *(Luis Aguiar 8, Renteria 46, Alan 87)*

Portsmouth (0) 0   12,000

Braga: Eduardo; Rodriguez, Moises, Evaldo, Frechaut, Luis Aguiar, Vandinho (Paulo Cesar 86), Renteria (Stelvio 83), Meyong, Alan, Matheus (Cesar Peixoto 63).

Portsmouth: James; Pamarot, Hreidarsson (Belhadj 46), Davis, Campbell, Distin, Little, Diop, Crouch, Defoe, Traore A (Kanu 62).

Thursday, 27 November 2008

Portsmouth (0) 2 *(Kaboul 62, Kanu 73)*

AC Milan (0) 2 *(Ronaldinho 84, Inzaghi 90)*   20,403

Portsmouth: James; Johnson, Belhadj, Hughes, Kaboul, Distin, Little (Mvuemba 65), Diop, Crouch, Kanu (Davis 81), Traore A.

AC Milan: Dida; Favalli, Senderos, Emerson, Gattuso (Seedorf 65), Zambrotta, Kaka (Ronaldinho 74), Antonini, Flamini, Inzaghi, Shevchenko (Pato 74).

Thursday, 4 December 2008

Wolfsburg (2) 3 *(Dzeko 3, Gentner 23, Misimovic 74)*

Portsmouth (2) 2 *(Defoe 11, Mvuemba 14)*   21,015

Wolfsburg: Benaglio; Zaccardo (Hasebe 37), Schafer, Ricardo Costa, Riether (Madlung 46), Barzagli, Josue, Misimovic, Dejagah (Simunek 88), Gentner, Dzeko.

Portsmouth: James; Johnson, Traore A, Davis, Campbell, Distin, Hughes, Mvuemba (Crouch 67), Belhadj (Pamarot 46), Defoe, Kranjcar (Kanu 77).

Wednesday, 17 December 2008

Portsmouth (2) 3 *(Crouch 40, 42, Hreidarsson 90)*

Heerenveen (0) 0   19,612

Portsmouth: Ashdown; Wilson, Belhadj, Mvuemba, Pamarot, Hreidarsson, Hughes, Diop (Davis 84), Crouch, Kanu, Traore A (Little 62).

Heerenveen: Vandenbussche; Nielsen, Breuer (Smarason 30), Dingsdag, Svec, Vayrynen, Beerens (Elyounoussi 46), Grindheim (Janmaat 84), Popov, Paulo Henrique, Sibon.

Group E Final Table	P	W	D	L	F	A	Pts
Wolfsburg	4	3	1	0	13	7	10
AC Milan	4	2	2	0	8	5	8
Braga	4	2	0	2	7	5	6
Portsmouth	4	1	1	2	7	8	4
Heerenveen	4	0	0	4	3	13	0

GROUP F

Aston Villa	(2) 2	Ajax	(1) 1
Zilina	(0) 1	Hamburg	(2) 2
Ajax	(1) 1	Zilina	(0) 0
Slavia Prague	(0) 0	Aston Villa	(1) 1
Hamburg	(0) 0	Ajax	(0) 1
Zilina	(0) 0	Slavia Prague	(0) 0
Aston Villa	(1) 1	Zilina	(2) 2
Slavia Prague	(0) 0	Hamburg	(1) 2
Ajax	(1) 2	Slavia Prague	(2) 2
Hamburg	(2) 3	Aston Villa	(0) 1

Thursday, 23 October 2008

Aston Villa (2) 2 *(Laursen 8, Barry 45)*

Ajax (1) 1 *(Vermaelen 22)* 36,657

Aston Villa: Friedel; Young L, Shorey, Reo-Coker (Gardner 81), Cuellar, Laursen, Petrov, Young A, Agbonlahor (Davies 90), Milner, Barry.
Ajax: Vermeer; Silva, Oleguer (Van der Wiel 78), Vermaelen, Vertonghen, Lindgren, Emanuelson, Gabri, Sarpong (Cvitanich 55), Huntelaar, Suarez (Leonardo 60).

Thursday, 6 November 2008

Slavia Prague (0) 0

Aston Villa (1) 1 *(Carew 26)* 20,322

Slavia Prague: Vaniak; Brabec, Hubacek (Senkerik 66), Suchy, Tavares, Jarolim, Smicer (Svento 41), Krajcik, Volesak (Belaid 46), Cerny, Necid.
Aston Villa: Guzan; Shorey, Cuellar, Davies, Knight, Salifou, Sidwell, Young A, Agbonlahor (Barry 89), Carew (Delfouneso 90), Gardner.

Thursday, 4 December 2008

Aston Villa (1) 1 *(Delfouneso 28)*

Zilina (2) 2 *(Leitner 16, Styvar 19)* 28,797

Aston Villa: Guzan; Young L, Salifou (Barry 68), Reo-Coker, Knight, Cuellar, Osbourne (Milner 65), Young A, Harewood, Delfouneso (Agbonlahor 76), Gardner.
Zilina: Pernis; Vomacka, Leitner■, Pekarik, Piacek, Sourek, Pecalka, Strba, Jez (Tesak 90), Adauto (Vladavic 70), Styvar (Rilke 86).

Wednesday, 17 December 2008

Hamburg (2) 3 *(Petric 18, Olic 30, 57)*

Aston Villa (0) 1 *(Delfouneso 83)* 49,121

Hamburg: Rost; Reinhardt, Mathijsen, Jansen, Boateng, Benjamin, Aogo, Jarolim, Trochowski (Ben-Hatira 89), Petric (Thiago Neves 78), Olic (Guerrero 67).
Aston Villa: Guzan; Young, Shorey, Salifou, Knight, Cuellar, Sidwell■, Reo-Coker, Harewood, Delfouneso, Gardner (Bannan 61).

Group F Final Table	P	W	D	L	F	A	Pts
Hamburg	4	3	0	1	7	3	9
Ajax	4	2	1	1	5	4	7
Aston Villa	4	2	0	2	5	6	6
Zilina	4	1	1	2	3	4	4
Slavia Prague	4	0	2	2	2	5	2

GROUP G

FC Copenhagen	(0) 1	St Etienne	(2) 3
Rosenborg	(0) 0	Club Brugge	(0) 0
St Etienne	(0) 3	Rosenborg	(0) 0
Valencia	(0) 1	FC Copenhagen	(0) 1
Club Brugge	(0) 1	St Etienne	(1) 1
Rosenborg	(0) 0	Valencia	(1) 4
FC Copenhagen	(0) 1	Rosenborg	(1) 1
Valencia	(0) 1	Club Brugge	(1) 1
Club Brugge	(0) 0	FC Copenhagen	(0) 1
St Etienne	(2) 2	Valencia	(1) 2

Group G Final Table	P	W	D	L	F	A	Pts
St Etienne	4	2	2	0	9	4	8
Valencia	4	1	3	0	8	4	6
FC Copenhagen	4	1	2	1	4	5	5
Club Brugge	4	0	3	1	2	3	3
Rosenborg	4	0	2	2	1	8	2

GROUP H

CSKA Moscow	(2) 3	La Coruna	(0) 0
Nancy	(0) 3	Feyenoord	(0) 0
Feyenoord	(1) 1	CSKA Moscow	(2) 3
Lech	(2) 2	Nancy	(1) 2
CSKA Moscow	(2) 2	Lech	(0) 1
La Coruna	(1) 3	Feyenoord	(0) 0
Lech	(1) 1	La Coruna	(1) 1
Nancy	(1) 3	CSKA Moscow	(2) 4
Feyenoord	(0) 0	Lech	(1) 1
La Coruna	(0) 1	Nancy	(0) 0

Group H Final Table	P	W	D	L	F	A	Pts
CSKA Moscow	4	4	0	0	12	5	12
La Coruna	4	2	1	1	5	4	7
Lech	4	1	2	1	5	5	5
Nancy	4	1	1	2	8	7	4
Feyenoord	4	0	0	4	1	10	0

THIRD ROUND, FIRST LEG

Aalborg	(0) 3	La Coruna	(0) 0
Aston Villa	(0) 1	CSKA Moscow	(1) 1
Bordeaux	(0) 0	Galatasaray	(0) 0
Braga	(2) 3	Standard Liege	(0) 0
Dynamo Kiev	(0) 1	Valencia	(1) 1
NEC Nijmegen	(0) 0	Hamburg	(2) 3
Olympiakos	(0) 1	St Etienne	(2) 3
Paris St Germain	(0) 2	Wolfsburg	(0) 0
Sampdoria	(0) 0	Metalist Kharkiv	(1) 1
Werder Bremen	(0) 1	AC Milan	(1) 1
Zenit	(2) 2	Stuttgart	(1) 1
FC Copenhagen	(0) 2	Manchester C	(1) 2
Fiorentina	(0) 0	Ajax	(0) 1
Lech	(0) 2	Udinese	(0) 2
Marseille	(0) 0	Twente	(1) 1
Shakhtar Donetsk	(0) 2	Tottenham H	(0) 0

Wednesday, 18 February 2009

Aston Villa (0) 1 *(Carew 69)*

CSKA Moscow (1) 1 *(Vagner Love 14)*   38,038

Aston Villa: Guzan; Young L, Shorey, Gardner, Davies, Knight, Petrov, Young A, Agbonlahor, Carew, Barry.
CSKA Moscow: Akinfeev; Ignashevich, Berezutski A, Berezutski V, Shchennikov, Krasic, Zhirkov (Mamaev 90), Aldonin (Erkin 90), Rahimic, Dzagoev (Daniel Carvalho 90), Vagner Love.

Thursday, 19 February 2009

FC Copenhagen (0) 2 *(Ailton 56, Vingaard 90)*
Manchester C (1) 2 *(Onuoha 29, Ireland 61)* 30,159

FC Copenhagen: Christiansen; Pospech, Laursen, Antonsson, Wendt, Norregaard (Gronkjaer 70), Kvist (Vingaard 60), Hutchinson, Kristensen, Ailton, Cesar Santin (N'Doye 59).
Manchester C: Given; Richards, Bridge, Kompany, Onuoha, Dunne, Zabaleta, Robinho (Caicedo 89), Bellamy, Ireland, Wright-Phillips.

Shakhtar Donetsk (0) 2 *(Seleznov 79, Jadson 88)*
Tottenham H (0) 0 25,000

Shakhtar Donetsk: Pyatov; Ilsinho (Luiz Adriano 68), Rat, Chigrinskiy, Ishchenko, Fernandinho, Jadson, Lewandowski, Willian, Srna, Gladkiy (Seleznov 78).
Tottenham H: Gomes; Chimbonda, Gunter, Zokora, Dawson, Parrett (Bostock 89), Bentley, Jenas, Campbell, Huddlestone, Giovani (Bent 69).

THIRD ROUND, SECOND LEG

AC Milan	(2) 2	Werder Bremen	(0) 2
Ajax	(0) 1	Fiorentina	(0) 1
CSKA Moscow	(0) 2	Aston Villa	(0) 0
Galatasaray	(2) 4	Bordeaux	(1) 3
Hamburg	(1) 1	NEC Nijmegen	(0) 0
La Coruna	(1) 1	Aalborg	(3) 3
Manchester City	(0) 2	FC Copenhagen	(0) 1
Metalist Kharkiv	(2) 2	Sampdoria	(0) 0
St Etienne	(1) 2	Olympiakos	(0) 1
Standard Liege	(0) 1	Braga	(0) 1
Stuttgart	(0) 1	Zenit	(1) 2
Tottenham Hotspur	(0) 1	Shakhtar Donetsk	(0) 1
Twente	(0) 0	Marseille	(1) 1
(aet; Marseille won 7-6 on penalties.)			
Udinese	(0) 2	Lech	(1) 1
Valencia	(1) 2	Dynamo Kiev	(1) 2
Wolfsburg	(0) 1	Paris St Germain	(1) 3

Thursday, 26 February 2009

CSKA Moscow (0) 2 *(Zhirkov 61, Vagner Love 90)*
Aston Villa (0) 0 25,650

CSKA Moscow: Akinfeev; Semberas, Ignashevich, Berezutski A, Berezutski V, Shchennikov, Krasic, Zhirkov, Rahimic, Dzagoev, Vagner Love.
Aston Villa: Guzan; Young L, Shorey, Salifou (Harewood 46), Davies (Osbourne 84), Knight, Gardner, Sidwell, Delfouneso, Bannan, Albrighton.

Manchester City (0) 2 *(Bellamy 73, 80)*
FC Copenhagen (0) 1 *(Vingaard 90)* 26,018

Manchester City: Given; Richards, Bridge, Kompany, Onuoha, Dunne, Zabaleta (Elano 82), Robinho, Bellamy, Ireland, Wright-Phillips.
FC Copenhagen: Christiansen; Pospech, Antonsson, Wendt, Jorgensen, Norregaard (Vingaard 76), Kvist, Hutchinson, Kristensen (Sionko 46), Ailton, N'Doye (Gronkjaer 59).

Tottenham Hotspur (0) 1 *(Giovani 55)*
Shakhtar Donetsk (0) 1 *(Fernandinho 86)* 30,595

Tottenham Hotspur: Gomes; Chimbonda, Bale, Palacios, Gunter, Huddlestone, Gilberto (Bostock 77), Obika, Giovani, Campbell, O'Hara (Parrett 71).
Shakhtar Donetsk: Pyatov; Ilsinho (Gay 80), Rat, Chigrinskiy, Ishchenko, Fernandinho, Jadson, Lewandowski, Willian (Hubschman 46), Srna, Gladkiy (Moreno 61).

FOURTH ROUND, FIRST LEG

CSKA Moscow	(0) 1	Shakhtar Donetsk	(0) 0
Dynamo Kiev	(0) 1	Metalist Kharkiv	(0) 0
Hamburg	(0) 1	Galatasaray	(1) 1
Manchester City	(2) 2	Aalborg	(0) 0
Marseille	(2) 2	Ajax	(1) 1
Paris St Germain	(0) 0	Braga	(0) 0
Udinese	(0) 2	Zenit	(0) 0
Werder Bremen	(1) 1	St Etienne	(0) 0

Thursday, 12 March 2009

Manchester City (2) 2 *(Caicedo 8, Wright-Phillips 30)*

Aalborg (0) 0   24,502

Manchester City: Given; Richards, Bridge, Caicedo (Evans 63), Onuoha, Dunne, Zabaleta, Ireland, Elano, Robinho, Wright-Phillips (Etuhu 87).
Aalborg: Zaza; Jakobsen (Nielsen 86), Beauchamp, Bogelund, Due (Curth 66), Johansson, Augustinussen, Caca, Enevoldsen (Risgard 76), Shelton, Kristensen.

FOURTH ROUND, SECOND LEG

Ajax	(1) 2	Marseille	(1) 2
St Etienne	(0) 2	Werder Bremen	(2) 2
Aalborg	(0) 2	Manchester City	(0) 0
(aet; Manchester City won 4-3 on penalties.)			
Braga	(0) 0	Paris St Germain	(0) 1
Galatasaray	(1) 2	Hamburg	(0) 3
Metalist Kharkiv	(1) 3	Dynamo Kiev	(0) 2
Shakhtar Donetsk	(0) 2	CSKA Moscow	(0) 0
Zenit	(1) 1	Udinese	(0) 0

Thursday, 19 March 2009

Aalborg (0) 2 *(Shelton 85, Jakobsen 90 (pen))*

Manchester City (0) 0   10,734

Aalborg: Zaza; Jakobsen, Beauchamp, Bogelund, Nielsen, Due (Nomvethe 46), Johansson, Augustinussen, Caca (Kristensen 106), Risgard (Tracy 77), Shelton.
Manchester City: Given; Richards, Bridge (Garrido 55), Kompany (Elano 107), Onuoha, Dunne, Zabaleta, Ireland, Evans, Robinho (Caicedo 96), Wright-Phillips.
aet; Manchester City won 4-3 on penalties: Jakobsen scored; Evans scored; Johansson scored; Elano scored; Augustinussen saved; Wright-Phillips scored; Nomvethe scored; Dunne scored; Shelton saved.

QUARTER-FINALS, FIRST LEG

Hamburg	(1) 3	Manchester City	(1) 1
Paris St Germain	(0) 0	Dynamo Kiev	(0) 0
Shakhtar Donetsk	(1) 2	Marseille	(0) 0
Werder Bremen	(1) 3	Udinese	(0) 1

Thursday, 9 April 2009

Hamburg (1) 3 *(Mathijsen 9, Trochowski 63 (pen), Guerrero 79)*

Manchester City (1) 1 *(Ireland 1)*   50,500

Hamburg: Rost; Mathijsen, Jansen, Gravgaard, Benjamin, Aogo, Jarolim, Trochowski, Pitriopa, Petric, Olic (Guerrero 71).
Manchester City: Given; Richards, Bridge (Garrido 46), Ireland, Onuoha, Dunne, Zabaleta, Robinho, Bellamy, Sturridge (Mwaruwari 62), Wright-Phillips (Gelson 83).

QUARTER-FINALS, SECOND LEG

Dynamo Kiev	(2) 3	Paris St Germain	(0) 0
Manchester City	(1) 2	Hamburg	(1) 1
Marseille	(1) 1	Shakhtar Donetsk	(1) 2
Udinese	(3) 3	Werder Bremen	(1) 3

Thursday, 16 April 2009

Manchester City (1) 2 *(Elano 16 (pen), Caicedo 50)*

Hamburg (1) 1 *(Guerrero 12)*   47,009

Manchester City: Given; Richards, Bridge, Kompany, Onuoha, Dunne■, Zabaleta (Gelson 77), Robinho, Elano (Sturridge 85), Caicedo, Ireland.
Hamburg: Rost; Mathijsen, Jansen, Gravgaard, Boateng, Aogo, Jarolim, Trochowski (Petric 73), Pitroipa, Guerrero, Olic.

SEMI-FINALS, FIRST LEG

Dynamo Kiev	(1) 1	Shakhtar Donetsk	(0) 1
Werder Bremen	(0) 0	Hamburg	(1) 1

SEMI-FINALS, SECOND LEG

Hamburg	(1) 2	Werder Bremen	(1) 3
Shakhtar Donetsk	(1) 2	Dynamo Kiev	(0) 1

UEFA CUP FINAL 2009

Wednesday, 20 May 2009

(in Istanbul, attendance 40,000)

Shakhtar Donetsk (1) 2 *(Luiz Adriano 26, Jadson 97)*

Werder Bremen (1) 1 *(Naldo 35)*

Shakhtar Donetsk: Pyatov; Kucher, Ilsinho (Gay 100), Rat, Chigrinskiy, Fernandinho, Jadson (Duljaj 112), Lewandowski, Willian, Srna, Luiz Adriano (Gladkiy 90).

Werder Bremen: Wiese; Boenisch, Naldo, Baumann, Fritz (Pasanen 95), Prodl, Ozil, Frings, Niemeyer (Tziolis 103), Rosenberg (Hunt 78), Pizarro.

(aet.)

Referee: Chantalejo (Spain).

PAST EUROPEAN CUP FINALS

Year	Winner		Runner-up	
1956	Real Madrid	4	Stade de Rheims	3
1957	Real Madrid	2	Fiorentina	0
1958	Real Madrid*	3	AC Milan	2
1959	Real Madrid	2	Stade de Rheims	0
1960	Real Madrid	7	Eintracht Frankfurt	3
1961	Benfica	3	Barcelona	2
1962	Benfica	5	Real Madrid	3
1963	AC Milan	2	Benfica	1
1964	Internazionale	3	Real Madrid	1
1965	Internazionale	1	SL Benfica	0
1966	Real Madrid	2	Partizan Belgrade	1
1967	Celtic	2	Internazionale	1
1968	Manchester U*	4	Benfica	1
1969	AC Milan	4	Ajax	1
1970	Feyenoord*	2	Celtic	1
1971	Ajax	2	Panathinaikos	0
1972	Ajax	2	Internazionale	0
1973	Ajax	1	Juventus	0
1974	Bayern Munich	1 4	Atletico Madrid	1 0
1975	Bayern Munich	2	Leeds U	0
1976	Bayern Munich	1	St Etienne	0
1977	Liverpool	3	Borussia Moenchengladbach	1
1978	Liverpool	1	FC Brugge	0
1979	Nottingham F	1	Malmö	0
1980	Nottingham F	1	Hamburg	0
1981	Liverpool	1	Real Madrid	0
1982	Aston Villa	1	Bayern Munich	0
1983	Hamburg	1	Juventus	0
1984	Liverpool†	1	Roma	1
1985	Juventus	1	Liverpool	0
1986	Steaua Bucharest†	0	Barcelona	0
1987	Porto	2	Bayern Munich	1
1988	PSV Eindhoven†	0	Benfica	0
1989	AC Milan	4	Steaua Bucharest	0
1990	AC Milan	1	Benfica	0
1991	Red Star Belgrade†	0	Marseille	0
1992	Barcelona	1	Sampdoria	0

PAST UEFA CHAMPIONS LEAGUE FINALS

Year	Winner		Runner-up	
1993	Marseille	1	AC Milan	0

(Marseille subsequently stripped of title)

Year	Winner		Runner-up	
1994	AC Milan	4	Barcelona	0
1995	Ajax	1	AC Milan	0
1996	Juventus†	1	Ajax	1
1997	Borussia Dortmund	3	Juventus	1
1998	Real Madrid	1	Juventus	0
1999	Manchester U	2	Bayern Munich	1
2000	Real Madrid	3	Valencia	0
2001	Bayern Munich†	1	Valencia	1
2002	Real Madrid	2	Leverkusen	1
2003	AC Milan†	0	Juventus	0
2004	Porto	3	Monaco	0
2005	Liverpool†	3	AC Milan	3
2006	Barcelona	2	Arsenal	1
2007	AC Milan	2	Liverpool	1
2008	Manchester U†	1	Chelsea	1
2009	Barcelona	2	Manchester U	0

† aet; won on penalties.   * aet.

PAST UEFA CUP FINALS

Year				Opponent		
1972	Tottenham H	2	1	Wolverhampton W	1	1
1973	Liverpool	3	0	Borussia Moenchengladbach	0	2
1974	Feyenoord	2	2	Tottenham H	2	0
1975	Borussia Moenchengladbach	0	5	Twente Enschede	0	1
1976	Liverpool	3	1	FC Brugge	2	1
1977	Juventus**	1	1	Athletic Bilbao	0	2
1978	PSV Eindhoven	0	3	SEC Bastia	0	0
1979	Borussia Moenchengladbach	1	1	Red Star Belgrade	1	0
1980	Borussia Moenchengladbach	3	0	Eintracht Frankfurt**	2	1
1981	Ipswich T	3	2	AZ 67 Alkmaar	0	4
1982	IFK Gothenburg	1	3	SV Hamburg	0	0
1983	Anderlecht	1	1	Benfica	0	1
1984	Tottenham H†	1	1	RSC Anderlecht	1	1
1985	Real Madrid	3	0	Videoton	0	1
1986	Real Madrid	5	0	Cologne	1	2
1987	IFK Gothenburg	1	1	Dundee U	0	1
1988	Bayer Leverkusen†	0	3	Espanol	3	0
1989	Napoli	2	3	Stuttgart	1	3
1990	Juventus	3	0	Fiorentina	1	0
1991	Internazionale	2	0	AS Roma	0	1
1992	Ajax**	0	2	Torino	0	2
1993	Juventus	3	3	Borussia Dortmund	1	0
1994	Internazionale	1	1	Salzburg	0	0
1995	Parma	1	1	Juventus	0	1
1996	Bayern Munich	2	3	Bordeaux	0	1
1997	Schalke*†	1	0	Internazionale	0	1
1998	Internazionale	3		Lazio	0	
1999	Parma	3		Marseille	0	
2000	Galatasaray†	0		Arsenal	0	
2001	Liverpool§	5		Alaves	4	
2002	Feyenoord	3		Borussia Dortmund	2	
2003	Porto*	3		Celtic	2	
2004	Valencia	2		Marseille	0	
2005	CSKA Moscow	3		Sporting Lisbon	1	
2006	Sevilla	4		Middlesbrough	0	
2007	Sevilla*†	2		Espanyol	2	
2008	Zenit St Petersburg	2		Rangers	0	
2009	Shakhtar Donetsk*	2		Werder Bremen	1	

*After extra time **Won on away goals †Won on penalties §Won on sudden death.

UEFA EUROPA LEAGUE 2009–2010

PARTICIPATING CLUBS Everton FC (ENG); Aston Villa FC (ENG); Villarreal CF (ESP); Valencia CF (ESP); S.S. Lazio (ITA) *; Genoa CFC (ITA); EA Guingamp (FRA) *; Toulouse FC (FRA); Werder Bremen (GER) *; Hertha BSC Berlin (GER); FC Amkar Perm (RUS); FC Zenit St. Petersburg (RUS); CFR 1907 Cluj (ROU); FC Dinamo 1948 Bucureşti (ROU); SL Benfica (POR); CD Nacional (POR); SC Heerenveen (NED) *; AFC Ajax (NED); Heart of Midlothian FC (SCO); Trabzonspor (TUR); FC Vorskla Poltava (UKR) *; KRC Genk (BEL) *; AEK Athens FC (GRE); FK Teplice (CZE) *; FC Sion (SUI) *; PFC Litex Lovech (BUL) *; Fulham FC (ENG); Athletic Club Bilbao (ESP) ** ; AS Roma (ITA); LOSC Lille Métropole (FRA); Hamburger SV (GER); PFC Krylya Sovetov Samara (RUS); SC Vaslui (ROU); SC Braga (POR); PSV Eindhoven (NED); Aberdeen FC (SCO); Fenerbahçe SK (TUR); FC Metalist Kharkiv (UKR); Club Brugge KV (BEL); PAOK FC (GRE); FC Slovan Liberec (CZE); BSC Young Boys (SUI); PFC CSKA Sofia (BUL); Vålerenga Fotball (NOR) *; Fredrikstad FK (NOR); Odense BK (DEN); FK Austria Wien (AUT) *; FK Vojvodina (SRB); Hapoel Tel-Aviv FC (ISR); IFK Göteborg (SWE) *; MFK Košice (SVK) *; KKS Lech Poznań (POL) *; Budapest Honvéd FC (HUN) *; HNK Hajduk Split (CRO); APOP/Kinyras Peyias FC (CYP) *; NK IB Ljubljana (SVN) *; FC Steaua Bucureşti (ROU); FC Paços de Ferreira (POR) **; NAC Breda (NED); Falkirk FC (SCO) **; Galatasaray AŞ (TUR) ; FC Metalurh Donetsk (UKR); KAA Gent (BEL); Larissa FC (GRE); SK Sigma Olomouc (CZE); FC Basel 1893 (SUI); PFC Cherno More Varna (BUL); Tromsø IL (NOR); Brøndby IF (DEN); Aalborg BK (DEN) **; SK Rapid Wien (AUT); SK Sturm Graz (AUT); FK Crvena Zvezda (SRB) *; FK Sevojno (SRB) **; Maccabi Netanya FC (ISR); IF Elfsborg (SWE) ; MŠK Žilina (SVK); Legia Warszawa (POL); Újpest FC (HUN); HNK Rijeka (CRO); AC Omonia (CYP); NK Gorica (SVN); HJK Helsinki (FIN) *; FC Honka Espoo (FIN); SK Liepājas Metalurgs (LVA); Skonto FC (LVA); FK Slavija Sarajevo (BIH) *; FK Sarajevo (BIH) ; FK Sūduva (LTU) *; FBK Kaunas (LTU); FC Dacia Chişinău (MDA) ; FC Iskra-Stali (MDA); Saint Patrick's Athletic FC (IRL); Derry City FC (IRL); FK Rabotnicki (MKD); FK Milano (MKD); KR Reykjavík (ISL) *; FC Dinamo Tbilisi (GEO) *; FC Vaduz (LIE) *; FC Naftan Novopolotsk (BLR) *; FC Flora (EST) *; FK Qarabağ (AZE) *; KS Flamurtari (ALB) *; FC Gandzasar Kapan (ARM); FC Tobol Kostanay (KAZ); Crusaders FC (NIR) *; Bangor City FC (WAL) *; HB Tórshavn (FRO); FC Differdange 03 (LUX); Sliema Wanderers FC (MLT) *; FK Petrovac (MNE) *; FC Santa Coloma (AND) *; AC Juvenes-Dogana (SMR) *; Randers FC (DEN) ***; Rosenborg BK (NOR) ***; Motherwell FC (SCO) ***; Bnei Yehuda Tel-Aviv FC (ISR); Helsingborgs IF (SWE); FC Spartak Trnava (SVK); KSP Polonia Warszawa (POL); Haladás FC (HUN); NK Slaven Koprivnica (CRO); Anorthosis Famagusta FC (CYP); NK Rudar Velenje (SVN); FC Lahti (FIN); FC Dinaburg (LVA); NK Široki Brijeg (BIH); FK Vėtra (LTU); FC Zimbru Chişinău (MDA); Sligo Rovers FC (IRL); FK Renova (MKD); Keflavík (ISL); Fram Reykjavík (ISL); FC Olimpi Rustavi (GEO); FC Zestafoni (GEO); FC Dinamo Minsk (BLR); FC MTZ-RIPO Minsk (BLR); JK Trans Narva (EST) ; JK Nõmme Kalju (EST); FC Inter Bakı (AZE); Simurq PFC (AZE); KS Vllaznia (ALB); KS Dinamo Tirana (ALB); FC MIKA (ARM); FC Banants (ARM) **; FC Irtysh Pavlodar (KAZ); FC Okzhetpes Kokshetau (KAZ); Linfield FC (NIR); Lisburn Distillery FC (NIR); Llanelli AFC (WAL); The New Saints FC (WAL); B36 Tórshavn (FRO) **; NSÍ Runavík (FRO); CS Grevenmacher (LUX); UN Käerjéng 97 (LUX) **; Valletta FC (MLT); Birkirkara FC (MLT); FK Budućnost Podgorica (MNE); FK Sutjeska (MNE).

* cup winners   ** losing cup finalists   *** Fair Play winners

PAST EUROPEAN CHAMPIONSHIP FINALS

Year	Winners		Runners-up		Venue	Attendance
1960	USSR	2	Yugoslavia	1	Paris	17,966
1964	Spain	2	USSR	1	Madrid	120,000
1968	Italy	2	Yugoslavia	0	Rome	60,000
	(After 1-1 draw)					75,000
1972	West Germany	3	USSR	0	Brussels	43,437
1976	Czechoslovakia	2	West Germany	2	Belgrade	45,000
	(Czechoslovakia won on penalties)					
1980	West Germany	2	Belgium	1	Rome	47,864
1984	France	2	Spain	0	Paris	48,000
1988	Holland	2	USSR	0	Munich	72,308
1992	Denmark	2	Germany	0	Gothenburg	37,800
1996	Germany	2	Czech Republic	1	Wembley	73,611
	(Germany won on sudden death)					
2000	France	2	Italy	1	Rotterdam	50,000
	(France won on sudden death)					
2004	Greece	1	Portugal	0	Lisbon	62,865
2008	Spain	1	Germany	0	Vienna	51,428

PAST WORLD CUP FINALS

Year	Winners		Runners-up		Venue	Att.	Referee
1930	Uruguay	4	Argentina	2	Montevideo	90,000	Langenus (B)
1934	Italy*	2	Czechoslovakia	1	Rome	50,000	Eklind (Se)
1938	Italy	4	Hungary	2	Paris	45,000	Capdeville (F)
1950	Uruguay	2	Brazil	1	Rio de Janeiro	199,854	Reader (E)
1954	West Germany	3	Hungary	2	Berne	60,000	Ling (E)
1958	Brazil	5	Sweden	2	Stockholm	49,737	Guigue (F)
1962	Brazil	3	Czechoslovakia	1	Santiago	68,679	Latychev (USSR)
1966	England*	4	West Germany	2	Wembley	93,802	Dienst (Sw)
1970	Brazil	4	Italy	1	Mexico City	107,412	Glockner (EG)
1974	West Germany	2	Holland	1	Munich	77,833	Taylor (E)
1978	Argentina*	3	Holland	1	Buenos Aires	77,000	Gonella (I)
1982	Italy	3	West Germany	1	Madrid	90,080	Coelho (Br)
1986	Argentina	3	West Germany	2	Mexico City	114,580	Filho (Br)
1990	West Germany	1	Argentina	0	Rome	73,603	Mendez (Mex)
1994	Brazil*	0	Italy	0	Los Angeles	94,194	Puhl (H)
	(Brazil won 3-2 on penalties)						
1998	France	3	Brazil	0	St-Denis	75,000	Belqola (Mor)
2002	Brazil	2	Germany	0	Yokohama	69,029	Collina (I)
2006	Italy*	1	France	1	Berlin	69,000	Elizondo (Arg)
	(Italy won 5-3 on penalties)						

*After extra time.

WORLD CUP 2010 QUALIFYING REVIEW

Short of a catastrophic loss of form in the remaining three matches, England have surely booked their place for the World Cup finals in South Africa next year. Seven wins on the trot for Fabio Capello in the competition is all that can be expected. All is well in Group Six at present it seems but the race to become second really is a three horse affair between Croatia, Ukraine and even Belarus.

As for the other British and Irish teams involved in the qualifying process, the Republic of Ireland would seem to be the next best placed to become one of the eight best of nine group runners-up. These eight are paired off for home and away ties, the four winners joining the group winners for the 13 European finalists.

For fairness, groups with six teams will not have matches counted against the sixth finishing team because Group Nine consists of just five countries. The draw for these play-offs will be held in October, the matches played in November. But as previously mentioned, the Republic have a good record at present which would enable it be among the eight.

This is a curious group indeed, with many drawn matches – the top three, Italy, Republic and Bulgaria still unbeaten, the bottom two Montenegro and Georgia striving to achieve their first victories.

Northern Ireland, too, are in second place in Group Three, but have played a game more than Poland who are three points behind with a game in hand. Crucially, too, the Irish have to go to Poland which is a crunch game for them. Even so Slovakia are just two points in front of Northern Ireland having played one fewer match. But what has happened to the Czech Republic, once a formidable east Europe outfit?

Wales in Group Four may be poorly positioned in fourth place, their position worsening after Russia won in Finland leaving them six points adrift of second place with one more game played.

For Scotland in the five-team Group Nine they have an excellent chance of finishing runners-up with Holland already the first European team to qualify for the finals with a perfect seven out of seven wins. The Scots have two matches in hand of Iceland, but Macedonia are level on points with them having beaten the Icelanders. Even so, Norway at the bottom are only four points from the Scots with only five matches played and the Norwegians host the Scots in August.

It is interesting to note that the current standings put the Republic of Ireland, Northern Ireland and Scotland in respectively sixth, seventh and eighth places in the list of runners-up.

As expected the Spaniards are leading the way in Group Five with another six out of six wins. The Euro 2008 title holders are almost in the finals and Bosnia have emerged as the surprise likely runners-up, with neither Turkey nor Belgium able to show any consistency of results.

Surprisingly France have been unable to dominate Group Seven, currently led by Serbia. Moreover the French must travel there in September. Shocks also in Group One where the Swedes have drawn three of their matches and trail behind Hungary and Portugal with unbeaten Denmark just favourites to qualify. For Hungary, if they manage to pip the Portuguese for a play-off spot, it would be a welcome return to international form after decades of poor performances.

In Group Two, Greece and Switzerland are neck and neck with Latvia the surprise package, clinging on in third place. As for the poorest team among the 53 entries San Marino take it with seven defeats out of seven with just one goal for their efforts and 32 conceded.

By mid-June four Asian countries succeeded in gaining final slots: Australia, Japan, North Korea and South Korea. South Africa as hosts qualify automatically.

In the marathon South America group which began two years ago, Brazil have recovered from a couple of indifferent results, but Argentina have slipped a little. After 14 matches with four to play only five points separate Brazil, Chile, Paraguay and the Argentines.

WORLD CUP 2010 QUALIFYING RESULTS

■ *Denotes player sent off.*

EUROPE

GROUP 1

Albania	(0) 0	Sweden	(0) 0
Hungary	(0) 0	Denmark	(0) 0
Malta	(0) 0	Portugal	(1) 4
Albania	(1) 3	Malta	(0) 0
Portugal	(1) 2	Denmark	(0) 3
Sweden	(0) 2	Hungary	(0) 1
Denmark	(2) 3	Malta	(0) 0
Hungary	(0) 2	Albania	(0) 0
Sweden	(0) 0	Portugal	(0) 0
Malta	(0) 0	Hungary	(1) 1
Portugal	(0) 0	Albania	(0) 0
Malta	(0) 0	Albania	(0) 0
Albania	(0) 0	Hungary	(1) 1
Malta	(0) 0	Denmark	(2) 3
Portugal	(0) 0	Sweden	(0) 0
Denmark	(2) 3	Albania	(0) 0
Hungary	(1) 3	Malta	(0) 0
Albania	(1) 1	Portugal	(1) 2
Sweden	(0) 0	Denmark	(1) 1
Sweden	(1) 4	Malta	(0) 0

Group 1 Table	P	W	D	L	F	A	Pts
Denmark	6	5	1	0	13	2	16
Hungary	6	4	1	1	8	2	13
Portugal	6	2	3	1	8	4	9
Sweden	6	2	3	1	6	2	9
Albania	8	1	3	4	4	8	6
Malta	8	0	1	7	0	21	1

GROUP 2

Israel	(0) 2	Switzerland	(1) 2
Luxembourg	(0) 0	Greece	(2) 3
Moldova	(0) 1	Latvia	(2) 2
Latvia	(0) 0	Greece	(1) 2
Moldova	(1) 1	Israel	(2) 2
Switzerland	(1) 1	Luxembourg	(1) 2
Greece	(2) 3	Moldova	(0) 0
Luxembourg	(1) 1	Israel	(1) 3
Switzerland	(0) 2	Latvia	(0) 1
Greece	(0) 1	Switzerland	(1) 2
Latvia	(0) 1	Israel	(0) 1
Luxembourg	(0) 0	Moldova	(0) 0
Israel	(0) 1	Greece	(1) 1
Luxembourg	(0) 0	Latvia	(1) 4
Moldova	(0) 0	Switzerland	(1) 2
Greece	(1) 2	Israel	(0) 1
Latvia	(1) 2	Luxembourg	(0) 0
Switzerland	(1) 2	Moldova	(0) 0

		P	W	D	L	F	A	Pts
Group 2 Table		P	W	D	L	F	A	Pts
Greece		6	4	1	1	12	4	13
Switzerland		6	4	1	1	11	6	13
Latvia		6	3	1	2	10	6	10
Israel		6	2	3	1	10	8	9
Luxembourg		6	1	1	4	3	13	4
Moldova		6	0	1	5	2	11	1

GROUP 3

Poland	(1) 1	Slovenia	(1) 1
Slovakia	(0) 2	Northern Ireland	(0) 1
Northern Ireland	(0) 0	Czech Republic	(0) 0
San Marino	(0) 0	Poland	(1) 2
Slovenia	(1) 2	Slovakia	(0) 1
Poland	(1) 2	Czech Republic	(0) 1
San Marino	(1) 1	Slovakia	(2) 3
Slovenia	(0) 2	Northern Ireland	(0) 0
Czech Republic	(0) 1	Slovenia	(0) 0
Northern Ireland	(2) 4	San Marino	(0) 0
Slovakia	(0) 2	Poland	(0) 1
San Marino	(0) 0	Czech Republic	(0) 3
San Marino	(0) 0	Northern Ireland	(2) 3
Northern Ireland	(1) 3	Poland	(1) 2
Slovenia	(0) 0	Czech Republic	(0) 0
Czech Republic	(1) 1	Slovakia	(1) 2
Northern Ireland	(0) 1	Slovenia	(0) 0
Poland	(4) 10	San Marino	(0) 0
Slovakia	(5) 7	San Marino	(0) 0

Bratislava, 6 September 2008, 5,445

Slovakia (0) 2 *(Skrtel 46, Hamsik 70)*

Northern Ireland (0) 1 *(Durica 81 (og))*

Slovakia: Senecky; Skrtel, Petras, Pekarik, Durica, Sapara, Kozak, Karhan (Zabavnik 75), Hamsik, Vittek (Mintal 84), Jakubko (Svento 59).
Northern Ireland: Taylor; Baird (Shiels 78), McCartney, Evans, Hughes, Craigan, Davis, Clingan, Gillespie (Feeney 53), Healy, Paterson (Brunt 66).
Referee: Ivanov (Russia).

Belfast, 10 September 2008, 12,882

Northern Ireland (0) 0

Czech Republic (0) 0

Northern Ireland: Taylor; Evans, Hughes, McCartney, Baird, Craigan, Brunt, Clingan (O'Connor 46), Feeney (Paterson 72), Gillespie (Shiels 83), Healy.
Czech Republic: Cech; Jankulovski, Kovac R, Rozehnal, Ujfalusi, Grygera, Plasil, Polak, Sionko (Pospech 67), Sirl, Baros (Slepicka 77).
Referee: Bebek (Croatia).

Maribor, 11 October 2008, 12,385

Slovenia (0) 2 *(Novakovic 84, Ljubijankic 85)*

Northern Ireland (0) 0

Slovenia: Handanovic; Suler, Kirm (Matic 90), Ilic, Cesar, Brecko, Koren, Komac, Sisic (Birsa 81), Novakovic, Dedic (Ljubijankic 69).
Northern Ireland: Taylor; Baird, McCartney, McAuley, Hughes, Evans, Gillespie, McCann (McGivern 73), Lafferty, Healy, Davis.
Referee: Gonzalez (Spain).

Belfast, 15 October 2008, 12,957

Northern Ireland (2) 4 *(Healy 31, McCann 43, Lafferty 56, Davis 75)*

San Marino (0) 0

Northern Ireland: Taylor; Baird, McCartney, McCann (Paterson 73), McAuley (McGivern 61), Hughes, Gillspie, O'Connor, Lafferty (Feeney 82), Healy, Davis.
San Marino: Valentini F; Della Valle, Vannucci, Valentini C, Bacciocchi, Albani N, Michele Marani, Mauro Marani[*], Bonini (Vitaioli F 77), Selva A (Vitaioli M 46), Manuel Marani (Cibelli 86).
Referee: Kari (Finland).

Serravalle, 11 February 2009, 1,942

San Marino (0) 0

Northern Ireland (2) 3 *(McAuley 7, McCann 33, Brunt 63)*

San Marino: Valentini F; Della Valle, Berretti, Bacciocchi (Vitaioli F 73), Vannucci, Valentini C, Simoncini D, Muccioli (Bugli 66), Michele Marani, Vitaioli M (Casadei 87), Manuel Marani[*].
Northern Ireland: Taylor; Hughes (McCourt 80), McCartney, McCann, McAuley, Craigan, Johnson, Davis, Lafferty (Brunt 55), Healy, Paterson (Feeney 77).
Referee: Stankovic (Serbia).

Belfast, 28 March 2009, 13,357

Northern Ireland (1) 3 *(Feeney 10, Evans 47, Michal Zewlakow 61 (og))*

Poland (1) 2 *(Jelen 27, Saganowski 90)*

Northern Ireland: Taylor; McAuley, Evans, Craigan, Hughes, Clingan, Johnson, McCann, Feeney (Baird 84), Healy (Little 90), Brunt.
Poland: Boruc; Wasilewski, Michal Zewlakow (Bosacki 65), Wawrzyniak, Roger, Bandrowski (Blaszczykowski 60), Lewandowski M, Krzynowek, Dudka, Jelen (Saganowski 71), Lewandowski R.
Referee: Hansson (Sweden).

Belfast, 1 April 2009, 15,000

Northern Ireland (0) 1 *(Feeney 73)*

Slovenia (0) 0

Northern Ireland: Taylor; Hughes, McCartney (McGivern 44), McCann, McAuley (Baird 16), Evans, Davis, Clingan, Feeney, Healy, Johnson.
Slovenia: Handanovic; Mavric, Kirm (Pecnik 77), Cesar, Brecko (Mejac 85), Koren, Komac, Jokic, Filekovic, Novakovic, Dedic (Ljubijankic 64).
Referee: Yefet (Israel).

Group 3 Table	P	W	D	L	F	A	Pts
Slovakia	6	5	0	1	17	6	15
Northern Ireland	7	4	1	2	12	6	13
Poland	6	3	1	2	18	7	10
Czech Republic	6	2	2	2	6	4	8
Slovenia	6	2	2	2	5	4	8
San Marino	7	0	0	7	1	32	0

GROUP 4

Liechtenstein	(0) 0	Germany	(1) 6
Wales	(0) 1	Azerbaijan	(0) 0
Azerbaijan	(0) 0	Liechtenstein	(0) 0
Finland	(2) 3	Germany	(2) 3
Russia	(1) 2	Wales	(0) 1
Finland	(0) 1	Azerbaijan	(0) 0
Germany	(2) 2	Russia	(0) 1
Wales	(1) 2	Liechtenstein	(0) 0
Germany	(0) 1	Wales	(0) 0
Russia	(1) 3	Finland	(0) 0

Germany	(2) 4	Liechtenstein	(0) 0
Russia	(1) 2	Azerbaijan	(0) 0
Wales	(0) 0	Finland	(1) 2
Liechtenstein	(0) 0	Russia	(1) 1
Wales	(0) 0	Germany	(1) 2
Azerbaijan	(0) 0	Wales	(1) 1
Finland	(1) 2	Liechtenstein	(1) 1
Finland	(0) 0	Russia	(1) 3

Cardiff, 6 September 2008, 17,106

Wales (0) 1 *(Vokes 83)*

Azerbaijan (0) 0

Wales: Hennessey; Morgan, Gunter, Williams A, Bale, Edwards D (Vokes 72), Ledley, Fletcher, Earnshaw (Evans C 62), Davies S, Koumas (Robinson 89).
Azerbaijan: Agayev; Yunisoglu, Malikov, Mammadov N (Nduka 78), Abbasov, Rashad Sadikhov, Mammadov E, Fabio■, Bakhshiyev, Subasic, Huseynov (Nabiyev 46).
Referee: Stavrev (Macedonia).

Moscow, 10 September 2008, 28,000

Russia (1) 2 *(Pavlyuchenko 22 (pen), Pogrebnyak 81)*

Wales (0) 1 *(Ledley 67)*

Russia: Akinfeev; Anyukov, Ignashevich (Bystrov 90), Kolodin, Semak (Pogrebnyak 74), Semshov, Torbinskiy (Saenko 61), Zhirkov, Zyryanov, Arshavin, Pavlyuchenko.
Wales: Hennessey; Morgan, Gunter, Bale, Robinson (Ricketts 46), Edwards D (Evans S 76), Fletcher, Ledley, Williams A, Davies S, Vokes (Evans C 62).
Referee: Skomina (Slovenia).

Cardiff, 11 October 2008, 13,356

Wales (1) 2 *(Edwards D 42, Frick M 80 (og))*

Liechtenstein (0) 0

Wales: Hennessey; Morgan, Gunter, Bale, Williams A, Koumas, Fletcher (Robinson 56), Edwards D, Davies S, Bellamy (Collins J 80), Vokes (Evans C 51).
Liechtenstein: Jehle; Martin Stocklasa, Ritzberger (Christen 67), D'Elia, Polverino (Buchel R 80), Gerster, Burgmeier, Buchel M, Frick M, Fischer, Beck T.
Referee: Vejlgaard (Denmark).

Moenchengladbach, 15 October 2008, 45,000

Germany (0) 1 *(Trochowski 72)*

Wales (0) 0

Germany: Adler; Westermann, Mertesacker, Lahm, Friedrich A (Fritz 65), Trochowski, Schweinsteiger, Hitzlsperger, Ballack, Podolski (Gomez 82), Klose (Helmes 46).
Wales: Hennessey; Gunter (Ricketts 86), Bale, Fletcher (Robinson 77), Morgan, Williams A, Davies S, Collins J, Bellamy, Koumas, Edwards D (Evans C 77).
Referee: Duhamel (France).

Cardiff, 28 March 2009, 22,604

Wales (0) 0

Finland (1) 2 *(Johansson 42, Kuqi S 90)*

Wales: Hennessey; Gunter, Bale, Edwards D (Ramsey 56), Nyatanga, Collins J, Koumas, Fletcher (Robinson 65), Bellamy, Davies S, Ledley (Earnshaw 71).
Finland: Jaaskelainen; Tihinen, Pasanen, Kallio, Hyypia, Eremenko R, Heikkinen, Eremenko A (Sjolund 78), Litmanen (Porokara 90), Johansson, Forssell (Kuqi S 89).
Referee: Gonzalez (Spain).

Cardiff, 1 April 2009, 26,064

Wales (0) 0

Germany (1) 2 *(Ballack 11, Williams A 48 (og))*

Wales: Hennessey; Ricketts (Gunter 54), Bale, Williams A, Nyatanga (Cotterill 75), Collins J, Davies S, Ramsey, Vokes (Evans C 62), Earnshaw, Ledley.
Germany: Enke; Tasci, Mertesacker, Lahm, Beck, Schweinsteiger (Helmes 86), Rolfes (Westermann 79), Hitzlsperger, Ballack, Podolski (Trochowski 72), Gomez.
Referee: Hauge (Norway).

Baku, 6 June 2009, 25,000

Azerbaijan (0) 0

Wales (1) 1 *(Edwards D 41)*

Azerbaijan: Veliyev; Shukurov, Melikov, Levin, Nabiyev (Huseynov 50), Rashad Sadikhov, Fabio (Subasic 46), Zeynalov, Bakhshiyev, Javadov, Akhtyamov (Nadyrov 60).
Wales: Hennessey; Gunter, Eardley, Nyatanga, Morgan, Williams A, Ramsey, Edwards D, Ledley, Earnshaw (Vokes 70), Church (Tudur-Jones 83).
Referee: Strombergsson (Sweden).

Group 4 Table	P	W	D	L	F	A	Pts
Germany	6	5	1	0	18	4	16
Russia	6	5	0	1	12	3	15
Finland	6	3	1	2	8	10	10
Wales	7	3	0	4	5	7	9
Azerbaijan	5	0	1	4	0	5	1
Liechtenstein	6	0	1	5	1	15	1

GROUP 5

Armenia	(0) 0	Turkey	(0) 2
Belgium	(1) 3	Estonia	(0) 2
Spain	(0) 1	Bosnia	(0) 0
Bosnia	(2) 7	Estonia	(0) 0
Spain	(2) 4	Armenia	(0) 0
Turkey	(0) 1	Belgium	(0) 1
Belgium	(2) 2	Armenia	(0) 0
Estonia	(0) 0	Spain	(2) 3
Turkey	(0) 2	Bosnia	(1) 1
Belgium	(1) 1	Spain	(1) 2
Bosnia	(2) 4	Armenia	(0) 1
Estonia	(0) 0	Turkey	(0) 0
Armenia	(1) 2	Estonia	(1) 2
Belgium	(0) 2	Bosnia	(1) 4
Spain	(0) 1	Turkey	(0) 0
Bosnia	(2) 2	Belgium	(0) 1
Estonia	(0) 1	Armenia	(0) 0
Turkey	(1) 1	Spain	(0) 2

Group 5 Table	P	W	D	L	F	A	Pts
Spain	6	6	0	0	13	2	18
Bosnia	6	4	0	2	18	7	12
Turkey	6	2	2	2	6	5	8
Belgium	6	2	1	3	10	11	7
Estonia	6	1	2	3	5	15	5
Armenia	6	0	1	5	3	15	1

GROUP 6

Kazakhstan	(3) 3	Andorra	(0) 0
Andorra	(0) 0	England	(0) 2

Croatia	(2) 3	Kazakhstan	(0) 0
Ukraine	(0) 1	Belarus	(0) 0
Andorra	(0) 1	Belarus	(1) 3
Croatia	(0) 1	England	(1) 4
Kazakhstan	(0) 1	Ukraine	(1) 3
England	(0) 5	Kazakhstan	(0) 1
Ukraine	(0) 0	Croatia	(0) 0
Belarus	(1) 1	England	(1) 3
Croatia	(2) 4	Andorra	(0) 0
Andorra	(0) 0	Croatia	(2) 2
England	(1) 2	Ukraine	(0) 1
Kazakhstan	(1) 1	Belarus	(0) 5
Belarus	(2) 5	Andorra	(0) 1
Croatia	(1) 2	Ukraine	(1) 2
Kazakhstan	(0) 0	England	(2) 4
England	(3) 6	Andorra	(0) 0
Ukraine	(1) 2	Kazakhstan	(1) 1

Barcelona, 6 September 2008, 10,300

Andorra (0) 0

England (0) 2 *(Cole J 48, 55)*

Andorra: Koldo; Lima T (Juli Fernandez 90), Lima I, Txema, Xavi, Vieira, Pujol (Vales 90), Ayala, Jimenez, Sonejee, Fernando Silva (Toscano 65).
England: James; Johnson G, Cole A, Barry, Terry, Lescott, Walcott, Lampard (Beckham 80), Rooney, Defoe (Heskey 46), Downing (Cole J 46).
Referee: Cuneyt (Turkey).

Zagreb, 10 September 2008, 35,218

Croatia (0) 1 *(Mandzukic 78)*

England (1) 4 *(Walcott 26, 59, 82, Rooney 63)*

Croatia: Pletikosa; Corluka, Simunic, Kovac R■, Srna, Rakitic, Pranjic, Modric, Kovac N (Pokrivac 62), Petric (Knezevic 56), Olic (Mandzukic 73).
England: James; Terry (Upson 89), Ferdinand, Cole A, Brown, Lampard, Cole J (Jenas 56), Barry, Walcott (Beckham 85), Rooney, Heskey.
Referee: Michel (Slovakia).

Wembley, 11 October 2008, 89,107

England (0) 5 *(Ferdinand 52, Rooney 76, 86, Defoe 90, Kuchma 64 (og))*

Kazakhstan (0) 1 *(Kukeyev 68)*

England: James; Brown, Cole A, Gerrard, Ferdinand, Upson, Walcott (Beckham 79), Lampard, Heskey, Rooney (Defoe 86), Barry (Wright-Phillips 46).
Kazakhstan: Mokin; Kuchma, Kislitsyn, Kirov (Sabalakov 85), Kukeyev, Baltiyev, Logvinenko, Ibrayev, Skorykh, Ostapenko (Maltsev 76), Nusserbayev.
Referee: Allaerts (Belgium).

Minsk, 15 October 2008, 32,000

Belarus (1) 1 *(Sitko 28)*

England (1) 3 *(Gerrard 11, Rooney 50, 74)*

Belarus: Zhevnov; Verkhovtsov, Filipenko, Omelyanchuk, Molosh, Kulchi, Sitko, Putsilo (Rodionov 67), Stasevich (Hleb V 90), Kutuzov (Strakanovich 77), Bulyga.
England: James; Brown, Bridge, Gerrard, Ferdinand, Upson, Walcott (Wright-Phillips 68), Lampard, Heskey (Crouch 70), Rooney (Beckham 87), Barry.
Referee: Hauge (Norway).

Wembley, 1 April 2009, 87,548

England (1) 2 *(Crouch 29, Terry 85)*

Ukraine (0) 1 *(Shevchenko 74)*

England: James; Johnson G, Cole A, Barry, Terry, Ferdinand (Jagielka 88), Lennon (Beckham 58), Lampard, Crouch (Wright-Phillips 79), Rooney, Gerrard.
Ukraine: Pyatov; Chigrinskiy, Shevchuk, Yarmash, Mikhalik, Valyaev (Nazarenko 61), Slyusar (Kalinichenko 89), Aliev, Tymoshchuk, Voronin (Shevchenko 55), Milevskiy.
Referee: Bo Larsen (Denmark).

Almaty, 6 June 2009, 24,000

Kazakhstan (0) 0

England (2) 4 *(Barry 39, Heskey 45, Rooney 72, Lampard 78 (pen))*

Kazakhstan: Mokin; Abdulin, Kirov, Kislitsyn, Karpovich, Logvinenko, Kukeev, Skorykh, Averchenko (Erbes 74), Ostapenko (Ibraev 27), Nuserbaev.
England: Green; Johnson G (Beckham 76), Cole A, Barry, Terry, Upson, Gerrard, Lampard, Heskey (Defoe 81), Rooney, Walcott (Wright-Phillips 46).
Referee: Jakobsson (Iceland).

Wembley, 10 June 2009, 57,897

England (3) 6 *(Rooney 4, 38, Lampard 29, Defoe 73, 75, Crouch 80)*

Andorra (0) 0

England: Green; Johnson G, Cole A (Bridge 63), Beckham, Terry, Lescott, Gerrard (Young A 46), Lampard, Crouch, Rooney (Defoe 46), Walcott.
Andorra: Koldo (Gomes 89); Lima T (Vales 47), Txema, Ayala, Lima I, Andorra, Vieira, Jimenez, Sonejee, Moreno, Fernando Silva (Juli Fernandez 79).
Referee: Nijhuis (Holland).

Group 6 Table	P	W	D	L	F	A	Pts
England	7	7	0	0	26	4	21
Croatia	6	3	2	1	12	6	11
Ukraine	6	3	2	1	9	6	11
Belarus	5	3	0	2	14	7	9
Kazakhstan	7	1	0	6	7	22	3
Andorra	7	0	0	7	2	25	0

GROUP 7

Austria	(2) 3	France	(0) 1
Romania	(0) 0	Lithuania	(1) 3
Serbia	(1) 2	Faeroes	(0) 0
Faeroes	(0) 0	Romania	(0) 1
France	(0) 2	Serbia	(0) 1
Lithuania	(0) 2	Austria	(0) 0
Faeroes	(0) 1	Austria	(0) 1
Romania	(2) 2	France	(1) 2
Serbia	(2) 3	Lithuania	(0) 0
Austria	(0) 1	Serbia	(3) 3
Lithuania	(1) 1	Faeroes	(0) 0
Lithuania	(0) 0	France	(0) 1
Romania	(0) 2	Serbia	(2) 3
Austria	(2) 2	Romania	(1) 1
France	(0) 1	Lithuania	(0) 0
Lithuania	(0) 0	Romania	(1) 1
Serbia	(1) 1	Austria	(0) 0
Faeroes	(0) 0	Serbia	(1) 2

	P	W	D	L	F	A	Pts
Serbia	7	6	0	1	15	5	18
France	5	3	1	1	7	6	10
Lithuania	7	3	0	4	6	6	9
Austria	6	2	1	3	7	9	7
Romania	6	2	1	3	7	10	7
Faeroes	5	0	1	4	1	7	1

GROUP 8

Cyprus	(1) 1	Italy	(1) 2
Georgia	(0) 1	Republic of Ireland	(1) 2
Montenegro	(0) 2	Bulgaria	(1) 2
Italy	(1) 2	Georgia	(0) 0
Montenegro	(0) 0	Republic of Ireland	(0) 0
Bulgaria	(0) 0	Italy	(0) 0
Georgia	(0) 1	Cyprus	(0) 1
Georgia	(0) 0	Bulgaria	(0) 0
Italy	(2) 2	Montenegro	(1) 1
Republic of Ireland	(1) 1	Cyprus	(0) 0
Republic of Ireland	(0) 2	Georgia	(1) 1
Cyprus	(1) 2	Georgia	(0) 1
Montenegro	(0) 0	Italy	(1) 2
Republic of Ireland	(1) 1	Bulgaria	(0) 1
Bulgaria	(1) 2	Cyprus	(0) 0
Georgia	(0) 0	Montenegro	(0) 0
Italy	(1) 1	Republic of Ireland	(0) 1
Bulgaria	(1) 1	Republic of Ireland	(1) 1
Cyprus	(2) 2	Montenegro	(0) 2

Mainz, 6 September 2008, 4,500

Georgia (0) 1 *(Kenia 90)*

Republic of Ireland (1) 2 *(Doyle K 13, Whelan 70)*

Georgia: Loria; Shashiashvili, Lobjanidze, Khizanishvili (Asatiani 83), Kaladze, Odikadze, Menteshashvili, Kobiashvili, Kenia, Aleksidze (Siradze 61), Iashvili (Mchedlidze 77).
Republic of Ireland: Given; Finnan (McShane 80), O'Shea, Dunne, Rowlands, Whelan, Kilbane, Hunt, Keane, Doyle K (Miller 77), McGeady (Keogh A 87).
Referee: Szabo (Hungary).

Podgorica, 10 September 2008, 12,000

Montenegro (0) 0

Republic of Ireland (0) 0

Montenegro: Poleksic; Batak, Jovanovic, Pavicevic, Tanasijevic, Zverotic, Bozovic (Vukcevic 54), Drincic, Pekovic, Jovetic, Vucinic.
Republic of Ireland: Given; Finnan, Hunt, Dunne, O'Shea, Whelan, Reid A, Doyle K, Keane, Kilbane, McGeady.
Referee: Kaldma (Estonia).

Dublin, 15 October 2008, 55,833

Republic of Ireland (1) 1 *(Keane 5)*

Cyprus (0) 0

Republic of Ireland: Given; McShane, Kilbane, Dunne, O'Shea, Whelan, Gibson, Doyle K (Folan 90), Keane, Duff, McGeady.
Cyprus: Georgallides; Elia, Constantinou, Marangos (Panagi 52), Charalambous, Lambrou (Papathanasiou 46), Makrides, Konstantinou (Yiasoumi 79), Garpozis, Christofi, Okkas.
Referee: Tudor (Romania).

Dublin, 11 February 2009, 45,000
Republic of Ireland (0) 2 *(Keane 73 (pen), 78)*
Georgia (1) 1 *(Iashvili 1)*
Republic of Ireland: Given; Kelly, O'Shea, Whelan, Dunne, Andrews, Duff (Hunt S 80), Doyle K, Keane, Kilbane, McGeady.
Georgia: Lomaia; Lobjanidze, Kvirkvelia, Khizanishvili, Kaladze, Siradze (Aleksidze 77), Menteshashvili (Khmaladze 70), Kobiashvili, Razmadze, Iashvili, Gotsiridze (Merebashvili 68).
Referee: Hyytia (Finland).

Dublin, 28 March 2009, 60,002
Republic of Ireland (1) 1 *(Dunne 1)*
Bulgaria (0) 1 *(Kilbane 74 (og))*
Republic of Ireland: Given; McShane, O'Shea, Whelan, Dunne, Andrews, Kilbane, Hunt S, Keane, Doyle K, McGeady (Keogh A 90).
Bulgaria: Ivankov; Manolev, Angelov S, Stoianov, Milanov (Kishishev 24), Tomasic, Petrov S, Georgiev (Makriev 66), Telkiyski, Popov I (Dimitrov 46), Rangelov.
Referee: Bebek (Croatia).

Bari, 1 April 2009, 41,000
Italy (1) 1 *(Iaquinta 9)*
Republic of Ireland (0) 1 *(Keane 89)*
Italy: Buffon; Grosso, Chiellini, Cannavaro, Zambrotta, Pirlo (Palombo 44), De Rossi, Brighi, Pepe (Dossena 55), Pazzini■, Iaquinta (Quagliarella 90).
Republic of Ireland: Given; McShane, O'Shea, Whelan, Dunne, Andrews (Gibson 54), Kilbane, Hunt S, Keane, Doyle K (Hunt N 63), McGeady.
Referee: Stark (Germany).

Sofia, 6 June 2009, 38,000
Bulgaria (1) 1 *(Telkiyski 29)*
Republic of Ireland (1) 1 *(Dunne 24)*
Bulgaria: Ivankov; Kishishev, Angelov S, Tomasic, Stoianov, Milanov, Telkiyski (Dimitrov 81), Petrov S, Petrov M (Georgiev 61), Bojinov (Makriev 59), Berbatov.
Republic of Ireland: Given; O'Shea (Kelly 82), Kilbane, Dunne, St Ledger-Hall, Whelan, Hunt S (McGeady 71), Andrews, Folan, Keane (Best 74), Duff.
Referee: Bo Larsen (Denmark).

Group 8 Table	P	W	D	L	F	A	Pts
Italy	6	4	2	0	9	3	14
Republic of Ireland	7	3	4	0	8	5	13
Bulgaria	6	1	5	0	6	4	8
Cyprus	6	1	2	3	6	9	5
Montenegro	6	0	4	2	5	8	4
Georgia	7	0	3	4	4	9	3

GROUP 9

Macedonia	(1) 1	Scotland	(0) 0
Norway	(1) 2	Iceland	(1) 2
Iceland	(0) 1	Scotland	(1) 2
Macedonia	(0) 1	Holland	(0) 2
Holland	(1) 2	Iceland	(0) 0
Scotland	(0) 0	Norway	(0) 0
Iceland	(1) 1	Macedonia	(0) 0
Norway	(0) 0	Holland	(0) 1
Holland	(2) 3	Scotland	(0) 0
Holland	(3) 4	Macedonia	(0) 0
Scotland	(1) 2	Iceland	(0) 1

Iceland	(0) 1	Holland	(2) 2
Macedonia	(0) 0	Norway	(0) 0
Holland	(1) 2	Norway	(0) 0
Macedonia	(1) 2	Iceland	(0) 0

Skopje, 6 September 2008, 9,000

Macedonia (1) 1 *(Naumoski 5)*

Scotland (0) 0

Macedonia: Milosevski; Sedloski, Petrov (Grncarov 79), Noveski, Mitreski, Lazarevski, Sumulikoski, Grozdanovski, Pandev (Tasevski 83), Naumoski (Trajanov 69), Maznov.
Scotland: Gordon; Alexander G, Naysmith, Hartley (Commons 66), Caldwell G, McManus, Fletcher D, Brown S, McFadden, Miller (Boyd 81), Robson (Maloney 76).
Referee: Kralovec (Czech Republic).

Reykjavik, 10 September 2008, 9,767

Iceland (0) 1 *(Gudjohnsen 77)*

Scotland (1) 2 *(Broadfoot 18, Robson 59)*

Iceland: Sturulson; Eiriksson (Sigurdsson I 46), Hreidarsson, Saevarsson (Gunnarsson V 78), Steinsson, Gislason, Gunnarsson A (Palmason 64), Sigurdsson K, Hallfredsson, Gudjohnsen E, Helguson.
Scotland: Gordon; Broadfoot, Naysmith, Brown S, Caldwell G, McManus■, Fletcher D, Maloney (Alexander G 79), McFadden (Hartley 79), Robson, Commons (Miller 63).
Referee: Gumienny (Belgium).

Glasgow, 11 October 2008, 50,205

Scotland (0) 0

Norway (0) 0

Scotland: Gordon; Broadfoot, Naysmith, Morrison (Fletcher S 56), Caldwell G, Weir, Robson, Brown, Fletcher D, McFadden (Iwelumo 56), Maloney.
Norway: Knudsen; Hoiland, Waehler, Hangeland, Riise JA, Grindheim, Stromstad (Pedersen 76), Riise BH (Braaten 56), Winsnes, Carew, Iversen.
Referee: Busacca (Switzerland).

Amsterdam, 28 March 2009, 49,552

Holland (2) 3 *(Huntelaar 30, Van Persie 45, Kuyt 76 (pen))*

Scotland (0) 0

Holland: Stekelenburg; Ooijer, Mathijsen, Van der Wiel, De Jong (Afellay 79), Van Bronckhorst, Van Bommel, Kuyt, Huntelaar (Schaars 79), Van Persie (Sneijder 64), Robben.
Scotland: McGregor; Alexander G (Hutton 73), Naysmith, Berra, Caldwell G, Ferguson, Teale (Morrison 84), Fletcher D, McCormack, Miller (Fletcher S 70), Brown S.
Referee: Duhamel (France).
Referee: Rasmussen (Denmark).

Glasgow, 1 April 2009, 42,259

Scotland (1) 2 *(McCormack 39, Fletcher S 65)*

Iceland (0) 1 *(Sigurdsson I 54)*

Scotland: Gordon; Hutton, Naysmith, Morrison (Rae 90), Caldwell G, McManus, Fletcher D, Brown S, Fletcher S (Teale 78), Miller, McCormack.
Iceland: Gunnleifsson; Eiriksson, Steinsson, Sigurdsson I (Bjarnason 81), Gunnarsson A (Jonsson E 70), Danielsson, Sigurdsson K, Palmason, Helguson, Gudjohnsen E, Smarason.
Referee: Einwaller (Austria).

271

Group 9 Table	P	W	D	L	F	A	Pts
Holland	7	7	0	0	16	2	21
Scotland	5	2	1	2	4	6	7
Macedonia	6	2	1	3	4	7	7
Iceland	7	1	1	5	6	12	4
Norway	5	0	3	2	2	5	3

SOUTH AMERICA

Argentina	(2) 2	Chile	(0) 0
Uruguay	(2) 5	Bolivia	(0) 0
Colombia	(0) 0	Brazil	(0) 0
Ecuador	(0) 0	Venezuela	(0) 1
Peru	(0) 0	Paraguay	(0) 0
Bolivia	(0) 0	Colombia	(0) 0
Venezuela	(0) 0	Argentina	(2) 2
Brazil	(1) 5	Ecuador	(0) 0
Chile	(1) 2	Peru	(0) 0
Paraguay	(1) 1	Uruguay	(0) 0
Argentina	(1) 3	Bolivia	(0) 0
Colombia	(0) 1	Venezuela	(0) 0
Paraguay	(2) 5	Ecuador	(0) 1
Peru	(0) 1	Brazil	(1) 1
Uruguay	(1) 2	Chile	(0) 2
Venezuela	(2) 5	Bolivia	(2) 3
Colombia	(0) 2	Argentina	(1) 1
Ecuador	(3) 5	Peru	(0) 1
Brazil	(1) 2	Uruguay	(1) 1
Chile	(0) 0	Paraguay	(2) 3
Uruguay	(1) 1	Venezuela	(0) 1
Argentina	(0) 1	Ecuador	(0) 1
Bolivia	(0) 0	Chile	(1) 2
Paraguay	(1) 2	Brazil	(0) 0
Peru	(1) 1	Colombia	(1) 1
Bolivia	(2) 4	Paraguay	(0) 2
Ecuador	(0) 0	Colombia	(0) 0
Uruguay	(2) 6	Peru	(0) 0
Brazil	(0) 0	Argentina	(0) 0
Venezuela	(0) 2	Chile	(0) 3
Argentina	(0) 1	Paraguay	(1) 1
Ecuador	(1) 3	Bolivia	(1) 1
Colombia	(0) 0	Uruguay	(1) 1
Peru	(1) 1	Venezuela	(0) 0
Chile	(0) 0	Brazil	(2) 3
Paraguay	(2) 2	Venezuela	(0) 0
Uruguay	(0) 0	Ecuador	(0) 0
Brazil	(0) 0	Bolivia	(0) 0
Chile	(2) 4	Colombia	(0) 0
Peru	(0) 1	Argentina	(0) 1
Argentina	(2) 2	Uruguay	(1) 1
Bolivia	(2) 3	Peru	(0) 0
Colombia	(0) 0	Paraguay	(1) 1
Ecuador	(0) 1	Chile	(0) 0
Venezuela	(0) 0	Brazil	(3) 4
Bolivia	(2) 2	Uruguay	(0) 2
Paraguay	(0) 1	Peru	(0) 0
Brazil	(0) 0	Colombia	(0) 0
Chile	(1) 1	Argentina	(0) 0
Venezuela	(0) 3	Ecuador	(1) 1

Argentina	(1) 4	Venezuela	(0) 0
Uruguay	(1) 2	Paraguay	(0) 0
Colombia	(1) 2	Bolivia	(0) 0
Ecuador	(0) 1	Brazil	(0) 1
Peru	(1) 1	Chile	(2) 3
Bolivia	(3) 6	Argentina	(1) 1
Ecuador	(0) 1	Paraguay	(0) 1
Venezuela	(0) 2	Colombia	(0) 0
Brazil	(2) 3	Peru	(0) 0
Chile	(0) 0	Uruguay	(0) 0
Argentina	(0) 1	Colombia	(0) 0
Bolivia	(0) 0	Venezuela	(1) 1
Uruguay	(0) 0	Brazil	(2) 4
Paraguay	(0) 0	Chile	(1) 2
Peru	(0) 1	Ecuador	(1) 2
Ecuador	(0) 2	Argentina	(0) 0
Brazil	(1) 2	Paraguay	(1) 1
Chile	(1) 4	Bolivia	(0) 0
Colombia	(1) 1	Peru	(0) 0
Venezuela	(1) 2	Uruguay	(0) 2

South America Table	P	W	D	L	F	A	Pts
Brazil	14	7	6	1	25	6	27
Chile	14	8	2	4	23	14	26
Paraguay	14	7	3	4	20	13	24
Argentina	14	6	4	4	19	15	22
Ecuador	14	5	5	4	18	20	20
Uruguay	14	4	6	4	23	16	18
Colombia	14	4	5	5	7	11	17
Venezuela	14	5	2	7	17	24	17
Bolivia	14	3	3	8	19	30	12
Peru	14	1	4	9	7	29	7

OCEANIA

GROUP A
Tahiti 0, New Caledonia 1; Fiji 16, Tuvalu 0; New Caledonia 1, Tuvalu 0; Fiji 4, Cook Islands 0; Tahiti 1, Tuvalu 1; New Caledonia 3, Cook Islands 0; Cook Islands 4, Tuvalu 1; Fiji 4, Tahiti 0; Fiji 1, New Caledonia 1; Tahiti 1, Cook Islands 0.
Fiji and New Caledonia qualify for semi-finals.

GROUP B
Solomon Islands 12, American Samoa 1; Samoa 0, Vanuatu 4; Solomon Islands 4, Tonga 0; Samoa 7, American Samoa 0; Vanuatu 15, American Samoa 0; Samoa 2, Tonga 1; Tonga 4, American Samoa 0; Solomon Islands 2, Vanuatu 0; Samoa 0, Solomon Islands 3; Vanuatu 4, Tonga 1.
Solomon Islands and Vanuatu qualify for semi-finals.

SEMI-FINALS
Solomon Islands 2, New Caledonia 3; Fiji 3, Vanuatu 0.

THIRD PLACE
Vanuatu 2, Solomon Islands 0.

FINAL
Fiji 0, New Caledonia 1.

FINAL ROUND
Fiji 0, New Zealand 2; Vanuatu 1, New Zealand 2; Fiji 3, New Caledonia 3; New Zealand 4, Vanuatu 1; New Caledonia 4, Fiji 0; New Zealand 1, New Caledonia 1; New Zealand 0, Fiji 2; New Caledonia 3, Vanuatu 0; Fiji 2, Vanuatu 0; New Caledonia 1, New Zealand 3; Vanuatu 2, Fiji 1; New Zealand 3, New Caledonia 0; New Zealand 0, Fiji 2.

ASIA

FIRST ROUND

Bangladesh 1, Tajikistan 1; Tajikistan 5, Bangladesh 0; Thailand 6, Macao 1; Macao 1, Thailand 7; Vietnam 0, UAE 1; UAE 5, Vietnam 0; Oman 2, Nepal 0; Nepal 0, Oman 2; Syria 3, Afganistan 0; Afganistan 1, Syria 2; Palestine 0, Singapore 4; Singapore v Palestine awarded 3-0; Lebanon 4, India 1; India 2, Lebanon 2; Yemen 3, Maldives 0; Maldives 2, Yemen 0; Cambodia 0, Turkmenistan 1; Turkmenistan 4, Cambodia 1; Uzbekistan 9, Taiwan 0; Taiwan 0, Uzbekistan 2; Kyrgyzstan 2, Jordan 0; Jordan 2, Kyrgyzstan 0 – *Jordan won 6-5 on penalties*; Mongolia 1, North Korea 4; North Korea 5, Mongolia 1; Timor-Leste 2, Hong Kong 3; Hong Kong 8, Timor-Leste 1; Sri Lanka 0, Qatar 1; Qatar 5, Sri Lanka 0; China 7, Myanmar 0; Myanmar 0, China 4; Bahrain 4, Malaysia 1; Malaysia 0, Bahrain 0; Pakistan 0, Iraq 7; Iraq 0, Pakistan 0.

SECOND ROUND

Singapore 2, Tajikistan 0; Tajikistan 1, Singapore 1; Indonesia 1, Syria 4; Syria 7, Indonesia 0; Yemen 1, Thailand 1; Thailand 1, Yemen 0; Hong Kong 0, Turkmenistan 0; Turkmenistan 3, Hong Kong 0.

GROUP 1

Australia 3, Qatar 0; Iraq 1, China 1; China 0, Australia 0; Qatar 2, Iraq 0; Australia 1, Iraq 0; Qatar 0, China 0; China 0, Qatar 1; Iraq 1, Australia 0; China 1, Iraq 2; Qatar1, Australia 3; Australia 0, China 1; Iraq 0, Qatar 1.

GROUP 2

Japan 4, Thailand 1; Oman 0, Bahrain 1; Thailand 0, Oman 2; Bahrain 1, Japan 0; Japan 3, Oman 0; Thailand 2, Bahrain 3; Oman 1, Japan 1; Bahrain 1, Thailand 1; Thailand 0, Japan 3; Bahrain 1, Oman 1; Japan 1, Bahrain 0; Oman 2, Thailand 1.

GROUP 3

South Korea 4, Turkmenistan 0; Jordan 0, North Korea 1; North Korea 0, South Korea 0; Turkmenistan 0, Jordan 2; South Korea 2, Jordan 0; Turkmenistan 0, North Korea 0; North Korea 1, Turkmenistan 0; Jordan 0, South Korea 1; North Korea 2, Jordan 0; Turkmenistan 1, South Korea 3; South Korea 0, North Korea 0; Jordan 2, Turkmenistan 0.

GROUP 4

Lebanon 0, Uzbekistan 1; Saudi Arabia 2, Singapore 0; Uzbekistan 3, Saudi Arabia 0; Singapore 2, Lebanon 0; Singapore 3, Uzbekistan 7; Saudi Arabia 4, Lebanon 1; Uzbekistan 1, Singapore 0; Lebanon 1, Saudi Arabia 2; Singapore 0, Saudi Arabia 2; Uzbekistan 3, Lebanon 0; Lebanon 1, Singapore 2; Saudi Arabia 4, Uzbekistan 0.

GROUP 5

Iran 0, Syria 0; UAE 2, Kuwait 0; Syria 1, UAE 1; Kuwait 2, Iran 2; Iran 0, UAE 0; Syria 1, Kuwait 0; UAE 0, Iran 1; Kuwait 4, Syria 2; Kuwait 2, UAE 3; Syria 0, Iran 2; Iran 2, Kuwait 0; UAE 1, Syria 3.

GROUP A

Bahrain 2, Japan 3; Qatar 3, Uzbekistan 0; Uzbekistan 0, Australia 1; Qatar 1, Bahrain 1; Australia 4, Qatar 0; Japan 1, Uzbekistan 1; Bahrain 0, Australia 1; Qatar 0, Japan 3; Japan 0, Australia 0; Uzbekistan 0, Bahrain 1; Japan 1, Bahrain 0; Uzbekistan 4, Qatar 0; Australia 2, Uzbekistan 0; Bahrain 1, Qatar 0; Uzbekistan 0, Japan 1; Qatar 0, Australia 0; Japan 1, Qatar 1; Australia 2, Bahrain 0; Bahrain 1, Uzbekistan 0; Australia 2, Japan 1.

GROUP B

UAE 1, North Korea 2; Saudi Arabia 1, Iran 1; North Korea 1, South Korea 1; UAE 1, Saudi Arabia 2; South Korea 4, UAE 1; Iran 2, North Korea 1; UAE 1, Iran 1; Saudi Arabia 0, South Korea 2; North Korea 1, Saudi Arabia 0; Iran 1, South Korea 1; North Korea 2, UAE 0; Iran 1, Saudi Arabia 2; South Korea 1, North Korea 0; Saudi Arabia 3, UAE 2; UAE 0, South Korea 2; North Korea 0, Saudi Arabia 0, UAE 2; UAE 0, South Korea 2; North Korea 0, Iran 0; South Korea 0, Saudi Arabia 0; Iran 1, UAE 0; South Korea 1, Iran 1; Saudi Arabia 0, North Korea 0.

CONCACAF

FIRST ROUND

Dominican Republic v Puerto Rico not played; Puerto Rico 1, Dominican Republic 0; US Virgin Islands v Grenada not played; Grenada 10, US Virgin Islands 0; Surinam v Monserrat not played; Monserrat 1, Surinam 7; Bermuda 1, Cayman Islands 1; Cayman Islands 1, Bermuda 3; Belize 3, St Kitts & Nevis 1; St Kitts & Nevis 1, Belize 1; Nicaragua 0, Netherlands Antilles 1; Netherlands Antilles 2, Nicaragua 0; Dominica 1, Barbados 1; Barbados 1, Dominica 0; Aruba 0, Antigua & Barbuda 3; Antigua & Barbuda 1, Aruba 0; Turks & Caicos 2, St Lucia 1; St Lucia 2, Turks & Caicos 0; El Salvador 12, Anguilla 0; Anguilla 0, El Salvador 4; Bahamas 1, British Virgin Islands 1; British Virgin Islands 2, Bahamas 2.

SECOND ROUND

Honduras 4, Puerto Rico 0; Puerto Rico 2, Honduras 2; Belize 0, Mexico 2; Mexico 7, Belize 0; Surinam 1, Guyana 0; Guyana 1, Surinam 2; Grenada 2, Costa Rica 2; Costa Rica 3, Grenada 0; Guatemala 6, St Lucia 1; St Lucia 1, Guatemala 3; St Vincent & the Grenadines 0, Canada 3; Canada 4, St Vincent & the Grenadines 1; Trinidad & Tobago 1, Bermuda 2; Bermuda 0, Trinidad & Tobago 2; Haiti 0, Netherlands Antilles 0; Netherlands Antilles 0, Haiti 1; USA 8, Barbados 0; Barbados 0, USA 1; Panama 1, El Salvador 0; El Salvador 3, Panama 1; Antigua & Barbuda 3, Cuba 4; Cuba 4, Antigua & Barbuda 0; Jamaica 7, Bahamas 0; Bahamas 0, Jamaica 6.

SEMI-FINAL

GROUP A

Cuba 1, Trinidad & Tobago 3; Guatemala 0, USA 1; Trinidad & Tobago 1, Guatemala 1; Cuba 0, USA 1; USA 3, Trinidad & Tobago 0; Guatemala 4, Cuba 1; USA 6, Cuba 1; Guatemala 0, Trinidad & Tobago 0; Cuba 2, Guatemala 1; Trinidad & Tobago 2, USA 1; USA 2, Guatemala 0; Trinidad & Tobago 3, Cuba 0.

GROUP B

Canada 1, Jamaica 1; Mexico 2, Honduras 1; Mexico 3, Jamaica 0; Canada 1, Honduras 2; Mexico 2, Canada 1; Honduras 2, Jamaica 0; Jamaica 1, Mexico 0; Honduras 3, Canada 1; Jamaica 1, Honduras 0; Canada 2, Mexico 2; Jamaica 3, Canada 0; Honduras 1, Mexico 0.

GROUP C

Haiti 2, Surinam 2; Costa Rica 1, El Salvador 0; Costa Rica 7, Surinam 0; El Salvador 5, Haiti 0; Surinam 0, El Salvador 2; Haiti 1, Costa Rica 3; Surinam 1, Costa Rica 4; Haiti 0, El Salvador 0; Costa Rica 2, Haiti 0; El Salvador 3, Surinam 0; El Salvador 1, Costa Rica 3; Surinam 1, Haiti 1.

FINAL ROUND

USA 2, Mexico 0; El Salvador 2, Trinidad & Tobago 2; Costa Rica 2, Honduras 0; Trinidad & Tobago 1, Honduras 1; Mexico 2, Costa Rica 0; El Salvador 2, USA 2; USA 3, Trinidad & Tobago 0; Honduras 3, Mexico 1; Costa Rica 1, El Salvador 0; Costa Rica 3, USA 1; Trinidad & Tobago 2, Costa Rica 3; El Salvador 2, Mexico 1; USA 2, Honduras 1; Mexico 2, Trinidad & Tobago 1; Honduras 1, El Salvador 0. *Remaining Fixtures:* Honduras v Costa Rica; Trinidad & Tobago v El Salvador; Mexico v USA; Honduras v Trinidad & Tobago; USA v El Salvador; Costa Rica v Mexico; El Salvador v Costa Rica; Mexico v Honduras; Trinidad & Tobago v USA; Costa Rica v Trinidad & Tobago; Mexico v El Salvador; Honduras v USA; USA v Costa Rica; Trinidad & Tobago v Mexico; El Salvador v Honduras.

AFRICA

FIRST ROUND

Madagascar 6, Comoros 2; Comoros 0, Madagascar 4; Sierra Leone 1, Guinea-Bissau 0; Guinea-Bissau 0, Sierra Leone 0; Djibouti 1, Somalia 0; Somalia v Djibouti not played.

GROUP 1

Tanzania 1, Mauritius 1; Cameroon 2, Cape Verde Islands 0; Cape Verde Islands 1, Tanzania 0; Mauritius 0, Cameroon 3; Tanzania 0, Cameroon 0; Mauritius 0, Cape Verde Islands 1; Cameroon 2, Tanzania 1; Cape Verde Islands 3, Mauritius 1; Mauritius 1, Tanzania 4; Cape Verde Islands 1, Cameroon 2; Tanzania 3, Cape Verde Islands 1; Cameroon 5, Mauritius 0.

GROUP 2

Namibia 2, Kenya 1; Guinea 0, Zimbabwe 0; Kenya 2, Guinea 0; Zimbabwe 2, Namibia 0; Kenya 2, Zimbabwe 0; Namibia 1, Guinea 2; Guinea 4, Namibia 0; Zimbabwe 0, Kenya 0; Kenya 1, Namibia 2; Zimbabwe 0, Guinea 0; Namibia 4, Zimbabwe 2; Guinea 3, Kenya 2.

GROUP 3

Uganda 1, Niger 0; Angola 3, Benin 0; Niger 1, Angola 2; Benin 4, Uganda 1; Uganda 3, Angola 1; Niger 0, Benin 2; Angola 0, Uganda 0; Benin 2, Niger 0; Benin 3, Angola 2; Niger 3, Uganda 1; Uganda 2, Benin 1; Angola 3, Niger 1.

GROUP 4

Equatorial Guinea 2, Sierra Leone 0; Nigeria 2, South Africa 0; South Africa 4, Equatorial Guinea 1; Sierra Leone 0, Nigeria 1; Sierra Leone 1, South Africa 0; Equatorial Guinea 0, Nigeria 1; Nigeria 2, Equatorial Guinea 0; South Africa 0, Sierra Leone 0; South Africa 1, Sierra Leone 2, Equatorial Guinea 1; Equatorial Guinea 0, South Africa 1; Nigeria 4, Sierra Leone 1.

GROUP 5

Gabon v Lesotho not played; Ghana 3, Libya 0; Libya 1, Gabon 0; Lesotho 2, Ghana 3; Gabon 2, Ghana 0; Lesotho 0, Libya 1; Ghana 2, Gabon 0; Libya 4, Lesotho 0; Gabon 2, Lesotho 0; Libya 1, Ghana 0; Lesotho 0, Gabon 3; Gabon 1, Libya 0; Ghana 3, Lesotho 0.

GROUP 6

Senegal 1, Algeria 0; Liberia 1, Gambia 1; Algeria 3, Liberia 0; Gambia 0, Senegal 0; Gambia 1, Algeria 0; Liberia 2, Senegal 2; Algeria 1, Gambia 0; Senegal 3, Liberia 1; Algeria 3, Senegal 2; Gambia 3, Liberia 0; Liberia 0, Algeria 0; Senegal 1, Gambia 1.

GROUP 7

Botswana 0, Madagascar 0; Ivory Coast 1, Mozambique 0; Madagascar 0, Ivory Coast 0; Mozambique 1, Botswana 2; Botswana 1, Ivory Coast 1; Madagascar 1, Mozambique 1; Ivory Coast 4, Botswana 0; Mozambique 3, Madagascar 0; Madagascar 1, Botswana 0; Mozambique 1, Ivory Coast 1; Botswana 0, Mozambique 1; Ivory Coast 3, Madagascar 0.

GROUP 8

Rwanda 1, Mauritania 0; Morocco 3, Ethiopia 0; Mauritania 1, Morocco 4; Ethiopia 1, Rwanda 2; Mauritania 0, Ethiopia 1; Rwanda 3, Morocco 1; Ethiopia 6, Mauritania 1; Morocco 2, Rwanda 0; Mauritania 0, Rwanda 1; Morocco 4, Mauritania 1.

GROUP 9

Burundi 1, Seychelles 0; Tunisia 1, Burkina Faso 2; Seychelles 0, Tunisia 2; Burkina Faso 2, Burundi 0; Seychelles 2, Burkina Faso 3; Burundi 0, Tunisia 1; Burkina Faso 4, Seychelles 1; Tunisia 2, Burundi 1; Seychelles 1, Burundi 2; Burkina Faso 0, Tunisia 0; Tunisia 5, Seychelles 0; Burundi 1, Burkina Faso 3.

GROUP 10

Sudan v Chad not played; Mali 4, Congo 2; Chad 1, Mali 2; Congo 1, Sudan 0; Chad 2, Congo 1; Sudan 3, Mali 2; Congo 2, Chad 0; Mali 3, Sudan 0; Sudan 1, Chad 2; Congo 1, Mali 0; Chad 1, Sudan 3; Sudan 2, Congo 0; Mali 2, Chad 1.

GROUP 11

Togo 1, Zambia 0; Swaziland 2, Togo 1; Swaziland 0, Zambia 0; Zambia 1, Swaziland 0; Zambia 1, Togo 0; Togo 6, Swaziland 0.

GROUP 12

Malawi 8, Djibouti 1; Egypt 2, Congo DR 1; Djibouti 0, Egypt 4; Congo DR 1, Malawi 0; Djibouti 0, Congo DR 6; Malawi 1, Egypt 0; Egypt 2, Malawi 0; Congo DR 5, Djibouti 1; Djibouti 0, Malawi 3; Congo DR 0, Egypt 1; Malawi 2, DR Congo 1; Egypt 4, Djibouti 0.

GROUP A

Togo 1, Cameroon 0; Morocco 1, Gabon 2; Cameroon 0, Morocco 0; Gabon 3, Togo 0; Morocco 0, Togo 0.
Remaining Fixtures: Gabon v Cameroon; Cameroon v Gabon; Togo v Morocco; Cameroon v Togo; Gabon v Morocco; Morocco v Cameroon; Togo v Gabon.

GROUP B

Kenya 1, Tunisia 2; Mozambique 0, Nigeria 0; Tunisia 2, Mozambique 0; Nigeria 3, Kenya 0; Tunisia 0, Nigeria 0; Kenya 2, Mozambique 1.
Remaining Fixtures: Mozambique v Kenya; Nigeria v Tunisia; Tunisia v Kenya; Nigeria v Mozambique; Kenya v Nigeria; Mozambique v Tunisia.

GROUP C

Rwanda 0, Algeria 0; Egypt 1, Zambia 1; Zambia 1, Rwanda 0; Algeria 3, Egypt 1; Zambia 0, Algeria 2.
Remaining Fixtures: Egypt v Rwanda; Algeria v Zambia; Rwanda v Egypt; Zambia v Egypt; Algeria v Rwanda; Egypt v Algeria; Rwanda v Zambia.

GROUP D

Sudan 1, Mali 1; Ghana 1, Benin 0; Benin 1, Sudan 0; Mali 0, Ghana 2; Mali 3, Benin 1; Sudan 0, Ghana 2.
Remaining Fixtures: Benin v Mali; Ghana v Sudan; Benin v Ghana; Mali v Sudan; Sudan v Benin; Ghana v Mali.

GROUP E

Burkina Faso 4, Guinea 2; Ivory Coast 5, Malawi 0; Malawi 0, Burkina Faso 1; Guinea1, Ivory Coast 2; Burkina Faso 2, Ivory Coast 3; Guinea 2, Malawi 1.
Remaining Fixtures: Ivory Coast v Burkina Faso; Malawi v Guinea; Guinea v Burkina Faso; Malawi v Ivory Coast; Burkina Faso v Malawi; Ivory Coast v Guinea.

WORLD CUP 2010 REMAINING FIXTURES

EUROPE

GROUP 1

05.09.09 Denmark v Portugal; Hungary v Sweden.
09.09.09 Albania v Denmark; Malta v Sweden; Hungary v Portugal.
10.10.09 Denmark v Sweden; Portugal v Hungary.
14.10.09 Sweden v Albania; Denmark v Hungary; Portugal v Malta.

GROUP 2

05.09.09 Switzerland v Greece; Israel v Latvia; Moldova v Luxembourg.
09.09.09 Moldova v Greece; Israel v Luxembourg; Latvia v Switzerland.
10.10.09 Greece v Latvia; Israel v Moldova; Luxembourg v Switzerland.
14.10.09 Greece v Luxembourg; Switzerland v Israel; Latvia v Moldova.

GROUP 3

19.08.09 Slovenia v San Marino.
05.09.09 Poland v Northern Ireland; Slovakia v Czech Republic.
09.09.09 Northern Ireland v Slovakia; Slovenia v Poland; Czech Republic v San Marino.
10.10.09 Czech Republic v Poland; Slovakia v Slovenia.
14.10.09 San Marino v Slovenia; Czech Republic v Northern Ireland; Poland v Slovakia.

GROUP 4

19.08.09 Azerbaijan v Germany.
05.09.09 Azerbaijan v Finland; Russia v Liechtenstein.
09.09.09 Wales v Russia; Germany v Azerbaijan; Liechtenstein v Finland.
10.10.09 Liechtenstein v Azerbaijan; Finland v Wales; Russia v Germany.
14.10.09 Azerbaijan v Russia; Germany v Finland; Liechtenstein v Wales.

GROUP 5

05.09.09 Armenia v Bosnia; Spain v Belgium; Turkey v Estonia.
09.09.09 Armenia v Belgium; Bosnia v Turkey; Spain v Estonia.
10.10.09 Armenia v Spain; Belgium v Turkey; Estonia v Bosnia.
14.10.09 Turkey v Armenia; Estonia v Belgium; Bosnia v Spain.

GROUP 6

19.08.09 Belarus v Croatia.
05.09.09 Ukraine v Andorra; Croatia v Belarus.
09.09.09 Andorra v Kazakhstan; Belarus v Ukraine; England v Croatia.
10.09.09 Ukraine v Kazakhstan.
10.10.09 Belarus v Kazakhstan; Ukraine v England.
14.10.09 Andorra v Ukraine; England v Belarus; Kazakhstan v Croatia.

GROUP 7

19.08.09 Faeroes v France.
05.09.09 Austria v Faeroes; France v Romania.
09.09.09 Faeroes v Lithuania; Serbia v France; Romania v Austria.
10.10.09 France v Faeroes; Austria v Lithuania; Serbia v Romania.
14.10.09 Romania v Faeroes; France v Austria; Lithuania v Serbia.

GROUP 8

10.09.08 Italy v Georgia; Montenegro v Eire.
11.10.08 Bulgaria v Italy; Georgia v Cyprus.
15.10.08 Georgia v Bulgaria; Eire v Cyprus; Italy v Montenegro.
11.02.09 Eire v Georgia.
28.03.09 Eire v Bulgaria; Cyprus v Georgia; Montenegro v Italy.
01.04.09 Georgia v Montenegro; Bulgaria v Cyprus; Italy v Eire.
06.06.09 Bulgaria v Eire; Cyprus v Montenegro.
05.09.09 Bulgaria v Montenegro; Georgia v Italy; Cyprus v Eire.
09.09.09 Italy v Bulgaria; Montenegro v Cyprus.
10.10.09 Montenegro v Georgia; Cyprus v Bulgaria; Eire v Italy.
14.10.09 Bulgaria v Georgia; Eire v Montenegro; Italy v Cyprus.

GROUP 9

19.08.09 Norway v Scotland.
05.09.09 Iceland v Norway; Scotland v Macedonia.
09.09.09 Norway v Macedonia; Scotland v Holland.

SOUTH AMERICA

05.09.09 Paraguay v Bolivia; Argentina v Brazil; Colombia v Ecuador; Peru v
          Uruguay; Chile v Venezuela.
09.09.09 Paraguay v Argentina; Brazil v Chile; Uruguay v Colombia; Bolivia v
          Ecuador; Venezuela v Peru.
10.10.09 Bolivia v Brazil; Colombia v Chile; Venezuela v Paraguay; Argentina v
          Peru; Ecuador v Uruguay.
14.10.09 Uruguay v Argentina; Peru v Bolivia; Paraguay v Colombia; Chile v
          Ecuador; Brazil v Venezuela.

WORLD CUP 2010 – OTHER QUALIFIERS

Denotes player sent off.

AUSTRALIAN GAMES

Melbourne, 6 February 2008, 50,969

Australia (3) 3 *(Kennedy 10, Cahill 18, Bresciano 33)*　　**Qatar (0) 0**

Australia: Schwarzer; Neill, Moore (Holman 77), Cahill (Valeri 67), Culina, Emerton, Wilkshire, Kennedy (Aloisi 70), McDonald, Carney, Bresciano.

Kunming, 26 March 2008, 32,000

China (0) 0　　Australia (0) 0

Australia: Schwarzer; Neill, North, Culina, Beauchamp, Valeri, Wilkshire, Thompson (Holman 10), Carney, Grella, Bresciano.

Brisbane, 1 June 2008, 48,678

Australia (0) 1 *(Kewell 47)*　　**Iraq (0) 0**

Australia: Schwarzer; Beauchamp, North, Culina, Emerton, Wilkshire, McDonald (Holman 65), Kewell (Djite 77), Carney, Grella, Bresciano (Valeri 62).

Dubai, 7 June 2008, 8,000

Iraq (0) 1 *(Mohammed 27)*　　**Australia (0) 0**

Australia: Schwarzer; Coyne (Kennedy 64), Beauchamp, North, Culina, Valeri, Emerton, Wilkshire, Kewell (McDonald), Carney, Grella (Holman 46).

Doha, 14 June 2008, 12,000

Qatar (0) 1 *(Al Khalfan 90)*　　**Australia (1) 3** *(Emerton 17, 56, Kewell 75)*

Australia: Schwarzer; Beauchamp, North, Culina, Valeri, Emerton, Wilkshire, Kewell (Djite 85), Carney, Holman, Bresciano.

Sydney, 22 June 2008, 70,054

Australia (0) 0　　China (1) 1 *(Sun 11)*

Australia: Petkovic; Topor-Stanley, Spiranovic, North, Zadkovich, Valeri, Jedinak (Kilkenny 79), Holland (Williams), Djite, Kewell, Troisi (Sarkies 83).

Tashkent, 10 September 2008, 34,000

Uzbekistan (0) 0　　Australia (1) 1 *(Chipperfield 26)*

Australia: Schwarzer; Neill, Chipperfield, Burns, Emerton, Wilkshire, Kewell (Djite 90), Coyne, Valeri, Holman (Sterjovski 77), Bresciano (Carney 73).

Brisbane, 15 October 2008, 34,320

Australia (2) 4 *(Cahill 8, Emerton 17 (pen), 58, Kennedy 76)*　　**Qatar (0) 0**

Australia: Schwarzer; Neill, Moore, Cahill, Culina, Emerton (Burns 86), Wilkshire, Kennedy, Carney, Chipperfield (Sterjovski 46), McDonald (Holman 68).

Manama, 19 November 2008, 10,000

Bahrain (0) 0　　Australia (0) 1 *(Bresciano 90)*

Australia: Schwarzer; Neill, Cahill (Sterjovski 86), Culina, Wilkshire, Kennedy, Kewell (Holman 71), Carney, Coyne (North 69), Valeri, Bresciano.

Yokohama, 11 February 2009, 66,000

Japan (0) 0　　Australia (0) 0

Japan: Tsuzuki; Nakazawa, Tanaka MT, Uchida, Endo, Matsui (Okubo 57), Tanaka T (Okazaki 83), Nakamura S, Tamada, Nagatomo, Hasebe.
Australia: Schwarzer; Neill, Moore, Cahill (Kennedy 85), Culina, Wilkshire, Chipperfield, Grella, Holman (Garcia 64), Valeri, Bresciano (Carney 90).

Sydney, 1 April 2009, 57,292

Australia (0) 2 *(Kennedy 66, Kewell 73 (pen))* **Uzbekistan (0) 0**

Australia: Schwarzer; Neill, Culina, Beauchamp, Wilkshire, Kewell (Holman 75), Chipperfield, Garcia, Valeri (Jedinak 82), McDonald (Kennedy 61), Bresciano.

Doha, 6 June 2009, 7,000

Qatar (0) 0 Australia (0) 0

Australia: Schwarzer; Neill, Cahill (Garcia 90), Culina, Coyne, Kennedy, Kewell, Chipperfield, Grella (North 73), Valeri, Bresciano (Holman 77).

Sydney, 10 June 2009, 39,540

Australia (0) 2 *(Sterjovski 55, Carney 88)* **Bahrain (0) 0**

Australia: Schwarzer; Milligan, Carney, Culina, Coyne (North 73), Jedinak (Grella 63), Wilkshire, Kewell, Holman (Carle 84), Sterjovski, McDonald.

Melbourne, 17 June 2009, 69,238

Australia (0) 2 *(Cahill 59, 77)* **Japan (1) 1** *(Tanaka MT 39)*

Australia: Schwarzer; Neill, Stefanutto, Cahill (Vidosic 84), Culina, Kennedy, Carle (Burns 77), Grella, Williams (McDonald 77), Sterjovski, North.
Japan: Narazaki; Abe, Tanaka MT, Uchida, Hashimoto (Kohrogi 84), Konno, Okazaki, Matsui (Yano 67), Tamada, Nakamura K, Nagatomo.

JAPANESE GAMES

Saitama, 6 February 2008, 35,130

Japan (1) 4 *(Endo 21, Okubo 54, Nakazawa 66, Maki 90)*
Thailand (1) 1 *(Winothai 22)*

Japan: Kawaguchi; Nakazawa, Komano, Abe, Endo, Uchida, Yamase (Maki 68), Suzuki, Nakamura K, Okubo (Hanyu 87), Takahara (Bando 77).

Manama, 26 March 2008, 26,000

Bahrain (0) 1 *(Hubail 78)* **Japan (0) 0**

Japan: Kawaguchi; Nakazawa, Komano, Yasuda (Yamagishi 71), Abe (Tamada 81), Maki, Suzuki, Nakamura K, Konno, Okubo.

Yokohama, 2 June 2008, 46,764

Japan (2) 3 *(Nakazawa 10, Okubo 22, Nakamura 49)* **Oman (0) 0**

Japan: Narazaki; Nakazawa, Komano, Tanaka MT, Nagatomo (Konno 83), Endo, Matsui, Nakamura S, Tamada (Maki 79), Okubo (Kagawa 72), Hasebe.

Muscat, 7 June 2008, 6,500

Oman (1) 1 *(Mubarak 12)* **Japan (0) 1** *(Endo 53 (pen))*

Japan: Narazaki; Nakazawa, Komano, Tanaka MT, Uchida (Konno 90), Endo, Matsui (Yamase 78), Nakamura S, Tamada (Yano 90), Okubo*, Hasebe.

Bangkok, 14 June 2008, 25,000

Thailand (0) 0 Japan (2) 3 *(Tanaka MT 23, Nakazawa 38, Nakamura K 88)*

Japan: Narazaki; Nakazawa, Komano, Tanaka MT, Uchida, Endo, Kagawa (Konno 82), Matsui (Nakamura K 70), Nakamura S (Yano 70), Tamada, Hasebe.

Saitama, 22 June 2008, 51,180

Japan (0) 1 *(Uchida 90)* **Bahrain (0) 0**

Japan: Narazaki; Nakazawa, Tanaka MT, Uchida, Endo, Sato (Yamase 64), Nakamura S, Tamada, Nakamura K, Yasuda (Konno 73), Honda (Maki 80).

Manama, 6 September 2008, 20,000

Bahrain (0) 2 *(Isa 87, Tanaka MT 89 (og))*   **Japan (2) 3** *(Nakamura S 18, Endo 44 (pen), Nakamura K 85)*

Japan: Narazaki; Nakazawa, Uchida, Tanaka MT, Abe, Endo, Matsui (Nakamura K 70), Nakamura S, Tamada, Tanaka T, Hasebe (Konno 84).

Saitama, 15 October 2008, 55,142

Japan (1) 1 *(Tamada 40)*   **Uzbekistan (1) 1** *(Shatskikh 27)*

Japan: Narazaki; Nakazawa, Tanaka MT, Abe, Endo, Nakamura S, Tamada (Kohrogi 81), Kagawa (Inamoto 76), Uchida, Okubo (Okazaki 62), Hasebe.

Doha, 19 November 2008, 13,000

Qatar (0) 0   Japan (1) 3 *(Tanaka T 19, Tamada 47, Tanaka MT 68)*

Japan: Kawaguchi; Terada, Uchida, Tanaka MT, Endo, Tanaka T (Matsui 71), Nakamura S, Tamada (Sato 90), Nagatomo, Okubo (Okazaki 86), Hasebe.

Saitama, 28 March 2009, 57,276

Japan (0) 1 *(Nakamura S 47)*   **Bahrain (0) 0**

Japan: Narazaki; Nakazawa, Tanaka MT, Uchida, Endo, Tanaka T (Okazaki 86), Nakamura S, Tamada (Matsui 79), Nagatomo, Okubo, Hasebe (Hashimoto 76).

Tashkent, 6 June 2009, 34,000

Uzbekistan (0) 0   Japan (1) 1 *(Okazaki 9)*

Japan: Narazaki; Nakazawa, Komano, Tanaka MT, Endo, Okazaki, Nakamura S (Abe 90), Nakamura K (Honda 66), Nagatomo, Okubo (Yano 69), Hasebe■.

Yokohama, 10 June 2009, 60,256

Japan (1) 1 *(Albinali 3 (og))*   **Qatar (0) 1** *(Yahya 53 (pen))*

Japan: Narazaki; Nakazawa, Tanaka MT, Abe (Matsui 58), Uchida, Hashimoto, Okazaki, Nakamura S (Honda 81), Tamada (Kohrogi 67), Nakamura K, Konno.

SOUTH KOREAN GAMES

Seoul, 6 February 2008, 25,738

South Korea (1) 4 *(Kwak TH 43, Seol 57, 85, Park JS 70)*   **Turkmenistan (0) 0**

South Korea: Jung; Oh BS, Cho YH (Park WJ 85), Kim N (Lee KW 77), Park JS, Park CY, Seol, Lee YP, Kang, Kwak TH, Yeom (Kim DH 31).

Shanghai, 26 March 2008, 20,000

North Korea (0) 0   South Korea (0) 0

North Korea: Ri MG; Ri J, Ri KH, An YH, Hong, Mun, Jong TS (Pak NC 90), Pak SC, Han (Cha 27), Kim YJ, Nam.
South Korea: Jung; Oh BS, Cho WH, Kim N (Kim DH 27), Park JS, Cho JJ (Yeom 46), Park CY, Seol (Han 81), Lee YP, Kang, Lee JS.

Seoul, 31 May 2008, 50,000

South Korea (1) 2 *(Park JS 39, Park CY 48)*   **Jordan (0) 2** *(Mahmoud 73, 81)*

South Korea: Jung; Oh BS, Cho WH, Kim N (Cho YH 76), Kwak HJ, Park JS, Park CY, Lee YP, Lee CY (Kim DH 55), Lee JS, Ahn (Ko 86).

Amman, 7 June 2008, 8,000

Jordan (0) 0   South Korea (1) 1 *(Park CY 24 (pen))*

South Korea: Jung; Oh BS, Cho WH, Kim N, Kwak HJ, Park JS, Park CY, Seol (Cho YH 46), Lee YP (Lee JS 68), Lee KH (Ahn 80), Kang.

Ashgabat, 14 June 2008, 11,000

Turkmenistan (0) 1 *(Ovekov 77 (pen))*   **South Korea (1) 3** *(Kim BH 14, 81, 90 (pen))*

South Korea: Jung; Oh BS (Lee JS 29), Cho WH (Choi HJ 46), Cho YH, Kim N, Lee KH (Lee CY 80), Kim DH, Park CY, Seol, Kim CW, Kang.

Seoul, 22 June 2008, 48,519

South Korea (0) 0   North Korea (0) 0

South Korea: Jung; Kim CW, Oh JE (Lee KH 78), Kim DH, Ahn (Park CY 60), Ko, Choi HJ, Kang, Lee JS, Kim JW (Kim N 71), Lee CY.
North Korea: Ri MG; Cha, Ri J, Ri KC, An YH, Hong (Choe 10), Mun, Jong TS, Pak CJ, Kim YJ (Pak NC 63), Nam.

Shanghai, 10 September 2008, 3,000

North Korea (0) 1 *(Hong 64 (pen))*   **South Korea (0) 1** *(Ki 69)*

North Korea: Ri MG; Cha, Ri J, Ri KC, An YH, Hong, Mun, Jong TS, Park CJ, Kim YJ (Choe 71) (Kim K 89), Nam.
South Korea: Jung; Oh BS (Choi HJ 79), Kim DJ, Kim N, Kim JK, Choi SK (Lee CS 60), Kim DH, Cho JJ (Seol 60), Kim CW, Kang, Ki.

Seoul, 15 October 2008, 30,000

South Korea (2) 4 *(Lee KH 20, 80, Park JS 26, Kwak TH 89)*
UAE (0) 1 *(Al Hammadi 72)*

South Korea: Jung; Cho YH, Kim DJ, Ki (Cho WH 80), Park JS, Lee CY (Kim HB 55), Lee KH (Shin 88), Lee YP, Kim JW, Jeong, Kwak TH.

Riyadh, 19 November 2008, 60,000

Saudi Arabia (0) 0   South Korea (0) 2 *(Lee KH 76, Park CY 90)*

South Korea: Lee WJ; Oh BS, Cho YH, Ki, Park JS, Kim JW, Jeong (Park CY 74), Lee KH (Yeom 89), Lee YP, Kang, Lee CY (Cho WH 90).

Tehran, 11 February 2009, 75,000

Iran (0) 1 *(Nekounam 58)*   **South Korea (0) 1** *(Park JS 81)*

South Korea: Lee WJ; Oh BS, Kang, Cho YH, Park JS (Park CY 84), Kim JW, Jeong (Yeom 41), Lee KH, Lee YP (Kim DJ 70), Ki, Lee CY.

Seoul, 1 April 2009, 48,000

South Korea (0) 1 *(Kim CW 86)*   **North Korea (0) 0**

South Korea: Lee WJ; Oh BS, Kang, Cho WH, Hwang (Lee JS 53), Park JS, Park CY, Lee KH (Kim CW 77), Lee YP (Kim DJ 59), Ki, Lee CY.
North Korea: Ri MK; Cha, Ri J, Pak NC, Ri KC, Ji (Nam SC 80), Hong, Mun, Jong TS, Pak CJ, Kim YJ (Choe 83).

Dubai, 6 June 2009, 4,000

UAE (0) 0   South Korea (2) 2 *(Park CY 9, Ki 37)*

South Korea: Lee WJ; Oh BS, Cho YH, Park JS, Kim JW■, Park CY (Bae 82), Lee KH (Cho WH 51), Lee YP (Kim DJ 59), Lee JS, Ki, Lee CY.

Seoul, 10 June 2009, 32,510

South Korea (0) 0   Saudi Arabia (0) 0

South Korea: Lee WJ; Cho WH, Cho YH, Kim DJ, Park JS, Park CY (Yang 73), Lee KH (Choi TU 84), Lee JS, Kim H, Ki, Lee CY.

Seoul, 17 June 2009, 40,000

South Korea (0) 1 *(Park JS 82)*   **Iran (0) 1** *(Shojaei 52)*

South Korea: Lee WJ; Oh BS, Cho YH, Kim DJ (Lee YP 70), Park JS, Kim JW, Park CY, Lee KH, Lee JS, Ki (Yang 75), Lee CY (Cho WH 46).

NORTH KOREAN GAMES

Ulaan-Baatar, 21 October 2007, 4,870
Mongolia (0) 1 *(Selenge 90)*   **North Korea (3) 4** *(Pak CM 14, Jong CM, 24, 32, 78)*
North Korea: Ri MG (Ju 46); Ri J, Pak NC, Pak CM, Pak SC, Jon, Ri CM (Jong SH 76), Jong CM, Kim KJ, Kim K (So 30), Yun.

Pyongyang, 28 October 2007, 5,000
North Korea (3) 5 *(Park CM 3, 74, Kim KJ 10, Jong CM 36, Jon 90)*
Mongolia (1) 1 *(Donorov 41)*
North Korea: Ju; Cha, Ri J (Ri KH 65), Pak NC, Pak CM, Pak SC, Jon, Ri CM*, Jong CM (So 79), Kim KJ (Ri HR 46), Yun.

Amman, 6 February 2008, 16,000
Jordan (0) 0   North Korea (1) 1 *(Hong 44)*
North Korea: Ri MG; Ri J, Ri KC, An YH, Hong, Mun, Jong TS, Pak CJ (Cha 60), Han, Kim YJ (Ryang 40) (Pak NC 90), Nam SC.

Ashgabat, 2 June 2008, 20,000
Turkmenistan (0) 0   North Korea (0) 0
North Korea: Ri MG; Cha (Han 57), Ri J, Ri KC, An YH, Hong, Mun, Jong TS, Pak CJ, Kim YJ (Pak NC 64), Nam SC.

Pyongyang, 7 June 2008, 25,000
North Korea (0) 1 *(Choe 72)*   **Turkmenistan (0) 0**
North Korea: Ri MG; Cha, Ri J, Pak NC, Ri KC, An YH (Kim YJ 60), Hong (Kim MW 87), Mun, Pak CJ (Han 28), Nam SC, Choe.

Pyongyang, 14 June 2008, 28,000
North Korea (1) 2 *(Hong 44, 72)*   **Jordan (0) 0**
North Korea: Ri MG; Cha, Ri J, Pak NC (Choe 88), Ri KC, An YH, Hong, Mun, Jong TS, Han, Nam SC.

Abu Dhabi, 6 September 2008, 10,000
UAE (0) 1 *(Basheer Saeed 85)*   **North Korea (0) 2** *(Choe 72, An 80)*
North Korea: Ri MG; Cha, Ri J, Ri KC, An YH, Hong (Kim K 71), Mun, Pak CJ, Kim YJ (An CH 29), Nam SC, Choe (Kim MW 86).

Tehran, 15 October 2008, 60,000
Iran (1) 2 *(Mahdavikia 9, Nekounam 63)*   **North Korea (0) 1** *(Jong TS 72)*
North Korea: Ri MG; Cha, Ri J, Ri KC, An YH, Hong, Mun (Pak NC 90), Jong TS, Pak CJ, Kim YJ (Choe 46), Nam SC.

Pyongyang, 11 February 2009, 48,000
North Korea (1) 1 *(Mun 29)*   **Saudi Arabia (0) 0**
North Korea: Ri MG; Cha, Ri J, Pak NC, Ri KC, Ji, An YH (An CH 67) (Kim MW 85), Hong, Mun, Jong TS, Pak CJ.

Pyongyang, 28 March 2009, 50,000
North Korea (0) 2 *(Pak NC 51, Mun 90)*   **UAE (0) 0**
North Korea: Ri MG; Cha, Ri J, Pak NC, Ri KC, Ji, An YH, Hong (Choe 88), Mun, Jong TS, Pak CJ.

Pyongyang, 6 June 2009, 30,000
North Korea (0) 0   Iran (0) 0
North Korea: Ri MG; Cha, Ri J, Pak NC, Ri KC, Ji, An YH, Hong, Mun (Kim YJ 88), Jong TS, Pak CJ.

Riyadh, 17 June 2009, 65,000
Saudi Arabia (0) 0   North Korea (0) 0
North Korea: Ri MG; Cha, Ri J, Pak NC, Ri KC, Ji, An YH, Hong (An CH 60), Mun (Kim K 74), Jong TS (Kim YJ* 89), Pak CJ.

CONFEDERATIONS CUP 2009

(in South Africa)

■ *Denotes player sent off.*

GROUP A

Johannesburg, 14 June 2009, 48,837

South Africa (0) 0   Iraq (0) 0

South Africa: Khune; Gaxa, Masilela, Mokoena, Mhlongo, Sibaya, Modise, Dikgacoi, Booth, Parker (Pienaar 85), Fanteni (Mashego 78).
Iraq: Mohammed Kassid; Mohammed Ali Kareem, Basem Abbas, Fareed Majeed, Nashat Akram, Emad Mohammed (Alaa Abdul Zahra 76), Younis Mahmoud, Karrar Jasim (Hawar Mulla Mohammed 74), Salam Shaker, Ali Hussein Rehema, Mahdi Kareem (Salih Sadir 88).

Rustenburg, 14 June 2009, 21,649

New Zealand (0) 0   Spain (4) 5 *(Torres 6, 14, 17, Fabregas 24, Villa 48)*

New Zealand: Moss; Lochhead, Vicelich, Elliott, Brown, Smeltz (James 76), Killen (Wright 85), Bertos, Brockie (Christie 27), Mulligan, Boyens.
Spain: Casillas; Sergio Ramos (Arbeloa 54), Albiol, Xabi Alonso, Puyol, Capdevila, Xavi (Cazorla 54), Fabregas, Torres (David Silva 70), Villa, Riera.

Mangaung/Bloemfontein, 17 June 2009, 30,512

Spain (0) 1 *(Villa 55)*   **Iraq (0) 0**

Spain: Casillas; Sergio Ramos, Pique, Xabi Alonso, Marchena, Capdevila, Xavi (Busquets 82), Mata, Torres, Villa (Guiza 74), Cazorla (David Silva 67).
Iraq: Mohammed Kassid; Mohammed Ali Kareem, Basem Abbas, Fareed Majeed, Nashat Akram, Hawar Mulla Mohammed (Karrar Jasim 69), Salam Shaker, Ali Hussein Rehema, Alaa Abdul Zahra (Younis Mahmoud 80), Samer Saeed (Mahdi Kareem 60).

Rustenburg, 17 June 2009, 36,598

South Africa (1) 2 *(Parker 21, 52)*   **New Zealand (0) 0**

South Africa: Khune; Gaxa, Masilela, Mokoena, Sibaya, Pienaar, Modise, Dikgacoi, Booth, Parker (Tshabalala 81), Fanteni (Mashego 62).
New Zealand: Moss; Lochhead, Vicelich, Elliott, Brown (Oughton 55), Smeltz, Killen (Wood 75), Bertos (James 66), Christie, Mulligan, Boyens.

Johannesburg, 20 June 2009, 23,295

Iraq (0) 0   New Zealand (0) 0

Iraq: Mohammed Kassid; Mohammed Ali Kareem, Basem Abbas, Nashat Akram, Emad Mohammed (Alaa Abdul Zahra 56), Younis Mahmoud, Hawar Mulla Mohammed (Fareed Majeed 46), Karrar Jasim, Salam Shaker, Ali Hussein Rehema, Mahdi Kareem (Salih Sadir 67).
New Zealand: Moss; Scott (Mulligan 85), Lochhead, Sigmund (Boyens 71), Vicelich, Elliott, Brown, Smeltz, Killen, Bertos, Brockie (Christie 68).

Mangaung/Bloemfontein, 20 June 2009, 38,212

Spain (0) 2 *(Villa 52, Llorente 72)*   **South Africa (0) 0**

Spain: Reina; Arbeloa, Pique, Albiol, Puyol, Busquets, Xavi, Fabregas, Torres (Llorente 60), Villa (Pablo Hernandez 60), Riera (Cazorla 81).
South Africa: Khune; Gaxa, Masilela, Mokoena, Mhlongo, Sibaya (Mashego 83), Pienaar, Modise, Dikgacoi, Booth, Parker (Tshabalala 90).

GROUP B

Mangaung/Bloemfontein, 15 June 2009, 27,851

Brazil (3) 4 *(Kaka 5, 90 (pen), Luis Fabiano 12, Juan 37)*

Egypt (1) 3 *(Zidan 9, 55, Shawky 54)*

Brazil: Julio Cesar; Lucio, Daniel Alves, Juan, Kleber (Andre Santos 83), Gilberto Silva, Kaka, Robinho (Ramires 62), Elano (Alexandre Pato 62), Luis Fabiano.
Egypt: El Hadary; Ahmed Said, Hani Said, Ahmed Fathi, Abd Rabbou (Al Muhamadi 75), Zidan, Shawky, Moawad, Ahmed Hassan (Ahmed Eid 51), Gomaa Aboutrika.

Tshwane/Pretoria, 15 June 2009, 34,341

USA (1) 1 *(Donovan 41 (pen))*   **Italy (0) 3** *(Rossi 58, 90, De Rossi 72)*

USA: Howard; Bornstein (Kljestan 86), Onyewu, Dempsey, Donovan, Bradley, Clark■, DeMerit, Altidore (Davies 66), Spector, Feilhaber (Beasley 72).
Italy: Buffon; Grosso, Chiellini, De Rossi, Legrottaglie, Zambrotta, Pirlo, Camoranesi (Rossi 57), Gattuso (Montolivo 57), Iaquinta, Gilardino (Toni 69).

Tshwane/Pretoria, 18 June 2009, 39,617

USA (0) 0   Brazil (2) 3 *(Felipe Melo 7, Robinho 20, Maicon 62)*

USA: Howard; Bornstein, Onyewu, Beasley (Casey 46), Dempsey, Donovan, Bradley, DeMerit, Kljestan■, Altidore (Feilhaber 60), Spector.
Brazil: Julio Cesar; Maicon, Lucio (Luisao 70), Felipe Melo, Miranda, Andre Santos, Gilberto Silva, Kaka (Julio Baptista 69), Robinho, Ramires, Luis Fabiano (Nilmar 89).

Johannesburg, 18 June 2009, 52,150

Egypt (1) 1 *(Homos 40)*   **Italy (0) 0**

Egypt: El Hadary; Ahmed Said, Hani Said, Ahmed Fathi (Ahmed Hassan 80), Abd Rabbou, Zidan (Ahmed Eid 57), Shawky, Homos, Moawad (Farag 69), Gomaa, Aboutrika.
Italy: Buffon; Zambrotta, Grosso, Chiellini, Cannavaro, De Rossi, Rossi (Montolivo 58), Pirlo, Gattuso (Toni 58), Quagliarella (Pepe 64), Iaquinta.

Tshwane/Pretoria, 21 June 2009, 41,195

Italy (0) 0   Brazil (3) 3 *(Luis Fabiano 37, 43, Dossena 45 (og))*

Italy: Buffon; Zambrotta, Dossena, Chiellini, Cannavaro, De Rossi, Camoranesi, Pirlo, Toni (Gilardino 57), Iaquinta (Rossi 38), Montolivo (Pepe 46).
Brazil: Julio Cesar; Maicon, Lucio, Juan (Luisao 24), Felipe Melo, Andre Santos, Gilberto Silva (Kleberson 84), Kaka, Robinho, Luis Fabiano, Ramires (Josue 86).

Rustenburg, 21 June 2009, 23,140

Egypt (0) 0   USA (1) 3 *(Davies 21, Bradley 63, Dempsey 71)*

Egypt: El Hadary; Al Muhamadi, Hani Said, Ahmed Fathi (Ahmed Said 56), Abd Rabbou, Ahmed Eid (Ahmed Hassan 50), Shawky, Farag, Abdelghani (Abougrisha 62), Gomaa, Aboutrika.
USA: Guzan; Bornstein, Onyewu, Dempsey, Davies (Casey 82), Donovan, Bradley, Clark, DeMerit, Altidore (Feilhaber 69), Spector.

SEMI-FINALS

Mangaung/Bloemfontein, 24 June 2009, 35,369

Spain (0) 0   USA (1) 2 *(Altidore 27, Dempsey 74)*

Spain: Casillas; Sergio Ramos, Pique, Capdevila, Xavi, Puyol, Xabi Alonso, Fabregas (Cazorla 68), Torres, Villa, Riera (Mata 78).
USA: Howard; Bocanegra, Onyewu, Dempsey (Bornstein 88), Davies (Feilhaber 69), Donovan, Bradley■, Clark, DeMerit, Altidore (Casey 83), Spector.

Johannesburg, 25 June 2009, 48,049

Brazil (0) 1 *(Daniel Alves 88)*   **South Africa (0) 0**

Brazil: Julio Cesar; Maicon, Lucio, Felipe Melo, Luisao, Gilberto Silva, Andre Santos (Daniel Alves 82), Ramires, Kaka, Robinho, Luis Fabiano (Kleberson 90).
South Africa: Khune; Gaxa, Masilela, Mokoena, Mhlongo, Tshabalala (Mashego 90), Pienaar (Van Heerden 90), Modise (Mphela 90), Dikgacoi, Booth, Parker.

MATCH FOR THIRD PLACE

Rustenburg, 28 June 2009, 31,788

Spain (0) 3 *(Guiza 68, 89, Xabi Alonso 107)*

South Africa (0) 2 *(Mphela 73, 90)*

Spain: Casillas; Albiol, Pique, Xabi Alonso, Arbeloa, Capdevila, Busquets (Llorente 81), Cazorla, Villa (Guiza 57), Torres (David Silva 57), Riera.
South Africa: Khune; Gaxa, Masilela, Mokoena, Sibaya, Tshabalala (Mhlongo 84), Pienaar (Mphela 90), Modise (Van Heerden 69), Dikgacoi, Booth, Parker.
aet.

FINAL

Johannesburg, 28 June 2009, 52,291

USA (2) 2 *(Dempsey 10, Donovan 27)*

Brazil (0) 3 *(Luis Fabiano 46, 74, Lucio 84)*

USA: Howard; Bocanegra, Onyewu, Dempsey, Davies, Donovan, Clark (Casey 88), DeMerit, Altidore (Bornstein 75), Spector, Feilhaber (Kljestan 75).
Brazil: Julio Cesar; Maicon, Lucio, Felipe Melo, Gilberto Silva, Luisao, Andre Santos (Daniel Alves 66), Kaka, Robinho, Ramires (Elano 67), Luis Fabiano.
Referee: M. Hansson (Sweden).

GOLDEN BALL WINNER
Kaka

GOLDEN SHOE WINNER
Luis Fabiano

GOLDEN GLOVE WINNER
Tim Howard

FIFA FAIR PLAY AWARD
Brazil

PREVIOUS TOURNAMENTS

Year	Winners	Runners-up	Venue
1992	Argentina 3,	Saudi Arabia 1	Saudi Arabia
1995	Denmark 2	Argentina 0	Saudi Arabia
1997	Brazil 6	Australia 0	Saudi Arabia
1999	Mexico 4	Brazil 3	Mexico
2001	France 1	Japan 0	Korea/Japan
2003	France 1	Cameroon 0	France
2005	Brazil 4	Argentina 1	Germany
2009	Brazil 3	USA 2	South Africa

EUROPEAN SUPER CUP

Played annually between the winners of the European Champions' Cup and the European Cup-Winners' Cup (UEFA Cup from 2000). AC Milan replaced Marseille in 1993–94.

EUROPEAN SUPER CUP 2008

29 August 2008, Monaco (attendance 18,064)

Manchester U (0) 1 *(Vidic 73)*

Zenit (1) 2 *(Pogrebnyak 44, Danny 59)*

Manchester U: Van der Sar; Neville, Evra, Anderson (Park 60), Ferdinand, Vidic, Fletcher (O'Shea 60), Scholes■, Rooney, Tevez, Nani.

Zenit: Malafeev; Krizanac (Radimov 71), Dominguez (Arshavin 46), Pogrebnyak, Sirl, Zyryanov, Danny, Anyukov, Denisov, Puygrenier (Shirokov 62), Tymoshchuk.

Referee: Bo Larsen (Denmark).　■*Denotes player sent off.*

Previous Matches

1972	Ajax beat Rangers 3-1, 3-2
1973	Ajax beat AC Milan 0-1, 6-0
1974	Not contested
1975	Dynamo Kiev beat Bayern Munich 1-0, 2-0
1976	Anderlecht beat Bayern Munich 4-1, 1-2
1977	Liverpool beat Hamburg 1-1, 6-0
1978	Anderlecht beat Liverpool 3-1, 1-2
1979	Nottingham F beat Barcelona 1-0, 1-1
1980	Valencia beat Nottingham F 1-0, 1-2
1981	Not contested
1982	Aston Villa beat Barcelona 0-1, 3-0
1983	Aberdeen beat Hamburg 0-0, 2-0
1984	Juventus beat Liverpool 2-0
1985	Juventus v Everton not contested due to UEFA ban on English clubs
1986	Steaua Bucharest beat Dynamo Kiev 1-0
1987	FC Porto beat Ajax 1-0, 1-0
1988	KV Mechelen beat PSV Eindhoven 3-0, 0-1
1989	AC Milan beat Barcelona 1-1, 1-0
1990	AC Milan beat Sampdoria 1-1, 2-0
1991	Manchester U beat Red Star Belgrade 1-0
1992	Barcelona beat Werder Bremen 1-1, 2-1
1993	Parma beat AC Milan 0-1, 2-0
1994	AC Milan beat Arsenal 0-0, 2-0
1995	Ajax beat Zaragoza 1-1, 4-0
1996	Juventus beat Paris St Germain 6-1, 3-1
1997	Barcelona beat Borussia Dortmund 2-0, 1-1
1998	Chelsea beat Real Madrid 1-0
1999	Lazio beat Manchester U 1-0
2000	Galatasaray beat Real Madrid 2-1
	(aet; Galatasaray won on sudden death.)
2001	Liverpool beat Bayern Munich 3-2
2002	Real Madrid beat Feyenoord 3-1
2003	AC Milan beat Porto 1-0
2004	Valencia beat Porto 2-1
2005	Liverpool beat CSKA Moscow 3-1
2006	Sevilla beat Barcelona 3-0
2007	AC Milan beat Sevilla 3-1
2008	Zenit beat Manchester U 2-1

FIFA CLUB WORLD CUP 2008–2009

Formerly known as the FIFA Club World Championship, this tournament is played annually between the champion clubs from all 6 continental confederations, although since 2007 the champions of Oceania must play a qualifying play-off against the champion club of the permanent host country Japan.

SEMI-FINAL

Pachuca (0) 0
Liga De Quito (2) 2 *(Bieler 4, Bolanos 26)*
33,366

Gamba Osaka (0) 3 *(Yamazaki 74, Endo 85
(pen), Hashimoto 90)* 67,618
Manchester United (2) 5 *(Vidic 28, Ronaldo
45, Rooney 75, 79, Fletcher 78)*

MATCH FOR THIRD PLACE

Pachuca (0) 0
Gamba Osaka (1) 1 *(Yamazaki 29)* 62,619

FIFA CLUB WORLD CUP FINAL 2008

Sunday 21 December, Yokohama, Japan (attendance 68,682)

Liga De Quito (0) 0   Manchester United (0) 1 *(Rooney 73)*

Liga De Quito: Cevallos; Araujo N, Calle (Ambrosi 77), Bolanos (Navia 87), Urrutia, Reasco (Larrea 82), Calderon, Araujo W, Bieler, Manso, Campos.

Manchester United: Van der Sar; Rafael (Neville 85), Evra, Carrick, Ferdinand, Vidic■, Ronaldo, Anderson (Fletcher 88), Rooney, Tevez, Evans (51), Park.

Referee: Irmatov (Uzbekistan). ■*Denotes player sent off.*

Previous Matches

2000	Corinthians beat Vaso de Gama 4-3 on penalties after 0-0 draw	2006	Internacional beat Barcelona 1-0
		2007	AC Milan beat Boca Juniors 4-2
2005	Sao Paulo beat Liverpool 1-0	2008	Manchester U beat Liga De Quito 1-0

WORLD CLUB CHAMPIONSHIP

Played annually up to 1974 and intermittently since then between the winners of the European Cup and the winners of the South American Champions Cup — known as the Copa Libertadores. In 1980 the winners were decided by one match arranged in Tokyo in February 1981 which remained the venue until 2004, after which the match was superseded by the FIFA World Club Championship. AC Milan replaced Marseille who had been stripped of their European Cup title in 1993.

1960 Real Madrid beat Penarol 0-0, 5-1; 1961 Penarol beat Benfica 0-1, 5-0, 2-1; 1962 Santos beat Benfica 3-2, 5-2; 1963 Santos beat AC Milan 2-4, 4-2, 1-0; 1964 Inter-Milan beat Independiente 0-1, 2-0, 1-0; 1965 Inter-Milan beat Independiente 3-0, 0-0; 1966 Penarol beat Real Madrid 2-0, 2-0; 1967 Racing Club beat Celtic 0-1, 2-1, 1-0; 1968 Estudiantes beat Manchester United 1-0, 1-1; 1969 AC Milan beat Estudiantes 3-0, 1-2; 1970 Feyenoord beat Estudiantes 2-2, 1-0; 1971 Nacional beat Panathinaikos* 1-1, 2-1; 1972 Ajax beat Independiente 1-1, 3-0; 1973 Independiente beat Juventus* 1-0; 1974 Atlético Madrid* beat Independiente 0-1, 2-0; 1975 Independiente and Bayern Munich could not agree dates; no matches.; 1976 Bayern Munich beat Cruzeiro 2-0, 0-0; 1977 Boca Juniors beat Borussia Moenchengladbach* 2-2, 3-0; 1978 Not contested; 1979 Olimpia beat Malmö* 1-0, 2-1; 1980 Nacional beat Nottingham Forest 1-0; 1981 Flamengo beat Liverpool 3-0; 1982 Penarol beat Aston Villa 2-0; 1983 Gremio Porto Alegre beat SV Hamburg 2-1; 1984 Independiente beat Liverpool 1-0; 1985 Juventus beat Argentinos Juniors 4-2 on penalties after a 2-2 draw; 1986 River Plate beat Steaua Bucharest 1-0; 1987 FC Porto beat Penarol 2-1 after extra time; 1988 Nacional (Uru) beat PSV Eindhoven 7-6 on penalties after 1-1 draw; 1989 AC Milan beat Atletico Nacional (Col) 1-0 after extra time; 1990 AC Milan beat Olimpia 3-0; 1991 Red Star Belgrade beat Colo Colo 3-0; 1992 Sao Paulo beat Barcelona 2-1; 1993 Sao Paulo beat AC Milan 3-2; 1994 Velez Sarsfield beat AC Milan 2-0; 1995 Ajax beat Gremio Porto Alegre 4-3 on penalties after 0-0 draw; 1996 Juventus beat River Plate 1-0; 1997 Borussia Dortmund beat Cruzeiro 2-0; 1998 Real Madrid beat Vasco da Gama 2-1; 1999 Manchester U beat Palmeiras 1-0; 2000 Boca Juniors beat Real Madrid 2-1; 2001 Bayern Munich beat Boca Juniors 1-0 after extra time; 2002 Real Madrid beat Olimpia 2-0; 2003 Boca Juniors beat AC Milan 3-1 on penalties after 1-1 draw; 2004 Porto beat Once Caldas 8-7 on penalties afer 0-0 draw. *European Cup runners-up; winners declined to take part.*

OTHER BRITISH AND IRISH INTERNATIONAL MATCHES 2008–2009

FRIENDLIES

Wembley, 20 August 2008, 69,738

England (1) 2 *(Brown 45, Cole J 90)*   **Czech Republic (1) 2** *(Baros 22, Jankulovski 48)*

England: James; Brown, Cole A, Barry, Ferdinand (Woodgate 58), Terry, Beckham (Jenas 79), Lampard (Bentley 79), Defoe (Heskey 46), Rooney (Downing 68), Gerrard (Cole J 58).

Czech Republic: Cech; Grygera (Pospech 46), Ujfalusi, Rozehnal, Jankulovski, Vlcek (Jarolim 46), Kovac R (Rajnoch 76), Polak, Plasil (Papadopoulos 90), Sirl (Kadlac 76), Baros (Sverkos 46).

Referee: T. Hauge (Norway).

Berlin, 19 November 2008, 74,244

Germany (0) 1 *(Helmes 63)*   **England (1) 2** *(Upson 23, Terry 84)*

Germany: Adler (Wiese 46); Friedrich (Tasci 68), Rolfes, Mertesacker, Westermann, Compper (Schafer 77), Schweinsteiger, Trochowski, Jones (Helmes 46), Klose (Marin 46), Gomez (Podolski 57).

England: James (Carson 46); Johnson, Bridge, Barry, Upson, Terry, Wright-Phillips (Crouch 90), Carrick, Defoe (Bent D 46), Agbonlahor (Young A 77), Downing.

Referee: Busacca (Switzerland).

Seville, 11 February 2009

Spain (1) 2 *(Villa 36, Llorente 82)*   **England (0) 0**

Spain: Casillas (Reina 46); Sergio Ramos, Albiol (Marchena 75), Pique, Xabi Alonso, Iniesta, Villa (Silva 56), Xavi (Guiza 85), Torres (Llorente 64), Capdevilla (Arbeloa 46), Senna.

England: James (Green 46); Johnson G, Cole A, Carrick, Jagielka (Upson 46), Terry, Wright-Phillips, Barry (Lampard 46), Agbonlahor (Cole C 75), Heskey (Crouch 46), Downing (Beckham 46).

Referee: S. Lannoy (France).

Wembley, 28 March 2009, 85,512

England (1) 4 *(Heskey 7, Rooney 70, 90, Lampard 82)*   **Slovakia (0) 0**

England: James (Foster 46); Johnson G, Cole A, Barry, Upson, Terry, Lennon (Beckham 46), Lampard, Heskey (Cole C 15), Crouch (Carrick 74), Rooney, Gerrard (Downing 46).

Slovakia: Senecky; Pekarik, Valachovic, Skrtel, Cech (Jendrisik 46), Karhan (Strba 83), Zabanik, Sestak (Jakubko 72), Kozak (Sapara 62), Hamsik (Mintal 79), Vittek (Holosko 46).

Referee: A. Hamer.

Hampden Park, 20 August 2008, 28,072

Scotland (0) 0   Northern Ireland (0) 0

Scotland: Gordon (McGregor 46); Alexander G, McManus (Barr 46), Weir (Berra 72), Naysmith, Brown S, Thomson (Robson 46), Fletcher D (Stewart 69), Morrison (Commons 62), Miller K, McFadden.

Northern Ireland: Taylor; McAuley (Duff 76), Evans J, Craigan, McGivern, Baird, Clingan (O'Connor 58), Davis, Brunt (Feeney 55), Healy, Paterson (Shiels 46).

Referee: N. Vollquartz (Denmark).

Hampden Park, 19 November 2008, 32,492

Scotland (0) 0   Argentina (0) 1 *(Rodriguez 8)*

Scotland: McGregor; Hutton, Broadfoot, Hartley (Maloney 59), Caldwell G, McManus (Berra 75), Brown S (Alexander G 83), Ferguson (Robertson 59), Iwelumo (Miller L 46), McFadden (Clarkson 67), Commons.
Argentina: Carrizo; Zanetti, Demichelis, Heinze, Papa (Cata Diaz 86), Rodriguez (Sosa 90), Mascherano, Gago, Gutierrez (Gonzalez 71), Lavezzi (Denis 75), Tevez.
Referee: F. Brych (Germany).

Liberty Stadium, Swansea, 20 August 2008, 6,435

Wales (1) 1 *(Koumas 16)*   **Georgia (0) 2** *(Kenia 66, Gotsiridze 90)*

Wales: Myhill; Erdley, Ricketts, Williams A, Morgan, Robinson, Davies S, Fletcher, Eastwood (Earnshaw 80), Koumas, Parry (Vaughan 70).
Georgia: Loria; Lobjanidze, Iashvili (Gotsiradze 79), Khizanishvili, Asatiani, Menteshashvili, Mujiri (Khmaladze 46), Kvakhadze, Odikadze (Devdariani 85), Kenia (Klimiashvili 77), Mchedlidze.
Referee: M. Jug (Slovenia).

Brondby, 19 November 2008, 10,271

Denmark (0) 0   Wales (0) 1 *(Bellamy 77)*

Denmark: Sorensen; Bogelund (Larsen 46), Kroldrup (Jorgensen 60), Agger, Rasmussen T (Andreasen 46), Norregaard, Kristensen (Retov 71), Nordstrand (Mtiliga 46), Bendtner, Romedahl, Krohn-Dehli (Vingaard 60).
Wales: Myhill; Gunter, Bale (Eardley 87), Williams A, Collins J, Nyatanga, Edwards D (Ricketts 46), Bellamy, Evans C (Vokes 60), Ramsey (Tudur-Jones 88), Collison.
Referee: M. Weiner (Germany).

Vila Real, 11 February 2009

Poland (0) 1 *(Guerreiro 79)*   **Wales (0) 0**

Poland: Fabianski (Boruc 46); Wawrzyniak, Lewandowski R (Pawel Brozek 62), Dudka, Krzynowek (Smolarek 46), Boguski (Lobodzinski 46), Murawski (Tralka 75), Wasilewski, Zewlakow, Gargula (Guerreiro 46), Lewandowski M.
Wales: Hennessey (Myhill 46); Gunter, Bale, Ricketts, Williams A, Nyatanga, Collison (Fletcher 46), Bellamy (Cotterill 46), Edwards D, Evans C (Vokes 46), Ledley (Ramsey 46).
Referee: B. Paixao (Portugal).

Llanelli, 29 May 2009, 4,071

Wales (1) 1 *(Earnshaw 26 (pen))*   **Estonia (0) 0**

Wales: Myhill (Hennessey 46); Gunter, Bale, Williams A, Morgan, Nyatanga, Ledley, Ramsey (Edwards D 67), Vokes (Church 59), Earnshaw (Evans C 59) (King A 88), Collison (Allen 80).
Estonia: Kotenko; Sisov, Morozov, Barengrub, Kruglov (Puri E 78), Teniste, Puri S (Kams 65), Dupikov (Marmor 72), Gussev (Konsa 65), Vunk, Vassiljev.
Referee: M. Thorisson (Iceland).

Oslo, 20 August 2008, 16,037

Norway (0) 1 *(Reginiussen 61)*   **Republic of Ireland (1) 1** *(Keane 44)*

Norway: Jarstein; Reginiussen, Hangeland, Winsnes, Riise JA, Stromstad (Haestad 44), Andresen, Hogli, Abdellaoui (Grindheim 80), Helstad (Nevland 57), Holm F (Pedersen 46).
Republic of Ireland: Given (Kiely 46); Finnan (Kelly 69), O'Shea, Dunne, Kilbane, Whelan, McGeady (Hunt S 69), Reid S, Duff, Doyle K (Murphy 64), Keane.
Referee: M. Whitery.

Dublin, 15 October 2008, 55,833

Republic of Ireland (1) 1 *(Keane 5)*   **Cyprus (0) 0**

Republic of Ireland: Given; McShane, O'Shea, Dunne, Kilbane, McGeady, Gibson, Whelan, Duff, Keane, Doyle K (Folan 90).
Cyprus: Georgallides; Elia, Constantinou A, Lambrou (Papathanasiou 46), Charalambous, Christofi, Maragkos (Panagi 52), Makridis, Garpozis, Okkas, Contantinou M (Yiasoumi 79).
Referee: A. Tudor (Romania).

Croke Park, 19 November 2008, 60,000

Republic of Ireland (0) 2 *(Hunt S 88 (pen), Andrews 90)*
Poland (2) 3 *(Lewandowski M 3, Lewandowski R 89, Guerreiro 47)*

Republic of Ireland: Given; McShane (Bruce 61), Kilbane, Whelan, O'Shea, Dunne, Keogh (Hunt S 61), Gibson (Andrews 73), Folan, Doyle K (Hunt N 60), Duff (Long 66).
Poland: Fabianski; Wasilewski, Dudka, Bosacki, Wawrzyniak, Blaszcyzkowski (Lewandowski R 46), Gargula, Lewandowski M, Krzynowek (Jodlowiec 81), Boguski (Peszko 70), Pavel Brozek (Guerreiro 46).
Referee: K. Jakobsson (Iceland).

Fulham, 29 May 2009

Nigeria (1) 1 *(Eneramo 30)*   **Republic of Ireland (1) 1** *(Keane 38)*

Nigeria: Ejide; Adefemi, Sodje, Mohammed, Olofinjana, Aluko (Obinna 61), Uche, Adeleye, Utaka, Akpala (Odemwingie 61), Eneramo.
Republic of Ireland: Given (Westwood 46); Foley (McShane 71), Dunne, St Ledger Hall, Nolan, Lawrence (Hunt S 81), Miller, Andrews (Whelan 59), Duff (McGeady 46), Keane (Long 46), Best.
Referee: W. Collum.

Windsor Park, 19 November 2008, 6,251

Northern Ireland (0) 0   Hungary (0) 2 *(Torghelle 57, Gera 71)*

Northern Ireland: Taylor (Tuffey 46); Duff (McGinn 54), McGivern, Baird, Evans J, Clingan, Gillespie, O'Connor (Feeney 82), Healy (Thompson 88), Lafferty (Shiels 46), Brunt (Paterson 70).
Hungary: Babos; Bodnar, Vanczak, Guhasz, Rudolf, Toth, Halmosi, Vadocz (Dardai 88), Torghelle (Feczesin 81), Gera, Huszti (Dzsudzsak 84).
Referee: R. Schoergenhofer (Austria).

Pisa, 6 June 2009

Italy (1) 3 *(Rossi 20, Foggia 52, Pellissier 72)*   **Northern Ireland (0) 0**

Italy: Marchetti; Santon, Gamberini, Legrottaglie, Grosso (Dossena 46), D'Agostino (Galloppa 75), Gattuso (Palombo 46), Montolivo (Brighi 46), Mascara (Foggia 46), Pazzini (Pellissier 62), Rossi.
Northern Ireland: Tuffey (Mannus 62); Johnson, Casement, Coates, McGivern, Little (Donnelly 82), O'Connor (Garrett 62), McCann, Evans C (Ferguson 78), Carson (Lawrie 70), Healy (McGinn 46).
Referee: K. Blom (Holland).

B INTERNATIONALS

Cumbernauld, 6 May 2009, 2,110

Scotland (1) 3 *(Webster 47, Boyd 75, Griffiths L 84)*   **Northern Ireland (0) 0**

Scotland: Marshall (Turner 78); Cuthbert (Ross 46), Hammell (Easton 46), Arfield (Black 46), Webster, Reynolds, Burke (Bannan 68), Hughes, Clarkson (Griffiths L 74), Naismith, Boyd.
Northern Ireland: Tuffey (Carson 53); Weir (Gibb 46), Casement, McGivern, Lafferty (Duffy 53), McGinn (Norwood 70), Evans C, O'Connor (Garrett 70), McCourt (Ferguson 70), McQuoid (Lawrie 35), Little.

ENGLAND UNDER-21 TEAMS 2008–2009

Denotes player sent off.

Hull, 19 August 2008, 9,733

England (2) 2 *(Richards 25, Milner 38)*

Slovenia (1) 1 *(Velikonja 12)*

England: Lewis (Heaton 46); Richards (Cranie 73), Taylor A, Huddlestone (Muamba 61), Mancienne, Onuoha (Wheater 84), Lennon (Johnson A 73), Noble, Derbyshire, Johnson M (Campbell 61), Milner (Kightly 46).

Wembley, 5 September 2008, 27,732

England (1) 2 *(Milner 44 (pen), Agbonlahor 63)*

Portugal (0) 0

England: Hart; Cranie, Taylor A, Muamba (Cattermole 56), Taylor S, Mancienne, Milner, Huddlestone, Agbonlahor (Campbell 76), Noble, Johnson A (Kightly 86).

Sheffield, 18 November 2008, 18,735

England (1) 2 *(Campbell 10, Gardner 55)*

Czech Republic (0) 0

England: Lewis (Fielding 31); Cranie (Norton 60), O'Hara (Bertrand 80), Muamba (Cork 60), Stearman, Onuoha, Lennon, Gardner (Delph 86), Campbell (Ebanks-Blake 69), Vaughan (Lallana 86), Kightly.

Malaga, 10 February 2009

Ecuador (0) 3 *(Guerron 53, Palacios 54, Caicedo 82)*

England (2) 2 *(Johnson A 14, Campbell 41)*

England: Heaton (Loach 88); Taylor S, Mattock (Gibbs 61), Mancienne, Richards (Cork 46), Stearman, Kightly (Gardner 61), Huddlestone, Campbell, Cattermole (Naughton 76), Johnson A (Welbeck).

Sandefjord, 27 March 2009, 2,014

Norway (0) 0

England (2) 5 *(Campbell 17, Johnson 29, Huddlestone 73, Derbyshire 78, 80)*

England: Hart (Loach 78); Gardiner, Taylor A (Gibbs 46), Muamba (Mancienne 46), Wheater, Onuoha (Derbyshire 46), Cattermole (Milner 67), Huddlestone, Campbell, O'Hara (Cranie 78), Johnson A.

Nottingham Forest, 31 March 2009, 23,632

England (0) 0

France (2) 2 *(Obertan 26, Sissoko 35)*

England: Hart; Cranie (Rodwell 85), Taylor A (O'Hara 85), Mancienne, Wheater (Muamba 46), Onuoha, Milner (Welbeck 71), Huddlestone, Derbyshire (Campbell 60), Noble (Gardner 71), Johnson A.

Milton Keynes, 8 June 2009, 12,020

England (3) 7 *(Mancienne 1, Sadigov 26 (og), Gardner 31, Cattermole 55, Gibbs 64, 70, Rodwell 90)*

Azerbaijan (0) 0

England: Hart (Loach 82); Cranie, Gibbs, Muamba (Rodwell 46), Tomkins, Mancienne, Gardner (Taylor A 46), Cattermole (Lewis 76), Campbell (Stearman 62), Noble (Rose 55), Johnson A.

Halmstad, 15 June 2009

England (1) 2 *(Cattermole 15, Richards 53)*

Finland (1) 1 *(Sparv 33 (pen))*

England: Hart; Cranie, Cattermole, Milner, Agbonlahor (Rodwell 86), Noble, Muamba, Walcott (Campbell 46), Richards (Tomkins 89), Mancienne, Gibbs.

Gothenburg, 18 June 2009

Spain (0) 0

England (0) 2 *(Campbell 67, Milner 73)*

England: Hart; Cranie, Gibbs, Noble, Richards, Onuoha, Milner (Gardner 84), Muamba, Agbonlahor (Campbell 39), Cattermole, Johnson A (Walcott 62).

Halmstad, 22 June 2009

Germany (1) 1 *(Castro 5)*

England (1) 1 *(Rodwell 30)*

England: Loach (Lewis 46); Stearman, Taylor A, Tomkins, Mancienne, Gardner, Johnson A, Rodwell, Campbell (Walcott 58), Rose, Driver (Gibbs 71).

Gothenburg, 26 June 2009

England (3) 3 *(Cranie 1, Onuoha 27, Bjarsmyr 38 (og))*

Sweden (0) 3 *(Berg 68, 81, Toivonen 75)*

aet; England won 5-4 on penalties.
England: Hart; Cranie, Gibbs, Noble (Rodwell 70), Richards, Onuoha, Milner, Muamba (Johnson A 116), Walcott, Agbonlahor (Campbell 60), Cattermole.

Malmo, 29 June 2009

Germany (1) 4 *(Castro 23, Ozil 48, Wagner 79, 84)*

England (0) 0

England: Loach; Cranie (Gardner 79), Gibbs, Noble, Richards, Onuoha (Mancienne 46), Milner, Cattermole, Walcott, Muamba (Rodwell 78), Johnson A.

UEFA UNDER-21 PLAY-OFF

FIRST LEG

Ninian Park, 10 October 2008, 10,500

Wales (2) 2 *(Church 13, 45)*

England (2) 3 *(Wheater 19, Johnson A 35, Agbonlahor 62)*

Wales: fon Williams; Eardley, Wiggins, Collison, Blake, Adams (Allen 59), King, Church, Ramsey, MacDonald (Brown 76), Nyatanga.
England: Hart; Wheater, O'Hara, Cattermole, Taylor S, Mancienne, Milner, Huddlestone, Agbonlahor (Campbell 76), Noble, Johnson A.

SECOND LEG

Villa Park, 14 October 2008, 23,812

England (2) 2 *(Huddlestone 14, Vokes 35 (og))*

Wales (2) 2 *(Ramsey 24, Church 29)*

England: Hart; Wheater, O'Hara, Cattermole (Muamba 31), Taylor S, Mancienne, Milner, Huddlestone*, Agbonlahor (Campbell 46), Noble, Johnson A.
Wales: fon Williams; Eardley, Wiggins, Collison, Blake, Jacobson, King (Bradley 60), Church, Ramsey, MacDonald (Adams 83), Vokes.

As at July 2009 (*Season of first cap given*)

ENGLAND

A'Court, A. (5) 1957/8 Liverpool
Adams, T. A. (66) 1986/7 Arsenal
Agbonlahor, G. (2) 2008/09 Aston
  Villa
Allen, C. (5) 1983/4 QPR, Tottenham
  H
Allen, R. (5) 1951/2 WBA
Allen, T. (3) 1959/60 Stoke C
Anderson, S. (2) 1961/2 Sunderland
Anderson, V. (30) 1978/9 Nottingham
  F, Arsenal, Manchester U
Anderton, D. R. (30) 1993/4
  Tottenham H
Angus, J. (1) 1960/1 Burnley
Armfield, J. (43) 1958/9 Blackpool
Armstrong, D. (3) 1979/80
  Middlesbrough, Southampton
Armstrong, K. (1) 1954/5 Chelsea
Ashton, D. (1) 2007/08 West Ham U
Astall, G. (2) 1955/6 Birmingham C
Astle, J. (5) 1968/9 WBA
Aston, J. (17) 1948/9 Manchester U
Atyeo, J. (6) 1955/6 Bristol C

Bailey, G. R. (2) 1984/5 Manchester U
Bailey, M. (2) 1963/4 Charlton
Baily, E. (9) 1949/50 Tottenham H
Baker, J. (8) 1959/60 Hibernian,
  Arsenal
Ball, A. (72) 1964/5 Blackpool,
  Everton, Arsenal
Ball, M. J. (1) 2000/01 Everton
Banks, G. (73) 1962/3 Leicester C,
  Stoke C
Banks, T. (6) 1957/8 Bolton W
Bardsley, D. (2) 1992/3 QPR
Barham, M. (2) 1982/3 Norwich C
Barlow, R. (1) 1954/5 WBA
Barmby, N. J. (23) 1994/5 Tottenham
  H, Middlesbrough, Everton,
  Liverpool
Barnes, J. (79) 1982/3 Watford,
  Liverpool
Barnes, P. (22) 1977/8 Manchester C,
  WBA, Leeds U
Barrass, M. (3) 1951/2 Bolton W
Barrett, E. D. (3) 1990/1 Oldham Ath,
  Aston Villa
Barry, G. (30) 1999/00 Aston Villa
Barton, J. (1) 2006/07 Manchester C
Barton, W. D. (3) 1994/5 Wimbledon,
  Newcastle

Batty, D. (42) 1990/1 Leeds U,
  Blackburn R, Newcastle U, Leeds U
Baynham, R. (3) 1955/6 Luton T
Beardsley, P. A. (59) 1985/6 Newcastle
  U, Liverpool, Newcastle U
Beasant, D. J. (2) 1989/90 Chelsea
Beattie, J. S. (5) 2002/03 Southampton
Beattie, T. K. (9) 1974/5 Ipswich T
Beckham, D. R. J. (112) 1996/7
  Manchester U, Real Madrid, LA
  Galaxy
Bell, C. (48) 1967/8 Manchester C
Bent, D. A. (4) 2005/06 Charlton Ath,
  Tottenham H
Bentley, D. M. (7) 2007/08 Blackburn
  R, Tottenham H
Bentley, R. (12) 1948/9 Chelsea
Berry, J. (4) 1952/3 Manchester U
Birtles, G. (3) 1979/80 Nottingham F
Blissett, L. (14) 1982/3 Watford, AC
  Milan
Blockley, J. (1) 1972/3 Arsenal
Blunstone, F. (5) 1954/5 Chelsea
Bonetti, P. (7) 1965/6 Chelsea
Bould, S. A. (2) 1993/4 Arsenal
Bowles, S. (5) 1973/4 QPR
Bowyer, L. D. (1) 2002/03 Leeds U
Boyer, P. (1) 1975/6 Norwich C
Brabrook, P. (3) 1957/8 Chelsea
Bracewell, P. W. (3) 1984/5 Everton
Bradford, G. (1) 1955/6 Bristol R
Bradley, W. (3) 1958/9 Manchester U
Bridge, W. M. (33) 2001/02
  Southampton, Chelsea, Manchester
  C
Bridges, B. (4) 1964/5 Chelsea
Broadbent, P. (7) 1957/8
  Wolverhampton W
Broadis, I. (14) 1951/2 Manchester C,
  Newcastle U
Brooking, T. (47) 1973/4 West Ham U
Brooks, J. (3) 1956/7 Tottenham H
Brown, A. (1) 1970/1 WBA
Brown, K. (1) 1959/60 West Ham U
Brown, W. M. (21) 1998/9 Manchester
  U
Bull, S. G. (13) 1988/9 Wolverhampton
  W
Butcher, T. (77) 1979/80 Ipswich T,
  Rangers
Butt, N. (39) 1996/7 Manchester U,
  Newcastle U

Byrne, G. (2) 1962/3 Liverpool
Byrne, J. (11) 1961/2 Crystal P, West Ham U
Byrne, R. (33) 1953/4 Manchester U

Callaghan, I. (4) 1965/6 Liverpool
Campbell, S. (73) 1995/6 Tottenham H, Arsenal, Portsmouth
Carragher, J. L. (34) 1998/9 Liverpool
Carrick, M. (17) 2000/01 West Ham U, Tottenham H, Manchester U
Carson, S. P. (3) 2007/08 Liverpool, WBA
Carter, H. (7) 1946/7 Derby Co
Chamberlain, M. (8) 1982/3 Stoke C
Channon, M. (46) 1972/3 Southampton, Manchester C
Charles, G. A. (2) 1990/1 Nottingham F
Charlton, J. (35) 1964/5 Leeds U
Charlton, R. (106) 1957/8 Manchester U
Charnley, R. (1) 1962/3 Blackpool
Cherry, T. (27) 1975/6 Leeds U
Chilton, A. (2) 1950/1 Manchester U
Chivers, M. (24) 1970/1 Tottenham H
Clamp, E. (4) 1957/8 Wolverhampton W
Clapton, D. (1) 1958/9 Arsenal
Clarke, A. (19) 1969/70 Leeds U
Clarke, H. (1) 1953/4 Tottenham H
Clayton, R. (35) 1955/6 Blackburn R
Clemence, R (61) 1972/3 Liverpool, Tottenham H
Clement, D. (5) 1975/6 QPR
Clough, B. (2) 1959/60 Middlesbrough
Clough, N. H. (14) 1988/9 Nottingham F
Coates, R. (4) 1969/70 Burnley, Tottenham H
Cockburn, H. (13) 1946/7 Manchester U
Cohen, G. (37) 1963/4 Fulham
Cole, Andy (15) 1994/5 Manchester U
Cole, Ashley (73) 2000/01 Arsenal, Chelsea
Cole, C. (2) 2008/09 West Ham U
Cole, J. J. (53) 2000/01 West Ham U, Chelsea
Collymore, S. V. (3) 1994/5 Nottingham F, Aston Villa
Compton, L. (2) 1950/1 Arsenal
Connelly, J. (20) 1959/60 Burnley, Manchester U
Cooper, C. T. (2) 1994/5 Nottingham F
Cooper, T. (20) 1968/9 Leeds U
Coppell, S. (42) 1977/8 Manchester U
Corrigan, J. (9) 1975/6 Manchester C

Cottee, A. R. (7) 1986/7 West Ham U, Everton
Cowans, G. (10) 1982/3 Aston Villa, Bari, Aston Villa
Crawford, R. (2) 1961/2 Ipswich T
Crouch, P. J. (34) 2004/05 Southampton, Liverpool, Portsmouth
Crowe, C. (1) 1962/3 Wolverhampton W
Cunningham, L. (6) 1978/9 WBA, Real Madrid
Curle, K. (3) 1991/2 Manchester C
Currie, A. (17) 1971/2 Sheffield U, Leeds U

Daley, A. M. (7) 1991/2 Aston Villa
Davenport, P. (1) 1984/5 Nottingham F
Deane, B. C. (3) 1990/1 Sheffield U
Deeley, N. (2) 1958/9 Wolverhampton W
Defoe, J. C. (34) 2003/04 Tottenham H, Portsmouth, Tottenham H
Devonshire, A. (8) 1979/80 West Ham U
Dickinson, J. (48) 1948/9 Portsmouth
Ditchburn, E. (6) 1948/9 Tottenham H
Dixon, K. M. (8) 1984/5 Chelsea
Dixon, L. M. (22) 1989/90 Arsenal
Dobson, M. (5) 1973/4 Burnley, Everton
Dorigo, A. R. (15) 1989/90 Chelsea, Leeds U
Douglas, B. (36) 1957/8 Blackburn R
Downing, S. (23) 2004/05 Middlesbrough
Doyle, M. (5) 1975/6 Manchester C
Dublin, D. (4) 1997/8 Coventry C, Aston Villa
Dunn, D. J. I. (1) 2002/03 Blackburn R
Duxbury, M. (10) 1983/4 Manchester U
Dyer, K. C. (33) 1999/00 Newcastle U, West Ham U

Eastham, G. (19) 1962/3 Arsenal
Eckersley, W. (17) 1949/50 Blackburn R
Edwards, D. (18) 1954/5 Manchester U
Ehiogu, U. (4) 1995/6 Aston Villa, Middlesbrough
Ellerington, W. (2) 1948/9 Southampton
Elliott, W. H. (5) 1951/2 Burnley

Fantham, J. (1) 1961/2 Sheffield W
Fashanu, J. (2) 1988/9 Wimbledon

Fenwick, T. (20) 1983/4 QPR, Tottenham H
Ferdinand, L. (17) 1992/3 QPR, Newcastle U, Tottenham H
Ferdinand, R. G. (73) 1997/8 West Ham U, Leeds U, Manchester U
Finney, T. (76) 1946/7 Preston NE
Flowers, R. (49) 1954/5 Wolverhampton W
Flowers, T. (11) 1992/3 Southampton, Blackburn R
Foster, B. (2) 2006/07 Manchester U
Foster, S. (3) 1981/2 Brighton
Foulkes, W. (1) 1954/5 Manchester U
Fowler, R. B. (26) 1995/6 Liverpool, Leeds U
Francis, G. (12) 1974/5 QPR
Francis, T. (52) 1976/7 Birmingham C, Nottingham F, Manchester C, Sampdoria
Franklin, N. (27) 1946/7 Stoke C
Froggatt, J. (13) 1949/50 Portsmouth
Froggatt, R. (4) 1952/3 Sheffield W

Gardner, A. (1) 2003/04 Tottenham H
Garrett, T. (3) 1951/2 Blackpool
Gascoigne, P. J. (57) 1988/9 Tottenham H, Lazio, Rangers, Middlesbrough
Gates, E. (2) 1980/1 Ipswich T
George, F. C. (1) 1976/7 Derby Co
Gerrard, S. G. (74) 1999/00 Liverpool
Gidman, J. (1) 1976/7 Aston Villa
Gillard, I. (3) 1974/5 QPR
Goddard, P. (1) 1981/2 West Ham U
Grainger, C. (7) 1955/6 Sheffield U, Sunderland
Gray, A. A. (1) 1991/2 Crystal P
Gray, M. (3) 1998/9 Sunderland
Greaves, J. (57) 1958/9 Chelsea, Tottenham H
Green, R. P. (4) 2004/05 Norwich C, West Ham U
Greenhoff, B. (18) 1975/6 Manchester U, Leeds U
Gregory, J. (6) 1982/3 QPR
Guppy, S. (1) 1999/00 Leicester C

Hagan, J. (1) 1948/9 Sheffield U
Haines, J. (1) 1948/9 WBA
Hall, J. (17) 1955/6 Birmingham C
Hancocks, J. (3) 1948/9 Wolverhampton W
Hardwick, G. (13) 1946/7 Middlesbrough
Harford, M. G. (2) 1987/8 Luton T
Hargreaves, O. (42) 2001/02 Bayern Munich, Manchester U

Harris, G. (1) 1965/6 Burnley
Harris, P. (2) 1949/50 Portsmouth
Hart, C. (1) 2007/08 Manchester C
Harvey, C. (1) 1970/1 Everton
Hassall, H. (5) 1950/1 Huddersfield T, Bolton W
Hateley, M. (32) 1983/4 Portsmouth, AC Milan, Monaco, Rangers
Haynes, J. (56) 1954/5 Fulham
Hector, K. (2) 1973/4 Derby Co
Hellawell, M. (2) 1962/3 Birmingham C
Hendrie, L. A. (1) 1998/9 Aston Villa
Henry, R. (1) 1962/3 Tottenham H
Heskey, E. W. (53) 1998/9 Leicester C, Liverpool, Birmingham C, Wigan Ath, Aston Villa
Hill, F. (2) 1962/3 Bolton W
Hill, G. (6) 1975/6 Manchester U
Hill, R. (3) 1982/3 Luton T
Hinchcliffe, A. G. (7) 1996/7 Everton, Sheffield W
Hinton, A. (3) 1962/3 Wolverhampton W, Nottingham F
Hirst, D. E. (3) 1990/1 Sheffield W
Hitchens, G. (7) 1960/1 Aston Villa, Internazionale
Hoddle, G. (53) 1979/80 Tottenham H, Monaco
Hodge, S. B. (24) 1985/6 Aston Villa, Tottenham H, Nottingham F
Hodgkinson, A. (5) 1956/7 Sheffield U
Holden, D. (5) 1958/9 Bolton W
Holliday, E. (3) 1959/60 Middlesbrough
Hollins, J. (1) 1966/7 Chelsea
Hopkinson, E. (14) 1957/8 Bolton W
Howe, D. (23) 1957/8 WBA
Howe, J. (3) 1947/8 Derby Co
Howey, S. N. (4) 1994/5 Newcastle U
Hudson, A. (2) 1974/5 Stoke C
Hughes, E. (62) 1969/70 Liverpool, Wolverhampton W
Hughes, L. (3) 1949/50 Liverpool
Hunt, R. (34) 1961/2 Liverpool
Hunt, S. (2) 1983/4 WBA
Hunter, N. (28) 1965/6 Leeds U
Hurst, G. (49) 1965/6 West Ham U

Ince, P. (53) 1992/3 Manchester U, Internazionale, Liverpool, Middlesbrough

Jagielka, P. N. (3) 2007/08 Everton
James, D. B. (48) 1996/7 Liverpool, Aston Villa, West Ham U, Manchester C, Portsmouth
Jeffers, F. (1) 2002/03 Arsenal

296

Jenas, J. A. (20) 2002/03 Newcastle U, Tottenham H

Jezzard, B. (2) 1953/4 Fulham

Johnson, A. (8) 2004/05 Crystal P, Everton

Johnson, D. (8) 1974/5 Ipswich T, Liverpool

Johnson, G. M. C. (15) 2003/04 Chelsea, Portsmouth

Johnson, S. A. M. (1) 2000/01 Derby Co

Johnston, H. (10) 1946/7 Blackpool

Jones, M. (3) 1964/5 Sheffield U, Leeds U

Jones, R. (8) 1991/2 Liverpool

Jones, W. H. (2) 1949/50 Liverpool

Kay, A. (1) 1962/3 Everton

Keegan, K. (63) 1972/3 Liverpool, SV Hamburg, Southampton

Kennedy, A. (2) 1983/4 Liverpool

Kennedy, R. (17) 1975/6 Liverpool

Keown, M. R. (43) 1991/2 Everton, Arsenal

Kevan, D. (14) 1956/7 WBA

Kidd, B. (2) 1969/70 Manchester U

King, L. B. (19) 2001/02 Tottenham H

Kirkland, C. E. (1) 2006/07 Liverpool

Knight, Z. (2) 2004/05 Fulham

Knowles, C. (4) 1967/8 Tottenham H

Konchesky, P. M. (2) 2002/03 Charlton Ath, West Ham U

Labone, B. (26) 1962/3 Everton

Lampard, F. J. (71) 1999/00 West Ham U, Chelsea

Lampard, F. R. G. (2) 1972/3 West Ham U

Langley, J. (3) 1957/8 Fulham

Langton, R. (11) 1946/7 Blackburn R, Preston NE, Bolton W

Latchford, R. (12) 1977/8 Everton

Lawler, C. (4) 1970/1 Liverpool

Lawton, T. (15) 1946/7 Chelsea, Notts Co

Lee, F. (27) 1968/9 Manchester C

Lee, J. (1) 1950/1 Derby C

Lee, R. M. (21) 1994/5 Newcastle U

Lee, S. (14) 1982/3 Liverpool

Lennon, A. J. (11) 2005/06 Tottenham H

Lescott, J. P. (7) 2007/08 Everton

Le Saux, G. P. (36) 1993/4 Blackburn R, Chelsea

Le Tissier, M. P. (8) 1993/4 Southampton

Lindsay, A. (4) 1973/4 Liverpool

Lineker, G. (80) 1983/4 Leicester C, Everton, Barcelona, Tottenham H

Little, B. (1) 1974/5 Aston Villa

Lloyd, L. (4) 1970/1 Liverpool, Nottingham F

Lofthouse, N. (33) 1950/1 Bolton W

Lowe, E. (3) 1946/7 Aston Villa

Mabbutt, G. (16) 1982/3 Tottenham H

Macdonald, M. (14) 1971/2 Newcastle U

Madeley, P. (24) 1970/1 Leeds U

Mannion, W. (26) 1946/7 Middlesbrough

Mariner, P. (35) 1976/7 Ipswich T, Arsenal

Marsh, R. (9) 1971/2 QPR, Manchester C

Martin, A. (17) 1980/1 West Ham U

Martyn, A. N. (23) 1991/2 Crystal P, Leeds U

Marwood, B. (1) 1988/9 Arsenal

Matthews, R. (5) 1955/6 Coventry C

Matthews, S. (37) 1946/7 Stoke C, Blackpool

McCann, G. P. (1) 2000/01 Sunderland

McDermott, T. (25) 1977/8 Liverpool

McDonald, C. (8) 1957/8 Burnley

McFarland, R. (28) 1970/1 Derby C

McGarry, W. (4) 1953/4 Huddersfield T

McGuinness, W. (2) 1958/9 Manchester U

McMahon, S. (17) 1987/8 Liverpool

McManaman, S. (37) 1994/5 Liverpool, Real Madrid

McNab, R. (4) 1968/9 Arsenal

McNeil, M. (9) 1960/1 Middlesbrough

Meadows, J. (1) 1954/5 Manchester C

Medley, L. (6) 1950/1 Tottenham H

Melia, J. (2) 1962/3 Liverpool

Merrick, G. (23) 1951/2 Birmingham C

Merson, P. C. (21) 1991/2 Arsenal, Middlesbrough, Aston Villa

Metcalfe, V. (2) 1950/1 Huddersfield T

Milburn, J. (13) 1948/9 Newcastle U

Miller, B. (1) 1960/1 Burnley

Mills, D. J. (19) 2000/01 Leeds U

Mills, M. (42) 1972/3 Ipswich T

Milne, G. (14) 1962/3 Liverpool

Milton, C. A. (1) 1951/2 Arsenal

Moore, R. (108) 1961/2 West Ham U

Morley, A. (6) 1981/2 Aston Villa

Morris, J. (3) 1948/9 Derby Co

Mortensen, S. (25) 1946/7 Blackpool

Mozley, B. (3) 1949/50 Derby Co

Mullen, J. (12) 1946/7 Wolverhampton W

Mullery, A. (35) 1964/5 Tottenham H
Murphy, D. B. (9) 2001/02 Liverpool

Neal, P. (50) 1975/6 Liverpool
Neville, G. A. (85) 1994/5 Manchester U
Neville, P. J. (59) 1995/6 Manchester U, Everton
Newton, K. (27) 1965/6 Blackburn R, Everton
Nicholls, J. (2) 1953/4 WBA
Nicholson, W. (1) 1950/1 Tottenham H
Nish, D. (5) 1972/3 Derby Co
Norman, M. (23) 1961/2 Tottenham H
Nugent, D. J. (1) 2006/07 Preston NE

O'Grady, M. (2) 1962/3 Huddersfield T, Leeds U
Osgood, P. (4) 1969/70 Chelsea
Osman, R. (11) 1979/80 Ipswich T
Owen, M. J. (89) 1997/8 Liverpool, Real Madrid, Newcastle U
Owen, S. (3) 1953/4 Luton T

Paine, T. (19) 1962/3 Southampton
Pallister, G. (22) 1987/8 Middlesbrough, Manchester U
Palmer, C. L. (18) 1991/2 Sheffield W
Parker, P. A. (19) 1988/9 QPR, Manchester U
Parker, S. M. (3) 2003/04 Charlton Ath, Chelsea, Newcastle U
Parkes, P. (1) 1973/4 QPR
Parlour, R. (10) 1998/9 Arsenal
Parry, R. (2) 1959/60 Bolton W
Peacock, A. (6) 1961/2 Middlesbrough, Leeds U
Pearce, S. (78) 1986/7 Nottingham F, West Ham U
Pearson, Stan (8) 1947/8 Manchester U
Pearson, Stuart (15) 1975/6 Manchester U
Pegg, D. (1) 1956/7 Manchester U
Pejic, M. (4) 1973/4 Stoke C
Perry, W. (3) 1955/6 Blackpool
Perryman, S. (1) 1981/2 Tottenham H
Peters, M. (67) 1965/6 West Ham U, Tottenham H
Phelan, M. C. (1) 1989/90 Manchester U
Phillips, K. (8) 1998/9 Sunderland
Phillips, L. (3) 1951/2 Portsmouth
Pickering, F. (3) 1963/4 Everton
Pickering, N. (1) 1982/3 Sunderland
Pilkington, B. (1) 1954/5 Burnley
Platt, D. (62) 1989/90 Aston Villa, Bari, Juventus, Sampdoria, Arsenal
Pointer, R. (3) 1961/2 Burnley

Powell, C. G. (5) 2000/01 Charlton Ath
Pye, J. (1) 1949/50 Wolverhampton W

Quixall, A. (5) 1953/4 Sheffield W

Radford, J. (2) 1968/9 Arsenal
Ramsey, A. (32) 1948/9 Southampton, Tottenham H
Reaney, P. (3) 1968/9 Leeds U
Redknapp, J. F. (17) 1995/6 Liverpool
Reeves, K. (2) 1979/80 Norwich C, Manchester C
Regis, C. (5) 1981/2 WBA, Coventry C
Reid, P. (13) 1984/5 Everton
Revie, D. (6) 1954/5 Manchester C
Richards, J. (1) 1972/3 Wolverhampton W
Richards, M. (11) 2006/07 Manchester C
Richardson, K. (1) 1993/4 Aston Villa
Richardon, K. E. (8) 2004/05 Manchester U
Rickaby, S. (1) 1953/4 WBA
Ricketts, M. B. (1) 2001/02 Bolton W
Rimmer, J. (1) 1975/6 Arsenal
Ripley, S. E. (2) 1993/4 Blackburn R
Rix, G. (17) 1980/1 Arsenal
Robb, G. (1) 1953/4 Tottenham H
Roberts, G. (6) 1982/3 Tottenham H
Robinson, P. W. (41) 2002/03 Leeds U, Tottenham H
Robson, B. (90) 1979/80 WBA, Manchester U
Robson, R. (20) 1957/8 WBA
Rocastle, D. (14) 1988/9 Arsenal
Rooney, W. (52) 2002/03 Everton, Manchester U
Rowley, J. (6) 1948/9 Manchester U
Royle, J. (6) 1970/1 Everton, Manchester C
Ruddock, N. (1) 1994/5 Liverpool

Sadler, D. (4) 1967/8 Manchester U
Salako, J. A. (5) 1990/1 Crystal P
Sansom, K. (86) 1978/9 Crystal P, Arsenal
Scales, J. R. (3) 1994/5 Liverpool
Scholes, P. (66) 1996/7 Manchester U
Scott, L. (17) 1946/7 Arsenal
Seaman, D. A. (75) 1988/9 QPR, Arsenal
Sewell, J. (6) 1951/2 Sheffield W
Shackleton, L. (5) 1948/9 Sunderland
Sharpe, L. S. (8) 1990/1 Manchester U
Shaw, G. (5) 1958/9 Sheffield U
Shearer, A. (63) 1991/2 Southampton, Blackburn R, Newcastle U
Shellito, K. (1) 1962/3 Chelsea

Sheringham, E. (51) 1992/3 Tottenham H, Manchester U, Tottenham H

Sherwood, T. A. (3) 1998/9 Tottenham H

Shilton, P. (125) 1970/1 Leicester C, Stoke C, Nottingham F, Southampton, Derby Co

Shimwell, E. (1) 1948/9 Blackpool

Shorey, N, (2) 2006/07 Reading

Sillett, P. (3) 1954/5 Chelsea

Sinclair, T. (12) 2001/02 West Ham U, Manchester C

Sinton, A. (12) 1991/2 QPR, Sheffield W

Slater, W. (12) 1954/5 Wolverhampton W

Smith, A. (19) 2000/01 Leeds U, Manchester U, Newcastle U

Smith, A. M. (13) 1988/9 Arsenal

Smith, L. (6) 1950/1 Arsenal

Smith, R. (15) 1960/1 Tottenham H

Smith, Tom (1) 1970/1 Liverpool

Smith, Trevor (2) 1959/60 Birmingham C

Southgate, G. (57) 1995/6 Aston Villa, Middlesbrough

Spink, N. (1) 1982/3 Aston Villa

Springett, R. (33) 1959/60 Sheffield W

Staniforth, R. (8) 1953/4 Huddersfield T

Statham, D. (3) 1982/3 WBA

Stein, B. (1) 1983/4 Luton T

Stepney, A. (1) 1967/8 Manchester U

Sterland, M. (1) 1988/9 Sheffield W

Steven, T. M. (36) 1984/5 Everton, Rangers, Marseille

Stevens, G. A. (7) 1984/5 Tottenham H

Stevens, M. G. (46) 1984/5 Everton, Rangers

Stewart, P. A. (3) 1991/2 Tottenham H

Stiles, N. (28) 1964/5 Manchester U

Stone, S. B. (9) 1995/6 Nottingham F

Storey-Moore, I. (1) 1969/70 Nottingham F

Storey, P. (19) 1970/1 Arsenal

Streten, B. (1) 1949/50 Luton T

Summerbee, M. (8) 1967/8 Manchester C

Sunderland, A. (1) 1979/80 Arsenal

Sutton, C. R. (1) 1997/8 Blackburn R

Swan, P. (19) 1959/60 Sheffield W

Swift, F. (19) 1946/7 Manchester C

Talbot, B. (6) 1976/7 Ipswich T, Arsenal

Tambling, R. (3) 1962/3 Chelsea

Taylor, E. (1) 1953/4 Blackpool

Taylor, J. (2) 1950/1 Fulham

Taylor, P. H. (3) 1947/8 Liverpool

Taylor, P. J. (4) 1975/6 Crystal P

Taylor, T. (19) 1952/3 Manchester U

Temple, D. (1) 1964/5 Everton

Terry, J. G. (53) 2002/03 Chelsea

Thomas, Danny (2) 1982/3 Coventry C

Thomas, Dave (8) 1974/5 QPR

Thomas, G. R. (9) 1990/1 Crystal P

Thomas, M. L. (2) 1988/9 Arsenal

Thompson, A. (1) 2003/04 Celtic

Thompson, P. (16) 1963/4 Liverpool

Thompson, P. B. (42) 1975/6 Liverpool

Thompson, T. (2) 1951/2 Aston Villa, Preston NE

Thomson, R. (8) 1963/4 Wolverhampton W

Todd, C. (27) 1971/2 Derby Co

Towers, T. (3) 1975/6 Sunderland

Tueart, D. (6) 1974/5 Manchester C

Ufton, D. (1) 1953/4 Charlton Ath

Unsworth, D. G. (1) 1994/5 Everton

Upson, M. J. (15) 2002/03 Birmingham C, West Ham U

Vassell, D. (22) 2001/02 Aston Villa

Venables, T. (2) 1964/5 Chelsea

Venison, B. (2) 1994/5 Newcastle U

Viljoen, C. (2) 1974/5 Ipswich T

Viollet, D. (2) 1959/60 Manchester U

Waddle, C. R. (62) 1984/5 Newcastle U, Tottenham H, Marseille

Waiters, A. (5) 1963/4 Blackpool

Walcott, T. J. (8) 2005/06 Arsenal

Walker, D. S. (59) 1988/9 Nottingham F, Sampdoria, Sheffield W

Walker, I. M. (4) 1995/6 Tottenham H, Leicester C

Wallace, D. L. (1) 1985/6 Southampton

Walsh, P. (5) 1982/3 Luton T

Walters, K. M. (1) 1990/1 Rangers

Ward, P. (1) 1979/80 Brighton

Ward, T. (2) 1947/8 Derby C

Warnock, S. (1) 2007/08 Blackburn R

Watson, D. (12) 1983/4 Norwich C, Everton

Watson, D. V. (65) 1973/4 Sunderland, Manchester C, Werder Bremen, Southampton, Stoke C

Watson, W. (4) 1949/50 Sunderland

Webb, N. (26) 1987/8 Nottingham F, Manchester U

Weller, K. (4) 1973/4 Leicester C

West, G. (3) 1968/9 Everton

Wheeler, J. (1) 1954/5 Bolton W

White, D. (1) 1992/3 Manchester C

Whitworth, S. (7) 1974/5 Leicester C

Whymark, T. (1) 1977/8 Ipswich T
Wignall, F. (2) 1964/5 Nottingham F
Wilcox, J. M. (3) 1995/6 Blackburn R, Leeds U
Wilkins, R. (84) 1975/6 Chelsea, Manchester U, AC Milan
Williams, B. (24) 1948/9 Wolverhampton W
Williams, S. (6) 1982/3 Southampton
Willis, A. (1) 1951/2 Tottenham H
Wilshaw, D. (12) 1953/4 Wolverhampton W
Wilson, R. (63) 1959/60 Huddersfield T, Everton
Winterburn, N. (2) 1989/90 Arsenal
Wise, D. F. (21) 1990/1 Chelsea
Withe, P. (11) 1980/1 Aston Villa
Wood, R. (3) 1954/5 Manchester U
Woodcock, A. (42) 1977/8 Nottingham F, FC Cologne, Arsenal

NORTHERN IRELAND

Aherne, T. (4) 1946/7 Belfast Celtic, Luton T
Anderson, T. (22) 1972/3 Manchester U, Swindon T, Peterborough U
Armstrong, G. (63) 1976/7 Tottenham H, Watford, Real Mallorca, WBA, Chesterfield

Baird, C. P. (40) 2002/03 Southampton, Fulham
Barr, H. (3) 1961/2 Linfield, Coventry C
Best, G. (37) 1963/4 Manchester U, Fulham
Bingham, W. (56) 1950/1 Sunderland, Luton T, Everton, Port Vale
Black, K. (30) 1987/8 Luton T, Nottingham F
Blair, R. (5) 1974/5 Oldham Ath
Blanchflower, D. (54) 1949/50 Barnsley, Aston Villa, Tottenham H
Blanchflower, J. (12) 1953/4 Manchester U
Blayney, A. (1) 2005/06 Doncaster R
Bowler, G. (3) 1949/50 Hull C
Braithwaite, R. (10) 1961/2 Linfield, Middlesbrough
Brennan, R. (5) 1948/9 Luton T, Birmingham C, Fulham
Briggs, R. (2) 1961/2 Manchester U, Swansea
Brotherston, N. (27) 1979/80 Blackburn R

Woodgate, J. S. (8) 1998/9 Leeds U, Newcastle U, Real Madrid, Tottenham H
Woods, C. C. E. (43) 1984/5 Norwich C, Rangers, Sheffield W
Worthington, F. (8) 1973/4 Leicester C
Wright, I. E. (33) 1990/1 Crystal P, Arsenal, West Ham U
Wright, M. (45) 1983/4 Southampton, Derby C, Liverpool
Wright, R. I. (2) 1999/00 Ipswich T, Arsenal
Wright, T. (11) 1967/8 Everton
Wright, W. (105) 1946/7 Wolverhampton W
Wright-Phillips, S. C. (25) 2004/05 Manchester C, Chelsea, Manchester C

Young, A. S. (5) 2007/08 Aston Villa
Young, G. (1) 1964/5 Sheffield W
Young, L. P. (7) 2004/05 Charlton Ath

Bruce, W. (2) 1960/1 Glentoran
Brunt, C. (23) 2004/05 Sheffield W, WBA

Campbell, A. (2) 1962/3 Crusaders
Campbell, D. A. (10) 1985/6 Nottingham F, Charlton Ath
Campbell, J. (2) 1950/1 Fulham
Campbell, R. M. (2) 1981/2 Bradford C
Campbell, W. (6) 1967/8 Dundee
Capaldi, A. C. (22) 2003/04 Plymouth Arg, Cardiff C
Carey, J. (7) 1946/7 Manchester U
Carroll, R. E. (19) 1996/7 Wigan Ath, Manchester U, West Ham U
Carson, S. (1) 2008/09 Coleraine
Casement, C. (1) 2008/09 Ipswich T
Casey, T. (12) 1954/5 Newcastle U, Portsmouth
Caskey, A. (8) 1978/9 Derby C, Tulsa Roughnecks
Cassidy, T. (24) 1970/1 Newcastle U, Burnley
Caughey, M. (2) 1985/6 Linfield
Clarke, C. J. (38) 1985/6 Bournemouth, Southampton, Portsmouth
Cleary, J. (5) 1981/2 Glentoran
Clements, D. (48) 1964/5 Coventry C, Sheffield W, Everton, New York Cosmos
Clingan, S. G. (21) 2005/06 Nottingham F, Norwich C

Clyde, M.G. (3) 2004/05
Wolverhampon W

Coates, C. (1) 2008/09 Crusaders

Cochrane, D. (10) 1946/7 Leeds U

Cochrane, T. (26) 1975/6 Coleraine,
Burnley, Middlesbrough,
Gillingham

Connell, T. E. (1) 1977/8 Coleraine

Coote, A. (6) 1998/9 Norwich C

Cowan, J. (1) 1969/70 Newcastle U

Coyle, F. (4) 1955/6 Coleraine,
Nottingham F

Coyle, L. (1) 1988/9 Derry C

Coyle, R. (5) 1972/3 Sheffield W

Craig, D. (25) 1966/7 Newcastle U

Craigan, S. (40) 2002/03 Partick T,
Motherwell

Crossan, E. (3) 1949/50 Blackburn R

Crossan, J. (24) 1959/60 Sparta
Rotterdam, Sunderland, Manchester
C, Middlesbrough

Cunningham, W. (30) 1950/1 St
Mirren, Leicester C, Dunfermline
Ath

Cush, W. (26) 1950/1 Glentoran, Leeds
U, Portadown

D'Arcy, S. (5) 1951/2 Chelsea,
Brentford

Davis, S. (34) 2004/05 Aston Villa,
Fulham, Rangers

Davison, A. J. (3) 1995/6 Bolton W,
Bradford C, Grimsby T

Dennison, R. (18) 1987/8
Wolverhampton W

Devine, J. (1) 1989/90 Glentoran

Dickson, D. (4) 1969/70 Coleraine

Dickson, T. (1) 1956/7 Linfield

Dickson, W. (12) 1950/1 Chelsea,
Arsenal

Doherty, L. (2) 1984/5 Linfield

Doherty, P. (6) 1946/7 Derby Co,
Huddersfield T, Doncaster R

Doherty, T. E. (9) 2002/03 Bristol C

Donaghy, M. (91) 1979/80 Luton T,
Manchester U, Chelsea

Donnelly, M. (1) 2008/09 Crusaders

Dougan, D. (43) 1957/8 Portsmouth,
Blackburn R, Aston Villa, Leicester
C, Wolverhampton W

Douglas, J. P. (1) 1946/7 Belfast Celtic

Dowd, H. (3) 1973/4 Glenavon,
Sheffield W

Dowie, I. (59) 1989/90 Luton T, West
Ham U, Southampton, Crystal P,
West Ham U, QPR

Duff, M. J. (22) 2001/02 Cheltenham
T, Burnley

Dunlop, G. (4) 1984/5 Linfield

Eglington, T. (6) 1946/7 Everton

Elder, A. (40) 1959/60 Burnley, Stoke
C

Elliott, S. (39) 2000/01 Motherwell,
Hull C

Evans, C. J. (1) 2008/09 Manchester U

Evans, J. G. (17) 2006/07 Manchester
U

Farrell, P. (7) 1946/7 Everton

Feeney, J. (2) 1946/7 Linfield, Swansea
T

Feeney, W. (1) 1975/6 Glentoran

Feeney, W. J. (32) 2001/02
Bournemouth, Luton T, Cardiff C

Ferguson, G. (5) 1998/9 Linfield

Ferguson, S. (1) 2008/09 Newcastle U

Ferguson, W. (2) 1965/6 Linfield

Ferris, R. (3) 1949/50 Birmingham

Fettis, A. (25) 1991/2 Hull C,
Nottingham F, Blackburn R

Finney, T. (14) 1974/5 Sunderland,
Cambridge U

Fleming, J. G. (31) 1986/7 Nottingham
F, Manchester C, Barnsley

Forde, T. (4) 1958/9 Ards

Gallogly, C. (2) 1950/1 Huddersfield T

Garrett, R. (1) 2008/09 Linfield

Garton, R. (1) 1968/9 Oxford U

Gault, M. (1) 2007/08 Linfield

Gillespie, K. R. (86) 1994/5
Manchester U, Newcastle U,
Blackburn R, Leicester C, Sheffield
U

Gorman, W. (4) 1946/7 Brentford

Graham, W. (14) 1950/1 Doncaster R

Gray, P. (26) 1992/3 Luton T,
Sunderland, Nancy, Luton T,
Burnley, Oxford U

Gregg, H. (25) 1953/4 Doncaster R,
Manchester U

Griffin, D. J. (29) 1995/6 St Johnstone,
Dundee U, Stockport Co

Hamill, R. (1) 1998/9 Glentoran

Hamilton, B. (50) 1968/9 Linfield,
Ipswich T, Everton, Millwall,
Swindon T

Hamilton, G. (5) 2002/03 Portadown

Hamilton, W. (41) 1977/8 QPR,
Burnley, Oxford U

Harkin, T. (5) 1967/8 Southport,
Shrewsbury T

Harvey, M. (34) 1960/1 Sunderland

Hatton, S. (2) 1962/3 Linfield

Healy, D. J. (74) 1999/00 Manchester U, Preston NE, Leeds U, Fulham, Sunderland

Healy, P. J. (4) 1981/2 Coleraine, Glentoran

Hegan, D. (7) 1969/70 WBA, Wolverhampton W

Hill, C. F. (27) 1989/90 Sheffield U, Leicester C, Trelleborg, Northampton T

Hill, J. (7) 1958/9 Norwich C, Everton

Hinton, E. (7) 1946/7 Fulham, Millwall

Holmes, S. P. (1) 2001/02 Wrexham

Horlock, K. (32) 1994/5 Swindon T, Manchester C

Hughes, A. W. (66) 1997/8 Newcastle U, Aston Villa, Fulham

Hughes, J. (2) 2005/06 Lincoln C

Hughes, M. A. (2) 2005/06 Oldham Ath

Hughes, M. E. (71) 1991/2 Manchester C, Strasbourg, West Ham U, Wimbledon, Crystal P

Hughes, P. (3) 1986/7 Bury

Hughes, W. (1) 1950/1 Bolton W

Humphries, W. (14) 1961/2 Ards, Coventry C, Swansea T

Hunter, A. (53) 1969/70 Blackburn R, Ipswich T

Hunter, B. V. (15) 1994/5 Wrexham, Reading

Hunter, V. (2) 1961/2 Coleraine

Ingham, M. G. (3) 2004/05 Sunderland, Wrexham

Irvine, R. (8) 1961/2 Linfield, Stoke C

Irvine, W. (23) 1962/3 Burnley, Preston NE, Brighton & HA

Jackson, T. (35) 1968/9 Everton, Nottingham F, Manchester U

Jamison, A. (1) 1975/6 Glentoran

Jenkins, I. (6) 1996/7 Chester C, Dundee U

Jennings, P. (119) 1963/4 Watford, Tottenham H, Arsenal, Tottenham H

Johnson, D. M. (52) 1998/9 Blackburn R, Birmingham C

Johnston, W. (2) 1961/2 Glenavon, Oldham Ath

Jones, J. (3) 1955/6 Glenavon

Jones, S. G. (29) 2002/03 Crewe Alex, Burnley

Keane, T. (1) 1948/9 Swansea T

Kee, P. V. (9) 1989/90 Oxford U, Ards

Keith, R. (23) 1957/8 Newcastle U

Kelly, H. (4) 1949/50 Fulham, Southampton

Kelly, P. (1) 1949/50 Barnsley

Kennedy, P. H. (20) 1998/9 Watford, Wigan Ath

Kirk, A. R. (8) 1999/00 Heart of Midlothian, Boston U, Northampton T

Lafferty, K. (20) 2005/06 Burnley, Rangers

Lawrie, J. (1) 2008/09 Port Vale

Lawther, I. (4) 1959/60 Sunderland, Blackburn R

Lennon, N. F. (40) 1993/4 Crewe Alex, Leicester C, Celtic

Little, A. (2) 2008/09 Rangers

Lockhart, N. (8) 1946/7 Linfield, Coventry C, Aston Villa

Lomas, S. M. (45) 1993/4 Manchester C, West Ham U

Lutton, B. (6) 1969/70 Wolverhampton W, West Ham U

Magill, E. (26) 1961/2 Arsenal, Brighton & HA

Magilton, J. (52) 1990/1 Oxford U, Southampton, Sheffield W, Ipswich T

Mannus, A. (4) 2003/04 Linfield

Martin, C. (6) 1946/7 Glentoran, Leeds U, Aston Villa

McAdams, W. (15) 1953/4 Manchester C, Bolton W, Leeds U

McAlinden, J. (2) 1946/7 Portsmouth, Southend U

McAuley, G. (16) 2004/05 Lincoln C, Leicester C

McBride, S. (4) 1990/1 Glenavon

McCabe, J. (6) 1948/9 Leeds U

McCann, G. S. (22) 2001/02 West Ham U, Cheltenham T, Barnsley, Scunthorpe U

McCarthy, J. D. (18) 1995/6 Port Vale, Birmingham C

McCartney, G. (31) 2001/02 Sunderland, West Ham U, Sunderland

McCavana, T. (3) 1954/5 Coleraine

McCleary, J. W. (1) 1954/5 Cliftonville

McClelland, J. (6) 1960/1 Arsenal, Fulham

McClelland, J. (53) 1979/80 Mansfield T, Rangers, Watford, Leeds U

McCourt, F. (6) 1951/2 Manchester C

McCourt, P. J. (2) 2001/02 Rochdale, Celtic

McCoy, R. (1) 1986/7 Coleraine

McCreery, D. (67) 1975/6 Manchester U, QPR, Tulsa Roughnecks, Newcastle U, Heart of Midlothian

McCrory, S. (1) 1957/8 Southend U

McCullough, W. (10) 1960/1 Arsenal, Millwall

McCurdy, C. (1) 1979/80 Linfield

McDonald, A. (52) 1985/6 QPR

McElhinney, G. (6) 1983/4 Bolton W

McEvilly, L. R. (1) 2001/02 Rochdale

McFaul, I. (6) 1966/7 Linfield, Newcastle U

McGarry, J. K. (3) 1950/1 Cliftonville

McGaughey, M. (1) 1984/5 Linfield

McGibbon, P. C. G. (7) 1994/5 Manchester U, Wigan Ath

McGivern, R. (6) 2008/09 Manchester C

McGrath, R. (21) 1973/4 Tottenham H, Manchester U

McIlroy, J. (55) 1951/2 Burnley, Stoke C

McIlroy, S. B. (88) 1971/2 Manchester U, Stoke C, Manchester C

McKeag, W. (2) 1967/8 Glentoran

McKenna, J. (7) 1949/50 Huddersfield T

McKenzie, R. (1) 1966/7 Airdrieonians

McKinney, W. (1) 1965/6 Falkirk

McKnight, A. (10) 1987/8 Celtic, West Ham U

McLaughlin, J. (12) 1961/2 Shrewsbury T, Swansea T

McLean, B. S. (1) 2005/06 Rangers

McMahon, G. J. (17) 1994/5 Tottenham H, Stoke C

McMichael, A. (39) 1949/50 Newcastle U

McMillan, S. (2) 1962/3 Manchester U

McMordie, E. (21) 1968/9 Middlesbrough

McMorran, E. (15) 1946/7 Belfast Celtic, Barnsley, Doncaster R

McNally, B. A. (5) 1985/6 Shrewsbury T

McParland, P. (34) 1953/4 Aston Villa, Wolverhampton W

McVeigh, P. (20) 1998/9 Tottenham H, Norwich C

Montgomery, F. J. (1) 1954/5 Coleraine

Moore, C. (1) 1948/9 Glentoran

Moreland, V. (6) 1978/9 Derby Co

Morgan, S. (18) 1971/2 Port Vale, Aston Villa, Brighton & HA, Sparta Rotterdam

Morrow, S. J. (39) 1989/90 Arsenal, QPR

Mullan, G. (4) 1982/3 Glentoran

Mulryne, P. P. (27) 1996/7 Manchester U, Norwich C, Cardiff C

Murdock, C. J. (34) 1999/00 Preston NE, Hibernian, Crewe Alex, Rotherham U

Napier, R. (1) 1965/6 Bolton W

Neill, T. (59) 1960/1 Arsenal, Hull C

Nelson, S. (51) 1969/70 Arsenal, Brighton & HA

Nicholl, C. (51) 1974/5 Aston Villa, Southampton, Grimsby T

Nicholl, J. M. (73) 1975/6 Manchester U, Toronto Blizzard, Sunderland, Rangers, WBA

Nicholson, J. (41) 1960/1 Manchester U, Huddersfield T

Nolan, I. R. (18) 1996/7 Sheffield W, Bradford C, Wigan Ath

O'Boyle, G. (13) 1993/4 Dunfermline Ath, St Johnstone

O'Connor, M. J. (6) 2007/08 Crewe Alex

O'Doherty, A. (2) 1969/70 Coleraine

O'Driscoll, J. (3) 1948/9 Swansea T

O'Kane, L. (20) 1969/70 Nottingham F

O'Neill, C. (3) 1988/9 Motherwell

O'Neill, H. M. (64) 1971/2 Distillery, Nottingham F, Norwich C, Manchester C, Norwich C, Notts Co

O'Neill, J. (1) 1961/2 Sunderland

O'Neill, J. P. (39) 1979/80 Leicester C

O'Neill, M. A. (31) 1987/8 Newcastle U, Dundee U, Hibernian, Coventry C

Parke, J. (13) 1963/4 Linfield, Hibernian, Sunderland

Paterson, M. A. (8) 2007/08 Scunthorpe U, Burnley

Patterson, D. J. (17) 1993/4 Crystal P, Luton T, Dundee U

Peacock, R. (31) 1951/2 Celtic, Coleraine

Penney, S. (17) 1984/5 Brighton & HA

Platt, J. A. (23) 1975/6 Middlesbrough, Ballymena U, Coleraine

Quinn, J. M. (46) 1984/5 Blackburn R, Swindon T, Leicester, Bradford C, West Ham U, Bournemouth, Reading

Quinn, S. J. (50) 1995/6 Blackpool, WBA, Willem II, Sheffield W, Peterborough U, Northampton T

Rafferty, P. (1) 1979/80 Linfield
Ramsey, P. (14) 1983/4 Leicester C
Rice, P. (49) 1968/9 Arsenal
Robinson, S. (7) 1996/7 Bournemouth, Luton T
Rogan, A. (18) 1987/8 Celtic, Sunderland, Millwall
Ross, E. (1) 1968/9 Newcastle U
Rowland, K. (19) 1994/5 West Ham U, QPR
Russell, A. (1) 1946/7 Linfield
Ryan, R. (1) 1949/50 WBA

Sanchez, L. P. (3) 1986/7 Wimbledon
Scott, J. (2) 1957/8 Grimsby T
Scott, P. (10) 1974/5 Everton, York C, Aldershot
Sharkey, P. (1) 1975/6 Ipswich T
Shields, J. (1) 1956/7 Southampton
Shiels, D. (8) 2005/06 Hibernian
Simpson, W. (12) 1950/1 Rangers
Sloan, D. (2) 1968/9 Oxford
Sloan, T. (3) 1978/9 Manchester U
Sloan, W. (1) 1946/7 Arsenal
Smith, A. W. (18) 2002/03 Glentoran, Preston NE
Smyth, S. (9) 1947/8 Wolverhampton W, Stoke C
Smyth, W. (4) 1948/9 Distillery
Sonner, D. J. (13) 1997/8 Ipswich T, Sheffield W, Birmingham C, Nottingham F, Peterborough U
Spence, D. (29) 1974/5 Bury, Blackpool, Southend U
Sproule, I. (11) 2005/06 Hibernian, Bristol C
Stevenson, A. (3) 1946/7 Everton
Stewart, A. (7) 1966/7 Glentoran, Derby
Stewart, D. (1) 1977/8 Hull C
Stewart, I. (31) 1981/2 QPR, Newcastle U
Stewart, T. (1) 1960/1 Linfield

Taggart, G. P. (51) 1989/90 Barnsley, Bolton W, Leicester C

SCOTLAND

Adam, C. G. (2) 2006/07 Rangers
Aird, J. (4) 1953/4 Burnley
Aitken, G. G. (8) 1948/9 East Fife, Sunderland
Aitken, R. (57) 1979/80 Celtic, Newcastle U, St Mirren
Albiston, A. (14) 1981/2 Manchester U
Alexander, G. (38) 2001/02 Preston NE, Burnley
Alexander, N. (3) 2005/06 Cardiff C

Taylor, M. S. (77) 1998/9 Fulham, Birmingham C
Thompson, P. (8) 2005/06 Linfield, Stockport Co
Todd, S. (11) 1965/6 Burnley, Sheffield W
Toner, C. (2) 2002/03 Leyton Orient
Trainor, D. (1) 1966/7 Crusaders
Tuffey, J. (2) 2008/09 Partick T
Tully, C. (10) 1948/9 Celtic

Uprichard, N. (18) 1951/2 Swindon T, Portsmouth

Vernon, J. (17) 1946/7 Belfast Celtic, WBA

Walker, J. (1) 1954/5 Doncaster R
Walsh, D. (9) 1946/7 WBA
Walsh, W. (5) 1947/8 Manchester C
Watson, P. (1) 1970/1 Distillery
Webb, S. M. (4) 2005/06 Ross Co
Welsh, S. (4) 1965/6 Carlisle U
Whiteside, N. (38) 1981/2 Manchester U, Everton
Whitley, Jeff (20) 1996/7 Manchester C, Sunderland, Cardiff C
Whitley, Jim (3) 1997/8 Manchester C
Williams, M. S. (36) 1998/9 Chesterfield, Watford, Wimbledon, Stoke C, Wimbledon, Milton Keynes D
Williams, P. (1) 1990/1 WBA
Wilson, D. J. (24) 1986/7 Brighton & HA, Luton, Sheffield W
Wilson, K. J. (42) 1986/7 Ipswich T, Chelsea, Notts C, Walsall
Wilson, S. (12) 1961/2 Glenavon, Falkirk, Dundee
Wood, T. J. (1) 1995/6 Walsall
Worthington, N. (66) 1983/4 Sheffield W, Leeds U, Stoke C
Wright, T. J. (31) 1988/9 Newcastle U, Nottingham F, Manchester C

Allan, T. (2) 1973/4 Dundee
Anderson, J. (1) 1953/4 Leicester C
Anderson, R. (11) 2002/03 Aberdeen, Sunderland
Archibald, S. (27) 1979/80 Aberdeen, Tottenham H, Barcelona
Auld, B. (3) 1958/9 Celtic

Baird, H. (1) 1955/6 Airdrieonians
Baird, S. (7) 1956/7 Rangers

Bannon, E. (11) 1979/80 Dundee U
Barr, D. (1) 2008/09 Falkirk
Bauld, W. (3) 1949/50 Heart of
  Midlothian
Baxter, J. (34) 1960/1 Rangers,
  Sunderland
Beattie, C. (7) 2005/06 Celtic, WBA
Bell, W. (2) 1965/6 Leeds U
Bernard, P. R. (2) 1994/5 Oldham Ath
Berra, C. (4) 2007/08 Heart of
  Midlothian, Wolverhampton W
Bett, J. (25) 1981/2 Rangers, Lokeren,
  Aberdeen
Black, E. (2) 1987/8 Metz
Black, I. (1) 1947/8 Southampton
Blacklaw, A. (3) 1962/3 Burnley
Blackley, J. (7) 1973/4 Hibernian
Blair, J. (1) 1946/7 Blackpool
Blyth, J. (2) 1977/8 Coventry C
Bone, J. (2) 1971/2 Norwich C
Booth, S. (21) 1992/3 Aberdeen,
  Borussia Dortmund, Twente
Bowman, D. (6) 1991/2 Dundee U
Boyd, K. (15) 2005/06 Rangers
Boyd, T. (72) 1990/1 Motherwell,
  Chelsea, Celtic
Brand, R. (8) 1960/1 Rangers
Brazil, A. (13) 1979/80 Ipswich T,
  Tottenham H
Bremner, D. (1) 1975/6 Hibernian
Bremner, W. (54) 1964/5 Leeds U
Brennan, F. (7) 1946/7 Newcastle U
Broadfood, K. (3) 2008/09 Rangers
Brogan, J. (4) 1970/1 Celtic
Brown, A. (14) 1949/50 East Fife,
  Blackpool
Brown, H. (3) 1946/7 Partick Th
Brown, J. (1) 1974/5 Sheffield U
Brown, R. (3) 1946/7 Rangers
Brown, S. (16) 2005/06 Hibernian,
  Celtic
Brown, W. (28) 1957/8 Dundee,
  Tottenham H
Brownlie, J. (7) 1970/1 Hibernian
Buchan, M. (34) 1971/2 Aberdeen,
  Manchester U
Buckley, P. (3) 1953/4 Aberdeen
Burchill, M. J. (6) 1999/00 Celtic
Burke, C. (2) 2005/06 Rangers
Burley, C. W. (46) 1994/5 Chelsea,
  Celtic, Derby Co
Burley, G. (11) 1978/9 Ipswich T
Burns, F. (1) 1969/70 Manchester U
Burns, K. (20) 1973/4 Birmingham C,
  Nottingham F
Burns, T. (8) 1980/1 Celtic

Calderwood, C. (36) 1994/5 Tottenham
  H, Aston Villa
Caldow, E. (40) 1956/7 Rangers
Caldwell, G. (33) 2001/02 Newcastle U,
  Hibernian, Celtic
Caldwell, S. (9) 2000/01 Newcastle U,
  Sunderland
Callaghan, W. (2) 1969/70
  Dunfermline
Cameron, C. (28) 1998/9 Heart of
  Midlothian, Wolverhampton W
Campbell, R. (5) 1946/7 Falkirk,
  Chelsea
Campbell, W. (5) 1946/7 Morton
Canero, P. (1) 2003/04 Leicester C
Carr, W. (6) 1969/70 Coventry C
Chalmers, S. (5) 1964/5 Celtic
Clark, J. (4) 1965/6 Celtic
Clark, R. (17) 1967/8 Aberdeen
Clarke, S. (6) 1987/8 Chelsea
Clarkson, D. (2) 2007/08 Motherwell
Collins, J. (58) 1987/8 Hibernian,
  Celtic, Monaco, Everton
Collins, R. (31) 1950/1 Celtic, Everton,
  Leeds U
Colquhoun, E. (9) 1971/2 Sheffield U
Colquhoun, J. (2) 1987/8 Heart of
  Midlothian
Combe, R. (3) 1947/8 Hibernian
Commons, K. (4) 2008/09 Derby Co
Conn, A. (1) 1955/6 Heart of
  Midlothian
Conn, A. (2) 1974/5 Tottenham H
Connachan, E. (2) 1961/2 Dunfermline
  Ath
Connelly, G. (2) 1973/4 Celtic
Connolly, J. (1) 1972/3 Everton
Connor, R. (4) 1985/6 Dundee,
  Aberdeen
Cooke, C. (16) 1965/6 Dundee,
  Chelsea
Cooper, D. (22) 1979/80 Rangers,
  Motherwell
Cormack, P. (9) 1965/6 Hibernian,
  Nottingham F
Cowan, J. (25) 1947/8 Morton
Cowie, D. (20) 1952/3 Dundee
Cox, C. (1) 1947/8 Heart of Midlothian
Cox, S. (24) 1947/8 Rangers
Craig, J. (1) 1976/7 Celtic
Craig, J. P. (1) 1967/8 Celtic
Craig, T. (1) 1975/6 Newcastle U
Crainey, S. (6) 2001/02 Celtic,
  Southampton
Crawford, S. (25) 1994/5 Raith R,
  Dunfermline Ath, Plymouth Arg
Crerand, P. (16) 1960/1 Celtic,
  Manchester U

Cropley, A. (2) 1971/2 Hibernian
Cruickshank, J. (6) 1963/4 Heart of
Midlothian
Cullen, M. (1) 1955/6 Luton T
Cumming, J. (9) 1954/5 Heart of
Midlothian
Cummings. W. (1) 2001/02 Chelsea
Cunningham, W. (8) 1953/4 Preston
NE
Curran, H. (5) 1969/70
Wolverhampton W

Dailly, C. (67) 1996/7 Derby Co,
Blackburn R, West Ham U, Rangers
Dalglish, K. (102) 1971/2 Celtic,
Liverpool
Davidson, C. I. (17) 1998/9 Blackburn
R, Leicester C
Davidson, J. (8) 1953/4 Partick Th
Dawson, A. (5) 1979/80 Rangers
Deans, D. (2) 1974/5 Celtic
Delaney, J. (4) 1946/7 Manchester U
Devlin, P. J. (10) 2002/03 Birmingham
C
Dick, J. (1) 1958/9 West Ham U
Dickov, P. (10) 2000/01 Manchester C,
Leicester C, Blackburn R
Dickson, W. (5) 1969/70 Kilmarnock
Dobie, R. S. (6) 2001/02 WBA
Docherty, T. (25) 1951/2 Preston NE,
Arsenal
Dodds, D. (2) 1983/4 Dundee U
Dodds, W. (26) 1996/7 Aberdeen,
Dundee U, Rangers
Donachie, W. (35) 1971/2 Manchester
C
Donnelly, S. (10) 1996/7 Celtic
Dougall, C. (1) 1946/7 Birmingham C
Dougan, R. (1) 1949/50 Heart of
Midlothian
Douglas, R. (19) 2001/02 Celtic,
Leicester C
Doyle, J. (1) 1975/6 Ayr U
Duncan, A. (6) 1974/5 Hibernian
Duncan, D. (3) 1947/8 East Fife
Duncanson, J. (1) 1946/7 Rangers
Durie, G. S. (43) 1987/8 Chelsea,
Tottenham H, Rangers
Durrant, I. (20) 1987/8 Rangers,
Kilmarnock

Elliott, M. S. (18) 1997/8 Leicester C
Evans, A. (4) 1981/2 Aston Villa
Evans, R. (48) 1948/9 Celtic, Chelsea
Ewing, T. (2) 1957/8 Partick Th

Farm, G. (10) 1952/3 Blackpool

Ferguson, B. (45) 1998/9 Rangers,
Blackburn R, Rangers
Ferguson, Derek (2) 1987/8 Rangers
Ferguson, Duncan (7) 1991/2 Dundee
U, Everton
Ferguson, I. (9) 1988/9 Rangers
Ferguson, R. (7) 1965/6 Kilmarnock
Fernie, W. (12) 1953/4 Celtic
Flavell, R. (2) 1946/7 Airdrieonians
Fleck, R. (4) 1989/90 Norwich C
Fleming, C. (1) 1953/4 East Fife
Fletcher, D. B. (42) 2003/04
Manchester U
Fletcher, S. (4) 2007/08 Hibernian
Forbes, A. (14) 1946/7 Sheffield U,
Arsenal
Ford, D. (3) 1973/4 Heart of
Midlothian
Forrest, J. (1) 1957/8 Motherwell
Forrest, J. (5) 1965/6 Rangers,
Aberdeen
Forsyth, A. (10) 1971/2 Partick Th,
Manchester U
Forsyth, C. (4) 1963/4 Kilmarnock
Forsyth, T. (22) 1970/1 Motherwell,
Rangers
Fraser, D. (2) 1967/8 WBA
Fraser, W. (2) 1954/5 Sunderland
Freedman, D. A. (2) 2001/02 Crystal P

Gabriel, J. (2) 1960/1 Everton
Gallacher, K. W. (53) 1987/8 Dundee
U, Coventry C, Blackburn R,
Newcastle U
Gallacher, P. (8) 2001/02 Dundee U
Gallagher, P. (1) 2003/04 Blackburn R
Galloway, M. (1) 1991/2 Celtic
Gardiner, W. (1) 1957/8 Motherwell
Gemmell, T. (2) 1954/5 St Mirren
Gemmell, T. (18) 1965/6 Celtic
Gemmill, A. (43) 1970/1 Derby Co,
Nottingham F, Birmingham C
Gemmill, S. (26) 1994/5 Nottingham F,
Everton
Gibson, D. (7) 1962/3 Leicester C
Gillespie, G. T. (13) 1987/8 Liverpool
Gilzean, A. (22) 1963/4 Dundee,
Tottenham H
Glass, S. (1) 1998/9 Newcastle U
Glavin, R. (1) 1976/7 Celtic
Glen, A. (2) 1955/6 Aberdeen
Goram, A. L. (43) 1985/6 Oldham Ath,
Hibernian, Rangers
Gordon, C. S. (36) 2003/04 Heart of
Midlothian, Sunderland
Gough, C. R. (61) 1982/3 Dundee U,
Tottenham H, Rangers
Gould, J. (2) 1999/00 Celtic

Govan, J. (6) 1947/8 Hibernian
Graham, A. (11) 1977/8 Leeds U
Graham, G. (12) 1971/2 Arsenal,
Manchester U
Grant, J. (2) 1958/9 Hibernian
Grant, P. (2) 1988/9 Celtic
Gray, A. (20) 1975/6 Aston Villa,
Wolverhampton W, Everton
Gray, A. D. (2) 2002/03 Bradford C
Gray, E. (12) 1968/9 Leeds U
Gray F. (32) 1975/6 Leeds U,
Nottingham F, Leeds U
Green, A. (6) 1970/1 Blackpool,
Newcastle U
Greig, J. (44) 1963/4 Rangers
Gunn, B. (6) 1989/90 Norwich C

Haddock, H. (6) 1954/5 Clyde
Haffey, F. (2) 1959/60 Celtic
Hamilton, A. (24) 1961/2 Dundee
Hamilton, G. (5) 1946/7 Aberdeen
Hamilton, W. (1) 1964/5 Hibernian
Hammell, S. (1) 2004/05 Motherwell
Hansen, A. (26) 1978/9 Liverpool
Hansen, J. (2) 1971/2 Partick Th
Harper, J. (4) 1972/3 Aberdeen,
Hibernian, Aberdeen
Hartford, A. (50) 1971/2 WBA,
Manchester C, Everton, Manchester
C
Hartley, P. J. (22) 2004/05 Heart of
Midlothian, Celtic
Harvey, D. (16) 1972/3 Leeds U
Haughney, M. (1) 1953/4 Celtic
Hay, D. (27) 1969/70 Celtic
Hegarty, P. (8) 1978/9 Dundee U
Henderson, J. (7) 1952/3 Portsmouth,
Arsenal
Henderson, W. (29) 1962/3 Rangers
Hendry, E. C. J. (51) 1992/3 Blackburn
R, Rangers, Coventry C, Bolton W
Herd, D. (5) 1958/9 Arsenal
Herd, G. (5) 1957/8 Clyde
Herriot, J. (8) 1968/9 Birmingham C
Hewie, J. (19) 1955/6 Charlton Ath
Holt, D. D. (5) 1962/3 Heart of
Midlothian
Holt, G. J. (10) 2000/01 Kilmarnock,
Norwich C
Holton, J. (15) 1972/3 Manchester U
Hope, R. (2) 1967/8 WBA
Hopkin, D. (7) 1996/7 Crystal P, Leeds
U
Houliston, W. (3) 1948/9 Queen of the
South
Houston, S. (1) 1975/6 Manchester U
Howie, H. (1) 1948/9 Hibernian
Hughes, J. (8) 1964/5 Celtic

Hughes, R. D. (5) 2003/04 Portsmouth
Hughes, W. (1) 1974/5 Sunderland
Humphries, W. (1) 1951/2 Motherwell
Hunter, A. (4) 1971/2 Kilmarnock,
Celtic
Hunter, W. (3) 1959/60 Motherwell
Husband, J. (1) 1946/7 Partick Th
Hutchison, D. (26) 1998/9 Everton,
Sunderland, West Ham U
Hutchison, T. (17) 1973/4 Coventry C
Hutton, A. (10) 2006/07 Rangers,
Tottenham H

Imlach, S. (4) 1957/8 Nottingham F
Irvine, B. (9) 1990/1 Aberdeen
Iwelumo, C. R. (2) 2008/09
Wolverhampton W

Jackson, C. (8) 1974/5 Rangers
Jackson, D. (28) 1994/5 Hibernian,
Celtic
Jardine, A. (38) 1970/1 Rangers
Jarvie, A. (3) 1970/1 Airdrieonians
Jess, E. (18) 1992/3 Aberdeen,
Coventry C, Aberdeen
Johnston, A. (18) 1998/9 Sunderland,
Rangers, Middlesbrough
Johnston, M. (38) 1983/4 Watford,
Celtic, Nantes, Rangers
Johnston, L. (2) 1947/8 Clyde
Johnston, W. (22) 1965/6 Rangers,
WBA
Johnstone, D. (14) 1972/3 Rangers
Johnstone, J. (23) 1964/5 Celtic
Johnstone, R. (17) 1950/1 Hibernian,
Manchester C
Jordan, J. (52) 1972/3 Leeds U,
Manchester U, AC Milan

Kelly, H. (1) 1951/2 Blackpool
Kelly, J. (2) 1948/9 Barnsley
Kennedy, Jim (6) 1963/4 Celtic
Kennedy, John (1) 2003/04 Celtic
Kennedy, S. (5) 1974/5 Rangers
Kennedy, S. (8) 1977/8 Aberdeen
Kerr, A. (2) 1954/5 Partick Th
Kerr, B. (3) 2002/03 Newcastle U
Kyle, K. (9) 2001/02 Sunderland

Lambert, P. (40) 1994/5 Motherwell,
Borussia Dortmund, Celtic
Law, D. (55) 1958/9 Huddersfield T,
Manchester C, Torino, Manchester
U, Manchester C
Lawrence, T. (3) 1962/3 Liverpool
Leggat, G. (18) 1955/6 Aberdeen,
Fulham

307

Leighton, J. (91) 1982/3 Aberdeen, Manchester U, Hibernian, Aberdeen
Lennox, R. (10) 1966/7 Celtic
Leslie, L. (5) 1960/1 Airdrieonians
Levein, C. (16) 1989/90 Heart of Midlothian
Liddell, W. (28) 1946/7 Liverpool
Linwood, A. (1) 1949/50 Clyde
Little, R. J. (1) 1952/3 Rangers
Logie, J. (1) 1952/3 Arsenal
Long, H. (1) 1946/7 Clyde
Lorimer, P. (21) 1969/70 Leeds U

Macari, L. (24) 1971/2 Celtic, Manchester U
Macaulay, A. (7) 1946/7 Brentford, Arsenal
MacDougall, E. (7) 1974/5 Norwich C
Mackay, D. (22) 1956/7 Heart of Midlothian, Tottenham H
Mackay, G. (4) 1987/8 Heart of Midlothian
Mackay, M. (5) 2003/04 Norwich C
Maloney, S. R. (15) 2005/06 Celtic, Aston Villa, Celtic
Malpas, M. (55) 1983/4 Dundee U
Marshall, D. J. (2) 2004/05 Celtic
Marshall, G. (1) 1991/2 Celtic
Martin, B. (2) 1994/5 Motherwell
Martin, F. (6) 1953/4 Aberdeen
Martin, N. (3) 1964/5 Hibernian, Sunderland
Martis, J. (1) 1960/1 Motherwell
Mason, J. (7) 1948/9 Third Lanark
Masson, D. (17) 1975/6 QPR, Derby C
Mathers, D. (1) 1953/4 Partick Th
Matteo, D. (6) 2000/01 Leeds U
McAllister, B. (3) 1996/7 Wimbledon
McAllister, G. (57) 1989/90 Leicester C, Leeds U, Coventry C
McAllister, J. R. (1) 2003/04 Livingston
McAvennie, F. (5) 1985/6 West Ham U, Celtic
McBride, J. (2) 1966/7 Celtic
McCall, S. M. (40) 1989/90 Everton, Rangers
McCalliog, J. (5) 1966/7 Sheffield W, Wolverhampton W
McCann, N. D. (26) 1998/9 Heart of Midlothian, Rangers, Southampton
McCann, R. (5) 1958/9 Motherwell
McClair, B. (30) 1986/7 Celtic, Manchester U
McCloy, P. (4) 1972/3 Rangers
McCoist, A. (61) 1985/6 Rangers, Kilmarnock

McColl, I. (14) 1949/50 Rangers
McCormack, R. (3) 20007/08 Motherwell, Cardiff C
McCreadie, E. (23) 1964/5 Chelsea
McCulloch, L. (15) 2004/05 Wigan Ath, Rangers
MacDonald, A. (1) 1975/6 Rangers
McDonald, J. (2) 1955/6 Sunderland
McEveley, J. (3) 2007/08 Derby Co
McFadden, J. (42) 2001/02 Motherwell, Everton, Birmingham C
McFarlane, W. (1) 1946/7 Heart of Midlothian
McGarr, E. (2) 1969/70 Aberdeen
McGarvey, F. (7) 1978/9 Liverpool, Celtic
McGhee, M. (4) 1982/3 Aberdeen
McGinlay, J. (13) 1993/4 Bolton W
McGrain, D. (62) 1972/3 Celtic
McGregor, A. (4) 2006/07 Rangers
McGrory, J. (3) 1964/5 Kilmarnock
McInally, A. (8) 1988/9 Aston Villa, Bayern Munich
McInally, J. (10) 1986/7 Dundee U
McInnes, D. (2) 2002/03 WBA
MacKay, D. (14) 1958/9 Celtic
McKean, R. (1) 1975/6 Rangers
MacKenzie, J. (9) 1953/4 Partick Th
McKimmie, S. (40) 1988/9 Aberdeen
McKinlay, T. (22) 1995/6 Celtic
McKinlay, W. (29) 1993/4 Dundee U, Blackburn R
McKinnon, Rob (3) 1993/4 Motherwell
McKinnon, Ronnie (28) 1965/6 Rangers
McLaren, Alan (24) 1991/2 Heart of Midlothian, Rangers
McLaren, Andy (4) 1946/7 Preston NE
McLaren, Andy (1) 2000/01 Kilmarnock
McLean, G. (1) 1967/8 Dundee
McLean, T. (6) 1968/9 Kilmarnock
McLeish, A. (77) 1979/80 Aberdeen
McLeod, J. (4) 1960/1 Hibernian
MacLeod, M. (20) 1984/5 Celtic, Borussia Dortmund, Hibernian
McLintock, F. (9) 1962/3 Leicester C, Arsenal
McManus, S. (18) 2006/07 Celtic
McMillan, I. (6) 1951/2 Airdrieonians, Rangers
McNamara, J. (33) 1996/7 Celtic, Wolverhampton W
McNamee, D. (4) 2003/04 Livingston
McNaught, W. (5) 1950/1 Raith R
McNaughton, K. (4) 2001/02 Aberdeen, Cardiff C

McNeill, W. (29) 1960/1 Celtic

McPhail, J. (5) 1949/50 Celtic

McPherson, D. (27) 1988/9 Heart of Midlothian, Rangers

McQueen, G. (30) 1973/4 Leeds U, Manchester U

McStay, P. (76) 1983/4 Celtic

McSwegan, G. (2) 1999/00 Heart of Midlothian

Millar, J. (2) 1962/3 Rangers

Miller, C. (1) 2000/01 Dundee U

Miller, K. (42) 2000/01 Rangers, Wolverhampton W, Celtic, Derby Co, Rangers

Miller, L. (2) 2005/06 Dundee U, Aberdeen

Miller, W. (6) 1946/7 Celtic

Miller, W. (65) 1974/5 Aberdeen

Mitchell, R. (2) 1950/1 Newcastle U

Mochan, N. (3) 1953/4 Celtic

Moir, W. (1) 1949/50 Bolton W

Moncur, R. (16) 1967/8 Newcastle U

Morgan, W. (21) 1967/8 Burnley, Manchester U

Morris, H. (1) 1949/50 East Fife

Morrison, J. C. (5) 2007/08 WBA

Mudie, J. (17) 1956/7 Blackpool

Mulhall, G. (3) 1959/60 Aberdeen, Sunderland

Munro, F. (9) 1970/1 Wolverhampton W

Munro, I. (7) 1978/9 St Mirren

Murdoch, R. (12) 1965/6 Celtic

Murray, I. (6) 2002/03 Hibernian, Rangers

Murray, J. (5) 1957/8 Heart of Midlothian

Murray, S. (1) 1971/2 Aberdeen

Murty, G. S. (4) 2003/04 Reading

Naismith, S. J. (2) 2006/07 Kilmarnock, Rangers

Narey, D. (35) 1976/7 Dundee U

Naysmith, G. A. (46) 1999/00 Heart of Midlothian, Everton, Sheffield U

Neilson, R. (1) 2006/07 Heart of Midlothian

Nevin, P. K. F. (28) 1985/6 Chelsea, Everton, Tranmere R

Nicholas, C. (20) 1982/3 Celtic, Arsenal, Aberdeen

Nicholson, B. (3) 2000/01 Dunfermline Ath

Nicol, S. (27) 1984/5 Liverpool

O'Connor, G. (15) 2001/02 Hibernian, Lokomotiv Moscow, Birmingham C

O'Donnell, P. (1) 1993/4 Motherwell

O'Hare, J. (13) 1969/70 Derby Co

O'Neil, B. (7) 1995/6 Celtic, Wolfsburg, Derby Co, Preston NE

O'Neil, J. (1) 2000/01 Hibernian

Ormond, W. (6) 1953/4 Hibernian

Orr, T. (2) 1951/2 Morton

Parker, A. (15) 1954/5 Falkirk, Everton

Parlane, D. (12) 1972/3 Rangers

Paton, A. (2) 1951/2 Motherwell

Pearson, S. P. (10) 2003/04 Motherwell, Celtic, Derby Co

Pearson, T. (2) 1946/7 Newcastle U

Penman, A. (1) 1965/6 Dundee

Pettigrew, W. (5) 1975/6 Motherwell

Plenderleith, J. (1) 1960/1 Manchester C

Pressley, S. J. (32) 1999/00 Heart of Midlothian

Provan, David (10) 1979/80 Celtic

Provan, Davie (5) 1963/4 Rangers

Quashie, N. F. (14) 2003/04 Portsmouth, Southampton, WBA

Quinn, P. (4) 1960/1 Motherwell

Rae, G. P. (14) 2000/01 Dundee, Rangers, Cardiff C

Redpath, W. (9) 1948/9 Motherwell

Reilly, L. (38) 1948/9 Hibernian

Ring, T. (12) 1952/3 Clyde

Rioch, B. (24) 1974/5 Derby Co, Everton, Derby Co

Riordan, D. G. (1) 2005/06 Hibernian

Ritchie, P. S. (7) 1998/9 Heart of Midlothian, Bolton W, Walsall

Ritchie, W. (1) 1961/2 Rangers

Robb, D. (5) 1970/1 Aberdeen

Robertson, A. (5) 1954/5 Clyde

Robertson, D. (3) 1991/2 Rangers

Robertson, H. (1) 1961/2 Dundee

Robertson, J. (16) 1990/1 Heart of Midlothian

Robertson, J. G. (1) 1964/5 Tottenham H

Robertson, J. N. (28) 1977/8 Nottingham F, Derby Co

Robertson, S. (1) 2008/09 Dundee U

Robinson, B. (4) 1973/4 Dundee

Robson, B. (6) 2007/08 Dundee U, Celtic

Ross, M. (13) 2001/02 Rangers

Rough, A. (53) 1975/6 Partick Th, Hibernian

Rougvie, D. (1) 1983/4 Aberdeen

Rutherford, E. (1) 1947/8 Rangers

St John, I. (21) 1958/9 Motherwell, Liverpool
Schaedler, E. (1) 1973/4 Hibernian
Scott, A. (16) 1956/7 Rangers, Everton
Scott, Jimmy (1) 1965/6 Hibernian
Scott, Jocky (2) 1970/1 Dundee
Scoular, J. (9) 1950/1 Portsmouth
Severin, S. D. (15) 2001/02 Heart of Midlothian, Aberdeen
Sharp, G. M. (12) 1984/5 Everton
Shaw, D. (8) 1946/7 Hibernian
Shaw, J. (4) 1946/7 Rangers
Shearer, D. (7) 1993/4 Aberdeen
Shearer, R. (4) 1960/1 Rangers
Simpson, N. (4) 1982/3 Aberdeen
Simpson, R. (5) 1966/7 Celtic
Sinclair, J. (1) 1965/6 Leicester C
Smith, D. (2) 1965/6 Aberdeen, Rangers
Smith, E. (2) 1958/9 Celtic
Smith, G. (18) 1946/7 Hibernian
Smith, H. G. (3) 1987/8 Heart of Midlothian
Smith, J. (4) 1967/8 Aberdeen, Newcastle U
Smith, J. (2) 2002/03 Celtic
Souness, G. (54) 1974/5 Middlesbrough, Liverpool, Sampdoria
Speedie, D. R. (10) 1984/5 Chelsea, Coventry C
Spencer, J. (14) 1994/5 Chelsea, QPR
Stanton, P. (16) 1965/6 Hibernian
Steel, W. (30) 1946/7 Morton, Derby C, Dundee
Stein, C. (21) 1968/9 Rangers, Coventry C
Stephen, J. (2) 1946/7 Bradford PA
Stewart, D. (1) 1977/8 Leeds U
Stewart, J. (2) 1976/7 Kilmarnock, Middlesbrough
Stewart, M. J. (4) 2001/02 Manchester U, Heart of Midlothian
Stewart, R. (10) 1980/1 West Ham U
Stockdale, R. K. (5) 2001/02 Middlesbrough
Strachan, G. (50) 1979/80 Aberdeen, Manchester U, Leeds U
Sturrock, P. (20) 1980/1 Dundee U
Sullivan, N. (28) 1996/7 Wimbledon, Tottenham H

Teale, G. (13) 2005/06 Wigan Ath, Derby Co
Telfer, P. N. (1) 1999/00 Coventry C
Telfer, W. (1) 1953/4 St Mirren
Thompson, S. (16) 2001/02 Dundee U, Rangers

Thomson, K. (1) 2008/09 Rangers
Thomson, W. (7) 1979/80 St Mirren
Thornton, W. (7) 1946/7 Rangers
Toner, W. (2) 1958/9 Kilmarnock
Turnbull, E. (8) 1947/8 Hibernian

Ure, I. (11) 1961/2 Dundee, Arsenal

Waddell, W. (17) 1946/7 Rangers
Walker, A. (3) 1987/8 Celtic
Walker, J. N. (2) 1992/3 Heart of Midlothian, Partick Th
Wallace, I. A. (3) 1977/8 Coventry C
Wallace, W. S. B. (7) 1964/5 Heart of Midlothian, Celtic
Wardhaugh, J. (2) 1954/5 Heart of Midlothian
Wark, J. (29) 1978/9 Ipswich T, Liverpool
Watson, J. (2) 1947/8 Motherwell, Huddersfield T
Watson, R. (1) 1970/1 Motherwell
Webster, A. (22) 2002/03 Heart of Midlothian
Weir, A. (6) 1958/9 Motherwell
Weir, D. G. (63) 1996/7 Heart of Midlothian, Everton, Rangers
Weir, P. (6) 1979/80 St Mirren, Aberdeen
White, J. (22) 1958/9 Falkirk, Tottenham H
Whyte, D. (12) 1987/8 Celtic, Middlesbrough, Aberdeen
Wilkie, L. (11) 2001/02 Dundee
Williams, G. (5) 2001/02 Nottingham F
Wilson, A. (1) 1953/4 Portsmouth
Wilson, D. (22) 1960/1 Rangers
Wilson, I. A. (5) 1986/7 Leicester C, Everton
Wilson, P. (1) 1974/5 Celtic
Wilson, R. (2) 1971/2 Arsenal
Winters, R. (1) 1998/9 Aberdeen
Wood, G. (4) 1978/9 Everton, Arsenal
Woodburn, W. (24) 1946/7 Rangers
Wright, K. (1) 1991/2 Hibernian
Wright, S. (2) 1992/3 Aberdeen
Wright, T. (3) 1952/3 Sunderland

Yeats, R. (2) 1964/5 Liverpool
Yorston, H. (1) 1954/5 Aberdeen
Young, A. (8) 1959/60 Heart of Midlothian, Everton
Young, G. (53) 1946/7 Rangers
Younger, T. (24) 1954/5 Hibernian, Liverpool

WALES

Aizlewood, M. (39) 1985/6 Charlton Ath, Leeds U, Bradford C, Bristol C, Cardiff C

Allchurch, I. (68) 1950/1 Swansea T, Newcastle U, Cardiff C, Swansea T

Allchurch, L. (11) 1954/5 Swansea T, Sheffield U

Allen, B. (2) 1950/1 Coventry C

Allen, J. M. (1) 2008/09 Swansea C

Allen, M. (14) 1985/6 Watford, Norwich C, Millwall, Newcastle U

Baker, C. (7) 1957/8 Cardiff C

Baker, W. (1) 1947/8 Cardiff C

Bale, G. (20) 2005/06 Southampton, Tottenham H

Barnard, D. S. (22) 1997/8 Barnsley, Grimsby

Barnes, W. (22) 1947/8 Arsenal

Bellamy, C. D. (56) 1997/8 Norwich C, Coventry C, Newcastle U, Blackburn R, Liverpool, West Ham U, Manchester C

Berry, G. (5) 1978/9 Wolverhampton W, Stoke C

Blackmore, C. G. (39) 1984/5 Manchester U, Middlesbrough

Blake, N. (29) 1993/4 Sheffield U, Bolton W, Blackburn R, Wolverhampton W

Bodin, P. J. (23) 1989/90 Swindon T, Crystal P, Swindon T

Bowen, D. (19) 1954/5 Arsenal

Bowen, J. P. (2) 1993/4 Swansea C, Birmingham C

Bowen, M. R. (41) 1985/6 Tottenham H, Norwich C, West Ham U

Boyle, T. (2) 1980/1 Crystal P

Brown, J. R. (2) 2005/06 Gillingham, Blackburn R

Browning, M. T. (5) 1995/6 Bristol R, Huddersfield T

Burgess, R. (32) 1946/7 Tottenham H

Burton, O. (9) 1962/3 Norwich C, Newcastle U

Cartwright, L. (7) 1973/4 Coventry C, Wrexham

Charles, J. (38) 1949/50 Leeds U, Juventus, Leeds U, Cardiff C

Charles, J. M. (19) 1980/1 Swansea C, QPR, Oxford U

Charles, M. (31) 1954/5 Swansea T, Arsenal, Cardiff C

Church, S. R. (2) 2008/09 Reading

Clarke, R. (22) 1948/9 Manchester C

Coleman, C. (32) 1991/2 Crystal P, Blackburn R, Fulham

Collins, D. L. (7) 2004/05 Sunderland

Collins, J. M. (29) 2003/04 Cardiff C, West Ham U

Collison, J. D. (5) 2007/08 West Ham U

Cornforth, J. M. (2) 1994/5 Swansea C

Cotterill, D. R. G. B. (13) 2005/06 Bristol C, Wigan Ath, Sheffield U

Coyne, D. (16) 1995/6 Tranmere R, Grimsby T, Leicester C, Burnley, Tranmere R

Crofts, A. L. (12) 2005/06 Gillingham

Crossley, M. G. (8) 1996/7 Nottingham F, Middlesbrough, Fulham

Crowe, V. (16) 1958/9 Aston Villa

Curtis, A. (35) 1975/6 Swansea C, Leeds U, Swansea C, Southampton, Cardiff C

Daniel, R. (21) 1950/1 Arsenal, Sunderland

Davies, A. (13) 1982/3 Manchester U, Newcastle U, Swansea C, Bradford C

Davies, A. R. (1) 2005/06 Yeovil T

Davies, C. (1) 1971/2 Charlton Ath

Davies, C. M. (5) 2005/06 Oxford U, Verona, Oldham Ath

Davies, D. (52) 1974/5 Everton, Wrexham, Swansea C

Davies, G. (16) 1979/80 Fulham, Manchester C

Davies, R. Wyn (34) 1963/4 Bolton W, Newcastle U, Manchester C, Manchester U, Blackpool

Davies, Reg (6) 1952/3 Newcastle U

Davies, Ron (29) 1963/4 Norwich C, Southampton, Portsmouth

Davies, S. (57) 2000/01 Tottenham H, Everton, Fulham

Davies, S. I. (1) 1995/6 Manchester U

Davis, G. (3) 1977/8 Wrexham

Deacy, N. (12) 1976/7 PSV Eindhoven, Beringen

Delaney, M. A. (36) 1999/00 Aston Villa

Derrett, S. (4) 1968/9 Cardiff C

Dibble, A. (3) 1985/6 Luton T, Manchester C

Duffy, R. M. (13) 2005/06 Portsmouth

Durban, A. (27) 1965/6 Derby C

Dwyer, P. (10) 1977/8 Cardiff C

Eardley, N. (10) 2007/08 Oldham Ath

Earnshaw, R. (45) 2001/02 Cardiff C, WBA, Norwich C, Derby Co, Nottingham F

Easter, J. M. (7) 2006/07 Wycombe W, Plymouth Arg

Eastwood, F. (10) 2007/08 Wolverhampton W

Edwards, C. N. H. (1) 1995/6 Swansea C

Edwards, D. (14) 2007/08 Luton T, Wolverhampton W

Edwards, G. (12) 1946/7 Birmingham C, Cardiff C

Edwards, I. (4) 1977/8 Chester, Wrexham

Edwards, R. O. (15) 2002/03 Aston Villa, Wolverhampton W

Edwards, R. W. (4) 1997/8 Bristol C

Edwards, T. (2) 1956/7 Charlton Ath

Emanuel, J. (2) 1972/3 Bristol C

England, M. (44) 1961/2 Blackburn R, Tottenham H

Evans, B. (7) 1971/2 Swansea C, Hereford U

Evans, C. M. (10) 2007/08 Manchester C

Evans, I. (13) 1975/6 Crystal P

Evans, P. S. (2) 2001/02 Brentford, Bradford C

Evans, R. (1) 1963/4 Swansea T

Evans, S. J. (7) 2006/07 Wrexham

Felgate, D. (1) 1983/4 Lincoln C

Fletcher, C. N. (36) 2003/04 Bournemouth, West Ham U, Crystal P

Flynn, B. (66) 1974/5 Burnley, Leeds U, Burnley

Ford, T. (38) 1946/7 Swansea T, Aston Villa, Sunderland, Cardiff C

Foulkes, W. (11) 1951/2 Newcastle U

Freestone, R. (1) 1999/00 Swansea C

Gabbidon, D. L. (40) 2001/02 Cardiff C, West Ham U

Garner, G. (1) 2005/06 Leyton Orient

Giggs, R. J. (64) 1991/2 Manchester U

Giles, D. (12) 1979/80 Swansea C, Crystal P

Godfrey, B. (3) 1963/4 Preston NE

Goss, J. (9) 1990/1 Norwich C

Green, C. (15) 1964/5 Birmingham C

Green, R. M. (2) 1997/8 Wolverhampton W

Griffiths, A. (17) 1970/1 Wrexham

Griffiths, H. (1) 1952/3 Swansea T

Griffiths, M. (11) 1946/7 Leicester C

Gunter, C. R. (16) 2006/07 Cardiff C, Tottenham H

Hall, G. D. (9) 1987/8 Chelsea

Harrington, A. (11) 1955/6 Cardiff C

Harris, C. (24) 1975/6 Leeds U

Harris, W. (6) 1953/4 Middlesbrough

Hartson, J. (51) 1994/5 Arsenal, West Ham U, Wimbledon, Coventry C, Celtic

Haworth, S. O. (5) 1996/7 Cardiff C, Coventry C

Hennessey, T. (39) 1961/2 Birmingham C, Nottingham F, Derby Co

Hennessey, W. R. (19) 2006/07 Wolverhampton W

Hewitt, R. (5) 1957/8 Cardiff C

Hill, M. (2) 1971/2 Ipswich T

Hockey, T. (9) 1971/2 Sheffield U, Norwich C, Aston Villa

Hodges, G. (18) 1983/4 Wimbledon, Newcastle U, Watford, Sheffield U

Holden, A. (1) 1983/4 Chester C

Hole, B. (30) 1962/3 Cardiff C, Blackburn R, Aston Villa, Swansea C

Hollins, D. (11) 1961/2 Newcastle U

Hopkins, J. (16) 1982/3 Fulham, Crystal P

Hopkins, M. (34) 1955/6 Tottenham H

Horne, B. (59) 1987/8 Portsmouth, Southampton, Everton, Birmingham C

Howells, R. (2) 1953/4 Cardiff C

Hughes, C. M. (8) 1991/2 Luton T, Wimbledon

Hughes, I. (4) 1950/1 Luton T

Hughes, L. M. (72) 1983/4 Manchester U, Barcelona, Manchester U, Chelsea, Southampton

Hughes, W. (3) 1946/7 Birmingham C

Hughes, W. A. (5) 1948/9 Blackburn R

Humphreys, J. (1) 1946/7 Everton

Jackett, K. (31) 1982/3 Watford

James, G. (9) 1965/6 Blackpool

James, L. (54) 1971/2 Burnley, Derby C, QPR, Burnley, Swansea C, Sunderland

James, R. M. (47) 1978/9 Swansea C, Stoke C, QPR, Leicester C, Swansea C

Jarvis, A. (3) 1966/7 Hull C

Jenkins, S. R. (16) 1995/6 Swansea C, Huddersfield T

Johnson, A. J. (15) 1998/9 Nottingham F, WBA

Johnson, M. (1) 1963/4 Swansea T

Jones, A. (6) 1986/7 Port Vale, Charlton Ath
Jones, Barrie (15) 1962/3 Swansea T, Plymouth Argyle, Cardiff C
Jones, Bryn (4) 1946/7 Arsenal
Jones, C. (59) 1953/4 Swansea T, Tottenham H, Fulham
Jones, D. (8) 1975/6 Norwich C
Jones, E. (4) 1947/8 Swansea T, Tottenham H
Jones, J. (72) 1975/6 Liverpool, Wrexham, Chelsea, Huddersfield T
Jones, K. (1) 1949/50 Aston Villa
Jones, M. A. (2) 2006/07 Wrexham
Jones, M. G. (13) 1999/00 Leeds U, Leicester C
Jones, P. L. (2) 1996/7 Liverpool, Tranmere R
Jones, P. S. (50) 1996/7 Stockport Co, Southampton, Wolverhampton W, QPR
Jones, R. (1) 1993/4 Sheffield W
Jones, T. G. (13) 1946/7 Everton
Jones, V. P. (9) 1994/5 Wimbledon
Jones, W. (1) 1970/1 Bristol R

Kelsey, J. (41) 1953/4 Arsenal
King, A. (1) 2008/09 Leicester C
King, J. (1) 1954/5 Swansea T
Kinsey, N. (7) 1950/1 Norwich C, Birmingham C
Knill, A. R. (1) 1988/9 Swansea C
Koumas, J. (34) 2000/01 Tranmere R, WBA, Wigan Ath
Krzywicki, R. (8) 1969/70 WBA, Huddersfield T

Lambert, R. (5) 1946/7 Liverpool
Law, B. J. (1) 1989/90 QPR
Lea, C. (2) 1964/5 Ipswich T
Ledley, J. C. (29) 2005/06 Cardiff C
Leek, K. (13) 1960/1 Leicester C, Newcastle U, Birmingham C, Northampton T
Legg, A. (6) 1995/6 Birmingham C, Cardiff C
Lever, A. (1) 1952/3 Leicester C
Lewis, D. (1) 1982/3 Swansea C
Llewellyn, C. M. (6) 1997/8 Norwich C, Wrexham
Lloyd, B. (3) 1975/6 Wrexham
Lovell, S. (6) 1981/2 Crystal P, Millwall
Lowndes, S. (10) 1982/3 Newport Co, Millwall, Barnsley
Lowrie, G. (4) 1947/8 Coventry C, Newcastle U
Lucas, M. (4) 1961/2 Leyton Orient
Lucas, W. (7) 1948/9 Swansea T

Maguire, G. T. (7) 1989/90 Portsmouth
Mahoney, J. (51) 1967/8 Stoke C, Middlesbrough, Swansea C
Mardon, P. J. (1) 1995/6 WBA
Margetson, M. W. (1) 2003/04 Cardiff C
Marriott, A. (5) 1995/6 Wrexham
Marustik, C. (6) 1981/2 Swansea C
Medwin, T. (30) 1952/3 Swansea T, Tottenham H
Melville, A. K. (65) 1989/90 Swansea C, Oxford U, Sunderland, Fulham, West Ham U
Mielczarek, R. (1) 1970/1 Rotherham U
Millington, A. (21) 1962/3 WBA, Crystal P, Peterborough U, Swansea C
Moore, G. (21) 1959/60 Cardiff C, Chelsea, Manchester U, Northampton T, Charlton Ath
Morgan, C. (15) 2006/07 Milton Keynes D, Peterborough U
Morris, W. (5) 1946/7 Burnley
Myhill, G. O. (5) 2007/08 Hull C

Nardiello, D. (2) 1977/8 Coventry C
Nardiello, D. A. (3) 2006/07 Barnsley, QPR
Neilson, A. B. (5) 1991/2 Newcastle U, Southampton
Nicholas, P. (73) 1978/9 Crystal P, Arsenal, Crystal P, Luton T, Aberdeen, Chelsea, Watford
Niedzwiecki, E. A. (2) 1984/5 Chelsea
Nogan, L. M. (2) 1991/2 Watford, Reading
Norman, A. J. (5) 1985/6 Hull C
Nurse, M. T. G. (12) 1959/60 Swansea T, Middlesbrough
Nyatanga, L. J. (27) 2005/06 Derby Co

O'Sullivan, P. (3) 1972/3 Brighton & HA
Oster, J. M. (13) 1997/8 Everton, Sunderland

Page, M. (28) 1970/1 Birmingham C
Page, R. J. (41) 1996/7 Watford, Sheffield U, Cardiff C, Coventry C
Palmer, D. (3) 1956/7 Swansea T
Parry, J. (1) 1950/1 Swansea T
Parry, P. I. (12) 2003/04 Cardiff C
Partridge, D. W. (7) 2004/05 Motherwell, Bristol C

313

Pascoe, C. (10) 1983/4 Swansea C, Sunderland
Paul, R. (33) 1948/9 Swansea T, Manchester C
Pembridge, M. A. (54) 1991/2 Luton T, Derby C, Sheffield W, Benfica, Everton, Fulham
Perry, J. (1) 1993/4 Cardiff C
Phillips, D. (62) 1983/4 Plymouth Argyle, Manchester C, Coventry C, Norwich C, Nottingham F
Phillips, J. (4) 1972/3 Chelsea
Phillips, L. (58) 1970/1 Cardiff C, Aston Villa, Swansea C, Charlton Ath
Pipe, D. R. (1) 2002/03 Coventry C
Pontin, K. (2) 1979/80 Cardiff C
Powell, A. (8) 1946/7 Leeds U, Everton, Birmingham C
Powell, D. (11) 1967/8 Wrexham, Sheffield U
Powell, I. (8) 1946/7 QPR, Aston Villa
Price, L. P. (6) 2005/06 Ipswich T, Derby Co
Price, P. (25) 1979/80 Luton T, Tottenham H
Pring, K. (3) 1965/6 Rotherham U
Pritchard, H. K. (1) 1984/5 Bristol C

Ramsey, A. (2) 2008/09 Arsenal
Rankmore, F. (l) 1965/6 Peterborough U
Ratcliffe, K. (59) 1980/1 Everton, Cardiff C
Ready, K. (5) 1996/7 QPR
Reece, G. (29) 1965/6 Sheffield U, Cardiff C
Reed, W. (2) 1954/5 Ipswich T
Rees, A. (1) 1983/4 Birmingham C
Rees, J. M. (1) 1991/2 Luton T
Rees, R. (39) 1964/5 Coventry C, WBA, Nottingham F
Rees, W. (4) 1948/9 Cardiff C, Tottenham H
Richards, S. (1) 1946/7 Cardiff C
Ricketts, S. (34) 2004/05 Swansea C, Hull C
Roberts, A. M. (2) 1992/3 QPR
Roberts, D. (17) 1972/3 Oxford U, Hull C
Roberts, G. W. (9) 1999/00 Tranmere R
Roberts, I. W. (15) 1989/90 Watford, Huddersfield T, Leicester C, Norwich C
Roberts, J. G. (22) 1970/1 Arsenal, Birmingham C
Roberts, J. H. (1) 1948/9 Bolton W

Roberts, N. W. (4) 1999/00 Wrexham, Wigan Ath
Roberts, P. (4) 1973/4 Portsmouth
Roberts, S. W. (1) 2004/05 Wrexham
Robinson, C. P. (52) 1999/00 Wolverhampton W, Portsmouth, Sunderland, Norwich C, Toronto Lynx
Robinson, J. R. C. (30) 1995/6 Charlton Ath
Rodrigues, P. (40) 1964/5 Cardiff C, Leicester C, Sheffield W
Rouse, V. (1) 1958/9 Crystal P
Rowley, T. (1) 1958/9 Tranmere R
Rush, I. (73) 1979/80 Liverpool, Juventus, Liverpool

Saunders, D. (75) 1985/6 Brighton & HA, Oxford U, Derby C, Liverpool, Aston Villa, Galatasaray, Nottingham F, Sheffield U, Benfica, Bradford C
Savage, R. W. (39) 1995/6 Crewe Alexandra, Leicester C, Birmingham C
Sayer, P. (7) 1976/7 Cardiff C
Scrine, F. (2) 1949/50 Swansea T
Sear, C. (1) 1962/3 Manchester C
Sherwood, A. (41) 1946/7 Cardiff C, Newport C
Shortt, W. (12) 1946/7 Plymouth Argyle
Showers, D. (2) 1974/5 Cardiff C
Sidlow, C. (7) 1946/7 Liverpool
Slatter, N. (22) 1982/3 Bristol R, Oxford U
Smallman, D. (7) 1973/4 Wrexham, Everton
Southall, N. (92) 1981/2 Everton
Speed, G. A. (85) 1989/90 Leeds U, Everton, Newcastle U, Bolton W
Sprake, G. (37) 1963/4 Leeds U, Birmingham C
Stansfield, F. (1) 1948/9 Cardiff C
Stevenson, B. (15) 1977/8 Leeds U, Birmingham C
Stevenson, N. (4) 1981/2 Swansea C
Stitfall, R. (2) 1952/3 Cardiff C
Sullivan, D. (17) 1952/3 Cardiff C
Symons, C. J. (37) 1991/2 Portsmouth, Manchester C, Fulham, Crystal P

Tapscott, D. (14) 1953/4 Arsenal, Cardiff C
Taylor, G. K. (15) 1995/6 Crystal P, Sheffield U, Burnley, Nottingham F
Thatcher, B. D. (7) 2003/04 Leicester C, Manchester C

314

Thomas, D. (2) 1956/7 Swansea T
Thomas, M. (51) 1976/7 Wrexham, Manchester U, Everton, Brighton & HA, Stoke C, Chelsea, WBA
Thomas, M. R. (1) 1986/7 Newcastle U
Thomas, R. (50) 1966/7 Swindon T, Derby C, Cardiff C
Thomas, S. (4) 1947/8 Fulham
Toshack, J. (40) 1968/9 Cardiff C, Liverpool, Swansea C
Trollope, P. J. (9) 1996/7 Derby Co, Fulham, Coventry C, Northampton T

Van Den Hauwe, P. W. R. (13) 1984/5 Everton
Vaughan, D. O. (14) 2002/03 Crewe Alex, Real Sociedad, Blackpool
Vaughan, N. (10) 1982/3 Newport Co, Cardiff C
Vearncombe, G. (2) 1957/8 Cardiff C
Vernon, R. (32) 1956/7 Blackburn R, Everton, Stoke C
Villars, A. (3) 1973/4 Cardiff C

Walley, T. (1) 1970/1 Watford
Walsh, I. (18) 1979/80 Crystal P, Swansea C
Ward, D. (2) 1958/9 Bristol R, Cardiff C
Ward, D. (5) 1999/00 Notts Co, Nottingham F
Webster, C. (4) 1956/7 Manchester U

Weston, R. D. (7) 1999/00 Arsenal, Cardiff C
Williams, A. (13) 1993/4 Reading, Wolverhampton R, Reading
Williams, A. E. (13) 2007/08 Stockport Co, Swansea C
Williams, A. P. (2) 1997/8 Southampton
Williams, D. G. 1987/8 13, Derby Co, Ipswich T
Williams, D. M. (5) 1985/6 Norwich C
Williams, G. (1) 1950/1 Cardiff C
Williams, G. E. (26) 1959/60 WBA
Williams, G. G. (5) 1960/1 Swansea T
Williams, G. J. (2) 2005/06 West Ham U, Ipswich T
Williams, H. (4) 1948/9 Newport Co, Leeds U
Williams, Herbert (3) 1064/5 Swansea T
Williams, S. (43) 1953/4 WBA, Southampton
Witcomb, D. (3) 1946/7 WBA, Sheffield W
Woosnam, P. (17) 1958/9 Leyton Orient, West Ham U, Aston Villa

Yorath, T. (59) 1969/70 Leeds U, Coventry C, Tottenham H, Vancouver Whitecaps
Young, E. (21) 1989/90 Wimbledon, Crystal P, Wolverhampton W

REPUBLIC OF IRELAND

Aherne, T. (16) 1945/6 Belfast Celtic, Luton T
Aldridge, J. W. (69) 1985/6 Oxford U, Liverpool, Real Sociedad, Tranmere R
Ambrose, P. (5) 1954/5 Shamrock R
Anderson, A. (16) 1979/80 Preston NE, Newcastle U
Andrews, K. J. (6) 2008/09 Blackburn R

Babb, P. (35) 1993/4 Coventry C, Liverpool, Sunderland
Bailham, E. (1) 1963/4 Shamrock R
Barber, E. (2) 1965/6 Shelbourne, Birmingham C
Barrett, G. (6) 2002/03 Arsenal, Coventry C
Beglin, J. (15) 1983/4 Liverpool
Bennett, A. J. (2) 2006/07 Reading
Best, L. J. B. (2) 2008/09 Coventry C
Bonner, P. (80) 1980/1 Celtic

Braddish, S. (1) 1977/8 Dundalk
Brady, T. R. (6) 1963/4 QPR
Brady, W. L. (72) 1974/5 Arsenal, Juventus, Sampdoria, Internazionale, Ascoli, West Ham U
Branagan, K. G. (1) 1996/7 Bolton W
Breen, G. (63) 1995/6 Birmingham C, Coventry C, West Ham U, Sunderland
Breen, T. (3) 1946/7 Shamrock R
Brennan, F. (1) 1964/5 Drumcondra
Brennan, S. A. (19) 1964/5 Manchester U, Waterford
Browne, W. (3) 1963/4 Bohemians
Bruce, A. (2) 2006/07 Ipswich T
Buckley, L. (2) 1983/4 Shamrock R, Waregem
Burke, F. (1) 1951/2 Cork Ath
Butler, P. J. (1) 1999/00 Sunderland
Butler, J. (2) 2002/03 Sunderland
Byrne, A. B. (14) 1969/70 Southampton

Byrne, J. (23) 1984/5 QPR, Le Havre, Brighton & HA, Sunderland, Millwall
Byrne, J. (2) 2003/04 Shelbourne
Byrne, P. (8) 1983/4 Shamrock R

Campbell, A. (3) 1984/5 Santander
Campbell, N. (11) 1970/1 St Patrick's Ath, Fortuna Cologne
Cantwell, N. (36) 1953/4 West Ham U, Manchester U
Carey, B. P. (3) 1991/2 Manchester U, Leicester C
Carey, J. J. (21) 1945/6 Manchester U
Carolan, J. (2) 1959/60 Manchester U
Carr, S. (44) 1998/9 Tottenham H, Newcastle U
Carroll, B. (2) 1948/9 Shelbourne
Carroll, T. R. (17) 1967/8 Ipswich T, Birmingham C
Carsley, L. K. (39) 1997/8 Derby Co, Blackburn R, Coventry C, Everton
Cascarino, A. G. (88) 1985/6 Gillingham, Millwall, Aston Villa, Celtic, Chelsea, Marseille, Nancy
Chandler, J. (2) 1979/80 Leeds U
Clarke, C. R. (2) 2003/04 Stoke C
Clarke, J. (1) 1977/8 Drogheda U
Clarke, K. (2) 1947/8 Drumcondra
Clarke, M. (1) 1949/50 Shamrock R
Clinton, T. J. (3) 1950/1 Everton
Coad, P. (11) 1946/7 Shamrock R
Coffey, T. (1) 1949/50 Drumcondra
Colfer, M. D. (2) 1949/50 Shelbourne
Colgan, N. (9) 2001/02 Hibernian, Barnsley
Conmy, O. M. (5) 1964/5 Peterborough U
Connolly, D. J. (41) 1995/6 Watford, Feyenoord, Wolverhampton W, Excelsior, Wimbledon, West Ham U, Wigan Ath
Conroy, G. A. (27) 1969/70 Stoke C
Conway, J. P. (20) 1966/7 Fulham, Manchester C
Corr, P. J. (4) 1948/9 Everton
Courtney, E. (1) 1945/6 Cork U
Coyle, O. (1) 1993/4 Bolton W
Coyne, T. (22) 1991/2 Celtic, Tranmere R, Motherwell
Crowe, G. (2) 2002/03 Bohemians
Cummins, G. P. (19) 1953/4 Luton T
Cuneen, T. (1) 1950/1 Limerick
Cunningham, K. (72) 1995/6 Wimbledon, Birmingham C
Curtis, D. P. (17) 1956/7 Shelbourne, Bristol C, Ipswich T, Exeter C
Cusack, S. (1) 1952/3 Limerick

Daish, L. S. (5) 1991/2 Cambridge U, Coventry C
Daly, G. A. (48) 1972/3 Manchester U, Derby C, Coventry C, Birmingham C, Shrewsbury T
Daly, M. (2) 1977/8 Wolverhampton W
Daly, P. (1) 1949/50 Shamrock R
Deacy, E. (4) 1981/2 Aston Villa
Delaney, D. F. (2) 2007/08 QPR
Delap, R. J. (11) 1997/8 Derby Co, Southampton
De Mange, K. J. P. P. (2) 1986/7 Liverpool, Hull C
Dempsey, J. T. (19) 1966/7 Fulham, Chelsea
Dennehy, J. (11) 1971/2 Cork Hibernian, Nottingham F, Walsall
Desmond, P. (4) 1949/50 Middlesbrough
Devine, J. (13) 1979/80 Arsenal, Norwich C
Doherty, G. M. T. (34) 1999/00 Luton T, Tottenham H, Norwich C
Donovan, D. C. (5) 1954/5 Everton
Donovan, T. (1) 1979/80 Aston Villa
Douglas, J. (8) 2003/04 Blackburn R, Leeds U
Doyle, C. (1) 1958/9 Shelbourne
Doyle, Colin (1) 2006/07 Birmingham C
Doyle, K. E. (26) 2005/06 Reading
Doyle, M. P. (1) 2003/04 Coventry C
Duff, D. A. (74) 1997/8 Blackburn R, Chelsea, Newcastle U
Duffy, B. (1) 1949/50 Shamrock R
Dunne, A. P. (33) 1961/2 Manchester U, Bolton W
Dunne, J. C. (1) 1970/1 Fulham
Dunne, P. A. J. (5) 1964/5 Manchester U
Dunne, R. P. (52) 1999/00 Everton, Manchester C
Dunne, S. (15) 1952/3 Luton T
Dunne, T. (3) 1955/6 St Patrick's Ath
Dunning, P. (2) 1970/1 Shelbourne
Dunphy, E. M. (23) 1965/6 York C, Millwall
Dwyer, N. M. (14) 1959/60 West Ham U, Swansea T

Eccles, P. (1) 1985/6 Shamrock R
Eglington, T. J. (24) 1945/6 Shamrock R, Everton
Elliott, S. W. (9) 2004/05 Sunderland
Evans, M. J. (1) 1997/8 Southampton

Fagan, E. (1) 1972/3 Shamrock R

316

Fagan, F. (8) 1954/5 Manchester C, Derby C

Fairclough, M. (2) 1981/2 Dundalk

Fallon, S. (8) 1950/1 Celtic

Farrell, P. D. (28) 1945/6 Shamrock R, Everton

Farrelly, G. (6) 1995/6 Aston Villa, Everton, Bolton W

Finnan, S. (53) 1999/00 Fulham, Liverpool, Espanyol

Finucane, A. (11) 1966/7 Limerick

Fitzgerald, F. J. (2) 1954/5 Waterford

Fitzgerald, P. J. (5) 1960/1 Leeds U, Chester

Fitzpatrick, K. (1) 1969/70 Limerick

Fitzsimons, A. G. (26) 1949/50 Middlesbrough, Lincoln C

Fleming, C. (10) 1995/6 Middlesbrough

Fogarty, A. (11) 1959/60 Sunderland, Hartlepool U

Folan, C. C. (4) 2008/09 Hull C

Foley, D. J. (6) 1999/00 Watford

Foley, K. P. (1) 2008/09 Wolverhampton W

Foley, T. C. (9) 1963/4 Northampton T

Fullam, J. 1960/1 Preston NE, Shamrock R

Gallagher, C. (2) 1966/7 Celtic

Gallagher, M. (1) 1953/4 Hibernian

Galvin, A. (29) 1982/3 Tottenham H, Sheffield W, Swindon T

Gamble, J. (2) 2006/07 Cork C

Gannon, E. (14) 1948/9 Notts Co, Sheffield W, Shelbourne K

Gannon, M. (1) 1971/2 Shelbourne

Gavin, J. T. (7) 1949/50 Norwich C, Tottenham H, Norwich C

Gibbons, A. (4) 1951/2 St Patrick's Ath

Gibson, D. T. D. (5) 2007/08 Manchester U

Gilbert, R. (1) 1965/6 Shamrock R

Giles, C. (1) 1950/1 Doncaster R

Giles, M. J. (59) 1959/60 Manchester U, Leeds U, WBA, Shamrock R

Given, S. J. J. (96) 1995/6 Blackburn R, Newcastle U, Manchester C

Givens, D. J. (56) 1968/9 Manchester U, Luton T, QPR, Birmingham C, Neuchatel Xamax

Gleeson, S. M. (2) 2006/07 Wolverhampton W

Glynn, D. (2) 1951/2 Drumcondra

Godwin, T. F. (13) 1948/9 Shamrock R, Leicester C, Bournemouth

Goodman, J. (4) 1996/7 Wimbledon

Goodwin, J. (1) 2002/03 Stockport Co

Gorman, W. C. (2) 1946/7 Brentford

Grealish, A. (45) 1975/6 Orient, Luton T, Brighton & HA, WBA

Gregg, E. (8) 1977/8 Bohemians

Grimes, A. A. (18) 1977/8 Manchester U, Coventry C, Luton T

Hale, A. (13) 1961/2 Aston Villa, Doncaster R, Waterford

Hamilton, T. (2) 1958/9 Shamrock R

Hand, E. K. (20) 1968/9 Portsmouth

Harte, I. P. (64) 1995/6 Leeds U, Levante

Hartnett, J. B. (2) 1948/9 Middlesbrough

Haverty, J. (32) 1955/6 Arsenal, Blackburn R, Millwall, Celtic, Bristol R, Shelbourne

Hayes, A. W. P. (1) 1978/9 Southampton

Hayes, W. E. (2) 1946/7 Huddersfield T

Hayes, W. J. (1) 1948/9 Limerick

Healey, R. (2) 1976/7 Cardiff C

Healy, C. (13) 2001/02 Celtic, Sunderland

Heighway, S. D. (34) 1970/1 Liverpool, Minnesota Kicks

Henderson, B. (2) 1947/8 Drumcondra

Henderson, W. C. P. (6) 2005/06 Brighton & HA, Preston NE

Hennessy, J. (5) 1964/5 Shelbourne, St Patrick's Ath

Herrick, J. (3) 1971/2 Cork Hibernians, Shamrock R

Higgins, J. (1) 1950/1 Birmingham C

Holland, M. R. (49) 1999/00 Ipswich T, Charlton Ath

Holmes, J. (30) 1970/1 Coventry C, Tottenham H, Vancouver Whitecaps

Hoolahan, W. (1) 2007/08 Blackpool

Houghton, R. J. (73) 1985/6 Oxford U, Liverpool, Aston Villa, Crystal P, Reading

Howlett, G. (1) 1983/4 Brighton & HA

Hughton, C. (53) 1979/80 Tottenham H, West Ham U

Hunt, N. (2) 2008/09 Reading

Hunt, S. P. (20) 2006/07 Reading

Hurley, C. J. (40) 1956/7 Millwall, Sunderland, Bolton W

Ireland, S. J. (6) 2005/06 Manchester C

Irwin, D. J. (56) 1990/1 Manchester U

Kavanagh, G. A. (16) 1997/8 Stoke C, Cardiff C, Wigan Ath

Keane, R. D. (90) 1997/8
Wolverhampton W, Coventry C,
Internazionale, Leeds U, Tottenham
H, Liverpool, Tottenham H
Keane, R. M. (67) 1990/1 Nottingham
F, Manchester U
Keane, T. R. (4) 1948/9 Swansea T
Kearin, M. (1) 1971/2 Shamrock R
Kearns, F. T. (1) 1953/4 West Ham U
Kearns, M. (18) 1969/70 Oxford U,
Walsall, Wolverhampton W
Kelly, A. T. (34) 1992/3 Sheffield U,
Blackburn R
Kelly, D. T. (26) 1987/8 Walsall, West
Ham U, Leicester C, Newcastle U,
Wolverhampton W, Sunderland,
Tranmere R
Kelly, G. (52) 1993/4 Leeds U
Kelly, J. A. (48) 1956/7 Drumcondra,
Preston NE
Kelly, J. P. V. (5) 1960/1
Wolverhampton W
Kelly, M. J. (4) 1987/8 Portsmouth
Kelly, N. (1) 1953/4 Nottingham F
Kelly, S. M. (14) 2005/06 Tottenham
H, Birmingham C
Kenna, J. J. (27) 1994/5 Blackburn R
Kennedy, M. (34) 1995/6 Liverpool,
Wimbledon, Manchester C,
Wolverhampton W
Kennedy, M. F. (2) 1985/6 Portsmouth
Kenny, P. (7) 2003/04 Sheffield U
Keogh, A. D. (11) 2006/07
Wolverhampton W
Keogh, J. (1) 1965/6 Shamrock R
Keogh, S. (1) 1958/9 Shamrock R
Kernaghan, A. N. (22) 1992/3
Middlesbrough, Manchester C
Kiely, D. L. (11) 1999/00 Charlton
Ath, WBA
Kiernan, F. W. (5) 1950/1 Shamrock R,
Southampton
Kilbane, K. D. (96) 1997/8 WBA,
Sunderland, Everton, Wigan Ath,
Hull C
Kinnear, J. P. (26) 1966/7 Tottenham
H, Brighton & HA
Kinsella, M. A. (48) 1997/8 Charlton
Ath, Aston Villa, WBA

Langan, D. (26) 1977/8 Derby Co,
Birmingham C, Oxford U
Lapira, J. (1) 2006/07 Notre Dame
Lawler, J. F. (8) 1952/3 Fulham
Lawlor, J. C. (3) 1948/9 Drumcondra,
Doncaster R
Lawlor, M. (5) 1970/1 Shamrock R
Lawrence, L. (1) 2008/09 Stoke C

Lawrenson, M. (39) 1976/7 Preston
NE, Brighton & HA, Liverpool
Lee, A. L. (10) 2002/03 Rotherham U,
Cardiff C, Ipswich T
Leech, M. (8) 1968/9 Shamrock R
Long, S. P. (10) 2006/07 Reading
Lowry, D. (1) 1961/2 St Patrick's Ath

McAlinden, J. (2) 1945/6 Portsmouth
McAteer, J. W. (52) 1993/4 Bolton W,
Liverpool, Blackburn R, Sunderland
McCann, J. (1) 1956/7 Shamrock R
McCarthy, M. (57) 1983/4 Manchester
C, Celtic, Lyon, Millwall
McConville, T. (6) 1971/2 Dundalk,
Waterford
McDonagh, Jim (25) 1980/1 Everton,
Bolton W, Notts C
McDonagh, Jacko (3) 1983/4
Shamrock R
McEvoy, M. A. (17) 1960/1 Blackburn
R
McGeady, A. (26) 2003/04 Celtic
McGee, P. (15) 1977/8 QPR, Preston
NE
McGoldrick, E. J. (15) 1991/2 Crystal
P, Arsenal
McGowan, D. (3) 1948/9 West Ham U
McGowan, J. (1) 1946/7 Cork U
McGrath, M. (22) 1957/8 Blackburn R,
Bradford Park Avenue
McGrath, P. (83) 1984/5 Manchester
U, Aston Villa, Derby C
McLoughlin, A. F. (42) 1989/90
Swindon T, Southampton,
Portsmouth
McMillan, W. (2) 1945/6 Belfast Celtic
McNally, J. B. (3) 1958/9 Luton T
McPhail, S. (10) 1999/00 Leeds U
McShane, P. D. (17) 2006/07 WBA,
Sunderland
Macken, A. (1) 1976/7 Derby Co
Macken, J. P. (1) 2004/05 Manchester
C
Mackey, G. (3) 1956/7 Shamrock R
Mahon, A. J. (2) 1999/00 Tranmere R
Malone, G. (1) 1948/9 Shelbourne
Mancini, T. J. (5) 1973/4 QPR, Arsenal
Martin, C. J. (30) 1945/6 Glentoran,
Leeds U, Aston Villa
Martin, M. P. (52) 1971/2 Bohemians,
Manchester U, WBA, Newcastle U
Maybury, A. (10) 1997/8 Leeds U,
Heart of Midlothian, Leicester C
Meagan, M. K. (17) 1960/1 Everton,
Huddersfield T, Drogheda
Miller, L. W. P. (20) 2003/04 Celtic,
Manchester U, Sunderland

Milligan, M. J. (1) 1991/2 Oldham Ath

Mooney, J. (2) 1964/5 Shamrock R

Moore, A. (8) 1995/6 Middlesbrough

Moran, K. (71) 1979/80 Manchester U, Sporting Gijon, Blackburn R

Moroney, T. (12) 1947/8 West Ham U, Evergreen U

Morris, C. B. (35) 1987/8 Celtic, Middlesbrough

Morrison, C. H. (36) 2001/02 Crystal P, Birmingham C, Crystal P

Moulson, G. B. (3) 1947/8 Lincoln C

Mucklan, C. (1) 1977/8 Drogheda

Mulligan, P. M. (50) 1968/9 Shamrock R, Chelsea, Crystal P, WBA, Shamrock R

Munroe, L. (1) 1953/4 Shamrock R

Murphy, A. (1) 1955/6 Clyde

Murphy, B. (1) 1985/6 Bohemians

Murphy, D. (9) 2006/07 Sunderland

Murphy, Jerry (1) 1979/80 Crystal P

Murphy, Joe (1) 2003/04 WBA

Murphy, P. M. (1) 2006/07 Carlisle U

Murray, T. (1) 1949/50 Dundalk

Newman, W. (1) 1968/9 Shelbourne

Nolan, E. W. (1) 2008/09 Preston NE

Nolan, R. (10) 1956/7 Shamrock R

O'Brien, A. (5) 2006/07 Newcastle U

O'Brien, A. J. (26) 2000/01 Newcastle U, Portsmouth

O'Brien, F. (3) 1979/80 Philadelphia Fury

O'Brien, J. M. (3) 2005/06 Bolton W

O'Brien, L. (16) 1985/6 Shamrock R, Manchester U, Newcastle U, Tranmere R

O'Brien, R. (5) 1975/6 Notts Co

O'Byrne, L. B. (1) 1948/9 Shamrock R

O'Callaghan, B. R. (6) 1978/9 Stoke C

O'Callaghan, K. (21) 1980/1 Ipswich T, Portsmouth

O'Cearuill, J. (2) 2006/07 Arsenal

O'Connnell, A. (2) 1966/7 Dundalk, Bohemians

O'Connor, T. (4) 1949/50 Shamrock R

O'Connor, T. (7) 1967/8 Fulham, Dundalk, Bohemians

O'Driscoll, J. F. (3) 1948/9 Swansea T

O'Driscoll, S. (3) 1981/2 Fulham

O'Farrell, F. (9) 1951/2 West Ham U, Preston NE

O'Flanagan, K. P. (3) 1946/7 Arsenal

O'Flanagan, M. (1) 1946/7 Bohemians

O'Halloran, S. E. (2) 2006/07 Aston Villa

O'Hanlon, K. G. (1) 1987/8 Rotherham U

O'Keefe, E. (5) 1980/1 Everton, Port Vale

O'Leary, D. (68) 1976/7 Arsenal

O'Leary, P. (7) 1979/80 Shamrock R

O'Neill, F. S. (20) 1961/2 Shamrock R

O'Neill, J. (17) 1951/2 Everton

O'Neill, J. (1) 1960/1 Preston NE

O'Neill, K. P. (13) 1995/6 Norwich C, Middlesbrough

O'Regan, K. (4) 1983/4 Brighton & HA

O'Reilly, J. (2) 1945/6 Cork U

O'Shea, J. F. (54) 2001/02 Manchester U

Peyton, G. (33) 1976/7 Fulham, Bournemouth, Everton

Peyton, N. (6) 1956/7 Shamrock R, Leeds U

Phelan, T. (42) 1991/2 Wimbledon, Manchester C, Chelsea, Everton, Fulham

Potter, D. M. (5) 2006/07 Wolverhampton W

Quinn, A. (8) 2002/03 Sheffield W, Sheffield U

Quinn, B. S. (4) 1999/00 Coventry C

Quinn, N. J. (91) 1985/6 Arsenal, Manchester C, Sunderland

Reid, A. M. (27) 2003/04 Nottingham F, Tottenham H, Charlton Ath, Sunderland

Reid, S. J. (23) 2001/02 Millwall, Blackburn R

Richardson, D. J. (3) 1971/2 Shamrock R, Gillingham

Ringstead, A. (20) 1950/1 Sheffield U

Robinson, M. (24) 1980/1 Brighton & HA, Liverpool, QPR

Roche, P. J. (8) 1971/2 Shelbourne, Manchester U

Rogers, E. (19) 1967/8 Blackburn R, Charlton Ath

Rowlands, M. C. (3) 2003/04 QPR

Ryan, G. (18) 1977/8 Derby Co, Brighton & HA

Ryan, R. A. (16) 1949/50 WBA, Derby C

Sadlier, R. T. (1) 2001/02 Millwall

Savage, D. P. T. (5) 1995/6 Millwall

Saward, P. (18) 1953/4 Millwall, Aston Villa, Huddersfield T

Scannell, T. (1) 1953/4 Southend U

319

Scully, P. J. (1) 1988/9 Arsenal
Sheedy, K. (46) 1983/4 Everton, Newcastle U
Sheridan, J. J. (34) 1987/8 Leeds U, Sheffield W
Slaven, B. (7) 1989/90 Middlesbrough
Sloan, J. W. (2) 1945/6 Arsenal
Smyth, M. (1) 1968/9 Shamrock R
Stapleton, F. (71) 1976/7 Arsenal, Manchester U, Ajax, Le Havre, Blackburn R
Staunton, S. (102) 1988/9 Liverpool, Aston Villa, Liverpool, Aston Villa
St. Ledger-Hall, S. P. (2) 2008/09 Preston NE
Stevenson, A. E. (6) 1946/7 Everton
Stokes, A. (3) 2006/07 Sunderland
Strahan, F. (5) 1963/4 Shelbourne
Swan, M. M. G. (1) 1959/60 Drumcondra
Synott, N. (3) 1977/8 Shamrock R

Taylor T. (1) 1958/9 Waterford
Thomas, P. (2) 1973/4 Waterford
Thompson, J. (1) 2003/04 Nottingham F
Townsend, A. D. (70) 1988/9 Norwich C, Chelsea, Aston Villa, Middlesbrough

Traynor, T. J. (8) 1953/4 Southampton
Treacy, R. C. P. (42) 1965/6 WBA, Charlton Ath, Swindon T, Preston NE, WBA, Shamrock R
Tuohy, L. (8) 1955/6 Shamrock R, Newcastle U, Shamrock R
Turner, P. (2) 1962/3 Celtic

Vernon, J. (2) 1945/6 Belfast Celtic

Waddock, G. (21) 1979/80 QPR, Millwall
Walsh, D. J. (20) 1945/6 Linfield, WBA, Aston Villa
Walsh, J. (1) 1981/2 Limerick
Walsh, M. (21) 1975/6 Blackpool, Everton, QPR, Porto
Walsh, M. (4) 1981/2 Everton
Walsh, W. (9) 1946/7 Manchester C
Waters, J. (2) 1976/7 Grimsby T
Westwood, K. (1) 2008/09 Coventry C
Whelan, G. D. (12) 2007/08 Stoke C
Whelan, R. (2) 1963/4 St Patrick's Ath
Whelan, R. (53) 1980/1 Liverpool, Southend U
Whelan, W. (4) 1955/6 Manchester U
Whittaker, R. (1) 1958/9 Chelsea

REPUBLIC OF IRELAND LEAGUE 2008

	P	W	D	L	F	A	Pts
Bohemians	33	27	4	2	55	13	85
St Patrick's Ath	33	20	6	7	48	24	66
Derry City	33	16	10	7	46	25	58
Sligo Rovers	33	12	12	9	41	28	48
Cork City*	33	15	11	7	45	28	46
Bray Wanderers	33	11	6	16	28	52	39
Shamrock Rovers	33	8	13	12	33	35	37
Drogheda United*	33	12	9	12	38	32	35
Galway United	33	8	8	17	34	49	32
Finn Harps	33	9	4	20	26	53	31
Cobh Ramblers	33	6	8	19	27	55	26
UCD	33	4	9	20	19	46	21

*Cork City and Drogheda United deducted 10 points for financial reasons.
Competition reduced to ten clubs for 2009.
Top scorers: Mooney (Cork City) 15, Quigley (St Patrick's Ath) 15, Farren (Derry C) 15.
Cup Final: Bohemians 2, Derry City 2.
(aet; Bohemians won 4-2 on penalties.)

BRITISH ISLES INTERNATIONAL GOALSCORERS SINCE 1946

ENGLAND

A'Court, A.	1
Adams, T.A.	5
Allen, R.	2
Anderson, V.	2
Anderton, D.R.	7
Astall, G.	1
Atyeo, P.J.W.	5
Baily, E.F.	5
Baker, J.H.	3
Ball, A.J.	8
Barmby, N.J.	4
Barnes, J.	11
Barnes, P.S.	4
Barry, G.	2
Beardsley, P.A.	9
Beattie, J.K.	1
Beckham, D.R.J.	17
Bell, C.	9
Bentley, R.T.F.	9
Blissett, L.	3
Bowles, S.	1
Bradford, G.R.W.	1
Bradley, W.	2
Bridge, W.M.	1
Bridges, B.J.	1
Broadbent, P.F.	2
Broadis, I.A.	8
Brooking, T.D.	5
Brooks, J.	2
Brown, W.M.	1
Bull, S.G.	4
Butcher, T.	3
Byrne, J.J.	8
Campbell, S.J.	1
Carter, H.S.	5
Chamberlain, M.	1
Channon, M.R.	21
Charlton, J.	6
Charlton, R.	49
Chivers, M.	13
Clarke, A.J.	10
Cole, A.	1
Cole, J.J.	10
Connelly, J.M.	7
Coppell, S.J.	7
Cowans, G.	2
Crawford, R.	1
Crouch, P.J.	16

Currie, A.W.	3
Defoe, J.C.	8
Dixon, L.M.	1
Dixon, K.M.	4
Douglas, B.	11
Eastham, G.	2
Edwards, D.	5
Ehiogu, U.	1
Elliott, W.H.	3
Ferdinand, L.	5
Ferdinand, R.G.	3
Finney, T.	30
Flowers, R.	10
Fowler, R.B.	7
Francis, G.C.J.	3
Francis, T.	12
Froggatt, J.	2
Froggatt, R.	2
Gascoigne, P.J.	10
Gerrard, S.G.	14
Goddard, P.	1
Grainger, C.	3
Greaves, J.	44
Haines, J.T.W.	2
Hancocks, J.	2
Hassall, H.W.	4
Hateley, M.	9
Haynes, J.N.	18
Heskey, E.W.	7
Hirst, D.E.	1
Hitchens, G.A.	5
Hoddle, G.	8
Hughes, E.W.	1
Hunt, R.	18
Hunter, N.	2
Hurst, G.C.	24
Ince P.E.C.	2
Jeffers, F.	1
Jenas, J.A.	1
Johnson, D.E.	6
Kay, A.H.	1
Keegan, J.K.	21
Kennedy, R.	3
Keown, M.R.	2
Kevan, D.T.	8

Kidd, B.	1
King, L.B.	1
Lampard, F.J.	17
Langton, R.	1
Latchford, R.D.	5
Lawler, C.	1
Lawton, T.	16
Lee, F.	10
Lee, J.	1
Lee, R.M.	2
Lee, S.	2
Le Saux, G.P.	1
Lineker, G.	48
Lofthouse, N.	30
Mabbutt, G.	1
McDermott, T.	3
Macdonald, M.	6
McManaman, S.	3
Mannion, W.J.	11
Mariner, P.	13
Marsh, R.W.	1
Matthews, S.	3
Medley, L.D.	1
Melia, J.	1
Merson, P.C.	3
Milburn, J.E.T.	10
Moore, R.F.	2
Morris, J.	3
Mortensen, S.H.	23
Mullen, J.	6
Mullery, A.P.	1
Murphy, D.B.	1
Neal, P.G.	5
Nicholls, J.	1
Nicholson, W.E.	1
Nugent, D.J.	1
O'Grady, M.	3
Owen, M.J.	40
Own goals	29
Paine, T.L.	7
Palmer, C.L.	1
Parry, R.A.	1
Peacock, A.	3
Pearce, S.	5
Pearson, J.S.	5
Pearson, S.C.	5
Perry, W.	2
Peters, M.	20

Pickering, F.	5
Platt, D.	27
Pointer, R.	2
Ramsay, A.E.	3
Redknapp, J.F.	1
Revie, D.G.	4
Richards, M.	1
Richardson, K.E.	2
Robson, B.	26
Robson, R.	4
Rooney, W.	24
Rowley, J.F.	6
Royle, J.	2
Sansom, K.	1
Scholes, P.	14
Sewell, J.	1
Shackleton, L.F.	5
Shearer, A.	30
Sheringham, E.P.	11
Smith, A.	1
Smith, A.M.	2
Smith, R.	13
Southgate, G.	2
Steven, T.M.	4
Stiles, N.P.	1
Stone, S.B.	2
Summerbee, M.G.	1
Tambling, R.V.	1
Taylor, P.J.	2
Taylor, T.	16
Terry, J.G.	6
Thompson, P.B.	1
Tueart, D.	2
Upson, M.J.	1
Vassell, D.	6
Viollet, D.S.	1
Waddle, C.R.	6
Walcott, T.J.	3
Wallace, D.L.	1
Walsh, P.	1
Watson, D.V.	4
Webb, N.	4
Weller, K.	1
Wignall, F.	2
Wilkins, R.G.	3
Wilshaw, D.J.	10
Wise, D.F.	1
Withe, P.	1
Woodcock, T.	16
Worthington, F.S.	2
Wright, I.E.	9
Wright, M.	1
Wright, W.A.	3
Wright-Phillips, S.C.	4

SCOTLAND

Aitken, R.	1
Archibald, S.	4
Baird, S.	2
Bannon, E.	1
Bauld, W.	2
Baxter, J.C.	3
Beattie, C.	1
Bett, J.	1
Bone, J.	1
Booth, S.	6
Boyd, R.	7
Boyd, T.	1
Brand, R.	8
Brazil, A.	1
Bremner, W.J.	3
Broadfoot, K.	1
Brown, A.D.	6
Buckley, P.	1
Burke, C.	2
Burley, C.W.	3
Burns, K.	1
Caldwell, G.	2
Calderwood, C.	1
Caldow, E.	4
Cameron, C.	2
Campbell, R.	1
Chalmers, S.	3
Clarkson, D.	1
Collins, J.	12
Collins, R.V.	10
Combe, J.R.	1
Conn, A.	1
Cooper, D.	6
Craig, J.	1
Crawford, S.	4
Curran, H.P.	1
Dailly, C.	6
Dalglish, K.	30
Davidson, J.A.	1
Dickov, P.	1
Dobie, R.S.	1
Docherty, T.H.	1
Dodds, D.	1
Dodds, W.	7
Duncan, D.M.	1
Durie, G.S.	7
Elliott, M.S.	1
Ferguson, B.	3
Fernie, W.	1
Flavell, R.	2
Fleming, C.	2
Fletcher, D.	4
Fletcher, S.	1
Freedman, D.A.	1
Gallacher, K.W.	9
Gemmell, T.K *(St Mirren)*	1
Gemmell, T.K *(Celtic)*	1
Gemmill, A.	8
Gemmill, S.	1
Gibson, D.W.	3
Gilzean, A.J.	12
Gough, C.R.	6
Graham, A.	2
Graham, G.	3
Gray, A.	7
Gray, E.	3
Gray, F.	1
Greig, J.	3
Hamilton, G.	4
Harper, J.M.	2
Hartford, R.A.	4
Hartley, P.J.	1
Henderson, J.G.	1
Henderson, W.	5
Hendry, E.C.J.	3
Herd, D.G.	3
Herd, G.	1
Hewie, J.D.	2
Holt, G.J.	1
Holton, J.A.	2
Hopkin, D.	2
Houliston, W.	2
Howie, H.	1
Hughes, J.	1
Hunter, W.	1
Hutchison, D.	6
Hutchison, T.	1
Jackson, C.	1
Jackson, D.	4
Jardine, A.	1
Jess, E.	2
Johnston, A.	2
Johnston, L.H.	1
Johnston, M.	14
Johnstone, D.	2
Johnstone, J.	4
Johnstone, R.	10
Jordan, J.	11
Kyle, K.	1

323

324

Quinn, J.M.	12	Dunne, R.P.	7	McEvoy, A.	6
Quinn, S.J.	4			McGee, P.	4
		Eglinton, T.	2	McGrath, P.	8
Rowland, K.	1	Elliott, S.W.	1	McLoughlin, A.	2
				McPhail, S.	1
Simpson, W.J.	5	Fagan, F.	5	Mancini, T.	1
Smyth, S.	5	Fallon, S.	2	Martin, C.	6
Spence, D.W.	3	Farrell, P.	3	Martin, M.	4
Sproule, I.	1	Finnan, S.	2	Miller, L.W.P.	1
Stewart, I.	2	Fitzgerald, J.	1	Mooney, J.	1
		Fitzgerald, P.	2	Moran, K.	6
Taggart, G.P.	7	Fitzsimons, A.	7	Moroney, T.	1
Tully, C.P.	3	Fogarty, A.	3	Morrison, C.H.	9
		Foley, D.	2	Mulligan, P.	1
Walker, J.	1	Fullam, J.	1		
Walsh, D.J.	5	Galvin, A.	1	O'Brien, A.J.	1
Welsh, E.	1	Gavin, J.	2	O'Callaghan, K.	1
Whiteside, N.	9	Giles, J.	5	O'Connor, T.	2
Whitley, Jeff	2	Givens, D.	19	O'Farrell, F.	2
Williams, M.S.	1	Glynn, D.	1	O'Keefe, E.	1
Wilson, D.J.	1	Grealish, T.	8	O'Leary, D.A.	1
Wilson, K.J.	6	Grimes, A.A.	1	O'Neill, F.	1
Wilson, S.J.	7			O'Neill, K.P.	4
		Hale, A.	2	O'Reilly, J.	1
EIRE		Hand, E.	2	O'Shea, J.F.	1
		Harte, I.P.	11	Own goals	10
Aldridge, J.	19	Haverty, J.	3		
Ambrose, P.	1	Healy, C.	1	Quinn, N.	21
Anderson, J.	1	Holland, M.R.	5		
Andrews, K.	1	Holmes, J.	1	Reid, A.M.	4
		Houghton, R.	6	Reid, S.J.	2
Barrett, G.	2	Hughton, C.	1	Ringstead, A.	7
Brady, L.	9	Hunt, S.P.	1	Robinson, M.	4
Breen, G.	7	Hurley, C.	2	Rogers, E.	5
Byrne, J.	4			Ryan, G.	1
		Ireland, S.J.	4	Ryan, R.	3
Cantwell, J.	14	Irwin, D.	4		
Carey, J.	3			Sheedy, K.	9
Carroll, T.	1	Kavanagh, G.A.	1	Sheridan, J.	5
Cascarino, A.	19	Keane, R.D.	39	Slaven, B.	1
Coad, P.	3	Keane, R.M.	9	Sloan, J.	1
Connolly, D.J.	9	Kelly, D.	9	Stapleton, F.	20
Conroy, T.	2	Kelly, G.	2	Staunton, S.	7
Conway, J.	3	Kennedy, M.	4	Strahan, F.	1
Coyne, T.	6	Keogh, A.	1		
Cummins, G.	5	Kernaghan, A.	1	Townsend, A.D.	7
Curtis, D.	8	Kilbane, K.D.	7	Treacy, R.	5
		Kinsella, M.A.	3	Tuohy, L.	4
Daly, G.	13				
Dempsey, J.	1	Lawrenson, M.	5	Waddock, G.	3
Dennehy, M.	2	Leech, M.	2	Walsh, D.	5
Doherty, G.M.T.	4	Long, S.P.	3	Walsh, M.	3
Doyle, K.E.	6			Waters, J.	1
Duff, D.A.	7	McAteer, J.W.	3	Whelan, G.D.	1
Duffy, B.	1	McCann, J.	1	Whelan, R.	3
		McCarthy, M.	2		

UEFA UNDER-21 CHAMPIONSHIP 2007–09

Qualifying competition

GROUP 1
Italy 4, Albania 0; Greece 4,
Azerbaijan 1; Croatia 2, Faeroes 0;
Croatia 3, Greece 2; Albania 1, Faeroes
0; Azerbaijan 0, Greece 2; Italy 2,
Faeroes 1; Albania 1, Croatia 0;
Albania 0, Italy 1; Croatia 3,
Azerbaijan 2; Faeroes 0, Greece 2;
Italy 2, Croatia 0; Faeroes 1,
Azerbaijan 0; Greece 2, Italy 2;
Azerbaijan 1, Albania 1; Faeroes 1,
Croatia 2; Italy 5, Azerbaijan 0;
Faeroes 0, Albania 5; Greece 3, Croatia
4; Azerbaijan 0, Croatia 1; Faeroes 0,
Italy 1; Greece 2, Albania 1;
Azerbaijan 0, Italy 2; Albania 1,
Greece 1; Croatia 4, Albania 0; Italy 1,
Greece 1; Azerbaijan 2, Faeroes 2;
Croatia 1, Italy 1; Greece 1, Faeroes 0;
Albania 0, Azerbaijan 0

GROUP 2
Armenia 1, Liechtenstein 0; Ukraine 1,
Turkey 2; Ukraine 4, Armenia 0;
Armenia 1, Czech Republic 1;
Liechtenstein 2, Turkey 3; Czech
Republic 8, Liechtenstein 0; Armenia 0,
Ukraine 2; Liechtenstein 0, Czech
Republic 4; Turkey 2, Ukraine 0;
Liechtenstein 1, Ukraine 3; Czech
Republic 3, Armenia 0; Czech Republic
1, Turkey 1; Ukraine 5, Liechtenstein 0;
Liechtenstein 1, Armenia 4; Ukraine 0,
Czech Republic 2; Turkey 3,
Liechtenstein 0; Armenia 2, Turkey 1;
Turkey 2, Czech Republic 0; Czech
Republic 0, Ukraine 1; Turkey 4,
Armenia 0

GROUP 3
Bulgaria 1, Montenegro 2; Republic of
Ireland 0, Portugal 2; Montenegro 0,
England 3; Bulgaria 0, England 2;
Portugal 4, Montenegro 0; Bulgaria 1,
Portugal 0; England 1, Montenegro 0;
Montenegro 1, Portugal 2; Republic of
Ireland 0, England 3; Montenegro 1,
Republic of Ireland 0; England 2,
Bulgaria 0; Republic of Ireland 1,
Bulgaria 0; Portugal 1, England 1;
England 3, Republic of Ireland 0;
Republic of Ireland 1, Montenegro 1;
Portugal 2, Bulgaria 0; Bulgaria 2,
Republic of Ireland 0; England 2,
Portugal 0; Montenegro 0, Bulgaria 0;
Portugal 2, Republic of Ireland 2

GROUP 4
Georgia 0, Spain 1; Kazakhstan 0,
Russia 3; Poland 3, Georgia 1; Georgia
2, Kazakhstan 1; Russia 1, Poland 0;
Poland 1, Kazakhstan 0; Spain 4,
Georgia 0; Russia 4, Kazakhstan 0;
Poland 0, Spain 2; Kazakhstan 4,
Georgia 1; Poland 0, Russia 1; Spain 3,
Poland 0; Georgia 2, Russia 0; Spain 5,
Kazakhstan 0; Kazakhstan 3, Poland 0;
Russia 1, Spain 2; Russia 4, Georgia 0;
Kazakhstan 1, Spain 2; Georgia 0,
Poland 5; Spain 2, Russia 0

GROUP 5
Estonia 0, Norway 1; Macedonia 0,
Holland 1; Norway 0, Holland 1;
Switzerland 1, Macedonia 1;
Macedonia 1, Estonia 0; Norway 2,
Switzerland 1; Estonia 0, Holland 3;
Macedonia 1, Norway 1; Estonia 0,
Switzerland 4; Holland 1, Macedonia 0;
Switzerland 5, Estonia 0; Norway 2,
Estonia 0; Macedonia 2, Switzerland 1;
Holland 3, Norway 0; Holland 0,
Switzerland 1; Estonia 1, Macedonia 1;
Switzerland 2, Norway 0; Holland 1,
Norway 1; Switzerland 1, Holland 0;
Norway 0, Macedonia 0

GROUP 6
Slovenia 2, Lithuania 1; Denmark 0,
Finland 1; Denmark 4, Lithuania 0;
Finland 3, Scotland 2; Lithuania 0,
Slovenia 0; Scotland 0, Denmark 0;
Scotland 3, Lithuania 0; Finland 1,
Slovenia 0; Slovenia 1, Denmark 3;
Lithuania 0, Finland 1; Lithuania 0,
Denmark 3; Slovenia 0, Scotland 4;
Denmark 1, Slovenia 0; Finland 2,
Lithuania 1; Scotland 2, Finland 1;
Lithuania 0, Scotland 3; Scotland 3,
Slovenia 1; Finland 2, Denmark 1;
Slovenia 0, Finland 0; Denmark 1,
Scotland 1

GROUP 7
Iceland 0, Cyprus 1; Slovakia 2, Iceland
2; Belgium 0, Austria 1; Slovakia 1,
Austria 1; Iceland 0, Belgium 0;
Austria 2, Cyprus 1; Belgium 4,
Slovakia 2; Iceland 1, Austria 1;
Slovakia 4, Cyprus 1; Cyprus 1,
Slovakia 2; Austria 3, Belgium 2;
Cyprus 1, Austria 2; Belgium 1, Iceland
2; Cyprus 2, Iceland 0; Cyprus 0,

Belgium 2; Austria 1, Slovakia 0; Slovakia 1, Belgium 1; Austria 1, Iceland 0; Iceland 1, Slovakia 1; Belgium 3, Cyprus 2

GROUP 8

Serbia 1, Latvia 1; Belarus 1, Hungary 0; Hungary 1, Latvia 0; San Marino 0, Belarus 3; Belarus 2, Latvia 1; San Marino 1, Hungary 6; Serbia 3, Belarus 1; Latvia 2, San Marino 0; Hungary 2, Serbia 1; Serbia 3, San Marino 0; Hungary 0, Belarus 1; Latvia 0, Serbia 2; Belarus 6, San Marino 0; Latvia 1, Hungary 0; Belarus 1, Serbia 1; San Marino 0, Serbia 5; Hungary 5, San Marino 0; San Marino 0, Latvia 1; Serbia 8, Hungary 0; Latvia 0, Belarus 0

GROUP 9

Moldova 0, Northern Ireland 1; Israel 3, Luxembourg 0; Northern Ireland 0, Germany 3; Moldova 1, Israel 0; Luxembourg 1, Northern Ireland 2; Israel 2, Germany 2; Luxembourg 0, Moldova 2; Germany 3, Moldova 0; Northern Ireland 1, Israel 3; Northern Ireland 5, Luxembourg 0; Luxembourg 0, Germany 7; Northern Ireland 3, Moldova 0; Israel 2, Northern Ireland

1; Germany 6, Luxembourg 0; Israel 1, Moldova 0; Moldova 1, Germany 0; Luxembourg 0, Israel 5; Germany 3, Northern Ireland 0; Moldova 2, Luxembourg 0; Germany 0, Israel 0

GROUP 10

France 1, Romania 1; Malta 0, Romania 1; France 1, Wales 0; Bosnia 4, Malta 0; Romania 3, Bosnia 0; Malta 0, France 2; France 4, Bosnia 0; Romania 0, France 0; Wales 3, Malta 1; Romania 4, Malta 0; Wales 4, Bosnia 0; Malta 2, Bosnia 1; Wales 4, France 2; Malta 0, Wales 4; Bosnia 1, Wales 2; Wales 0, Romania 1; France 5, Malta 0; Bosnia 1, Romania 1; Romania 0, Wales 3; Bosnia 0, France 1

PLAY-OFFS FIRST LEG

Wales 2, England 3; Germany 1, France 1; Turkey 1, Belarus 0; Austria 2, Finland 1; Switzerland 2, Spain 1; Denmark 0, Serbia 1; Italy 0, Israel 0

PLAY-OFFS SECOND LEG

Spain 3, Switzerland 1; England 2, Wales 2; Belarus 2, Turkey 0; Finland 2, Austria 1; Israel 1, Italy 3; France 0, Germany 1; Serbia 1, Denmark 0

Final Tournament (in Sweden)

GROUP A

Sweden 5, Belarus 1
Italy 0, Serbia 0
Sweden 1, Italy 2
Belarus 0, Serbia 0
Serbia 1, Sweden 3
Belarus1, Italy 2

GROUP B

England 2, Finland 1
Spain 0, Germany 0
Germany 2, Finland 0
Spain 0, England 2
Finland 0, Spain 2
Germany 1, England 1

SEMI-FINALS

England 3, Sweden 3
England won 5-4 on penalties: Milner missed; Berg saved; Hart scored; Elm scored; Cattermole scored; Bjarsmyr scored; Johnson scored; Lustig scored; Walcott scored; Bengtsson R scored; Gibbs scored; Molins hit post.
Italy 0, Germany 1

FINAL

Malmo, 29 June 2009, 18,769

Germany (1) 4 *(Castro 23, Ozil 48, Wagner 79, 84)*

England (0) 0

Germany: Neuer; Beck, Boenisch, Howedes, Boateng, Khedira, Ozil (Schmelzer 89), Wagner, Johnson (Schwaab 69), Hummels (Aogo 83), Castro.
England: Loach; Cranie (Gardner 79), Gibbs, Cattermole, Richards, Onuoha (Mancienne 46), Milner, Noble, Walcott, Johnson A, Muamba (Rodwell 78).
Referee: B. Kuipers (Holland).

UEFA UNDER-19 CHAMPIONSHIP 2008–09

Elite Round

GROUP 1
Hungary v Austria		2-3
Serbia v Finland		1-1
Finland v Hungary		1-2
Serbia v Austria		3-0
Hungary v Serbia		0-1
Austria v Finland		0-2

GROUP 2
Russia v Slovenia		3-3
Holland v Belarus		0-0
Russia v Belarus		2-2
Slovenia v Holland		1-1
Holland v Russia		2-1
Belarus v Slovenia		0-2

GROUP 3
Turkey v Greece		1-0
Portugal v Denmark		3-0
Turkey v Denmark		1-0
Greece v Portugal		0-1
Portugal v Turkey		0-4
Denmark v Greece		1-0

GROUP 4
Belgium v Republic of Ireland		1-0
Switzerland v Sweden		3-1
Belgium v Sweden		5-0
Republic of Ireland v Switzerland		1-6
Switzerland v Belgium		1-1
Sweden v Republic of Ireland		1-2

GROUP 5
Romania v Lativa		2-0
France v Norway		1-2
France v Latvia		4-1
Norway v Romania		1-1
Romania v France		0-3
Latvia v Norway		0-0

GROUP 6
Scotland v Slovakia		2-1
England v Bosnia		2-0
Scotland v Bosnia		3-0
Slovakia v England		1-4
England v Scotland		2-1
Bosnia v Slovakia		0-1

GROUP 7
Spain v Czech Republic		5-1
Germany v Estonia		5-0
Germany v Czech Republic		1-0
Estonia v Spain		0-3
Spain v Germany		1-0
Czech Republic v Estonia		5-1

Competition still being played.

UEFA UNDER-17 CHAMPIONSHIP 2008–09

(Finals in Germany)

GROUP A
Spain 0, Italy 0
France 1, Switzerland 1
Spain 0, France 0
Italy 1, Switzerland 3
Switzerland 0, Spain 0
Italy 2, France 1

GROUP B
England 1, Holland 1
Germany 3, Turkey 1
Germany 4, England 0
Turkey 1, Holland 2
Holland 0, Germany 2
Turkey 1, England 0

SEMI-FINALS
Switzerland 1, Holland 2
Germany 2, Italy 0

FINAL
Holland 1, Germany 2 *(aet.)*

BLUE SQUARE PREMIER 2008–2009

			Home				Away				Total					
		P	W	D	L	F	A	W	D	L	F	A	W	D	L	F	A	GD	Pts
1	Burton Alb	46	15	5	3	48	23	12	2	9	33	29	27	7	12	81	52	29	88
2	Cambridge U	46	14	6	3	34	15	10	8	5	31	24	24	14	8	65	39	26	86
3	Histon	46	14	8	1	41	18	9	6	8	37	30	23	14	9	78	48	30	83
4	Torquay U	46	11	7	5	38	23	12	7	4	34	24	23	14	9	72	47	25	83
5	Stevenage B	46	12	8	3	41	23	11	4	8	32	31	23	12	11	73	54	19	81
6	Kidderminster H	46	16	2	5	40	18	7	8	8	29	30	23	10	13	69	48	21	79
7	Oxford U*	46	16	3	4	42	20	8	7	8	30	31	24	10	12	72	51	21	77
8	Kettering T	46	12	5	6	26	19	9	8	6	24	18	21	13	12	50	37	13	76
9	Crawley T*	46	13	5	5	48	26	6	9	8	29	29	19	14	13	77	55	22	70
10	Wrexham	46	11	7	5	39	22	7	5	11	25	26	18	12	16	64	48	16	66
11	Rushden & D	46	11	5	7	30	24	5	10	8	31	26	15	15	16	61	50	11	63
12	Mansfield T*	46	14	5	4	35	19	5	4	14	22	36	19	9	18	57	55	2	62
13	Eastbourne B	46	11	3	9	29	27	7	3	13	29	43	18	6	22	58	70	–12	60
14	Ebbsfleet U	46	10	9	4	28	19	6	1	16	24	41	16	10	20	52	60	–8	58
15	Altrincham	46	9	7	7	30	29	6	4	13	19	37	15	11	20	49	66	–17	56
16	Salisbury C	46	8	6	9	29	33	6	7	10	25	31	14	13	19	54	64	–10	55
17	York C	46	8	6	9	26	26	3	10	10	21	31	11	19	16	47	51	–4	52
18	Forest Green R	46	7	6	10	39	40	5	10	8	31	36	12	16	18	70	76	–6	52
19	Grays Ath	46	12	5	6	31	24	2	5	16	13	40	14	10	22	44	64	–20	52
20	Barrow	46	7	10	6	27	26	5	5	13	24	39	12	15	19	51	65	–14	51
21	Woking	46	6	8	9	21	29	4	6	13	16	31	10	14	22	37	60	–23	44
22	Northwich Vic	46	7	5	11	29	26	4	5	14	27	49	11	10	25	56	75	–19	43
23	Weymouth	46	5	6	12	27	53	6	4	13	18	33	11	10	25	45	86	–41	43
24	Lewes	46	5	2	16	15	41	1	4	18	13	48	6	6	34	28	89	–61	24

Oxford U deducted 5 points, Crawley T deducted 1 point, Mansfield T deducted 4 points.

Leading Goalscorers 2008–09

League Games only

Andrew Mangan	(Forest Green Rovers)	26
James Constable	(Oxford United)	23
Steve Morison	(Stevenage Borough)	22
Charlie Griffin	(Salisbury City)	21
Matthew Barnes-Homer	(Kidderminster Harriers)	20
Justin Richards	(Kidderminster Harriers)	20
Greg Pearson	(Burton Albion)	18
Richard Brodie	(York City)	15
Shaun Harrad	(Burton Albion)	15
Jefferson Louis	(Wrexham)	15
Gareth Seddon	(Kettering Town)	15
Stuart Beavon	(Weymouth)	14
Tim Sills	(Torquay United)	14

BLUE SQUARE PREMIER RESULTS 2008–2009

Home \ Away	Altrincham	Barrow	Burton Alb	Cambridge U	Crawley T	Eastbourne B	Ebbsfleet U	Forest Green R	Grays Ath	Histon	Kettering T	Kidderminster H	Lewes	Mansfield T	Northwich Vic	Oxford U	Rushden & D	Salisbury C	Stevenage B	Torquay U	Weymouth	Woking	Wrexham	York C
Altrincham	—	2-2	1-3	1-0	2-2	2-2	2-1	0-3	2-0	0-1	3-1	2-2	1-0	2-0	0-1	1-0	0-4	0-0	1-2	0-1	4-0	1-0	1-1	1-1
Barrow	2-2	—	0-0	2-0	2-0	1-0	1-0	1-0	0-0	0-1	0-1	1-1	2-1	1-0	2-1	0-1	2-1	1-2	2-1	1-0	0-2	1-0	2-1	0-0
Burton Alb	1-1	0-0	—	3-1	2-0	1-2	0-1	2-3	0-1	3-1	0-1	2-1	4-0	2-1	0-3	0-1	3-0	0-0	2-0	0-1	2-0	3-2	2-1	2-1
Cambridge U	0-0	2-0	3-1	—	1-1	2-1	3-1	1-0	2-1	0-1	1-0	2-0	1-0	2-1	0-1	1-1	0-0	4-0	0-2	0-3	2-1	0-0	2-0	1-0
Crawley T	4-0	2-0	1-1	1-1	—	1-0	2-1	1-0	0-0	2-2	3-3	0-2	0-3	0-3	2-1	2-1	0-0	0-3	2-1	4-2	3-0	2-2	1-0	0-1
Eastbourne B	4-0	1-0	2-0	2-1	1-0	—	1-0	4-4	3-3	0-1	0-2	0-2	6-3	2-0	1-1	2-1	1-0	2-2	2-1	1-2	1-0	0-0	1-0	0-0
Ebbsfleet U	1-0	0-3	3-1	3-1	2-1	1-0	—	0-1	5-2	1-2	2-2	2-0	5-2	2-0	3-0	0-1	0-0	4-0	1-2	1-2	4-2	0-2	1-0	1-1
Forest Green R	1-3	1-0	2-3	1-0	1-0	4-4	0-1	—	4-1	2-0	1-4	3-2	2-0	1-1	1-1	0-1	4-0	1-2	0-3	1-2	4-1	0-2	2-3	1-0
Grays Ath	2-1	0-0	0-1	2-1	0-0	3-3	5-2	1-0	—	1-4	1-2	1-1	4-1	0-4	2-0	1-2	1-0	3-1	1-2	0-3	2-1	1-1	1-0	4-2
Histon	1-0	0-1	3-1	0-1	2-2	0-1	1-2	2-0	1-0	—	1-1	1-2	2-2	1-2	2-1	0-4	2-1	1-0	1-4	2-1	1-0	3-0	0-1	2-0
Kettering T	3-1	0-1	0-1	1-0	3-3	0-2	2-2	1-4	0-0	1-1	—	2-4	0-1	3-0	3-0	1-2	2-1	3-2	0-3	1-3	0-1	0-1	1-0	1-0
Kidderminster H	4-0	1-1	2-1	2-0	0-2	0-2	2-0	3-2	1-0	2-1	1-1	—	1-1	0-1	1-2	2-2	0-4	3-0	3-2	2-4	1-0	0-1	0-2	2-2
Lewes	2-0	2-1	4-0	1-0	0-3	6-3	5-2	2-0	4-1	1-2	2-2	1-0	—	1-3	1-2	1-1	1-0	1-0	1-1	2-0	0-2	2-0	1-2	1-0
Mansfield T	0-1	1-0	2-1	2-1	0-3	2-0	2-0	1-1	0-0	2-0	2-0	2-0	0-1	—	0-1	2-3	1-2	3-0	2-1	1-3	2-3	0-0	1-2	2-0
Northwich Vic	1-0	2-1	0-3	0-1	2-1	1-1	3-0	1-1	2-1	0-2	0-1	1-1	1-2	2-1	—	2-3	2-3	2-1	3-0	2-1	0-2	3-1	1-0	1-1
Oxford U	2-0	0-1	0-1	1-1	2-1	2-1	0-1	0-1	1-0	3-3	1-0	0-1	1-1	2-0	1-2	—	5-2	2-1	5-2	2-1	0-3	1-0	1-1	1-1
Rushden & D	0-0	2-1	3-0	0-0	0-0	1-0	0-0	4-0	0-1	0-1	1-0	0-2	3-2	2-1	1-1	1-3	—	0-0	2-1	2-2	0-0	2-1	1-4	3-3
Salisbury C	3-0	1-2	0-0	4-0	0-3	2-2	4-0	1-2	0-0	0-2	1-1	1-2	1-0	3-0	1-1	1-1	3-1	—	3-2	3-1	0-4	0-1	1-2	1-1
Stevenage B	2-0	2-1	2-0	0-2	2-1	2-1	1-2	0-3	1-2	1-4	2-4	1-0	0-0	2-1	3-0	5-2	1-1	2-0	—	0-1	0-2	2-1	1-3	1-2
Torquay U	3-1	1-0	0-1	0-3	4-2	1-2	1-2	1-2	1-2	2-1	1-1	1-2	1-0	2-1	1-3	2-2	3-1	0-4	3-0	—	1-1	1-1	1-2	1-1
Weymouth	2-0	0-2	2-0	2-1	3-0	1-0	4-2	4-1	2-1	1-0	1-2	0-2	1-0	1-0	5-2	0-3	0-0	0-2	0-1	0-2	—	1-1	0-2	2-0
Woking	1-0	1-0	3-2	0-0	2-2	0-0	0-2	0-2	1-1	3-0	1-1	0-1	2-0	0-0	3-1	1-0	2-1	0-1	2-1	1-1	1-1	—	1-3	3-1
Wrexham	1-2	2-1	2-1	2-0	1-0	1-0	1-0	2-3	1-0	0-1	1-0	1-2	3-0	1-2	1-0	2-0	0-3	1-1	1-1	1-2	0-2	2-0	—	1-0
York C	1-0	0-0	2-1	1-0	0-1	0-0	1-1	1-0	4-2	2-0	1-2	2-2	2-2	2-1	1-1	0-0	2-0	1-1	1-2	1-2	0-2	2-0	1-0	—

BLUE SQUARE PREMIER PLAY-OFFS 2008–2009

BLUE SQUARE PREMIER SEMI-FINALS FIRST LEG

Stevenage B	(0) 3	Cambridge U	(0) 1
Torquay U	(1) 2	Histon	(0) 0

BLUE SQUARE PREMIER SEMI-FINALS SECOND LEG

Cambridge U	(0) 3	Stevenage B	(0) 0
Histon	(1) 1	Torquay U	(0) 0

BLUE SQUARE PREMIER FINAL (at Wembley)

Sunday, 17 May 2009

Cambridge U (0) 0

Torquay U (1) 2 *(Hargreaves 35, Sills 75)*   35,089

Cambridge U: Bartlett; Gleeson, Tonkin, Bolland■, Hatswell, Wilmott (Holroyd), Reason, Carden (Challinor), Rendell, Phillips, Pitt (Parkinson).
Torquay U: Poke; Mansell, Nicholson, Hargreaves, Todd, Robertson, Carlisle (Carayol), Wroe, Benyon (Thompson), Sills, Stevens (Hodges).
Referee: G. Sutton (Lincolnshire).

ATTENDANCES BY CLUB 2008–2009

	Aggregate 2008–09	Average 2008–09	Highest Attendance 2008–09
Oxford United	112,228	4,879	10,298 v Northwich Victoria
Cambridge United	82,117	3,570	7,090 v Altrincham
Wrexham	75,730	3,293	5,173 v York City
Mansfield Town	55,721	2,423	3,614 v Stevenage Borough
Burton Albion	55,229	2,401	6,192 v Oxford United
York City	52,794	2,295	2,703 v Burton Albion
Torquay United	51,578	2,243	4,528 v Burton Albion
Stevenage Borough	45,756	1,989	3,700 v Oxford United
Woking	39,739	1,728	3,791 v Oxford United
Kidderminster Harriers	38,835	1,688	3,025 v Burton Albion
Kettering Town	37,150	1,615	2,897 v Rushden & Diamonds
Barrow	35,900	1,561	2,790 v Oxford United
Rushden & Diamonds	34,715	1,509	3,406 v Kettering Town
Eastbourne Borough	31,905	1,387	3,105 v Cambridge United
Ebbsfleet United	27,667	1,203	1,872 v Mansfield Town
Crawley Town	27,467	1,194	2,207 v Kettering Town
Salisbury City	26,306	1,144	2,418 v Oxford United
Histon	25,763	1,120	2,716 v Kettering Town
Weymouth	25,096	1,091	2,323 v Torquay United
Altrincham	24,863	1,081	2,619 v Wrexham
Forest Green Rovers	21,970	955	2,027 v Oxford United
Northwich Victoria	18,112	787	1,709 v Wrexham
Lewes	16,537	719	2,232 v Eastbourne Borough
Grays Athletic	15,793	687	1,246 v Forest Green Rovers

APPEARANCES AND GOALSCORERS 2008–2009

ALTRINCHAM

League Appearances: Acton, 2; Banim, 2+1; Battersby, 5; Coburn, 40; Danylyk, 39+3; Denham, 10+8; Densmore, 33; Doughty, 42+1; Elam, 11+10; Hadfield, 1+3; Johnson, 31+13; Lane, 30+4; Lawton, 35+1; Little, 41+2; McGregor, 41+1; Meechan, 7+13; O'Neill, 4+24; Peyton, 19+21; Ralph, 4+1; Senior, 23+7; Smith, 24; Street, 3+2; Thornley, 0+3; Tierney, 0+3; Waterfall, 0+1; Welch, 9+4; Wilkinson, 6+3; Young, 44+1.

Goals: League (49): Little 16 (2 pens), Senior 7, Densmore 4, Johnson 4, O'Neill 3 (1 pen), Welch 3, Denham 2, Doughty 2 (1 pen), Meechan 2, Young 2, Banim 1, Lawton 1, McGregor 1, Peyton 1.

FA Cup (2): Lane 1, Little 1.

BARROW

League Appearances: Black, 5+2; Bond, 34+5; Boyd, 39; Brodie, 3; Brown, D. 11; Brown, P. 21+12; Curtis, 2; Deasy, 26+1; Elderton, 3; Henney, 28+2; Holness, 11+1; Horne, 1; Hunt, 18+8; Jelleyman, 9; Jones, 44; Joyce, 5; Kerr, 12+7; Logan, 43+1; Martin, 20+1; McEvilly, 6; McGill, 17+1; McNulty, 36+1; Pearson, 21+1; Rogan, 8+24; Sharry, 4; Sheridan, 8; Spender, 12; Steele, 4+3; Tait, 6+19; Thompson, 0+1; walker, 35+6; Winn, 13+5; Woodyatt, 1.

Goals: League (51): Walker 12, Boyd 5, Brown P 5, Rogan 5, Henney 4, McNulty 4 (3 pens), Brown D 3 (1 pen), Jones 3, Bond 2 (1 pen), Hunt 2, Logan 2, Tait 2, McEvilly 1, own goal 1.

FA Cup (11): Brodie 3, Brown D 2 (2 pens), Henney 2, Brown P 1, Logan 1, McNulty 1, Walker 1.

BURTON ALBION

League Appearances: Armstrong, 1+2; Austin, 19+15; Bailey, 6+4; Banim, 8+7; Brayford, 6; Butler, 3+9; Buxton, 41; Byrne, 3+4; Corbett, 45; Deeney, 8; Gilroy, 38+1; Goodfellow, 18+12; Harrad, 28+13; Holmes, 6+10; James, 29; McGrath, 46; Morris, 16+13; Newby, 10+12; Pearson, 34+6; Poole, 38; Simmons, 1+1; Simpson, 40+1; Stride, 17+12; Webster, 36+2; Yates, 9+1.

Goals: League (81): Pearson 18 (7 pens), Harrad 15 (3 pens), Morris 7,

Webster 7, Goodfellow 6, McGrath 6, Gilroy 5, Simpson 3, Austin 2, Butler 2, Corbett 2, Stride 2, Armstrong 1, Brayford 1, Buxton 1, Yates 1, own goals 2.

FA Cup (0).

CAMBRIDGE UNITED

League Appearances: Ainge, 1+1; Beesley, 23+5; Bolland, 40; Brown, 6; Carden, 40; Challinor, 26+7; Collins, 1; Convery, 10+2; Coulson, 10+2; Crow, 13+9; Farrell, 10+4; Gleeson, 37; Hatswell, 44; Holroyd, 24+11; Ives, 0+1; Jardim, 14+8; Jones, 2+6; McAuley, 3; McEvilly, 17+1; McMahon, 8+1; Parkinson, 5+6; Phillips, 2+3; Pitt, 13+7; Potter, 46; Reason, 15; Rendell, 24+2; Tonkin, 42; Willmott, 30+7.

Goals: League (65): Rendell 13 (2 pens), Holroyd 10 (3 pens), McEvilly 8 (2 pens), Willmott 6, Beesley 4, Hatswell 4, Crow 3, Challinor 2, Jardim 2, Pitt 2, Reason 2, Bolland 1, Brown 1, Carden 1, Convery 1, Farrell 1, Parkinson 1, Phillips 1, own goals 2.

FA Cup (3): Crow 1, Willmott 1, own goal 1.

Play-Offs (4): Rendell 2, Phillips 1, Willmott 1.

CRAWLEY TOWN

League Appearances: Anton, 0+9; Bulman, 44+1; Chalmers, 4; Cook, 27+5; Dark, 0+1; Dayton, 1+2; Douglas, 0+1; Fletcher, 4+16; Forrest, 31+7; Gaia, 9+1; Giles, 18+8; Gill, 1+1; Hurren, 3+2; Killeen, 19+10; Lake-Edwards, 1; Malcolm, 25+3; Matthews, 15+4; Mills, 0+2; Napper, 1+1; Nayee, 0+1; Nayee, 0+1; Pinault, 26+2; Pittman, 22+3; Quinn, 37; Rankin, 6+12; Rayner, 46; Raynor, 0+1; Rents, 36+3; Shaw, 12+5; Stevens, 4+2; Thomas, 3+6; Weatherstone, 34+5; Wilson, 36+4; Wright, 41.

Goals: League (77): Cook 13 (5 pens), Pittman 10, Quinn 7, Weatherstone 6, Killeen 5, Shaw 5, Malcolm 4, Wilson 4, Bulman 3, Matthews 3, Pinault 3 (2 pens), Rankin 3, Rents 3 (1 pen), Fletcher 2, Forrest 2, Gaia 1, Giles 1, own goals 2.

FA Cup (0).

EASTBOURNE BOROUGH

League Appearances: Armstrong, 38; Atkin, 21+10; Austin, 42+2; Baker, 42; Barnes, 8; Brown, 23+1; Budd, 0+6; Crabb, M. 36+3; Crabb, N. 14+21; Gargan, 3+3; Goulding, 1+2; Harding, 14+18; Harkin, 6+5; Hook, 44; Illugason, 0+3; Jeffery, 7+6; Jenkins, 43; Johnson, 0+1; Jordan, 2; Lovett, 28+12; Mingle, 1+2; Osborne, 3; Pullan, 44; Sigere, 3+2; Smart, 37+3; Smith, 13; Tait, 21+5; Taylor, 1+3; Wormull, 11+18.

Goals: *League (58):* Armstrong 9 (3 pens), Atkin 8, Crabb M 6, Barnes 5, Crabb N 5, Smart 4, Austin 3, Jeffery 3, Smith 3, Harding 2, Tait 2, Wormull 2, Brown 1, Gargan 1, Lovett 1, Osborne 1, Pullan 1, Taylor 1.

FA Cup (1): Baker 1.

EBBSFLEET UNITED

League Appearances: Akinde, 1+4; Appiah, 1+2; Barrett, 29; Bowes, 0+2; Charles, 35+1; Cronin, 46; Crooks, 16; Cumbers, 2; Delicate, 3; Duncan, 6+2; Gash, 40; Hand, 17+6; Hawkins, 9+2; Henry, 1+1; Ibe, 7+19; Judge, 1; Long, 43+2; Martin, 7; McCarthy, 19; Moore, 34+2; Murray, 5+3; Opinel, 31+2; Pooley, 12+5; Purcell, 12+17; Ricketts, 34+2; Shakes, 23+11; Slatter, 10+11; Smith, 18+2; Sole, 8+5; Stevens, 8+1; Stone, 16+7; West, 8+2; Yussuff, 4+4.

Goals: *League (52):* Gash 11, Barrett 6, Moore 6 (1 pen), Ibe 5, Sole 5 (2 pens), Long 4 (1 pen), Shakes 4, Akinde 2, Smith 2, Appiah 1, Cumbers 1, McCarthy 1, Pooley 1, Purcell 1, Ricketts 1, Yussuff 1.

FA Cup (3): Moore 2 (2 pens), Ibe 1.

FOREST GREEN ROVERS

League Appearances: Afful, 8+16; Ashford, 0+2; Ayres, 19+1; Baldwin, 1+3; Brown, 16+2; Burton, 27; Casey, 1+1; Clist, 21; Courtney, 0+1; Else, 1+3; Fowler, 38+2; Gill, 20; Hardiker, 11; Jones, 39; Kempson, 5; Lawless, 32; Lloyd, 11+5; Low, 3+1; Mangan, 38+3; McDonald, 17+7; Mohamed, 17+10; Molyneux, 2+2; Palmer, 0+4; Pitman, 2; Platt, 27+12; Preece, 32+3; Pugh, 1; Rigoglioso, 14+11; Robinson, 19+1; Simpson, 0+3; Smith, 33+9; Stonehouse, 37+3; Symonds, 7+10; Thomas, 7+2.

Goals: *League (70):* Mangan 26 (4 pens), Platt 6 (2 pens), Smith 6, Lawless 5, Rigoglioso 5, Brown 3, Hardiker 3, Mohamed 3, Ayres 2, Jones 2, Palmer 2, Preece 2, Clist 1, Fowler 1, Lloyd 1, Symonds 1, own goal 1.

FA Cup (10): Mohamed 3, Afful 2, Smith 2, Lawless 1, Low 1, Stonehouse 1.

GRAYS ATHLETIC

League Appearances: Arnold, 17+1; Ashton, 15+2; Bailey, 9+6; Batchelor, 0+1; Batt, 9+1; Beavan, 18+1; Beckwith, 7; Berry, 2+7; Black, 7+1; Bodkin, 2; Butcher, 3; Button, 13; Campana, 2+3; Candrain, 1+1; Cogan, 38+5; Davis, 17+8; Dayes, 5; Deany, 1; Dinning, 8+1; Dixon, 1+3; Elliott, 22+4; Flitney, 6; Forrester, 6+2; Gier, 16+2; Gray, 0+1; Gross, 6; Hickie, 6+4; Hudson-Odoi, 8+2; Ide, 4+3; Jones, 2; Kedwell, 7+1; Lindie, 1+4; Long, 3+3; McCollin, 3; McKenzie, 1; Molesley, 6+4; Pugh, 16+1; Quistin, 1+1; Reid, 0+3; Rigg, 6; Slabber, 15+10; Sloma, 19+3; St Aimie, 4+2; Stuart, 46; Sweeney, 0+1; Tabiri, 3; Taylor, 15+2; Thomas, 10; Thurgood, 35+2; Welsh, 33+7; Wilnis, 31+2.

Goals: *League (44):* Pugh 7, Cogan 6, Slabber 3, Sloma 3, Taylor 3, Thurgood 3, Welsh 3, Dinning 2, Molesley 2, St Aimie 2, Stuart 2, Thomas 2, Beavan 1, Berry 1, Black 1, Elliott 1, Forrester 1, own goal 1.

FA Cup (3): Cogan 1 (pen), Elliott 1, Stuart 1.

HISTON

League Appearances: Ada, 41; Andrews, 8+24; Barker, 25+5; Bygrave, 2; Campbell, 0+1; Coker, 0+1; Gwillim, 41; Kennedy, 4+3; Knight-Percival, 36+5; Langston, 45; Midson, 46; Mitchell-King, 38+1; Murray, 39+2; Naisbitt, 43; Nightingale, 1+4; Okay, 5+3; Oyebanjo, 37+3; Pacquette, 1+2; Patterson, 1; Pope, 12+4; Reeves, 12+8; Roache, 0+12; Rose, 0+1; Simpson, 32; Welch, 34+1; Wright, 34+3.

Goals: *League (78):* Midson 20, Wright 10 (4 pens), Knight-Percival 9, Murray 9, Barker 8, Reeves 5, Simpson 5, Langston 3, Gwillim 2, Mitchell-King 2, Andrews 1, Oyebanjo 1, own goals 3.

FA Cup (10): Simpson 4, Wright 3, Midson 2, Langston 1.

Play-Offs (1): Andrews 1.

KETTERING TOWN

League Appearances: Arther, 1+3; Artus, 5; Beardsley, 14+23; Bennett, 16+1; Boucaud, 40+2; Branam-Barrett, 2; Branston, 39; Charles, 6+3; Christie, 11+2; Dempster, 27+9; Eaden, 20; Geohaghan, 44; Graham, 11+6; Harper, 46; Jaszczun, 22; Lee, 2+6; Lorougnon, 0+4; Marna, 20+19; Potter, A. 29+9; Potter, L. 22; Rawle, 1; Seddon, 34+6; Smith, 0+1; Solkhon, 21+16; Taylor, 0+2; Warlow, 3+1; Westcarr, 33+6; Wrack, 31+5; Wright, 6+5.

Goals: *League (50):* Seddon 15 (4 pens), Marna 9, Christie 5 (1 pen), Dempster 5, Beardsley 4, Westcarr 4, Wright 3, Charles 1, Lee 1, Lorougnon 1, Potter A 1, Solkhon 1.

FA Cup (13): Westcarr 4 (1 pen), Seddon 3, Solkhon 2, Christie 1, Dempster 1, Geohagan 1, Potter A 1.

KIDDERMINSTER HARRIERS

League Appearances: Armstrong, 7; Baker, 36+1; Barnes-Homer, 41+5; Bartlett, 46; Beardsley, 0+3; Bennett, 25+12; Bignot, 2+1; Bowler, 3; Brittain, 30+12; Carr, 2+6; Creighton, 43+1; Ferrell, 28+3; Jones, 23+8; Knights, 21+16; Lowe, 43; MacKenzie, 2+2; McDermott, 6+17; McGrath, 0+1; McPhee, 16; Moore, 5+12; Penn, 38+4; Reilly, 26; Richards, 38+1; Russell, 3; Smikle, 22+19.

Goals: *League (69):* Barnes-Homer 20, Richards 16 (2 pens), Smikle 8, Brittain 4, Lowe 4, McPhee 3, Penn 3, Reilly 3, Creighton 1, Ferrell 1, Jones 1, Knights 1, MacKenzie 1, Moore 1, own goals 2.

FA Cup (8): Richards 2 (1 pen), Barnes-Homer 1, Brittain 1, Creighton 1, Moore 1, Penn 1, Smikle 1.

LEWES

League Appearances: Baidoo, 2+3; Banks, 44; Banks-Smith, 1; Barness, 43; Beda, 1; Bell, 0+3; Breach, 38; Butters, 7; Charles, 5; Clark, 0+1; Compton, 3; Cox, 18+17; Cullip, 33; Davis, 2; Elliott, 4+5; Fenelon, 8+9; Fisk, 16; Foreman, 10+9; Fraser, 4; Gargan, 8; Geard, 4+2; Graves, 4+1; Greaves, 0+1; Hall, 4+1; Henry, 4+3; Hinshelwood, 4; Jirbandey, 5; Keehan, 44; Klein-Davies, 8+1; Liburd, 0+2; Lyons, 1+2; Mayo, 6; Osborne, 0+2; Pearson, 2; Richards, 6+1; Rivers, 10+6; Rooney, 6; Rowland,

9+4; Ruddy, 2+1; Sackey, 1+3; St Aimie, 5; Standing, 35+1; Storrie, 6+3; Sutton, 0+8; Tabiri, 9; Taylor, 19; Thomas, 14; Timms, 2; Wallis-Taylor, 22+2; Wheeler, 15+4; Wilkinson, A. 4+2; Wilkinson, S. 8.

Goals: *League (28):* Keehan 8 (1 pen), Taylor 5, Gargan 3, Standing 3 (2 pens), Fenelon 2, Breach 1, Henry 1, Jirbandey 1, Tabiri 1, Wheeler 1, own goals 2.

FA Cup (2): Cox 1, Wheeler 1.

MANSFIELD TOWN

League Appearances: Ahmed, 9; Ameobi, 1+4; Annerson, 2; Arnold, 38+4; Blackwood, 20+5; Briscoe, 10+8; Chanot, 5; Clare, 4+5; D'Laryea, 39+2; Duffy, 20+1; Gamble, 24; Garner, 11+3; Havern, 12; Higginson, 0+1; Hotchkiss, 6; Howell, 0+2; Hurren, 9+5; Jeannin, 25+1; Kay, 4+1; Lee, 13+8; MacKenzie, 3+5; Marriott, 18; Mayo, 12; Moses, 42; Naylor, 1; O'Connor, 21+18; O'Hare, 24+1; Robinson, 1+12; Ryan, 0+1; Shaw, 2+1; Silk, 40+1; Sinclair, 9+1; Somner, 33+2; Stallard, 18+10; Wedgbury, 1; White, 3+1; Williams, 12+2; Woodhouse, 11+1.

Goals: *League (57):* Duffy 9 (3 pens), O'Connor 8, Stallard 8 (2 pens), Arnold 5, Garner 4, Sinclair 4, Blackwood 3, Lee 3, Ahmed 2 (1 pen), D'Laryea 2, Briscoe 1, Clare 1, Hurren 1, Mayo 1, O'Hare 1, Silk 1, Somner 1, Williams 1, own goal 1.

FA Cup (2): Arnold 1, Hurren 1.

NORTHWICH VICTORIA

League Appearances: Allan, 31+3; Almeida, 0+1; Antwi, 5; Aspin, 30+2; Bailey, 20+6; Barnes, 0+1; Barrett, 2+5; Benjamin, 0+2; Birch, 1; Brown, 30+2; Burns, 18+6; Byrne, 5+6; Byrom, 23+5; Carr, 3+1; Clarke, 22+1; Connett, 5; Conroy, 1+1; Crowell, 38+5; Elam, 21+1; Farran, 0+2; Flynn, 11+6; Grand, 34; Horrocks, 8+4; Jones, 4; Joyce, 12; King, 1; Lodge, 6+4; Marsh, M. 1; Marsh, P. 0+5; McDonald, 2; Meadowcroft, 8+1; Mullan, 18+14; Murray, 5; Perry, 7; Price, 2; Reeves, 7+2; Richards, 0+4; Riley, 1+5; Roberts, 20; Robinson, 9; Stamp, 15+11; Steele, 12+6; Stevens, 6+1; Sutton, 4; Tynan, 19; Wagstaff, 5; Welch, 12+2; Whitley, 5; Williams, 8; Winn, 9; Yussuff, 7.

Goals: *League (56):* Allan 8, Stamp 6,

Grand 5, Burns 4, Byrom 4, Crowell 4,
Bailey 3, Steele 3, Joyce 2, Mullan 2,
Perry 2, Brown 1, Elam 1, Flynn 1, Hor-
rocks 1, McDonald 1, Reeves 1, Roberts
1, Robinson 1, Wagstaff 1, Welch 1,
Williams 1 (pen), Winn 1, own goal 1.
FA Cup (0).

OXFORD UNITED

League Appearances: Batt, 16; Burnell,
21; Carruthers, 31+4; Chapman, 20;
Clarke, 12+2; Clist, 14; Cole, 4; Constable, 41+1; Davies, 1; Day, 15+3; Deering, 8+11; Evans, 2+1; Farrell, 7+7;
Fisher, 0+4; Foster, 39; Groves, 0+1;
Guy, 18+3; Haldane, 34+9; Hinchliffe,
5+2; Husbands, 1+1; Hutchinson, 12+16;
Killock, 3; Murray, 45+1; Nelthorpe,
14+2; Odubade, 20+23; Osbourne, 6;
Quinn, 15; Reid, 5+5; Sandwith, 9+3;
Sappleton, 1+3; Taylor, 0+4; Trainer,
16+1; Turley, 37; Willmott, 34+3.
Goals: *League (72):* Constable 23 (6
pens), Murray 7, Odubade 6 (2 pens),
Trainer 4, Clist 3, Haldane 3, Chapman
2, Deering 2, Farrell 2, Guy 2, Hutchin-
son 2, Nelthorpe 2, Quinn 2, Reid 2,
Willmott 2, Burnell 1, Day 1, Fisher 1,
Foster 1, Sandwith 1, Sappleton 1, own
goals 2.
FA Cup (5): Constable 2, Guy 1,
Odubade 1, Trainer 1.

RUSHDEN & DIAMONDS

League Appearances: Arthur, 1+1;
Beecroft, 15+10; Boden, 2+2; Bolasie,
5+2; Broadbent, 2+1; Brown, 2+1;
Burgess, 38+2; Burton, 8+3; Clare, 10+2;
Cochrane, 4; Corcoran, 30+7; Cousins,
11+9; Downer, 16+1; Fortune, 1; Gul-
liver, 6+2; Hilliard, 0+1; Hope, 46; Jel-
leyman, 14+3; Kelly, 28+11; Knight,
10+2; Marriott, 12; McDonald, 3;
McGuinness, 0+5; McNamara, 2+3;
Moloney, 4; Osano, 39; Panther, 3;
Phillips, 13+7; Rankine, 24+11; Roberts,
37; Robinson, 20; Roget, 1; Smith, 7+26;
Tomlin, 36+5; Wolleaston, 36+5; Wood-
house, 20.
Goals: *League (61):* Smith 8, Tomlin 8,
Wolleaston 8, Rankine 7 (2 pens), Clare
5, Hope 5, Knight 4, Burgess 3, Kelly 3,
Corcoran 2, Phillips 2, Beecroft 1,
Cousins 1, McDonald 1, Osano 1,
Robinson 1, Woodhouse 1 (pen).
FA Cup (0).

SALISBURY CITY

League Appearances: Ademeno, 17+3;
Bartlett, 19+3; Bass, 32+4; Beavan, 2+1;
Bittner, 46; Bond, 10+2; Brough, 13;
Clarke, D. 28+11; Clohessy, 35+1;
Cook, 17+2; Cox, 0+1; Davies, 3+4;
Dutton, 18+9; Feeney, 20+3; Fowler,
25+3; Griffin, 32+13; Herring, 35+2;
Hill, 2+3; Maher, 1+2; Martin, 1+1;
Matthews, 2+11; Osman, 0+2; Pearce,
5+1; Robinson, 12+1; Ruddick, 20+4;
Sandell, 16; Sangare, 16+1; Sinclair,
10+4; Spence, 4; Todd, 8; Tubbs, 27+5;
Turk, 15+3; Webb, 11+9; Winfield, 4.
Goals: *League (54):* Griffin 21 (1 pen),
Ademeno 6, Sandell 5 (1 pen) Clarke D
4, Clohessy 3, Tubbs 3 (1 pen), Dutton
2, Feeney 2, Sangare 2, Fowler 1,
Robinson 1, Sinclair 1, Todd 1, Webb 1,
own goal 1.
FA Cup (0).

STEVENAGE BOROUGH

League Appearances: Albrighton, 25+4;
Anaclet, 9+8; Anderson, 0+7; Ashton,
10+1; Bayes, 5+1; Black, 3+3; Bostwick,
39; Boylan, 25+7; Bridges, 15; Christie,
2+1; Cole, 36+6; Day, 41; Drury, 23+2;
Henry, 40+1; Laird, 42; Maamria, 0+1;
Martin, 11; McMahon, 11+2; Mendes,
3+3; Mills, 21+9; Morison, 40+1; Murphy, 10+2; Murray, 1; Nurse, 0+2;
Oliver, 18+4; Roberts, 25; St Aimie,
0+1; Thomas, 5+6; Upson, 0+1; Vincenti, 10+16; Willock, 12+17; Wilson,
24+11.
Goals: *League (73):* Morison 22 (3
pens), Cole 12 (2 pens), Boylan 10,
Drury 5, Vincenti 4, Willock 4, Bostwick 3, Bridges 3, Roberts 2, Albrighton
1, Anaclet 1, Laird 1, Mendes 1, Murphy 1, Murray 1, Wilson 1, own goal 1.
FA Cup (6): Willock 2, Cole 1, Laird 1,
McMahon 1, Morison 1.
Play-Offs (3): Morison 2, Roberts 1.

TORQUAY UNITED

League Appearances: Adams, 1+2;
Benyon, 17+17; Bevan, 34; Brough, 2+1;
Carayol, 14+16; Carlisle, 34+3; Charran,
0+1; Christie, 2+4; D'Sane, 22+5; Ellis,
8+1; Green, 15+14; Hargreaves, 44;
Hodges, 31+4; Mansell, 41+1; Nichol-
son, 38+2; Poke, 12+1; Robertson, 27+3;
Sills, 43+2; Stevens, 15+14; Sturrock,
6+1; Thompson, 17+6; Todd, 16;
Woods, 27; Wroe, 40; Yeoman, 0+1.

335

Goals: *League (72):* Sills 14 (3 pens), Benyon 9, D'Sane 9, Carlisle 8 (1 pen), Wroe 6, Stevens 5, Green 4, Hargreaves 4, Nicholson 3, Robertson 3, Sturrock 2, Christie 1, Ellis 1, Thompson 1, Todd 1, Woods 1.

FA Cup (9): Sills 4, Benyon 2, Thompson 2, Green 1.

Play-Offs (4): Sills 2, Hargreaves 1, Wroe 1.

WEYMOUTH

League Appearances: Agera, 1+1; Akurang, 8; Appiah, 4; Babson, 1; Bansenbe, 1; Beavon, 26+1; Bernard, 14; Browning, 3+2; Bygrave, 13+3; Collins, 8+3; Cooke, 2+2; Coutts, 23+10; Critchell, 8; Crook, 6; Cutler, 22+7; Dickson, 3+1; Doe, 29; Evans, 6; Frampton, 1+1; Gaia, 24+1; Gill, 9; Gwinnett, 2+2; Hart, 5+3; Hoyte, 14; Hyde, 6; Joseph-Dubois, 10+11; Knowles, 17; Legzdins, 8; Luther, 1; Malcolm, 14+3; Mawer, 34+2; McKechnie, 1+3; McPhee, 30; Merella, 6+1; Onibuje, 5+4; Palmer, 4+4; Phillips, 5; Poole, 0+1; Prodomo, 1; Reed, 31+1; Richardson, 1+7; Robins, 1; Robinson, 28+1; Ryan, 3; Sandwith, 30; Strickland, 1; Tribe, 1+2; Tubbs, 0+1; Vincent, 6; Webb, 1+3; Williams, 28+3.

Goals: *League (45):* Beavon 14 (4 pens), McPhee 7, Malcolm 6, Coutts 3, Joseph-Dubois 3, Akurang 2, Williams 2, Bygrave 1, Doe 1, Phillips 1, Reed 1, Robinson 1, Vincent 1, own goals 2.

FA Cup (1): Beavon 1.

WOKING

League Appearances: Anderson, 14; Bossman, 7+1; Bozanic, 18; Bunce, 22+3; Denton, 3+2; Domoraud, 35+2; Eastwood, 12; El Kholti, 15; Elvins, 7; Gindre, 2; Hutchinson, 17+1; Hyde, 4; Kamara, 14+1; Knowles, 12; Lambu, 19+10; Ledgister, 19+12; Lorraine, 33+3; Magunda, 8+2; Marum, 26+14; McNerney, 0+3; Miles, 30; Mondon-Konan, 37+4; Moone, 2+10; Pattison, 34+7; Pidgeley, 16; Quamina, 28+4; Rhodes, 2+1; Salau, 1+1; Sam-Yorke, 5+12; Sintim, 6+4; Sole, 17+4; Spence, 11; Thorpe, 1; Vernazza, 21+4; Williams, 4+8; Worner, 4.

Goals: *League (37):* Domoraud 8, Sole 5 (1 pen), Ledgister 4, Marum 4, Lorraine 3, Bozanic 2, Denton 2, Anderson 1,

Elvins 1, Kamara 1, Lambu 1, Miles 1, Pattison 1, Rhodes 1, Spence 1, Vernazza 1.

FA Cup (2): Domoraud 1, Marum 1.

WREXHAM

League Appearances: Abbott, 1+1; Aiston, 11+8; Allen, 2; Anoruo, 4+7; Assoumani, 3; Baynes, 15+13; Brown, J. 16+5; Brown, N. 6+1; Brown, S. 10+3; Collin, 10+2; Critchell, 2; Crofts, 16; Curtis, 13; De Laet, 8; Edwards, 0+1; Evans, G. 0+1; Evans, S. 11+3; Fairhurst, 15+5; Fleming, 24; Flynn, 21+4; Jansen, 3; Kearney, 13+2; Kempson, 15; Louis, 38+4; Mackin, 13+3; Maxwell, 4; McCluskey, 3+5; Neilsen, 5; Pejic, 1; Proctor, 8+10; Smith, 2+6; Spann, 7+6; Spender, 12+1; Suffo, 1+13; Taylor, 18+8; Tremarco, 17; Tsiaklis, 6; Ward, 32; Westwood, 31; Whalley, 14+2; Williams, A. 5; Williams, Marc 19+3; Williams, Mike 25+2; Williamson, 23+3; Woolfe, 8+2.

Goals: *League (64):* Louis 15, Marc Williams 13, Flynn 4, Whalley 4, Brown J 3, Anoruo 2 (1 pen), Baynes 2, Brown S 2 (1 pen), Evans S 2, Fairhurst 2, Suffo 2 (2 pens), Taylor 2, Mike Williams 2, Allen 1, Crofts 1, Jansen 1, Kearney 1, Mackin 1, Proctor 1, Smith 1, Westwood 1, Woolfe 1.

FA Cup (0).

YORK CITY

League Appearances: Bore, 2+2; Boyes, 10+13; Brodie, 29+9; Brown, 11+6; Critchell, 6; Dyer, 2; Farrell, 15+10; Greaves, 27+8; Henderson, 4+2; Hogg, 8+1; Holmes, 5; Ingham, 40; Kelly, 8+2; Krysiak, 2; Mackin, 15; McBreen, 31+7; McGurk, 35+2; McWilliams, 14+5; Mimms, 4+2; Parslow, 45; Pejic, 15; Purkiss, 38+1; Robinson, 37; Rothery, 0+1; Rusk, 35+2; Russell, 15+8; Shepherd, 1+7; Smith, A. 9+8; Smith, C. 14+1; Sodje, 17+19; Torpey, 1+1; Wilkinson, 11+10.

Goals: *League (47):* Brodie 15, Sodje 7, McBreen 5, Farrell 3, Greaves 3, Boyes 2, Robinson 2 (1 pen), Smith A 2, Smith C 2, Wilkinson 2, Holmes 1, Purkiss 1, own goals 2.

FA Cup (0).

BLUE SQUARE NORTH 2008–2009

FINAL LEAGUE TABLE

			Home					Away					Total					
	P	W	D	L	F	A	W	D	L	F	A	W	D	L	F	A	GD	Pts
1 Tamworth	42	12	5	4	32	18	12	8	1	38	23	24	13	5	70	41	29	85
2 Gateshead	42	14	5	2	50	19	10	3	8	31	29	24	8	10	81	48	33	80
3 Alfreton T	42	12	6	3	46	25	8	11	2	35	23	20	17	5	81	48	33	77
4 AFC Telford U	42	13	6	2	36	13	9	4	8	29	21	22	10	10	65	34	31	76
5 Southport	42	13	4	4	41	20	8	9	4	22	16	21	13	8	63	36	27	76
6 Stalybridge Celtic	42	8	6	7	42	33	12	4	5	29	17	20	10	12	71	50	21	70
7 Droylsden	42	12	6	3	35	18	6	8	7	29	26	18	14	10	64	44	20	68
8 Fleetwood T	42	12	4	5	32	23	5	7	9	38	43	17	11	14	70	66	4	62
9 Harrogate T	42	11	6	4	39	23	6	4	11	27	34	17	10	15	66	57	9	61
10 Hinckley U	42	10	3	8	29	21	6	6	9	27	38	16	9	17	56	59	–3	57
11 Vauxhall Motors	42	7	8	6	28	29	7	3	11	23	38	14	11	17	51	67	–16	53
12 Workington	42	8	5	8	31	30	5	7	9	23	25	13	12	17	54	55	–1	51
13 Gainsborough Trinity	42	5	7	9	25	31	7	7	7	32	32	12	14	16	57	63	–6	50
14 Redditch U	42	6	7	8	23	28	6	7	8	26	33	12	14	16	49	61	–12	50
15 Blyth Spartans	42	11	3	7	35	23	3	4	14	15	35	14	7	21	50	58	–8	49
16 Solihull Moors	42	9	6	6	34	31	4	4	13	15	42	13	10	19	49	73	–24	49
17 King's Lynn	42	5	10	6	28	30	5	8	8	22	30	10	18	14	50	60	–10	48
18 Stafford R	42	6	5	10	15	20	6	7	8	26	36	12	12	18	41	56	–15	48
19 Farsley Celtic	42	10	3	8	42	29	4	2	15	16	36	14	5	23	58	65	–7	47
20 Hyde U	42	6	6	9	31	36	5	3	13	26	44	11	9	22	57	80	–23	42
21 Burscough	42	3	5	13	20	35	7	1	13	23	45	10	6	26	43	80	–37	36
22 Hucknall T	42	2	7	12	20	36	3	6	12	19	48	5	13	24	39	84	–45	28

BLUE SQUARE SETANTA SHIELD FINAL 2008–09

at Forest Green
Attendance 2,323

Forest Green Rovers (0) 0
AFC Telford United (0) 0
aet; AFC Telford United won 3-0 on penalties.

Forest Green Rovers: Burton; Smith, Stonehouse (McDonald), Preece, Jones, Fowler, Lawless (Baldwin), Rigoglioso, Mangan, Platt, Mohamed (Lloyd).

AFC Telford United: Young; Vaughan, Khela, Cowan, Whitehead, Nwadike, Jagielka (Blakeman), Rodgers, Danks, Brown (Lewis), Moore (Adams).

Penalties: Mangan saved; Adams scored; Platt saved; Danks scored; Lloyd saved; Cowan scored.

Referee: S. Creighton (Berkshire).

BLUE SQUARE NORTH RESULTS 2008–2009

	AFC Telford U	Alfreton T	Blyth Spartans	Burscough	Droylsden	Farsley Celtic	Fleetwood T	Gainsborough T	Gateshead	Harrogate T	Hinckley U	Hucknall T	Hyde U	King's Lynn	Redditch U	Solihull Moors	Southport	Stafford Rangers	Stalybridge C	Tamworth	Vauxhall Motors	Workington
AFC Telford U	—	0-0	2-0	0-2	1-0	1-0	1-2	0-2	2-0	0-5	0-4	0-1	4-1	1-0	2-0	0-0	2-0	2-2	3-0	0-0	5-1	0-0
Alfreton T	0-0	—	2-2	1-3	2-0	3-3	1-1	0-2	3-0	2-2	1-1	1-1	0-2	1-2	0-4	2-2	1-1	1-2	1-1	1-1	1-1	0-0
Blyth Spartans	2-0	2-3	—	0-2	2-3	5-0	3-0	1-1	0-1	3-4	3-4	3-0	3-0	2-4	1-0	3-0	2-3	2-1	2-0	0-4	0-1	3-1
Burscough	3-0	0-0	0-2	—	3-1	0-0	3-3	3-2	0-0	0-2	0-2	5-1	2-2	1-0	2-2	1-2	0-3	0-1	2-3	0-1	0-1	2-1
Droylsden	1-3	2-0	3-0	3-1	—	0-0	1-3	0-3	2-4	0-2	0-2	1-3	2-2	1-0	2-2	1-2	0-0	0-1	1-1	1-3	1-2	0-5
Farsley Celtic	1-0	3-3	3-0	5-1	1-1	—	4-1	2-2	0-2	1-0	1-0	1-0	2-1	3-2	1-2	0-1	5-1	4-0	2-3	0-4	1-1	1-0
Fleetwood T	1-2	1-1	3-0	0-4	1-0	4-1	—	1-0	0-0	1-3	2-3	2-0	6-3	4-0	1-1	4-1	1-1	0-3	3-3	1-1	2-0	1-2
Gainsborough T	2-2	0-2	1-1	4-1	1-1	2-2	3-4	—	1-0	2-0	1-2	4-0	2-1	0-1	4-2	1-1	0-1	0-3	0-1	5-1	1-1	1-1
Gateshead	0-1	3-0	2-3	3-0	1-0	0-2	5-2	0-3	—	2-0	1-3	0-0	2-1	2-0	1-1	4-0	0-3	3-3	0-1	2-2	2-0	1-1
Harrogate T	2-0	2-2	3-1	2-0	1-1	1-0	3-2	1-2	1-0	—	2-0	0-0	0-1	1-1	1-1	0-2	0-0	3-3	2-3	1-3	2-0	1-0
Hinckley U	0-5	1-1	1-1	0-1	3-2	1-2	3-2	2-2	2-2	1-1	—	2-2	1-0	1-2	2-3	2-0	0-0	4-0	2-0	2-3	2-3	0-0
Hucknall T	0-4	0-2	2-1	3-3	2-0	3-1	5-3	2-0	2-5	1-1	1-3	—	2-0	2-1	3-3	3-0	0-0	4-0	1-0	1-2	0-1	4-4
Hyde U	0-1	1-2	2-1	4-0	0-3	2-1	0-0	1-3	2-3	2-3	0-0	4-0	—	0-1	2-3	3-0	0-1	0-1	0-2	1-2	3-1	1-3
King's Lynn	4-1	1-2	2-1	6-2	2-0	3-2	3-1	2-3	2-0	1-0	3-1	2-2	1-0	—	1-2	5-0	0-2	4-0	2-0	1-2	1-1	2-0
Redditch U	1-0	0-4	1-0	2-0	0-3	1-2	0-0	1-1	2-3	1-0	7-1	4-1	2-0	2-1	—	3-0	0-1	3-3	2-0	1-2	3-1	2-0
Solihull Moors	0-0	2-2	1-1	0-1	2-0	0-1	1-1	0-1	4-1	0-4	0-0	2-3	2-0	1-3	2-2	—	0-0	4-0	2-0	0-1	3-2	2-0
Southport	2-0	1-1	1-3	3-3	0-3	1-0	2-0	0-1	1-2	0-0	3-1	1-0	2-0	1-1	0-2	3-0	—	0-3	1-2	2-2	5-2	2-0
Stafford Rangers	2-2	1-2	2-1	4-0	2-0	2-0	0-1	1-3	4-1	3-1	0-4	2-2	2-0	1-1	2-2	5-0	0-0	—	0-1	0-1	0-0	0-0
Stalybridge C	3-0	1-1	2-0	0-1	1-1	2-3	3-3	0-1	1-2	3-1	2-0	2-2	2-0	2-1	2-0	1-0	1-0	1-1	—	0-3	1-0	1-0
Tamworth	2-1	1-1	0-4	0-1	1-3	0-4	1-1	5-1	2-2	1-3	2-3	1-2	1-2	0-1	0-1	0-1	2-2	2-0	0-3	—	1-0	3-0
Vauxhall Motors	0-0	2-2	0-1	0-1	1-2	2-1	2-0	1-1	2-0	2-3	0-1	3-1	1-1	1-3	0-1	2-2	0-1	1-2	2-2	1-4	—	3-0
Workington	1-0	0-3	0-1	4-1	1-1	0-2	1-3	0-1	2-1	1-0	1-3	0-0	2-2	1-1	2-0	2-1	0-1	2-2	0-2	1-4	3-1	—

338

BLUE SQUARE SOUTH 2008–2009

FINAL LEAGUE TABLE

			Home					Away					Total						
		P	W	D	L	F	A	W	D	L	F	A	W	D	L	F	A	GD	Pts
1	AFC Wimbledon	42	17	2	2	49	14	9	8	4	37	22	26	10	6	86	36	50	88
2	Hampton & Richmond B	42	13	5	3	38	16	12	5	4	36	21	25	10	7	74	37	37	85
3	Eastleigh	42	15	4	2	37	18	10	4	7	32	31	25	8	9	69	49	20	83
4	Hayes & Yeading U	42	14	3	4	39	19	10	6	5	35	24	24	9	9	74	43	31	81
5	Chelmsford C	42	12	6	3	42	24	11	2	8	30	28	23	8	11	72	52	20	77
6	Maidenhead U	42	11	3	7	28	23	10	5	6	29	23	21	8	13	57	46	11	71
7	Welling U	42	9	6	6	32	25	10	5	6	29	19	19	11	12	61	44	17	68
8	Bath C	42	11	4	6	28	24	9	4	8	28	21	20	8	14	56	45	11	68
9	Bishop's Stortford	42	9	4	8	28	28	8	4	9	32	32	17	8	17	60	60	0	59
10	Newport Co	42	10	3	8	31	29	6	8	7	19	22	16	11	15	50	51	–1	59
11	Team Bath	42	9	1	11	30	29	7	6	8	32	35	16	7	19	62	64	–2	55
12	St Albans C	42	8	6	7	35	26	6	6	9	21	24	14	12	16	56	50	6	54
13	Bromley	42	9	5	7	36	30	6	4	11	24	34	15	9	18	60	64	–4	54
14	Braintree T	42	7	5	9	23	24	7	5	9	34	30	14	10	18	57	54	3	52
15	Havant & Waterlooville	42	6	10	5	34	28	5	5	11	25	30	11	15	16	59	58	1	48
16	Worcester C	42	4	8	9	18	25	8	3	10	20	28	12	11	19	38	53	–15	47
17	Weston Super Mare	42	5	7	9	24	34	7	4	10	19	34	12	11	19	43	68	–25	47
18	Basingstoke T	42	4	11	6	17	19	6	5	10	19	36	10	16	16	36	55	–19	46
19	Dorchester T	42	6	6	9	23	30	4	6	11	16	31	10	12	20	39	61	–22	42
20	Thurrock	42	6	5	10	25	23	3	8	10	29	37	9	13	20	54	60	–6	40
21	Bognor Regis T	42	4	6	11	19	38	3	6	12	14	30	7	12	23	33	68	–35	26
22	Fisher Ath	42	3	1	17	9	47	2	2	17	13	53	5	3	34	22	100	–78	18

BLUE SQUARE SOUTH RESULTS 2008–2009

	AFC Wimbledon	Basingstoke T	Bath C	Bishop's Stortford	Bognor Regis T	Braintree T	Bromley	Chelmsford C	Dorchester T	Eastleigh	Fisher Ath	Hampton & Richmond B	Havant & Waterlooville	Hayes & Yeading U	Maidenhead U	Newport Co	St Albans C	Team Bath	Thurrock	Welling U	Weston Super Mare	Worcester C
AFC Wimbledon	–	1-0	3-2	4-1	3-1	5-1	3-1	3-1	2-0	0-2	3-0	3-0	2-0	3-1	3-0	3-0	3-0	2-0	2-1	0-1	1-1	2-0
Basingstoke T	0-1	–	1-0	1-1	0-0	2-2	0-1	1-2	0-0	0-1	1-0	1-1	0-1	0-1	0-1	0-0	1-2	1-3	1-3	1-0	2-1	1-0
Bath C	2-2	1-0	–	2-3	0-2	0-2	1-1	2-1	0-0	2-3	2-0	2-1	2-1	0-0	1-0	2-1	1-1	1-0	1-2	2-1	3-0	0-0
Bishop's Stortford	4-1	1-1	2-3	–	2-0	0-3	1-1	2-1	0-0	3-4	1-0	1-3	0-1	1-0	1-0	2-0	0-5	4-3	2-2	2-0	1-1	3-0
Bognor Regis T	1-5	3-2	0-2	2-0	–	1-1	1-0	2-1	0-2	0-0	0-1	0-1	1-1	2-4	0-1	0-1	0-1	3-0	1-1	0-4	1-1	1-2
Braintree T	0-2	2-3	0-0	1-1	1-1	–	2-0	2-2	1-0	5-1	3-0	1-2	1-0	0-2	2-1	3-2	2-3	4-1	3-3	0-5	3-0	1-1
Bromley	3-2	0-1	2-0	2-0	2-0	2-0	–	0-1	0-1	1-1	3-0	1-0	1-5	0-2	0-1	1-0	1-1	0-1	4-3	1-1	4-1	2-0
Chelmsford C	2-1	0-1	2-3	1-1	1-0	2-2	0-1	–	2-1	5-1	3-0	2-0	1-2	0-3	0-1	0-1	1-1	1-1	3-1	4-1	0-2	0-2
Dorchester T	0-3	2-2	0-2	1-2	2-1	1-4	1-0	2-1	–	0-4	3-0	3-2	1-2	0-1	3-2	3-2	0-1	1-3	0-3	2-3	0-0	3-1
Eastleigh	0-0	1-0	2-0	3-3	3-1	1-1	2-0	1-1	0-4	–	0-4	0-1	1-0	0-1	1-3	1-3	0-4	1-1	1-1	1-2	1-0	1-0
Fisher Ath	2-1	0-0	2-0	2-1	0-1	1-0	1-0	0-1	4-0	0-4	–	2-1	2-0	0-1	2-0	0-0	0-6	1-3	3-1	1-2	2-0	0-1
Hampton & Richmond B	0-4	3-1	0-1	1-1	1-3	0-1	1-3	0-2	1-4	2-2	1-3	–	2-1	3-3	0-1	2-1	3-0	3-0	2-1	0-0	1-0	1-2
Havant & Waterlooville	2-1	0-0	2-2	0-3	1-0	0-1	1-0	2-1	2-2	2-2	3-4	1-4	–	1-0	0-1	2-0	0-4	0-3	2-1	2-3	2-1	3-1
Hayes & Yeading U	0-4	5-1	2-2	0-1	3-0	0-2	2-1	1-2	3-3	0-5	4-0	0-0	1-5	–	3-3	0-1	0-1	1-0	2-1	2-1	3-0	3-1
Maidenhead U	0-4	2-2	2-1	3-1	1-0	3-2	0-1	1-2	1-2	1-0	4-0	0-3	1-0	3-3	–	1-1	2-0	4-2	1-1	0-0	1-0	1-0
Newport Co	1-2	1-2	2-1	1-0	0-0	2-0	0-1	0-1	2-0	1-3	4-1	1-0	0-2	2-2	1-1	–	1-0	0-0	4-1	2-3	3-2	0-2
St Albans C	1-1	3-0	1-1	0-2	0-1	2-1	2-1	4-1	2-0	2-2	2-1	0-2	1-1	1-5	1-2	1-1	–	2-0	0-0	0-0	0-2	2-0
Team Bath	0-1	1-0	0-1	1-3	1-1	1-0	1-1	0-3	2-0	0-1	5-0	2-1	4-1	1-1	2-0	0-0	2-0	–	1-2	1-1	2-0	0-2
Thurrock	1-2	6-0	2-1	3-1	0-0	4-0	1-1	0-1	4-1	0-0	2-1	1-0	1-0	2-1	2-0	0-0	0-0	1-2	–	0-0	3-2	1-3
Welling U	2-1	1-1	2-1	1-1	4-1	3-1	4-0	3-1	0-2	2-1	3-1	0-3	1-2	2-2	0-0	2-1	1-1	0-1	4-1	–	2-0	0-2
Weston Super Mare	1-1	0-3	2-0	1-0	2-0	1-1	1-2	1-4	1-0	3-2	3-1	0-2	1-2	1-2	2-2	1-1	1-1	1-1	2-1	2-0	–	1-3
Worcester C	3-2	1-0	0-1	3-0	2-0	1-2	1-0	0-1	0-0	1-0	1-1	1-2	0-3	1-1	1-0	1-0	2-0	0-2	2-0	0-1	1-2	–

UNIBOND LEAGUE 2008–2009

Premier Division

Premier Division	P	Home					Away					Total						
		W	D	L	F	A	W	D	L	F	A	W	D	L	F	A	GD	Pts
1 Eastwood Town	42	15	5	1	49	19	10	7	4	33	18	25	12	5	82	37	45	87
2 Ilkeston Town	42	13	5	3	35	17	10	8	3	24	17	23	13	6	59	34	25	82
3 Nantwich Town	42	12	4	5	43	23	10	6	5	40	18	22	10	10	83	41	42	76
4 Guiseley	42	11	6	4	46	27	11	6	4	52	33	22	10	10	98	60	38	76
5 Kendal Town	42	11	5	5	50	30	10	6	5	35	33	21	11	10	85	63	22	74
6 FC United of Man	42	11	6	4	47	29	10	3	8	35	29	21	9	12	82	58	24	72
7 Bradford Park Av	42	12	5	4	39	23	8	7	6	35	29	20	12	10	74	52	22	72
8 Hednesford Town	42	10	3	8	39	27	11	3	7	39	25	21	6	15	78	52	26	69
9 Ashton United	42	11	7	3	45	26	5	3	13	26	49	16	10	16	71	75	-4	58
10 North Ferriby U	42	9	4	8	44	29	7	2	12	23	36	16	6	20	67	65	2	54
11 Frickley Athletic	42	7	10	4	25	23	6	5	10	29	31	13	15	14	50	58	-8	54
12 Ossett Town	42	8	5	8	38	38	7	3	11	33	36	15	8	19	71	74	-3	53
13 Marine	42	7	4	10	28	34	8	2	11	26	41	15	6	21	54	75	-21	51
14 Buxton	42	7	7	7	25	23	6	3	12	31	35	13	10	19	56	58	-2	49
15 Matlock Town	42	9	6	6	35	28	3	7	11	30	46	12	13	17	65	74	-9	49
16 Boston United	42	6	5	10	22	27	6	8	7	16	25	12	13	17	38	52	-14	49
17 Worksop Town	42	6	7	8	24	38	6	5	10	24	49	12	12	18	52	87	-39	48
18 Cammell Laird	42	7	5	9	29	30	5	6	10	29	40	12	11	19	58	70	-12	47
19 Whitby Town	42	8	4	9	27	28	4	6	11	31	43	12	10	20	58	71	-13	46
20 Witton Albion	42	6	4	11	29	36	6	2	13	24	37	12	6	24	53	73	-20	42
21 Leigh Genesis	42	5	2	14	19	54	6	5	10	23	34	11	7	24	42	88	-46	40
22 Prescot Cables	42	4	4	13	28	49	1	8	12	24	58	5	12	25	52	107	-55	27

SOUTHERN LEAGUE DIVISION 2008–2009

Premier Division

Premier Division	P	Home			Away			Total						
		W	D	L	W	D	L	W	D	L	F	A	GD	Pts
1 Corby Town	42	10	6	5	15	3	3	25	9	8	85	38	47	84
2 Farnborough	42	14	5	2	9	9	3	23	14	5	67	36	31	83
3 Gloucester City	42	12	4	5	9	8	4	21	12	9	80	45	35	75
4 Cambridge City	42	14	1	6	7	9	5	21	10	11	62	40	22	73
5 Hemel Hempstead Town	42	12	5	4	9	2	10	21	7	14	71	48	23	70
6 Oxford City	42	11	4	6	8	6	7	19	10	13	76	55	21	67
7 Merthyr Tydfil	42	11	5	5	8	5	8	19	10	13	66	55	11	67
8 Chippenham Town*	42	12	5	4	8	3	10	20	8	14	64	51	13	65
9 Evesham United	42	8	8	5	8	5	8	16	13	13	48	39	9	61
10 Halesowen Town*	42	11	2	8	8	4	9	19	6	17	65	73	-8	60
11 Brackley Town	42	10	4	7	5	8	8	15	12	15	69	62	7	57
12 Tiverton Town	42	7	6	8	9	3	9	16	9	17	51	50	1	57
13 Swindon Supermarine	42	7	7	7	8	5	8	15	12	15	59	61	-2	57
14 Bashley	42	10	6	5	5	6	10	15	12	15	52	58	-6	57
15 Bedford Town	42	10	7	4	4	1	16	14	8	20	44	55	-11	50
16 Stourbridge	42	8	6	7	5	5	11	13	11	18	62	78	-16	50
17 Rugby Town	42	7	5	9	4	5	12	11	10	21	63	71	-8	43
18 Clevedon Town	42	7	4	10	4	6	11	11	10	21	51	80	-29	43
19 Banbury United	42	10	3	8	1	5	15	11	8	23	43	83	-40	41
20 Hitchin Town	42	5	9	7	5	1	15	10	10	22	57	79	-22	40
21 Yate Town	42	7	4	10	2	5	14	9	9	24	54	91	-37	36
22 Mangotsfield United	42	7	2	12	3	4	14	10	6	26	39	80	-41	36

* 3 points deducted for breach of rules.

RYMAN LEAGUE 2008–2009

Premier Division		Home					Away					Total						
	P	W	D	L	F	A	W	D	L	F	A	W	D	L	F	A	GD	Pts
1 Dover Athletic	42	18	2	1	55	17	15	3	3	36	17	33	5	4	91	34	57	104
2 Staines Town	42	15	5	1	45	18	8	8	5	30	23	23	13	6	75	41	34	82
3 Tonbridge Angels	42	10	5	6	40	28	10	8	3	42	26	20	13	9	82	54	28	73
4 Carshalton Ath	42	6	5	10	26	39	13	6	2	38	24	19	11	12	64	63	1	68
5 Sutton United	42	11	9	1	33	19	7	4	10	24	34	18	13	11	57	53	4	67
6 AFC Hornchurch	42	12	2	7	32	21	7	6	8	28	30	19	8	15	60	51	9	65
7 Wealdstone	42	11	4	6	37	22	7	4	10	33	34	18	8	16	70	56	14	62
8 Dartford	42	9	6	6	39	24	8	5	8	23	25	17	11	14	62	49	13	62
9 Tooting & Mitcham U	42	10	4	7	36	28	6	6	9	21	29	16	10	16	57	57	0	58
10 Ashford Town (Mx)	42	11	2	8	34	27	7	0	14	30	39	18	2	22	64	66	-2	56
11 Billericay Town	42	9	8	4	34	27	6	3	12	20	39	15	11	16	54	66	-12	56
12 Canvey Island	42	10	4	7	39	31	6	3	12	26	39	16	7	19	65	70	-5	55
13 Horsham	42	8	4	9	24	25	8	3	10	25	35	16	7	19	49	60	-11	55
14 Harrow Borough	42	7	6	8	33	34	7	6	8	23	39	14	12	16	56	73	-17	54
15 Maidstone United	42	6	6	9	18	24	8	5	7	28	27	14	11	17	46	51	-5	53
16 Hendon	42	8	6	9	38	27	7	2	12	31	38	15	6	21	69	65	4	51
17 Hastings United	42	6	4	11	23	33	8	3	10	29	35	14	7	21	52	68	-16	49
18 Boreham Wood	42	6	2	13	20	28	6	10	5	28	33	12	12	18	48	61	-13	48
19 Margate	42	8	4	9	29	29	5	3	13	22	35	13	7	22	51	64	-13	46
20 Harlow Town (-3)*	42	5	4	12	31	37	8	2	11	30	40	13	6	23	61	77	-16	42
21 Heybridge Swifts	42	4	6	11	20	34	6	5	10	21	29	10	11	21	41	63	-22	41
22 Ramsgate (-4)*	42	5	5	11	26	37	3	6	12	21	42	8	11	23	47	79	-32	31

* points deducted for breach of rules.

CUP FINALS AND PLAY-OFFS 2008–2009

UNIBOND LEAGUE

CHALLENGE CUP FINAL 2008–09
Guiseley 3, Ilkeston Town 2

PRESIDENT'S CUP FINAL
Trafford 2, Quorn 0

PLAY-OFF FINALS
Premier Division
Ilkeston 2, Nantwich Town 1 (aet.)

First Division North
Newcastle Blue Star 4 Curzon Ashton 1

First Division South
Stocksbridge Park Steels 1, Belper Town 0

SOUTHERN LEAGUE

ERREA SOUTHERN LEAGUE CUP

Final First Leg
Atherstone Town 2, Bridgwater Town 1

Final Second Leg
Bridgwater Town 1, Atherstone Town 3

PLAY-OFF FINALS
Premier Division
Farnborough 0, Gloucester City 1

Division One Midlands
Nuneaton Town 1, Chasetown 0

Division One South & West
AFC Totton 1 Didcot Town 2

RYMAN LEAGUE

ISTHMIAN LEAGUE CUP
Tilbury 2, Harrow Borough 0

PLAY-OFF FINALS
Premier Division
Staines Town 1, Carshalton Athletic 0

Division One North
Waltham Abbey 1, Concord Rangers 1
Waltham Abbey won 5-4 on penalties.

Division One South
Cray Wanderers 1, Metropolitan Police 0

TOTESPORT.COM RESERVE LEAGUE 2008–2009

CENTRAL DIVISION

	P	W	D	L	F	A	GD	Pts
Shrewsbury T	16	12	3	1	49	13	26	39
Nottingham F	16	10	4	2	37	12	25	34
Sheffield U	16	6	3	7	27	25	2	21
Sheffield W	16	6	3	7	24	27	–3	21
Walsall	16	6	3	7	23	31	–8	21
Port Vale	16	6	3	7	23	31	–8	21
Lincoln C	16	6	2	8	24	26	–2	20
Macclesfield T	16	5	4	7	28	35	–7	19
Mansfield T	16	3	5	8	21	47	–26	14
	16	4	1	11	15	32	–17	13

WEST DIVISION

	P	W	D	L	F	A	GD	Pts
Burnley	18	11	4	3	42	18	24	37
Manchester C	18	10	1	7	39	27	12	31
Morecambe	18	9	3	6	31	29	2	30
Carlisle U	18	8	5	5	38	27	11	29
Preston NE	18	8	3	7	28	19	9	27
Blackpool	18	6	4	8	33	43	–10	22
Rochdale	18	6	4	8	28	44	–16	22
Tranmere R	18	4	7	7	25	30	–5	19
Bury	18	4	5	9	19	32	–13	17
Accrington S	18	4	4	10	21	35	–14	16

EAST DIVISION

	P	W	D	L	F	A	GD	Pts
Leeds U	16	13	0	3	27	8	19	39
Huddersfield T	16	11	4	1	46	22	24	37
Hartlepool U	16	10	2	4	40	30	10	32
Scunthorpe U	16	5	5	6	29	24	5	20
Bradford C	16	5	1	10	27	26	1	16
Rotherham U	16	4	4	8	27	37	–10	16
Barnsley	16	4	4	8	33	45	–12	16
Grimsby T	16	4	3	9	27	39	–12	15
York C	16	3	3	10	21	46	–25	12

TOTESPORT.COM LEAGUE CUP 2008–09

GROUP ONE

	P	W	D	L	F	A	GD	Pts
Sunderland	3	3	0	0	15	0	15	9
Newcastle U	3	2	0	1	8	5	3	6
Carlisle U	4	2	0	2	8	5	3	6
Sheffield U	4	1	1	2	5	8	–3	4
Hartlepool U	4	0	1	3	4	12	–8	1

GROUP TWO

	P	W	D	L	F	A	GD	Pts
Grimsby T	3	2	1	0	5	3	2	7
Middlesbrough	3	1	2	0	7	5	2	5
Sheffield W	3	1	1	1	5	7	–2	3
Bradford C	3	0	1	2	2	7	–5	1

GROUP THREE

	P	W	D	L	F	A	GD	Pts
Derby Co	3	2	1	0	10	6	4	7
Oldham Ath	3	2	0	1	5	5	0	6
Walsall	3	1	1	1	6	6	0	4
Mansfield T	3	0	0	3	6	10	–4	0

GROUP FOUR

	P	W	D	L	F	A	GD	Pts
Accrington S	3	3	0	0	8	4	4	9
Rochdale	4	1	2	1	6	6	0	5
Morecambe	4	1	1	2	10	11	–1	4
Tranmere R	3	1	1	1	6	7	–1	4
Macclesfield T	3	1	0	3	6	8	–2	3

Unplayed matches declared void.

SEMI–FINALS
Accrington S 0, Sunderland 2
Derby Co 3, Grimsby T 1

FINAL
Derby Co 1, Sunderland 3

TOTESPORT.COM COMBINATION 2008–2009

CENTRAL DIVISION

	P	W	D	L	GD	Pts
Reading	18	13	3	2	52	42
Millwall	18	11	1	6	23	34
Crystal Palace	18	10	2	6	4	32
Southampton	18	9	3	6	–2	30
Brighton & HA	18	9	2	7	2	29
QPR	18	8	4	6	1	28
Charlton Ath	18	7	2	9	0	23
Aldershot T	18	4	5	9	–2	17
Gillingham	18	3	6	9	–15	15
Lewes	18	1	2	15	–63	5

EAST DIVISION

	P	W	D	L	GD	Pts
Luton T	18	8	7	3	10	31
Watford	18	9	3	6	4	30
Wycombe W	18	7	7	4	2	28
Ipswich T	18	7	5	6	22	26
Peterborough U	18	6	6	6	7	24
Colchester U	18	7	2	9	2	23
Southend U	18	7	2	9	–11	23
Leyton Orient	18	6	4	8	–14	22
Northampton T	18	6	3	9	–6	21
Stevenage B	18	6	3	9	–16	21

WALES & WEST DIVISION

	P	W	D	L	GD	Pts
Plymouth Arg	18	11	5	2	19	38
Swindon T	18	9	6	3	13	33
Bristol C	18	9	4	5	18	31
Exeter C	18	10	0	8	10	30
Bournemouth	18	7	4	7	–7	25
Swansea C	18	6	5	7	–5	23
Salisbury C	18	6	3	9	–16	21
Forest Green R	18	6	2	10	–21	20
Yeovil T	18	6	1	11	–1	19
Cheltenham T	18	4	2	12	–10	14

CUP COMPETITION
GROUP A

	P	W	D	L	GD	Pts
Reading	4	3	1	0	10	10
Bristol C	4	2	1	1	4	7
Southampton	4	2	0	2	–2	6
Plymouth Arg	4	1	1	2	–4	4
Swansea C	4	0	1	3	–8	1

GROUP B

	P	W	D	L	GD	Pts
Crystal Palace	3	3	0	0	6	9
Charlton Ath	4	1	2	1	2	5
Ipswich T	3	1	1	1	0	4
Watford	3	1	0	2	–5	3
QPR	3	0	1	2	–3	1

Unplayed matches cancelled.

FA ACADEMY UNDER-18 LEAGUE 2008–2009

GROUP A

	P	W	D	L	GD	Pts
Arsenal	28	22	4	2	40	70
Norwich C	28	13	6	9	4	45
Ipswich T	28	14	2	12	2	44
Crystal Palace	28	12	4	12	4	40
West Ham U	28	10	8	10	13	38
Southampton	28	12	2	14	–7	38
Portsmouth	28	10	5	13	–4	35
Chelsea	28	10	4	14	–8	34
Fulham	28	8	9	11	–1	33
Charlton Ath	28	6	4	18	–33	22

GROUP B

	P	W	D	L	GD	Pts
Tottenham H	28	19	7	2	49	64
Leicester C	28	19	3	6	42	60
Aston Villa	28	16	6	6	24	54
Coventry C	28	15	8	5	16	53
Reading	28	10	5	13	–8	35
Bristol C	28	9	6	13	–4	33
Cardiff C	28	7	7	14	–15	28
Watford	28	7	4	17	–15	25
Birmingham C	28	7	4	17	–34	25
Milton Keynes D	28	3	4	21	–55	13

GROUP C

	P	W	D	L	GD	Pts
Manchester C	28	22	6	0	55	72
Manchester U	28	15	8	5	31	53
WBA	28	13	5	10	18	44
Liverpool	28	13	5	10	7	44
Everton	28	11	8	9	10	41
Stoke C	28	11	7	10	–11	40
Wolverhampton W	28	10	9	9	–3	39
Crewe Alex	28	11	5	12	1	38
Blackburn R	28	8	6	14	–14	30
Bolton W	28	7	2	19	–29	23

GROUP D

	P	W	D	L	GD	Pts
Sunderland	28	22	2	4	32	68
Newcastle U	28	13	7	8	9	46
Derby Co	28	11	7	10	4	40
Sheffield U	28	8	11	9	–9	35
Nottingham F	28	10	3	15	–10	33
Leeds U	28	9	5	14	–2	32
Barnsley	28	7	7	14	–30	28
Sheffield W	28	6	6	16	–20	24
Huddersfield T	28	5	9	14	–32	24
Middlesbrough	28	5	8	15	–17	23

SEMI-FINALS
Sunderland 1, Tottenham H 2
Manchester C 1, Arsenal 2

FINAL
Tottenham H 0, Arsenal 1

FA PREMIER RESERVE LEAGUES
2008–2009
NORTH SECTION

	P	W	D	L	GD	Pts
Sunderland	20	13	4	3	18	43
Manchester U	20	10	6	4	16	36
Blackburn R	20	9	6	5	11	33
Newcastle U	20	9	5	6	4	32
Manchester C	20	10	0	10	3	30
Wigan Ath	20	7	3	10	–11	24
Liverpool	20	5	7	8	0	22
Everton	20	5	7	8	–6	22
Hull C	20	6	4	10	–16	22
Middlesbrough	20	6	3	11	–7	21
Bolton W	20	6	3	11	–16	21

Leading Goalscorers *(excludes Play-off)*

Federico Macheda	Manchester U	9
Thomas Craddock	Middlesbrough	7
Nile Ranger	Newcastle U	7
David Ball	Manchester C	6
Mark Doninger	Newcastle U	6
David Dowson	Sunderland	6
Tomasz Cywka	Wigan Ath	6
Alan Judge	Blackburn R	5
Carlos Villanueva Rolland	Blackburn R	5
James Vaughan	Everton	5
Andrew Carroll	Newcastle U	5

SOUTH SECTION

	P	W	D	L	GD	Pts
Aston Villa	16	11	3	2	16	36
Tottenham H	16	10	1	5	7	31
Fulham	16	7	5	4	8	26
Portsmouth	16	8	1	7	–7	25
West Ham U	16	7	1	8	–7	22
Arsenal	16	5	4	7	–5	19
Chelsea	16	5	3	8	2	18
Stoke C	16	4	2	10	–5	14
WBA	16	4	2	10	–9	14

Leading Goalscorers *(excludes Play-off)*

Thomas Kilbey	Portsmouth	5
Fred Sears	West Ham U	5
Mark Randall	Arsenal	4
Jonathan Hogg	Aston Villa	4
Fabio Borini	Chelsea	4
Michael Uwezu	Fulham	4
Giles Barnes	Fulham	4
Adel Taarabt	Tottenham H	4
Lateef Elford-Alliyu	WBA	4

Play-off (at Villa Park)
Aston Villa 3, Sunderland 1

WOMEN'S FOOTBALL 2008–2009

WOMEN'S PREMIER LEAGUE
NATIONAL DIVISION

	P	W	D	L	F	A	GD	Pts
Arsenal	22	20	1	1	89	14	75	61
Everton	22	20	1	1	68	10	58	61
Chelsea	22	16	2	4	55	23	32	50
Doncaster R Belles	22	9	6	7	43	36	7	33
Birmingham C	22	10	3	9	39	43	-4	33
Leeds Carnegie	22	8	4	10	32	40	-8	28
Watford	22	7	4	11	31	40	-9	25
Bristol Academy	22	5	8	9	39	49	-10	23
Blackburn R	22	5	3	14	27	52	-25	18
Nottingham F	22	5	2	15	25	59	-34	17
Liverpool	22	4	4	14	28	63	-35	16
WFC Fulham	22	1	6	15	17	64	-47	9

NORTHERN DIVISION

	P	W	D	L	F	A	GD	Pts
Sunderland	22	17	2	3	95	16	79	53
Ooh Lincoln	22	16	4	2	79	15	64	52
Manchester C	22	13	4	5	42	22	20	43
Newcastle U	22	12	5	5	58	28	30	41
Leicester C	22	12	4	6	54	33	21	40
Reading	22	9	6	7	43	31	12	33
Aston Villa	22	10	2	10	49	50	-1	32
Preston NE	22	7	3	12	37	51	-14	24
Sheffield W	22	6	0	16	37	72	-35	18
Curzon Ashton	22	4	4	14	35	70	-35	16
Tranmere R	22	4	2	16	28	76	-48	14
Rotherham U	22	3	2	17	17	110	-93	11

SOUTHERN DIVISION

	P	W	D	L	F	A	GD	Pts
Millwall Lionesses	22	17	3	2	61	14	47	54
Barnet	22	11	7	4	58	33	25	40
West Ham U	22	10	9	3	41	20	21	39
Charlton Ath	22	10	6	6	37	28	9	36
Portsmouth	22	9	6	7	50	36	14	33
Colchester U	22	8	6	8	37	41	-4	30
Cardiff C	22	8	5	9	40	38	2	29
Keynsham T	22	8	3	11	34	49	-15	27
Crystal Palace	22	5	8	9	31	43	-12	23
Brighton & HA	22	5	5	12	28	44	-16	20
Ipswich T	22	5	3	14	19	64	-45	18
Truro C	22	3	5	14	32	58	-26	14

FA WOMEN'S CUP FINAL 2008–2009

Monday, 4 May 2009

(at Derby Co)

Arsenal 2 *(Chapman 32, Little 89)*

Sunderland 1 *(McDougall 90)*   23,291

Arsenal: Byrne; Bassett (White 90), Grant C, Flaherty, Fahey, Davison (Ross 82), Ludlow, Chapman, Yankey, Little, Grant S (Lander 62).

Sunderland: Alderson; Bronze, Greenwell, Bannon, Halliday, Staniforth, McDougall, Nobbs, Williams (Devine 62), Gutteridge (Danby 83), Stokes.

Referee: A. Ihringova.

ENGLAND WOMEN'S INTERNATIONAL MATCHES 2008–2009

EUROPEAN CHAMPIONSHIP QUALIFIERS

28 Sept (in Prague)

Czech Republic 1 *(Doskova 28)*   **England 5** *(Westwood 61, Smith K 79, 86, Carney 81, Scott J 83)*   1054

England: Brown; Scott A, Stoney (Unitt 84), Scott J, Johnson, Asante, Carney, Williams, Sanderson (Westwood 46), Smith K, Yankey (Smith S 64).

2 Oct (in Zamora)

Spain 2 *(Boquette 9, Bermudez 42)*   **England 2** *(Carney 55, Smith K 77)*

England: Brown; Scott A, Stoney, Scott J, Johnson, Asante, Carney, Williams, Aluko (Westwood 46), Smith K, Yankey (Smith S 82).

6 Apr

Spain 2 *(Lambarri 58, Gonzalez 63)*   **England 0**

7 Apr

England 0   Czech Republic 1 *(Vonkova 18)*

FRIENDLIES

17 July (in Unterhaching)

Germany 3 *(Smisek 15, Prinz 55, Behringer 70 (pen))*
England 0   9185

England: Brown; Scott A (Johnson 60), Stoney, Williams, White, Asante, Carney (Smith S 77), Scott J, Sanderson (Westwood 61), Smith K, Yankey.

9 Feb (in Larnaca)

England 2 *(Smith K 2 (pen), Sanderson 3)*   **Finland 2** *(Puranen, Makinen)*

England: Telford; Stoney (Houghton), Unitt, Asante, Johnson, Bassett, Carney, Williams, Sanderson (Handley), Smith K (Scott A), Smith S.

13 Feb (in Larnaca)

England 4 *(White 40, Westwood 42, Smith K 44 (pen), Yankey 55)*   **Finland 1**

England: Brown; Scott A, Yorston (Hickmott), Williams, White (Asante), Houghton, Carney, Westwood (Johnson), Sanderson, Smith K (Smith S), Yankey.

23 Apr (at Shrewsbury)

England 3 *(Williams 18, 81, Johnson 39)*   **Norway 0** 4468

(at Shrewsbury).
England: Brown; Scott A, Stoney, Williams, Johnson, Asante, Carney, Scott J, Aluko (Chapman 66), Smith K, Smith S (Clarke 79).

CYPRUS CUP (in Larnaca)

6 Mar

England 6 *(Williams 18, Sanderson 19, Smith K 42, Houghton 87, Chapman 90)*
South Africa 0

England: Chamberlain; Scott A, Stoney, Williams, Asante, Houghton, Carney (Clarke 62), Scott J (Chapman 46), Sanderson (Aluko 74), Smith K (Westwood 46) (Buet 72), Smith S (Yankey 46).

7 Mar

England 2 *(Carney 28, Stoney 75)*   **France 2** *(Franco 15, Thomis 72)*

England: Brown; Johnson (Scott A 46), Stoney, Asante, Houghton, Scott J, Williams, Carney, Westwood (Chapman 68), Smith S, Smith K (Aluko 56).

11 Mar

England 3 *(Aluko 40, Westwood 66, Clarke 83)*   **Scotland 0**

England: Chamberlain; Scott A, Johnson, Yorston, Unitt, Chapman, Buet, Clarke, Westwood, Yankey, Aluko (Sanderson 82).

12 Mar

England 3 *(Sanderson 32, Smith K 40, Williams 45)*   **Canada 1** *(Sinclair 14)*

England: Brown; Scott A, Stoney, Williams, Asante, Houghton, Carney, Scott J, Sanderson (Aluko 71), Smith K, Smith S.

WOMEN'S UNDER-23 CHAMPIONSHIP

2 Feb

England 2 *(Clarke 2)*   **Norway 0**

6 Feb

England 0   USA 3

FIFA UNDER-20 WOMEN'S WORLD CUP (in Chile)

Chile 0   England 2 *(Chaplen 54, Duggan 80)*
Nigeria 1 *(Orji 71)*   **England 1** *(Dowie 45)*
New Zealand 1 *(McLaughlin 27)*   **England 1** *(Duggan 90)*
USA 3 *(Winters 53, Leroux 81, 90)*   **England 0**
England fielded Under-19 team.

UEFA UNDER-17 WOMEN'S CHAMPIONSHIP

Greece 0   England 4 *(Cole 7, Bruton 28, Carter 47, Eli 69)*
Estonia 0   England 3 *(Bruton 16, Gardener 70, Carter 80)*
Norway 2 *(Haavi 42, Vassbo 47)*   **England 1** *(Eli 85)*

FIFA UNDER-17 WOMEN'S WORLD CUP
(in New Zealand)

Brazil 0   England 3 *(Carter 71, 89, Bruton 75)*
Nigeria 0   England 1 *(Holbrook 79)*
South Korea 3 *(So Yun 8, Kyung Yeon 16, Ari 71)*   **England 0**
Japan 2 *(Kira 8, Iwabuchi 82)*   **England 2** *(Staniforth 45, Christiansen 90)*
England won 5-4 on penalties.
North Korea 2 *(Ho Un Byol 19, Jon Myong Hwa 44)*   **England 1** *(Jane 75)*
Germany 3 *(Wesely 11, Knaak 74, Mester 88)*   **England 0**

THE FA TROPHY 2008–2009

FINAL (at Wembley) – Saturday, 9 May 2009

Stevenage Borough (0) 2 *(Morison 69, Boylan 90)*

York City (0) 0   27,198

Stevenage Borough: Day; Wilson, Roberts, Bostwick, Henry, Murphy, Drury, Mills, Morison, Boylan, Vincenti (Anaclet 86).
York City: Ingham; Purkiss, Pejic, Mackin, McGurk, Parslow, Rusk (Russell 77), Greaves (McWilliams 72), McBreen (Sodje 60), Brodie, Boyes.
Referee: M. Jones (Cheshire).

THE FA VASE 2008–2009

FINAL (at Wembley) – Sunday, 10 May 2009

Glossop North End (0) 0

Whitley Bay (2) 2 *(Kerr 36, Chow 45)*   12,212

Glossop North End: Cooper; Young, Kay, Lugsden, Yates, Gorton, Bailey R (Hind 56), Morris, Allen (Balfe 65), Hamilton (Bailey T 72), Hodges.
Whitley Bay: Burke; Taylor, Picton, McFarlane (Fawcett 59), Coulson, Ryan, Moore, Robson, Kerr, Chow (Robinson 73), Johnstone (Bell 59).
Referee: K. Friend (Leicestershire).

THE FA YOUTH CUP 2008–2009

FINAL (First Leg) – Friday, 22 May 2009

Arsenal (2) 4 *(Sunu 21, Wilshere 35 (pen), Watt 57, Emmanuel-Thomas 66)*

Liverpool (1) 1 *(Kacaniklic 37)*   33,662

Arsenal: Shea; Eastmond, Cruise, Frimpong (Watt 17), Bartley, Ayling, Lansbury, Coquelin, Sunu (Murphy 75), Wilshere (Henderson 90), Emmanuel-Thomas.
Liverpool: Bouzanis; Clair, Buchtmann, Ayala, Kennedy, Wisdom, Amoo, Irwin, Dalla Valle (Robinson 80), Ince, Kacaniklic (Eccleston 64).
Referee: L. Mason (Lancashire).

FINAL (Second Leg) – Tuesday, 26 May 2009

Liverpool (0) 1 *(Dalla Valle 52)*

Arsenal (1) 2 *(Watt 25, Ayala 70 (og))*   7,792

Liverpool: Bouzanis; Irwin, Robinson (Clair 83), Ayala, Kennedy, Wisdom, Amoo, Buchtmann, Della Valle, Ince, Kacaniklic (Eccleston 46).
Arsenal: Shea; Eastmond, Cruise, Wilshere, Bartley, Ayling (Cooper 83), Lansbury, Coquelin (Ozyakup 83), Sunu (Murphy 68), Watt, Emannuel-Thomas (Henderson 83).
Referee: L. Mason (Lancashire).

THE FA SUNDAY CUP 2008–2009

FINAL (at Liverpool FC)

Scots Grey 4 *(Bignall 16, Staples 90, Jeffries 98, 118)*

Oyster Martyrs 3 *(Latham 35, Rooney 57, Lipson 120)*   2,559
(aet.)

THE FA COUNTY YOUTH CUP 2008–2009

FINAL (at Gillingham FC)

Kent (1) 1 *(Cliff 40)*

Birmingham (1) 2 *(Johnson 4, Doyle 82)*

NATIONAL LIST OF REFEREES FOR SEASON 2009–2010

Draft

Atkinson, M (Martin) – W. Yorkshire
Attwell, SB (Stuart) – Warwickshire
Bates, A (Tony) – Staffordshire
Bennett, SG (Steve) – Kent
Booth, R (Russell) – Nottinghamshire
Boyeson, C (Carl) – E. Yorkshire
Bratt, SJ (Steve) – West Midlands
Clattenburg, M (Mark) – Tyne & Wear
Cook, SD (Steven) – Surrey
Crossley, PT (Phil) – Kent
Deadman, D (Darren) – Cambs.
Dean, ML (Mike) – Wirral
Dowd, P (Phil) – Staffordshire
D'urso, AP (Andy) – Essex
East, R (Roger) – Wiltshire
Eltringham, G (Geoff) – Tyne & Wear
Evans, KG (Karl) – Lancashire
Foster, D (David) – Tyne & Wear
Foy, CJ (Chris) – Merseyside
Friend, KA (Kevin) – Leicestershire
Gibbs, PN (Phil) – W. Midlands
Graham, F (Fred) – Essex
Haines, A (Andy) – Tyne & Wear
Hall, AR (Andy) – W. Midlands
Halsey, MR (Mark) – Lancashire
Haywood, M (Mark) – W. Yorkshire
Hegley, GK (Grant) – Hertfordshire
Hill, KD (Keith) – Hertfordshire
Hooper, SA (Simon) – Wiltshire
Horwood, GD (Graham) – Bedfordshire
Ilderton, EL (Eddie) – Tyne & Wear
Jones, MJ (Michael) – Cheshire
Kettle, TM (Trevor) – Rutland
Langford, O (Oliver) – W. Midlands
Laws, G (Graham) – Tyne & Wear
Linington, JJ (James) – Isle of Wight
McDermid, D (Danny) – Middlesex
Marriner, AM (Andre) – W. Midlands
Mason, LS (Lee) – Lancashire

Mathieson, SW (Scott) – Cheshire
Miller, NS (Nigel) – Co. Durham
Miller, P (Pat) – Bedfordshire
Moss, J (Jon) – W. Yorkshire
Oliver, CW (Clive) – Northumberland
Oliver, M (Michael) – Northumberland
Pawson, CL (Craig) – S. Yorkshire
Penn, AM (Andy) – W. Midlands
Phillips, DJ (David) – W. Sussex
Probert, LW (Lee) – Wiltshire
Quinn, P (Peter) – Cleveland
Rushton, SJ (Steve) – Staffordshire
Russell, MP (Mike) – Hertfordshire
Salisbury, G (Graham) – Lancashire
Sarginson, CD (Chris) – Staffordshire
Scott, GD (Graham) – Oxfordshire
Sheldrake, D (Darren) – Surrey
Shoebridge, RL (Rob) – Derbyshire
Singh, J (Jarnail) – Middlesex
Stroud, KP (Keith) – Hampshire
Sutton, GJ (Gary) – Lincolnshire
Swarbrick, ND (Neil) – Lancashire
Tanner, SJ (Steve) – Somerset
Taylor, A (Anthony) – Cheshire
Taylor, P (Paul) – Hertfordshire
Thorpe, M (Mike) – Suffolk
Tierney, P (Paul) – Lancashire
Walton, P (Peter) – Northamptonshire
Ward, GL (Gavin) – Surrey
Waugh, J (Jock) – S. Yorkshire
Webb, D (David) – Co. Durham
Webb, HM (Howard) – S. Yorkshire
Webster, CH (Colin) – Tyne & Wear
Whitestone, D (Dean) –
  Northamptonshire
Wiley, AG (Alan) – Staffordshire
Williamson, IG (Iain) – Berkshire
Woolmer, KA (Andy) –
  Northamptonshire
Wright, KK (Kevin) – Cambridgeshire

ENGLISH LEAGUE FIXTURES 2009–2010

Reproduced under licence from Football DataCo Limited. All rights reserved.
Licence number PRINT/PLAFANNU/16996a

Copyright © and Database Right 2009[/10] The Football Association Premier League Ltd / The Football League Ltd. All rights reserved. No part of this publication may be reproduced, stored in a retrieval system or transmitted in any way or by any means (including photocopying, recording or storing it in any medium by electronic means), without the written permission of the copyright/database right owner. Applications for written permission should be addressed c/o Football DataCo Ltd, 30 Gloucester Place, London W1U 8PL.

*Sky Sports   All fixtures subject to change.

Friday, 7 August 2009
Coca-Cola Football League
Championship
Middlesbrough v Sheffield U* (8.00)

Saturday, 8 August 2009
Coca-Cola Football League
Championship
Cardiff C v Scunthorpe U
Crystal Palace v Plymouth Arg
Derby Co v Peterborough U
Leicester C v Swansea C
Preston NE v Bristol C
QPR v Blackpool
Reading v Nottingham F
Sheffield W v Barnsley
Watford v Doncaster R
WBA v Newcastle U

Coca-Cola Football League One
Brighton & HA v Walsall
Bristol R v Leyton Orient
Carlisle U v Brentford
Charlton Ath v Wycombe W
Gillingham v Swindon T
Leeds U v Exeter C
Milton Keynes D v Hartlepool U
Norwich C v Colchester U
Oldham Ath v Stockport Co
Southampton v Millwall* (12.45)
Southend v Huddersfield T
Yeovil T v Tranmere R

Coca-Cola Football League Two
Aldershot T v Darlington
Bury v Bournemouth
Cheltenham T v Grimsby T
Crewe Alex v Dagenham & R
Lincoln C v Barnet
Morecambe v Hereford U
Northampton T v Macclesfield T
Notts Co v Bradford C
Port Vale v Rochdale
Rotherham U v Accrington S
Shrewsbury T v Burton Albion
Torquay U v Chesterfield

Sunday, 9 August 2009
Coca-Cola Football League
Championship
Coventry C v Ipswich T* (12.45)

Saturday, 15 August 2009
Barclays Premier League
Aston Villa v Wigan Ath
Blackburn R v Manchester C
Bolton W v Sunderland
Chelsea v Hull C* (12.45)
Everton v Arsenal
Portsmouth v Fulham
Stoke C v Burnley
Wolverhampton W v West Ham U

Coca-Cola Football League
Championship
Barnsley v Coventry C
Blackpool v Cardiff C
Bristol C v Crystal Palace
Doncaster R v Preston NE
Ipswich T v Leicester C
Newcastle U v Reading* (5.20)
Nottingham F v WBA
Peterborough U v Sheffield W
Plymouth Arg v QPR
Scunthorpe U v Derby Co
Sheffield U v Watford
Swansea C v Middlesbrough

Coca-Cola Football League One
Brentford v Brighton & HA
Colchester U v Yeovil T
Exeter C v Norwich C
Hartlepool U v Charlton Ath
Huddersfield T v Southampton
Leyton Orient v Oldham Ath
Millwall v Carlisle U
Stockport Co v Bristol R
Swindon T v Milton Keynes D
Tranmere R v Gillingham
Walsall v Southend
Wycombe W v Leeds U

352

Coca-Cola Football League Two
Accrington S v Lincoln C
Barnet v Shrewsbury T
Bournemouth v Rotherham U
Bradford C v Port Vale
Burton Albion v Morecambe
Chesterfield v Northampton T
Dagenham & R v Torquay U
Darlington v Bury
Grimsby T v Crewe Alex
Hereford U v Cheltenham T
Macclesfield T v Notts Co
Rochdale v Aldershot T

Sunday, 16 August 2009
Barclays Premier League
Manchester U v Birmingham C* (1.30)
Tottenham H v Liverpool* (4.00)

Tuesday, 18 August 2009
Barclays Premier League
Arsenal v Bolton W
Birmingham C v Portsmouth
Burnley v Manchester U
Fulham v Blackburn R
Hull C v Tottenham H
Sunderland v Chelsea
West Ham U v Aston Villa
Wigan Ath v Wolverhampton W

Coca-Cola Football League Championship
Barnsley v Preston NE
Blackpool v Derby Co
Bristol C v QPR
Doncaster R v Coventry C
Ipswich T v Crystal Palace
Nottingham F v Watford
Peterborough U v WBA
Plymouth Arg v Cardiff C
Scunthorpe U v Middlesbrough
Sheffield U v Leicester C
Swansea C v Reading

Coca-Cola Football League One
Brentford v Norwich C
Colchester U v Gillingham
Exeter C v Yeovil T
Hartlepool U v Bristol R
Huddersfield T v Brighton & HA
Leyton Orient v Charlton Ath
Millwall v Oldham Ath
Stockport Co v Carlisle U
Swindon T v Southampton
Tranmere R v Milton Keynes D
Walsall v Leeds U
Wycombe W v Southend

Coca-Cola Football League Two
Accrington S v Northampton T

Barnet v Morecambe
Bournemouth v Aldershot T
Bradford C v Lincoln C
Burton Albion v Torquay U
Dagenham & R v Shrewsbury T
Darlington v Crewe Alex
Grimsby T v Rotherham U
Hereford U v Bury
Macclesfield T v Port Vale
Rochdale v Cheltenham T

Wednesday, 19 August 2009
Barclays Premier League
Liverpool v Stoke C
Manchester C v Everton

Coca-Cola Football League Championship
Newcastle U v Sheffield W

Coca-Cola Football League Two
Chesterfield v Notts Co

Saturday, 22 August 2009
Barclays Premier League
Arsenal v Portsmouth
Birmingham C v Stoke C
Burnley v Everton
Hull C v Bolton W
Liverpool v Aston Villa
Manchester C v Wolverhampton W
Sunderland v Blackburn R
West Ham U v Tottenham H
Wigan Ath v Manchester U

Coca-Cola Football League Championship
Cardiff C v Bristol C
Coventry C v Swansea C
Crystal Palace v Newcastle U
Derby Co v Plymouth Arg
Leicester C v Barnsley
Middlesbrough v Doncaster R
Preston NE v Peterborough U
QPR v Nottingham F
Reading v Sheffield U
Sheffield W v Scunthorpe U
Watford v Blackpool
WBA v Ipswich T* (5.20)

Coca-Cola Football League One
Brighton & HA v Stockport Co
Bristol R v Huddersfield T
Carlisle U v Exeter C
Charlton Ath v Walsall
Gillingham v Hartlepool U
Leeds U v Tranmere R
Milton Keynes D v Colchester U
Norwich C v Wycombe W

Oldham Ath v Swindon T
Southampton v Brentford
Southend v Millwall
Yeovil T v Leyton Orient

Coca-Cola Football League Two
Aldershot T v Accrington S
Bury v Grimsby T
Cheltenham T v Bradford C
Crewe Alex v Hereford U
Lincoln C v Burton Albion
Morecambe v Macclesfield T
Northampton T v Bournemouth
Notts Co v Dagenham & R
Port Vale v Darlington
Rotherham U v Rochdale
Shrewsbury T v Chesterfield
Torquay U v Barnet

Sunday, 16 August 2009
Barclays Premier League
Fulham v Chelsea* (4.00)

Saturday, 29 August 2009
Barclays Premier League
Blackburn R v West Ham U
Bolton W v Liverpool
Chelsea v Burnley
Everton v Wigan Ath
Manchester U v Arsenal* (5.15)
Stoke C v Sunderland
Tottenham H v Birmingham C
Wolverhampton W v Hull C

Coca-Cola Football League Championship
Barnsley v Reading
Blackpool v Coventry C
Bristol C v Middlesbrough
Doncaster R v Cardiff C
Ipswich T v Preston NE
Nottingham F v Derby Co
Plymouth Arg v Sheffield W
Scunthorpe U v QPR
Sheffield U v WBA
Swansea C v Watford

Coca-Cola Football League One
Brentford v Oldham Ath
Colchester U v Leeds U
Exeter C v Milton Keynes D
Hartlepool U v Norwich C
Huddersfield T v Yeovil T
Leyton Orient v Carlisle U
Millwall v Brighton & HA
Stockport Co v Southampton
Swindon T v Southend
Tranmere R v Charlton Ath
Walsall v Gillingham
Wycombe W v Bristol R

Coca-Cola Football League Two
Accrington S v Shrewsbury T
Barnet v Notts Co
Bournemouth v Crewe Alex
Bradford C v Torquay U
Burton Albion v Northampton T
Chesterfield v Morecambe
Dagenham & R v Lincoln C
Darlington v Cheltenham T
Grimsby T v Aldershot T
Hereford U v Port Vale
Macclesfield T v Rotherham U
Rochdale v Bury

Sunday, 30 August 2009
Barclays Premier League
Portsmouth v Manchester C* (1.30)
Aston Villa v Fulham* (4.00)

Monday, 31 August 2009
Coca-Cola Football League Championship
Peterborough U v Crystal Palace* (5.15)
Newcastle U v Leicester C* (7.45)

Saturday, 5 September 2009
Coca-Cola Football League One
Brighton & HA v Wycombe W
Bristol R v Millwall
Carlisle U v Tranmere R
Charlton Ath v Brentford* (12.15)
Gillingham v Exeter C
Leeds U v Stockport Co
Milton Keynes D v Huddersfield T
Norwich C v Walsall
Oldham Ath v Hartlepool U
Southampton v Colchester U
Southend v Leyton Orient
Yeovil T v Swindon T

Coca-Cola Football League Two
Aldershot T v Hereford U
Bury v Accrington S
Cheltenham T v Dagenham & R
Crewe Alex v Macclesfield T
Lincoln C v Darlington
Morecambe v Rochdale
Northampton T v Barnet
Notts Co v Burton Albion
Port Vale v Grimsby T
Rotherham U v Chesterfield
Shrewsbury T v Bradford C
Torquay U v Bournemouth

Saturday, 12 September 2009
Barclays Premier League
Blackburn R v Wolverhampton W
Liverpool v Burnley
Manchester C v Arsenal

Portsmouth v Bolton W
Stoke C v Chelsea
Sunderland v Hull C
Tottenham H v Manchester U
Wigan Ath v West Ham U

Coca-Cola Football League Championship
Coventry C v Bristol C
Crystal Palace v Scunthorpe U
Derby Co v Sheffield U
Leicester C v Blackpool
Middlesbrough v Ipswich T
Preston NE v Swansea C
QPR v Peterborough U
Reading v Doncaster R
Sheffield W v Nottingham F
Watford v Barnsley
WBA v Plymouth Arg

Coca-Cola Football League One
Bristol R v Oldham Ath
Carlisle U v Brighton & HA
Charlton Ath v Southampton
Gillingham v Millwall
Hartlepool U v Wycombe W
Huddersfield T v Brentford
Leyton Orient v Exeter C
Southend v Leeds U
Swindon T v Colchester U
Tranmere R v Walsall
Yeovil T v Stockport Co

Coca-Cola Football League Two
Accrington S v Darlington
Aldershot T v Port Vale
Bournemouth v Lincoln C
Bradford C v Burton Albion
Bury v Cheltenham T
Dagenham & R v Chesterfield
Grimsby T v Hereford U
Macclesfield T v Barnet
Notts Co v Northampton T
Rochdale v Torquay U
Rotherham U v Morecambe
Shrewsbury T v Crewe Alex

Sunday, 13 September 2009
Barclays Premier League
Birmingham C v Aston Villa* (12.00)
Fulham v Everton* (4.15)

Coca-Cola Football League Championship
Cardiff C v Newcastle U* (2.05)

Monday, 14 September 2009
Coca-Cola Football League One
Milton Keynes D v Norwich C* (7.45)

Tuesday, 15 September 2009
Coca-Cola Football League Championship
Coventry C v Sheffield U
Derby Co v Barnsley
Ipswich T v Nottingham F
Leicester C v Peterborough U
Plymouth Arg v Watford
QPR v Crystal Palace
Reading v Cardiff C
Scunthorpe U v Preston NE
Sheffield W v Middlesbrough
Swansea C v Bristol C
WBA v Doncaster R

Wednesday, 16 September 2009
Coca-Cola Football League Championship
Blackpool v Newcastle U

Friday, 18 September 2009
Coca-Cola Football League Championship
Sheffield U v Sheffield W* (7.45)

Saturday, 19 September 2009
Barclays Premier League
Arsenal v Wigan Ath
Aston Villa v Portsmouth
Bolton W v Stoke C
Burnley v Sunderland* (12.45)
Everton v Blackburn R
Hull C v Birmingham C
West Ham U v Liverpool
Wolverhampton W v Fulham

Coca-Cola Football League Championship
Barnsley v Swansea C
Bristol C v Scunthorpe U
Cardiff C v QPR
Crystal Palace v Derby Co
Doncaster R v Ipswich T
Middlesbrough v WBA
Newcastle U v Plymouth Arg
Nottingham F v Blackpool
Peterborough U v Reading
Preston NE v Coventry C
Watford v Leicester C

Coca-Cola Football League One
Brentford v Bristol R
Brighton & HA v Southend
Colchester U v Hartlepool U
Exeter C v Tranmere R
Leeds U v Gillingham
Millwall v Huddersfield T
Norwich C v Charlton Ath
Oldham Ath v Carlisle U
Southampton v Yeovil T

Stockport Co v Leyton Orient
Walsall v Swindon T
Wycombe W v Milton Keynes D

Coca-Cola Football League Two
Barnet v Bradford C
Burton Albion v Dagenham & R
Cheltenham T v Rotherham U
Chesterfield v Macclesfield T
Crewe Alex v Aldershot T
Darlington v Bournemouth
Hereford U v Accrington S
Lincoln C v Shrewsbury T
Morecambe v Notts Co
Northampton T v Rochdale
Port Vale v Bury
Torquay U v Grimsby T

Sunday, 20 September 2009
Barclays Premier League
Manchester U v Manchester C* (1.30)
Chelsea v Tottenham H* (4.00)

Saturday, 26 September 2009
Barclays Premier League
Birmingham C v Bolton W
Blackburn R v Aston Villa
Fulham v Arsenal
Liverpool v Hull C
Manchester C v West Ham U
Portsmouth v Everton* (12.45)
Stoke C v Manchester U
Tottenham H v Burnley
Wigan Ath v Chelsea

Coca-Cola Football League
Championship
Blackpool v Peterborough U
Coventry C v Middlesbrough
Derby Co v Bristol C
Ipswich T v Newcastle U
Leicester C v Preston NE
QPR v Barnsley
Reading v Watford
Scunthorpe U v Doncaster R
Sheffield W v Cardiff C
Swansea C v Sheffield U
WBA v Crystal Palace

Coca-Cola Football League One
Bristol R v Brighton & HA
Carlisle U v Southampton
Charlton Ath v Exeter C
Gillingham v Norwich C
Hartlepool U v Walsall
Huddersfield T v Stockport Co
Leyton Orient v Millwall
Milton Keynes D v Leeds U
Southend v Oldham Ath
Swindon T v Wycombe W

Tranmere R v Colchester U
Yeovil T v Brentford

Coca-Cola Football League Two
Accrington S v Crewe Alex
Aldershot T v Cheltenham T
Bournemouth v Burton Albion
Bradford C v Chesterfield
Bury v Lincoln C
Dagenham & R v Morecambe
Grimsby T v Darlington
Macclesfield T v Torquay U
Notts Co v Port Vale
Rochdale v Hereford U
Rotherham U v Barnet
Shrewsbury T v Northampton T

Sunday, 27 September 2009
Barclays Premier League
Sunderland v Wolverhampton W*
(4.00)

Coca-Cola Football League
Championship
Plymouth Arg v Nottingham F* (1.15)

Tuesday, 29 September 2009
Coca-Cola Football League
Championship
Barnsley v WBA
Bristol C v Blackpool
Cardiff C v Derby Co
Crystal Palace v Sheffield W
Doncaster R v Swansea C
Middlesbrough v Leicester C
Nottingham F v Scunthorpe U
Peterborough U v Plymouth Arg
Preston NE v Reading
Sheffield U v Ipswich T
Watford v Coventry C

Coca-Cola Football League One
Brentford v Southend
Brighton & HA v Gillingham
Colchester U v Charlton Ath
Exeter C v Swindon T
Leeds U v Carlisle U
Millwall v Yeovil T
Norwich C v Leyton Orient
Oldham Ath v Milton Keynes D
Southampton v Bristol R
Stockport Co v Hartlepool U
Walsall v Huddersfield T
Wycombe W v Tranmere R

Coca-Cola Football League Two
Barnet v Dagenham & R
Burton Albion v Macclesfield T
Cheltenham T v Shrewsbury T
Crewe Alex v Bury

Darlington v Rochdale
Hereford U v Bournemouth
Lincoln C v Notts Co
Morecambe v Bradford C
Northampton T v Rotherham U
Port Vale v Accrington S
Torquay U v Aldershot T

Wednesday, 30 September 2009
Coca-Cola Football League Championship
Newcastle U v QPR

Coca-Cola Football League Two
Chesterfield v Grimsby T

Saturday, 3 October 2009
Barclays Premier League
Aston Villa v Manchester C
Bolton W v Tottenham H
Burnley v Birmingham C
Everton v Stoke C
Hull C v Wigan Ath
Manchester U v Sunderland
West Ham U v Fulham
Wolverhampton W v Portsmouth

Coca-Cola Football League Championship
Barnsley v Ipswich T
Coventry C v Leicester C
Crystal Palace v Blackpool
Derby Co v Sheffield W
Newcastle U v Bristol C
Peterborough U v Nottingham F
Plymouth Arg v Scunthorpe U
Preston NE v WBA* (12.45)
Reading v Middlesbrough
Sheffield U v Doncaster R
Swansea C v QPR
Watford v Cardiff C

Coca-Cola Football League One
Brentford v Swindon T
Brighton & HA v Milton Keynes D
Colchester U v Huddersfield T
Exeter C v Hartlepool U
Leeds U v Charlton Ath
Millwall v Tranmere R
Norwich C v Bristol R
Oldham Ath v Yeovil T
Southampton v Gillingham
Stockport Co v Southend
Walsall v Carlisle U
Wycombe W v Leyton Orient

Coca-Cola Football League Two
Barnet v Grimsby T
Burton Albion v Rochdale
Cheltenham T v Notts Co

Chesterfield v Accrington S
Crewe Alex v Rotherham U
Darlington v Macclesfield T
Hereford U v Dagenham & R
Lincoln C v Aldershot T
Morecambe v Shrewsbury T
Northampton T v Bradford C
Port Vale v Bournemouth
Torquay U v Bury

Sunday, 4 October 2009
Barclays Premier League
Arsenal v Blackburn R* (1.30)
Chelsea v Liverpool* (4.00)

Saturday, 10 October 2009
Coca-Cola Football League One
Bristol R v Leeds U
Carlisle U v Norwich C
Charlton Ath v Oldham Ath
Gillingham v Wycombe W
Hartlepool U v Brentford
Huddersfield T v Exeter C
Leyton Orient v Colchester U
Milton Keynes D v Walsall
Southend v Southampton
Swindon T v Millwall
Yeovil T v Brighton & HA

Coca-Cola Football League Two
Accrington S v Cheltenham T
Aldershot T v Morecambe
Bournemouth v Chesterfield
Bradford C v Crewe Alex
Bury v Northampton T
Dagenham & R v Darlington
Grimsby T v Burton Albion
Macclesfield T v Lincoln C
Notts Co v Torquay U
Rochdale v Barnet
Rotherham U v Hereford U
Shrewsbury T v Port Vale

Monday, 12 October 2009
Coca-Cola Football League One
Tranmere R v Stockport Co* (7.45)

Saturday, 17 October 2009
Barclays Premier League
Arsenal v Birmingham C
Aston Villa v Chelsea* (12.45)
Everton v Wolverhampton W
Fulham v Hull C
Manchester U v Bolton W
Portsmouth v Tottenham H
Stoke C v West Ham U
Sunderland v Liverpool

Coca-Cola Football League Championship
Blackpool v Plymouth Arg
Bristol C v Peterborough U
Cardiff C v Crystal Palace
Doncaster R v Barnsley
Ipswich T v Swansea C
Leicester C v Derby Co
Middlesbrough v Watford
Nottingham F v Newcastle U* (5.20)
QPR v Preston NE
Scunthorpe U v Sheffield U
Sheffield W v Coventry C
WBA v Reading

Coca-Cola Football League One
Charlton Ath v Huddersfield T
Leyton Orient v Brentford
Milton Keynes D v Gillingham
Oldham Ath v Southampton
Southend v Bristol R
Stockport Co v Millwall
Swindon T v Hartlepool U
Tranmere R v Brighton & HA
Walsall v Exeter C
Wycombe W v Colchester U
Yeovil T v Carlisle U

Coca-Cola Football League Two
Accrington S v Bournemouth
Aldershot T v Bury
Burton Albion v Barnet
Cheltenham T v Macclesfield T
Crewe Alex v Port Vale
Dagenham & R v Bradford C
Darlington v Shrewsbury T
Grimsby T v Rochdale
Hereford U v Chesterfield
Northampton T v Lincoln C
Rotherham U v Notts Co
Torquay U v Morecambe

Sunday, 18 October 2009
Barclays Premier League
Blackburn R v Burnley* (1.00)
Wigan Ath v Manchester C* (4.00)

Monday, 19 October 2009
Coca-Cola Football League One
Leeds U v Norwich C* (7.45)

Tuesday, 20 October 2009
Coca-Cola Football League Championship
Blackpool v Sheffield U
Bristol C v Plymouth Arg
Cardiff C v Coventry C
Doncaster R v Peterborough U
Ipswich T v Watford
Leicester C v Crystal Palace

Middlesbrough v Derby Co
Nottingham F v Barnsley
QPR v Reading
Scunthorpe U v Newcastle U
Sheffield W v Preston NE
WBA v Swansea C

Saturday, 24 October 2009
Barclays Premier League
Birmingham C v Sunderland
Bolton W v Everton
Burnley v Wigan Ath
Chelsea v Blackburn R
Hull C v Portsmouth
Manchester C v Fulham
Tottenham H v Stoke C
Wolverhampton W v Aston Villa*
  (12.45)

Coca-Cola Football League Championship
Barnsley v Bristol C
Coventry C v WBA
Crystal Palace v Nottingham F
Derby Co v QPR
Newcastle U v Doncaster R
Peterborough U v Scunthorpe U
Plymouth Arg v Ipswich T
Preston NE v Middlesbrough
Reading v Leicester C
Sheffield U v Cardiff C
Swansea C v Blackpool
Watford v Sheffield W

Coca-Cola Football League One
Brentford v Stockport Co
Brighton & HA v Oldham Ath
Bristol R v Yeovil T
Carlisle U v Southend
Colchester U v Walsall
Exeter C v Wycombe W
Gillingham v Charlton Ath
Hartlepool U v Tranmere R
Huddersfield T v Leyton Orient
Millwall v Leeds U
Norwich C v Swindon T
Southampton v Milton Keynes D

Coca-Cola Football League Two
Barnet v Darlington
Bournemouth v Grimsby T
Bradford C v Hereford U
Bury v Rotherham U
Chesterfield v Burton Albion
Lincoln C v Torquay U
Macclesfield T v Dagenham & R
Morecambe v Northampton T
Notts Co v Crewe Alex
Port Vale v Cheltenham T
Rochdale v Accrington S
Shrewsbury T v Aldershot T

Sunday, 25 October 2009
Barclays Premier League
Liverpool v Manchester U* (2.00)
West Ham U v Arsenal* (4.15)

Saturday, 31 October 2009
Barclays Premier League
Arsenal v Tottenham H* (12.45)
Bolton W v Chelsea
Burnley v Hull C
Everton v Aston Villa
Fulham v Liverpool
Manchester U v Blackburn R
Portsmouth v Wigan Ath
Stoke C v Wolverhampton W
Sunderland v West Ham U

Coca-Cola Football League
Championship
Bristol C v Sheffield W
Cardiff C v Nottingham F
Coventry C v Reading
Doncaster R v Blackpool
Ipswich T v Derby Co
Middlesbrough v Plymouth Arg
Peterborough U v Barnsley
Preston NE v Crystal Palace
QPR v Leicester C
Scunthorpe U v Swansea C
WBA v Watford

Coca-Cola Football League One
Brighton & HA v Hartlepool U
Carlisle U v Charlton Ath
Exeter C v Brentford
Leeds U v Yeovil T
Leyton Orient v Southampton
Millwall v Colchester U
Milton Keynes D v Bristol R
Oldham Ath v Huddersfield T
Southend v Gillingham
Stockport Co v Norwich C
Tranmere R v Swindon T
Wycombe W v Walsall

Coca-Cola Football League Two
Bournemouth v Rochdale
Burton Albion v Bury
Cheltenham T v Crewe Alex
Chesterfield v Barnet
Dagenham & R v Port Vale
Grimsby T v Accrington S
Hereford U v Darlington
Macclesfield T v Bradford C
Morecambe v Lincoln C
Notts Co v Shrewsbury T
Rotherham U v Aldershot T
Torquay U v Northampton T

Sunday, 1 November 2009
Barclays Premier League
Birmingham C v Manchester C* (4.00)

Monday, 2 November 2009
Coca-Cola Football League
Championship
Sheffield U v Newcastle U* (7.45)

Friday, 6 November 2009
Coca-Cola Football League
Championship
Derby Co v Coventry C* (7.45)

Saturday, 7 November 2009
Barclays Premier League
Aston Villa v Bolton W
Blackburn R v Portsmouth
Liverpool v Birmingham C
Manchester C v Burnley
Tottenham H v Sunderland
West Ham U v Everton
Wigan Ath v Fulham
Wolverhampton W v Arsenal

Coca-Cola Football League
Championship
Barnsley v Sheffield U
Blackpool v Scunthorpe U
Crystal Palace v Middlesbrough
Leicester C v WBA
Newcastle U v Peterborough U
Nottingham F v Bristol C
Plymouth Arg v Doncaster R
Reading v Ipswich T
Sheffield W v QPR
Swansea C v Cardiff C* (12.45)
Watford v Preston NE

Sunday, 8 November 2009
Barclays Premier League
Hull C v Stoke C* (1.30)
Chelsea v Manchester U* (4.00)

Saturday, 14 November 2009
Coca-Cola Football League One
Brentford v Millwall
Bristol R v Carlisle U
Charlton Ath v Milton Keynes D
Colchester U v Exeter C
Gillingham v Oldham Ath
Hartlepool U v Leyton Orient
Huddersfield T v Wycombe W
Norwich C v Tranmere R
Southampton v Brighton & HA
Swindon T v Leeds U
Walsall v Stockport Co
Yeovil T v Southend

Coca-Cola Football League Two
Accrington S v Dagenham & R
Aldershot T v Macclesfield T
Barnet v Hereford U
Bradford C v Bournemouth
Bury v Notts Co
Crewe Alex v Morecambe
Darlington v Burton Albion
Lincoln C v Cheltenham T
Northampton T v Grimsby T
Port Vale v Rotherham U
Rochdale v Chesterfield
Shrewsbury T v Torquay U

Saturday, 21 November 2009
Barclays Premier League
Birmingham C v Fulham
Burnley v Aston Villa
Chelsea v Wolverhampton W
Hull C v West Ham U
Liverpool v Manchester C* (12.45)
Manchester U v Everton
Sunderland v Arsenal
Tottenham H v Wigan Ath

Coca-Cola Football League
Championship
Barnsley v Cardiff C
Coventry C v Crystal Palace
Doncaster R v QPR
Ipswich T v Sheffield W
Leicester C v Plymouth Arg
Middlesbrough v Nottingham F
Preston NE v Newcastle U
Reading v Blackpool
Sheffield U v Peterborough U
Swansea C v Derby Co
Watford v Scunthorpe U
WBA v Bristol C

Coca-Cola Football League One
Brentford v Walsall
Brighton & HA v Leeds U
Bristol R v Gillingham
Carlisle U v Swindon T
Huddersfield T v Hartlepool U
Leyton Orient v Tranmere R
Millwall v Wycombe W
Oldham Ath v Colchester U
Southampton v Norwich C
Southend v Milton Keynes D
Stockport Co v Exeter C
Yeovil T v Charlton Ath

Coca-Cola Football League Two
Barnet v Port Vale
Bradford C v Accrington S
Burton Albion v Hereford U
Chesterfield v Darlington
Dagenham & R v Rochdale

Lincoln C v Grimsby T
Macclesfield T v Bournemouth
Morecambe v Cheltenham T
Northampton T v Crewe Alex
Notts Co v Aldershot T
Shrewsbury T v Bury
Torquay U v Rotherham U

Sunday, 22 November 2009
Barclays Premier League
Bolton W v Blackburn R* (1.30)
Stoke C v Portsmouth* (4.00)

Tuesday, 24 November 2009
Coca-Cola Football League One
Charlton Ath v Bristol R
Colchester U v Stockport Co
Exeter C v Millwall
Gillingham v Yeovil T
Hartlepool U v Southampton
Leeds U v Leyton Orient
Milton Keynes D v Carlisle U
Norwich C v Brighton & HA
Swindon T v Huddersfield T
Tranmere R v Southend
Walsall v Oldham Ath
Wycombe W v Brentford

Coca-Cola Football League Two
Accrington S v Macclesfield T
Aldershot T v Northampton T
Bournemouth v Dagenham & R
Bury v Chesterfield
Cheltenham T v Barnet
Crewe Alex v Burton Albion
Darlington v Morecambe
Grimsby T v Bradford C
Hereford U v Shrewsbury T
Port Vale v Torquay U
Rochdale v Notts Co
Rotherham U v Lincoln C

Saturday, 28 November 2009
Barclays Premier League
Aston Villa v Tottenham H
Blackburn R v Stoke C
Fulham v Bolton W
Manchester C v Hull C
Portsmouth v Manchester U
West Ham U v Burnley
Wigan Ath v Sunderland
Wolverhampton W v Birmingham C

Coca-Cola Football League
Championship
Blackpool v Preston NE
Bristol C v Sheffield U
Cardiff C v Ipswich T
Crystal Palace v Watford
Derby Co v Reading

Newcastle U v Swansea C
Nottingham F v Doncaster R
Peterborough U v Middlesbrough
Plymouth Arg v Barnsley
QPR v Coventry C
Scunthorpe U v Leicester C
Sheffield W v WBA

Sunday, 29 November 2009
Barclays Premier League
Everton v Liverpool* (1.30)
Arsenal v Chelsea* (4.00)

Tuesday, 1 December 2009
Coca-Cola Football League One
Brentford v Colchester U
Brighton & HA v Charlton Ath
Bristol R v Exeter C
Carlisle U v Hartlepool U
Huddersfield T v Tranmere R
Leyton Orient v Gillingham
Millwall v Milton Keynes D
Oldham Ath v Leeds U
Southampton v Wycombe W
Southend v Norwich C
Stockport Co v Swindon T
Yeovil T v Walsall

Coca-Cola Football League Two
Barnet v Bournemouth
Bradford C v Rochdale
Burton Albion v Accrington S
Dagenham & R v Aldershot T
Lincoln C v Port Vale
Macclesfield T v Grimsby T
Morecambe v Bury
Northampton T v Hereford U
Notts Co v Darlington
Shrewsbury T v Rotherham U
Torquay U v Cheltenham T

Wednesday, 2 December 2009
Coca-Cola Football League Two
Chesterfield v Crewe Alex

Saturday, 5 December 2009
Barclays Premier League
Arsenal v Stoke C
Aston Villa v Hull C
Blackburn R v Liverpool
Everton v Tottenham H
Fulham v Sunderland
Manchester C v Chelsea
Portsmouth v Burnley
West Ham U v Manchester U
Wigan Ath v Birmingham C
Wolverhampton W v Bolton W

**Coca-Cola Football League
Championship**
Blackpool v Barnsley
Bristol C v Ipswich T
Cardiff C v Preston NE
Crystal Palace v Doncaster R
Derby Co v WBA
Newcastle U v Watford
Nottingham F v Leicester C
Peterborough U v Swansea C
Plymouth Arg v Sheffield U
QPR v Middlesbrough
Scunthorpe U v Coventry C
Sheffield W v Reading

Coca-Cola Football League One
Charlton Ath v Southend
Colchester U v Bristol R
Exeter C v Brighton & HA
Gillingham v Carlisle U
Hartlepool U v Millwall
Leeds U v Huddersfield T
Milton Keynes D v Yeovil T
Norwich C v Oldham Ath
Swindon T v Leyton Orient
Tranmere R v Brentford
Walsall v Southampton
Wycombe W v Stockport Co

Coca-Cola Football League Two
Accrington S v Torquay U
Aldershot T v Chesterfield
Bournemouth v Shrewsbury T
Bury v Barnet
Cheltenham T v Northampton T
Crewe Alex v Lincoln C
Darlington v Bradford C
Grimsby T v Dagenham & R
Hereford U v Notts Co
Port Vale v Morecambe
Rochdale v Macclesfield T
Rotherham U v Burton Albion

Tuesday, 8 December 2009
**Coca-Cola Football League
Championship**
Barnsley v Scunthorpe U
Coventry C v Newcastle U
Doncaster R v Sheffield W
Ipswich T v Peterborough U
Leicester C v Bristol C
Middlesbrough v Blackpool
Preston NE v Derby Co
Reading v Crystal Palace
Sheffield U v Nottingham F
Swansea C v Plymouth Arg
Watford v QPR
WBA v Cardiff C

Saturday, 12 December 2009
Barclays Premier League
Birmingham C v West Ham U
Bolton W v Manchester C
Burnley v Fulham
Chelsea v Everton
Hull C v Blackburn R
Liverpool v Arsenal
Manchester U v Aston Villa
Stoke C v Wigan Ath
Sunderland v Portsmouth
Tottenham H v Wolverhampton W

Coca-Cola Football League Championship
Barnsley v Newcastle U
Coventry C v Peterborough U
Doncaster R v Bristol C
Ipswich T v Blackpool
Leicester C v Sheffield W
Middlesbrough v Cardiff C
Preston NE v Plymouth Arg
Reading v Scunthorpe U
Sheffield U v Crystal Palace
Swansea C v Nottingham F
Watford v Derby Co
WBA v QPR

Coca-Cola Football League One
Brentford v Leeds U
Brighton & HA v Colchester U
Bristol R v Swindon T
Carlisle U v Wycombe W
Huddersfield T v Gillingham
Leyton Orient v Milton Keynes D
Millwall v Walsall
Oldham Ath v Exeter C
Southampton v Tranmere R
Southend v Hartlepool U
Stockport Co v Charlton Ath
Yeovil T v Norwich C

Coca-Cola Football League Two
Barnet v Crewe Alex
Bradford C v Rotherham U
Burton Albion v Aldershot T
Chesterfield v Cheltenham T
Dagenham & R v Bury
Lincoln C v Rochdale
Macclesfield T v Hereford U
Morecambe v Bournemouth
Northampton T v Port Vale
Notts Co v Accrington S
Shrewsbury T v Grimsby T
Torquay U v Darlington

Tuesday, 15 December 2009
Barclays Premier League
Birmingham C v Blackburn R
Bolton W v West Ham U

Burnley v Arsenal
Hull C v Everton
Manchester U v Wolverhampton W
Stoke C v Fulham
Sunderland v Aston Villa
Tottenham H v Manchester C

Wednesday, 16 December 2009
Barclays Premier League
Chelsea v Portsmouth
Liverpool v Wigan Ath

Saturday, 19 December 2009
Barclays Premier League
Arsenal v Hull C
Aston Villa v Stoke C
Blackburn R v Tottenham H
Everton v Birmingham C
Fulham v Manchester U
Manchester C v Sunderland
Portsmouth v Liverpool
West Ham U v Chelsea
Wigan Ath v Bolton W
Wolverhampton W v Burnley

Coca-Cola Football League Championship
Blackpool v WBA
Bristol C v Reading
Cardiff C v Leicester C
Crystal Palace v Barnsley
Derby Co v Doncaster R
Newcastle U v Middlesbrough
Nottingham F v Preston NE
Peterborough U v Watford
Plymouth Arg v Coventry C
QPR v Sheffield U
Scunthorpe U v Ipswich T
Sheffield W v Swansea C

Coca-Cola Football League One
Charlton Ath v Millwall
Colchester U v Carlisle U
Exeter C v Southend
Gillingham v Stockport Co
Hartlepool U v Yeovil T
Leeds U v Southampton
Milton Keynes D v Brentford
Norwich C v Huddersfield T
Swindon T v Brighton & HA
Tranmere R v Bristol R
Walsall v Leyton Orient
Wycombe W v Oldham Ath

Coca-Cola Football League Two
Accrington S v Barnet
Aldershot T v Bradford C
Bournemouth v Notts Co
Bury v Macclesfield T
Cheltenham T v Burton Albion

362

Crewe Alex v Torquay U
Darlington v Northampton T
Grimsby T v Morecambe
Hereford U v Lincoln C
Port Vale v Chesterfield
Rochdale v Shrewsbury T
Rotherham U v Dagenham & R

Saturday, 26 December 2009
Barclays Premier League
Arsenal v Aston Villa
Birmingham C v Chelsea
Burnley v Bolton W
Fulham v Tottenham H
Hull C v Manchester U
Liverpool v Wolverhampton W
Manchester C v Stoke C
Sunderland v Everton
West Ham U v Portsmouth
Wigan Ath v Blackburn R

Coca-Cola Football League Championship
Cardiff C v Plymouth Arg
Coventry C v Doncaster R
Crystal Palace v Ipswich T
Derby Co v Blackpool
Leicester C v Sheffield U
Middlesbrough v Scunthorpe U
Preston NE v Barnsley
QPR v Bristol C
Reading v Swansea C
Sheffield W v Newcastle U
Watford v Nottingham F
WBA v Peterborough U

Coca-Cola Football League One
Brighton & HA v Leyton Orient
Bristol R v Walsall
Carlisle U v Huddersfield T
Charlton Ath v Swindon T
Gillingham v Brentford
Leeds U v Hartlepool U
Milton Keynes D v Stockport Co
Norwich C v Millwall
Oldham Ath v Tranmere R
Southampton v Exeter C
Southend v Colchester U
Yeovil v Wycombe W

Coca-Cola Football League Two
Aldershot T v Barnet
Bury v Bradford C
Cheltenham T v Bournemouth
Crewe Alex v Rochdale
Lincoln C v Chesterfield
Morecambe v Accrington S
Northampton T v Dagenham & R
Notts Co v Grimsby T
Port Vale v Burton Albion

Rotherham U v Darlington
Shrewsbury T v Macclesfield T
Torquay U v Hereford U

Monday, 28 December 2009
Barclays Premier League
Aston Villa v Liverpool
Blackburn R v Sunderland
Bolton W v Hull C
Chelsea v Fulham
Everton v Burnley
Manchester U v Wigan Ath
Portsmouth v Arsenal
Stoke C v Birmingham C
Tottenham H v West Ham U
Wolverhampton W v Manchester C

Coca-Cola Football League Championship
Barnsley v Middlesbrough
Blackpool v Sheffield W
Bristol C v Watford
Doncaster R v Leicester C
Ipswich T v QPR
Newcastle U v Derby Co
Nottingham F v Coventry C
Peterborough U v Cardiff C
Plymouth Arg v Reading
Scunthorpe U v WBA
Sheffield U v Preston NE
Swansea C v Crystal Palace

Coca-Cola Football League One
Brentford v Charlton Ath
Colchester U v Southampton
Exeter C v Gillingham
Hartlepool U v Oldham Ath
Huddersfield T v Milton Keynes D
Leyton Orient v Southend
Millwall v Bristol R
Stockport Co v Leeds U
Swindon T v Yeovil T
Tranmere R v Carlisle U
Walsall v Norwich C
Wycombe W v Brighton & HA

Coca-Cola Football League Two
Accrington S v Bury
Barnet v Northampton T
Bournemouth v Torquay U
Bradford C v Shrewsbury T
Burton Albion v Notts Co
Chesterfield v Rotherham U
Dagenham & R v Cheltenham T
Darlington v Lincoln C
Grimsby T v Port Vale
Hereford U v Aldershot T
Macclesfield T v Crewe Alex
Rochdale v Morecambe

Saturday, 2 January 2010

Coca-Cola Football League One
Brentford v Southampton
Colchester U v Milton Keynes D
Exeter C v Carlisle U
Hartlepool U v Gillingham
Huddersfield T v Bristol R
Leyton Orient v Yeovil T
Millwall v Southend
Stockport Co v Brighton & HA
Swindon T v Oldham Ath
Tranmere R v Leeds U
Walsall v Charlton Ath
Wycombe W v Norwich C

Coca-Cola Football League Two
Accrington S v Aldershot T
Barnet v Torquay U
Bournemouth v Northampton T
Bradford C v Cheltenham T
Burton Albion v Lincoln C
Chesterfield v Shrewsbury T
Dagenham & R v Notts Co
Darlington v Port Vale
Grimsby T v Bury
Hereford U v Crewe Alex
Macclesfield T v Morecambe
Rochdale v Rotherham U

Saturday, 9 January 2010

Barclays Premier League
Arsenal v Everton
Birmingham C v Manchester U
Burnley v Stoke C
Fulham v Portsmouth
Hull C v Chelsea
Liverpool v Tottenham H
Manchester C v Blackburn R
Sunderland v Bolton W
West Ham U v Wolverhampton W
Wigan Ath v Aston Villa

Coca-Cola Football League Championship
Cardiff C v Blackpool
Coventry C v Barnsley
Crystal Palace v Bristol C
Derby Co v Scunthorpe U
Leicester C v Ipswich T
Middlesbrough v Swansea C
Preston NE v Doncaster R
QPR v Plymouth Arg
Reading v Newcastle U
Sheffield W v Peterborough U
Watford v Sheffield U
WBA v Nottingham F

Coca-Cola Football League One
Brighton & HA v Brentford
Bristol R v Stockport Co

Carlisle U v Millwall
Charlton Ath v Hartlepool U
Gillingham v Tranmere R
Leeds U v Wycombe W
Milton Keynes D v Swindon T
Norwich C v Exeter C
Oldham Ath v Leyton Orient
Southampton v Huddersfield T
Southend v Walsall
Yeovil T v Colchester U

Coca-Cola Football League Two
Aldershot T v Rochdale
Bury v Darlington
Cheltenham T v Hereford U
Crewe Alex v Grimsby T
Lincoln C v Accrington S
Morecambe v Burton Albion
Northampton T v Chesterfield
Notts Co v Macclesfield T
Port Vale v Bradford C
Rotherham U v Bournemouth
Shrewsbury T v Barnet
Torquay U v Dagenham & R

Saturday, 16 January 2010

Barclays Premier League
Aston Villa v West Ham U
Blackburn R v Fulham
Bolton W v Arsenal
Chelsea v Sunderland
Everton v Manchester C
Manchester U v Burnley
Portsmouth v Birmingham C
Stoke C v Liverpool
Tottenham H v Hull C
Wolverhampton W v Wigan Ath

Coca-Cola Football League Championship
Barnsley v Sheffield W
Blackpool v QPR
Bristol C v Preston NE
Doncaster R v Watford
Ipswich T v Coventry C
Newcastle U v WBA
Nottingham F v Reading
Peterborough U v Derby Co
Plymouth Arg v Crystal Palace
Scunthorpe U v Cardiff C
Sheffield U v Middlesbrough
Swansea C v Leicester C

Coca-Cola Football League One
Brentford v Carlisle U
Colchester U v Norwich C
Exeter C v Leeds U
Hartlepool U v Milton Keynes D
Huddersfield T v Southend
Leyton Orient v Bristol R

Millwall v Southampton
Stockport Co v Oldham Ath
Swindon T v Gillingham
Tranmere R v Yeovil T
Walsall v Brighton & HA
Wycombe W v Charlton Ath

Coca-Cola Football League Two
Accrington S v Rotherham U
Barnet v Lincoln C
Bournemouth v Bury
Bradford C v Notts Co
Burton Albion v Shrewsbury T
Chesterfield v Torquay U
Dagenham & R v Crewe Alex
Darlington v Aldershot T
Grimsby T v Cheltenham T
Hereford U v Morecambe
Macclesfield T v Northampton T
Rochdale v Port Vale

Saturday, 23 January 2010
Coca-Cola Football League One
Brighton & HA v Huddersfield T
Bristol R v Hartlepool U
Carlisle U v Stockport Co
Charlton Ath v Leyton Orient
Gillingham v Colchester U
Leeds U v Walsall
Milton Keynes D v Tranmere R
Norwich C v Brentford
Oldham Ath v Millwall
Southampton v Swindon T
Southend v Wycombe W
Yeovil T v Exeter C

Coca-Cola Football League Two
Aldershot T v Bournemouth
Bury v Hereford U
Cheltenham T v Rochdale
Crewe Alex v Darlington
Lincoln C v Bradford C
Morecambe v Barnet
Northampton T v Accrington S
Notts Co v Chesterfield
Port Vale v Macclesfield T
Rotherham U v Grimsby T
Shrewsbury T v Dagenham & R
Torquay U v Burton Albion

Tuesday, 26 January 2010
Barclays Premier League
Bolton W v Burnley
Manchester U v Hull C
Portsmouth v West Ham U
Stoke C v Manchester C
Tottenham H v Fulham
Wolverhampton W v Liverpool

Coca-Cola Football League Championship
Barnsley v Leicester C
Blackpool v Watford
Bristol C v Cardiff C
Doncaster R v Middlesbrough
Ipswich T v WBA
Nottingham F v QPR
Peterborough U v Preston NE
Plymouth Arg v Derby Co
Scunthorpe U v Sheffield W
Sheffield U v Reading
Swansea C v Coventry C

Wednesday, 27 January 2010
Barclays Premier League
Aston Villa v Arsenal
Blackburn R v Wigan Ath
Chelsea v Birmingham C
Everton v Sunderland

Coca-Cola Football League Championship
Newcastle U v Crystal Palace

Saturday, 30 January 2010
Barclays Premier League
Arsenal v Manchester U
Birmingham C v Tottenham H
Burnley v Chelsea
Fulham v Aston Villa
Hull C v Wolverhampton W
Liverpool v Bolton W
Manchester C v Portsmouth
Sunderland v Stoke C
West Ham U v Blackburn R
Wigan Ath v Everton

Coca-Cola Football League Championship
Cardiff C v Doncaster R
Coventry C v Blackpool
Crystal Palace v Peterborough U
Derby Co v Nottingham F
Leicester C v Newcastle U
Middlesbrough v Bristol C
Preston NE v Ipswich T
QPR v Scunthorpe U
Reading v Barnsley
Sheffield W v Plymouth Arg
Watford v Swansea C
WBA v Sheffield U

Coca-Cola Football League One
Brighton & HA v Millwall
Bristol R v Wycombe W
Carlisle U v Leyton Orient
Charlton Ath v Tranmere R
Gillingham v Walsall
Leeds U v Colchester U

Milton Keynes D v Exeter C
Norwich C v Hartlepool U
Oldham Ath v Brentford
Southampton v Stockport Co
Southend v Swindon T
Yeovil T v Huddersfield T

Coca-Cola Football League Two
Aldershot T v Grimsby T
Bury v Rochdale
Cheltenham T v Darlington
Crewe Alex v Bournemouth
Lincoln C v Dagenham & R
Morecambe v Chesterfield
Northampton T v Burton Albion
Notts Co v Barnet
Port Vale v Hereford U
Rotherham U v Macclesfield T
Shrewsbury T v Accrington S
Torquay U v Bradford C

Saturday, 6 February 2010
Barclays Premier League
Birmingham C v Wolverhampton W
Bolton W v Fulham
Burnley v West Ham U
Chelsea v Arsenal
Hull C v Manchester C
Liverpool v Everton
Manchester U v Portsmouth
Stoke C v Blackburn R
Sunderland v Wigan Ath
Tottenham H v Aston Villa

**Coca-Cola Football League
Championship**
Barnsley v Watford
Blackpool v Leicester C
Bristol C v Coventry C
Doncaster R v Reading
Ipswich T v Middlesbrough
Newcastle U v Cardiff C
Nottingham F v Sheffield W
Peterborough U v QPR
Plymouth Arg v WBA
Scunthorpe U v Crystal Palace
Sheffield U v Derby Co
Swansea C v Preston NE

Coca-Cola Football League One
Brentford v Gillingham
Colchester U v Southend
Exeter C v Southampton
Hartlepool U v Leeds U
Huddersfield T v Carlisle U
Leyton Orient v Brighton & HA
Millwall v Norwich C
Stockport Co v Milton Keynes D
Swindon T v Charlton Ath
Tranmere R v Oldham Ath

Walsall v Bristol R
Wycombe W v Yeovil T

Coca-Cola Football League Two
Accrington S v Morecambe
Barnet v Aldershot T
Bournemouth v Cheltenham T
Bradford C v Bury
Burton Albion v Port Vale
Chesterfield v Lincoln C
Dagenham & R v Northampton T
Darlington v Rotherham U
Grimsby T v Notts Co
Hereford U v Torquay U
Macclesfield T v Shrewsbury T
Rochdale v Crewe Alex

Tuesday, 9 February 2010
Barclays Premier League
Arsenal v Liverpool
Fulham v Burnley
Portsmouth v Sunderland
West Ham U v Birmingham C
Wigan Ath v Stoke C
Wolverhampton W v Tottenham H

**Coca-Cola Football League
Championship**
Cardiff C v Peterborough U
Coventry C v Nottingham F
Crystal Palace v Swansea C
Derby Co v Newcastle U
Leicester C v Doncaster R
Middlesbrough v Barnsley
Preston NE v Sheffield U
QPR v Ipswich T
Reading v Plymouth Arg
Sheffield W v Blackpool
Watford v Bristol C
WBA v Scunthorpe U

Wednesday, 10 February 2010
Barclays Premier League
Aston Villa v Manchester U
Blackburn R v Hull C
Everton v Chelsea
Manchester C v Bolton W

Saturday, 13 February 2010
**Coca-Cola Football League
Championship**
Barnsley v Plymouth Arg
Coventry C v QPR
Doncaster R v Nottingham F
Ipswich T v Cardiff C
Leicester C v Scunthorpe U
Middlesbrough v Peterborough U
Preston NE v Blackpool
Reading v Derby Co
Sheffield U v Bristol C

Swansea C v Newcastle U
Watford v Crystal Palace
WBA v Sheffield W

Coca-Cola Football League One
Brentford v Wycombe W
Brighton & HA v Norwich C
Bristol R v Charlton Ath
Carlisle U v Milton Keynes D
Huddersfield T v Swindon T
Leyton Orient v Leeds U
Millwall v Exeter C
Oldham Ath v Walsall
Southampton v Hartlepool U
Southend v Tranmere R
Stockport Co v Colchester U
Yeovil T v Gillingham

Coca-Cola Football League Two
Barnet v Cheltenham T
Bradford C v Grimsby T
Burton Albion v Crewe Alex
Chesterfield v Bury
Dagenham & R v Bournemouth
Lincoln C v Rotherham U
Macclesfield T v Accrington S
Morecambe v Darlington
Northampton T v Aldershot T
Notts Co v Rochdale
Shrewsbury T v Hereford U
Torquay U v Port Vale

Tuesday, 16 February 2010
Coca-Cola Football League Championship
Blackpool v Middlesbrough
Bristol C v Leicester C
Cardiff C v WBA
Crystal Palace v Reading
Derby Co v Preston NE
Nottingham F v Sheffield U
Peterborough U v Ipswich T
Plymouth Arg v Swansea C
QPR v Watford
Scunthorpe U v Barnsley
Sheffield W v Doncaster R

Wednesday, 17 February 2010
Coca-Cola Football League Championship
Newcastle U v Coventry C

Saturday, 20 February 2010
Barclays Premier League
Arsenal v Sunderland
Aston Villa v Burnley
Blackburn R v Bolton W
Everton v Manchester U
Fulham v Birmingham C
Manchester C v Liverpool

Portsmouth v Stoke C
West Ham U v Hull C
Wigan Ath v Tottenham H
Wolverhampton W v Chelsea

Coca-Cola Football League Championship
Blackpool v Reading
Bristol C v WBA
Cardiff C v Barnsley
Crystal Palace v Coventry C
Derby Co v Swansea C
Newcastle U v Preston NE
Nottingham F v Middlesbrough
Peterborough U v Sheffield U
Plymouth Arg v Leicester C
QPR v Doncaster R
Scunthorpe U v Watford
Sheffield W v Ipswich T

Coca-Cola Football League One
Charlton Ath v Yeovil T
Colchester U v Oldham Ath
Exeter C v Stockport Co
Gillingham v Bristol R
Hartlepool U v Huddersfield T
Leeds U v Brighton & HA
Milton Keynes D v Southend
Norwich C v Southampton
Swindon T v Carlisle U
Tranmere R v Leyton Orient
Walsall v Brentford
Wycombe W v Millwall

Coca-Cola Football League Two
Accrington S v Bradford C
Aldershot T v Notts Co
Bournemouth v Macclesfield T
Bury v Shrewsbury T
Cheltenham T v Morecambe
Crewe Alex v Northampton T
Darlington v Chesterfield
Grimsby T v Lincoln C
Hereford U v Burton Albion
Port Vale v Barnet
Rochdale v Dagenham & R
Rotherham U v Torquay U

Tuesday, 23 February 2010
Coca-Cola Football League One
Charlton Ath v Brighton & HA
Colchester U v Brentford
Exeter C v Bristol R
Gillingham v Leyton Orient
Hartlepool U v Carlisle U
Leeds U v Oldham Ath
Milton Keynes D v Millwall
Norwich C v Southend
Swindon T v Stockport Co
Tranmere R v Huddersfield T

Walsall v Yeovil T
Wycombe W v Southampton

Coca-Cola Football League Two
Accrington S v Burton Albion
Aldershot T v Dagenham & R
Bournemouth v Barnet
Bury v Morecambe
Cheltenham T v Torquay U
Crewe Alex v Chesterfield
Darlington v Notts Co
Grimsby T v Macclesfield T
Hereford U v Northampton T
Port Vale v Lincoln C
Rochdale v Bradford C
Rotherham U v Shrewsbury T

Saturday, 27 February 2010
Barclays Premier League
Birmingham C v Wigan Ath
Bolton W v Wolverhampton W
Burnley v Portsmouth
Chelsea v Manchester C
Hull C v Aston Villa
Liverpool v Blackburn R
Manchester U v West Ham U
Stoke C v Arsenal
Sunderland v Fulham
Tottenham H v Everton

Coca-Cola Football League Championship
Barnsley v Blackpool
Coventry C v Scunthorpe U
Doncaster R v Crystal Palace
Ipswich T v Bristol C
Leicester C v Nottingham F
Middlesbrough v QPR
Preston NE v Cardiff C
Reading v Sheffield W
Sheffield U v Plymouth Arg
Swansea C v Peterborough U
Watford v Newcastle U
WBA v Derby Co

Coca-Cola Football League One
Brentford v Tranmere R
Brighton & HA v Exeter C
Bristol R v Colchester U
Carlisle U v Gillingham
Huddersfield T v Leeds U
Leyton Orient v Swindon T
Millwall v Hartlepool U
Oldham Ath v Norwich C
Southampton v Walsall
Southend v Charlton Ath
Stockport Co v Wycombe W
Yeovil T v Milton Keynes D

Coca-Cola Football League Two
Barnet v Bury
Bradford C v Darlington
Burton Albion v Rotherham U
Chesterfield v Aldershot T
Dagenham & R v Grimsby T
Lincoln C v Crewe Alex
Macclesfield T v Rochdale
Morecambe v Port Vale
Northampton T v Cheltenham T
Notts Co v Hereford U
Shrewsbury T v Bournemouth
Torquay U v Accrington S

Saturday, 6 March 2010
Barclays Premier League
Arsenal v Burnley
Aston Villa v Sunderland
Blackburn R v Birmingham C
Everton v Hull C
Fulham v Stoke C
Manchester C v Tottenham H
Portsmouth v Chelsea
West Ham U v Bolton W
Wigan Ath v Liverpool
Wolverhampton W v Manchester U

Coca-Cola Football League Championship
Blackpool v Ipswich T
Bristol C v Doncaster R
Cardiff C v Middlesbrough
Crystal Palace v Sheffield U
Derby Co v Watford
Newcastle U v Barnsley
Nottingham F v Swansea C
Peterborough U v Coventry C
Plymouth Arg v Preston NE
QPR v WBA
Scunthorpe U v Reading
Sheffield W v Leicester C

Coca-Cola Football League One
Charlton Ath v Stockport Co
Colchester U v Brighton & HA
Exeter C v Oldham Ath
Gillingham v Huddersfield T
Hartlepool U v Southend
Leeds U v Brentford
Milton Keynes D v Leyton Orient
Norwich C v Yeovil T
Swindon T v Bristol R
Tranmere R v Southampton
Walsall v Millwall
Wycombe W v Carlisle U

Coca-Cola Football League Two
Accrington S v Notts Co
Aldershot T v Burton Albion
Bournemouth v Morecambe

Bury v Dagenham & R
Cheltenham T v Chesterfield
Crewe Alex v Barnet
Darlington v Torquay U
Grimsby T v Shrewsbury T
Hereford U v Macclesfield T
Port Vale v Northampton T
Rochdale v Lincoln C
Rotherham U v Bradford C

Saturday, 13 March 2010
Barclays Premier League
Birmingham C v Everton
Bolton W v Wigan Ath
Burnley v Wolverhampton W
Chelsea v West Ham U
Hull C v Arsenal
Liverpool v Portsmouth
Manchester U v Fulham
Stoke C v Aston Villa
Sunderland v Manchester C
Tottenham H v Blackburn R

Coca-Cola Football League Championship
Barnsley v Crystal Palace
Coventry C v Plymouth Arg
Doncaster R v Derby Co
Ipswich T v Scunthorpe U
Leicester C v Cardiff C
Middlesbrough v Newcastle U
Preston NE v Nottingham F
Reading v Bristol C
Sheffield U v QPR
Swansea C v Sheffield W
Watford v Peterborough U
WBA v Blackpool

Coca-Cola Football League One
Brentford v Milton Keynes D
Brighton & HA v Swindon T
Bristol R v Tranmere R
Carlisle U v Colchester U
Huddersfield T v Norwich C
Leyton Orient v Walsall
Millwall v Charlton Ath
Oldham Ath v Wycombe W
Southampton v Leeds U
Southend v Exeter C
Stockport Co v Gillingham
Yeovil T v Hartlepool U

Coca-Cola Football League Two
Barnet v Accrington S
Bradford C v Aldershot T
Burton Albion v Cheltenham T
Chesterfield v Port Vale
Dagenham & R v Rotherham U
Lincoln C v Hereford U
Macclesfield T v Bury

Morecambe v Grimsby T
Northampton T v Darlington
Notts Co v Bournemouth
Shrewsbury T v Rochdale
Torquay U v Crewe Alex

Tuesday, 16 March 2010
Coca-Cola Football League Championship
Barnsley v Nottingham F
Coventry C v Cardiff C
Crystal Palace v Leicester C
Derby Co v Middlesbrough
Peterborough U v Doncaster R
Plymouth Arg v Bristol C
Preston NE v Sheffield W
Reading v QPR
Sheffield U v Blackpool
Swansea C v WBA
Watford v Ipswich T

Wednesday, 17 March 2010
Coca-Cola Football League Championship
Newcastle U v Scunthorpe U

Saturday, 20 March 2010
Barclays Premier League
Arsenal v West Ham U
Aston Villa v Wolverhampton W
Blackburn R v Chelsea
Everton v Bolton W
Fulham v Manchester C
Manchester U v Liverpool
Portsmouth v Hull C
Stoke C v Tottenham H
Sunderland v Birmingham C
Wigan Ath v Burnley

Coca-Cola Football League Championship
Blackpool v Crystal Palace
Bristol C v Newcastle U
Cardiff C v Watford
Doncaster R v Sheffield U
Ipswich T v Barnsley
Leicester C v Coventry C
Middlesbrough v Reading
Nottingham F v Peterborough U
QPR v Swansea C
Scunthorpe U v Plymouth Arg
Sheffield W v Derby Co
WBA v Preston NE

Coca-Cola Football League One
Charlton Ath v Gillingham
Leeds U v Millwall
Leyton Orient v Huddersfield T
Milton Keynes D v Southampton
Oldham Ath v Brighton & HA

Southend v Carlisle U
Stockport Co v Brentford
Swindon T v Norwich C
Tranmere R v Hartlepool U
Walsall v Colchester U
Wycombe W v Exeter C
Yeovil T v Bristol R

Coca-Cola Football League Two
Accrington S v Rochdale
Aldershot T v Shrewsbury T
Burton Albion v Chesterfield
Cheltenham T v Port Vale
Crewe Alex v Notts Co
Dagenham & R v Macclesfield T
Darlington v Barnet
Grimsby T v Bournemouth
Hereford U v Bradford C
Northampton T v Morecambe
Rotherham U v Bury
Torquay U v Lincoln C

Tuesday, 23 March 2010
Coca-Cola Football League
Championship
Blackpool v Swansea C
Bristol C v Barnsley
Cardiff C v Sheffield U
Doncaster R v Newcastle U
Ipswich T v Plymouth Arg
Leicester C v Reading
Middlesbrough v Preston NE
Nottingham F v Crystal Palace
QPR v Derby Co
Scunthorpe U v Peterborough U
Sheffield W v Watford
WBA v Coventry C

Saturday, 27 March 2010
Barclays Premier League
Birmingham C v Arsenal
Bolton W v Manchester U
Burnley v Blackburn R
Chelsea v Aston Villa
Hull C v Fulham
Liverpool v Sunderland
Manchester C v Wigan Ath
Tottenham H v Portsmouth
West Ham U v Stoke C
Wolverhampton W v Everton

Coca-Cola Football League
Championship
Barnsley v Doncaster R
Coventry C v Sheffield W
Crystal Palace v Cardiff C
Derby Co v Leicester C
Newcastle U v Nottingham F
Peterborough U v Bristol C
Plymouth Arg v Blackpool
Preston NE v QPR

Reading v WBA
Sheffield U v Scunthorpe U
Swansea C v Ipswich T
Watford v Middlesbrough

Coca-Cola Football League One
Brentford v Leyton Orient
Brighton & HA v Tranmere R
Bristol R v Southend
Carlisle U v Yeovil T
Colchester U v Wycombe W
Exeter C v Walsall
Gillingham v Milton Keynes D
Hartlepool U v Swindon T
Huddersfield T v Charlton Ath
Millwall v Stockport Co
Norwich C v Leeds U
Southampton v Oldham Ath

Coca-Cola Football League Two
Barnet v Burton Albion
Bournemouth v Accrington S
Bradford C v Dagenham & R
Bury v Aldershot T
Chesterfield v Hereford U
Lincoln C v Northampton T
Macclesfield T v Cheltenham T
Morecambe v Torquay U
Notts Co v Rotherham U
Port Vale v Crewe Alex
Rochdale v Grimsby T
Shrewsbury T v Darlington

Saturday, 3 April 2010
Barclays Premier League
Arsenal v Wolverhampton W
Birmingham C v Liverpool
Bolton W v Aston Villa
Burnley v Manchester C
Everton v West Ham U
Fulham v Wigan Ath
Manchester U v Chelsea
Portsmouth v Blackburn R
Stoke C v Hull C
Sunderland v Tottenham H

Coca-Cola Football League
Championship
Bristol C v Nottingham F
Cardiff C v Swansea C
Coventry C v Derby Co
Doncaster R v Plymouth Arg
Ipswich T v Reading
Middlesbrough v Crystal Palace
Peterborough U v Newcastle U
Preston NE v Watford
QPR v Sheffield W
Scunthorpe U v Blackpool
Sheffield U v Barnsley
WBA v Leicester C

Coca-Cola Football League One
Brighton & HA v Southampton
Carlisle U v Bristol R
Exeter C v Colchester U
Leeds U v Swindon T
Leyton Orient v Hartlepool U
Millwall v Brentford
Milton Keynes D v Charlton Ath
Oldham Ath v Gillingham
Southend v Yeovil T
Stockport Co v Walsall
Tranmere R v Norwich C
Wycombe W v Huddersfield T

Coca-Cola Football League Two
Bournemouth v Bradford C
Burton Albion v Darlington
Cheltenham T v Lincoln C
Chesterfield v Rochdale
Dagenham & R v Accrington S
Grimsby T v Northampton T
Hereford U v Barnet
Macclesfield T v Aldershot T
Morecambe v Crewe Alex
Notts Co v Bury
Rotherham U v Port Vale
Torquay U v Shrewsbury T

Monday, 5 April 2010
Coca-Cola Football League Championship
Barnsley v Peterborough U
Blackpool v Doncaster R
Crystal Palace v Preston NE
Derby Co v Ipswich T
Leicester C v QPR
Newcastle U v Sheffield U
Nottingham F v Cardiff C
Plymouth Arg v Middlesbrough
Reading v Coventry C
Sheffield W v Bristol C
Swansea C v Scunthorpe U
Watford v WBA

Coca-Cola Football League One
Brentford v Exeter C
Bristol R v Milton Keynes D
Charlton Ath v Carlisle U
Colchester U v Millwall
Gillingham v Southend
Hartlepool U v Brighton & HA
Huddersfield T v Oldham Ath
Norwich C v Stockport Co
Southampton v Leyton Orient
Swindon T v Tranmere R
Walsall v Wycombe W
Yeovil T v Leeds U

Coca-Cola Football League Two
Accrington S v Grimsby T
Aldershot T v Rotherham U

Barnet v Chesterfield
Bradford C v Macclesfield T
Bury v Burton Albion
Crewe Alex v Cheltenham T
Darlington v Hereford U
Lincoln C v Morecambe
Northampton T v Torquay U
Port Vale v Dagenham & R
Rochdale v Bournemouth
Shrewsbury T v Notts Co

Saturday, 10 April 2010
Barclays Premier League
Aston Villa v Everton
Blackburn R v Manchester U
Chelsea v Bolton W
Hull C v Burnley
Liverpool v Fulham
Manchester C v Birmingham C
Tottenham H v Arsenal
West Ham U v Sunderland
Wigan Ath v Portsmouth
Wolverhampton W v Stoke C

Coca-Cola Football League Championship
Barnsley v Derby Co
Bristol C v Swansea C
Cardiff C v Reading
Crystal Palace v QPR
Doncaster R v WBA
Middlesbrough v Sheffield W
Newcastle U v Blackpool
Nottingham F v Ipswich T
Peterborough U v Leicester C
Preston NE v Scunthorpe U
Sheffield U v Coventry C
Watford v Plymouth Arg

Coca-Cola Football League One
Brentford v Huddersfield T
Brighton & HA v Carlisle U
Colchester U v Swindon T
Exeter C v Leyton Orient
Leeds U v Southend
Millwall v Gillingham
Norwich C v Milton Keynes D
Oldham Ath v Bristol R
Southampton v Charlton Ath
Stockport Co v Yeovil T
Walsall v Tranmere R
Wycombe W v Hartlepool U

Coca-Cola Football League Two
Barnet v Macclesfield T
Burton Albion v Bradford C
Cheltenham T v Bury
Chesterfield v Dagenham & R
Crewe Alex v Shrewsbury T
Darlington v Accrington S
Hereford U v Grimsby T

Lincoln C v Bournemouth
Morecambe v Rotherham U
Northampton T v Notts Co
Port Vale v Aldershot T
Torquay U v Rochdale

Tuesday, 13 April 2010
Coca-Cola Football League One
Bristol R v Southampton
Carlisle U v Leeds U
Charlton Ath v Colchester U
Gillingham v Brighton & HA
Hartlepool U v Stockport Co
Huddersfield T v Walsall
Leyton Orient v Norwich C
Milton Keynes D v Oldham Ath
Southend v Brentford
Swindon T v Exeter C
Tranmere R v Wycombe W
Yeovil T v Millwall

Coca-Cola Football League Two
Accrington S v Port Vale
Aldershot T v Torquay U
Bournemouth v Hereford U
Bradford C v Morecambe
Bury v Crewe Alex
Dagenham & R v Barnet
Grimsby T v Chesterfield
Macclesfield T v Burton Albion
Notts Co v Lincoln C
Rochdale v Darlington
Rotherham U v Northampton T
Shrewsbury T v Cheltenham T

Saturday, 17 April 2010
Barclays Premier League
Birmingham C v Hull C
Blackburn R v Everton
Fulham v Wolverhampton W
Liverpool v West Ham U
Manchester C v Manchester U
Portsmouth v Aston Villa
Stoke C v Bolton W
Sunderland v Burnley
Tottenham H v Chelsea
Wigan Ath v Arsenal

Coca-Cola Football League Championship
Blackpool v Nottingham F
Coventry C v Preston NE
Derby Co v Crystal Palace
Ipswich T v Doncaster R
Leicester C v Watford
Plymouth Arg v Newcastle U
QPR v Cardiff C
Reading v Peterborough U
Scunthorpe U v Bristol C
Sheffield W v Sheffield U
Swansea C v Barnsley
WBA v Middlesbrough

Coca-Cola Football League One
Bristol R v Brentford
Carlisle U v Oldham Ath
Charlton Ath v Norwich C
Gillingham v Leeds U
Hartlepool U v Colchester U
Huddersfield T v Millwall
Leyton Orient v Stockport Co
Milton Keynes D v Wycombe W
Southend v Brighton & HA
Swindon T v Walsall
Tranmere R v Exeter C
Yeovil T v Southampton

Coca-Cola Football League Two
Accrington S v Hereford U
Aldershot T v Crewe Alex
Bournemouth v Darlington
Bradford C v Barnet
Bury v Port Vale
Dagenham & R v Burton Albion
Grimsby T v Torquay U
Macclesfield T v Chesterfield
Notts Co v Morecambe
Rochdale v Northampton T
Rotherham U v Cheltenham T
Shrewsbury T v Lincoln C

Saturday, 24 April 2010
Barclays Premier League
Arsenal v Manchester C
Aston Villa v Birmingham C
Bolton W v Portsmouth
Burnley v Liverpool
Chelsea v Stoke C
Everton v Fulham
Hull C v Sunderland
Manchester U v Tottenham H
West Ham U v Wigan Ath
Wolverhampton W v Blackburn R

Coca-Cola Football League Championship
Barnsley v QPR
Bristol C v Derby Co
Cardiff C v Sheffield W
Crystal Palace v WBA
Doncaster R v Scunthorpe U
Middlesbrough v Coventry C
Newcastle U v Ipswich T
Nottingham F v Plymouth Arg
Peterborough U v Blackpool
Preston NE v Leicester C
Sheffield U v Swansea C
Watford v Reading

Coca-Cola Football League One
Brentford v Yeovil T
Brighton & HA v Bristol R
Colchester U v Tranmere R
Exeter C v Charlton Ath

Leeds U v Milton Keynes D
Millwall v Leyton Orient
Norwich C v Gillingham
Oldham Ath v Southend
Southampton v Carlisle U
Stockport Co v Huddersfield T
Walsall v Hartlepool U
Wycombe W v Swindon T

Coca-Cola Football League Two
Barnet v Rotherham U
Burton Albion v Bournemouth
Cheltenham T v Aldershot T
Chesterfield v Bradford C
Crewe Alex v Accrington S
Darlington v Grimsby T
Hereford U v Rochdale
Lincoln C v Bury
Morecambe v Dagenham & R
Northampton T v Shrewsbury T
Port Vale v Notts Co
Torquay U v Macclesfield T

Saturday, 1 May 2010
Barclays Premier League
Birmingham C v Burnley
Blackburn R v Arsenal
Fulham v West Ham U
Liverpool v Chelsea
Manchester C v Aston Villa
Portsmouth v Wolverhampton W
Stoke C v Everton
Sunderland v Manchester U
Tottenham H v Bolton W
Wigan Ath v Hull C

Coca-Cola Football League One
Bristol R v Norwich C
Carlisle U v Walsall
Charlton Ath v Leeds U
Gillingham v Southampton
Hartlepool U v Exeter C
Huddersfield T v Colchester U
Leyton Orient v Wycombe W
Milton Keynes D v Brighton & HA
Southend v Stockport Co
Swindon T v Brentford
Tranmere R v Millwall
Yeovil T v Oldham Ath

Coca-Cola Football League Two
Accrington S v Chesterfield
Aldershot T v Lincoln C
Bournemouth v Port Vale
Bradford C v Northampton T
Bury v Torquay U
Dagenham & R v Hereford U
Grimsby T v Barnet
Macclesfield T v Darlington
Notts Co v Cheltenham T
Rochdale v Burton Albion

Rotherham U v Crewe Alex
Shrewsbury T v Morecambe

Sunday, 2 May 2010
Coca-Cola Football League Championship
Blackpool v Bristol C
Coventry C v Watford
Derby Co v Cardiff C
Ipswich T v Sheffield U
Leicester C v Middlesbrough
Plymouth Arg v Peterborough U
QPR v Newcastle U
Reading v Preston NE
Scunthorpe U v Nottingham F
Sheffield W v Crystal Palace
Swansea C v Doncaster R
WBA v Barnsley

Saturday, 8 May 2010
Coca-Cola Football League One
Brentford v Hartlepool U
Brighton & HA v Yeovil T
Colchester U v Leyton Orient
Exeter C v Huddersfield T
Leeds U v Bristol R
Millwall v Swindon T
Norwich C v Carlisle U
Oldham Ath v Charlton Ath
Southampton v Southend
Stockport Co v Tranmere R
Walsall v Milton Keynes D
Wycombe W v Gillingham

Coca-Cola Football League Two
Barnet v Rochdale
Burton Albion v Grimsby T
Cheltenham T v Accrington S
Chesterfield v Bournemouth
Crewe Alex v Bradford C
Darlington v Dagenham & R
Hereford U v Rotherham U
Lincoln C v Macclesfield T
Morecambe v Aldershot T
Northampton T v Bury
Port Vale v Shrewsbury T
Torquay U v Notts Co

Sunday, 9 May 2010
Barclays Premier League
Arsenal v Fulham
Aston Villa v Blackburn R
Bolton W v Birmingham C
Burnley v Tottenham H
Chelsea v Wigan Ath
Everton v Portsmouth
Hull C v Liverpool
Manchester U v Stoke C
West Ham U v Manchester C
Wolverhampton W v Sunderland

BLUE SQUARE PREMIER FIXTURES 2009–2010

Saturday, 8 August 2009
AFC Wimbledon v Luton T
Altrincham T v Ebbsfleet U
Cambridge U v Barrow
Forest Green R v Kettering T
Gateshead v Histon
Grays Ath v Chester C
Kidderminster H v Hayes & Yeading U
Mansfield T v Crawley T
Oxford U v York C
Rushden & D'monds v Salisbury C
Stevenage B v Tamworth
Wrexham v Eastbourne B

Tuesday, 11 August 2009
Barrow v Altrincham T
Chester C v Gateshead
Crawley T v Forest Green R
Eastbourne B v AFC Wimbledon
Ebbsfleet U v Cambridge U
Hayes & Yeading U v Stevenage B
Histon v Grays Ath
Kettering T v Oxford U
Luton T v Mansfield T
Salisbury C v Kidderminster H
Tamworth v Wrexham
York C v Rushden & D'monds

Saturday, 15 August 2009
Barrow v Stevenage B
Chester C v Cambridge U
Crawley T v Wrexham
Eastbourne B v Rushden & D'monds
Ebbsfleet U v Kidderminster H
Hayes & Yeading U v Altrincham T
Histon v Oxford U
Kettering T v AFC Wimbledon
Luton T v Gateshead
Salisbury C v Mansfield T
Tamworth v Grays Ath
York C v Forest Green R

Tuesday, 18 August 2009
AFC Wimbledon v Salisbury C
Altrincham T v Histon
Cambridge U v Crawley T
Forest Green R v Luton T
Gateshead v Tamworth
Grays Ath v Eastbourne B
Kidderminster H v Kettering T
Mansfield T v Barrow
Oxford U v Chester C
Rushden & D'monds v Hayes & Yeading U
Stevenage B v Ebbsfleet U
Wrexham v York C

Saturday, 22 August 2009
Altrincham T v AFC Wimbledon
Crawley T v Gateshead
Eastbourne B v Barrow
Grays Ath v Kidderminster H
Hayes & Yeading U v York C
Histon v Salisbury C
Luton T v Chester C
Mansfield T v Ebbsfleet U
Oxford U v Stevenage B
Rushden & D'monds v Forest Green R
Tamworth v Cambridge U
Wrexham v Kettering T

Saturday, 29 August 2009
AFC Wimbledon v Oxford U
Barrow v Tamworth
Cambridge U v Gateshead
Chester C v Mansfield T
Crawley T v Grays Ath
Ebbsfleet U v Hayes & Yeading U
Forest Green R v Wrexham
Kettering T v Luton T
Kidderminster H v Altrincham T
Salisbury C v Eastbourne B
Stevenage B v Rushden & D'monds
York C v Histon

Monday, 31 August 2009
Altrincham T v Chester C
Eastbourne B v Ebbsfleet U
Gateshead v York C
Grays Ath v AFC Wimbledon
Hayes & Yeading U v Salisbury C
Histon v Stevenage B
Mansfield T v Kettering T
Oxford U v Forest Green R
Rushden & D'monds v Cambridge U
Tamworth v Kidderminster H
Wrexham v Barrow

Tuesday, 1 September 2009
Luton T v Crawley T

Saturday, 5 September 2009
Barrow v Rushden & D'monds
Cambridge U v Forest Green R
Chester C v Histon
Ebbsfleet U v Oxford U
Gateshead v Hayes & Yeading U
Grays Ath v Mansfield T
Kettering T v Altrincham T
Kidderminster H v Eastbourne B
Salisbury C v Luton T
Stevenage B v Wrexham
Tamworth v AFC Wimbledon
York C v Crawley T

Tuesday, 8 September 2009
AFC Wimbledon v Wrexham
Barrow v York C
Cambridge U v Altrincham T
Chester C v Tamworth
Crawley T v Histon
Ebbsfleet U v Rushden & D'monds
Forest Green R v Hayes & Yeading U
Kettering T v Gateshead
Kidderminster H v Mansfield T
Oxford U v Luton T
Salisbury C v Grays Ath
Stevenage B v Eastbourne B

Saturday, 12 September 2009
AFC Wimbledon v Cambridge U
Altrincham T v Crawley T
Eastbourne B v Chester C
Forest Green R v Ebbsfleet U
Gateshead v Salisbury C
Hayes & Yeading U v Tamworth
Histon v Kidderminster H
Luton T v Barrow
Mansfield T v Stevenage B
Rushden & D'monds v Grays Ath
Wrexham v Oxford U
York C v Kettering T

Saturday, 19 September 2009
Barrow v Forest Green R
Cambridge U v Wrexham
Chester C v Stevenage B
Crawley T v Kettering T
Ebbsfleet U v AFC Wimbledon
Grays Ath v Altrincham T
Hayes & Yeading U v Histon
Kidderminster H v Gateshead
Luton T v York C
Oxford U v Eastbourne B
Rushden & D'monds v Mansfield T
Tamworth v Salisbury C

Tuesday, 22 September 2009
AFC Wimbledon v Crawley T
Altrincham T v Tamworth
Eastbourne B v Hayes & Yeading U
Forest Green R v Kidderminster H
Gateshead v Rushden & D'monds
Histon v Ebbsfleet U
Kettering T v Barrow
Mansfield T v Oxford U
Salisbury C v Chester C
Stevenage B v Grays Ath
Wrexham v Luton T
York C v Cambridge U

Saturday, 26 September 2009
AFC Wimbledon v Histon
Cambridge U v Luton T
Crawley T v Rushden & D'monds

Eastbourne B v Tamworth
Forest Green R v Grays Ath
Gateshead v Oxford U
Kettering T v Ebbsfleet U
Mansfield T v Hayes & Yeading U
Salisbury C v Barrow
Stevenage B v Altrincham T
Wrexham v Chester C
York C v Kidderminster H

Tuesday, 29 September 2009
Altrincham T v Gateshead
Barrow v Mansfield T
Chester C v Forest Green R
Ebbsfleet U v Salisbury C
Grays Ath v Cambridge U
Hayes & Yeading U v Kettering T
Histon v Eastbourne B
Kidderminster H v Wrexham
Luton T v Stevenage B
Oxford U v Crawley T
Rushden & D'monds v
   AFC Wimbledon
Tamworth v York C

Saturday, 3 October 2009
AFC Wimbledon v Kidderminster H
Barrow v Oxford U
Eastbourne B v Kettering T
Ebbsfleet U v Crawley T
Grays Ath v Gateshead
Hayes & Yeading U v Chester C
Histon v Cambridge U
Luton T v Tamworth
Mansfield T v Forest Green R
Rushden & D'monds v Altrincham T
Wrexham v Salisbury C
York C v Stevenage B

Saturday, 10 October 2009
Altrincham T v Mansfield T
Cambridge U v Ebbsfleet U
Chester C v Rushden & D'monds
Crawley T v Barrow
Forest Green R v AFC Wimbledon
Gateshead v Eastbourne B
Kettering T v Wrexham
Kidderminster H v Luton T
Oxford U v Grays Ath
Salisbury C v York C
Stevenage B v Hayes & Yeading U
Tamworth v Histon

Saturday, 17 October 2009
AFC Wimbledon v Kettering T
Altrincham T v Luton T
Barrow v Ebbsfleet U
Eastbourne B v Mansfield T
Gateshead v Chester C
Hayes & Yeading U v Cambridge U

Histon v Forest Green R
Kidderminster H v Crawley T
Rushden & D'monds v Tamworth
Stevenage B v Salisbury C
Wrexham v Grays Ath
York C v Oxford U

Saturday, 31 October 2009
Cambridge U v Kidderminster H
Chester C v AFC Wimbledon
Crawley T v York C
Ebbsfleet U v Wrexham
Forest Green R v Eastbourne B
Grays Ath v Barrow
Kettering T v Stevenage B
Luton T v Rushden & D'monds
Mansfield T v Histon
Oxford U v Altrincham T
Salisbury C v Gateshead
Tamworth v Hayes & Yeading U

Saturday, 14 November 2009
Altrincham T v Forest Green R
Barrow v AFC Wimbledon
Cambridge U v Kettering T
Crawley T v Mansfield T
Eastbourne B v Salisbury C
Grays Ath v Luton T
Kidderminster H v Oxford U
Rushden & D'monds v Histon
Stevenage B v Gateshead
Tamworth v Chester C
Wrexham v Hayes & Yeading U
York C v Ebbsfleet U

Saturday, 21 November 2009
AFC Wimbledon v York C
Chester C v Altrincham T
Ebbsfleet U v Tamworth
Forest Green R v Stevenage B
Gateshead v Grays Ath
Hayes & Yeading U v Crawley T
Histon v Wrexham
Kettering T v Kidderminster H
Luton T v Cambridge U
Mansfield T v Eastbourne B
Oxford U v Barrow
Salisbury C v Rushden & D'monds

Tuesday, 24 November 2009
AFC Wimbledon v Ebbsfleet U
Barrow v Grays Ath
Cambridge U v Rushden & D'monds
Crawley T v Salisbury C
Eastbourne B v Histon
Forest Green R v Oxford U
Kettering T v Hayes & Yeading U
Mansfield T v Luton T
Stevenage B v Chester C
Tamworth v Altrincham T

Wrexham v Kidderminster H
York C v Gateshead

Saturday, 28 November 2009
Altrincham T v Kettering T
Chester C v Eastbourne B
Ebbsfleet U v Mansfield T
Gateshead v Crawley T
Grays Ath v Tamworth
Hayes & Yeading U v Forest Green R
Histon v York C
Kidderminster H v Barrow
Luton T v AFC Wimbledon
Oxford U v Cambridge U
Rushden & D'monds v Wrexham
Salisbury C v Stevenage B

Tuesday, 1 December 2009
Altrincham T v Barrow
Cambridge U v Chester C
Crawley T v Oxford U
Ebbsfleet U v Stevenage B
Gateshead v Mansfield T
Grays Ath v Histon
Hayes & Yeading U v Eastbourne B
Kidderminster H v Tamworth
Luton T v Kettering T
Rushden & D'monds v York C
Salisbury C v AFC Wimbledon
Wrexham v Forest Green R

Saturday, 5 December 2009
AFC Wimbledon v Gateshead
Barrow v Hayes & Yeading U
Chester C v Luton T
Eastbourne B v Cambridge U
Forest Green R v Rushden & D'monds
Histon v Altrincham T
Kettering T v Salisbury C
Mansfield T v Grays Ath
Oxford U v Ebbsfleet U
Stevenage B v Kidderminster H
Tamworth v Crawley T
York C v Wrexham

Tuesday, 8 December 2009
Oxford U v Hayes & Yeading U

Saturday, 19 December 2009
Altrincham T v Eastbourne B
Cambridge U v Oxford U
Crawley T v AFC Wimbledon
Ebbsfleet U v Histon
Gateshead v Kettering T
Grays Ath v York C
Hayes & Yeading U v Kidderminster H
Luton T v Forest Green R
Rushden & D'monds v Chester C
Salisbury C v Tamworth

Stevenage B v Barrow
Wrexham v Mansfield T

Saturday, 26 December 2009
AFC Wimbledon v Hayes & Yeading U
Barrow v Gateshead
Cambridge U v Stevenage B
Crawley T v Eastbourne B
Ebbsfleet U v Grays Ath
Forest Green R v Salisbury C
Kettering T v Tamworth
Kidderminster H v Chester C
Luton T v Histon
Oxford U v Rushden & D'monds
Wrexham v Altrincham T
York C v Mansfield T

Monday, 28 December 2009
Altrincham T v York C
Chester C v Barrow
Eastbourne B v Luton T
Gateshead v Wrexham
Grays Ath v Crawley T
Hayes & Yeading U v Ebbsfleet U
Histon v Kettering T
Mansfield T v Cambridge U
Rushden & D'monds v
  Kidderminster H
Salisbury C v Oxford U
Stevenage B v AFC Wimbledon
Tamworth v Forest Green R

Friday, 1 January 2010
Altrincham T v Wrexham
Chester C v Kidderminster H
Eastbourne B v Crawley T
Gateshead v Barrow
Grays Ath v Ebbsfleet U
Hayes & Yeading U v AFC Wimbledon
Histon v Luton T
Mansfield T v York C
Rushden & D'monds v Oxford U
Salisbury C v Forest Green R
Stevenage B v Cambridge U
Tamworth v Kettering T

Saturday, 16 January 2010
AFC Wimbledon v Mansfield T
Barrow v Histon
Cambridge U v Eastbourne B
Crawley T v Chester C
Ebbsfleet U v Altrincham T
Forest Green R v Gateshead
Kettering T v Rushden & D'monds
Kidderminster H v Grays Ath
Luton T v Salisbury C
Oxford U v Tamworth
Wrexham v Stevenage B
York C v Hayes & Yeading U

Tuesday, 19 January 2010
AFC Wimbledon v Grays Ath
Barrow v Wrexham
Chester C v Salisbury C
Eastbourne B v Stevenage B
Forest Green R v Crawley T
Histon v Rushden & D'monds
Kettering T v Cambridge U
Kidderminster H v Ebbsfleet U
Mansfield T v Altrincham T
Tamworth v Gateshead
York C v Luton T

Saturday, 23 January 2010
Altrincham T v Hayes & Yeading U
Cambridge U v York C
Crawley T v Kidderminster H
Ebbsfleet U v Forest Green R
Gateshead v Luton T
Grays Ath v Oxford U
Mansfield T v Chester C
Rushden & D'monds v Barrow
Salisbury C v Histon
Stevenage B v Kettering T
Tamworth v Eastbourne B
Wrexham v AFC Wimbledon

Saturday, 30 January 2010
AFC Wimbledon v Barrow
Altrincham T v Stevenage B
Chester C v Grays Ath
Eastbourne B v Gateshead
Forest Green R v Mansfield T
Hayes & Yeading U v Rushden &
  D'monds
Histon v Tamworth
Kettering T v Crawley T
Kidderminster H v Cambridge U
Luton T v Ebbsfleet U
Oxford U v Wrexham
York C v Salisbury C

Tuesday, 2 February 2010
Gateshead v Altrincham T

Saturday, 6 February 2010
AFC Wimbledon v Forest Green R
Altrincham T v Salisbury C
Barrow v Luton T
Chester C v Ebbsfleet U
Crawley T v Cambridge U
Eastbourne B v Wrexham
Grays Ath v Rushden & D'monds
Histon v Hayes & Yeading U
Kettering T v York C
Mansfield T v Gateshead
Oxford U v Kidderminster H
Tamworth v Stevenage B

Tuesday, 9 February 2010
Ebbsfleet U v Kettering T
Forest Green R v Chester C
Hayes & Yeading U v Grays Ath
Kidderminster H v AFC Wimbledon
Luton T v Oxford U
Rushden & D'monds v Eastbourne B
Salisbury C v Crawley T
Stevenage B v Mansfield T
Wrexham v Tamworth
York C v Barrow

Saturday, 13 February 2010
Barrow v Kettering T
Cambridge U v AFC Wimbledon
Chester C v Wrexham
Crawley T v Altrincham T
Ebbsfleet U v York C
Grays Ath v Salisbury C
Hayes & Yeading U v Gateshead
Kidderminster H v Forest Green R
Luton T v Eastbourne B
Oxford U v Histon
Rushden & D'monds v Stevenage B
Tamworth v Mansfield T

Saturday, 20 February 2010
AFC Wimbledon v Tamworth
Barrow v Kidderminster H
Eastbourne B v Altrincham T
Forest Green R v Cambridge U
Gateshead v Ebbsfleet U
Histon v Chester C
Kettering T v Grays Ath
Mansfield T v Rushden & D'monds
Salisbury C v Hayes & Yeading U
Stevenage B v Oxford U
Wrexham v Crawley T

Tuesday, 23 February 2010
Grays Ath v Hayes & Yeading U
Oxford U v AFC Wimbledon
York C v Chester C

Saturday, 27 February 2010
Altrincham T v Grays Ath
Cambridge U v Tamworth
Chester C v Oxford U
Crawley T v Luton T
Ebbsfleet U v Barrow
Gateshead v Forest Green R
Hayes & Yeading U v Mansfield T
Kidderminster H v Histon
Rushden & D'monds v Kettering T
Salisbury C v Wrexham
York C v Eastbourne B

Saturday, 6 March 2010
AFC Wimbledon v Altrincham T
Barrow v Cambridge U

Eastbourne B v Kidderminster H
Forest Green R v York C
Hayes & Yeading U v Luton T
Histon v Gateshead
Kettering T v Chester C
Mansfield T v Salisbury C
Stevenage B v Crawley T
Tamworth v Rushden & D'monds
Wrexham v Ebbsfleet U

Saturday, 13 March 2010
AFC Wimbledon v Eastbourne B
Cambridge U v Histon
Chester C v Hayes & Yeading U
Crawley T v Ebbsfleet U
Forest Green R v Barrow
Grays Ath v Stevenage B
Kidderminster H v York C
Luton T v Wrexham
Mansfield T v Tamworth
Oxford U v Kettering T
Rushden & D'monds v Gateshead
Salisbury C v Altrincham T

Tuesday, 16 March 2010
Cambridge U v Salisbury C
Luton T v Kidderminster H
Stevenage B v Histon

Saturday, 20 March 2010
Altrincham T v Rushden & D'monds
Barrow v Crawley T
Eastbourne B v Grays Ath
Ebbsfleet U v Luton T
Gateshead v Stevenage B
Histon v Mansfield T
Kettering T v Forest Green R
Tamworth v Oxford U
Wrexham v Cambridge U
York C v AFC Wimbledon

Saturday, 27 March 2010
AFC Wimbledon v Rushden & D'monds
Barrow v Eastbourne B
Cambridge U v Grays Ath
Crawley T v Stevenage B
Ebbsfleet U v Chester C
Forest Green R v Altrincham T
Kettering T v Mansfield T
Kidderminster H v Salisbury C
Luton T v Hayes & Yeading U
Oxford U v Gateshead
Wrexham v Histon
York C v Tamworth

Saturday, 3 April 2010
Altrincham T v Kidderminster H
Chester C v York C
Eastbourne B v Forest Green R

Gateshead v Cambridge U
Grays Ath v Kettering T
Hayes & Yeading U v Oxford U
Histon v AFC Wimbledon
Mansfield T v Wrexham
Rushden & D'monds v Crawley T
Salisbury C v Ebbsfleet U
Stevenage B v Luton T
Tamworth v Barrow

Monday, 5 April 2010
AFC Wimbledon v Stevenage B
Barrow v Chester C
Cambridge U v Mansfield T
Crawley T v Hayes & Yeading U
Ebbsfleet U v Eastbourne B
Forest Green R v Tamworth
Kettering T v Histon
Kidderminster H v Rushden &
    D'monds
Luton T v Grays Ath
Oxford U v Salisbury C
Wrexham v Gateshead
York C v Altrincham T

Saturday, 10 April 2010
Altrincham T v Oxford U
Chester C v Kettering T
Eastbourne B v York C
Gateshead v Kidderminster H
Grays Ath v Wrexham
Hayes & Yeading U v Barrow
Histon v Crawley T

Mansfield T v AFC Wimbledon
Rushden & D'monds v Ebbsfleet U
Salisbury C v Cambridge U
Stevenage B v Forest Green R
Tamworth v Luton T

Saturday, 17 April 2010
AFC Wimbledon v Chester C
Barrow v Salisbury C
Cambridge U v Hayes & Yeading U
Crawley T v Tamworth
Ebbsfleet U v Gateshead
Forest Green R v Histon
Kettering T v Eastbourne B
Kidderminster H v Stevenage B
Luton T v Altrincham T
Oxford U v Mansfield T
Wrexham v Rushden & D'monds
York C v Grays Ath

Saturday, 24 April 2010
Altrincham T v Cambridge U
Chester C v Crawley T
Eastbourne B v Oxford U
Gateshead v AFC Wimbledon
Grays Ath v Forest Green R
Hayes & Yeading U v Wrexham
Histon v Barrow
Mansfield T v Kidderminster H
Rushden & D'monds v Luton T
Salisbury C v Kettering T
Stevenage B v York C
Tamworth v Ebbsfleet U

OTHER FIXTURES — SEASON 2009–2010

JULY 2009
15 Wed UEFA Champions Lge 2Q (1)
        UEFA Europa Lge 2Q (1)
22 Wed UEFA Champions Lge 2Q (2)
        UEFA Europa Lge 2Q (2)
29 Wed UEFA Champions Lge 3Q (1)
        UEFA Europa Lge 3Q (1)

AUGUST 2009
05 Wed UEFA Champions Lge 3Q (2)
        UEFA Europa Lge 3Q (2)
08 Sat Football Lge commences
09 Sun FA Community Shield
12 Wed Holland v England –
        International Friendly
        Football Lge Cup 1
15 Sat The FA Cup Sponsored by
        E.On EP
        Premier Lge commences

19 Wed UEFA Champions Lge
        Play-Off (1)
        UEFA Europa Lge Play-Off (1)
26 Wed UEFA Champions Lge Play-Off
        (2)
        UEFA Europa Lge Play-Off (2)
        Football Lge Cup 2
28 Fri UEFA Super Cup
29 Sat The FA Cup Sponsored by
        E.On P

SEPTEMBER 2009
02 Wed Football Lge Trophy 1
05 Sat England v Slovenia –
        International Qualifier
        The FA Carlsberg Vase 1Q
07 Mon The FA Youth Cup Sponsored
        by E.On P†
09 Wed England v Croatia – World Cup
        Qualifier

12 Sat The FA Cup Sponsored by
        E.On 1Q
13 Sun The FA Women's Cup
        Sponsored by E.On P
16 Wed UEFA Champions Lge MD1
        UEFA Europa Lge MD1
19 Sat The FA Carlsberg Vase 2Q
20 Sun The FA Carlsberg Sunday Cup
        P
21 Mon The FA Youth Cup Sponsored
        by E.On 1Q†
23 Wed Football Lge Cup 3
26 Sat The FA Cup Sponsored by
        E.On 2Q
        The FA Carlsberg National Lge
        System Cup 1*
27 Sun The FA Women's Cup
        Sponsored by E.On 1Q
30 Wed UEFA Champions Lge MD2
        UEFA Europa Lge MD2

OCTOBER 2009

03 Sat The FA Carlsberg Trophy P
        The FA Carlsberg Vase 1p
05 Mon The FA Youth Cup Sponsored
        by E.On 2Q†
07 Wed Football Lge Trophy 2
10 Sat Ukraine v England – World
        Cup Qualifier
        The FA Cup Sponsored by
        E.On 3Q
11 Sun The FA Women's Cup
        Sponsored by E.On 2Q
14 Wed England v Belarus – World Cup
        Qualifier
17 Sat The FA Carlsberg Trophy 1Q
18 Sun The FA Carlsberg Sunday Cup 1
        The FA County Youth Cup 1*
19 Mon The FA Youth Cup Sponsored
        by E.On 3Q†
21 Wed UEFA Champions Lge MD3
        UEFA Europa Lge MD3
24 Sat The FA Cup Sponsored by
        E.On 4Q
25 Sun The FA Women's Cup
        Sponsored by E.On 3Q
28 Wed Football Lge Cup 4
31 Sat The FA Carlsberg Trophy 2Q

NOVEMBER 2009

04 Wed UEFA Champions Lge MD4
        UEFA Europa Lge MD4
07 Sat The FA Cup Sponsored by
        E.On 1p
        The FA Youth Cup Sponsored
        by E.On 1p*
08 Sun The FA Women's Cup
        Sponsored by E.On 1p

11 Wed Football Lge Trophy AQF
14 Sat International Play-Off Matches
        The FA Carlsberg Vase 2p
15 Sun The FA Carlsberg Sunday Cup 2
        The FA County Youth Cup 2*
18 Wed International Play-Off Matches
        The FA Cup Sponsored by
        E.On 1p Replay
21 Sat The FA Carlsberg Trophy 3Q
        The FA Youth Cup Sponsored
        by E.On 2p*
25 Wed UEFA Champions Lge MD5
28 Sat The FA Cup Sponsored by
        E.On 2p
29 Sun The FA Women's Cup
        Sponsored by E.On 2p

DECEMBER 2009

02 Wed UEFA Europa Lge MD5
        Football Lge Cup 5
05 Sat The FA Carlsberg Vase 3p
06 Sun The FA Carlsberg Sunday Cup 3
09 Wed UEFA Champions Lge MD6
        The FA Cup Sponsored by
        E.On 2p Replay
12 Sat The FA Carlsberg Trophy 1p
        The FA Youth Cup Sponsored
        by E.On 3p*
        The FA Carlsberg National Lge
        System Cup 2*
13 Sun The FA Women's Cup
        Sponsored by E.On 3p
16 Wed UEFA Europa Lge MD6
        Football Lge Trophy Asf
20 Sun The FA County Youth Cup 3*

JANUARY 2010

02 Sat The FA Cup Sponsored by
        E.On 3p
06 Wed Football Lge Cup SF1
09 Sat The FA Carlsberg Trophy 2p
10 Sun The FA Women's Cup
        Sponsored by E.On 4p
13 Wed The FA Cup Sponsored by
        E.On 3p Replay
16 Sat The FA Carlsberg Vase 4p
        The FA Youth Cup Sponsored
        by E.On 4p*
17 Sun The FA Carlsberg Sunday Cup 4
20 Wed Football Lge Cup SF2
        Football Lge Trophy Af1
23 Sat The FA Cup Sponsored by
        E.On 4p
24 Sun The FA County Youth Cup 4*
        The FA Women's Cup
        Sponsored by E.On 5p

| 30 Sat | The FA Carlsberg Trophy 3p |
| | The FA Youth Cup Sponsored by E.On 5p* |

FEBRUARY 2010

03 Wed	The FA Cup Sponsored by E.On 4p Replay
06 Sat	The FA Carlsberg Vase 5p
13 Sat	The FA Cup Sponsored by E.On 5p
	The FA Youth Cup Sponsored by E.On 6p*
14 Sun	The FA Women's Cup Sponsored by E.On 6p
17 Wed	UEFA Champions Lge 16
	UEFA Europa Lge 32 (1)
	Football Lge Trophy Af2
20 Sat	The FA Carlsberg Trophy 4p
	The FA Carlsberg National Lge System Cup 3*
21 Sun	The FA Carlsberg Sunday Cup 5
24 Wed	UEFA Champions Lge 16
	UEFA Europa Lge 32 (2)
	The FA Cup Sponsored by E.On 5p Replay
27 Sat	The FA Carlsberg Vase 6p
28 Sun	Football Lge Cup Final
	The FA County Youth Cup SF*

MARCH 2010

03 Wed	International Friendly
06 Sat	The FA Cup Sponsored by E.On 6p
	The FA Youth Cup Sponsored by E.On SF1*
10 Wed	UEFA Champions Lge 16
	UEFA Europa Lge 16 (1)
13 Sat	The FA Carlsberg Trophy SF1
14 Sun	The FA Women's Cup Sponsored by E.On SF
17 Wed	UEFA Champions Lge 16
	UEFA Europa Lge 16 (2)
	The FA Cup Sponsored by E.On 6p Replay
20 Sat	The FA Carlsberg Trophy SF2
	The FA Youth Cup Sponsored by E.On SF2*
21 Sun	The FA Carlsberg Sunday Cup SF
27 Sat	The FA Carlsberg Vase SF1
28 Sun	Football Lge Trophy Final
31 Wed	UEFA Champions Lge Qf (1)
	UEFA Europa Lge Qf (1)

APRIL 2010

03 Sat	The FA Carlsberg Vase SF2
07 Wed	UEFA Champions Lge Qf (2)
	UEFA Europa Lge Qf (2)
10 Sat	The FA Cup Sponsored by E.On SF
11 Sun	The FA Cup Sponsored by E.On SF
21 Wed	UEFA Champions Lge SF (1)
	UEFA Europa Lge SF (1)
24 Sat	The FA County Youth Cup Final (Prov)
25 Sun	The FA Carlsberg Sunday Cup Final (Prov)
28 Wed	UEFA Champions Lge SF (2)
	UEFA Europa Lge SF (2)

MAY 2010

01 Sat	The FA County Youth Cup Final (Prov)
02 Sun	Championship Season Finish
	The FA Carlsberg Sunday Cup Final (Prov)
	The FA Women's Cup Sponsored by E.On Final
08 Sat	The FA Carlsberg Trophy Final (Prov)
	Championship Play-Off SF1
	Lge 1 & Lge 2 Finishes
09 Sun	Premier Lge Season Finish
	The FA Carlsberg Vase Final (Prov)
10 Mon	The FA Carlsberg National Lge System Cup SF*
12 Wed	UEFA Europa Lge Final
	Championship Play-Off SF2
15 Sat	The FA Cup Sponsored by E.On Final
	Lge 1 & Lge 2 Play-Off SF1
19 Wed	Lge 1 & Lge 2 Play-Off SF2
22 Sat	UEFA Champions Lge Final
	Championship Play-Off Final (Prov)
	FA Youth Cup Final 1st leg
23 Sun	Championship Play-Off Final (Prov)
26 Wed	FA Youth Cup Final 2nd leg
29 Sat	Lge 1 Play-Off Final
30 Sun	Lge 2 Play-Off Final

JUNE 2010

| 11 Fri | World Cup Commences |

† Ties to be played in week commencing
* Closing date of round

381

STOP PRESS

Summer transfers completed and pending:

Premier League: Arsenal: Thomas Vermaelen (Ajax) undisclosed. **Birmingham C:** Cristian Benitez (Santos Laguna) undisclosed; Giovanni Espinoza (Barcelona SC) undisclosed; Roger Johnson (Cardiff C) £5m; Scott Dann (Coventry C) undisclosed; Joe Hart (Manchester C) Loan; Lee Bowyer (West Ham U) Free. **Blackburn R:** Gael Givet (Marseille) undisclosed; Steven N'Zonzi (Amiens) undisclosed; Elrio Van Heerden (Club Brugge) Free; Lars Jacobsen (Everton) Free. **Bolton W:** Sean Davis (Portsmouth) Free; Paul Robinson (WBA) Loan. **Burnley:** Tyrone Mears (Derby Co) undisclosed; Steven Fletcher (Hibernian) £3m; David Edgar (Newcastle U) Free. **Chelsea:** Daniel Sturridge (Manchester C) undisclosed; Ross Turnbull (Middlesbrough) Free; Yuri Zhirkov (CSKA Moscow) undisclosed. **Everton:** Anton Peterlin (Ventura County Fusion) Free; Jo (Manchester C) Loan. **Fulham:** Stephen Kelly (Birmingham C) undisclosed. **Hull C:** Steven Mouvokolo (Bologne) undisclosed. **Liverpool:** Glen Johnson (Portsmouth) undisclosed. **Manchester C:** Gareth Barry (Aston Villa) £12m; Roque Santa Cruz (Blackburn R) £17m; Stuart Taylor (Aston Villa) undisclosed. **Manchester U:** Michael Owen (Newcastle U) Free; Antonio Valencia (Wigan Ath) undisclosed; Gabriel Obertan (Bordeaux) undisclosed. **Portsmouth:** Aaron Mokoena (Blackburn R) Free. **Sunderland:** Fraizer Campbell (Manchester U) £3,500,000. **West Ham U:** Luis Jimenez (Internazionale) Loan; Herita Ilunga (Toulouse) undisclosed; Peter Kurucz (Ujpest) undisclosed. **Wigan Ath:** Hendry Thomas (Olimpia) undisclosed; Jordi Gomez (Espanyol) undisclosed. **Wolverhampton W:** Ronald Zubar (Marseille) undisclosed; Greg Halford (Sunderland) undisclosed; Nenad Milijas (Red Star Belgrade) undisclosed; Marcus Hahnemann (Reading) Free; Andrew Surman (Southampton) undisclosed; Kevin Doyle (Reading) undisclosed.

Football League Championship: Barnsley: Onome Sodje (York C) Free. **Bristol C:** Dean Gerken (Colchester U) undisclosed; Andre Blackman (Portsmouth) Free; Paul Hartley (Celtic) Free; David Clarkson (Motherwell) Free. **Cardiff C:** Paul Quinn (Motherwell) undisclosed; Anthony Gerrard (Walsall) undisclosed; Mark Hudson (Charlton Ath) undisclosed; David Marshall (Norwich C) undisclosed; Michael Chopra (Sunderland) £4m. **Crystal Palace:** Freddie Sears (West Ham U) Loan; Darren Ambrose (Charlton Ath) Free. **Derby Co:** Lee Croft (Norwich C) Free; Dean Moxey (Exeter C) undisclosed; Jake Buxton (Burton Alb) undisclosed. **Ipswich T:** Damien Delaney (QPR) undisclosed; Lee Martin (Manchester U) undisclosed. **Leicester C:** Chris Weale (Bristol C) Free; Dany N'Guessan (Lincoln C) undisclosed; Richard Wellens (Doncaster R) £1,200,000; Wayne Brown (Hull C) Free; Robbie Neilson (Hearts) Free; Jack Hobbs (Liverpool) undisclosed. **Middlesbrough:** Mark Yeates (Colchester U) undisclosed; Danny Coyne (Tranmere R) Free. **Nottingham F:** Lee Camp (QPR) undisclosed; David McGoldrick (Southampton) undisclosed; Paul Anderson (Liverpool) £250,000; Dele Adebola (Bristol C) Free. **Peterborough U:** Tommy Rowe (Stockport Co) undisclosed; Lee Frecklington (Lincoln C) undisclosed; Toumani Diagouraga (Hereford U) undisclosed. **Plymouth Arg:** Carl Fletcher (Crystal Palace) Free. **Scunthorpe U:** Rob Jones (Hibernian) undisclosed; Josh Wright (Charlton Ath) Free; Michael O'Connor (Crewe Alex) undisclosed. **Sheffield U:** Kyel Reid (West Ham U) Free; Lee Williamson (Watford) undisclosed. **Sheffield W:** Tommy Miller (Ipswich T) Free; Darren Purse (Cardiff C) Free; Darren Potter (Wolverhampton W) undisclosed. **Swansea C:** Steven Dobbie (Queen of the South) Free. **Watford:** Danny Graham (Carlisle U) Free; Scott Severin (Aberdeen) Free. **WBA:** Simon Cox (Swindon T) £1,500,000.

Football League 1: Brentford: Myles Weston (Notts Co) undisclosed; Sam Saunders, Danny Foster and Ben Strevens (all Dagenham & R) Free. **Brighton & HA:** Mark Wright (Milton Keynes D) Free; Gary Dicker (Stockport Co) Free; Graeme Smith (Motherwell) Free; James Tunnicliffe (Stockport Co) undisclosed. **Bristol R:** Dominic Blizzard (Stockport Co) Free. **Carlisle U:** Adam Collin (Workington) Free; Matty Robson (Hartlepool U) Free; Tom Taiwo (Chelsea) Loan; Tony Kane (Blackburn R) Free. **Charlton Ath:** Miguel Angel Llera (Milton Keynes D) Free; Frazer Richardson (Leeds U) Free. **Colchester U:** Lee Beevers (Lincoln C) Free. **Exeter C:** Scott Golbourne (Reading) Free; Barry Corr (Swindon T) Free; Joe Burnell (Oxford U) Free. **Gillingham:** Kevin Maher (Oldham Ath) Free; Chris Palmer (Walsall) Free. **Hartlepool U:** Peter Hartley (Sunderland) Free; Scott Flinders (Crystal Palace) Free; Neil Austin (Darlington) Free. **Huddersfield T:** Theo Robinson (Watford) undisclosed; Antony Kay (Tranmere R) Free; Peter Clarke (Southend U) Free; Lee Peltier (Yeovil T) undisclosed; Robbie Simpson (Coventry C) undisclosed. **Leeds U:** Shane Higgs (Cheltenham T) Free; Jason Crowe (Northampton T) Free. **Leyton Orient:** Scott McGleish (Wycombe W) Free; Jimmy Smith (Chelsea) Free. **Millwall:** John Sullivan (Brighton & HA) undisclosed; Jason Price (Doncaster R) Free. **Milton Keynes D:** Dan Woodards (Crewe Alex) Free; David McCracken (Wycombe W) Free. **Norwich C:** Owain Tudur-Jones (Swansea C) undisclosed; Michael Nelson (Hartlepool U) Free; Matthew Gill (Exeter C) Free; Michael Theoklitos (Melbourne Victory) Free. **Oldham Ath:** Jon Worthington (Huddersfield T) Free; Joe Jacobson (Bristol R) Free; Pawel Abbott (Darlington) Free; Robert Purdie (Darlington) Free. **Swindon T:** Gordon Greer (Doncaster R) Free; David Lucas (Leeds U) Free; Jonathan Douglas (Leeds U) Free; Alan O'Brien (Hibernian) Free. **Tranmere R:** Alan Mahon (Burnley) Free; Ryan France (Hull C) Free; John Welsh (Hull C) Free. **Walsall:** Steve Jones (Burnley) Free; Mark Hughes (Northampton T) Free. **Wycombe W:** Michael Duberry (Reading) Free; Chris Westwood (Peterborough U) Free. **Yeovil T:** Stefan Stam (Oldham Ath) Free; Scott Murray (Bristol C) Free.

Football League 2: Accrington S: Michael Symes (Shrewsbury T) Free; Luke Joyce (Carlisle U) Free. **Barnet:** Micah Hyde (Woking) Free; Jake Cole (QPR) Free. **Bradford C:** Gareth Evans (Macclesfield T) undisclosed; Zesh Rehman (QPR) Free; Simon Ramsden (Rochdale) Free. **Burton Albion:** Paul Boertien (Walsall) Free; Richard Walker (Bristol R) Free; Robin Shroot (Birmingham C) Loan; Martin Butler (Grimsby T) undisclosed. **Bury:** Danny Carlton (Carlisle U) Free. **Cheltenham T:** Justin Richards (Kidderminster H) Free. **Chesterfield:** Ian Breckin (Nottingham F) Free. **Crewe Alexandra:** Patrick Ada (Histon) undisclosed. **Dagenham & R:** Danny Green (Bishop's Stortford) undisclosed; Joshua Scott (Hayes & Yeading) Free; Stuart Thurgood (Grays Ath) Free. **Darlington:** Dean Windass (Hull C) Free. **Grimsby T:** Peter Sweeney (Leeds U) Free; Joe Widdowson (West Ham U) Free; Michael Leary (Barnet) Free. **Hereford U:** Glen Southam (Dagenham & R) Free; Adam Bartlett (Kidderminster H) Free; Marc Pugh (Shrewsbury T) Free; Kenny Lunt (Sheffield W) Free; Jamie Tolley (Macclesfield T) Free; Darren Jones (Forest Green R) undisclosed. **Lincoln C:** Joe Heath (Nottingham F) Loan. **Macclesfield T:** Paul Morgan (Bury) Free; Ben Wright (Lincoln C) Free; Steve Reed (Weymouth) undisclosed; Nat Brown (Wrexham) Free; Hamza Bencherif (Nottingham F) Free; Ross Draper (Hednesford T) undisclosed; Colin Daniel (Crewe Alex) Free. **Northampton T:** Dean Beckwith (Hereford U) Free; Steve Guinan (Hereford U) Free. **Notts Co:** Ben Davies (Shrewsbury T) Free; Graeme Lee (Bradford C) undisclosed; Brendan Moloney (Nottingham F) Loan. **Port Vale:** Doug Loft (Brighton & HA) Free; Adam Yates (Morecambe) Free; Tommy Fraser (Brighton & HA) undisclosed. **Rochdale:** Kenny Arthur (Accrington S) Free; Matthew Edwards (Leeds U) Free. **Rotherham U:** Jamie Annerson (Sheffield U) Free; Nicky Law (Sheffield U) Free. **Shrewsbury T:** Lewis Neal (Carlisle U) Free; Chris Neal (Preston NE) nominal; Dean Holden (Falkirk) Free.

Scottish Premier League: Celtic: Marc-Antoine Fortune (Nancy) undisclosed; Lukasz Zaluska (Dundee u) Free. **Dundee U:** Danny Cadamarteri (Huddersfield T) Free; Jennison Myrie-Williams (Bristol C) Free; Steve Banks (Hearts) Free. **Falkirk:** Brian McLean (Motherwell) Free; Sean Fraser (Coventry C) Free; Alex MacDonald (Burnley) Loan; Mark Twaddle (Partick T) undisclosed; Ryan Flynn (Liverpool) Loan. **Hibernian:** Kevin McBride (Falkirk) Free. **Kilmarnock:** Graeme Owens (Middlesbrough) Free. **St Johnstone:** Collin Samuel (Toronto) undisclosed; Euan McLean (Dundee U) undisclosed; Gavin Swankie (Dundee) undisclosed; Graham Gartland (Drogheda U) undisclosed; Graeme Smith (Rangers) Free. **St Mirren:** Lee Mair (Aberdeen) undisclosed; Michael Higdon (Falkirk) Free.

Leaving the country: **Arsenal:** Havard Nordtveit (Lillestrom) Loan. **Blackburn R:** Matt Derbyshire (Olympiakos) undisclosed; Andre Ooijer (PSV Eindhoven) Free. **Chelsea:** Ben Sahar (Espanyol) undisclosed; Slobodan Rajkovic (Twente) Loan. **Fulham:** Collins John (Roeselare) Free. **Liverpool:** Jermaine Pennant (Real Zaragoza) Free; Sebastian Leto (Panathinaikos) £1,300,000. **Manchester C:** Gelson (St Etienne) undisclosed; Darius Vassell (Ankaragucu) Free. **Manchester U:** Cristiano Ronaldo (Real Madrid) £80,000,000; Rodrigo Possebon (Braga) Loan. **Portsmouth:** Andrea Mbuyi-Mutombo (Standard Liege) Free. **Barnsley:** Dennis Souza (Katar) Free. **Bristol C:** Peter Styvar (Xanthi) Loan. **Derby Co:** Emanuel Villa (Cruz Azul) undisclosed. **Plymouth Arg:** Emile Mpenza (Sion) Free. **Crewe Alex:** Julien Baudet (Colorado Rapids) Free. **Celtic:** Shunsuke Nakamura (Espanyol) Free.

Now you can buy any of these other bestselling sports titles from your bookshop or *direct from the publisher.*

FREE P&P AND UK DELIVERY
(Overseas and Ireland £3.50 per book)

Sky Sports Football Yearbook 2009–2010	Glenda Rollin and Jack Rollin	£20.00
1966 and All That	Geoff Hurst	£7.99
Psycho	Stuart Pearce	£7.99
Vinnie	Vinnie Jones	£7.99
Left Foot Forward	Garry Nelson	£6.99
The Doc	Tommy Docherty	£8.99
The Autobiography	Niall Quinn	£7.99
Black and Blue	Paul Canoville	£7.99
Cloughie	Brian Clough	£7.99
Determined	Norman Whiteside	£7.99
Gazza: My Story	Paul Gascoigne	£7.99
My Manchester United Years	Bobby Charlton	£8.99
My England Years	Bobby Charlton	£7.99
My Defence	Ashley Cole	£7.99
Fallen Idle	Peter Marinello	£6.99
Being Gazza	Paul Gascoigne	£6.99
The Autobiography	Alan Mullery	£7.99

TO ORDER SIMPLY CALL THIS NUMBER

01235 400 414

or visit our website:
www.headline.co.uk
Prices and availability subject to change without notice.